D1162635

VISUAL
dictionary

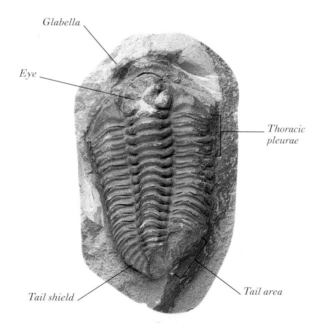

Glabella

Eye

Thoracic
pleurae

Tail shield

Tail area

PREHISTORIC TRILOBITE

DIGITAL VIDEO CAMERA

Liquid crystal display (LCD)

Viewfinder

Power switch

Cassette compartment lid

Battery

OVERHEAD VIEW OF OUR GALAXY

Location of Solar System

Nucleus

First electron shell

Second electron shell

Nucleus

ANATOMY OF A FLUORINE-19 ATOM

Fault plane

Dip of fault plane

Hade of fault plane

STRUCTURE OF A FAULT

Openable windscreen

Steering wheel

Radiator

Headlamp

Exhaust port

Floral design

VELOCETTE OHV ENGINE

MOSAIC DESIGN

MODEL T FORD

VISUAL
dictionary

Pedicel
(flower stalk)

Sepal

Achene
(one-seeded
dry fruit)

Remains
of stigma
and style

STRAWBERRY

A DORLING KINDERSLEY BOOK

DK

LONDON, NEW YORK, MUNICH, MELBOURNE, AND DELHI

THIS EDITION

DK LONDON

Editorial Consultants Ian Graham, Darren Naish, Carole Stott
Picture Researcher Karen VanRoss
Jacket Designer Silke Spingies
Digital Conversion Coordinator Linda Zacharia
Production Editor Joanna Byrne
Production Controller Linda Dare
Managing Editor Julie Ferris
Managing Art Editor Owen Peyton Jones
Art Director Philip Ormerod
Associate Publishing Director Liz Wheeler
Publishing Director Jonathan Metcalf

DK DELHI

Managing Art Editor Arunesh Talapatra
Managing Editor Saloni Talwar
Deputy Managing Art Editor Priyabrata Roy Chowdhury
Senior Art Editor Rajnish Kashyap
Senior Editor Neha Gupta
Art Editors Arijit Ganguly, Pooja Pipil
Assistant Art Editor Pooja Pawwar
DTP Manager Balwant Singh
DTP Designer Jaypal Singh Chauhan
Managing Director Aparna Sharma

Anatomical And Botanical Models Supplied By Somso Modelle, Coburg, Germany

ORIGINAL EDITION (*Ultimate Visual Dictionary*)

Project Art Editors Heather McCarry, Johnny Pau, Chris Walker, Kevin Williams
Designer Simon Murrell
Project Editors Luisa Caruso, Peter Jones, Jane Mason, Geoffrey Stalker
Editor Jo Evans
DTP Designer Zirrinia Austin
Picture Researcher Charlotte Bush
Managing Art Editor Toni Kay
Senior Editor Roger Tritton
Managing Editor Sean Moore
Production Manager Hilary Stephens

FIRST PUBLISHED IN GREAT BRITAIN IN 1994
UNDER THE TITLE *ULTIMATE VISUAL DICTIONARY* BY
DORLING KINDERSLEY LIMITED
80 STRAND, LONDON WC2R 0RL
A PENGUIN COMPANY

PENGUIN GROUP (UK)
2 4 6 8 10 9 7 5 3
003–178144–Nov/11
REVISED EDITIONS IN 1996, 1997, 1998, 1999, 2000, 2002, 2006, 2011

COPYRIGHT © 1994, 1996, 1997, 1998, 1999, 2000, 2002, 2006, 2011 DORLING KINDERSLEY LIMITED, LONDON

A CIP CATALOGUE RECORD FOR THIS BOOK IS AVAILABLE FROM THE BRITISH LIBRARY

ISBN 978-1-4053-6390-7

COLOUR REPRODUCTION BY Colourscan, Singapore
PRINTED AND BOUND IN Hong Kong

See our complete catalogue at www.dk.com

Prosoma (cephalothorax)

Spinneret

Leg

EXTERNAL FEATURES OF A SPIDER

Canopy

Fin

G-BNHB

Main landing gear

SIDE VIEW OF ARV SUPER 2 AEROPLANE

Heat shield

Third stage motor

Delta II launch vehicle second stage

MARS PATHFINDER

Barrel

Permanent black ink

FOUNTAIN PEN AND INK

CONTENTS

Face light emitting diodes (LEDs)

Movable tail

SONY AIBO ROBOT DOG

Low pressure gases

Central electrode

BALL CONTAINING HIGH TEMPERATURE GAS (PLASMA)

Parallel bands

ONYX

Non-breakable plastic

Shock absorber

AMERICAN FOOTBALL HELMET

Introduction

THE VISUAL DICTIONARY is a completely new kind of reference book. It provides a link between pictures and words in a way that no ordinary dictionary ever has. Most dictionaries simply tell you what a word means, but the *VISUAL DICTIONARY* shows you – through a combination of detailed annotations, explicit photographs, and illustrations. In the *VISUAL DICTIONARY*, pictures define the annotations around them. You do not read definitions of the annotated words, you see them. The highly accessible format of the *VISUAL DICTIONARY*, the thoroughness of its annotations, and the range of its subject matter make it a unique and helpful reference tool.

How to use the VISUAL DICTIONARY

You will find the *VISUAL DICTIONARY* simple to use. Instead of being organized alphabetically, it is divided by subject into 14 sections – THE UNIVERSE, PREHISTORIC EARTH, PLANTS, ANIMALS, THE HUMAN BODY, etc. Each section begins with a table of contents listing the major entries within that section. For example, The Visual Arts section has entries on *Drawing, Tempera, Fresco, Oils, Watercolour, Pastels, Acrylics, Calligraphy, Printmaking, Mosaic,* and *Sculpture*. Every entry has a short introduction explaining the purpose of the photographs and illustrations, and the significance of the annotations.

If you know what something looks like, but don't know its name, find the term you need by turning to the annotations surrounding the pictures; if you know a word, but don't know what it refers to, use the comprehensive index to direct you to the appropriate page.

Suppose that you want to know what the bone at the end of your little finger is called. With a standard dictionary, you wouldn't know where to begin. But with the *VISUAL DICTIONARY* you simply turn to the entry called *Hands* – within THE HUMAN BODY section – where you will find four fully annotated, colour photographs showing the skin, muscles, and bones of the human hand. In this entry you will quickly find that the bone you are searching for is called the distal phalanx, and for good measure you will discover that it is attached to the middle phalanx by the distal interphalangeal joint.

Perhaps you want to know what a catalytic converter looks like. If you look up "catalytic converter" in an ordinary dictionary, you will be told what it is and possibly what it does – but you will not be able to tell what shape it is or what it is made of. However, if you look up "catalytic converter" in the index of the *VISUAL DICTIONARY*, you will be directed to the *Modern engines* entry on page 344 – where the introduction gives you basic information about what a catalytic converter is – and to page 350 – where there is a spectacular exploded-view photograph of the mechanics of a Renault Clio. From these pages you will find out not only what a catalytic converter looks like, but also that it is attached at one end to an exhaust downpipe and at the other to a silencer.

Whatever it is that you want to find a name for, or whatever name you want to find a picture for, you will find it quickly and easily in the *VISUAL DICTIONARY*. Perhaps you need to know where the vamp on a shoe is; or how to tell obovate and lanceolate leaves apart; or what a spiral galaxy looks like; or whether birds have nostrils. With the *VISUAL DICTIONARY* at hand, the answers to each of these questions, and thousands more, are readily available.

The *VISUAL DICTIONARY* does not just tell you what the names of the different parts of an object are. The photographs, illustrations, and annotations are all specially arranged to help you understand which parts relate to one another and how objects function.

With the *VISUAL DICTIONARY* you can find in seconds the words or pictures that you are looking for; or you can simply browse through the pages of the book for your own pleasure. The *VISUAL DICTIONARY* is not intended to replace a standard dictionary or conventional encyclopedia, but is instead a stimulating and valuable companion to ordinary reference volumes. Giving you instant access to the language that is used by astronomers and architects, musicians and mechanics, scientists and sportspeople, it is the ideal reference book for specialists and generalists of all ages.

Sections of the VISUAL DICTIONARY

The 14 sections of the *VISUAL DICTIONARY* contain a total of more than 30,000 terms, encompassing a wide range of topics:

• In the first section, THE UNIVERSE, spectacular photographs and illustrations are used to show the names of the stars and planets and to explain the structure of solar systems, galaxies, nebulae, comets, and black holes.

• PREHISTORIC EARTH tells the story in annotations of how our own planet has evolved since its formation. It includes examples of prehistoric flora and fauna, and fascinating dinosaur models – some with parts of the body stripped away to show anatomical sections.

• PLANTS covers a huge range of species – from the familiar to the exotic. In addition to the colour photographs of plants included in this section, there is a series of micrographic photographs illustrating plant details – such as pollen grains, spores, and cross-sections of stems and roots – in close-up.

• In the ANIMALS section, skeletons, anatomical diagrams, and different parts of animals' bodies have been meticulously annotated. This section provides a comprehensive guide to the vocabulary of zoological classification and animal physiology.

• The structure of the human body, its parts, and its systems are presented in THE HUMAN BODY. The section includes lifelike, three-dimensional models and the latest false-colour images. Clear and authoritative annotations indicate the correct anatomical terms.

• GEOLOGY, GEOGRAPHY, AND METEOROLOGY describes the structure of the Earth – from the inner core to the exosphere – and the physical phenomena – such as volcanoes, rivers, glaciers, and climate – that shape its surface.

• PHYSICS AND CHEMISTRY is a visual journey through the fundamental principles underlying the physical universe, and provides the essential vocabulary of these sciences.

• In RAIL AND ROAD, a wide range of trains, trams and buses, cars, bicycles, and motorcycles are described. Exploded-view photographs show mechanical details with striking clarity.

• SEA AND AIR gives the names for hundreds of parts of ships and aeroplanes. The section includes civil and fighting craft, both historical and modern.

• THE VISUAL ARTS shows the equipment and materials used by painters, sculptors, printers, and other artists. Well-known compositions have been chosen to illustrate specific artistic techniques and effects.

• ARCHITECTURE includes photographs of exemplary architectural models and illustrates dozens of additional features such as columns, domes, and arches.

• MUSIC provides a visual introduction to the special language of music and musical instruments. It includes clearly annotated photographs of each of the major groups of traditional instruments – brass, woodwind, strings, and percussion – together with modern electronic instruments.

• The SPORTS section is a guide to the playing areas, formations, equipment, and techniques needed for many of today's most popular sports.

• In THE MODERN WORLD, items that are a familiar part of our daily lives are taken apart to reveal their inner workings and give access to the language used by their manufacturers. It also includes systems and concepts, such as the Internet, that increasingly influence our 21st century world.

THE UNIVERSE

Anatomy of the Universe

Fireball of rapidly expanding, extremely hot gas lasting about one million years

THE UNIVERSE CONTAINS EVERYTHING that exists, from the tiniest subatomic particles to galactic superclusters (the largest structures known). Nobody knows how big the Universe is, but astronomers estimate that it contains at least 125 billion galaxies, each comprising an average of 100 billion stars. The most widely accepted theory about the origin of the Universe is the Big Bang theory, which states that the Universe came into being in a huge explosion – the Big Bang – that took place between 10 and 20 billion years ago. The Universe initially consisted of a very hot, dense fireball of expanding, cooling gas. After about one million years, the gas began to condense into localized clumps called protogalaxies. During the next five billion years, the protogalaxies continued condensing, forming galaxies in which stars were being born. Today, billions of years later, the Universe as a whole is still expanding, although there are localized areas in which objects are held together by gravity; for example, many galaxies are found in clusters. The Big Bang theory is supported by the discovery of faint, cool background radiation coming evenly from all directions. This radiation is believed to be the remnant of the radiation produced by the Big Bang. Small "ripples" in the temperature of the cosmic background radiation are thought to be evidence of slight fluctuations in the density of the early Universe, which resulted in the formation of galaxies. Astronomers do not yet know if the Universe is "closed", which means it will eventually stop expanding and begin to contract, or if it is "open", which means it will continue expanding forever.

FALSE-COLOUR MICROWAVE MAP OF COSMIC BACKGROUND RADIATION

Pink indicates "warm ripples" in background radiation

Pale blue indicates "cool ripples" in background radiation

Low-energy microwave radiation corresponding to about -270°C

Deep blue indicates background radiation corresponding to -270°C (remnant of the Big Bang)

Red and pink band indicates radiation from our galaxy

High-energy gamma radiation corresponding to about 3,000°C

ORIGIN AND EXPANSION OF THE UNIVERSE

Quasar (probably the centre
of a galaxy containing a
massive black hole)

Universe about five
billion years after
Big Bang

Protogalaxy
(condensing gas cloud)

Galaxy spinning and
flattening to become
spiral shaped

Dark cloud
(dust and gas
condensing
to form a
protogalaxy)

Elliptical
galaxy in
which stars
form rapidly

Universe today
(13–17 billion years
after Big Bang)

Cluster of
galaxies held
together by gravity

Elliptical galaxy
containing old stars
and little gas and dust

Irregular galaxy

Spiral galaxy
containing gas,
dust, and young stars

OBJECTS IN THE UNIVERSE

CLUSTER OF
GALAXIES IN VIRGO

FALSE-COLOUR IMAGE
OF 3C273 (QUASAR)

NGC 4406
(ELLIPTICAL GALAXY)

NGC 5236
(BARRED SPIRAL GALAXY)

NGC 6822
(IRREGULAR GALAXY)

THE ROSETTE NEBULA
(EMISSION NEBULA)

THE JEWEL BOX
(STAR CLUSTER)

THE SUN
(MAIN SEQUENCE STAR)

EARTH

THE MOON

Galaxies

SOMBRERO,
A SPIRAL GALAXY

A GALAXY IS A HUGE MASS OF STARS, nebulae, and interstellar material. The smallest galaxies contain about 100,000 stars, while the largest contain up to 3,000 billion stars. There are three main types of galaxy, classified according to their shape: elliptical, which are oval shaped; spiral, which have arms spiralling outwards from a central bulge (those whose arms spiral from a bar-shaped bulge are called spirals); and irregular, which have no obvious shape. Sometimes, the shape of a galaxy is distorted by a collision with another galaxy. Quasars (quasi-stellar objects) are thought to be galactic nuclei but are so far away that their exact nature is still uncertain. They are compact, highly luminous objects in the outer reaches of the known Universe: while the furthest known "ordinary" galaxies are about 12 billion light years away, the furthest known quasar is about 13 billion light years away. Active galaxies, such as Seyfert galaxies and radio galaxies, emit intense radiation. In a Seyfert galaxy, this radiation comes from the galactic nucleus; in a radio galaxy, it also comes from huge lobes on either side of the galaxy. The radiation from active galaxies and quasars is thought to be caused by material falling into central black holes (see pp. 28-29).

OPTICAL IMAGE OF NGC 4486 (ELLIPTICAL GALAXY)

Globular cluster containing very old red giants

Central region containing old red giants

Less densely populated region

Neighbouring galaxy

OPTICAL IMAGE OF LARGE MAGELLANIC CLOUD (IRREGULAR GALAXY)

Tarantula Nebula

Dust cloud obscuring light from stars

Emission nebula

Light from stars

OPTICAL IMAGE OF NGC 2997 (SPIRAL GALAXY)

Glowing nebula in spiral arm

Spiral arm containing young stars

Galactic nucleus containing old stars

Dust in spiral arm reflecting blue light from hot young stars

Hot, ionized hydrogen gas emitting red light

Dust lane

OPTICAL IMAGE OF CENTAURUS A (RADIO GALAXY)

Dust lane crossing elliptical galaxy

Galactic nucleus containing powerful source of radiation

Light from old stars

FALSE-COLOUR RADIO IMAGE OF CENTAURUS A

Radio lobe

Radio lobe

Red indicates high-intensity radio waves

Blue indicates low-intensity radio waves

Radiation from galactic nucleus

Outline of optical image of Centaurus A

Yellow indicates medium-intensity radio waves

FALSE-COLOUR RADIO IMAGE OF 3C 273 (QUASAR)

Radiation from jet of high-energy particles moving away from quasar

Blue indicates low-intensity radio waves

Quasar nucleus

White indicates high-intensity radio waves

OPTICAL IMAGE OF NGC 1566 (SEYFERT GALAXY)

Nebula in spiral arm

Compact nucleus emitting intense radiation

Spiral arm

FALSE-COLOUR OPTICAL IMAGE OF NGC 5754 (TWO COLLIDING GALAXIES)

Blue indicates low-intensity radiation

Red indicates medium-intensity radiation

Spiral arm distorted by gravitational influence of smaller galaxy

Large spiral galaxy

Smaller galaxy colliding with large galaxy

Yellow indicates high-intensity radiation

The Milky Way

VIEW TOWARDS
GALACTIC CENTRE

THE MILKY WAY IS THE NAME GIVEN TO THE FAINT BAND OF LIGHT that stretches across the night sky. This light comes from stars and nebulae in our galaxy, known as the Milky Way Galaxy or simply as "the Galaxy". The Galaxy is believed to be a barred spiral, with a dense central bar of stars encircled by four arms spiralling outwards and surrounded by a less dense halo. We cannot see the spiral shape because the Solar System is in one of the spiral arms, the Orion Arm (also called the Local Arm). From our position, the centre of the Galaxy is completely obscured by dust clouds; as a result, optical maps give only a limited view of the Galaxy. However, a more complete picture can be obtained by studying radio, infra-red, and other radiation. The central part of the Galaxy is relatively small and dense and contains mainly older red and yellow stars. The halo is a less dense region in which the oldest stars are situated; some of these stars are as old as the Galaxy itself (possibly 13 billion years). The spiral arms contain main sequence stars and hot, young, blue stars, as well as nebulae (clouds of dust and gas inside which stars are born). The Galaxy is vast, about 100,000 light years across (a light year is about 9,460 billion kilometres); in comparison, the Solar System seems small, at about 12 light hours across (about 13 billion kilometres). The entire Galaxy is rotating in space, although the inner stars travel faster than those further out. The Sun, which is about two-thirds out from the centre, completes one lap of the Galaxy about every 220 million years.

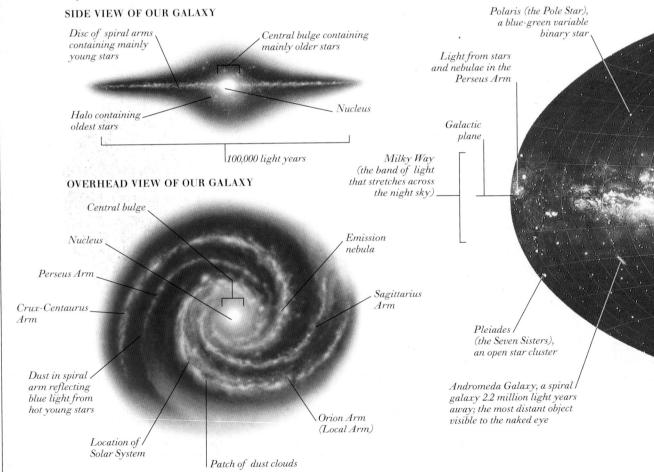

SIDE VIEW OF OUR GALAXY

Disc of spiral arms containing mainly young stars

Central bulge containing mainly older stars

Halo containing oldest stars

Nucleus

100,000 light years

OVERHEAD VIEW OF OUR GALAXY

Central bulge

Nucleus

Perseus Arm

Crux-Centaurus Arm

Emission nebula

Sagittarius Arm

Dust in spiral arm reflecting blue light from hot young stars

Location of Solar System

Patch of dust clouds

Orion Arm (Local Arm)

PANORAMIC OPTICAL MAP OF OUR GALAXY AND NEARBY GALAXIES

Polaris (the Pole Star), a blue-green variable binary star

Light from stars and nebulae in the Perseus Arm

Galactic plane

Milky Way (the band of light that stretches across the night sky)

Pleiades (the Seven Sisters), an open star cluster

Andromeda Galaxy, a spiral galaxy 2.2 million light years away; the most distant object visible to the naked eye

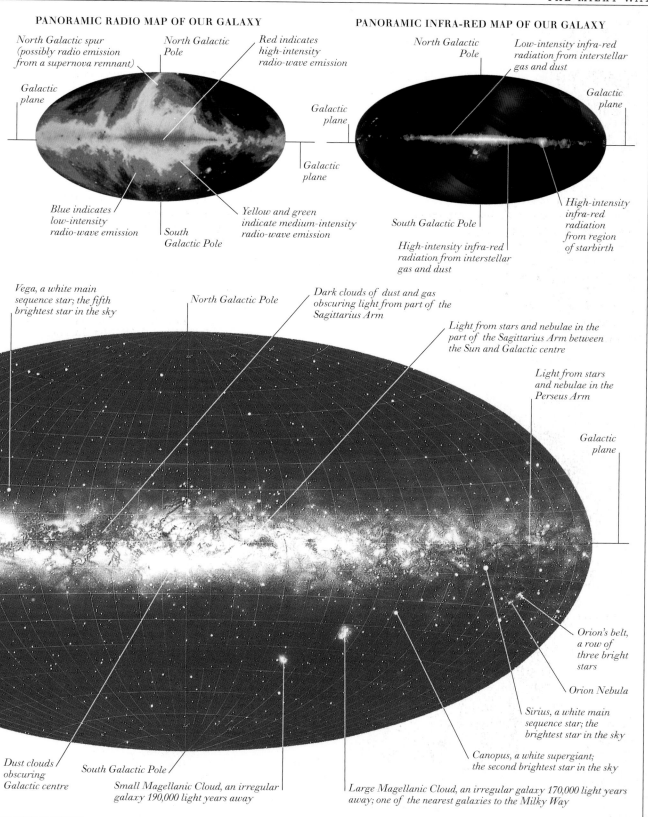

PANORAMIC RADIO MAP OF OUR GALAXY

North Galactic spur (possibly radio emission from a supernova remnant)

North Galactic Pole

Red indicates high-intensity radio-wave emission

Galactic plane

Galactic plane

Galactic plane

Blue indicates low-intensity radio-wave emission

South Galactic Pole

Yellow and green indicate medium-intensity radio-wave emission

PANORAMIC INFRA-RED MAP OF OUR GALAXY

North Galactic Pole

Low-intensity infra-red radiation from interstellar gas and dust

Galactic plane

High-intensity infra-red radiation from region of starbirth

South Galactic Pole

High-intensity infra-red radiation from interstellar gas and dust

Vega, a white main sequence star; the fifth brightest star in the sky

North Galactic Pole

Dark clouds of dust and gas obscuring light from part of the Sagittarius Arm

Light from stars and nebulae in the part of the Sagittarius Arm between the Sun and Galactic centre

Light from stars and nebulae in the Perseus Arm

Galactic plane

Orion's belt, a row of three bright stars

Orion Nebula

Sirius, a white main sequence star; the brightest star in the sky

Canopus, a white supergiant; the second brightest star in the sky

Dust clouds obscuring Galactic centre

South Galactic Pole

Small Magellanic Cloud, an irregular galaxy 190,000 light years away

Large Magellanic Cloud, an irregular galaxy 170,000 light years away; one of the nearest galaxies to the Milky Way

Nebulae and star clusters

HODGE 11, A
GLOBULAR CLUSTER

A NEBULA IS A CLOUD OF DUST AND GAS inside a galaxy. Nebulae become visible if the gas glows, or if the cloud reflects starlight or obscures light from more distant objects. Emission nebulae shine because their gas emits light when it is stimulated by radiation from hot young stars. Reflection nebulae shine because their dust reflects light from stars in or around the nebula. Dark nebulae appear as silhouettes because they block out light from shining nebulae or stars behind them. Two types of nebula are associated with dying stars: planetary nebulae and supernova remnants. Both consist of expanding shells of gas that were once the outer layers of a star. A planetary nebula is a gas shell drifting away from a dying stellar core. A supernova remnant is a gas shell moving away from a stellar core at great speed following a violent explosion called a supernova (see pp. 26-27). Stars are often found in groups known as clusters. Open clusters are loose groups of a few thousand young stars that were born from the same cloud and are drifting apart. Globular clusters are densely packed, roughly spherical groups of hundreds of thousands of older stars.

TRIFID NEBULA (EMISSION NEBULA)

Reflection nebula

Emission nebula

Dust lane

Starbirth region (area in which dust and gas clump together to form stars)

PLEIADES (OPEN STAR CLUSTER) WITH A REFLECTION NEBULA

Wisps of dust and hydrogen gas. The cluster is passing through a region of inter-stellar material

Young star in an open cluster of more than 1,000 stars

Reflection nebula

HORSEHEAD NEBULA (DARK NEBULA)

Glowing filament of hot, ionized hydrogen gas

Alnitak (star in Orion's belt)

Dust lane

Emission nebula

Star near southern end of Orion's belt

Emission nebula

Horsehead Nebula

Reflection nebula

Dark nebula obscuring light from distant stars

ORION NEBULA (DIFFUSE EMISSION NEBULA)

Glowing cloud of dust and hydrogen gas forming part of Orion Nebula

Gas cloud emitting light due to ultraviolet radiation from the four young Trapezium stars

Dust cloud

Trapezium (group of four young stars)

Green light from hot, ionized oxygen gas

Glowing filament of hot, ionized hydrogen gas

Red light from hot, ionized hydrogen gas

VELA SUPERNOVA REMNANT

Supernova remnant (gas shell consisting of outer layers of star thrown off in supernova explosion)

Hydrogen gas emitting red light due to being heated by supernova explosion

Glowing filament of hot, ionized hydrogen gas

HELIX NEBULA (PLANETARY NEBULA)

Planetary nebula (gas shell expanding outwards from dying stellar core)

Remnant of core with a surface temperature of about 100,000°C

Red light from hot, ionized hydrogen gas

Blue-green light from hot, ionized oxygen and nitrogen gases

Stars of northern skies

WHEN YOU LOOK AT THE NORTHERN SKY, you look away from the densely populated Galactic centre, so the northern sky generally appears less bright than the southern sky (see pp. 20-21). Among the best-known sights in the northern sky are the constellations Ursa Major (the Great Bear) and Orion. Some ancient civilizations believed that the stars were fixed to a celestial sphere surrounding the Earth, and modern maps of the sky are based on a similar idea. The North and South Poles of this imaginary celestial sphere are directly above the North and South Poles of the Earth, at the points where the Earth's axis of rotation intersects the sphere. The celestial North Pole is at the centre of the map shown here, and Polaris (the Pole Star) lies very close to it. The celestial equator marks a projection of the Earth's equator on the sphere. The ecliptic marks the path of the Sun across the sky as the Earth orbits the Sun. The Moon and planets move against the background of the stars because the stars are much more distant; the nearest star outside the Solar System (Proxima Centauri) is more than 50,000 times further away than the planet Jupiter.

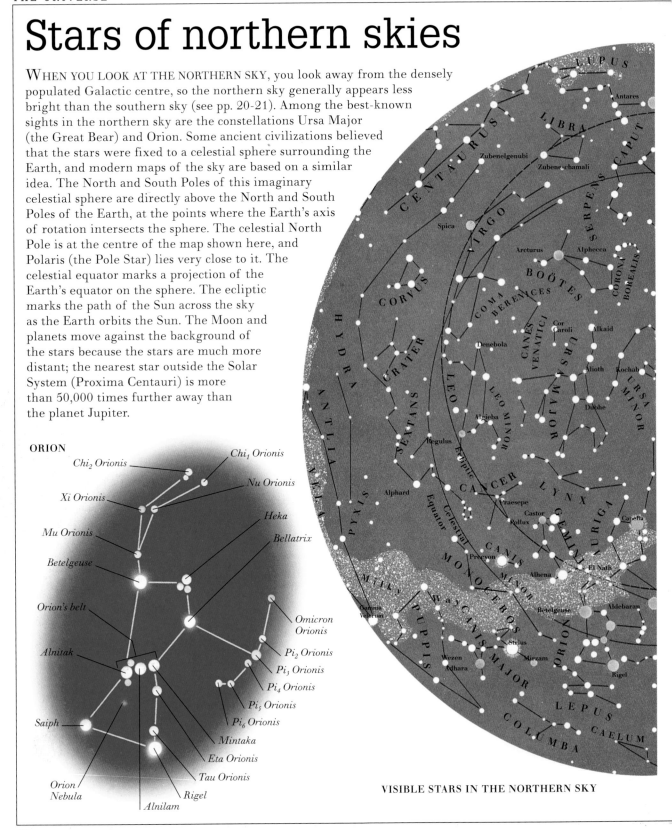

ORION

Chi₂ Orionis → $Chi_2\ Orionis$
Chi₁ Orionis → $Chi_1\ Orionis$
Nu Orionis
Xi Orionis
Heka
Mu Orionis
Bellatrix
Betelgeuse
Omicron Orionis
Orion's belt
$Pi_2\ Orionis$
$Pi_3\ Orionis$
Alnitak
$Pi_4\ Orionis$
$Pi_5\ Orionis$
$Pi_6\ Orionis$
Saiph
Mintaka
Eta Orionis
Tau Orionis
Orion Nebula
Rigel
Alnilam

VISIBLE STARS IN THE NORTHERN SKY

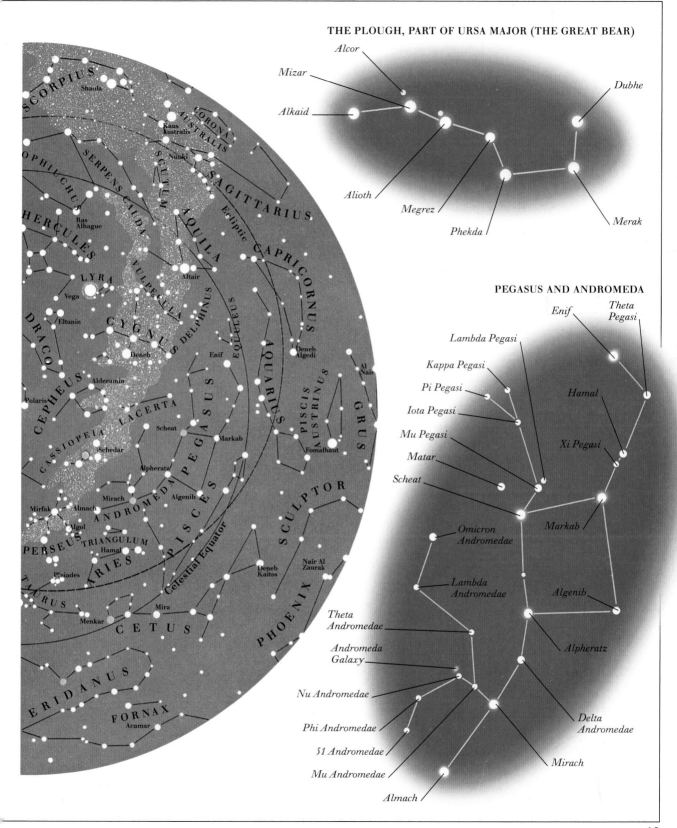

THE PLOUGH, PART OF URSA MAJOR (THE GREAT BEAR)

Alcor
Mizar
Alkaid
Dubhe
Alioth
Megrez
Phekda
Merak

PEGASUS AND ANDROMEDA

Enif
Theta Pegasi
Lambda Pegasi
Kappa Pegasi
Pi Pegasi
Iota Pegasi
Hamal
Mu Pegasi
Xi Pegasi
Matar
Scheat
Markab
Omicron Andromedae
Algenib
Lambda Andromedae
Theta Andromedae
Alpheratz
Andromeda Galaxy
Nu Andromedae
Delta Andromedae
Phi Andromedae
51 Andromedae
Mirach
Mu Andromedae
Almach

SCORPIUS
Shaula
CORONA AUSTRALIS
Kaus Australis
Nunki
SERPENS CAUDA
SCUTUM
SAGITTARIUS
AQUILA
Altair
CAPRICORNUS
Ecliptic
OPHIUCHUS
HERCULES
Ras Alhague
LYRA
VULPECULA
Vega
Eltanin
CYGNUS
DELPHINUS
Deneb
EQUULEUS
AQUARIUS
Deneb Algedi
PISCIS AUSTRINUS
Al Nair
GRUS
DRACO
CEPHEUS
Alderamin
Polaris
LACERTA
Scheat
PEGASUS
Enif
Markab
Fomalhaut
CASSIOPEIA
Schedar
ANDROMEDA
Alpheratz
Algenib
SCULPTOR
Mirfak
Almach
Mirach
PERSEUS
Algol
TRIANGULUM
PISCES
Celestial Equator
Nair Al Zaurak
Pleiades
Hamal
ARIES
Deneb Kaitos
TAURUS
Mira
PHOENIX
Menkar
CETUS
ERIDANUS
FORNAX
Acamar

19

Stars of southern skies

WHEN YOU LOOK AT THE SOUTHERN SKY, you look towards the Galactic centre, which has a huge population of stars. As a result, the Milky Way appears brighter in the southern sky than in the northern sky (see pp. 18-19). The southern sky is rich in nebulae and star clusters. It contains the Large and Small Magellanic Clouds, which are two of the nearest galaxies to our own. Stars make fixed patterns in the sky called constellations. However, the constellations are only apparent groupings of stars, since the distances to the stars in a constellation may vary enormously. The shapes of constellations may change over many thousands of years due to the relative motions of stars. The movement of the constellations across the sky is due to the Earth's motion in space. The daily rotation of the Earth causes the constellations to move across the sky from east to west, and the orbit of the Earth around the Sun causes different areas of sky to be visible in different seasons. The visibility of areas of sky also depends on the location of the observer. For instance, stars near the celestial equator may be seen from either hemisphere at some time during the year, whereas stars close to the celestial poles (the celestial South Pole is at the centre of the map shown here) can never be seen from the opposite hemisphere.

HYDRUS (THE WATER SNAKE) AND MENSA (THE TABLE)

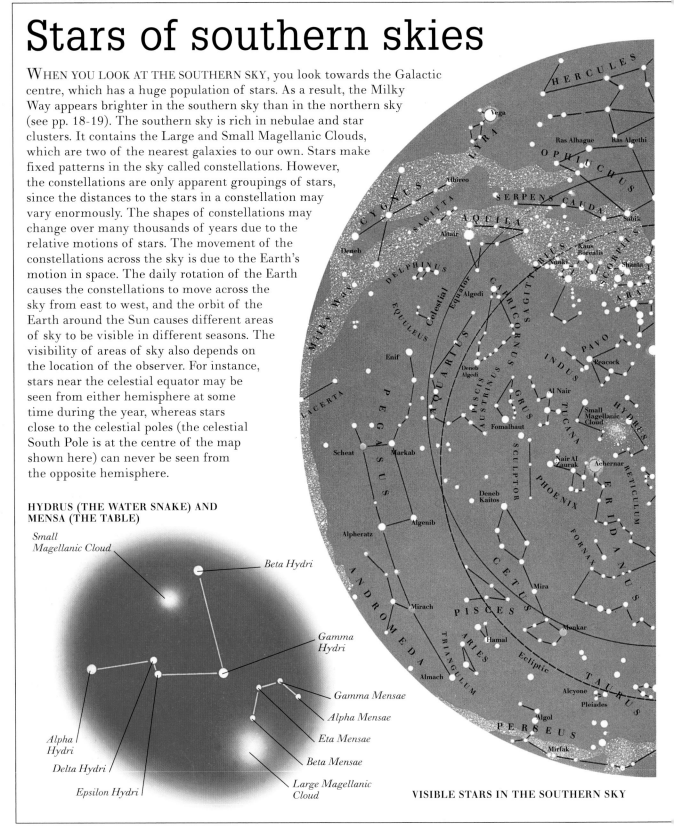

VISIBLE STARS IN THE SOUTHERN SKY

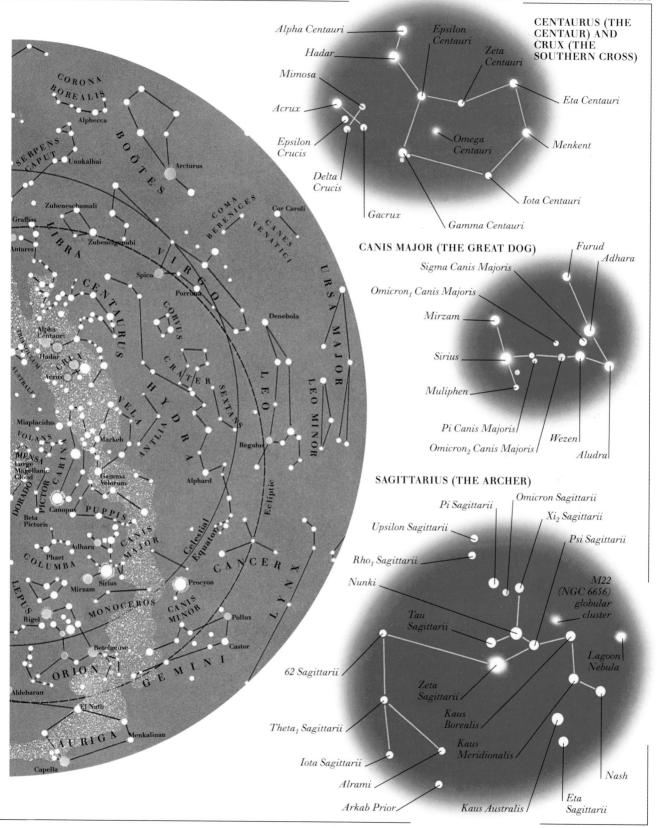

CENTAURUS (THE CENTAUR) AND CRUX (THE SOUTHERN CROSS)

Alpha Centauri
Hadar
Mimosa
Acrux
Epsilon Crucis
Delta Crucis
Gacrux
Epsilon Centauri
Zeta Centauri
Eta Centauri
Menkent
Omega Centauri
Iota Centauri
Gamma Centauri

CANIS MAJOR (THE GREAT DOG)

Sigma Canis Majoris
Omicron₁ Canis Majoris
Mirzam
Sirius
Muliphen
Pi Canis Majoris
Omicron₂ Canis Majoris
Furud
Adhara
Wezen
Aludra

SAGITTARIUS (THE ARCHER)

Pi Sagittarii
Upsilon Sagittarii
Rho₁ Sagittarii
Nunki
Tau Sagittarii
62 Sagittarii
Theta₁ Sagittarii
Iota Sagittarii
Alrami
Arkab Prior
Omicron Sagittarii
Xi₂ Sagittarii
Psi Sagittarii
M22 (NGC 6656) globular cluster
Lagoon Nebula
Zeta Sagittarii
Kaus Borealis
Kaus Meridionalis
Kaus Australis
Eta Sagittarii
Nash

Left map labels:
CORONA BOREALIS
Alphecca
BOÖTES
SERPENS CAPUT
Unukalhai
Arcturus
Zubeneschamali
Graffias
LIBRA
Zubenelgenubi
Antares
COMA BERENICES
CANES VENATICI
Cor Caroli
VIRGO
Spica
Porrima
Denebola
URSA MAJOR
CENTAURUS
Alpha Centauri
Hadar
CRUX
Acrux
TRIANGULUM AUSTRALE
VELA
CORVUS
CRATER
SEXTANS
HYDRA
LEO
LEO MINOR
Miaplacidus
VOLANS
ANTLIA
Markeb
Regulus
MENSA
Large Magellanic Cloud
DORADO
PICTOR
CARINA
PUPPIS
Gamma Velorum
Canopus
Beta Pictoris
Alphard
Adhara
CANIS MAJOR
COLUMBA
Phact
Mirzam
Sirius
MONOCEROS
CANIS MINOR
Procyon
Pollux
Castor
LYNX
CANCER
Celestial Equator
Ecliptic
LEPUS
Rigel
Betelgeuse
ORION
GEMINI
Aldebaran
El Natb
AURIGA
Menkalinan
Capella

Stars

OPEN STAR CLUSTER AND DUST CLOUD

STARS ARE BODIES of hot, glowing gas that are born in nebulae (see pp. 24-27). They vary enormously in size, mass, and temperature: diameters range from about 450 times smaller to over 1,000 times bigger than that of the Sun; masses range from about a twentieth to over 50 solar masses; and surface temperatures range from about 3,000°C to over 50,000°C. The colour of a star is determined by its temperature: the hottest stars are blue and the coolest are red. The Sun, with a surface temperature of 5,500°C, is between these extremes and appears yellow. The energy emitted by a shining star is usually produced by nuclear fusion in the star's core. The brightness of a star is measured in magnitudes – the brighter the star, the lower its magnitude. There are two types of magnitude: apparent magnitude, which is the brightness seen from Earth, and absolute magnitude, which is the brightness that would be seen from a standard distance of 10 parsecs (32.6 light years). The light emitted by a star may be split to form a spectrum containing a series of dark lines (absorption lines). The patterns of lines indicate the presence of particular chemical elements, enabling astronomers to deduce the composition of the star's atmosphere. The magnitude and spectral type (colour) of stars may be plotted on a graph called a Hertzsprung-Russell diagram, which shows that stars tend to fall into several well-defined groups. The principal groups are main sequence stars (those which are fusing hydrogen to form helium), giants, supergiants, and white dwarfs.

STAR SIZES

Red giant (diameters between about 15 million and 150 million km)

The Sun (main sequence star with diameter about 1.4 million km)

White dwarf (diameters between about 3,000 and 50,000 km)

ENERGY EMISSION FROM THE SUN

Nuclear fusion in core produces gamma rays and neutrinos

Neutrinos travel to Earth directly from Sun's core in about 8 minutes

Lower-energy radiation travels to Earth in about 8 minutes

Sun

Earth

Lower-energy radiation (mainly ultraviolet, infra-red, and light rays) leaves surface

High-energy radiation (gamma rays) loses energy while travelling to surface over 2 million years

STAR MAGNITUDES

APPARENT MAGNITUDE

Brighter stars

-9

0

+9

Fainter stars

ABSOLUTE MAGNITUDE

Sirius: apparent magnitude of -1.46

Rigel: apparent magnitude of +0.12

Objects of magnitude higher than about +6.0 cannot be seen by the naked eye

Rigel: absolute magnitude of -7.1

Sirius: absolute magnitude of +1.4

NUCLEAR FUSION IN MAIN SEQUENCE STARS LIKE THE SUN

Positron

Deuterium nucleus

Proton

Neutron

Proton (hydrogen nucleus)

Neutrino

Gamma rays

Helium-3 nucleus

Helium-4 nucleus

HERTZSPRUNG-RUSSELL DIAGRAM

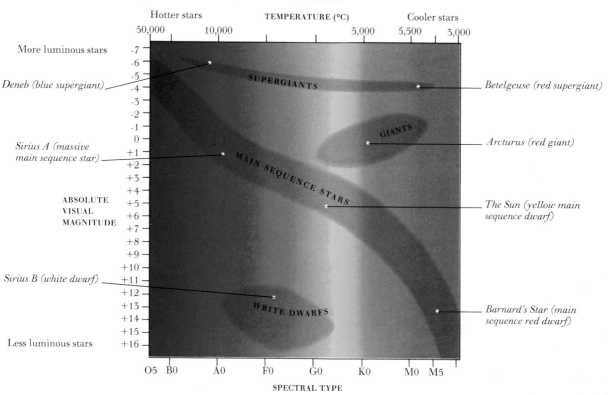

Hotter stars   TEMPERATURE (°C)   Cooler stars

50,000   10,000   5,000   5,500   3,000

More luminous stars

Deneb (blue supergiant)

SUPERGIANTS

Betelgeuse (red supergiant)

GIANTS

Sirius A (massive
main sequence star)

MAIN SEQUENCE STARS

Arcturus (red giant)

The Sun (yellow main
sequence dwarf)

ABSOLUTE
VISUAL
MAGNITUDE

Sirius B (white dwarf)

WRITE DWARFS

Less luminous stars

Barnard's Star (main
sequence red dwarf)

O5   B0   A0   F0   G0   K0   M0   M5

SPECTRAL TYPE

STELLAR SPECTRAL ABSORPTION LINES

Calcium line   Hydrogen
gamma line   Hydrogen
beta line   Helium line   Sodium
lines   Hydrogen
alpha line

STAR OF SPECTRAL
TYPE A (e.g., SIRIUS)

STAR OF SPECTRAL
TYPE G (e.g., THE SUN)

Hydrogen
beta line   Magnesium
lines   Sodium
lines   Hydrogen
alpha line

Small stars

REGION OF STAR FORMATION IN ORION

SMALL STARS HAVE A MASS of up to about one and a half times that of the Sun. They begin to form when a region of higher density in a nebula condenses into a huge globule of gas and dust that contracts under its own gravity. Within a globule, regions of condensing matter heat up and begin to glow, forming protostars. If a protostar contains enough matter, the central temperature reaches about 8 million °C. At this temperature, nuclear reactions in which hydrogen fuses to form helium can start. This process releases energy, which prevents the star from contracting further and also causes it to shine; it is now a main sequence star. A star of about one solar mass remains on the main sequence for about 10 billion years, until much of the hydrogen in the star's core has been converted into helium. The helium core then contracts, and nuclear reactions continue in a shell around the core. The core becomes hot enough for helium to fuse to form carbon, while the outer layers of the star expand and cool. The expanding star is known as a red giant. When the helium in the core runs out, the outer layers of the star may be blown away as an expanding gas shell called a planetary nebula. The remaining core (about 80 per cent of the original star) is now in its final stages. It becomes a white dwarf star that gradually cools and dims. When it finally stops shining altogether, the dead star will become a black dwarf.

STRUCTURE OF A MAIN SEQUENCE STAR

Core containing hydrogen fusing to form helium

Radiative zone

Convective zone

Surface temperature about 5,500°C

Core temperature about 15 million °C

STRUCTURE OF A NEBULA

Young main sequence star

Dense region of dust and gas (mainly hydrogen) condensing under gravity to form globules

Hot, ionized hydrogen gas emitting red light due to being stimulated by radiation from hot young stars

Dark globule of dust and gas (mainly hydrogen) contracting to form protostars

LIFE OF A SMALL STAR OF ABOUT ONE SOLAR MASS

Cool cloud of gas (mainly hydrogen) and dust

Dense globule condensing to form protostars

NEBULA

Glowing ball of gas (mainly hydrogen)

Natal cocoon (shell of dust blown away by radiation from protostar)

PROTOSTAR
Duration: 50 million years

About 1.4 million km

Star producing energy by nuclear fusion in core

MAIN SEQUENCE STAR
Duration: 10 billion years

STRUCTURE OF A RED GIANT

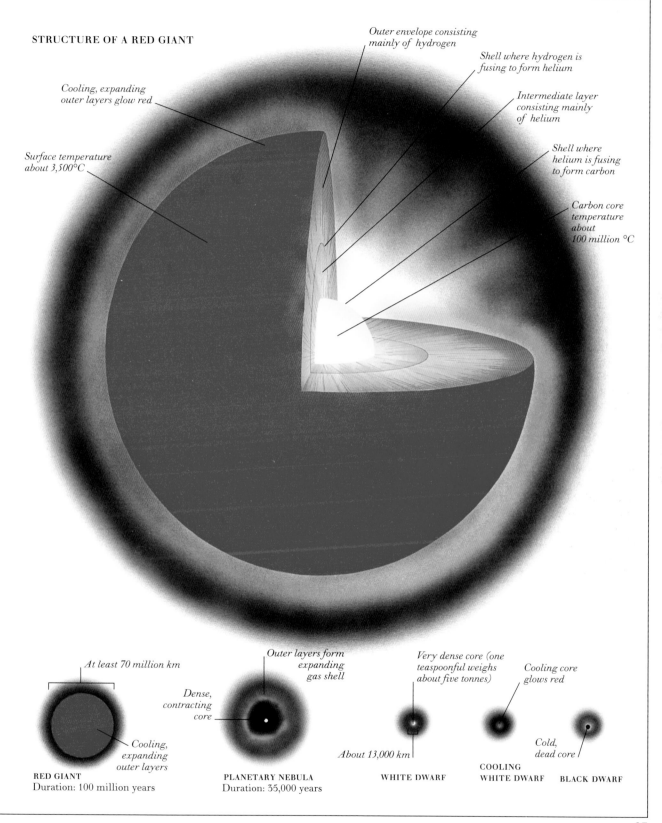

Outer envelope consisting
mainly of hydrogen

Shell where hydrogen is
fusing to form helium

Intermediate layer
consisting mainly
of helium

Shell where
helium is fusing
to form carbon

Carbon core
temperature
about
100 million °C

Cooling, expanding
outer layers glow red

Surface temperature
about 3,500°C

At least 70 million km

Cooling,
expanding
outer layers

RED GIANT
Duration: 100 million years

Outer layers form
expanding
gas shell

Dense,
contracting
core

PLANETARY NEBULA
Duration: 35,000 years

Very dense core (one
teaspoonful weighs
about five tonnes)

About 13,000 km

WHITE DWARF

Cooling core
glows red

Cold,
dead core

COOLING
WHITE DWARF

BLACK DWARF

Massive stars

MASSIVE STARS HAVE A MASS AT LEAST THREE TIMES that of the Sun, and some stars are as massive as about 50 Suns. A massive star evolves in a similar way to a small star until it reaches the main sequence stage (see pp. 24-25). During its life as a main sequence star, it shines steadily until the hydrogen in its core has fused to form helium. This process takes billions of years in a small star, but only millions of years in a massive star. A massive star then becomes a red supergiant, which initially consists of a helium core surrounded by outer layers of cooling, expanding gas. Over the next few million years, a series of nuclear reactions form different elements in shells around an iron core. The core eventually collapses in less than a second, causing a massive explosion called a supernova, in which a shock wave blows away the outer layers of the star. Supernovae shine brighter than an entire galaxy for a short time. Sometimes, the core survives the supernova explosion. If the surviving core is between about one and a half and three solar masses, it contracts to become a tiny, dense neutron star. If the core is greater than three solar masses, it contracts to become a black hole (see pp. 28-29).

SUPERNOVA

TARANTULA NEBULA BEFORE
SUPERNOVA

STRUCTURE
OF A RED SUPERGIANT

Outer envelope consisting
mainly of hydrogen

Layer consisting
mainly of helium

Layer consisting
mainly of carbon

Layer consisting
mainly of oxygen

Layer consisting
mainly of silicon

Shell of hydrogen
fusing to form
helium

Shell of helium
fusing to form
carbon

Shell of carbon
fusing to form
oxygen

Shell of oxygen fusing
to form silicon

Shell of silicon fusing
to form iron core

Surface temperature
about 3,000°C

Cooling, expanding
outer layers glow red

Core of mainly iron at a
temperature of 3-5 billion °C

LIFE OF A MASSIVE STAR OF
ABOUT 10 SOLAR MASSES

Dense globule
condensing to
form protostars

Cool cloud of gas
(mainly hydrogen)
and dust

NEBULA

Glowing
ball of gas
(mainly hydrogen)

Natal cocoon (shell
of dust blown away
by radiation from
protostar)

PROTOSTAR
Duration: a few hundred
thousand years

Star producing
energy by nuclear
fusion in
core

About 3 million km

MAIN SEQUENCE STAR
Duration: 10 million years

FEATURES OF A SUPERNOVA

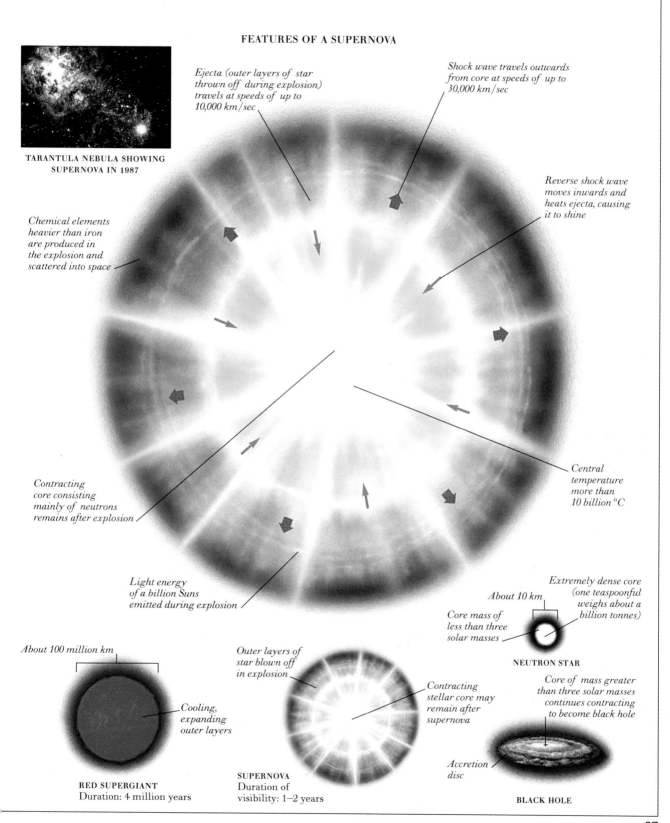

TARANTULA NEBULA SHOWING
SUPERNOVA IN 1987

*Ejecta (outer layers of star
thrown off during explosion)
travels at speeds of up to
10,000 km/sec*

*Shock wave travels outwards
from core at speeds of up to
30,000 km/sec*

*Reverse shock wave
moves inwards and
heats ejecta, causing
it to shine*

*Chemical elements
heavier than iron
are produced in
the explosion and
scattered into space*

*Central
temperature
more than
10 billion °C*

*Contracting
core consisting
mainly of neutrons
remains after explosion*

*Light energy
of a billion Suns
emitted during explosion*

*Extremely dense core
(one teaspoonful
weighs about a
billion tonnes)*

About 10 km

*Core mass of
less than three
solar masses*

NEUTRON STAR

About 100 million km

*Cooling,
expanding
outer layers*

*Outer layers of
star blown off
in explosion*

*Contracting
stellar core may
remain after
supernova*

*Core of mass greater
than three solar masses
continues contracting
to become black hole*

*Accretion
disc*

RED SUPERGIANT
Duration: 4 million years

SUPERNOVA
Duration of
visibility: 1–2 years

BLACK HOLE

27

Neutron stars and black holes

NEUTRON STARS AND BLACK HOLES form from the stellar cores that remain after stars have exploded as supernovae (see pp. 26-27). If the remaining core is between about one and a half and three solar masses, it contracts to form a neutron star. If the remaining core is greater than about three solar masses, it contracts to form a black hole. Neutron stars are typically only about 10 kilometres in diameter and consist almost entirely of subatomic particles called neutrons. Such stars are so dense that a teaspoonful would weigh about a billion tonnes. Neutron stars are observed as pulsars, so-called because they rotate rapidly and emit two beams of radio waves, which sweep across the sky and are detected as short pulses. Black holes are characterized by their extremely strong gravity, which is so powerful that not even light can escape; as a result, black holes are invisible. However, they can be detected if they have a close companion star. The gravity of the black hole pulls gas from the other star, forming an accretion disc that spirals around the black hole at high speed, heating up and emitting radiation. Eventually, the matter spirals in to cross the event horizon (the boundary of the black hole), thereby disappearing from the visible Universe.

Nebula of gas and dust surrounds pulsar

Rapidly rotating pulsar

Beam of radiation from pulsar

X-RAY IMAGE OF PULSAR AND CENTRAL REGION OF CRAB NEBULA (SUPERNOVA REMNANT)

PULSAR (ROTATING NEUTRON STAR)

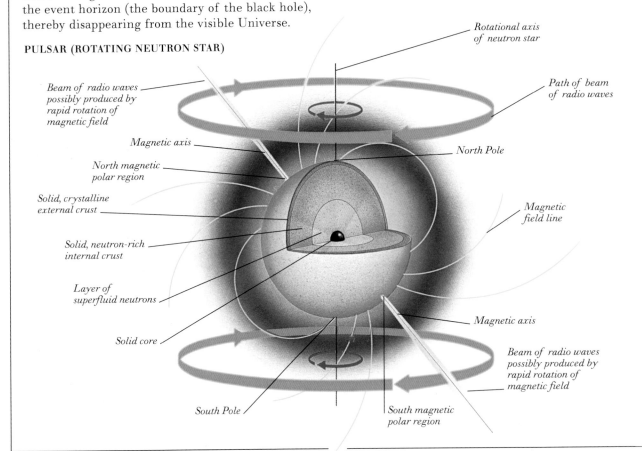

Rotational axis of neutron star

Beam of radio waves possibly produced by rapid rotation of magnetic field

Path of beam of radio waves

Magnetic axis

North Pole

North magnetic polar region

Solid, crystalline external crust

Magnetic field line

Solid, neutron-rich internal crust

Layer of superfluid neutrons

Solid core

Magnetic axis

Beam of radio waves possibly produced by rapid rotation of magnetic field

South Pole

South magnetic polar region

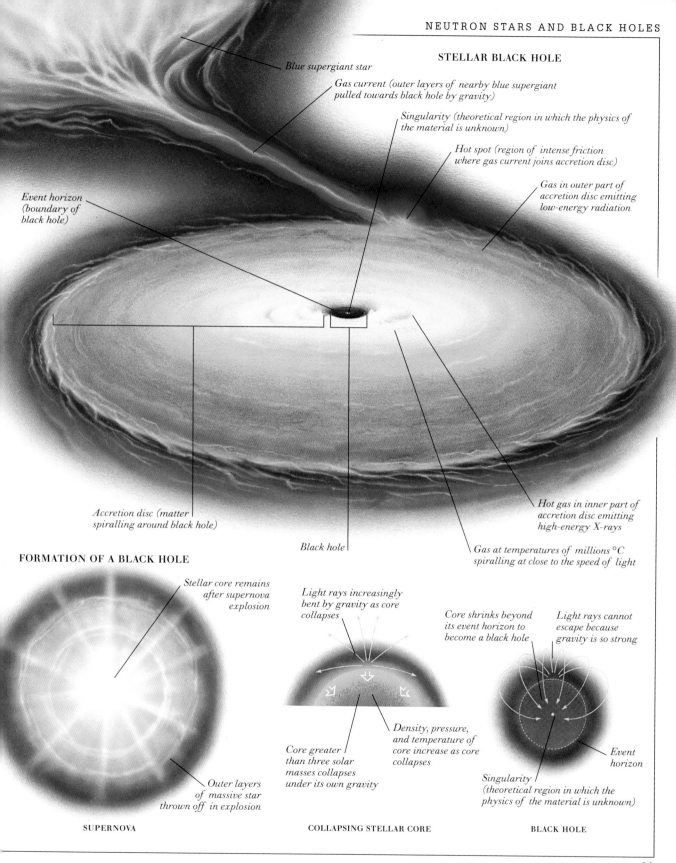

STELLAR BLACK HOLE

Blue supergiant star

Gas current (outer layers of nearby blue supergiant pulled towards black hole by gravity)

Singularity (theoretical region in which the physics of the material is unknown)

Hot spot (region of intense friction where gas current joins accretion disc)

Gas in outer part of accretion disc emitting low-energy radiation

Event horizon (boundary of black hole)

Accretion disc (matter spiralling around black hole)

Black hole

Hot gas in inner part of accretion disc emitting high-energy X-rays

Gas at temperatures of millions °C spiralling at close to the speed of light

FORMATION OF A BLACK HOLE

Stellar core remains after supernova explosion

Light rays increasingly bent by gravity as core collapses

Core shrinks beyond its event horizon to become a black hole

Light rays cannot escape because gravity is so strong

Outer layers of massive star thrown off in explosion

Core greater than three solar masses collapses under its own gravity

Density, pressure, and temperature of core increase as core collapses

Singularity (theoretical region in which the physics of the material is unknown)

Event horizon

SUPERNOVA

COLLAPSING STELLAR CORE

BLACK HOLE

The Solar System

THE SUN

THE SOLAR SYSTEM consists of a central star (the Sun) and the bodies that orbit it. These bodies include eight planets and their more than 160 known moons; dwarf planets; Kuiper Belt objects; asteroids; comets; and meteoroids. The Solar System also contains interplanetary gas and dust. The planets fall into two groups: four small rocky planets near the Sun (Mercury, Venus, Earth, and Mars); and four planets further out, the giants (Jupiter, Saturn, Uranus, and Neptune). Between the rocky planets and giants is the asteroid belt, which contains thousands of chunks of rock orbiting the Sun. Beyond Neptune is the Kuiper Belt and, more distant, the Oort Cloud. Most of the bodies in the planetary part of the Solar System move around the Sun in elliptical orbits located in a thin disc around the Sun's equator. All the planets orbit the Sun in the same direction (anticlockwise when viewed from above) and all but Venus and Uranus also spin about their axes in this direction. Moons also spin as they, in turn, orbit their planets. The entire Solar System orbits the centre of our galaxy, the Milky Way (see pp. 14-15).

PLANETARY ORBIT (EXAGGERATED)

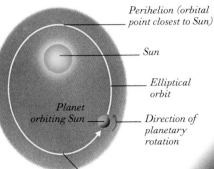

Perihelion (orbital point closest to Sun)

Sun

Elliptical orbit

Planet orbiting Sun

Direction of planetary rotation

Aphelion (orbital point furthest from Sun)

Aphelion of Neptune: 4,545 million km

ORBITS OF INNER PLANETS

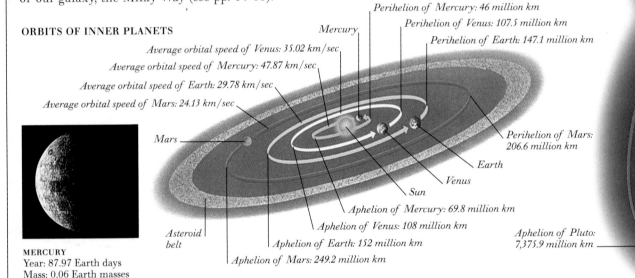

Average orbital speed of Venus: 35.02 km/sec

Average orbital speed of Mercury: 47.87 km/sec

Average orbital speed of Earth: 29.78 km/sec

Average orbital speed of Mars: 24.13 km/sec

Mars

Mercury

Perihelion of Mercury: 46 million km

Perihelion of Venus: 107.5 million km

Perihelion of Earth: 147.1 million km

Perihelion of Mars: 206.6 million km

Earth

Venus

Sun

Aphelion of Mercury: 69.8 million km

Aphelion of Venus: 108 million km

Aphelion of Pluto: 7,375.9 million km

Asteroid belt

Aphelion of Earth: 152 million km

Aphelion of Mars: 249.2 million km

MERCURY
Year: 87.97 Earth days
Mass: 0.06 Earth masses
Diameter: 4,878 km

VENUS
Year: 224.7 Earth days
Mass: 0.81 Earth masses
Diameter: 12,103 km

EARTH
Year: 365.26 days
Mass: 1 Earth mass
Diameter: 12,756 km

MARS
Year: 1.88 Earth years
Mass: 0.11 Earth masses
Diameter: 6,786 km

JUPITER
Year: 11.87 Earth years
Mass: 317.83 Earth masses
Diameter: 142,984 km

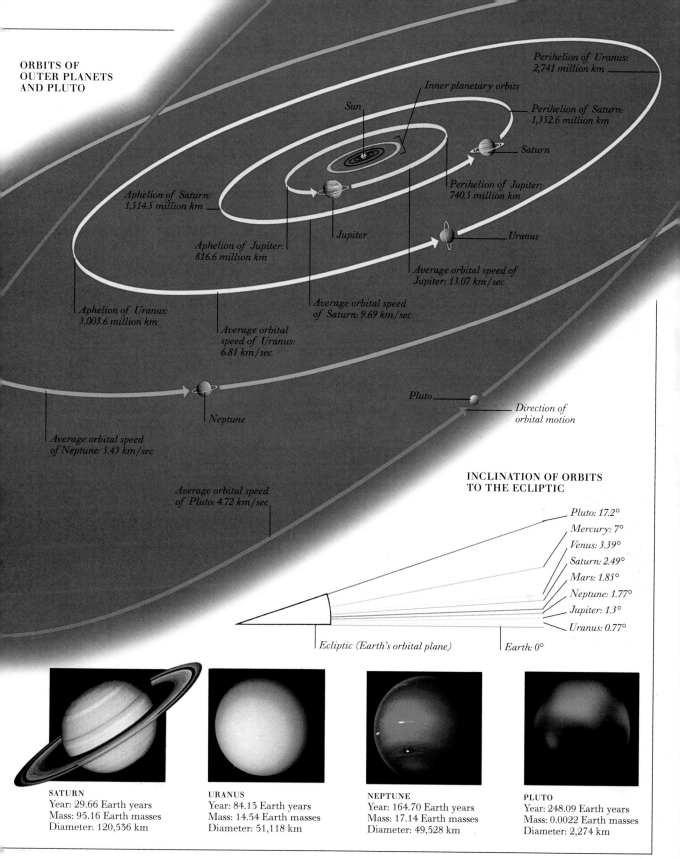

ORBITS OF OUTER PLANETS AND PLUTO

Perihelion of Uranus: 2,741 million km

Inner planetary orbits

Sun

Perihelion of Saturn: 1,352.6 million km

Saturn

Perihelion of Jupiter: 740.5 million km

Aphelion of Saturn: 1,514.5 million km

Jupiter

Uranus

Aphelion of Jupiter: 816.6 million km

Average orbital speed of Jupiter: 13.07 km/sec

Aphelion of Uranus: 3,003.6 million km

Average orbital speed of Saturn 9.69 km/sec

Average orbital speed of Uranus: 6.81 km/sec

Pluto

Direction of orbital motion

Neptune

Average orbital speed of Neptune: 5.43 km/sec

INCLINATION OF ORBITS TO THE ECLIPTIC

Average orbital speed of Pluto: 4.72 km/sec

Pluto: 17.2°
Mercury: 7°
Venus: 3.39°
Saturn: 2.49°
Mars: 1.85°
Neptune: 1.77°
Jupiter: 1.3°
Uranus: 0.77°

Ecliptic (Earth's orbital plane)   *Earth: 0°*

SATURN
Year: 29.66 Earth years
Mass: 95.16 Earth masses
Diameter: 120,536 km

URANUS
Year: 84.13 Earth years
Mass: 14.54 Earth masses
Diameter: 51,118 km

NEPTUNE
Year: 164.70 Earth years
Mass: 17.14 Earth masses
Diameter: 49,528 km

PLUTO
Year: 248.09 Earth years
Mass: 0.0022 Earth masses
Diameter: 2,274 km

The Sun

THE SUN IS THE STAR AT THE CENTRE of the Solar System. It is about five billion years old and will continue to shine as it does now for about another five billion years. The Sun is a yellow main sequence star (see pp. 22-23) about 1.4 million kilometres in diameter. It consists almost entirely of hydrogen and helium. In the Sun's core, hydrogen is converted to helium by nuclear fusion, releasing energy in the process. The energy travels from the core, through the radiative and convective zones, to the photosphere (visible surface), where it leaves the Sun in the form of heat and light. On the photosphere there are often dark, relatively cool areas called sunspots, which usually appear in pairs or groups and are caused by the cooling effect of the magnetic field. Other types of solar activity are flares, which are usually associated with sunspots, and prominences. Flares are sudden discharges of high-energy radiation and atomic particles. Prominences are huge loops or filaments of gas extending into the solar atmosphere; some last for hours, others for months. Beyond the photosphere is the chromosphere (inner atmosphere) and the extremely rarified corona (outer atmosphere), which extends millions of kilometres into space. Tiny particles that escape from the corona give rise to the solar wind, which streams through space at hundreds of kilometres per second. The chromosphere and corona can be seen from Earth when the Sun is totally eclipsed by the Moon.

SOLAR
PHOTOSPHERE

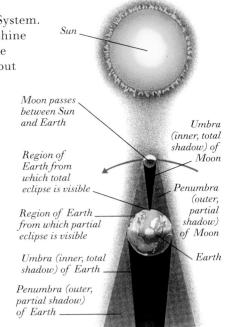

Sun

Moon passes
between Sun
and Earth

Umbra
(inner, total
shadow) of
Moon

Region of
Earth from
which total
eclipse is visible

Penumbra
(outer,
partial
shadow)
of Moon

Region of Earth
from which partial
eclipse is visible

Earth

Umbra (inner, total
shadow) of Earth

Penumbra (outer,
partial shadow)
of Earth

SURFACE FEATURES

Gas loop (looped
prominence)

Prominence (jet of gas at
edge of Sun's disc up to
hundreds of thousands of
kilometres high)

Spicule
(vertical
jet of gas)

Photosphere
(visible surface)

Chromosphere
(inner atmosphere)

TOTAL SOLAR ECLIPSE

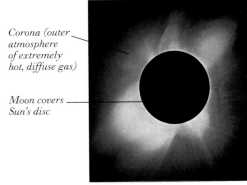

Corona (outer
atmosphere
of extremely
hot, diffuse gas)

Moon covers
Sun's disc

SUNSPOTS

Granulated surface
of Sun

Penumbra
(lighter, outer region)
containing radial fibrils

Umbra (darker, inner
region) temperature
about 2,700°C

Photosphere
temperature
about 5,500°C

EXTERNAL FEATURES AND
INTERNAL STRUCTURE OF THE SUN

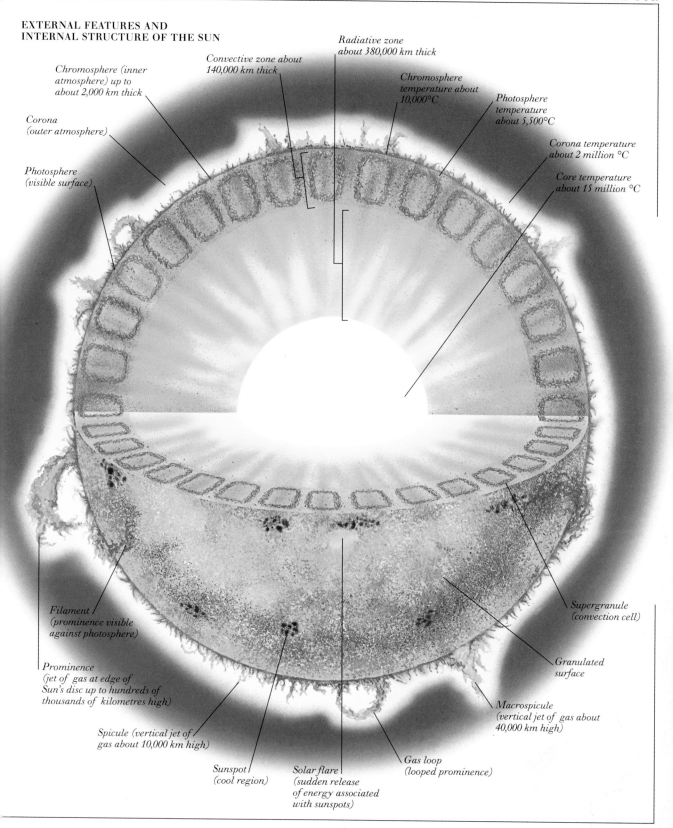

Chromosphere (inner atmosphere) up to about 2,000 km thick

Convective zone about 140,000 km thick

Radiative zone about 380,000 km thick

Chromosphere temperature about 10,000°C

Photosphere temperature about 5,500°C

Corona temperature about 2 million °C

Core temperature about 15 million °C

Corona (outer atmosphere)

Photosphere (visible surface)

Filament (prominence visible against photosphere)

Prominence (jet of gas at edge of Sun's disc up to hundreds of thousands of kilometres high)

Spicule (vertical jet of gas about 10,000 km high)

Sunspot (cool region)

Solar flare (sudden release of energy associated with sunspots)

Gas loop (looped prominence)

Macrospicule (vertical jet of gas about 40,000 km high)

Granulated surface

Supergranule (convection cell)

Mercury

MERCURY

MERCURY IS THE NEAREST PLANET to the Sun, orbiting at an average distance of about 58 million kilometres. Because Mercury is the closest planet to the Sun, it moves faster than any other planet, travelling at an average speed of nearly 48 kilometres per second and completing an orbit in just under 88 days. Mercury is very small (only 40 per cent bigger than the Moon) and rocky. Most of the surface has been heavily cratered by the impact of meteorites, although there are also smooth, sparsely cratered lava-covered plains. The Caloris Basin is the largest crater, measuring about 1,300 kilometres across. It is thought to have been formed when a 60-kilometre-diameter asteroid hit the planet, and is surrounded by concentric rings of mountains thrown up by the impact. The surface also has many cliff-like ridges (called rupes) that are thought to have been formed when the hot core of the young planet cooled and shrank about four billion years ago, buckling the planet's surface in the process. The planet rotates about its axis very slowly, taking nearly 59 Earth days to complete one rotation. As a result, a solar day (sunrise to sunrise) on Mercury is about 176 Earth days – twice as long as the 88-day Mercurian year. Mercury has extreme surface temperatures, ranging from a maximum of 430°C on the sunlit side to -170°C on the dark side. At nightfall, the temperature drops very quickly because the planet's atmosphere is almost non-existent. It consists only of minute amounts of helium and hydrogen captured from the solar wind, plus traces of other gases.

TILT AND ROTATION OF MERCURY

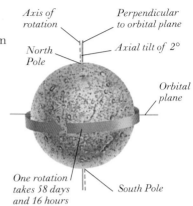

Axis of rotation

Perpendicular to orbital plane

North Pole

Axial tilt of 2°

Orbital plane

One rotation takes 58 days and 16 hours

South Pole

DEGAS AND BRONTË (RAY CRATERS)

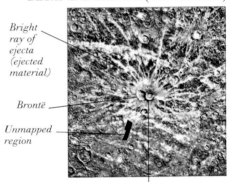

Bright ray of ejecta (ejected material)

Brontë

Unmapped region

Degas with central peak

FORMATION OF A RAY CRATER

Debris thrown out by impact

Path of meteorite colliding with planet

Wall of rock thrown up around crater

Impact forms saucer-shaped crater

Fractured rock

METEORITE IMPACT

Path of rocky ejecta (ejected material)

Ejecta forms secondary craters

Loose debris on crater floor

SECONDARY CRATERING

Wall of rock forms ring of mountains

Ray of ejecta (ejected material)

Small secondary crater

Loose ejected rock

Central mountain rings form if floor of large crater recoils from meteorite impact

Falling debris forms ridges on side of wall

RAY CRATER

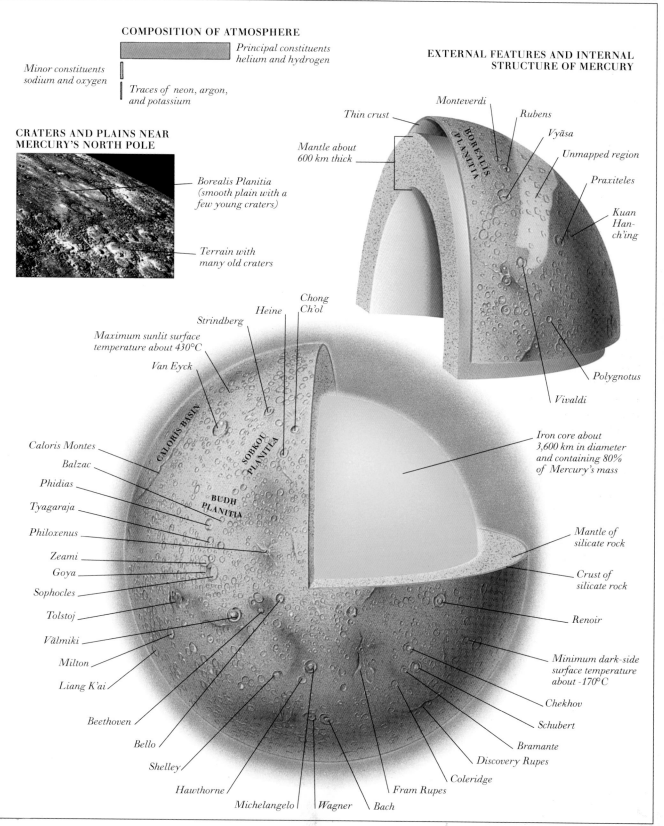

COMPOSITION OF ATMOSPHERE

Principal constituents helium and hydrogen

Minor constituents sodium and oxygen

Traces of neon, argon, and potassium

CRATERS AND PLAINS NEAR MERCURY'S NORTH POLE

Borealis Planitia (smooth plain with a few young craters)

Terrain with many old craters

EXTERNAL FEATURES AND INTERNAL STRUCTURE OF MERCURY

Thin crust

Mantle about 600 km thick

Monteverdi

Rubens

Vyāsa

Unmapped region

Praxiteles

Kuan Han-ch'ing

BOREALIS PLANITIA

Polygnotus

Vivaldi

Iron core about 3,600 km in diameter and containing 80% of Mercury's mass

Mantle of silicate rock

Crust of silicate rock

Renoir

Minimum dark-side surface temperature about -170°C

Chekhov

Schubert

Bramante

Discovery Rupes

Coleridge

Fram Rupes

Bach

Wagner

Michelangelo

Hawthorne

Shelley

Bello

Beethoven

Liang K'ai

Milton

Vālmiki

Tolstoj

Sophocles

Goya

Zeami

Philoxenus

Tyagaraja

Phidias

Balzac

Caloris Montes

Maximum sunlit surface temperature about 430°C

Van Eyck

Strindberg

Heine

Chong Ch'ol

CALORIS BASIN

SOBKOU PLANITIA

BUDH PLANITIA

Venus

RADAR IMAGE OF VENUS

VENUS IS A ROCKY PLANET and the second planet from the Sun. Venus spins slowly backwards as it orbits the Sun, causing its rotational period to be the longest in the Solar System, at about 243 Earth days. It is slightly smaller than Earth and probably has a similar internal structure, consisting of a semi-solid metal core, surrounded by a rocky mantle and crust. Venus is the brightest object in the sky after the Sun and Moon because its clouds reflect sunlight strongly. The main component of the atmosphere is carbon dioxide, which traps heat in a greenhouse effect far stronger than that on Earth. As a result, Venus is the hottest planet, with a maximum surface temperature of about 480°C. The thick cloud layers contain droplets of sulphuric acid and are driven around the planet by winds at speeds of up to 360 kilometres per hour. Although the planet takes 243 Earth days to rotate once, the high-speed winds cause the clouds to circle the planet in only four Earth days. The high temperature, acidic clouds, and enormous atmospheric pressure (about 90 times greater at the surface than that on Earth) make the environment extremely hostile. However, space probes have managed to land on Venus and photograph its dry, dusty surface. The Venusian surface has also been mapped by probes with radar equipment that can "see" through the cloud layers. Such radar maps reveal a terrain with craters, mountains, volcanoes, and areas where craters have been covered by plains of solidified volcanic lava. There are two large highland regions called Aphrodite Terra and Ishtar Terra.

TILT AND ROTATION OF VENUS

Axis of rotation

Perpendicular to orbital plane

Axial tilt of 2°

North Pole

Orbital plane

One rotation takes 243 days and 14 minutes

South Pole

CLOUD FEATURES

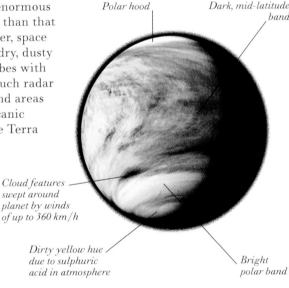

Polar hood

Dark, mid-latitude band

Cloud features swept around planet by winds of up to 360 km/h

Dirty yellow hue due to sulphuric acid in atmosphere

Bright polar band

VENUSIAN CRATERS

Danilova

Ejecta (ejected material)

Central peak

Howe

FALSE-COLOUR RADAR MAP OF THE SURFACE OF VENUS

Metis Regio

Maxwell Montes

Bell Regio

Tethus Regio

Sedna Planitia

Eisila Regio

Guinevere Planitia

Phoebe Regio

Alpha Regio

Themis Regio

Lavinia Planitia

Helen Planitia

ISHTAR TERRA

APHRODITE TERRA

Atalanta Planitia

Leda Planitia

Tellus Regio

Niobe Planitia

Ovda Regio

Thetis Regio

Aino Planitia

Lada Terra

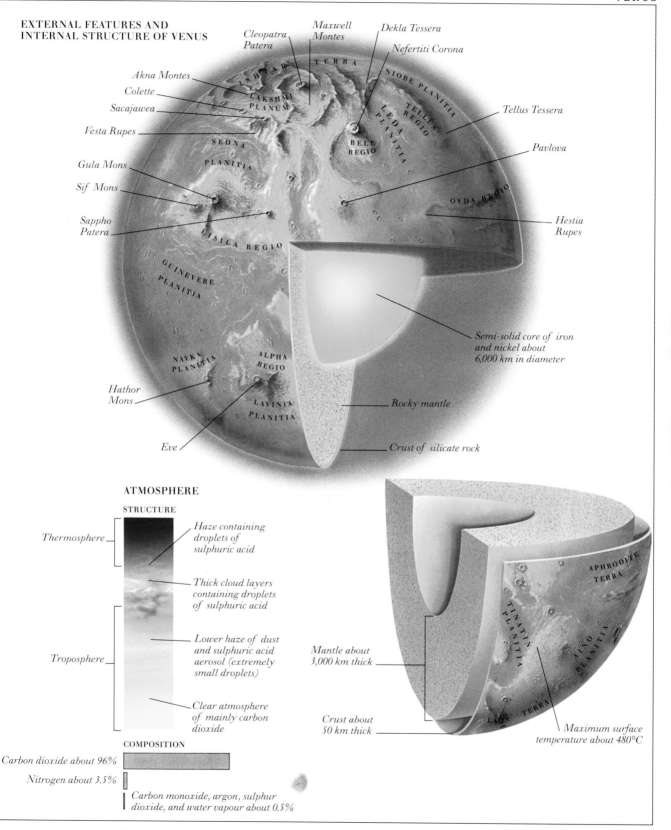

EXTERNAL FEATURES AND INTERNAL STRUCTURE OF VENUS

Cleopatra Patera
Maxwell Montes
Dekla Tessera
Nefertiti Corona
Akna Montes
Colette
Sacajawea
Vesta Rupes
Gula Mons
Sif Mons
Sappho Patera
Hathor Mons
Eve

ISHTAR TERRA
LAKSHMI PLANUM
SEDNA PLANITIA
EISILA REGIO
GUINEVERE PLANITIA
NAVKA PLANITIA
ALPHA REGIO
LAVINIA PLANITIA

NIOBE PLANITIA
TELLUS REGIO
LEDA PLANITIA
BELL REGIO
OVDA REGIO

Tellus Tessera
Pavlova
Hestia Rupes

Semi-solid core of iron and nickel about 6,000 km in diameter
Rocky mantle
Crust of silicate rock

ATMOSPHERE

STRUCTURE

Thermosphere

Troposphere

Haze containing droplets of sulphuric acid

Thick cloud layers containing droplets of sulphuric acid

Lower haze of dust and sulphuric acid aerosol (extremely small droplets)

Clear atmosphere of mainly carbon dioxide

COMPOSITION

Carbon dioxide about 96%

Nitrogen about 3.5%

Carbon monoxide, argon, sulphur dioxide, and water vapour about 0.5%

APHRODITE TERRA
TINATIN PLANITIA
LADA TERRA
AINO PLANITIA

Mantle about 3,000 km thick

Crust about 50 km thick

Maximum surface temperature about 480°C

The Earth

THE EARTH

THE EARTH IS THE THIRD of the eight planets that orbit the Sun. It is the largest and densest rocky planet, and the only one known to support life. About 70 per cent of the Earth's surface is covered by water, which is not found in liquid form on the surface of any other planet. There are four main layers: the inner core, the outer core, the mantle, and the crust. At the heart of the planet the solid inner core has a temperature of about 6,600°C. The heat from this inner core causes material in the molten outer core and mantle to circulate in convection currents. It is thought that these convection currents generate the Earth's magnetic field, which extends into space as the magnetosphere. The Earth's atmosphere helps screen out some of the harmful radiation from the Sun, stops most meteoroids from reaching the planet's surface, and traps enough heat to prevent extremes of cold. The Earth has one natural satellite, the Moon, which is thought to have formed when a huge asteroid impacted Earth in the distant past.

TILT AND ROTATION OF THE EARTH

Axis of rotation

Axial tilt of 23.4°

North Pole

Orbital plane

South Pole

One rotation takes 23 hours and 56 minutes

Perpendicular to orbital plane

THE FORMATION OF THE EARTH

The heat of the collisions caused the planet to glow red

The cloud formed a disc of material around the young Sun's equator. The disc material stuck together to form planets

Micro-organisms began to photosynthesize, creating a build up of oxygen

4,600 MILLION YEARS AGO, THE SOLAR SYSTEM FORMED FROM A CLOUD OF ROCK, ICE, AND GAS

THE EARTH WAS FORMED FROM COLLIDING ROCKS

4,500 MILLION YEARS AGO THE SURFACE COOLED TO FORM THE CRUST

THE CONTINENTS BROKE UP AND REFORMED, GRADUALLY MOVING TO THEIR PRESENT POSITIONS

Solar wind enters atmosphere and produces aurora

Magnetosphere (region affected by magnetic field)

Solar wind (stream of electrically charged particles)

THE EARTH'S MAGNETOSPHERE

Axis of geographic poles

Axis of magnetic poles

Van Allen radiation belt

Earth

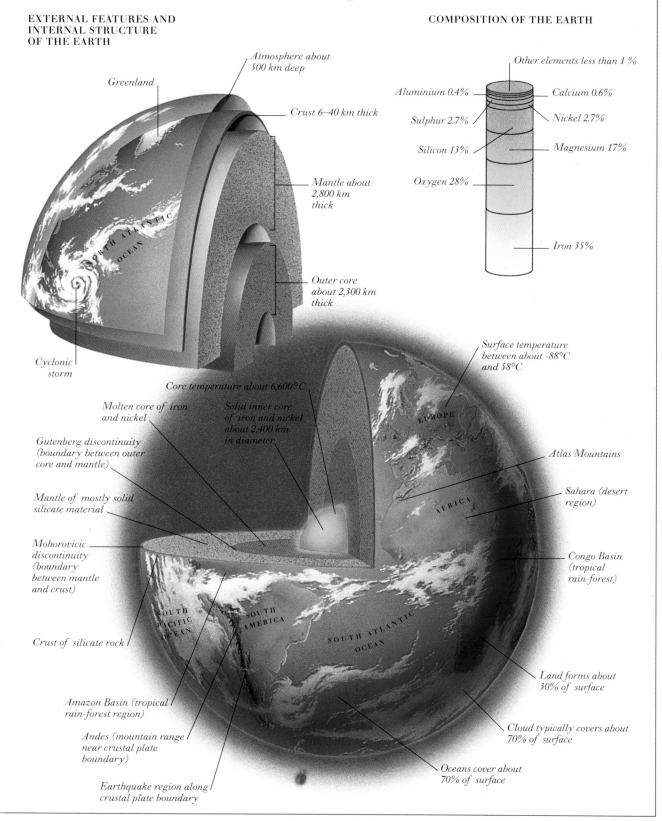

EXTERNAL FEATURES AND
INTERNAL STRUCTURE
OF THE EARTH

COMPOSITION OF THE EARTH

Atmosphere about
500 km deep

Greenland

Crust 6–40 km thick

Mantle about
2,800 km
thick

NORTH ATLANTIC
OCEAN

Outer core
about 2,300 km
thick

Cyclonic
storm

Other elements less than 1 %

Aluminium 0.4%

Calcium 0.6%

Sulphur 2.7%

Nickel 2.7%

Silicon 13%

Magnesium 17%

Oxygen 28%

Iron 35%

Surface temperature
between about -88°C
and 58°C

Core temperature about 6,600°C

Molten core of iron
and nickel

Solid inner core
of iron and nickel
about 2,400 km
in diameter

EUROPE

Atlas Mountains

Gutenberg discontinuity
(boundary between outer
core and mantle)

AFRICA

Sahara (desert
region)

Mantle of mostly solid
silicate material

Mohorovicic
discontinuity
(boundary
between mantle
and crust)

Congo Basin
(tropical
rain-forest)

SOUTH
PACIFIC
OCEAN

SOUTH
AMERICA

SOUTH ATLANTIC
OCEAN

Crust of silicate rock

Amazon Basin (tropical
rain-forest region)

Land forms about
30% of surface

Andes (mountain range
near crustal plate
boundary)

Cloud typically covers about
70% of surface

Earthquake region along
crustal plate boundary

Oceans cover about
70% of surface

The Moon

THE MOON FROM EARTH

THE MOON IS THE EARTH'S only natural satellite. It is relatively large for a moon, with a diameter of about 3,470 kilometres – just over a quarter that of the Earth. The Moon takes the same time to rotate on its axis as it takes to orbit the Earth (27.3 days), and so the same side (the near side) always faces us. However, the amount of the surface we can see – the phase of the Moon – depends on how much of the near side is in sunlight. The Moon is dry and barren, with negligible atmosphere and water. It consists mainly of solid rock, although its core may contain molten rock or iron. The surface is dusty, with highlands covered in craters caused by meteorite impacts, and lowlands in which large craters have been filled by solidified lava to form dark areas called maria or "seas". Maria occur mainly on the near side, which has a thinner crust than the far side. Many of the craters are rimmed by mountain ranges that form the crater walls and can be thousands of metres high.

TILT AND ROTATION OF THE MOON

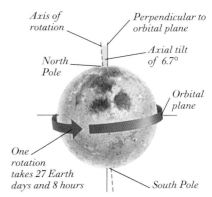

Axis of rotation

Perpendicular to orbital plane

North Pole

Axial tilt of 6.7°

Orbital plane

One rotation takes 27 Earth days and 8 hours

South Pole

CRATERS ON OCEANUS PROCELLARUM

Aristarchus

Cobra Head (head of Schröter's Valley)

Herodotus

NEAR SIDE OF THE MOON

De la Rue
Aristoteles
Aristillus
Plato
Archimedes
Montes Jura
Sinus Iridum
Bright rays of ejected material
Copernicus
Aristarchus
Kepler
Encke
Flamsteed
Fra Mauro
Grimaldi
Letronne
Gassendi
Mersenius
Pitatus
Schickard
Alphonsus
Bailly
Tycho
Clavius
Maginus

Hercules
Atlas
Montes Apenninus
Cleomedes
Macrobius
Julius Caesar
Langrenus
Vendelinus
Cyrillus
Petavius
Fracastorius
Furnerius
Catharina
Rupes Altai
Albategnius
Ptolemaeus
Arzachel
Walter
Stöfler
Deslandres

MARE FRIGORIS
MARE IMBRIUM
MARE SERENITATIS
MARE VAPORUM
MARE TRANQUILLITATIS
OCEANUS PROCELLARUM
MARE NUBIUM
MARE HUMORUM

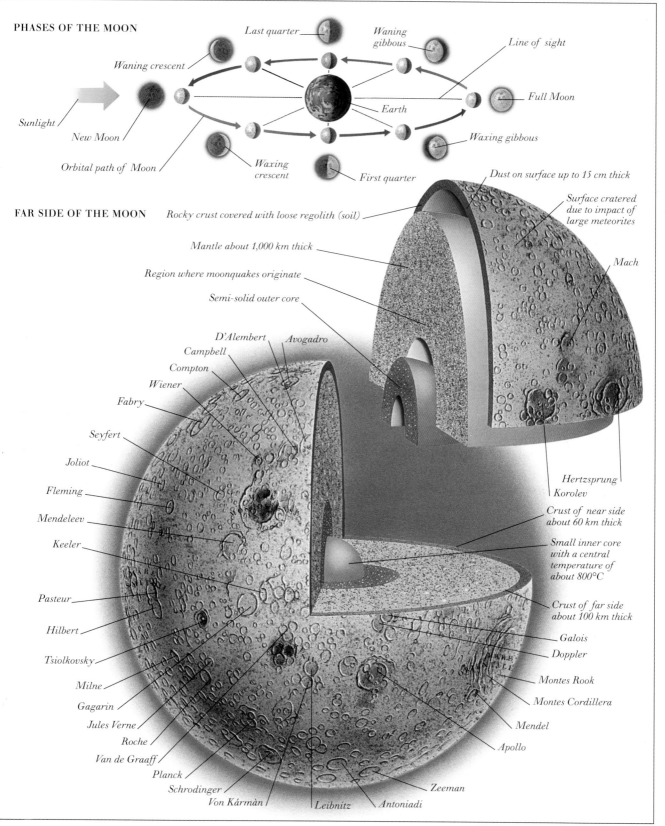

PHASES OF THE MOON

Last quarter

Waning gibbous

Waning crescent

Line of sight

Sunlight

New Moon

Earth

Full Moon

Orbital path of Moon

Waxing crescent

First quarter

Waxing gibbous

FAR SIDE OF THE MOON

Dust on surface up to 15 cm thick

Surface cratered due to impact of large meteorites

Rocky crust covered with loose regolith (soil)

Mantle about 1,000 km thick

Region where moonquakes originate

Semi-solid outer core

Mach

D'Alembert

Avogadro

Campbell

Compton

Wiener

Fabry

Seyfert

Joliot

Fleming

Mendeleev

Keeler

Hertzsprung

Korolev

Crust of near side about 60 km thick

Small inner core with a central temperature of about 800°C

Pasteur

Hilbert

Crust of far side about 100 km thick

Tsiolkovsky

Galois

Milne

Doppler

Gagarin

Montes Rook

Jules Verne

Montes Cordillera

Roche

Mendel

Van de Graaff

Apollo

Planck

Schrodinger

Zeeman

Von Kármàn

Leibnitz

Antoniadi

41

Mars

MARS

MARS, KNOWN AS THE RED PLANET, is the fourth planet from the Sun and the outermost rocky planet. In the 19th century, astronomers first observed what were thought to be signs of life on Mars. These signs included apparent canal-like lines on the surface, and dark patches that were thought to be vegetation. It is now known that the "canals" are an optical illusion, and the dark patches are areas where the red dust that covers most of the planet has been blown away. The fine dust particles are often whipped up by winds into dust storms that occasionally obscure almost all the surface. Residual fine dust in the atmosphere gives the Martian sky a pinkish hue. The northern hemisphere of Mars has many large plains formed of solidified volcanic lava, whereas the southern hemisphere has many craters and large impact basins. There are also several huge, extinct volcanoes, including Olympus Mons, which, at 600 kilometres across and 25 kilometres high, is the largest known volcano in the Solar System. The surface also has many canyons and branching channels. The canyons were formed by movements of the surface crust, but the channels are thought to have been formed by flowing water that has now dried up. The Martian atmosphere is much thinner than Earth's, with only a few clouds and morning mists. Mars has two tiny, irregularly shaped moons called Phobos and Deimos. Their small size indicates that they may be asteroids that have been captured by the gravity of Mars.

TILT AND ROTATION OF MARS

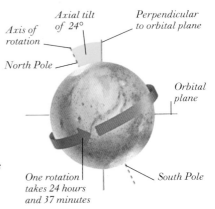

Axis of rotation

Axial tilt of 24°

Perpendicular to orbital plane

North Pole

Orbital plane

One rotation takes 24 hours and 37 minutes

South Pole

SURFACE FEATURES OF MARS

Bright water-ice fog

Fog in canyon about 20 km wide at end of Valles Marineris

Syria Planum

NOCTIS LABYRINTHUS (CANYON SYSTEM)

Summit caldera consisting of overlapping collapsed volcanic craters

Gentle slope produced by lava flow

Cloud formation

OLYMPUS MONS (EXTINCT SHIELD VOLCANO)

THE SURFACE OF MARS

Dark area where dust has been blown away by wind

South polar ice-cap

Surface covered with red-coloured iron oxide dust

MOONS OF MARS

PHOBOS
Average diameter: 22 km
Average distance from planet: 9,400 km

DEIMOS
Average diameter: 13 km
Average distance from planet: 23,500 km

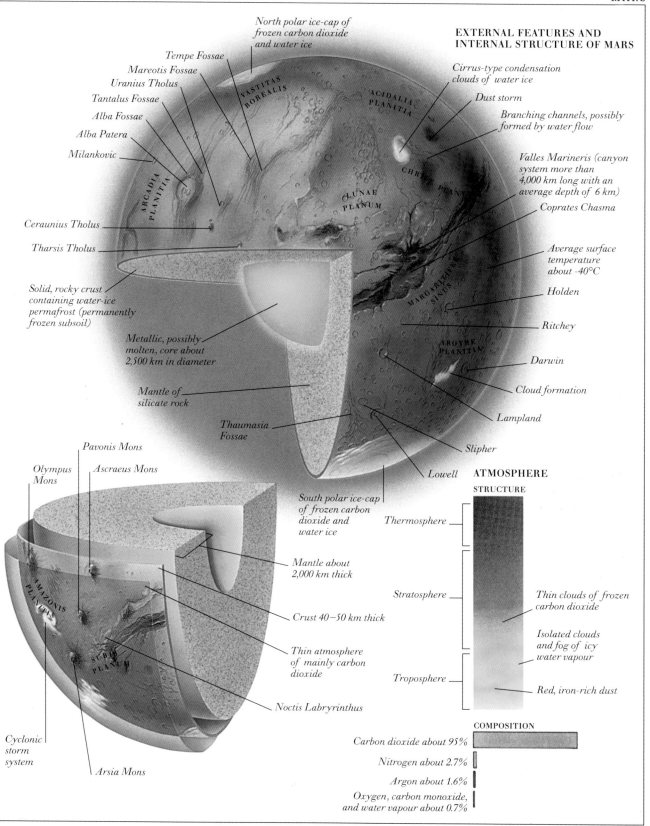

EXTERNAL FEATURES AND INTERNAL STRUCTURE OF MARS

North polar ice-cap of frozen carbon dioxide and water ice

Tempe Fossae

Mareotis Fossae

Uranius Tholus

Tantalus Fossae

Alba Fossae

Alba Patera

Milankovic

Ceraunius Tholus

Tharsis Tholus

Solid, rocky crust containing water-ice permafrost (permanently frozen subsoil)

Metallic, possibly molten, core about 2,500 km in diameter

Mantle of silicate rock

Thaumasia Fossae

VASTITAS BOREALIS

ACIDALIA PLANITIA

ARCADIA PLANITIA

LUNAE PLANUM

CHRYSE PLANITIA

MARGARITIFER SINUS

ARGYRE PLANITIA

Cirrus-type condensation clouds of water ice

Dust storm

Branching channels, possibly formed by water flow

Valles Marineris (canyon system more than 4,000 km long with an average depth of 6 km)

Coprates Chasma

Average surface temperature about -40°C

Holden

Ritchey

Darwin

Cloud formation

Lampland

Slipher

Lowell

South polar ice-cap of frozen carbon dioxide and water ice

Olympus Mons

Pavonis Mons

Ascraeus Mons

Mantle about 2,000 km thick

Crust 40−50 km thick

Thin atmosphere of mainly carbon dioxide

Noctis Labryrinthus

AMAZONIS PLANITIA

SYRIA PLANUM

Cyclonic storm system

Arsia Mons

ATMOSPHERE

STRUCTURE

Thermosphere

Stratosphere

Troposphere

Thin clouds of frozen carbon dioxide

Isolated clouds and fog of icy water vapour

Red, iron-rich dust

COMPOSITION

Carbon dioxide about 95%

Nitrogen about 2.7%

Argon about 1.6%

Oxygen, carbon monoxide, and water vapour about 0.7%

Jupiter

JUPITER

JUPITER IS THE FIFTH PLANET from the Sun and the innermost of the four giant planets. It is the largest and the most massive planet, with a diameter about 11 times that of the Earth and a mass about 2.5 times the combined mass of the seven other planets. Jupiter is thought to have a small rocky core surrounded by an inner mantle of metallic hydrogen (liquid hydrogen that acts like a metal). Outside the inner mantle is an outer mantle of liquid hydrogen and helium that merges into the gaseous atmosphere. Jupiter's rapid rate of rotation causes the clouds in its atmosphere to form belts and zones that encircle the planet parallel to the equator. Belts are dark, low-lying, relatively warm cloud layers, and zones are bright, high-altitude, cooler cloud layers. Within the belts and zones, turbulence causes the formation of cloud features such as white ovals and red spots, both of which are huge storm systems. The most prominent cloud feature is a storm called the Great Red Spot, which consists of a spiralling column of clouds three times wider than the Earth that rises about eight kilometres above the upper cloud layer. Jupiter has a thin, faint, main ring, inside which is a tenuous halo ring of tiny particles. Beyond the main ring's outer edge is a broad and faint two-part gossamer ring. There are 63 known Jovian moons. The four largest moons (called the Galileans) are Ganymede, Callisto, Io, and Europa. Ganymede and Callisto are cratered and icy. Europa is smooth and icy and is thought to have a subsurface water ocean. Io is covered in bright red, orange, and yellow splotches. This colouring is caused by sulphurous material from active volcanoes that shoot plumes of lava hundreds of kilometres above the surface.

TILT AND ROTATION OF JUPITER

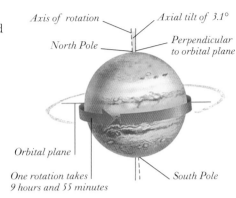

Axis of rotation

Axial tilt of 3.1°

North Pole

Perpendicular to orbital plane

Orbital plane

One rotation takes 9 hours and 55 minutes

South Pole

GREAT RED SPOT AND WHITE OVAL

Great Red Spot (anticyclonic storm system)

Red colour probably due to phosphorus

White oval (temporary anticyclonic storm system)

GALILEAN MOONS OF JUPITER

EUROPA
Diameter: 3,130 km
Average distance from planet: 670,900 km

CALLISTO
Diameter: 4,806 km
Average distance from planet: 1,883,000 km

GANYMEDE
Diameter: 5,268 km
Average distance from planet: 1,070,000 km

IO
Diameter: 3,642 km
Average distance from planet: 421,800 km

INNER RINGS OF JUPITER

Main ring

Halo ring

ATMOSPHERE

STRUCTURE

EXTERNAL FEATURES AND INTERNAL STRUCTURE OF JUPITER

Stratosphere

Troposphere

White clouds of ammonia crystals

Dark orange clouds of ammonium hydrosulphide crystals

Bluish clouds of water ice and water droplets

COMPOSITION

Hydrogen about 90%

Helium about 10%

Traces of ammonia, methane, and water vapour

Atmosphere of mainly hydrogen and helium

Outer mantle merging into atmosphere

Inner mantle about 30,000 km thick

Zone (high-pressure region of rising gases)

Red-coloured storm

Plume (trailing cloud)

High-altitude white cloud

North polar aurora

North Temperate Zone

North Temperate Belt

North Tropical Zone

North Equatorial Belt

Equatorial Zone

South Equatorial Belt

South Tropical Zone

South Temperate Belt

South Temperate Zone

Flash of lightning

Outer mantle of liquid hydrogen and helium

Inner mantle of metallic hydrogen

Rocky core about 28,000 km in diameter

Core temperature about 30,000°C

Belt (low-pressure region of sinking gases)

White oval (temporary anticyclonic storm system)

Great Red Spot (anticyclonic storm system)

Cloud-top temperature about -120°C

45

Saturn

SATURN IS THE SIXTH PLANET from the Sun. It is a gas giant almost as big as Jupiter, with an equatorial diameter of about 120,500 kilometres. Saturn is thought to consist of a small core of rock and ice surrounded by an inner mantle of metallic hydrogen (liquid hydrogen that acts like a metal). Outside the inner mantle is an outer mantle of liquid hydrogen that merges into a gaseous atmosphere. Saturn's clouds form belts and zones similar to those on Jupiter, but obscured by overlying haze. Storms and eddies, seen as red or white ovals, occur in the clouds. Saturn has an extremely thin but wide system of rings that is less than one kilometre thick but extends outwards to about 420,000 kilometres from the planet's surface. The main rings comprise thousands of narrow ringlets, each made of icy rock lumps that range in size from tiny particles to chunks several metres across. The D, E, and G rings are very faint, the F ring is brighter, and the A, B, and C rings are bright enough to be seen from Earth with binoculars. In 2009, a huge dust ring was discovered 6 kilometres (4 million miles) beyond the main system. Saturn has more than 60 known moons, some of which orbit inside the rings and are thought to exert a gravitational influence on the shapes of the rings. Unusually, seven of the moons are co-orbital – they share an orbit with another moon. Astronomers believe that such co-orbital moons may have originated from a single satellite that broke up.

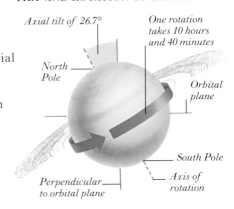

FALSE-COLOUR
IMAGE OF SATURN

TILT AND ROTATION OF SATURN

Axial tilt of 26.7°

One rotation takes 10 hours and 40 minutes

North Pole

Orbital plane

South Pole

Axis of rotation

Perpendicular to orbital plane

FALSE-COLOUR IMAGE OF SATURN'S CLOUD FEATURES

Ribbon-shaped striation caused by winds of up to 540 km/h

Oval (rotating storm system)

INNER RINGS OF SATURN

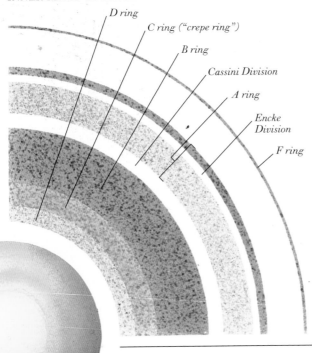

D ring

C ring ("crepe ring")

B ring

Cassini Division

A ring

Encke Division

F ring

MOONS OF SATURN

ENCELADUS
Diameter: 498 km
Average distance from planet: 238,000 km

TETHYS
Diameter: 1,066 km
Average distance from planet: 295,000 km

DIONE
Diameter: 1,123 km
Average distance from planet: 377,000 km

MIMAS
Diameter: 397 km
Average distance from planet: 186,000 km

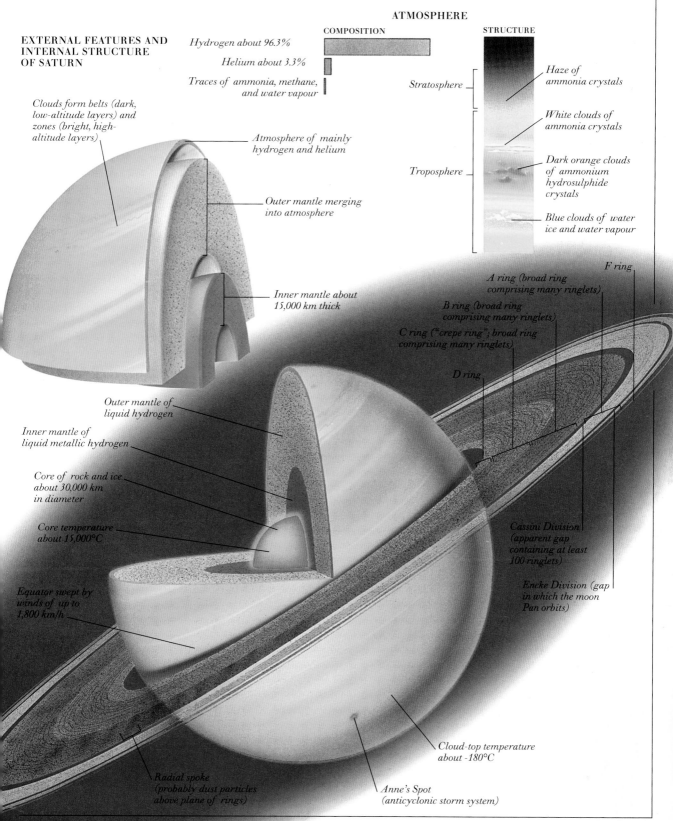

EXTERNAL FEATURES AND
INTERNAL STRUCTURE
OF SATURN

ATMOSPHERE

COMPOSITION

Hydrogen about 96.3%

Helium about 3.3%

Traces of ammonia, methane,
and water vapour

STRUCTURE

Stratosphere

Haze of
ammonia crystals

White clouds of
ammonia crystals

Troposphere

Dark orange clouds
of ammonium
hydrosulphide
crystals

Blue clouds of water
ice and water vapour

Clouds form belts (dark,
low-altitude layers) and
zones (bright, high-
altitude layers)

Atmosphere of mainly
hydrogen and helium

Outer mantle merging
into atmosphere

Inner mantle about
15,000 km thick

F ring

A ring (broad ring
comprising many ringlets)

B ring (broad ring
comprising many ringlets)

C ring ("crepe ring"; broad ring
comprising many ringlets)

D ring

Outer mantle of
liquid hydrogen

Inner mantle of
liquid metallic hydrogen

Core of rock and ice
about 30,000 km
in diameter

Core temperature
about 15,000°C

Cassini Division
(apparent gap
containing at least
100 ringlets)

Encke Division (gap
in which the moon
Pan orbits)

Equator swept by
winds of up to
1,800 km/h

Cloud-top temperature
about -180°C

Radial spoke
(probably dust particles
above plane of rings)

Anne's Spot
(anticyclonic storm system)

Uranus

FALSE-COLOUR
IMAGE OF URANUS

URANUS IS THE SEVENTH PLANET from the Sun
and the third largest, with a diameter of about
51,000 kilometres. It is thought to consist of
a dense mixture of different types of ice and
gas around a solid core. Its atmosphere contains
traces of methane, giving the planet a blue-green
hue, and the temperature at the cloud tops is
about -210°C. Uranus is the most featureless
planet to have been closely observed: only a
few icy clouds of methane have been seen so far. Uranus is unique
among the planets in that its axis of rotation lies close to its orbital
plane. As a result of its strongly tilted rotational axis, Uranus rolls on
its side along its orbital path around the Sun, whereas other planets spin
more or less upright. Uranus is encircled by main rings that consist of rocks
interspersed with dust lanes and too distant outer rings made of dust. The rings
contain some of the darkest matter in the Solar System and are extremely
narrow, making them difficult to detect: most of them are less than 10
kilometres wide, whereas most of Saturn's rings are thousands of kilometres in
width. There are 27 known Uranian moons, all of which are icy and most of
which are further out than the rings. The 13 inner moons are small and dark,
with diameters of less than 160 kilometres, and the five major moons are
between about 470 and 1,600 kilometres in diameter. The major moons have a
wide variety of surface features. Miranda has the most varied surface, with
cratered areas broken up by huge ridges and cliffs 20 kilometres high. Beyond
these are nine much more distant moons with diameters less than 150 km.

TILT AND ROTATION OF URANUS

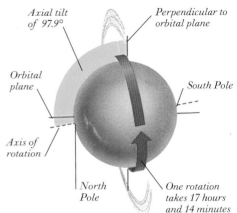

Axial tilt
of 97.9°

Perpendicular to
orbital plane

Orbital
plane

South Pole

Axis of
rotation

North
Pole

One rotation
takes 17 hours
and 14 minutes

MAJOR MOONS

MIRANDA
Diameter: 470 km
Average distance from
planet: 129,800 km

RINGS OF URANUS

Epsilon ring

Lambda ring

Delta ring

Gamma ring

Eta ring

Beta ring

Alpha ring

Rings 4 and 5

Ring 6

Zeta ring

RINGS AND DUST LANES

ARIEL
Diameter: 1,158 km
Average distance from
planet: 191,200 km

TITANIA
Diameter: 1,578 km
Average distance from
planet: 435,800 km

UMBRIEL
Diameter: 1,170 km
Average distance from
planet: 266,000 km

OBERON
Diameter: 1,523 km
Average distance from
planet: 583,600 km

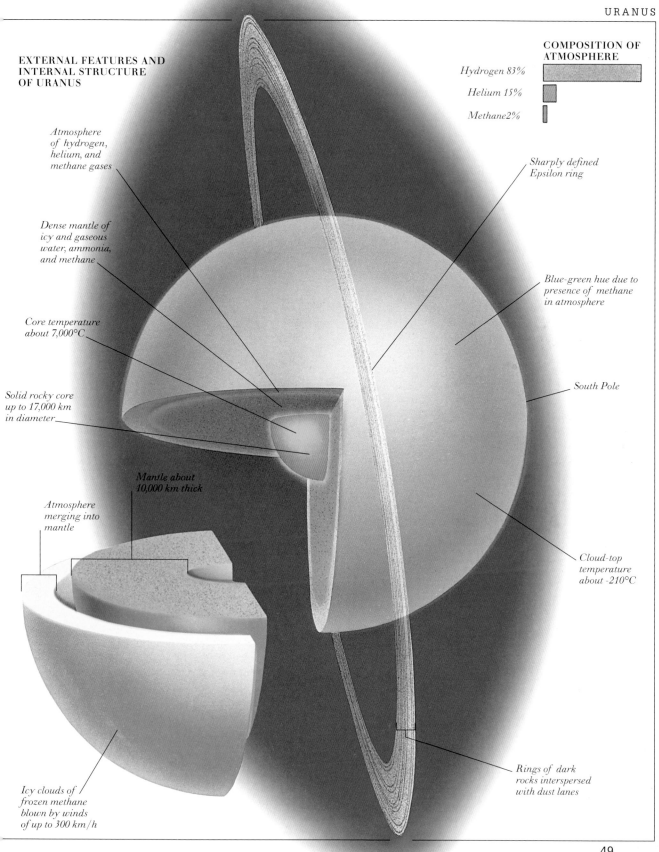

EXTERNAL FEATURES AND
INTERNAL STRUCTURE
OF URANUS

COMPOSITION OF
ATMOSPHERE

Hydrogen 83%

Helium 15%

Methane 2%

Atmosphere
of hydrogen,
helium, and
methane gases

Dense mantle of
icy and gaseous
water, ammonia,
and methane

Core temperature
about 7,000°C

Solid rocky core
up to 17,000 km
in diameter

Atmosphere
merging into
mantle

Mantle about
10,000 km thick

Icy clouds of
frozen methane
blown by winds
of up to 300 km/h

Sharply defined
Epsilon ring

Blue-green hue due to
presence of methane
in atmosphere

South Pole

Cloud-top
temperature
about -210°C

Rings of dark
rocks interspersed
with dust lanes

Neptune and Pluto

FALSE-COLOUR IMAGE OF NEPTUNE

NEPTUNE IS the furthest planet from the Sun, at an average distance of about 4,500 million kilometres. Neptune is the smallest of the giant planets and is thought to consist of a small rocky core surrounded by a mixture of liquids and gases. Several transient cloud features have been observed in its atmosphere. The largest of these were the Great Dark Spot, which was as wide as the Earth, the Small Dark Spot, and the Scooter. The Great and Small Dark Spots were huge storms that were swept around the planet by winds of about 2,000 kilometres per hour. The Scooter was a large area of cirrus cloud. Neptune has six tenuous rings and 13 known moons. Triton is the largest Neptunian moon and the coldest object in the Solar System, with a temperature of -240°C. Unlike most moons in the Solar System, Triton orbits its mother planet in the opposite direction to the planet's rotation. The region extending out from Neptune's orbit is populated by Kuiper Belt objects and dwarf planets. They make a dough-nut shaped belt called the Kuiper Belt. The Kuiper Belt objects are a mix of rock and ice, irregular in shape, and less than 1,000 kilometres across. The larger dwarf planets, which include Pluto, are almost round bodies. Pluto was the first object discovered beyond Neptune and was considered a planet until the dwarf planet category was introduced in 2006. It is made of rock and ice and is 2,274 kilometres across. It has three known moons. The largest, Charon, is about half Pluto's size and the two probably had a common origin.

TILT AND ROTATION OF NEPTUNE

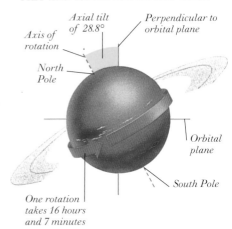

Axial tilt of 28.8°

Perpendicular to orbital plane

Axis of rotation

North Pole

Orbital plane

South Pole

One rotation takes 16 hours and 7 minutes

CLOUD FEATURES OF NEPTUNE

Great Dark Spot (anticyclonic wind storm)

Scooter (cirrus cloud)

Small Dark Spot (cyclonic wind storm)

RINGS OF NEPTUNE

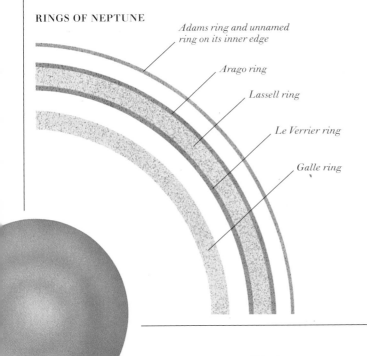

Adams ring and unnamed ring on its inner edge

Arago ring

Lassell ring

Le Verrier ring

Galle ring

HIGH-ALTITUDE CLOUDS

Methane cirrus clouds 40 km above main cloud deck

Cloud shadow

Main cloud deck blown by winds at speeds of about 2,000 km/h

MOONS OF NEPTUNE

TRITON
Diameter: 2,705 km
Average distance from planet: 354,800 km

PROTEUS
Diameter: 416 km
Average distance from planet: 117,600 km

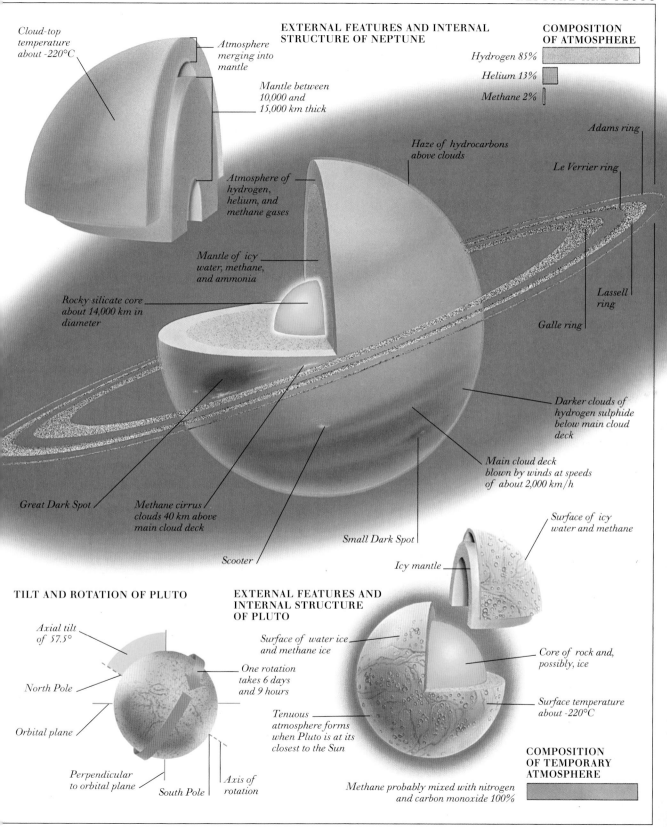

EXTERNAL FEATURES AND INTERNAL
STRUCTURE OF NEPTUNE

COMPOSITION
OF ATMOSPHERE

Hydrogen 85%

Helium 13%

Methane 2%

Cloud-top
temperature
about -220°C

Atmosphere
merging into
mantle

Mantle between
10,000 and
15,000 km thick

Atmosphere of
hydrogen,
helium, and
methane gases

Haze of hydrocarbons
above clouds

Adams ring

Le Verrier ring

Mantle of icy
water, methane,
and ammonia

Rocky silicate core
about 14,000 km in
diameter

Lassell
ring

Galle ring

Darker clouds of
hydrogen sulphide
below main cloud
deck

Main cloud deck
blown by winds at speeds
of about 2,000 km/h

Great Dark Spot

Methane cirrus
clouds 40 km above
main cloud deck

Scooter

Small Dark Spot

Surface of icy
water and methane

Icy mantle

TILT AND ROTATION OF PLUTO

EXTERNAL FEATURES AND
INTERNAL STRUCTURE
OF PLUTO

Axial tilt
of 57.5°

North Pole

Orbital plane

Perpendicular
to orbital plane

South Pole

Axis of
rotation

Surface of water ice
and methane ice

One rotation
takes 6 days
and 9 hours

Tenuous
atmosphere forms
when Pluto is at its
closest to the Sun

Core of rock and,
possibly, ice

Surface temperature
about -220°C

COMPOSITION
OF TEMPORARY
ATMOSPHERE

Methane probably mixed with nitrogen
and carbon monoxide 100%

51

Asteroids, comets, and meteoroids

ASTEROID 951 GASPRA

ASTEROIDS, COMETS, AND METEOROIDS are all debris remaining from the nebula from which the Solar System formed 4.6 billion years ago. Asteroids are rocky bodies up to about 1,000 kilometres in diameter, although most are much smaller. Most of them orbit the Sun in the asteroid belt, which lies between the orbits of Mars and Jupiter. Cometary nuclei exist in a huge cloud (called the Oort Cloud) that surrounds the planetary part of the Solar System. They are made of frozen water and dust, and are a few kilometres in diameter. Occasionally, a comet is deflected from the Oort Cloud on to a long, elliptical path that brings it much closer to the Sun. As the comet approaches the Sun, the cometary nucleus starts to vaporize in the heat, producing both a brightly shining coma (a huge sphere of gas and dust around the nucleus), and a gas tail, and a dust tail. Meteoroids are small chunks of stone or stone and iron, which are fragments of asteroids or comets. Meteoroids range in size from tiny dust particles to objects tens of metres across. If a meteoroid enters the Earth's atmosphere, it is heated by friction and appears as a glowing streak of light called a meteor (also known as a shooting star). Meteor showers occur when the Earth passes through the trail of dust particles left by a comet. Most meteoroids burn up in the atmosphere. The remnants of the few that are large enough to reach the Earth's surface are termed meteorites.

OPTICAL IMAGE OF HALLEY'S COMET

FALSE-COLOUR IMAGE OF HALLEY'S COMET

High-intensity light emission

Nucleus

Medium-intensity light emission

Low-intensity light emission

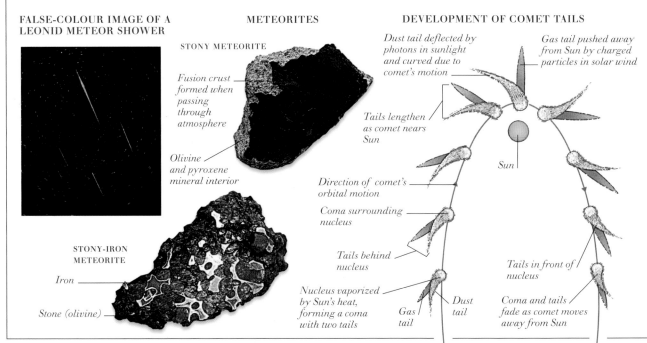

FALSE-COLOUR IMAGE OF A LEONID METEOR SHOWER

METEORITES

STONY METEORITE

Fusion crust formed when passing through atmosphere

Olivine and pyroxene mineral interior

STONY-IRON METEORITE

Iron

Stone (olivine)

DEVELOPMENT OF COMET TAILS

Dust tail deflected by photons in sunlight and curved due to comet's motion

Gas tail pushed away from Sun by charged particles in solar wind

Tails lengthen as comet nears Sun

Direction of comet's orbital motion

Coma surrounding nucleus

Tails behind nucleus

Nucleus vaporized by Sun's heat, forming a coma with two tails

Gas tail

Dust tail

Sun

Tails in front of nucleus

Coma and tails fade as comet moves away from Sun

FEATURES OF A COMET

Comet tails up to 100 million km long

Thin, straight gas tail

Gas molecules excited by Sun and emitting light

...ead ...oma and ...ucleus)

Thin, straight gas tail blown by solar wind

Coma surrounding nucleus

Broad, curved dust tail

Nucleus a few kilometres across

...TRUCTURE OF ... COMET

...lowing coma up ... 1 million km ...ross surrounding ...cleus

...st layer ...th active ...eas emitting ...s of gas ...d dust

...et of gas and ...ust produced by ...aporization ...n sunlit side ...f nucleus

...es, mainly water ice, but ...so frozen carbon dioxide, ...ethane, and ammonia

Broad curved dust tail

Dust particles reflecting sunlight

PREHISTORIC EARTH

The changing Earth

THE EARTH FORMED FROM A CLOUD OF DUST and gas drifting through space about 4,600 million years ago. Dense minerals sank to the centre while lighter ones formed a thin rocky crust. However, the first known life-forms – bacteria and blue-green algae – did not appear until about 3,400 million years ago, and it was only about 700 million years ago that more complex plants and animals began to develop. Since then, thousands of animal and plant species have evolved; some, such as the dinosaurs, survived for many millions of years, while others died out quickly. The Earth itself is continually changing. Although continents neared their present locations about 50 million years ago, they are still drifting slowly over the planet's surface, and mountain ranges such as the Himalayas – which began to form 40 million years ago – are continually being built up and worn away. Climate is also subject to change: the Earth has undergone a series of ice ages interspersed with warmer periods (the most recent glacial period was at its height about 20,000 years ago).

Small mammals appeared (e.g., Crusafontia)

Dinosaurs became extinct

Global mountain building occurred

Multicellular soft-bodied animals appeared (e.g., worms and jellyfish)

Shelled invertebrates appeared (e.g., trilobites)

Marine plants flourished

Land plants appeared (e.g., Cooksonia)

Unicellular organisms appeared (e.g., blue-green algae)

Earth formed

Coral reefs appeared

Vertebrates appeared (e.g., Hemicyclaspis)

More complex types of algae appeared

Amphibians appeared (e.g., Ichthyostega)

CRETACEOUS

ORDOVICIAN

CAMBRIAN

PRECAMBRIAN TIME

SILURIAN

DEVONIAN

GEOLOGICAL TIMESCALE

MILLIONS OF
YEARS AGO (MYA)

4,600	570	510	439	409	363	323	2
	CAMBRIAN	ORDOVICIAN	SILURIAN	DEVONIAN		MISSISSIPPIAN (NORTH AMERICA)	PENNSYLVANIAN (NORTH AMERICA)
						CARBONIFEROUS	
PRECAMBRIAN TIME	PALAEOZOIC						

EVOLUTION OF THE EARTH

Birds appeared
(e.g., Archaeopteryx)

Dinosaurs
flourished

Marine reptiles
appeared (e.g.,
Mixosaurus)

JURASSIC

TRIASSIC

Flowering plants
appeared (e.g.,
Magnolia)

Oil and gas
deposits formed

Himalayas
began to form

Large mammals
appeared (e.g.,
Arsinoitherium)

Coal-forming
forests flourished

Early
desertification
occurred

PERMIAN

Conifers
appeared

TERTIARY

ONIFEROUS

Last glacial
period occurred

Colorado River
began to cut out
the Grand Canyon

Uplift of the
Sierra Nevada
began

QUATERNARY

Modern humans
(Homo sapiens)
appeared

	65	56.5	35.5	23.5	5.2	1.64		0.01		0	MYA
	PALAEOCENE	EOCENE	OLIGOCENE	MIOCENE	PLIOCENE		PLEISTOCENE		HOLOCENE		EPOCH

90	250		200		145					
PERMIAN	TRIASSIC		JURASSIC		CRETACEOUS		TERTIARY		QUATERNARY	PERIOD
			MESOZOIC				CENOZOIC			ERA

The Earth's crust

THE EARTH'S CRUST IS THE SOLID outer shell of the Earth. It includes continental crust (about 40 kilometres thick) and oceanic crust (about six kilometres thick). The crust and the topmost layer of the mantle form the lithosphere. The lithosphere consists of semi-rigid plates that move relative to each other on the underlying asthenosphere (a partly molten layer of the mantle). This process is known as plate tectonics and helps explain continental drift. Where two plates move apart, there are rifts in the crust. In mid-ocean, this movement results in sea-floor spreading and the formation of ocean ridges; on continents, crustal spreading can form rift valleys. When plates move towards each other, one may be subducted beneath (forced under) the other. In mid-ocean, this causes ocean trenches, seismic activity, and arcs of volcanic islands. Where oceanic crust is subducted beneath continental crust or where continents collide, land may be uplifted and mountains formed (see pp. 62–65). Plates may also slide past each other – along the San Andreas fault, for example. Crustal movement on continents may result in earthquakes, while movement under the seabed can lead to tidal waves.

ELEMENTS IN THE EARTH'S CRUST

Other elements 2%
Potassium 2.6%
Calcium 3.6%
Aluminium 8%
Magnesium 2%
Sodium 2.8%
Iron 5%
Silicon 28%
Oxygen 46%

FEATURES OF PLATE MOVEMENTS

Ocean trench formed where oceanic crust is forced under continental crust

Subduction zone

Ridge where magma is rising to form new oceanic crust

Region of sea-floor spreading

Rift formed where two plates are moving apart

Magma rises to form a hot spot

Magma (molten rock) erupts at rift

Volcano develops over hot spot and builds up to form an island

Volcanic island that originally formed over hot spot

Oceanic crust melts

Magma rises to form a volcano

MAJOR PLATES OF THE EARTH'S CRUST

North American plate

Hellenic plate

Eurasian plate

Plates sliding past each other

Pacific plate

Cocos plate

Philippine plate

Caribbean plate

Plates converging

Nazca plate

South American plate

African plate

Indo-Australian plate

Plates moving apart

MOVEMENT OF LAND ALONG OCEANIC RIDGES

Boundary along which two plates slide past each other

Land moves apart at a constant rate, perpendicular to ridge

STRAIGHT OCEANIC RIDGE

Mountain range uplifted where subducting oceanic crust compresses and deforms edge of continental crust

Land moves apart at a constant rate, perpendicular to curve

CURVED OCEANIC RIDGE

Staggered parallel ridge sections take shape of curve

Transform fault

Lithosphere (crust and topmost layer of mantle)

Asthenosphere (upper part of mantle)

STRESSES RESOLVE INTO SECTIONS

59

Faults and folds

THE CONTINUOUS MOVEMENT of the Earth's crustal plates (see pp. 58–59) can squeeze, stretch, or break rock strata, deforming them and producing faults and folds. A fault is a fracture in a rock along which there is movement of one side relative to the other. The movement can be vertical, horizontal, or oblique (vertical and horizontal). Faults develop when rocks are subjected to compression or tension. They tend to occur in hard, rigid rocks, which are more likely to break than bend. The smallest faults occur in single mineral crystals and are microscopically small, whereas the largest – the Great Rift Valley in Africa, which formed between 5 million and 100,000 years ago – is more than 9,000 kilometres long. A fold is a bend in a rock layer caused by compression. Folds occur in elastic rocks, which tend to bend rather than break. The two main types of fold are anticlines (upfolds) and synclines (downfolds). Folds vary in size from a few millimetres long to folded mountain ranges hundreds of kilometres long, such as the Himalayas (see pp. 62–63) and the Alps, which are repeatedly folding. In addition to faults and folds, other features associated with rock deformations include boudins, mullions, and *en échelon* fractures.

STRUCTURE OF A FOLD

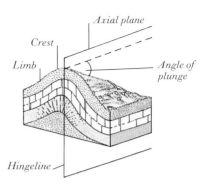

Axial plane

Crest

Limb

Angle of plunge

Hingeline

STRUCTURE OF A FAULT

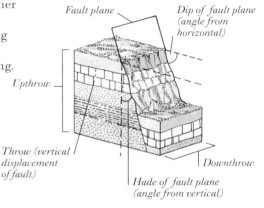

Fault plane

Dip of fault plane (angle from horizontal)

Upthrow

Throw (vertical displacement of fault)

Downthrow

Hade of fault plane (angle from vertical)

STRUCTURE OF A SLOPE

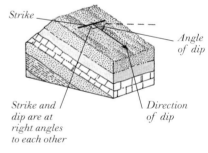

Strike

Angle of dip

Strike and dip are at right angles to each other

Direction of dip

FOLDED ROCK

Steeply dipping limbs

Crest of anticline

Plunge

SECTION THROUGH FOLDED ROCK STRATA THAT HAVE BEEN ERODED

Dipping bed

Anticlinal fold

Monoclinal fold

Mineral-filled fault

Upper Carboniferous Millstone Grit

Lower Carboniferous Limestone

EXAMPLES OF FOLDS

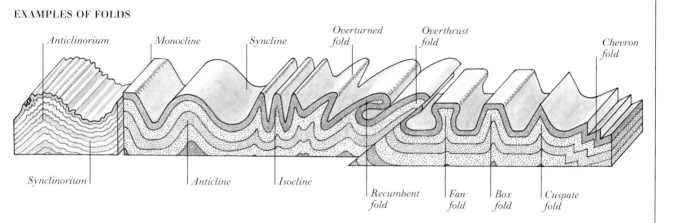

Anticlinorium
Monocline
Syncline
Overturned fold
Overthrust fold
Chevron fold
Synclinorium
Anticline
Isocline
Recumbent fold
Fan fold
Box fold
Cuspate fold

EXAMPLES OF FAULTS

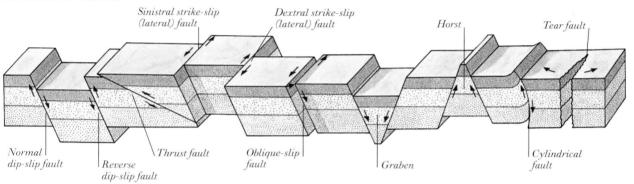

Sinistral strike-slip (lateral) fault
Dextral strike-slip (lateral) fault
Horst
Tear fault
Normal dip-slip fault
Reverse dip-slip fault
Thrust fault
Oblique-slip fault
Graben
Cylindrical fault

SMALL-SCALE ROCK DEFORMATIONS

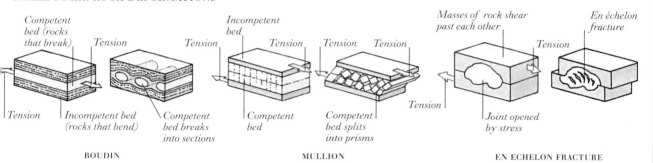

Competent bed (rocks that break)
Tension
Tension
Tension
Incompetent bed
Tension
Tension
Tension
Masses of rock shear past each other
Tension
En échelon fracture
Tension
Incompetent bed (rocks that bend)
Competent bed breaks into sections
Competent bed
Competent bed splits into prisms
Joint opened by stress

BOUDIN
MULLION
EN ECHELON FRACTURE

Mineral-filled fault
Dipping bed
Gently folded bed
Horizontal bed
Mineral-filled fault
Dipping bed

Upper Carboniferous Millstone Grit
Upper Carboniferous Coal Measures

Mountain building

THE PROCESSES INVOLVED in mountain building – termed orogenesis – occur
as a result of the movement of the Earth's crustal plates (see pp. 58–59).
There are three main types of mountains: volcanic mountains, fold
mountains, and block mountains. Most volcanic mountains have been
formed along plate boundaries where plates have come together or
moved apart and lava and other debris have been ejected onto the
Earth's surface. The lava and debris may have built up to form a
dome around the vent of a volcano. Fold mountains are formed
where plates push together and
cause the rock to buckle upwards.
Where oceanic crust meets less dense
continental crust, the oceanic crust
is forced under the continental crust. The
continental crust is buckled by the impact.
This is how folded mountain ranges, such as the
Appalachian Mountains in North America, were
formed. Fold mountains are also formed where
two areas of continental crust meet. The
Himalayas, for example, began to form when
India collided with Asia, buckling the sediments
and parts of the oceanic crust between them. Block mountains are formed when a block
of land is uplifted between two faults as a result of compression or tension in the Earth's
crust (see pp. 60–61). Often, the movement along faults has taken place gradually over
millions of years. However, two plates may cause an earthquake by suddenly sliding past
each other along a faultline.

BHAGIRATHI PARBAT,
HIMALAYAS

Asia

Himalayas
formed by
buckling of
sediment and
part of the
oceanic crust
between two
colliding
continents

India moves
north

India collides
with Asia about 40
million years ago

EXAMPLES OF MOUNTAINS

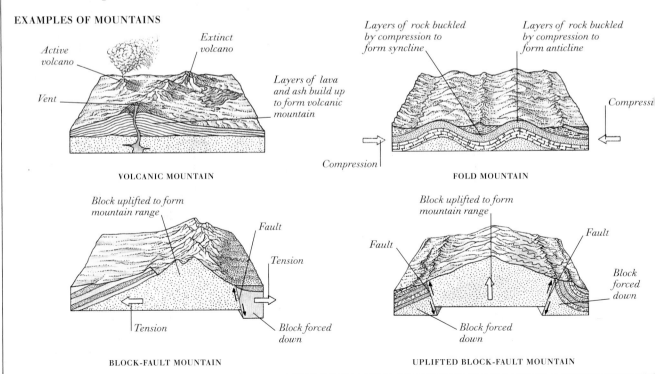

Active
volcano

Extinct
volcano

Vent

Layers of lava
and ash build up
to form volcanic
mountain

VOLCANIC MOUNTAIN

Layers of rock buckled
by compression to
form syncline

Layers of rock buckled
by compression to
form anticline

Compressi

Compression

FOLD MOUNTAIN

Block uplifted to form
mountain range

Fault

Tension

Tension

Block forced
down

BLOCK-FAULT MOUNTAIN

Block uplifted to form
mountain range

Fault

Fault

Block
forced
down

Block forced
down

UPLIFTED BLOCK-FAULT MOUNTAIN

STAGES IN THE FORMATION OF THE HIMALAYAS

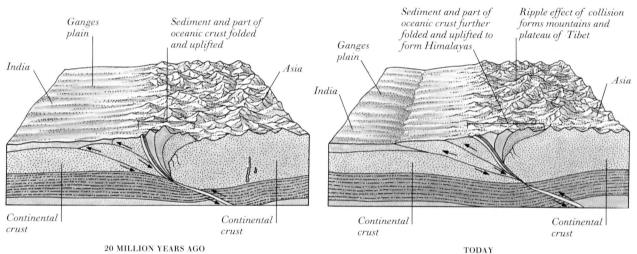

Sediment

Ocean area becomes smaller as plates converge

India moves towards Asia

Sediment

Asia

Volcano

Continental crust

Continental crust

Oceanic crust forced under continental crust

Magma rises to form volcanoes

60 MILLION YEARS AGO

Sediment and part of oceanic crust folded by continental collision

India

Asia

Continental crust

Oceanic crust forced further under continental crust

Continental crust

40 MILLION YEARS AGO

Ganges plain

India

Sediment and part of oceanic crust folded and uplifted

Asia

Continental crust

Continental crust

20 MILLION YEARS AGO

Sediment and part of oceanic crust further folded and uplifted to form Himalayas

Ripple effect of collision forms mountains and plateau of Tibet

Ganges plain

India

Asia

Continental crust

Continental crust

TODAY

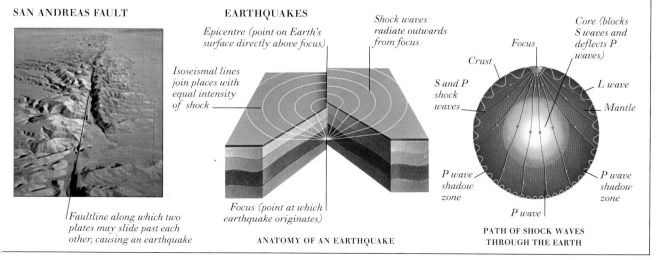

SAN ANDREAS FAULT

Faultline along which two plates may slide past each other, causing an earthquake

EARTHQUAKES

Epicentre (point on Earth's surface directly above focus)

Isoseismal lines join places with equal intensity of shock

Shock waves radiate outwards from focus

Focus (point at which earthquake originates)

ANATOMY OF AN EARTHQUAKE

Focus

Crust

S and P shock waves

Core (blocks S waves and deflects P waves)

L wave

Mantle

P wave shadow zone

P wave

P wave shadow zone

PATH OF SHOCK WAVES THROUGH THE EARTH

Precambrian to Devonian periods

WHEN THE EARTH FORMED about 4,600 million years ago, its atmosphere consisted of volcanic gases with little oxygen, making it hostile to most forms of life. One large supercontinent, Gondwana, was situated over the southern polar region, while other smaller continents were spread over the rest of the world. Constant movement of the earth's crustal plates carried continents across the earth's surface. The first primitive life-forms emerged around 3,400 million years ago in shallow, warm seas. The build up of oxygen began to form a shield of ozone around the earth, protecting living organisms from the sun's harmful rays and helping to establish an atmosphere in which life could sustain itself. The first vertebrates appeared about 470 million years ago, during the Ordovician period (510–439 million years ago), the first land plants appeared around 400 million years ago during the Devonian period (409–363 million years ago), and the first land animals about 30 million years later.

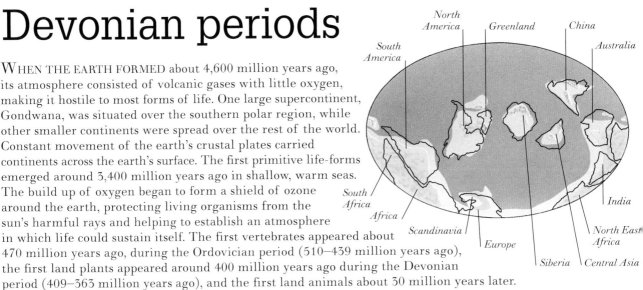

MIDDLE ORDOVICIAN POSITIONS
OF PRESENT-DAY LAND-MASSES

North America
Greenland
China
Australia
South America
India
South Africa
Africa
North East Africa
Scandinavia
Europe
Siberia
Central Asia

EXAMPLES OF PRECAMBRIAN TO DEVONIAN PLANT GROUPS

A PRESENT-DAY CLUBMOSS
(*Lycopodium* sp.)

A PRESENT-DAY
LAND PLANT
(*Asparagus setaceous*)

FOSSIL OF AN EXTINCT LAND PLANT
(*Cooksonia hemisphaerica*)

FOSSIL OF AN EXTINCT SWAMP PLANT
(*Zosterophyllum llanoveranum*)

EXAMPLES OF PRECAMBRIAN TO DEVONIAN TRILOBITES

ACADAGNOSTUS
Group: Agnostidae
Length: 8 mm (⅓ in)

PHACOPS
Group: Phacopidae
Length: 4.5 cm (1¾ in)

OLENELLUS
Group: Olenellidae
Length: 6 cm (2½ in)

ELRATHIA
Group: Ptychopariidae
Length: 2 cm (¾ in)

THE EARTH DURING THE MIDDLE ORDOVICIAN PERIOD

EXAMPLES OF EARLY MARINE INVERTEBRATES

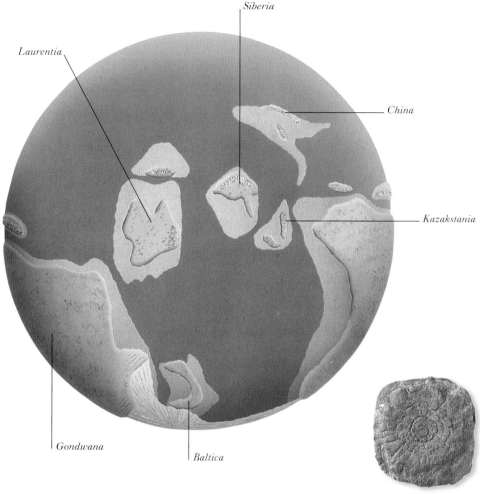

Siberia

Laurentia

China

Kazakstania

Gondwana

Baltica

FOSSIL NAUTILOID
(*Estonioceras perforatum*)

FOSSIL BRACHIOPOD
(*Dicoelosia bilobata*)

TRACE FOSSIL
(*Mawsonites spriggi*)

FOSSIL GRAPTOLITE
(*Monograptus convolutus*)

EXAMPLES OF DEVONIAN FISH

RHAMPHODOPSIS
Group: Ptyctodontidae
Length: 15 cm (6 in)

PTERASPIS
Group: Pteraspidae
Length: 25 cm (10 in)

COCCOSTEUS
Group: Coccosteidae
Length: 35 cm (14 in)

BOTHRIOLEPIS
Group: Bothriolepididae
Length: 40 cm (16 in)

CHEIRACANTHUS
Group: Acanthodidae
Length: 30 cm (12 in)

PTERICHTHYODES
Group: Asterolepididae
Length: 15 cm (6 in)

CHEIROLEPIS
Group: Cheirolepidae
Length: 17 cm (6¾ in)

CEPHALASPIS
Group: Cephalaspidae
Length: 22 cm (8¾ in)

Carboniferous to Permian periods

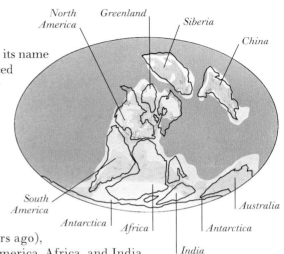

THE CARBONIFEROUS PERIOD (363–290 million years ago) takes its name from the thick, carbon-rich layers – now coal – that were produced during this period as swampy tropical forests were repeatedly drowned by shallow seas. The humid climate across northern and equatorial continents throughout Carboniferous times produced the first dense plant cover on Earth. During the early part of this period, the first reptiles appeared. Their development of a waterproof egg with a protective internal structure ended animal life's dependence on an aquatic environment. Towards the end of Carboniferous times, the earth's continents Laurasia and Gondwana collided, resulting in the huge land-mass of Pangaea. Glaciers smothered much of the southern hemisphere during the Permian period (290–245 million years ago), covering Antarctica, parts of Australia, and much of South America, Africa, and India. Ice locked up much of the world's water and large areas of the northern hemisphere experienced a drop in sea-level. Away from the poles, deserts and a hot dry climate predominated. As a result of these conditions, the Permian period ended with the greatest mass extinction of life on earth ever.

EXAMPLES OF CARBONIFEROUS AND PERMIAN PLANT GROUPS

A PRESENT-DAY FIR
(Abies concolor)

FOSSIL OF AN EXTINCT FERN
(Zeilleria frenzlii)

FOSSIL OF AN EXTINCT HORSETAIL
(Equisetites sp.)

FOSSIL OF AN EXTINCT CLUBMOSS
(Lepidodendron sp.)

EXAMPLES OF CARBONIFEROUS AND PERMIAN TREES

PECOPTERIS
Group: Marattiaceae
Height: 4 m (13 ft)

PARIPTERIS
Group: Medullosaceae
Height: 5 m (16 ft 6 in)

MARIOPTERIS
Group: Lyginopteridales
Height: 5 m (16 ft 6 in)

MEDULLOSA
Group: Medullosaceae
Height: 5 m (16 ft 6 in)

THE EARTH DURING THE LATE CARBONIFEROUS PERIOD

Siberia

Laurussia

China

Ural Mountains

Caledonian Mountains

Appalachian Mountains

Gondwana

EXAMPLES OF CARBONIFEROUS AND PERMIAN ANIMALS

SKULL OF AN EXTINCT SYNAPSID
(Dimetrodon loomisi)

FOSSIL TEETH OF AN EXTINCT SHARK
(Helicoprion bessonowi)

MODEL OF AN EXTINCT EARLY REPTILE-LIKE ANIMAL
(Westlothiana lizziae)

LEPIDODENDRON
Group: Lepidodendraceae
Height: 30 m (100 ft)

CORDAITES
Group: Cordaitacea
Height: 10 m (33 ft)

GLOSSOPTERIS
Group: Glossopteridaceae
Height: 8 m (26 ft)

ALETHOPTERIS
Group: Medullosaceae
Height: 5 m (16 ft 6 in)

Triassic period

THE TRIASSIC PERIOD (250–200 million years ago) marked the beginning of what is known as the Age of the Dinosaurs (the Mesozoic era). During this period, the present-day continents were massed together, forming one huge continent known as Pangaea. This land-mass experienced extremes of climate, with lush green areas around the coast or by lakes and rivers, and arid deserts in the interior. The only forms of plant life were non-flowering plants, such as conifers, ferns, cycads, and ginkgos; flowering plants had not yet evolved. The principal forms of animal life included diverse, often gigantic, amphibians, rhynchosaurs ("beaked lizards"), and primitive crocodilians. Dinosaurs first appeared about 230 million years ago, at the beginning of the Late Triassic period. Among the earliest dinosaurs were the carnivorous (flesh-eating) herrerasaurids, such as *Herrerasaurus* and *Staurikosaurus*. Early herbivorous (plant-eating) dinosaurs first appeared in Late Triassic times and included *Plateosaurus* and *Technosaurus*. By the end of the Triassic period, dinosaurs dominated Pangaea, possibly contributing to the extinction of many other reptiles.

TRIASSIC POSITIONS OF PRESENT-DAY LAND-MASSES

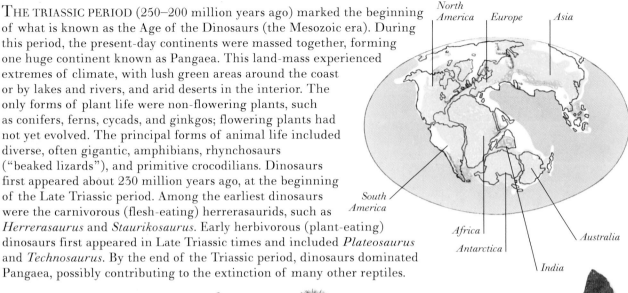

North America
Europe
Asia
South America
Africa
Antarctica
India
Australia

EXAMPLES OF TRIASSIC PLANT GROUPS

A PRESENT-DAY CYCAD
(*Cycas revoluta*)

A PRESENT-DAY GINKGO
(*Ginkgo biloba*)

A PRESENT-DAY CONIFER
(*Araucaria araucana*)

FOSSIL OF AN EXTINCT FERN
(*Pachypteris sp.*)

FOSSIL LEAF OF AN EXTINCT CYCAD
(*Cycas sp.*)

EXAMPLES OF TRIASSIC DINOSAURS

MELANOROSAURUS
Group: Melanorosauridae
Length: 12.2 m (40 ft)

MUSSAURUS
Group: Sauropodomorpha
Length: 2–3 m (6 ft 6 in–10 ft)

HERRERASAURUS
Group: Herrerasauridae
Length: 3 m (10 ft)

PISANOSAURUS
Group: Ornithischia
Length: 90 cm (3 ft)

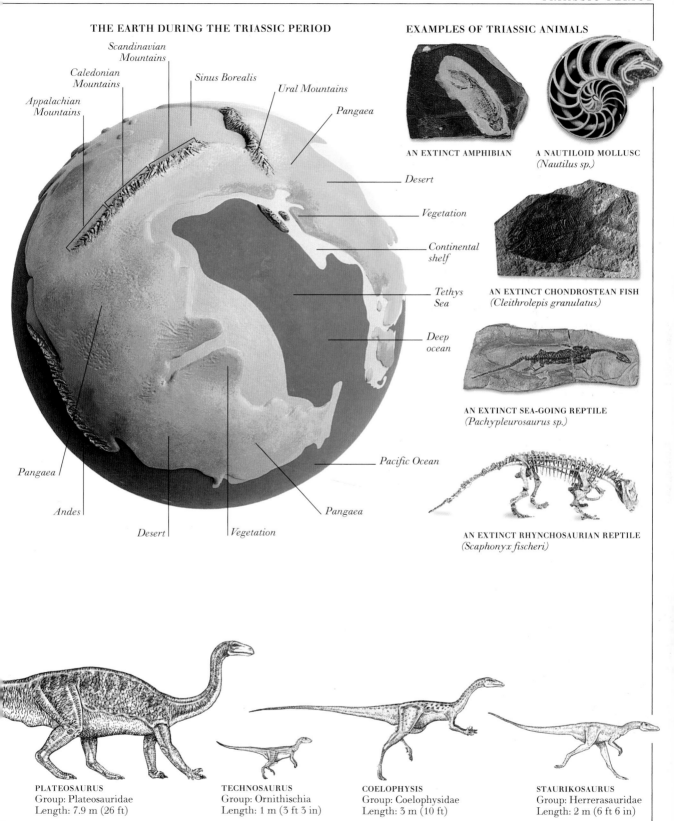

THE EARTH DURING THE TRIASSIC PERIOD

Appalachian Mountains
Caledonian Mountains
Scandinavian Mountains
Sinus Borealis
Ural Mountains
Pangaea
Desert
Vegetation
Continental shelf
Tethys Sea
Deep ocean
Pacific Ocean
Pangaea
Pangaea
Andes
Desert
Vegetation

EXAMPLES OF TRIASSIC ANIMALS

AN EXTINCT AMPHIBIAN

A NAUTILOID MOLLUSC
(*Nautilus sp.*)

AN EXTINCT CHONDROSTEAN FISH
(*Cleithrolepis granulatus*)

AN EXTINCT SEA-GOING REPTILE
(*Pachypleurosaurus sp.*)

AN EXTINCT RHYNCHOSAURIAN REPTILE
(*Scaphonyx fischeri*)

PLATEOSAURUS
Group: Plateosauridae
Length: 7.9 m (26 ft)

TECHNOSAURUS
Group: Ornithischia
Length: 1 m (3 ft 3 in)

COELOPHYSIS
Group: Coelophysidae
Length: 3 m (10 ft)

STAURIKOSAURUS
Group: Herrerasauridae
Length: 2 m (6 ft 6 in)

Jurassic period

THE JURASSIC PERIOD, the middle part of the Mesozoic era, lasted from 199 to 145 million years ago. During Jurassic times, the land-mass of Pangaea broke up into the continents of Gondwana and Laurasia, and sea-levels rose, flooding areas of lower land. The Jurassic climate was warm and moist. Plants such as ginkgos, horsetails, and conifers thrived, and giant redwood trees appeared, as did the first flowering plants. The abundance of plant food coincided with the proliferation of herbivorous (plant-eating) dinosaurs, such as the large sauropods (e.g., *Diplodocus*) and stegosaurs (e.g., *Stegosaurus*). Carnivorous (flesheating) dinosaurs, such as *Compsognathus* and *Allosaurus*, also flourished by hunting the many animals that existed – among them other dinosaurs. Further Jurassic animals included shrew-like mammals, and pterosaurs (flying reptiles), as well as plesiosaurs and ichthyosaurs (both marine reptiles).

JURASSIC POSITIONS OF PRESENT-DAY LAND-MASSES

North America
Europe
Arabia
Asia
South America
Africa
Antarctica
India
Australia

EXAMPLES OF JURASSIC PLANT GROUPS

A PRESENT-DAY FERN
(*Dicksonia antarctica*)

A PRESENT-DAY HORSETAIL
(*Equisetum arvense*)

A PRESENT-DAY CONIFER
(*Taxus baccata*)

FOSSIL LEAF OF AN EXTINCT CONIFER
(*Taxus sp.*)

FOSSIL LEAF OF AN EXTINCT REDWOOD
(*Sequoiadendron affinis*)

EXAMPLES OF JURASSIC DINOSAURS

DIPLODOCUS
Group: Diplodocidae
Length: 26.8 m (88 ft)

CAMPTOSAURUS
Group: Iguanodontia
Length: 4.9–7 m (16–23 ft)

DRYOSAURUS
Group: Dryosauridae
Length: 3–4 m (10–13 ft)

THE EARTH DURING THE JURASSIC PERIOD

EXAMPLES OF JURASSIC ANIMALS

North Atlantic Ocean

Laurasia

Laurasia

Ural Mountains

Turgai Strait

North American Cordillera

Vegetation

Laurasia

Desert

Tethys Sea

Deep ocean

Continental shelf

Desert

Vegetation

Andes

Gondwana

Gondwana

Pacific Ocean

AN EXTINCT PTEROSAUR
(*Rhamphorhynchus sp.*)

**AN EXTINCT
BELEMNITE MOLLUSC**
(*Belemnoteuthis sp.*)

**AN EXTINCT
RHYNCHOSAURIAN REPTILE**
(*Homeosaurus pulchellus*)

AN EXTINCT PLESIOSAUR
(*Peloneustes philarcus*)

AN EXTINCT ICHTHYOSAUR
(*Stenopterygius megacephalus*)

ALLOSAURUS
Group: Allosauroidea
Length: 11 m (36 ft)

SCELIDOSAURUS
Group: Thyreophora
Length: 4 m (13 ft)

STEGOSAURUS
Group: Stegosauridae
Length: 9.1 m (30 ft)

Cretaceous period

THE MESOZOIC ERA ENDED WITH the Cretaceous period, which lasted from 146 to 65 million years ago. During this period, Gondwana and Laurasia were breaking up into smaller land-masses that more closely resembled the modern continents. The climate remained mild and moist but the seasons became more marked. Flowering plants, including deciduous trees, replaced many cycads, seed ferns, and conifers. Animal species became more varied, with the evolution of new mammals, insects, fish, crustaceans, and turtles. Dinosaurs evolved into a wide variety of species during Cretaceous times; more than half of all known dinosaurs – including *Iguanodon*, *Deinonychus*, *Tyrannosaurus*, and *Hypsilophodon* – lived during this period. At the end of the Cretaceous period, however, most dinosaurs became extinct. The reason for this mass extinction is unknown but it is thought to have been caused by climatic changes due to either a catastrophic meteor impact with the Earth or extensive volcanic eruptions.

CRETACEOUS POSITIONS OF PRESENT-DAY LAND-MASSES

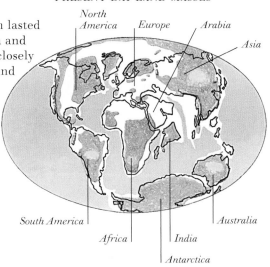

North America
Europe
Arabia
Asia
South America
Africa
India
Antarctica
Australia

EXAMPLES OF CRETACEOUS PLANT GROUPS

A PRESENT-DAY CONIFER
(*Pinus muricata*)

A PRESENT-DAY DECIDUOUS TREE
(*Magnolia sp.*)

FOSSIL OF AN EXTINCT FERN
(*Sphenopteris latiloba*)

FOSSIL OF AN EXTINCT GINKGO
(*Ginkgo pluripartita*)

FOSSIL LEAVES OF AN EXTINCT DECIDUOUS TREE
(*Cercidyphyllum sp.*)

EXAMPLES OF CRETACEOUS DINOSAURS

SALTASAURUS
Group: Saltasauridae
Length: 12.2 m (40 ft)

TOROSAURUS
Group: Ceratopsidae
Length: 7.6 m (25 ft)

HYPSILOPHODON
Group: Ornithopoda
Length: 1.4–2.3 m (4 ft 6 in–7 ft 6 in)

THE EARTH DURING THE CRETACEOUS PERIOD

EXAMPLES OF CRETACEOUS ANIMALS

West Africa

North America

Rocky Mountains

Africa

Greenland

Europe

Continental Sea

Ural Mountains

Desert

Tethys Sea

Asia

India

Indian Ocean

Australia

Pacific Ocean

North Atlantic Ocean

Andes

South America

South Atlantic Ocean

Antarctica

Vegetation

AN EXTINCT INSECT
(*Libellulium longialatum*)

AN EXTINCT MARINE TURTLE
(*Plesiochelys latiscutata*)

AN EXTINCT CRUSTACEAN
(*Homarus sp.*)

AN EXTINCT CROCODILIAN

AN EXTINCT HOLOSTEAN FISH
(*Lepidotes maximus*)

TYRANNOSAURUS
Group: Tyrannosauridae
Length: 12.2 m (40 ft)

DEINONYCHUS
Group: Dromaeosauridae
Length: 2.4–3.4 m (8–11 ft)

IGUANODON
Group: Iguanodontia
Length: 9.1 m (30 ft)

Tertiary period

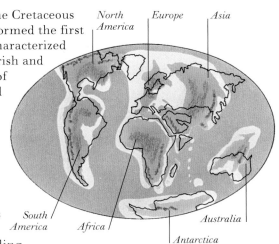

North America · Europe · Asia · South America · Africa · Australia · Antarctica

FOLLOWING THE DEMISE OF THE DINOSAURS at the end of the Cretaceous period, the Tertiary period (65–1.6 million years ago), which formed the first part of the Cenozoic era (65 million years ago–present), was characterized by a huge expansion of mammal life. Placental mammals nourish and maintain the young in the mother's uterus; only a few groups of placental mammals existed during Cretaceous times, compared with several tens of groups during the Tertiary period. One of these tens included the early human (see pp.108–109), *Ardipithecus*, which appeared in Africa. By the beginning of the Tertiary period, the continents had almost reached their present position. The Tethys Sea, which had separated the northern continents from Africa and India, began to close up, forming the Mediterranean Sea and allowing the migration of terrestrial animals between Africa and western Europe. India's collision with Asia led to the formation of the Himalayas. During the middle part of the Tertiary period, the forest-dwelling and browsing mammals were replaced by mammals such as the horses, better suited to grazing the open savannahs that began to dominate. Repeated cool periods throughout the Tertiary period established the Antarctic as an icy island continent.

EXAMPLES OF TERTIARY PLANT GROUPS

A PRESENT-DAY OAK
(*Quercus palustris*)

A PRESENT-DAY BIRCH
(*Betula grossa*)

**FOSSIL LEAF OF AN
EXTINCT BIRCH**
(*Betulites sp.*)

**FOSSILIZED STEM OF
AN EXTINCT PALM**
(*Palmoxylon sp.*)

EXAMPLES OF TERTIARY
ANIMAL GROUPS

HYAENODON
Group: Hyaenodontidae
Length: 2 m (6 ft 6 in)

TITANOHYRAX
Group: Pliohyracidae
Length: 2 m (6 ft 6 in)

PHORUSRHACOS
Group: Phorusrhacidae
Length: 1.5 m (5 ft)

SAMOTHERIUM
Group: Giraffidae
Length: 3 m (10 ft)

THE EARTH DURING THE TERTIARY PERIOD

EXAMPLES OF TERTIARY ANIMALS

North America

Appalachian Mountains

Rocky Mountains

Pyrenees

Europe

Alps

Asia

Continental sea

Sierra Nevada

Zagros Mountains

Himalayas

Tethys Sea

Australia

India

Indian Ocean

Andes

South America

Atlantic Ocean

Atlas Mountains

Africa

Antarctica

Vegetation

AN EXTINCT MAMMAL
(Arsinoitherium)

AN EXTINCT MAMMAL
(Merycoidodon culbertsonii)

AN EXTINCT PRIMATE
(Aegyptopithecus sp.)

AN EXTINCT
GASTROPOD MOLLUSC
(Ecphora quadricostata)

MAMMUT
Group: Mammutidae
Length: 2.5 m (8 ft)

TETRALOPHODON
Group: Gomphotheriidae
Length: 2.5 m (8 ft)

75

Quaternary period

THE QUATERNARY PERIOD (1.6 million years ago–present) forms the second part of the Cenozoic era (65 million years ago–present): it has been characterized by alternating cold (glacial) and warm (interglacial) periods. During cold periods, ice sheets and glaciers have formed repeatedly on northern and southern continents. The cold environments in North America and Eurasia, and to a lesser extent in southern South America and parts of Australia, have caused the migration of many life forms towards the Equator. Only the specialized ice age mammals such as *Mammuthus* and *Coelodonta*, with their thick wool and fat insulation, were suited to life in very cold climates. Humans developed throughout the Pleistocene period (1.6 million–10,000 years ago) in Africa and migrated northward into Europe and Asia. Modern humans, *Homo sapiens*, lived on the cold European continent 30,000 years ago and hunted other mammals. The end of the last ice age and the climatic changes that occurred about 10,000 years ago brought extinction to many Pleistocene mammals, but enabled humans to flourish.

QUATERNARY POSITIONS OF PRESENT-DAY LAND-MASSES

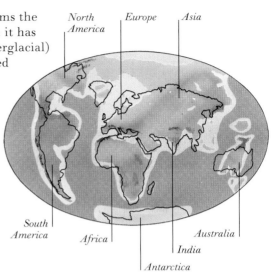

North America · Europe · Asia · South America · Africa · Australia · India · Antarctica

EXAMPLES OF QUATERNARY PLANT GROUPS

A PRESENT-DAY BIRCH
(*Betula lenta*)

A PRESENT-DAY SWEEETGUM
(*Liquidambar styraciflua*)

FOSSIL LEAF OF A SWEETGUM
(*Liquidambar europeanum*)

FOSSIL LEAF OF A BIRCH
(*Betula sp.*)

EXAMPLES OF QUATERNARY ANIMAL GROUPS

PROCOPTODON
Group: Macropodidae
Length: 3 m (10 ft)

DIPROTODON
Group: Diprotodontidae
Length: 3 m (10 ft)

TOXODON
Group: Toxodontidae
Length: 3 m (10 ft)

MAMMUTHUS
Group: Elephantidae
Length: 3 m (10 ft)

THE EARTH DURING THE QUATERNARY PERIOD

EXAMPLES OF QUATERNARY ANIMALS

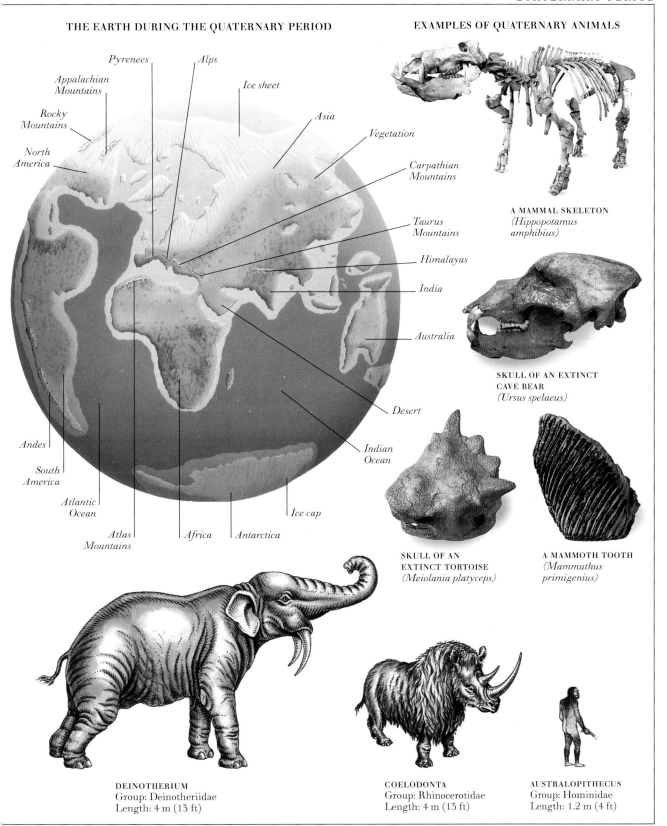

Pyrenees

Alps

Appalachian
Mountains

Ice sheet

Rocky
Mountains

Asia

North
America

Vegetation

Carpathian
Mountains

Taurus
Mountains

Himalayas

India

Australia

Andes

South
America

Desert

Atlantic
Ocean

Indian
Ocean

Atlas
Mountains

Africa

Antarctica

Ice cap

A MAMMAL SKELETON
(*Hippopotamus
amphibius*)

**SKULL OF AN EXTINCT
CAVE BEAR**
(*Ursus spelaeus*)

**SKULL OF AN
EXTINCT TORTOISE**
(*Meiolania platyceps*)

A MAMMOTH TOOTH
(*Mammuthus
primigenius*)

DEINOTHERIUM
Group: Deinotheriidae
Length: 4 m (13 ft)

COELODONTA
Group: Rhinocerotidae
Length: 4 m (13 ft)

AUSTRALOPITHECUS
Group: Hominidae
Length: 1.2 m (4 ft)

Early signs of life

STROMATOLITIC LIMESTONE

FOR ALMOST A THOUSAND MILLION YEARS after its formation, there was no known life on Earth. The first simple, sea-dwelling organic structures appeared about 3,500 million years ago; they may have formed when certain chemical molecules joined together. Prokaryotes, single-celled micro-organisms such as blue-green algae, were able to photosynthesize (see pp. 138–139), and thus produce oxygen. A thousand million years later, sufficient oxygen had built up in the earth's atmosphere to allow multicellular organisms to proliferate in the Precambrian seas (before 570 million years ago). Soft-bodied jellyfish, corals, and seaworms flourished about 700 million years ago. Trilobites, the first animals with hard body frames, developed during the Cambrian period (570–510 million years ago). However, it was not until the beginning of the Devonian period (409–363 million years ago) that early land plants, such as *Asteroxylon*, formed a water-retaining cuticle, which ended their dependence on an aquatic environment. About 360 million years ago, the first amphibians (see pp. 80–81) crawled onto the land, although they probably still returned to the water to lay their soft eggs. By the time the first reptiles and synapsids appeared late in the Carboniferous, animals with backbones had become fully independent of water.

Alternate layers of mud and sand

Layers bound by algae

Layered structure

Limestone

Long, beak-like snout

Growth line

Dorsal plate

Dorsal spine base

Fixed lateral plate

Bony dorsal shield

FOSSILIZED JAWLESS FISH

Glabella

Eye

Thoracic pleurae

Tail shield

Tail area

FOSSILIZED TRILOBITE

Ambulacral groove

Small ossicles of upper surface

Central disc

Iron pyrites

FOSSILIZED STARFISH

Row of ossicles

Broad disc

UPPER SURFACE OF FOSSILIZED STARFISH

Row of ossicles

Short arm

LOWER SURFACE OF FOSSILIZED STARFISH

Jointed leg

Chelicera (jointed pincer)

Jointed leg with oar-shaped paddle

Segmented abdomen

UNDERSIDE OF FOSSILIZED EURYPTERID

Telson (tail spine)

Abdominal segments

Shell contains eight somites (thoracic segments)

Hingeless, bivalved shell

FOSSIL OF AN EXTINCT SHRIMP

Growing tip

Disc-shaped sporangium (spore-case)

Leaf-like scale

Stem

RECONSTRUCTION OF ASTEROXYLON

Amphibians and reptiles

THE EARLIEST KNOWN AMPHIBIANS, such as *Acanthostega* and *Ichthyostega*, lived about 363 million years ago at the end of the Devonian period (409–363 million years ago). Their limbs may have evolved from the muscular fins of lungfish-like creatures. These fish can use their fins to push themselves along the bottom of lakes and some can breathe at the water's surface. While amphibians (see pp. 182–183) can exist on land, they are dependent on a wet environment because their skin does not retain moisture and most species must return to the water to lay their eggs. Evolving from amphibians, reptiles (see pp. 184–187) first appeared during the Carboniferous period (363–290 million years ago): *Westlothiana*, a possible early reptile, lived on land 338 million years ago. The development of the amniotic egg, with an embryo enclosed in its own wet environment (the amnion) and protected by a waterproof shell, freed reptiles from the amphibian's dependence on a wet habitat. A scaly skin protected the reptile from desiccation on land and enabled it to exploit ways of life closed to its amphibian ancestors. Reptiles include the dinosaurs, which came to dominate life on land during the Mesozoic era (245–65 million years ago).

Orbit

Sculpted or pitted bone surface

Pocket enclosing nostril

Spiracle to draw in water

Mandible

Small tooth

FOSSIL SKULL OF ACANTHOSTEGA

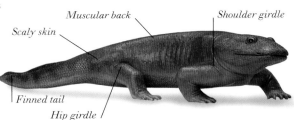

Muscular back

Shoulder girdle

Scaly skin

Finned tail

Hip girdle

MODEL OF ICHTHYOSTEGA

Dorsal vertebra

Scapula

Cleithrum

Cervical vertebra

Cranium

Orbit

Maxilla

Naris

Rib

Glenoid cavity

Humerus

Elbow joint

Mandible

Clavicle

Radius

Ulna

Phalanges

Metacarpals

Sharp tooth

SKELETON OF ERYOPS

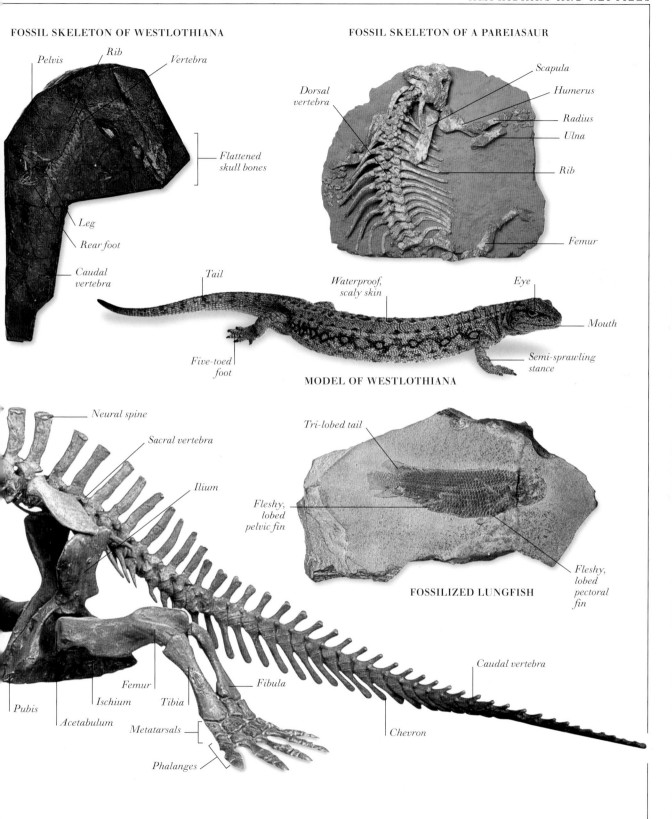

FOSSIL SKELETON OF WESTLOTHIANA

Pelvis

Rib

Vertebra

Flattened skull bones

Leg

Rear foot

Caudal vertebra

FOSSIL SKELETON OF A PAREIASAUR

Dorsal vertebra

Scapula

Humerus

Radius

Ulna

Rib

Femur

Tail

Waterproof, scaly skin

Eye

Mouth

Five-toed foot

Semi-sprawling stance

MODEL OF WESTLOTHIANA

Neural spine

Sacral vertebra

Ilium

Tri-lobed tail

Fleshy, lobed pelvic fin

Fleshy, lobed pectoral fin

FOSSILIZED LUNGFISH

Pubis

Acetabulum

Ischium

Femur

Tibia

Metatarsals

Phalanges

Fibula

Chevron

Caudal vertebra

The dinosaurs

THE DINOSAURS WERE A LARGE GROUP of reptiles that were the dominant land vertebrates (animals with backbones) for most of the Mesozoic era (245–65 million years ago). They appeared some 230 million years ago and were distinguished from other scaly, egg-laying reptiles by an important feature: dinosaurs had an erect limb stance. This enabled them to keep their bodies well above the ground, unlike the sprawling and semi-sprawling stance of other reptiles. The head of the dinosaur's femur (thigh-bone) fitted into a socket in its pelvis (hip-bone), producing efficient and mobile locomotion. Dinosaurs are categorized into two groups according to the structure of their pelvis: saurischian (lizard-hipped) and ornithischian (bird-hipped) dinosaurs. In the case of most saurischians, the pubis (part of the pelvis) jutted forward, while in ornithischians it slanted back, parallel to the ischium (another part of the pelvis). Dinosaurs ranged in size from smaller than a domestic cat to the biggest land animals ever known. The Dinosauria were the most successful land vertebrates ever, and survived for 165 million years, until most became extinct 65 million years ago.

STRUCTURE OF SAURISCHIAN PELVIS

Ilium

Hook of preacetabular process

Postacetabular process

Ilio-pubic joint

Acetabulum

Ilio-ischial joint

Pubis

Ischium

Pubic foot

GALLIMIMUS
A saurischian dinosaur

POSITION OF PELVIS IN A SAURISCHIAN DINOSAUR

STRUCTURE OF ORNITHISCHIAN PELVIS

Ilium

Postacetabular process

Preacetabular process

Ilio-ischial joint

Ilio-pubic joint

Prepubis

Acetabulum

Pubis

Ischium

HYPSILOPHODON
An ornithischian dinosaur

POSITION OF PELVIS IN AN ORNITHISCHIAN DINOSAUR

BAROSAURUS
A saurischian dinosaur

COMPARISON OF ANIMAL STANCES

SPRAWLING STANCE
The thighs and upper arms project straight out from the body so that the knees and elbows are bent at right angles.

COMMON IGUANA
(*Iguana iguana*)
A present-day reptile

ERECT STANCE
The thighs and upper arms project straight down from the body so that the knees and elbows are straight.

SEMI-SPRAWLING STANCE
The thighs and upper arms project downwards and outwards so that the knees and elbows are slightly bent.

DWARF CROCODILE
(*Osteolaemus tetraspis*)
A present-day reptile

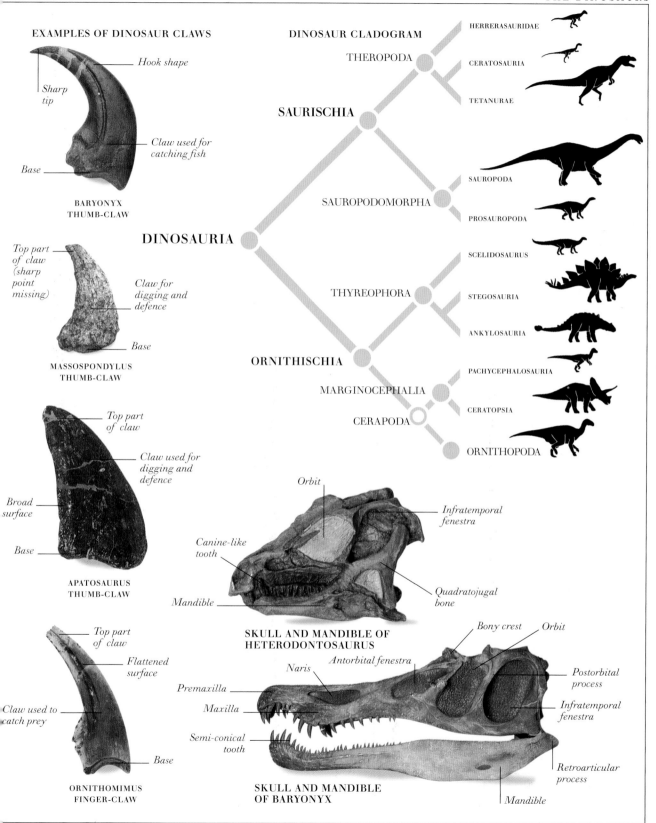

EXAMPLES OF DINOSAUR CLAWS

Hook shape

Sharp tip

Claw used for catching fish

Base

BARYONYX THUMB-CLAW

Top part of claw (sharp point missing)

Claw for digging and defence

Base

MASSOSPONDYLUS THUMB-CLAW

Top part of claw

Claw used for digging and defence

Broad surface

Base

APATOSAURUS THUMB-CLAW

Top part of claw

Flattened surface

Claw used to catch prey

Base

ORNITHOMIMUS FINGER-CLAW

DINOSAUR CLADOGRAM

THEROPODA

SAURISCHIA

DINOSAURIA

SAUROPODOMORPHA

THYREOPHORA

ORNITHISCHIA

MARGINOCEPHALIA

CERAPODA

HERRERASAURIDAE

CERATOSAURIA

TETANURAE

SAUROPODA

PROSAUROPODA

SCELIDOSAURUS

STEGOSAURIA

ANKYLOSAURIA

PACHYCEPHALOSAURIA

CERATOPSIA

ORNITHOPODA

Orbit

Infratemporal fenestra

Canine-like tooth

Quadratojugal bone

Mandible

SKULL AND MANDIBLE OF HETERODONTOSAURUS

Bony crest

Orbit

Antorbital fenestra

Naris

Premaxilla

Maxilla

Semi-conical tooth

Postorbital process

Infratemporal fenestra

Retroarticular process

Mandible

SKULL AND MANDIBLE OF BARYONYX

Theropods 1

AN ENORMOUSLY SUCCESSFUL SUBGROUP of the Saurischia,
the bipedal (two-footed) theropods ("beast feet") emerged
230 million years ago in Late Triassic times; the oldest known
example comes from South America. Theropods spanned the
age of most dinosaurs (230–65 million years ago) and beyond,
and included most of the known predatory dinosaurs. The
typical theropod had smallish arms with sharp, clawed fingers;
powerful jaws lined with sharp teeth; an S-shaped neck; long,
muscular hind limbs; and clawed, usually four-toed feet. Many
theropods may have been warm-blooded; most were exclusively
carnivorous. Theropods ranged from animals no larger than
a chicken to huge creatures, such as *Tyrannosaurus* and
Baryonyx. The group also included ostrich-like omnivores
and herbivores with toothless beaks, such as *Struthiomimus*
and *Gallimimus*. Birds are dinosaurs and evolved from
within a group of tetanuran theropods called maniraptorans.
Archaeopteryx, small and feathered, was the first known
bird and lived alongside other dinosaurs.

INTERNAL ANATOMY OF
ALBERTOSAURUS LEG

Ilio-tibial muscle
Ilio-femoral muscle
Femoro-tibial muscle
Internal tibial flexor muscle
Femur
Ilio-fibular muscle
Gastrocnemius muscle
Digital flexor muscle
Fibula
Tarsal
Metatarsal
Ambiens muscle
Femoro-tibial muscle
Anterior tibial muscle
Common digital extensor muscle
Toe
Claw

Cranium
Supraoccipital crest
Orbit
Naris
Cervical vertebrae
Dorsal vertebrae
Ilium
Cervical rib
Scapula
Shoulder joint
Ulna
Mandible
Phalanges
Serrated tooth
Metacarpals
Wrist joint
Elbow joint
Coracoid
Rib
Humerus
Femur
Ischium
Hip joint
Pubis
Knee joint
Tibia
Fibula
Ankle joint

SKELETON OF
TYRANNOSAURUS

Naris
Eye
Thigh
Scaly skin
Tail
Forelimb
Hand
Knee
Ankle
Hind limb
Toe
Foot
Metatarsals
Phalanges
Hallux (first toe)
Claw

EXTERNAL FEATURES OF TYRANNOSAURUS

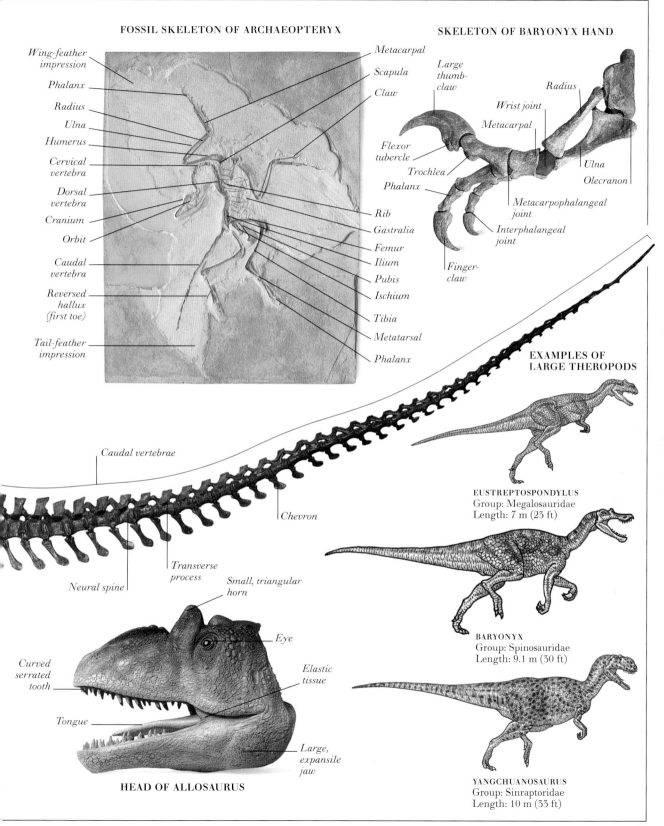

FOSSIL SKELETON OF ARCHAEOPTERYX

Wing-feather impression
Phalanx
Radius
Ulna
Humerus
Cervical vertebra
Dorsal vertebra
Cranium
Orbit
Caudal vertebra
Reversed hallux (first toe)
Tail-feather impression

Metacarpal
Scapula
Claw
Rib
Gastralia
Femur
Ilium
Pubis
Ischium
Tibia
Metatarsal
Phalanx

SKELETON OF BARYONYX HAND

Large thumb-claw
Radius
Wrist joint
Metacarpal
Flexor tubercle
Trochlea
Phalanx
Ulna
Olecranon
Metacarpophalangeal joint
Interphalangeal joint
Finger-claw

EXAMPLES OF LARGE THEROPODS

Caudal vertebrae
Chevron
Neural spine
Transverse process

Small, triangular horn
Eye
Curved serrated tooth
Elastic tissue
Tongue
Large, expansile jaw

HEAD OF ALLOSAURUS

EUSTREPTOSPONDYLUS
Group: Megalosauridae
Length: 7 m (23 ft)

BARYONYX
Group: Spinosauridae
Length: 9.1 m (30 ft)

YANGCHUANOSAURUS
Group: Sinraptoridae
Length: 10 m (33 ft)

Theropods 2

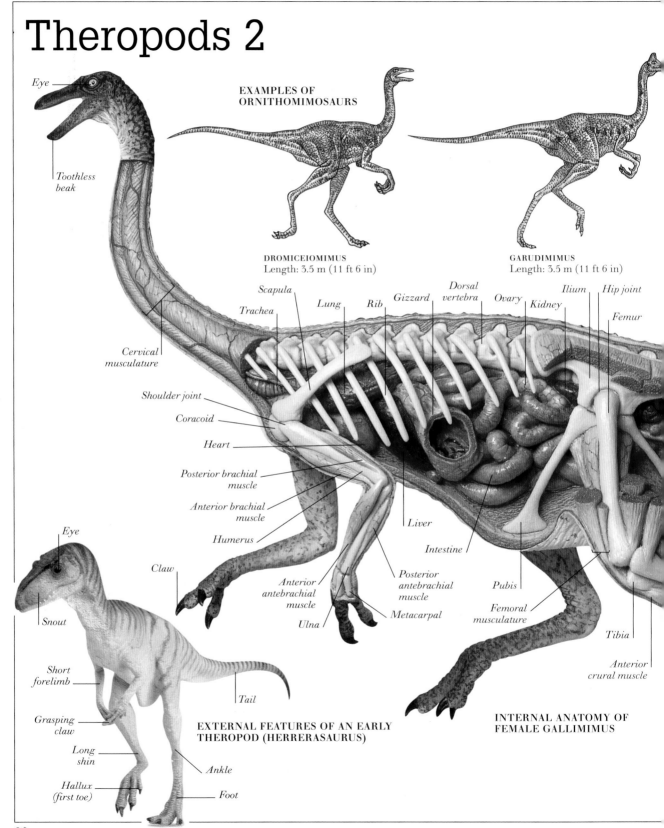

Eye

Toothless
beak

**EXAMPLES OF
ORNITHOMIMOSAURS**

DROMICEIOMIMUS
Length: 3.5 m (11 ft 6 in)

GARUDIMIMUS
Length: 3.5 m (11 ft 6 in)

Cervical
musculature

Scapula

Trachea

Lung

Rib

Gizzard

Dorsal
vertebra

Ovary

Kidney

Ilium

Hip joint

Femur

Shoulder joint

Coracoid

Heart

Posterior brachial
muscle

Anterior brachial
muscle

Humerus

Liver

Intestine

Pubis

Femoral
musculature

Tibia

Anterior
crural muscle

Anterior
antebrachial
muscle

Posterior
antebrachial
muscle

Metacarpal

Ulna

Claw

Eye

Snout

Short
forelimb

Grasping
claw

Long
shin

Hallux
(first toe)

Foot

Ankle

Tail

**EXTERNAL FEATURES OF AN EARLY
THEROPOD (HERRERASAURUS)**

**INTERNAL ANATOMY OF
FEMALE GALLIMIMUS**

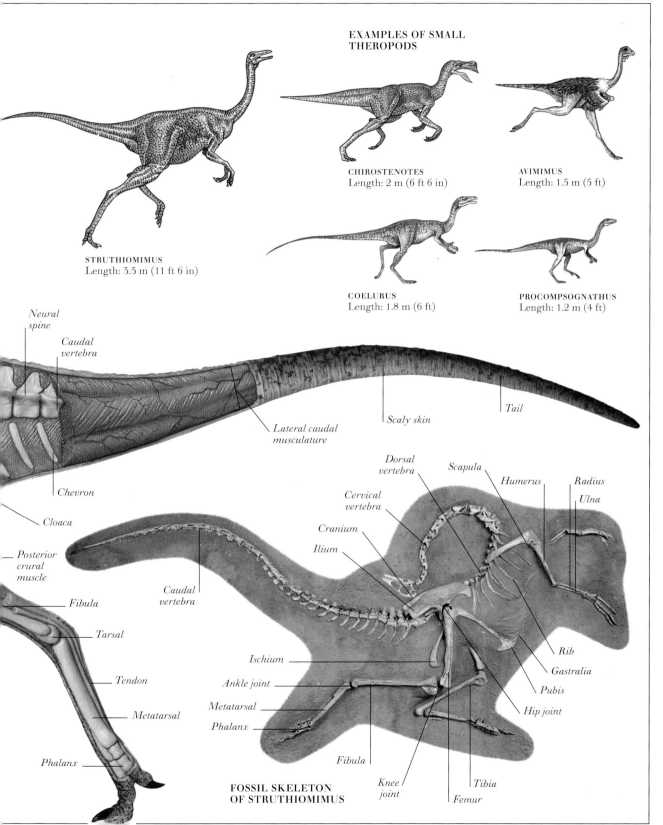

EXAMPLES OF SMALL
THEROPODS

CHIROSTENOTES
Length: 2 m (6 ft 6 in)

AVIMIMUS
Length: 1.5 m (5 ft)

STRUTHIOMIMUS
Length: 3.5 m (11 ft 6 in)

COELURUS
Length: 1.8 m (6 ft)

PROCOMPSOGNATHUS
Length: 1.2 m (4 ft)

Neural
spine

Caudal
vertebra

Lateral caudal
musculature

Scaly skin

Tail

Chevron

Cloaca

Posterior
crural
muscle

Fibula

Tarsal

Tendon

Metatarsal

Phalanx

Caudal
vertebra

Dorsal
vertebra

Scapula

Humerus

Radius

Ulna

Cervical
vertebra

Cranium

Ilium

Rib

Gastralia

Pubis

Hip joint

Ischium

Ankle joint

Metatarsal

Phalanx

Fibula

Knee
joint

Femur

Tibia

**FOSSIL SKELETON
OF STRUTHIOMIMUS**

Sauropodomorphs 1

THECODONTOSAURUS

THE SAUROPODOMORPHA ("lizard-feet forms") were herbivorous, usually quadrupedal (four-footed) dinosaurs. A clade within Saurischia, they were characterized by small heads, bulky bodies, and long necks and tails. Sauropodomorphs have often been split into two groups: prosauropods and sauropods. Prosauropods lived from Late Triassic to Early Jurassic times (225–180 million years ago) and included beasts such as the small *Anchisaurus* and one of the first very large dinosaurs, *Plateosaurus*. By Middle Jurassic times (about 165 million years ago), sauropods had replaced prosauropods and spread worldwide. They included the heaviest and longest land animals ever, such as *Diplodocus* and *Brachiosaurus*. Sauropods persisted to the end of the Cretaceous period (65 million years ago). Many of these dinosaurs moved in herds, protected from predatory theropods by their huge bulk and powerful tails, which they could use to lash out at attackers. Sauropodomorphs were the most common large herbivores until Late Jurassic times (about 145 million years ago), and appear to have survived in both southern and northern continents until the end of the Cretaceous period.

SKULL AND MANDIBLE OF PLATEOSAURUS

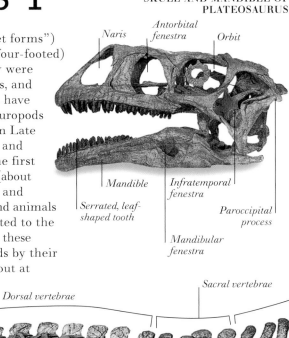

Naris
Antorbital fenestra
Orbit
Mandible
Infratemporal fenestra
Paroccipital process
Serrated, leaf-shaped tooth
Mandibular fenestra

SKELETON OF PLATEOSAURUS

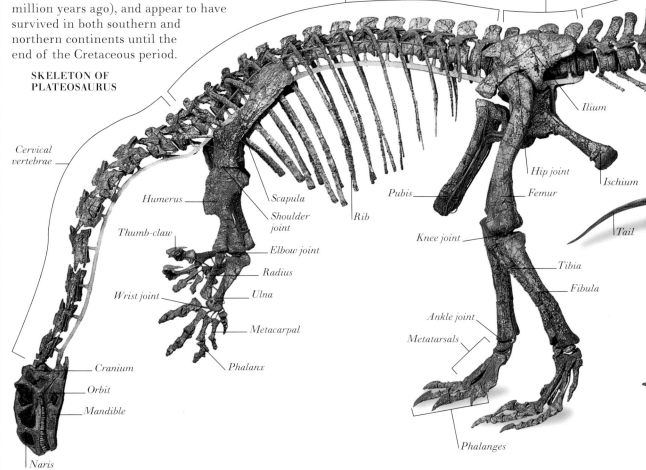

Dorsal vertebrae
Sacral vertebrae
Ilium
Hip joint
Ischium
Cervical vertebrae
Pubis
Femur
Humerus
Scapula
Tail
Shoulder joint
Rib
Thumb-claw
Knee joint
Elbow joint
Tibia
Radius
Fibula
Wrist joint
Ulna
Ankle joint
Metatarsals
Metacarpal
Cranium
Orbit
Phalanx
Mandible
Phalanges
Naris

THUMB-CLAW OF MASSOSPONDYLUS

Top part of claw (sharp point missing)

Curved body of claw

Base of claw

Caudal vertebrae

Neural spine

Chevron

Transverse process

EXAMPLES OF PROSAUROPODS

MASSOSPONDYLUS
Group: Massospondylidae
Length: 5 m (16 ft)

LUFENGOSAURUS
Group: Massospondylidae
Length: 6.1 m (20 ft)

RIOJASAURUS
Group: Riojasauridae
Length: 11 m (36 ft)

MELANOROSAURUS
Group: Melanorosauridae
Length: 7 m (23 ft)

EXTERNAL FEATURES OF ANCHISAURUS

Thigh

Toe

Claw

Forelimb

Hind limb

Slender snout

TOP VIEW OF ANCHISAURUS

Naris

Eye

Leaf-shaped tooth

Long, flexible neck

Long body

Hip

Scaly skin

Thigh

Tail

Knee

Ankle

Hind limb

Hallux (first toe)

Foot

Toe

Claw

Shoulder

Forelimb

Elbow

Hand

Large, curved thumb-claw

Finger

SIDE VIEW OF ANCHISAURUS

Sauropodomorphs 2

SKULL AND MANDIBLE OF DIPLODOCUS

Cranium
Orbit
Antorbital fenestra
Maxillary fenestra
Maxilla
Peg-shaped tooth
Sclerotic ring
Infratemporal fenestra
Mandible

FOREFOOT OF ELEPHANT

Wrist
Nail

FOREFOOT BONES OF ELEPHANT

Radius
Ulna
Carpals
Metacarpals
Phalanges

COMPARISON OF THE FOREFEET OF AN ELEPHANT AND DIPLODOCUS

FOREFOOT BONES OF DIPLODOCUS

Radius
Ulna
Carpals
Metacarpals
Phalanges

MIDDLE SECTION OF DIPLODOCUS SKELETON

Coracoid
Dorsal vertebra
Scapula
Sacral vertebra
Ilium
Caudal vertebra
Ischium
Hip joint
Femur
Humerus
Rib
Elbow joint
Knee joint
Ulna
Radius
Tibia
Fibula
Ankle joint
Wrist joint
Phalanges
Metacarpals

Neural spine
Small intestine
Dorsal vertebra
Ovary
Kidney
Rib
Large intestine
Hip joint
Caecum
Pubis
Femur
Oviduct
Cloaca
Thigh musculature
Posterior crural musculature
Fibula
Ankle joint
Anterior crural muscle
Metatarsal
Caudal musculature

FOSSIL EGG OF SALTASAURID

Fossil eggshell fragment

Fossil egg

Fossil eggshell fragment

Outer ear

Naris

Eye

Mouth

Orbit

Antorbital fenestra

Naris

Cranium

Maxilla

Infratemporal fenestra

Spoon-shaped tooth

Mandible

SKULL AND MANDIBLE OF CAMARASAURUS

INTERNAL ANATOMY OF FEMALE BRACHIOSAURUS

Cervical vertebra

Scapula

Trachea

Oesophagus

Intercostal muscle

Scapular muscle

Shoulder joint

Lung

Humerus

Gizzard

Anterior brachial muscle

Posterior brachial musculature

Elbow joint

Radius

Ulna

Posterior antebrachial musculature

Wrist joint

Metacarpal

CETIOSAURUS
Group: Cetisauridae
Length: 18 m (59 ft)

SHUNOSAURUS
Group: Eusauropoda
Length: 10 m (33 ft)

SALTASAURUS
Group: Saltasauridae
Length: 12.2 m (40 ft)

DIPLODOCUS
Group: Diplodocidae
Length: 27.4 m (90 ft)

Thyreophorans 1

THYREOPHORANS ("SHIELD BEARERS") were a group of quadrupedal armoured dinosaurs. They were one clade among several within the Ornithischia (bird-hipped dinosaurs), they were characterized by rows of bony studs, plates, or spikes along the back, which protected some from predators and may have helped others regulate body temperature. Up to 9 m (30 ft) long, with a small head and small cheek teeth, thyreophorans had shorter forelimbs than hind limbs and probably browsed on low-level vegetation. The earliest thyreophorans were small and lived in Early Jurassic times (about 200 million years ago) in Europe, North America, and China. Stegosaurs, such as *Stegosaurus* and *Kentrosaurus*, replaced these older forms. The earliest stegosaur remains come mainly from China. Several genera of stegosaurs survived into the Early Cretaceous period (145–100 million years ago). Ankylosaurs, with a combination of beak and teeth in close proximity, and cheek teeth adapted for cropping vegetation, appeared at the same time as stegosaurs. They originated in the Late Jurassic period (155 million years ago) and in North America survived until 65 million years ago.

TUOJIANGOSAURUS
Group: Stegosauridae
Length: 7 m (23 ft)

Dorsal plate

Hip

Thigh

Cervical plate

Eye

Naris

Beak

Cheek

Neck

Outer ear

Knee

Shoulder

Long
hind limb

Short forelimb

Elbow

Nail

Wrist

Ankle

Hind foot

**EXTERNAL FEATURES OF
STEGOSAURUS**

Nail

Forefoot

EXAMPLES OF STEGOSAURS

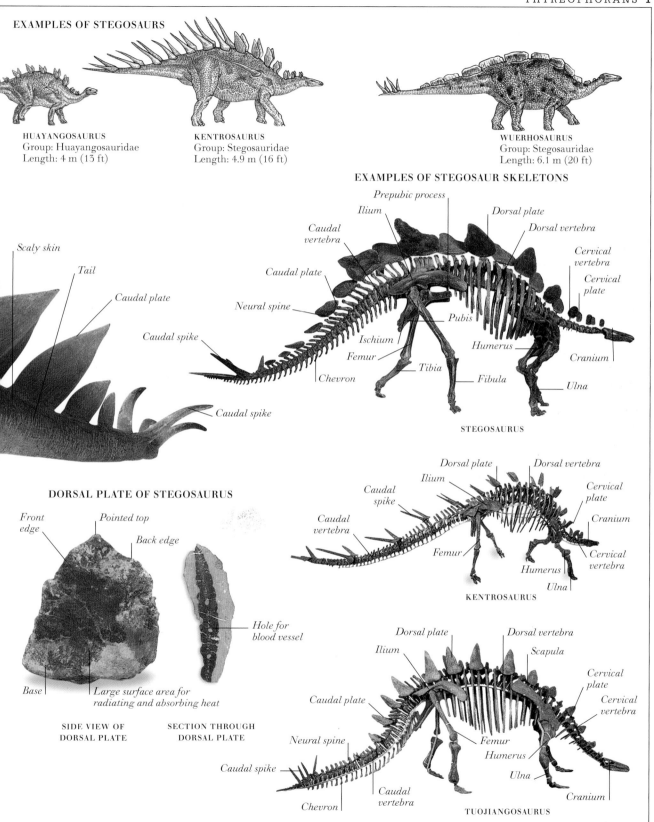

HUAYANGOSAURUS
Group: Huayangosauridae
Length: 4 m (13 ft)

KENTROSAURUS
Group: Stegosauridae
Length: 4.9 m (16 ft)

WUERHOSAURUS
Group: Stegosauridae
Length: 6.1 m (20 ft)

EXAMPLES OF STEGOSAUR SKELETONS

Scaly skin

Tail

Caudal plate

Caudal spike

Caudal spike

Prepubic process

Ilium

Caudal vertebra

Dorsal plate

Dorsal vertebra

Cervical vertebra

Cervical plate

Caudal plate

Neural spine

Pubis

Ischium

Femur

Tibia

Chevron

Humerus

Fibula

Cranium

Ulna

STEGOSAURUS

DORSAL PLATE OF STEGOSAURUS

Front edge

Pointed top

Back edge

Hole for blood vessel

Base

Large surface area for radiating and absorbing heat

SIDE VIEW OF DORSAL PLATE

SECTION THROUGH DORSAL PLATE

Dorsal plate

Ilium

Caudal spike

Caudal vertebra

Dorsal vertebra

Cervical plate

Cranium

Femur

Humerus

Cervical vertebra

Ulna

KENTROSAURUS

Dorsal plate

Ilium

Caudal plate

Neural spine

Caudal spike

Chevron

Caudal vertebra

Dorsal vertebra

Scapula

Cervical plate

Cervical vertebra

Femur

Humerus

Ulna

Cranium

TUOJIANGOSAURUS

Thyreophorans 2

EXAMPLES OF
ANKYLOSAUR
SKULLS

Maxilla

Orbit

Posterolateral horn

Naris

Beak

Cranium

Tooth

Mandible

Jugal plate

SKULL AND MANDIBLE OF EUOPLOCEPHALUS

Nasal bone

Maxilla

Posterolateral horn

Cranium

Orbit

Naris

Beak

Tooth

Mandible

SKULL AND MANDIBLE OF ANKYLOSAURUS

Orbit

Nasal bone

Beak

Naris

Cranium

Infratemporal fenestra

Mandible

**SKULL AND MANDIBLE
OF PANOPLOSAURUS**

Dorsal vertebra

Rib

Small intestine

Gizzard

Ilio-tibial muscle

Scapula

Lung

Ilium

Reproductive canal

Ischium

Coracoid

Cervical musculature

Head horn

Shoulder spike

Humerus

Radius

Wrist joint

Heart

Liver

Ilio-tibial muscle

Femur

Knee joint

Metacarpal

Toothless beak

Large intestine

Fibula

Gastrocnemius muscle

Ventral antebrachial muscle

Ulna

Elbow joint

Digital extensor muscle

Ankle joint

Metatarsal

INTERNAL ANATOMY OF FEMALE EUOPLOCEPHALUS

94

EXTERNAL FEATURES OF EDMONTONIA

EXAMPLES OF ANKYLOSAURS

Hind limb

Flank spike

Dorsal scute

Dermal armour

Scaly skin

Nuchal ring

Shoulder spike

Broad, flat snout

Ankle

Elbow

Forelimb

Naris

Caudal vertebra

Neural spine

Ureter

Forefoot

Blunt nail

Terminal plate

Chevron

Cloaca

Lateral caudal musculature

Lateral plate

PINACOSAURUS
Group: Ankylosauridae
Length: 16 ft 6 in (5 m)

MINMI
Group: Ankylosauria
Length: 8 ft (2.4 m)

POLACANTHUS
Group: Polacanthidae
Length: 13 ft (4 m)

FOSSIL OF ANKYLOSAURUS TAIL CLUB

Ossified caudal vertebra

Tail club

Ornithopods 1

ORNITHOPODS ("BIRD FEET") were a group of ornithischian ("bird-hipped") dinosaurs. These bipedal and quadrupedal herbivores had a horny beak, plant-cutting or grinding cheek teeth, and a pelvic and tail region stiffened by bony tendons. They evolved teeth and jaws adapted to pulping vegetation and flourished

IGUANODON TOOTH

from the Middle Jurassic to the Late Cretaceous period (165–65 million years ago) in North America, Europe, Africa, China, Australia, and Antarctica. Some ornithopods were no larger than a dog, while others were immense creatures up to 15 m (49 ft) long. Iguanodonts, an ornithopod group, had a broad, toothless beak at the end of a long snout, large jaws with long rows of ridged, closely packed teeth for grinding vegetation, a bulky body, and a heavy tail. *Iguanodon* and some other iguanodonts had large thumb-spikes that were strong enough to stab attackers. Another group, the hadrosaurs, such as *Gryposaurus* and *Hadrosaurus*, lived in Late Cretaceous times (97–65 million years ago) and with their broad beaks are sometimes known as "duckbills". They were characterized by their deep skulls and closely packed rows of teeth, while some, such as *Corythosaurus* and *Lambeosaurus*, had tall, hollow, bony head crests.

SKELETON OF IGUANODON

- Orbit
- Cranium
- Naris
- Mandible
- Cervical vertebra
- Cervical rib
- Scapula
- Humerus
- Sternal bone
- Radius
- Dorsal vertebra
- Ulna
- Prepubic process
- Femur
- Pubis
- Tibia
- Sacral vertebra
- Caudal vertebra
- Neural spine
- Ilium
- Chevron
- Ischium
- Fibula
- Metatarsal

EXTERNAL FEATURES OF MANTELLISAURUS

- Thigh
- Heavy, stiff tail
- Knee
- Hind limb
- Ankle
- Toe
- Foot
- Hoof-like nail

SKULL AND MANDIBLE OF YOUNG MANTELLISAURUS

- Maxilla
- Cheek tooth
- Orbit
- Cranium
- Premaxilla
- Paroccipital process
- Jugal bone
- Coronoid process
- Predentary bone
- Dentary bone
- Mandible

EXAMPLES OF IGUANODONTS

OURANOSAURUS
Group: Iguanodontia
Length: 7 m (23 ft)

CAMPTOSAURUS
Group: Camptosauridae
Length: 4.9–7 m (16–23 ft)

MUTTABURRASAURUS
Group: Iguanodontia
Length: 7 m (23 ft)

PROBACTROSAURUS
Group: Hadrosauroidea
Length: 6.1 m (20 ft)

Shoulder

Eye

Naris

Neck

Beak

Tongue

Scaly skin

Forelimb

Elbow

Wrist

Hand

Finger

Thumb-spike

Hoof-like nail

**INTERNAL ANATOMY OF
HIND LEG OF IGUANODON**

Ilium

Ilio-femoral
muscle

Ilio-tibial
muscle

Ambiens
muscle

Short
caudo-
femoral
muscle

External pubo-ischio-
femoral muscle

Tibial flexor
muscle

Femur

Ilio-fibular
muscle

Gastrocnemius
muscle

Common digital
extensor muscle

Anterior tibial
muscle

Tibia

Fibula

Tarsal

Metatarsal

Toe

Hoof-like nail

97

Ornithopods 2

BRACHYLOPHOSAURUS
Length: 7m (23 ft)

LAMBEOSAURUS
Length: 14.9 m (49 ft)

Caudal vertebrae

Sacral
vertebrae

Neural spine

Chevron

Rounded top
end of egg

Emerging
hatchling

Hatchling

Plant material
to protect and
warm eggs

Eggshell
fragment

Ilium

Unhatched
egg

Raised nest
scooped out
of soil

Hip joint

Ischium

Prepubic process

MODEL OF MAIASAURA NEST

Bony crest

Naris

Femur

Eye

Knee joint

Cheek pouch

Neck

Thigh

**FOSSIL SKELETON OF
PARASAUROLOPHUS**

Tongue

Toothless
beak

Scaly skin

Shoulder

Forelimb

Elbow

Long, thick
tail

Ankle joint

Tubercle

Wrist

Knee

Hind limb

Metatarsal

Nail

Ankle

Toe

**EXTERNAL FEATURES
OF CORYTHOSAURUS**

Nail

Foot

EXAMPLES OF HADROSAURS

HYPACROSAURUS
Length: 9.1 m (30 ft)

HADROSAURUS
Length: 7.9–10 m (26–33 ft)

GRYPOSAURUS
Length: 7.9–10 m (26–33 ft)

Dorsal
vertebrae

Bony crest

Air passage

Cranium

Infratemporal fenestra

Orbit

Cervical
vertebrae

Mandible

Naris

Scapula

Shoulder joint

Tibia

Rib

Humerus

Elbow joint

Fibula

Radius

Wrist joint

Ulna

Phalanges

Metacarpal

Phalanges

Orbit

Infratemporal
fenestra

Air passage

Naris

Mandible

Tooth

**SKULL AND MANDIBLE
OF JUVENILE
LAMBEOSAURUS**

Sclerotic ring

Bony
crest

Cranium

Orbit

Naris

Infratemporal
fenestra

Mandible

Premaxilla

**SKULL AND MANDIBLE OF
ADULT LAMBEOSAURUS**

Marginocephalians 1

MARGINOCEPHALIA ("margined heads") were a group of bipedal and quadrupedal ornithischian dinosaurs with a narrow shelf or deep, bony frill at the back of the skull. Marginocephalians were probably descended from the same ancestor as the ornithopods and lived in what are now North America, Africa, Asia, and Europe during the Cretaceous period (145–65 million years ago). They were divided into two groups: Pachycephalosauria ("thickheaded lizards"), such as *Pachycephalosaurus* and *Stegoceras*, and Ceratopsia ("horned faces"), such as *Triceratops* and *Psittacosaurus*. The thick skulls of Pachycephalosauria may have protected their brains during possible head-butting contests fought to win territory and mates; their hips and spines may also have been strengthened to withstand the shock. The bony frill of Ceratopsia would have added to their frightening appearance when charging; the neck was strengthened for impact and to support the huge head, with its snipping beak and powerful slicing toothed jaws. A charging ceratopsian would have been a formidable opponent for even the largest predators. Ceratopsians were among the most abundant herbivorous dinosaurs of the Late Cretaceous period (97–65 million years ago).

HEAD-BUTTING PRENOCEPHALES

Labels on skeleton: Thick, high-domed cranium · Supraorbital ridge · Orbit · Naris · Mandible · Neural spine · Cervical rib · Humerus · Ulna · Radius · Wrist joint · Metacarpal · Phalanx · Pubis · Ilium · Ischium · Metatarsals · Phalanges

EXAMPLES OF SKULLS OF PACHYCEPHALOSAURS

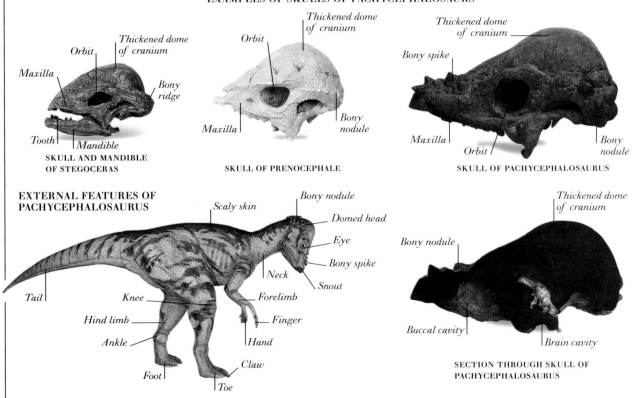

Labels (Stegoceras skull): Orbit · Thickened dome of cranium · Maxilla · Bony ridge · Tooth · Mandible

SKULL AND MANDIBLE OF STEGOCERAS

Labels (Prenocephale skull): Orbit · Thickened dome of cranium · Maxilla · Bony nodule

SKULL OF PRENOCEPHALE

Labels (Pachycephalosaurus skull): Thickened dome of cranium · Bony spike · Maxilla · Orbit · Bony nodule

SKULL OF PACHYCEPHALOSAURUS

EXTERNAL FEATURES OF PACHYCEPHALOSAURUS

Labels: Scaly skin · Bony nodule · Domed head · Eye · Bony spike · Neck · Snout · Tail · Knee · Hind limb · Ankle · Forelimb · Finger · Hand · Foot · Claw · Toe

Labels (section): Thickened dome of cranium · Bony nodule · Buccal cavity · Brain cavity

SECTION THROUGH SKULL OF PACHYCEPHALOSAURUS

EXAMPLES OF PACHYCEPHALOSAURS

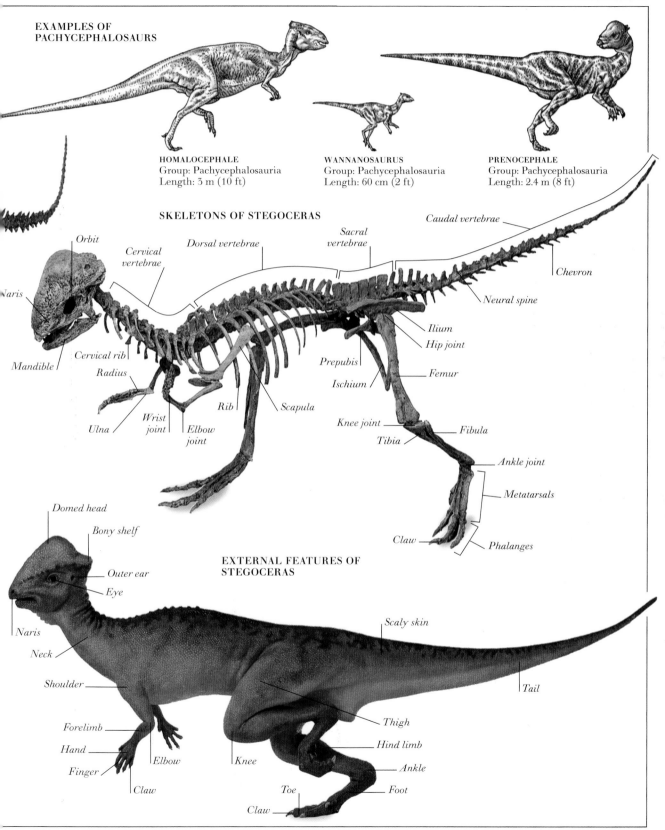

HOMALOCEPHALE
Group: Pachycephalosauria
Length: 3 m (10 ft)

WANNANOSAURUS
Group: Pachycephalosauria
Length: 60 cm (2 ft)

PRENOCEPHALE
Group: Pachycephalosauria
Length: 2.4 m (8 ft)

SKELETONS OF STEGOCERAS

Orbit

Cervical vertebrae

Dorsal vertebrae

Sacral vertebrae

Caudal vertebrae

Chevron

Neural spine

Naris

Ilium

Hip joint

Mandible

Cervical rib

Prepubis

Femur

Radius

Ischium

Scapula

Rib

Ulna

Wrist joint

Elbow joint

Knee joint

Fibula

Tibia

Ankle joint

Metatarsals

Claw

Phalanges

EXTERNAL FEATURES OF STEGOCERAS

Domed head

Bony shelf

Outer ear

Eye

Scaly skin

Naris

Neck

Tail

Shoulder

Forelimb

Thigh

Hand

Hind limb

Finger

Elbow

Knee

Ankle

Claw

Toe

Foot

Claw

Marginocephalians 2

SKULL AND MANDIBLE OF STYRACOSAURUS

Parietal fenestra
Epoccipital bone
Parietosquamosal frill
Nose horn core
Supraorbital ridge
Naris
Orbit
Cranium
Mandible

EXTERNAL FEATURES OF TRICERATOPS

Parietosquamosal frill
Epoccipital bone
Brow horn
Nose horn
Thick, scaly skin
Thigh
Tail
Ankle
Hind limb
Elbow
Nail
Forelimb
Wrist
Eye
Naris
Toothless beak

SKULL AND MANDIBLE OF PROTOCERATOPS

Parietosquamosal frill
Cranium
Postorbital bone
Parietal fenestra
Nasal bone
Orbit
Lacrimal bone
Naris
Infratemporal fenestra
Beak
Rostral bone
Jugal bone
Predentary bone
Surangular bone
Dentary bone
Tooth
Angular bone
Mandible

SKELETON OF TRICERATOPS

Pubis
Ilium
Hip joint
Dorsal vertebrae
Rib
Scapula
Humerus
Ischium
Femur
Knee joint
Fibula
Tibia
Ankle joint
Metatarsals
Phalanges
Caudal vertebra
Chevron
Neural spine
Elbow joint
Ulna
Sternal bone
Coracoid
Shoulder joint
Radius

EXTERNAL FEATURES
OF PSITTACOSAURUS

Eye

Cheek horn

Beak

Claw

Finger

Scaly skin

Thigh

Forelimb

Elbow

Knee

Claw

Toe

Ankle

Hind limb

Parietosquamosal
frill

Tail

Cranium

Orbit

Brow horn
core

Nose horn
core

Naris

Cervical
rib

Infratemporal
fenestra

Jugal bone

Tooth

Mandible

Metacarpals

Phalanges

Predentary
bone

Rostral bone

EXAMPLES OF CERATOPSIA

PROTOCERATOPS
Group: Protoceratopsidae
Length: 2.7 m (9 ft)

STYRACOSAURUS
Group: Centrosaurinae
Length: 5.5 m (18 ft)

TRICERATOPS
Group: Chasmosaurinae
Length: 9.1 m (30 ft)

PACHYRHINOSAURUS
Group: Centrosaurinae
Length: 5.5 m (18 ft)

LEPTOCERATOPS
Group: Leptoceratopsidae
Length: 2.1 m (7 ft)

Mammals 1

TETRALOPHODON CHEEK TEETH

Long tail aids balance

Insulating hair

SINCE THE EXTINCTION of most of the dinosaurs 65 million years ago, mammals (along with birds) have been the dominant vertebrates on land. This class includes terrestrial, aerial, and aquatic forms. Having developed from the therapsids, the first true mammals – small, nocturnal, shrew-like creatures, such as *Megazostrodon*-appeared over 200 million years ago during the Triassic period (250–200 million years ago). Mammals had several features that differed from those of their ancestors: an efficient four-chambered heart allowed these warm-blooded animals to sustain high levels of activity; a covering of hair helped them maintain a constant body temperature; an improved limb structure gave them more efficient locomotion; and the birth of live young and the immediate supply of food from the mother's milk aided their rapid growth. Since the end of the Mesozoic era (65 million years ago), the number of major mammal groups and the abundance of species in each have varied dramatically. For example, the Perissodactyla (the group that includes *Coelodonta* and modern horses) was a common group during the Early Tertiary period (about 54 million years ago). Today, the mammalian groups with the most species include the Rodentia (rats and mice), the Chiroptera (bats), the Primates (monkeys and apes), the Carnivora (bears, cats, and dogs), and the Artiodactyla (cattle, deer, and pigs), while the Proboscidea group, which formerly included many genera, such as *Phiomia*, *Moeritherium*, *Tetralophodon*, and *Mammuthus*, now has only three species of elephant. In Australia and South America, millions of years of continental isolation led to increased diversity of the marsupials, a group of mammals distinct from the placentals (see p. 74) that existed elsewhere.

Neural spine

Scapula

Cervical vertebra

Humerus

Nasal horn

Naris

Orbit

Mandible

Premaxilla bone

Radius

Ulna

Chisel-edged molar

Metacarpal

Phalanx

UPPER JAWBONE (MAXILLA) OF A HORSE

Molars

Premolars

HOOFBONE (THIRD PHALANX) OF A HORSE

Articular surface

Tendon insertion

Cranium

Naris

Premaxilla bone

Molar tooth

SKULL AND MANDIBLE OF A MOERITHERIUM

Upper jaw tusk

Shovel-shaped tusk

Molar tooth

SKULL AND MANDIBLE OF A PHIOMIA

Trunk

Thick hide

Short tusk used for rooting up plants

MODEL OF A PHIOMIA

Dorsal vertebra

Ilium

Ball and socket joint

Pubis

Rib

Caudal vertebra

Femur

Tibia

Fibula

Metatarsal

Phalanx

SKELETON OF AN ARSINOITHERIUM

Mandible

Cranium

Teeth

Elongated digit

Humerus

Hind limb bone

FOSSIL SKELETON OF A BAT

Mammals 2

LOWER JAW OF A BEAR

Articulation with skull

Large canine

Diastema

Low cusp

Premolar

Molar

SKELETON OF A TOXODON

Scapula

Neural spine

Cervical vertebra

Zygomatic arch

Cranium

Orbit

Maxilla

Nasal bone

Incisor

Mandible

Molar

Incisor

Occipital region

Humerus

Radius

Ulna

Metacarpals

Large breastbone

Phalanx

SKULL OF AN OPOSSUM

Orbit

Cranium

Naris

Occipital region

Canine

Infraorbital foramen

Molar

**FOSSIL SKULL OF
AN HYAENODON**

Orbit

Sagittal crest

Naris

Cranium

Canine

Neck
insertion

Infraorbital
foramen

Mandible

Molar

**LOWER JAW OF AN
AUSTRALOPITHECUS**

Expanded
occlusal
surface

Premolar

Molar

SKULL OF A SMILODON

Orbit

Muscle scar

Naris

Sagittal crest

Infraorbital
foramen

Occipital
condyle

Canine

Dentary
bone

Slicing
tooth

Zygomatic
arch

Ilium

Femur

Rib

Knee
joint

Tibia

Fibula

Metatarsals

Phalanx

Thick,
insulating
coat

Ivory tusk

Woolly
underhair

Hairy trunk

RECONSTRUCTION OF A MAMMOTH

The first humans

MODERN HUMANS BELONG TO THE MAMMALIAN order of primates
(see pp. 202–203), which originated about 55 million years ago;
primates included the only extant hominid species. The earliest
members of the human clade include *Ardipithecus* ("ground ape")
and *Australopithecus* ("southern ape"), both small-brained intermediates
between apes and humans that were capable of standing and walking
upright. *Homo habilis*, the earliest member of the genus Homo, appeared
at least 2 million years ago. This larger-brained "handy man" began making
tools for hunting. *Homo ergaster* first appeared in Africa about 1.8 million
years ago and spread into Asia about 800,000 years later. Smaller-toothed than
Homo habilis, H. ergaster – followed by Homo erectus – developed fire as a tool,
which enabled it to cook food. Neanderthals, a near relative of modern humans,
originated about 200,000 years ago, and *Homo sapiens* (modern humans) appeared
in Africa about 100,000 years later. The two co-existed for thousands of years, but by
30,000 years ago, *Homo sapiens* had become dominant and the Neanderthals had died
out. Classification of *Homo sapiens* in relation to its ancestors is enormously problematic:
modern humans must be classified not only by bone structure, but also by specific
behaviour – the ability to plan future action; to follow traditions; and to use
symbolic communication, including complex language and the ability to use
and recognize symbols.

**JAWBONE OF AUSTRALOPITHECUS
(SOUTHERN APE)**

*Larger jawbone
than modern
human*

*Large back
tooth*

*Jutting brow
ridge*

Cranium

Orbit

Naris

*Jutting
jawbone*

**SKULL OF AUSTRALOPITHECUS
(SOUTHERN APE)**

Orbit

Naris

**SKULL OF HOMO HABILIS
(FIRST MEMBER OF HOMO GENUS)**

*Larger braincase than
Australopithecus*

Orbit

Naris

External auditory meatus

SKULL OF HOMO ERECTUS (UPRIGHT MAN)

*Well-rounded
cranium*

*Small brow
ridge*

Orbit

Naris

Small tooth

*External
auditory meatus*

SKULL OF HOMO SAPIENS (MODERN HUMAN)

108

FLINT TOOL MADE ABOUT 250,000 YEARS AGO

Point

Sharp edge used to cut meat

Flint may have been carved by Homo erectus

FLINT HANDAXE

FLINT FLAKE

EXAMPLES OF TOOLS USED BY HOMO SAPIENS

Axe used to clear land

Leather binding

FIRE-MAKING TOOLS

Wooden mouthpiece held drill securely

WOODEN MOUTHPIECE

Wooden drill turned in drill hole to create spark

Bone

Leather bow kept drill upright

BOW DRILL

DRY STRAW

Drill hole

WOODEN HEARTH

Hammer head used to detach chips of flint

Head used to mine flint

Handle

Handle

Handle

ANTLER HAMMER

RED DEER ANTLER HAMMER

FARMING AXE

EXAMPLES OF PREHISTORIC FOODS

MINT

WHEAT GRAINS

SALMON

SPEAR AND ARROW HEADS

Antler

HARPOON POINT

Twine binding

FISHING TACKLE

Wooden point hardened by fire

WOODEN ARROW

Flint glued into groove cut in shaft

FLINT ARROW

PLANTS

Plant variety

THE ARE MORE THAN 300,000 SPECIES of plants.
They show a wide diversity of forms and life-styles, ranging, for example,
from delicate liverworts, adapted for life in a damp habitat, to cacti, capable of surviving
in the desert, and from herbaceous plants, such as corn, which completes its life-cycle in one year,
to the giant redwood tree, which can live for thousands of years. This diversity reflects the adaptations
of plants to survive in a wide range of habitats. This is seen most clearly in the flowering plants (phylum
Angiospermophyta), which are the most numerous, with over 250,000 species, and the most widespread,
being found from the tropics to the poles. Despite their diversity, plants share certain characteristics: typically,
plants are green, and make their food by photosynthesis; and most plants live in or on a substrate, such as
soil, and do not actively move. Algae (kingdom Protista) and fungi (kingdom Fungi) have
some plant-like characteristics and are often studied alongside plants, although they
are not true plants.

FLOWERING PLANT
Bromeliad
(*Acanthostachys strobilacea*)

Leaf

GREEN ALGA
Micrograph of desmid
(*Micrasterias sp.*)

Pyrenoid
(*small protein
body*)

Chloroplast

Sinus
(*division between
two halves of cell*)

Cell wall

FERN
Tree fern
(*Dicksonia antarctica*)

Rachis
(*main axis
of pinnate leaf*)

Petiole
(*leaf stalk*)

Ramentum
(*brown scale*)

Base of dead
frond (*leaf*)

Trunk

Adventitious
root

Epiphytic
fern growing
at base

BRYOPHYTE
Moss
(*Bryum sp.*)

Seta
(*stalk*)

Immature capsule

Sporophyte
(*spore-
producing
plant*)

Capsule
(*site of spore
production*)

"Leaf"

Gametophyte
(*gamete-producing
plant*)

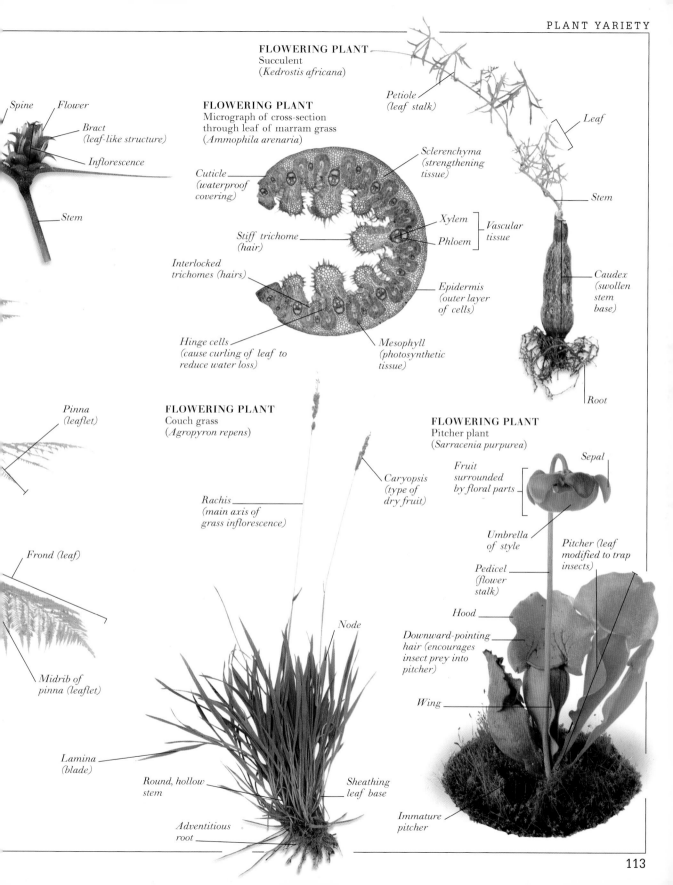

FLOWERING PLANT
Succulent
(*Kedrostis africana*)

Petiole
(leaf stalk)

Leaf

Stem

FLOWERING PLANT
Micrograph of cross-section
through leaf of marram grass
(*Ammophila arenaria*)

Sclerenchyma
(strengthening
tissue)

Cuticle
(waterproof
covering)

Xylem

Vascular
tissue

Stiff trichome
(hair)

Phloem

Interlocked
trichomes (hairs)

Epidermis
(outer layer
of cells)

Caudex
(swollen
stem
base)

Hinge cells
(cause curling of leaf to
reduce water loss)

Mesophyll
(photosynthetic
tissue)

Root

Spine

Flower

Bract
(leaf-like structure)

Inflorescence

Stem

Pinna
(leaflet)

FLOWERING PLANT
Couch grass
(*Agropyron repens*)

Caryopsis
(type of
dry fruit)

Rachis
(main axis of
grass inflorescence)

FLOWERING PLANT
Pitcher plant
(*Sarracenia purpurea*)

Sepal

Fruit
surrounded
by floral parts

Umbrella
of style

Pitcher (leaf
modified to trap
insects)

Pedicel
(flower
stalk)

Node

Frond (leaf)

Hood

Downward-pointing
hair (encourages
insect prey into
pitcher)

Midrib of
pinna (leaflet)

Wing

Lamina
(blade)

Round, hollow
stem

Sheathing
leaf base

Adventitious
root

Immature
pitcher

113

Fungi and lichens

FUNGI WERE ONCE THOUGHT OF AS PLANTS but are now classified as a separate kingdom. This kingdom includes not only the familiar mushrooms, puffballs, stinkhorns, and moulds, but also yeasts, smuts, rusts, and lichens. Most fungi are multicellular, consisting of a mass of thread-like hyphae that together form a mycelium. However, the simpler fungi (e.g., yeasts) are microscopic, single-celled organisms. Typically, fungi reproduce by means of spores. Most fungi feed on dead or decaying matter, or on living organisms. A few fungi obtain their food from plants or algae, with which they have a symbiotic (mutually advantageous) relationship. Lichens are a symbiotic partnership between algae and fungi. Of the six types of lichens the three most common are crustose (flat and crusty), foliose (leafy), and fruticose (shrub-like). Some lichens (e.g., *Cladonia floerkeana*) are a combination of types. Lichens reproduce by means of spores or soredia (powdery vegetative fragments).

Emerging sporophore (spore-bearing structure)

Pileus (cap) continuous with stipe (stalk)

Bark of dead beech tree

Inrolled margin of pileus (cap)

Gill (site of spore production)

Sporophore (spore-bearing structure)

Stipe (stalk)

Hyphae (fungal filaments)

OYSTER FUNGUS
(*Pleurotus pulmonarius*)

EXAMPLES OF LICHENS

Secondary fruticose thallus

Branched, hollow stem

Apothecium (spore-producing body)

FRUTICOSE
Cladonia portentosa

Soredia (powdery vegetative fragments) produced at end of lobe

Tree bark

Foliose thallus

FOLIOSE
Hypogymnia physodes

Soredia (powdery vegetative fragments) released onto surface of squamulose thallus

Apothecium (spore-producing body)

Basal scale of primary squamulose thallus

Moss

Podetium (granular stalk) of secondary fruticose thallus

SQUAMULOSE (SCALY) AND FRUTICOSE THALLUS
Cladonia floerkeana

Gleba (spore-producing tissue found in this type of fungus)

Sporophore (spore-bearing structure)

Porous stipe (stalk)

Volva (remains of universal veil)

STINKHORN
(*Phallus impudicus*)

Toothed branchlet

Branch

Sporophore (spore-bearing structure)

Stipe (stalk)

RAMARIA FORMOSA

SECTION THROUGH FOLIOSE LICHEN SHOWING REPRODUCTION BY SOREDIA

Soredium (powdery vegetative fragment involved in propagation) released from lichen

Algal cell

Fungal hypha

Upper cortex

Algal layer

Medulla of fungal hyphae (mycelium)

Lower cortex

Rhizine (bundle of absorptive hyphae)

Soralium (pore in upper surface of thallus)

Upper surface of thallus

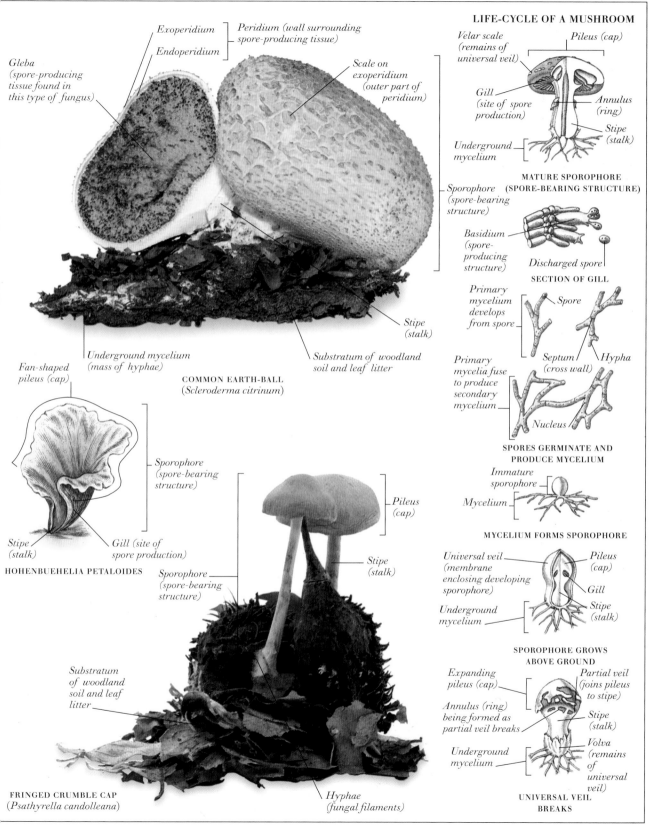

LIFE-CYCLE OF A MUSHROOM

Exoperidium

Endoperidium

Peridium (wall surrounding spore-producing tissue)

Gleba (spore-producing tissue found in this type of fungus)

Scale on exoperidium (outer part of peridium)

Velar scale (remains of universal veil)

Pileus (cap)

Gill (site of spore production)

Annulus (ring)

Stipe (stalk)

Underground mycelium

MATURE SPOROPHORE (SPORE-BEARING STRUCTURE)

Sporophore (spore-bearing structure)

Basidium (spore-producing structure)

Discharged spore

SECTION OF GILL

Stipe (stalk)

Underground mycelium (mass of hyphae)

Substratum of woodland soil and leaf litter

COMMON EARTH-BALL (Scleroderma citrinum)

Primary mycelium develops from spore

Spore

Septum (cross wall)

Hypha

Primary mycelia fuse to produce secondary mycelium

Nucleus

SPORES GERMINATE AND PRODUCE MYCELIUM

Fan-shaped pileus (cap)

Sporophore (spore-bearing structure)

Immature sporophore

Mycelium

MYCELIUM FORMS SPOROPHORE

Stipe (stalk)

Gill (site of spore production)

HOHENBUEHELIA PETALOIDES

Pileus (cap)

Sporophore (spore-bearing structure)

Stipe (stalk)

Universal veil (membrane enclosing developing sporophore)

Pileus (cap)

Gill

Underground mycelium

Stipe (stalk)

SPOROPHORE GROWS ABOVE GROUND

Substratum of woodland soil and leaf litter

Expanding pileus (cap)

Partial veil (joins pileus to stipe)

Annulus (ring) being formed as partial veil breaks

Stipe (stalk)

Underground mycelium

Volva (remains of universal veil)

FRINGED CRUMBLE CAP (Psathyrella candolleana)

Hyphae (fungal filaments)

UNIVERSAL VEIL BREAKS

Algae and seaweeds

ALGAE ARE NOT TRUE PLANTS. They form a diverse group of plant-like organisms that belong to the kingdom Protista. Like plants, algae possess the green pigment chlorophyll and make their own food by photosynthesis (see pp. 138-139). Many algae also possess other pigments by which they can be classified; for example, the brown pigment fucoxanthin is found in the brown algae. Some of the ten phyla of algae are exclusively unicellular (single-celled); others also contain aggregates of cells in filaments or colonies. Three phyla – the Chlorophyta (green algae), Rhodophyta (red algae), and Phaeophyta (brown algae) – contain larger, multicellular, thalloid (flat), marine organisms commonly known as seaweeds. Most algae can reproduce sexually. For example, in the brown seaweed *Fucus vesiculosus*, gametes (sex cells) are produced in conceptacles (chambers) in the receptacles (fertile tips of fronds); after their release into the sea, antherozoids (male gametes) and oospheres (female gametes) fuse; the resulting zygote settles on a rock and develops into a new seaweed.

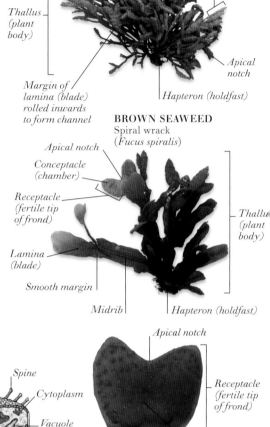

BROWN SEAWEED
Channelled wrack
(*Pelvetia canaliculata*)

Receptacle
(fertile tip
of frond)

Thallus
(plant
body)

Apical
notch

Margin of
lamina (blade)
rolled inwards
to form channel

Hapteron (holdfast)

BROWN SEAWEED
Spiral wrack
(*Fucus spiralis*)

Apical notch

Conceptacle
(chamber)

Receptacle
(fertile tip
of frond)

Lamina
(blade)

Smooth margin

Midrib

Hapteron (holdfast)

Thallus
(plant
body)

EXAMPLES OF ALGAE

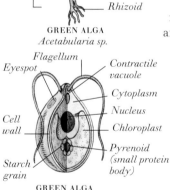

Reproductive
chamber

Cap

Sterile whorl

Cell wall

Stalk

Rhizoid

GREEN ALGA
Acetabularia sp.

Flagellum

Eyespot

Contractile
vacuole

Cytoplasm

Nucleus

Cell
wall

Chloroplast

Pyrenoid
(small protein
body)

Starch
grain

GREEN ALGA
Chlamydomonas sp.

Coenobium
(colony of cells)

Daughter
coenobium

Gelatinous
sheath

Biflagellate cell

GREEN ALGA
Volvox sp.

Spine

Cytoplasm

Girdle

Vacuole

Nucleus

Plastid
(photosynthetic
organelle)

DIATOM
Thalassiosira sp.

Apical notch

Receptacle
(fertile tip
of frond)

Conceptacle
(chamber)
containing
reproductive
structures

Lamina
(blade)

Midrib

RECEPTACLE
Spiral wrack
(*Fucus spiralis*)

BROWN SEAWEED
Oarweed
(*Laminaria digitata*)

Thallus (plant body)

Lamina (blade)
palmately
divided

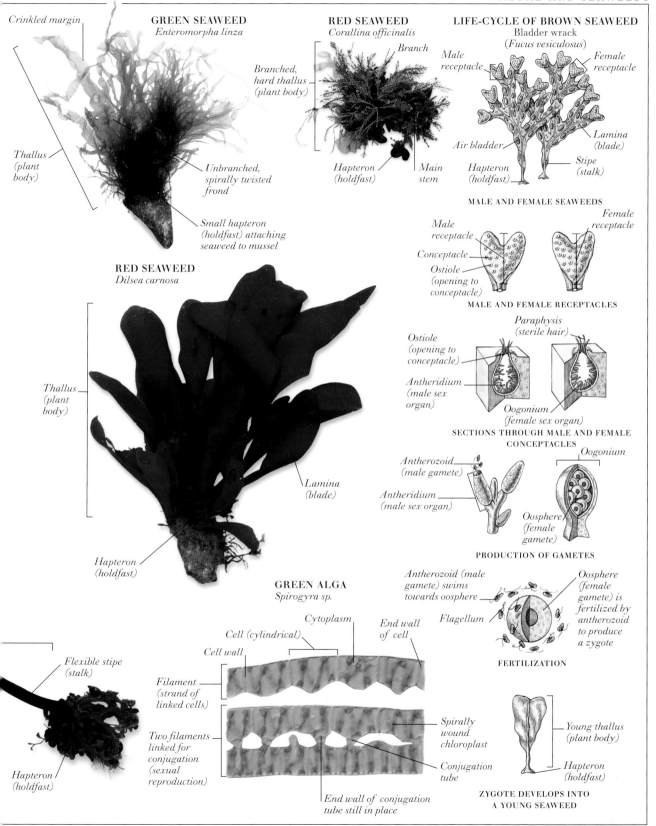

GREEN SEAWEED
Enteromorpha linza

Crinkled margin

Thallus
(plant
body)

Unbranched,
spirally twisted
frond

Small hapteron
(holdfast) attaching
seaweed to mussel

RED SEAWEED
Corallina officinalis

Branch

Branched,
hard thallus
(plant body)

Hapteron
(holdfast)

Main
stem

LIFE-CYCLE OF BROWN SEAWEED
Bladder wrack
(*Fucus vesiculosus*)

Male
receptacle

Female
receptacle

Air bladder

Lamina
(blade)

Hapteron
(holdfast)

Stipe
(stalk)

MALE AND FEMALE SEAWEEDS

Male
receptacle

Female
receptacle

Conceptacle

Ostiole
(opening to
conceptacle)

MALE AND FEMALE RECEPTACLES

Paraphysis
(sterile hair)

Ostiole
(opening to
conceptacle)

Antheridium
(male sex
organ)

Oogonium
(female sex organ)

**SECTIONS THROUGH MALE AND FEMALE
CONCEPTACLES**

Antherozoid
(male gamete)

Oogonium

Antheridium
(male sex organ)

Oosphere
(female
gamete)

PRODUCTION OF GAMETES

RED SEAWEED
Dilsea carnosa

Thallus
(plant
body)

Lamina
(blade)

Hapteron
(holdfast)

Antherozoid (male
gamete) swims
towards oosphere

Flagellum

Oosphere
(female
gamete) is
fertilized by
antherozoid
to produce
a zygote

FERTILIZATION

GREEN ALGA
Spirogyra sp.

Cytoplasm

Cell (cylindrical)

End wall
of cell

Cell wall

Filament
(strand of
linked cells)

Flexible stipe
(stalk)

Hapteron
(holdfast)

Two filaments
linked for
conjugation
(sexual
reproduction)

Spirally
wound
chloroplast

Conjugation
tube

End wall of conjugation
tube still in place

Young thallus
(plant body)

Hapteron
(holdfast)

**ZYGOTE DEVELOPS INTO
A YOUNG SEAWEED**

Liverworts and mosses

LIVERWORTS AND MOSSES ARE SMALL, LOW-GROWING PLANTS that belong to the phylum Bryophyta. Bryophytes do not have true stems, leaves, or roots (they are anchored to the ground by rhizoids), nor do they have the vascular tissues (xylem and phloem) that transport water and nutrients in higher plants. With no outer, waterproof cuticle, bryophytes are susceptible to drying out, and most grow in moist habitats. The bryophyte life-cycle has two stages. In stage one, the green plant (gametophyte) produces male and female gametes (sex cells), which fuse to form a zygote. In stage two, the zygote develops into a sporophyte that remains attached to the gametophyte. The sporophyte produces spores, which are released and germinate into new green plants. Liverworts (class Hepaticae) grow horizontally and may be thalloid (flat and ribbon-like) or "leafy". Mosses (class Musci) typically have an upright "stem" with spirally arranged "leaves".

A LEAFY LIVERWORT
Scapania undulata

"Stem"

"Leaf"

Rhizoid

A THALLOID LIVERWORT
Marchantia polymorpha

Archegoniophore (stalked structure carrying archegonia)

Disc

Lobe

Stalk

Disc

Lobe

Stalk

Lobe

Ray (radial groove)

Stalk

Disc

ARCHEGONIOPHORE FROM BELOW

Gemma cup

Gemma (detachable tissue that produces new plants)

Thallus (plant body)

Toothed margin of cup

Thallus (plant body)

Apical notch

Rhizoid

SIDE VIEW OF ARCHEGONIOPHORE

Stalk

DETAIL OF GEMMA CUP

FEMALE GAMETOPHYTE

Pore

Ray (radial groove)

MICROGRAPH OF LOBE

Gemma cup

Thallus (plant body)

Midrib

Archegoniophore (stalked structure carrying archegonia)

MICROGRAPH OF THALLUS
Conocephalum conicum

Position of air chamber

Pore for exchange of gases

Upper surface

Rhizoid

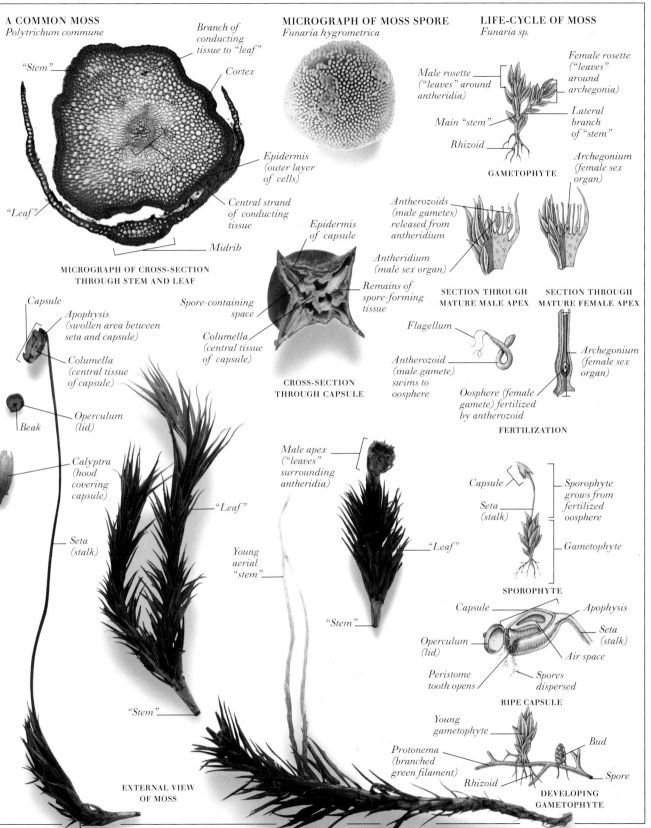

A COMMON MOSS
Polytrichum commune

"Stem"

Branch of
conducting
tissue to "leaf"

Cortex

Epidermis
(outer layer
of cells)

Central strand
of conducting
tissue

"Leaf"

Midrib

**MICROGRAPH OF CROSS-SECTION
THROUGH STEM AND LEAF**

MICROGRAPH OF MOSS SPORE
Funaria hygrometrica

LIFE-CYCLE OF MOSS
Funaria sp.

Male rosette
("leaves" around
antheridia)

Female rosette
("leaves"
around
archegonia)

Main "stem"

Lateral
branch
of "stem"

Rhizoid

GAMETOPHYTE

Archegonium
(female sex
organ)

Antherozoids
(male gametes)
released from
antheridium

Antheridium
(male sex organ)

**SECTION THROUGH
MATURE MALE APEX**

**SECTION THROUGH
MATURE FEMALE APEX**

Archegonium
(female sex
organ)

Flagellum

Antherozoid
(male gamete)
swims to
oosphere

Oosphere (female
gamete) fertilized
by antherozoid

FERTILIZATION

Epidermis
of capsule

Spore-containing
space

Remains of
spore-forming
tissue

Columella
(central tissue
of capsule)

**CROSS-SECTION
THROUGH CAPSULE**

Capsule

Apophysis
(swollen area between
seta and capsule)

Columella
(central tissue
of capsule)

Beak

Operculum
(lid)

Calyptra
(hood
covering
capsule)

Seta
(stalk)

"Leaf"

"Stem"

Young
aerial
"stem"

Male apex
("leaves"
surrounding
antheridia)

"Leaf"

"Stem"

Capsule

Seta
(stalk)

Sporophyte
grows from
fertilized
oosphere

Gametophyte

SPOROPHYTE

Capsule

Apophysis

Operculum
(lid)

Seta
(stalk)

Air space

Peristome
tooth opens

Spores
dispersed

RIPE CAPSULE

Young
gametophyte

Bud

Protonema
(branched
green filament)

Rhizoid

Spore

**DEVELOPING
GAMETOPHYTE**

**EXTERNAL VIEW
OF MOSS**

119

Horsetails, clubmosses, and ferns

HORSETAILS, CLUBMOSSES, AND FERNS are primitive land plants, which, like higher plants, have stems, roots, and leaves, and vascular systems that transport water, minerals, and food. However, unlike higher plants, they do not produce seeds when reproducing. Their life-cycles involve two stages. In stage one, the sporophyte (green plant) produces spores in sporangia. In stage two, the spores germinate, developing into small, short-lived gametophyte plants that produce male and female gametes (sex cells); the gametes fuse to form a zygote from which a new sporophyte plant develops. Horsetails (phylum Sphenophyta) have erect, green stems with branches arranged in whorls; some stems are fertile and have a single spore-producing strobilus (group of sporangia) at the tip. Clubmosses (phylum Lycopodophyta) typically have small leaves arranged spirally around the stem, with spore-producing strobili at the tip of some stems. Ferns (phylum Filicinophyta) typically have large, pinnate fronds (leaves); sporangia, grouped together in sori, develop on the underside of fertile fronds.

FROND
Male fern
(*Dryopteris filix-mas*)

CLUBMOSS
Lycopodium sp.

Stem with spirally arranged leaves

Branch

Strobilus (group of sporangia)

CLUBMOSS
Selaginella sp.

Epidermis (outer layer of cells)

Cortex (layer between epidermis and vascular tissue)

Vascular tissue — Phloem / Xylem

Lacuna (air space)

MICROGRAPH OF CROSS-SECTION THROUGH CLUBMOSS STEM

Shoot apex

Branch

Rhizophore (leafless branch)

Creeping stem with spirally arranged leaves

HORSETAIL
Common horsetail
(*Equisetum arvense*)

Apex of sterile shoot

Sporangiophore (structure carrying sporangia)

Strobilus (group of sporangia)

Non-photosynthetic fertile stem

Collar of small brown leaves

Young shoot

Lateral branch

Photosynthetic sterile stem

Node

Internode

Node

Tuber

Rhizome

Adventitious root

Endodermis (inner layer of cortex)

Vascular tissue

Sclerenchyma (strengthening tissue)

Chlorenchyma (photosynthetic tissue)

Epidermis (outer layer of cells)

Parenchyma (packing tissue)

Cortex (layer between epidermis and vascular tissue)

Hollow pith cavity

Vallecular canal (longitudinal channel)

Carinal canal (longitudinal channel)

MICROGRAPH OF CROSS-SECTION THROUGH HORSETAIL STEM

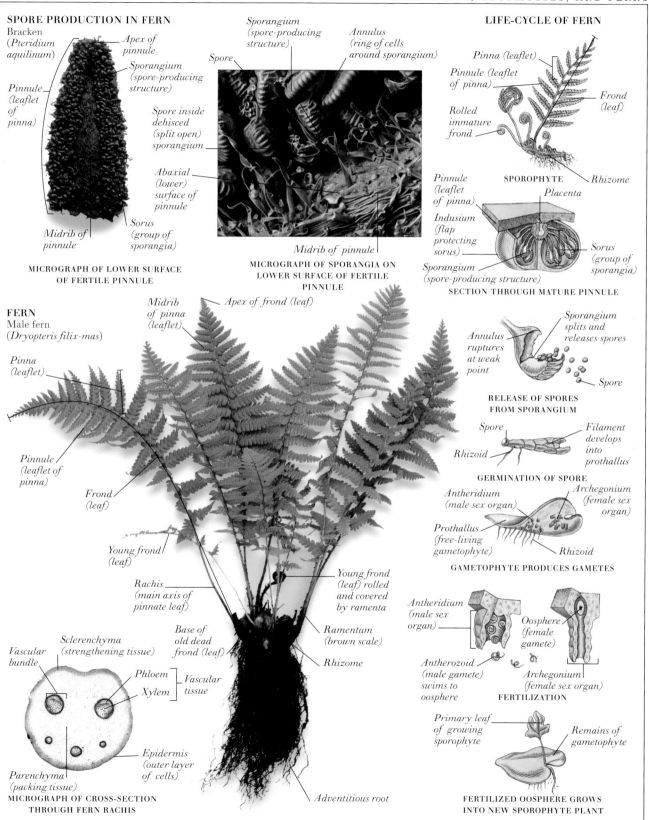

SPORE PRODUCTION IN FERN

Bracken
(*Pteridium aquilinum*)

Apex of pinnule

Sporangium (spore-producing structure)

Pinnule (leaflet of pinna)

Spore inside dehisced (split open) sporangium

Abaxial (lower) surface of pinnule

Midrib of pinnule

Sorus (group of sporangia)

MICROGRAPH OF LOWER SURFACE OF FERTILE PINNULE

Sporangium (spore-producing structure)

Annulus (ring of cells around sporangium)

Spore

Abaxial (lower) surface of pinnule

Midrib of pinnule

MICROGRAPH OF SPORANGIA ON LOWER SURFACE OF FERTILE PINNULE

LIFE-CYCLE OF FERN

Pinna (leaflet)

Pinnule (leaflet of pinna)

Rolled immature frond

Frond (leaf)

SPOROPHYTE

Rhizome

Pinnule (leaflet of pinna)

Placenta

Indusium (flap protecting sorus)

Sporangium (spore-producing structure)

Sorus (group of sporangia)

SECTION THROUGH MATURE PINNULE

Sporangium splits and releases spores

Annulus ruptures at weak point

Spore

RELEASE OF SPORES FROM SPORANGIUM

Spore

Filament develops into prothallus

Rhizoid

GERMINATION OF SPORE

Antheridium (male sex organ)

Archegonium (female sex organ)

Prothallus (free-living gametophyte)

Rhizoid

GAMETOPHYTE PRODUCES GAMETES

Antheridium (male sex organ)

Oosphere (female gamete)

Antherozoid (male gamete) swims to oosphere

Archegonium (female sex organ)

FERTILIZATION

Primary leaf of growing sporophyte

Remains of gametophyte

FERTILIZED OOSPHERE GROWS INTO NEW SPOROPHYTE PLANT

FERN

Male fern
(*Dryopteris filix-mas*)

Midrib of pinna (leaflet)

Apex of frond (leaf)

Pinna (leaflet)

Pinnule (leaflet of pinna)

Frond (leaf)

Young frond (leaf)

Rachis (main axis of pinnate leaf)

Base of old dead frond (leaf)

Young frond (leaf) rolled and covered by ramenta

Ramentum (brown scale)

Rhizome

Sclerenchyma (strengthening tissue)

Vascular bundle

Phloem

Xylem

Vascular tissue

Epidermis (outer layer of cells)

Parenchyma (packing tissue)

Adventitious root

MICROGRAPH OF CROSS-SECTION THROUGH FERN RACHIS

Gymnosperms 1

THE GYMNOSPERMS ARE FOUR RELATED PHYLA of seed-producing plants; their seeds, however, lack the protective, outer covering which surrounds the seeds of flowering plants. Typically, gymnosperms are woody, perennial shrubs or trees, with stems, leaves, and roots, and a well-developed vascular (transport) system. The reproductive structures in most gymnosperms are cones: male cones produce microspores in which male gametes (sex cells) develop; female cones produce megaspores in which female gametes develop. Microspores are blown by the wind to female cones, male and female gametes fuse during fertilization, and a seed develops. The four gymnosperm phyla are the conifers (phylum Coniferophyta), mostly tall trees; cycads (phylum Cycadophyta), small palm-like trees; the ginkgo or maidenhair tree (phylum Ginkgophyta), a tall tree with bilobed leaves; and gnetophytes (phylum Gnetophyta), a diverse group of plants, mainly shrubs, but also including the horizontally growing welwitschia.

LIFE-CYCLE OF SCOTS PINE
(*Pinus sylvestris*)

Needle (foliage leaf)

Cone

Ovuliferous scale (ovule- then seed-bearing structure)

MALE CONES **YOUNG FEMALE CONE**

Pollen grain in micropyle (entrance to ovule)

Ovuliferous scale

Pollen grain

Nucleus

Air sac

Ovule (contains female gamete)

POLLINATION

Integument (outer part of ovule)

Pollen tube (carries male gamete from pollen grain to ovum)

Archegonium (containing female gamete)

FERTILIZATION

SCALE AND SEEDS
Pine
(*Pinus sp.*)

Ovuliferous scale (ovule- then seed-bearing structure)

Wing scar

Wing of seed derived from ovuliferous scale

Seed

Seed

Seed scar

Point of attachment to axis of cone

OVULIFEROUS SCALE FROM THIRD-YEAR FEMALE CONE

Ovuliferous scale (ovule- then seed-bearing structure)

Seed

Seed

Wing

MATURE FEMALE CONE AND WINGED SEED

Microsporangium (structure in which pollen grains are formed)

Microsporophyll (modified leaf carrying microsporangia)

Ovule (contains female gametes)

Bract scale

Axis of cone

Scale leaf

Ovuliferous scale (ovule- then seed-bearing structure)

Axis of cone

MICROGRAPH OF LONGITUDINAL SECTION THROUGH YOUNG MALE CONE

MICROGRAPH OF LONGITUDINAL SECTION THROUGH SECOND-YEAR FEMALE CONE

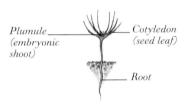

Plumule (embryonic shoot)

Cotyledon (seed leaf)

Root

GERMINATION OF PINE SEEDLING

WELWITSCHIA
(*Welwitschia mirabilis*)

Frayed end of leaf

SMOOTH CYPRESS
(*Cupressus glabra*)

Immature female cone

Ovuliferous scale (ovule- then seed-bearing structure)

Scale-like leaf

Mature female cone

Immature male cone

Stem

Ovuliferous scale

Ovule (contains female gamete)

CROSS-SECTION THROUGH IMMATURE CONE

Ovuliferous scale (ovule- then seed-bearing structure)

Seed

CROSS-SECTION THROUGH MATURE CONE

Woody scale

Opening between woody scales through which seeds are released

DISCARDED CONE

YEW
(*Taxus baccata*)

Single ovule (contains female gamete)

Scale

Female "cone"

Scale

Developing seed

Scale

FEMALE "CONES" AT VARIOUS STAGES OF DEVELOPMENT

Seed

Aril (fleshy outgrowth from seed)

Stem

Needle (foliage leaf)

CYCAD
Sago palm
(*Cycas revoluta*)

Pinna (leaflet)

Pinnate leaf

Scale leaf

Old leaf base

Stem covered by scale leaves

MAIDENHAIR TREE
(*Ginkgo biloba*)

Girdle scar

Stem

Petiole (leaf stalk)

Bilobed leaf

Continuously growing leaf

Site of cone growth

Adaxial (upper) surface of leaf

Abaxial (lower) surface of leaf

Frayed end of leaf

Immature cone

Stalk scar

Woody stem

123

Gymnosperms 2

BRANCH OF BISHOP PINE
(*Pinus muricata*)

Second-year female cone

Ovuliferous scale
(ovule- then seed-bearing
structure)

Needle
(foliage leaf)

Ovuliferous scale
(ovule- then seed-
bearing structure)

Bud
scale

Cone

Cone stalk

Stem

Dwarf shoot

Scale leaf scar

Apical bud

**FEMALE CONE
(FIRST YEAR)**

Stem

Male cone

Needle (foliage leaf)

Dwarf shoot

Margin
of needle
(foliage leaf)

Upper surface
of needle
(foliage leaf)

Needle
(foliage leaf)

Apical bud

Scar of
dwarf shoot

Stem

Dwarf shoot

TERMINAL ZONE OF BRANCH

Stoma
(pore)

Female
cone

Woody ovuliferous
scale (ovule- then
seed-bearing structure)

Vascular tissue

Phloem

Xylem

Mesophyll
(photosynthetic tissue)

Stoma
(pore)

Epidermis
(outer
layer of
cells)

Endodermis
(inner layer
of cortex)

Resin canal

Cuticle
(waterproof
covering)

**FEMALE CONE
(THIRD YEAR)**

**MICROGRAPH OF CROSS-SECTION
THROUGH NEEDLE (FOLIAGE LEAF)**

**MICROGRAPH OF NEEDLE
(FOLIAGE LEAF) OF PINE**
(*Pinus sp.*)

CROSS-SECTION THROUGH MATURE STEM OF BISHOP PINE
(*Pinus muricata*)

Apical bud scale

Apical bud

Shoot apex

Immature needle
(foliage leaf)

Needle
(foliage
leaf) bud

Bud scale

Scale leaf

MICROGRAPH OF LONGITUDINAL SECTION
THROUGH SHOOT APEX OF PINE
(*Pinus sp.*)

Annual ring

Heartwood
(supportive,
inactive
secondary
xylem)

Branch trace
(vascular bundle
supplying branch)

Pith

Sapwood
(active secondary
xylem)

Medullary ray
(extension of pith)

Pith

Hypodermis
(cell layer below
epidermis)

Cortex
(layer between
epidermis and
vascular tissue)

Base of dwarf shoot

Dwarf shoot trace
(vascular bundle
supplying dwarf
shoot)

Secondary
xylem

Epidermis
(outer layer
of cells)

Vascular
tissue

Phloem

Primary
xylem

Resin canal

Phloem

Bark

Periderm
(outer layer
of bark)

MICROGRAPH OF CROSS-SECTION
THROUGH YOUNG STEM OF PINE
(*Pinus sp.*)

Cortex
(layer between
phellem and
vascular tissue)

Resin canal

Cortex
(layer between
phellem and
vascular tissue)

Secondary
xylem

Primary
xylem

Endodermis
(inner layer
of cortex)

Phellem
(protective
outer layer)

Phloem

Secondary
xylem

Phellem
(protective
outer layer)

Primary
xylem

Phloem

Resin canal

MICROGRAPH OF CROSS-SECTION
THROUGH YOUNG ROOT OF PINE
(*Pinus sp.*)

MICROGRAPH OF CROSS-SECTION
THROUGH MATURE ROOT OF PINE
(*Pinus sp.*)

Monocotyledons and dicotyledons

FLOWERING PLANTS (PHYLUM ANGIOSPERMOPHYTA) are divided into two classes: monocotyledons (class Monocotyledoneae) and dicotyledons (class Dicotyledoneae). Typically, monocotyledons have seeds with one cotyledon (seed leaf); their foliage leaves are narrow with parallel veins; the flower components occur in multiples of three; sepals and petals are indistinguishable and are known as tepals; vascular (transport) tissues are scattered in random bundles throughout the stem; and, since they lack stem cambium (actively dividing cells that produce wood), most monocotyledons are herbaceous (see pp. 128-129). Dicotyledons have seeds with two cotyledons; leaves are broad with a central midrib and branched veins; flower parts occur in multiples of four or five; sepals are generally small and green; petals are large and colourful; vascular bundles are arranged in a ring around the edge of the stem; and, because many dicotyledons possess wood-producing stem cambium, there are woody forms (see pp. 130-131) as well as herbaceous ones.

CROSS-SECTION THROUGH MONOCOTYLEDONOUS LEAF BASES

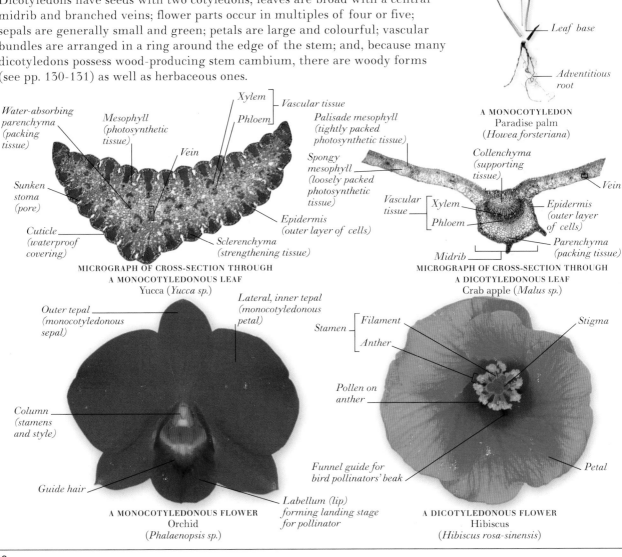

Vein (parallel venation)

Leaflet

Petiole (leaf stalk)

Emerging leaf

Leaf base

Adventitious root

A MONOCOTYLEDON
Paradise palm
(*Howea forsteriana*)

Water-absorbing parenchyma (packing tissue)

Mesophyll (photosynthetic tissue)

Xylem

Phloem

Vascular tissue

Vein

Sunken stoma (pore)

Cuticle (waterproof covering)

Epidermis (outer layer of cells)

Sclerenchyma (strengthening tissue)

MICROGRAPH OF CROSS-SECTION THROUGH A MONOCOTYLEDONOUS LEAF
Yucca (*Yucca sp.*)

Palisade mesophyll (tightly packed photosynthetic tissue)

Spongy mesophyll (loosely packed photosynthetic tissue)

Collenchyma (supporting tissue)

Vein

Vascular tissue

Xylem

Phloem

Epidermis (outer layer of cells)

Parenchyma (packing tissue)

Midrib

MICROGRAPH OF CROSS-SECTION THROUGH A DICOTYLEDONOUS LEAF
Crab apple (*Malus sp.*)

Outer tepal (monocotyledonous sepal)

Lateral, inner tepal (monocotyledonous petal)

Stamen

Filament

Anther

Stigma

Pollen on anther

Column (stamens and style)

Funnel guide for bird pollinators' beak

Petal

Guide hair

Labellum (lip) forming landing stage for pollinator

A MONOCOTYLEDONOUS FLOWER
Orchid
(*Phalaenopsis sp.*)

A DICOTYLEDONOUS FLOWER
Hibiscus
(*Hibiscus rosa-sinensis*)

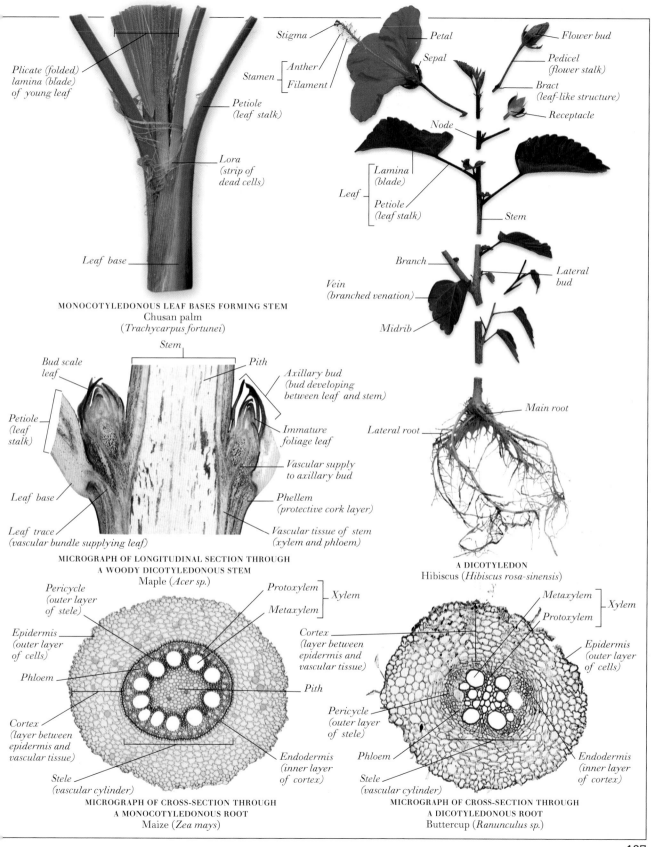

Plicate (folded)
lamina (blade)
of young leaf

Petiole
(leaf stalk)

Lora
(strip of
dead cells)

Leaf base

MONOCOTYLEDONOUS LEAF BASES FORMING STEM
Chusan palm
(*Trachycarpus fortunei*)

Stigma

Stamen {
Anther
Filament
}

Petal

Sepal

Flower bud

Pedicel
(flower stalk)

Bract
(leaf-like structure)

Receptacle

Node

Leaf {
Lamina
(blade)
Petiole
(leaf stalk)
}

Stem

Branch

Lateral
bud

Vein
(branched venation)

Midrib

Main root

Lateral root

A DICOTYLEDON
Hibiscus (*Hibiscus rosa-sinensis*)

Bud scale
leaf

Stem

Pith

Axillary bud
(bud developing
between leaf and stem)

Petiole
(leaf
stalk)

Immature
foliage leaf

Vascular supply
to axillary bud

Leaf base

Leaf trace
(vascular bundle supplying leaf)

Phellem
(protective cork layer)

Vascular tissue of stem
(xylem and phloem)

**MICROGRAPH OF LONGITUDINAL SECTION THROUGH
A WOODY DICOTYLEDONOUS STEM**
Maple (*Acer sp.*)

Pericycle
(outer layer
of stele)

Epidermis
(outer layer
of cells)

Phloem

Cortex
(layer between
epidermis and
vascular tissue)

Stele
(vascular cylinder)

Protoxylem

Metaxylem
} Xylem

Pith

Endodermis
(inner layer
of cortex)

**MICROGRAPH OF CROSS-SECTION THROUGH
A MONOCOTYLEDONOUS ROOT**
Maize (*Zea mays*)

Cortex
(layer between
epidermis and
vascular tissue)

Metaxylem

Protoxylem
} Xylem

Epidermis
(outer layer
of cells)

Pericycle
(outer layer
of stele)

Phloem

Stele
(vascular cylinder)

Endodermis
(inner layer
of cortex)

**MICROGRAPH OF CROSS-SECTION THROUGH
A DICOTYLEDONOUS ROOT**
Buttercup (*Ranunculus sp.*)

Herbaceous flowering plants

HERBACEOUS FLOWERING PLANTS TYPICALLY HAVE GREEN, NON-WOODY STEMS, and tend to be relatively short-lived. Many herbaceous plants live for only one or two years. Annuals (e.g., sweet peas) grow from seed, produce flowers and then seeds, and die within a single year. Biennials (e.g., carrots) have a two-year life cycle. In the first year, seeds grow into plants, which produce leaves and store food in underground storage organs; the stems and foliage then die back in winter. In the second year, new stems grow from the storage organs, produce leaves, flowers, and seeds, and then die. Some herbaceous plants (e.g., potatoes) are perennial. They grow back year after year, producing shoots and flowers in spring, storing food in underground tubers or rhizomes during summer, dying back in autumn, and surviving underground during winter.

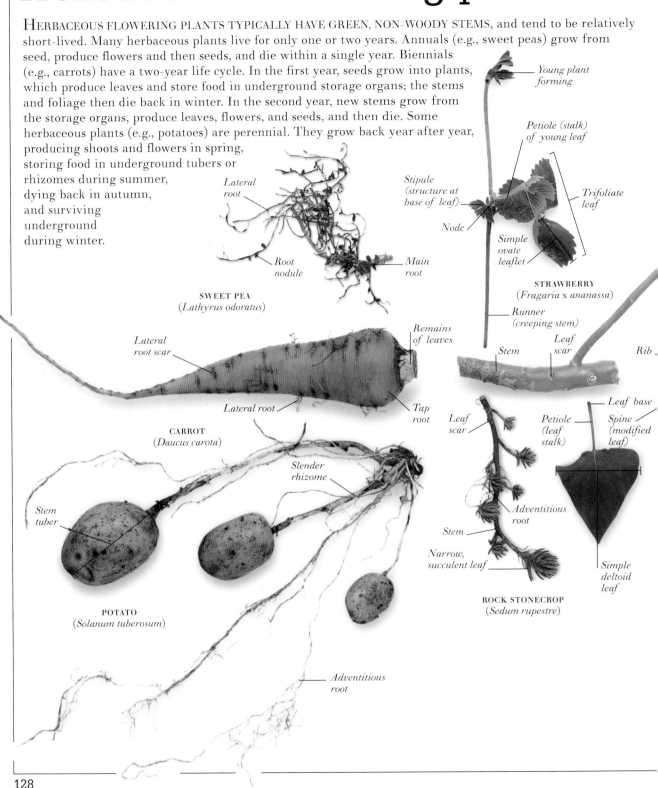

Young plant forming

Petiole (stalk) of young leaf

Lateral root

Stipule (structure at base of leaf)

Trifoliate leaf

Node

Simple ovate leaflet

Root nodule

Main root

SWEET PEA
(*Lathyrus odoratus*)

STRAWBERRY
(*Fragaria* x *ananassa*)

Runner (creeping stem)

Remains of leaves

Leaf scar

Lateral root scar

Stem

Rib

Lateral root

Tap root

Leaf base

CARROT
(*Daucus carota*)

Leaf scar

Petiole (leaf stalk)

Spine (modified leaf)

Slender rhizome

Adventitious root

Stem tuber

Stem

Narrow, succulent leaf

Simple deltoid leaf

ROCK STONECROP
(*Sedum rupestre*)

POTATO
(*Solanum tuberosum*)

Adventitious root

PARTS OF HERBACEOUS FLOWERING PLANTS

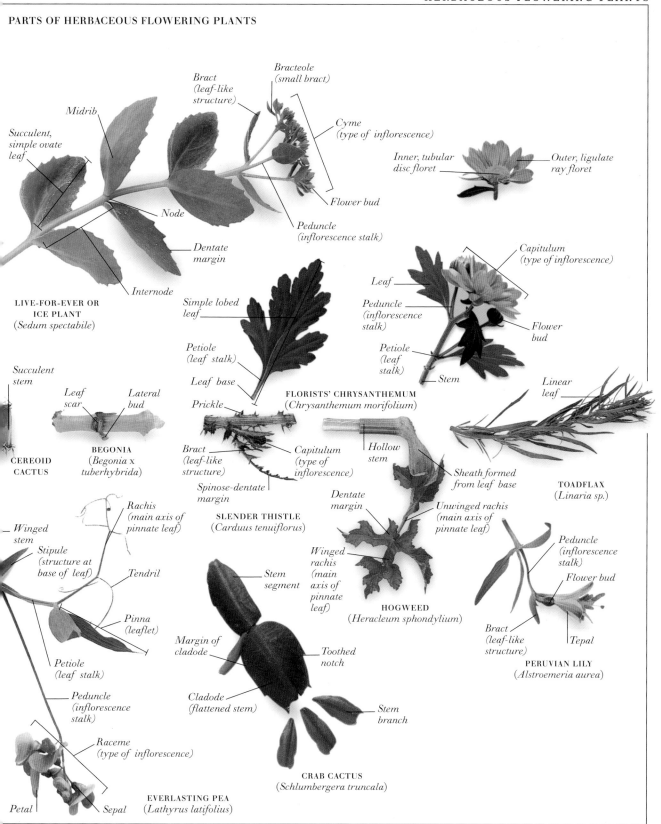

Midrib

Succulent, simple ovate leaf

Bract (leaf-like structure)

Bracteole (small bract)

Cyme (type of inflorescence)

Inner, tubular disc floret

Outer, ligulate ray floret

Node

Flower bud

Dentate margin

Peduncle (inflorescence stalk)

Internode

LIVE-FOR-EVER OR ICE PLANT (*Sedum spectabile*)

Simple lobed leaf

Petiole (leaf stalk)

Leaf base

Prickle

Leaf

Capitulum (type of inflorescence)

Peduncle (inflorescence stalk)

Petiole (leaf stalk)

Flower bud

Stem

Linear leaf

FLORISTS' CHRYSANTHEMUM (*Chrysanthemum morifolium*)

Succulent stem

Leaf scar

Lateral bud

CEREOID CACTUS

BEGONIA (*Begonia x tuberhybrida*)

Bract (leaf-like structure)

Capitulum (type of inflorescence)

Spinose-dentate margin

Hollow stem

Sheath formed from leaf base

TOADFLAX (*Linaria sp.*)

SLENDER THISTLE (*Carduus tenuiflorus*)

Dentate margin

Unwinged rachis (main axis of pinnate leaf)

Winged stem

Rachis (main axis of pinnate leaf)

Stipule (structure at base of leaf)

Tendril

Winged rachis (main axis of pinnate leaf)

Peduncle (inflorescence stalk)

Pinna (leaflet)

Stem segment

Flower bud

HOGWEED (*Heracleum sphondylium*)

Petiole (leaf stalk)

Margin of cladode

Toothed notch

Bract (leaf-like structure)

Tepal

Peduncle (inflorescence stalk)

Cladode (flattened stem)

Stem branch

PERUVIAN LILY (*Alstroemeria aurea*)

Raceme (type of inflorescence)

CRAB CACTUS (*Schlumbergera truncala*)

Petal

Sepal

EVERLASTING PEA (*Lathyrus latifolius*)

Woody flowering plants

WOODY FLOWERING PLANTS ARE PERENNIAL, that is, they continue to grow and reproduce for many years. They have one or more permanent stems above ground, and numerous smaller branches. The stems and branches have a strong woody core that supports the plant and contains vascular tissue for transporting water and nutrients. Outside the woody core is a layer of tough, protective bark, which has lenticels (tiny pores) in it to enable gases to pass through. Woody flowering plants may be shrubs, which have several stems arising from the soil; bushes, which are shrubs with dense branching and foliage; or trees, which typically have a single upright stem (the trunk) that bears branches. Deciduous woody plants (e.g., roses) shed all their leaves once a year and remain leafless during winter. Evergreen woody plants (e.g., ivy) shed their leaves gradually, so retaining full leaf cover throughout the year.

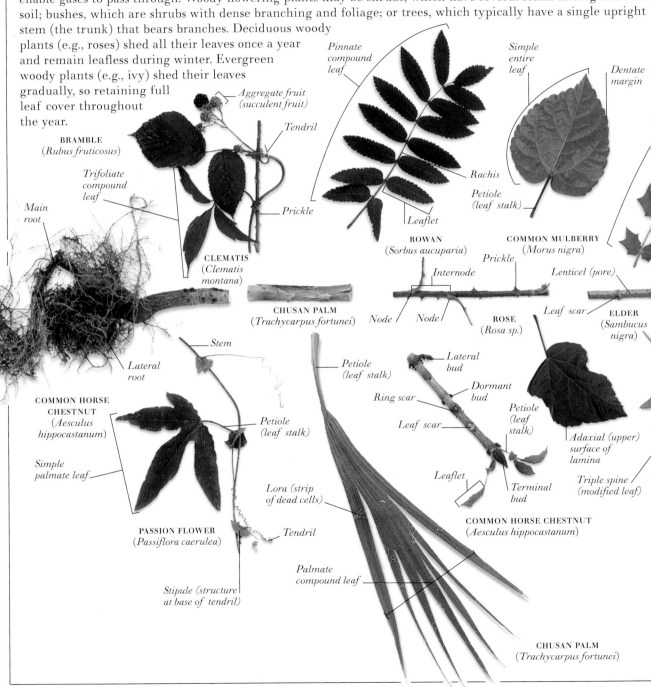

Aggregate fruit (succulent fruit)

Tendril

BRAMBLE
(*Rubus fruticosus*)

Trifoliate compound leaf

Prickle

CLEMATIS
(*Clematis montana*)

Main root

Lateral root

COMMON HORSE CHESTNUT
(*Aesculus hippocastanum*)

Simple palmate leaf

Stem

Petiole (leaf stalk)

PASSION FLOWER
(*Passiflora caerulea*)

Lora (strip of dead cells)

Tendril

Stipule (structure at base of tendril)

Pinnate compound leaf

Rachis

Petiole (leaf stalk)

Leaflet

ROWAN
(*Sorbus aucuparia*)

CHUSAN PALM
(*Trachycarpus fortunei*)

Node

Node

Internode

Prickle

ROSE
(*Rosa sp.*)

Simple entire leaf

Dentate margin

COMMON MULBERRY
(*Morus nigra*)

Lenticel (pore)

Leaf scar

ELDER
(*Sambucus nigra*)

Petiole (leaf stalk)

Lateral bud

Dormant bud

Ring scar

Leaf scar

Petiole (leaf stalk)

Adaxial (upper) surface of lamina

Leaflet

Terminal bud

Triple spine (modified leaf)

COMMON HORSE CHESTNUT
(*Aesculus hippocastanum*)

Palmate compound leaf

CHUSAN PALM
(*Trachycarpus fortunei*)

130

PARTS OF WOODY FLOWERING PLANTS

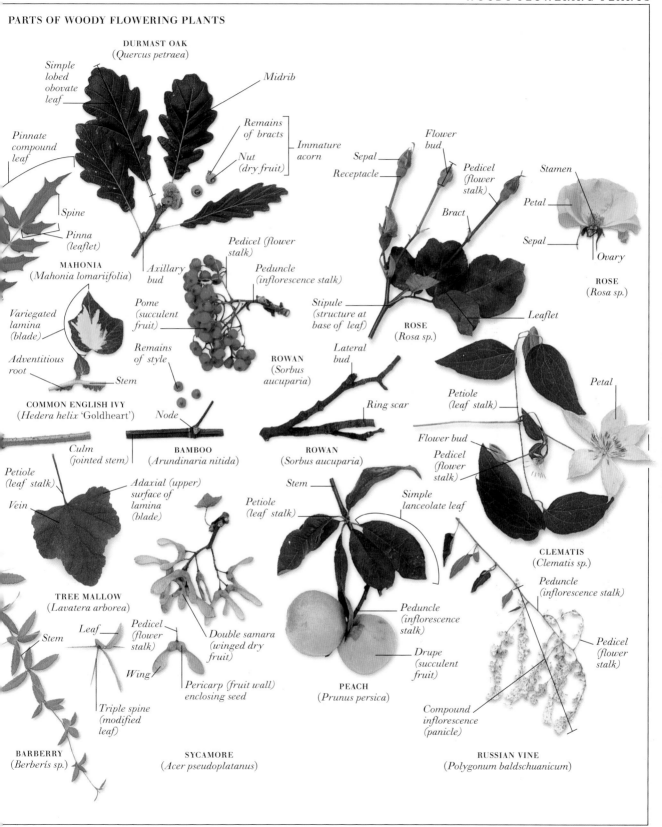

DURMAST OAK
(*Quercus petraea*)

Simple
lobed
obovate
leaf

Midrib

Remains
of bracts

Nut
(dry fruit)

Immature
acorn

Pinnate
compound
leaf

Spine

Pinna
(leaflet)

MAHONIA
(*Mahonia lomariifolia*)

Axillary
bud

Pome
(succulent
fruit)

Pedicel (flower
stalk)

Peduncle
(inflorescence stalk)

Remains
of style

Variegated
lamina
(blade)

Adventitious
root

Stem

COMMON ENGLISH IVY
(*Hedera helix* 'Goldheart')

Node

Culm
(jointed stem)

BAMBOO
(*Arundinaria nitida*)

Petiole
(leaf stalk)

Vein

Adaxial (upper)
surface of
lamina
(blade)

TREE MALLOW
(*Lavatera arborea*)

Stem

Leaf

Pedicel
(flower
stalk)

Wing

Double samara
(winged dry
fruit)

Pericarp (fruit wall)
enclosing seed

Triple spine
(modified
leaf)

BARBERRY
(*Berberis sp.*)

SYCAMORE
(*Acer pseudoplatanus*)

Sepal

Receptacle

Flower
bud

Pedicel
(flower
stalk)

Bract

Stamen

Petal

Sepal

Ovary

ROSE
(*Rosa sp.*)

Stipule
(structure at
base of leaf)

ROWAN
(*Sorbus
aucuparia*)

ROSE
(*Rosa sp.*)

Leaflet

Lateral
bud

Ring scar

ROWAN
(*Sorbus aucuparia*)

Petiole
(leaf stalk)

Petal

Flower bud

Pedicel
(flower
stalk)

Stem

Petiole
(leaf stalk)

Simple
lanceolate leaf

CLEMATIS
(*Clematis sp.*)

Peduncle
(inflorescence
stalk)

Drupe
(succulent
fruit)

PEACH
(*Prunus persica*)

Peduncle
(inflorescence
stalk)

Pedicel
(flower
stalk)

Compound
inflorescence
(panicle)

RUSSIAN VINE
(*Polygonum baldschuanicum*)

Roots

ROOTS ARE THE UNDERGROUND PARTS OF PLANTS. They have three main functions. First, they anchor the plant in the soil. Second, they absorb water and minerals from the spaces between soil particles; the roots' absorptive properties are increased by root hairs, which grow behind the root tip, allowing maximum uptake of vital substances. Third, the root is part of the plant's transport system: xylem carries water and minerals from the roots to the stem and leaves, and phloem carries nutrients from the leaves to all parts of the root system. In addition, some roots (e.g., carrots) are food stores. Roots have an outer epidermis covering a cortex of parenchyma (packing tissue), and a central cylinder of vascular tissue. This arrangement helps the roots resist the forces of compression as they grow through the soil.

CARROT
(*Daucus carota*)

MICROGRAPH OF PRIMARY ROOT DEVELOPMENT
Cabbage (*Brassica sp.*)

Split in testa as seed germinates

Cotyledon (seed leaf)

Primary root

Testa (seed coat)

Root hair

Root tip (region of cell division)

FEATURES OF A TYPICAL ROOT
Buttercup
(*Ranunculus sp.*)

Stele (vascular cylinder)

Phloem sieve tube (through which nutrients are transported)

Pericycle (outer layer of stele)

Companion cell (cell associated with phloem sieve tube)

Root hair

Cortex (layer between epidermis and vascular tissue)

Air space (allowing gas diffusion in the root)

Root hair

Epidermis (outer layer of cells)

Xylem vessel (through which water and minerals are transported)

Endodermis (inner layer of cortex)

Cell wall

Nucleus

Cytoplasm

Parenchyma (packing) cell

PRIMARY ROOT AND MICROGRAPHS OF SECTIONS THROUGH ROOTS

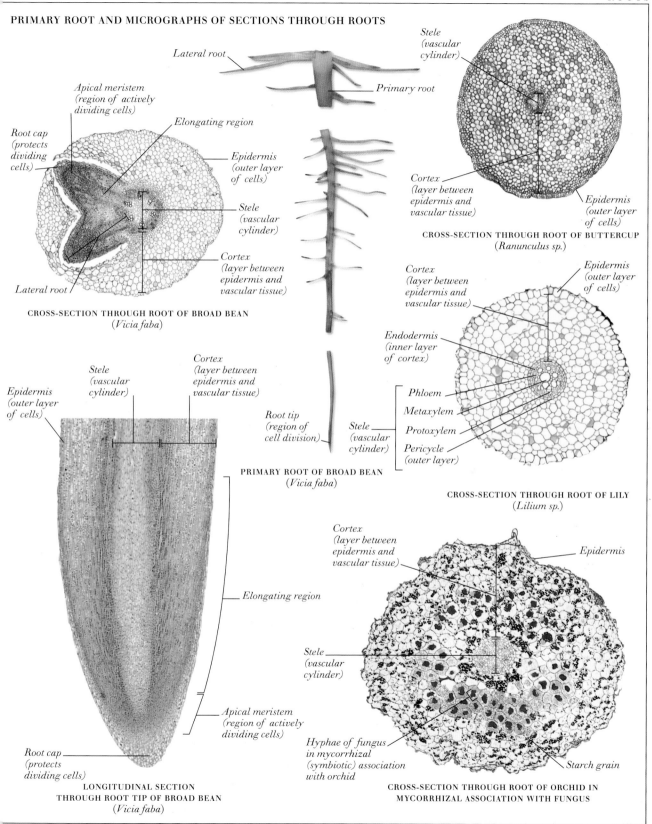

Lateral root

Primary root

Stele (vascular cylinder)

Apical meristem (region of actively dividing cells)

Elongating region

Root cap (protects dividing cells)

Epidermis (outer layer of cells)

Stele (vascular cylinder)

Cortex (layer between epidermis and vascular tissue)

Cortex (layer between epidermis and vascular tissue)

Epidermis (outer layer of cells)

Lateral root

CROSS-SECTION THROUGH ROOT OF BUTTERCUP
(*Ranunculus sp.*)

CROSS-SECTION THROUGH ROOT OF BROAD BEAN
(*Vicia faba*)

Cortex (layer between epidermis and vascular tissue)

Epidermis (outer layer of cells)

Endodermis (inner layer of cortex)

Phloem

Metaxylem

Protoxylem

Pericycle (outer layer)

Stele (vascular cylinder)

Stele (vascular cylinder)

Cortex (layer between epidermis and vascular tissue)

Epidermis (outer layer of cells)

Root tip (region of cell division)

PRIMARY ROOT OF BROAD BEAN
(*Vicia faba*)

CROSS-SECTION THROUGH ROOT OF LILY
(*Lilium sp.*)

Elongating region

Apical meristem (region of actively dividing cells)

Root cap (protects dividing cells)

Cortex (layer between epidermis and vascular tissue)

Epidermis

Stele (vascular cylinder)

Hyphae of fungus in mycorrhizal (symbiotic) association with orchid

Starch grain

LONGITUDINAL SECTION
THROUGH ROOT TIP OF BROAD BEAN
(*Vicia faba*)

CROSS-SECTION THROUGH ROOT OF ORCHID IN
MYCORRHIZAL ASSOCIATION WITH FUNGUS

Stems

THE STEM IS THE MAIN SUPPORTIVE PART OF A PLANT that grows above ground. Stems bear leaves (organs of photosynthesis), which grow at nodes; buds (shoots covered by protective scales), which grow at the stem tip (apical or terminal buds) and in the angle between a leaf and the stem (axillary or lateral buds); and flowers (reproductive structures). The stem forms part of the plant's transport system: xylem tissue in the stem transports water and minerals from the roots to the aerial parts of the plant, and phloem tissue transports nutrients manufactured in the leaves to other parts of the plant. Stem tissues are also used for storing water and food. Herbaceous (non-woody) stems have an outer protective epidermis covering a cortex that consists mainly of parenchyma (packing tissue) but also has some collenchyma (supporting tissue). The vascular tissue of such stems is arranged in bundles, each of which consists of xylem, phloem, and sclerenchyma (strengthening tissue). Woody stems have an outer protective layer of tough bark, which is perforated with lenticels (pores) to allow gas exchange. Inside the bark is a ring of secondary phloem, which surrounds an inner core of secondary xylem.

MICROGRAPH OF LONGITUDINAL SECTION THROUGH APEX OF STEM
Coleus sp.

Apical meristem (region of actively dividing cells)

Developing bud

Pith

Procambial strand (cells that produce vascular tissue)

Leaf primordium (developing leaf)

Cortex (layer between epidermis and vascular tissue)

Vascular tissue

Epidermis (outer layer of cells)

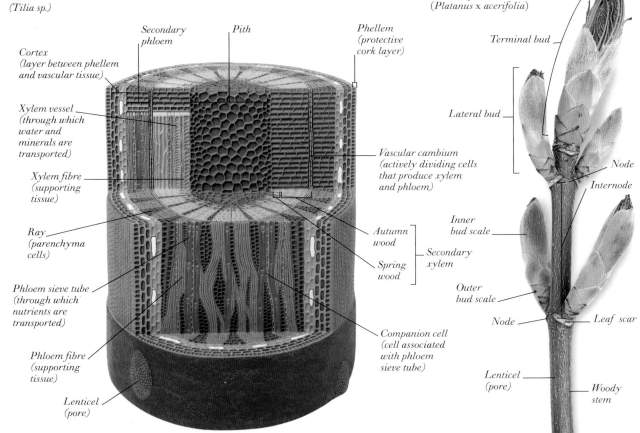

YOUNG WOODY STEM
Lime
(Tilia sp.)

Secondary phloem

Pith

Phellem (protective cork layer)

Cortex (layer between phellem and vascular tissue)

Xylem vessel (through which water and minerals are transported)

Xylem fibre (supporting tissue)

Ray (parenchyma cells)

Phloem sieve tube (through which nutrients are transported)

Phloem fibre (supporting tissue)

Lenticel (pore)

Vascular cambium (actively dividing cells that produce xylem and phloem)

Autumn wood

Spring wood

Secondary xylem

Companion cell (cell associated with phloem sieve tube)

EMERGENT BUDS
London plane
(Platanus x acerifolia)

Young leaves emerging

Terminal bud

Lateral bud

Node

Internode

Inner bud scale

Outer bud scale

Node

Leaf scar

Lenticel (pore)

Woody stem

MICROGRAPHS OF CROSS-SECTIONS THROUGH VARIOUS STEMS

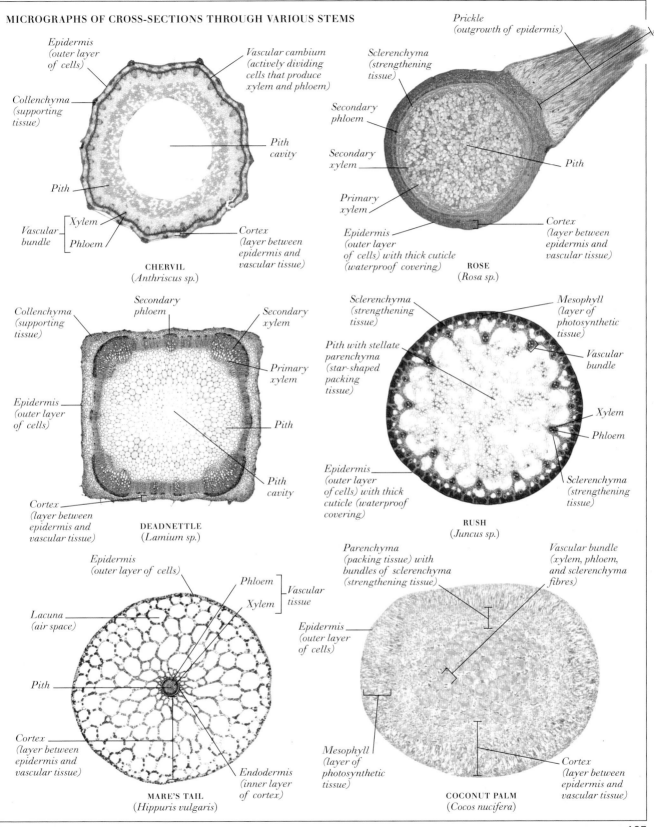

Epidermis (outer layer of cells)

Collenchyma (supporting tissue)

Pith

Vascular bundle

Xylem

Phloem

Vascular cambium (actively dividing cells that produce xylem and phloem)

Pith cavity

Cortex (layer between epidermis and vascular tissue)

CHERVIL (*Anthriscus sp.*)

Prickle (outgrowth of epidermis)

Sclerenchyma (strengthening tissue)

Secondary phloem

Secondary xylem

Primary xylem

Epidermis (outer layer of cells) with thick cuticle (waterproof covering)

Pith

Cortex (layer between epidermis and vascular tissue)

ROSE (*Rosa sp.*)

Collenchyma (supporting tissue)

Secondary phloem

Secondary xylem

Primary xylem

Epidermis (outer layer of cells)

Cortex (layer between epidermis and vascular tissue)

Pith

Pith cavity

DEADNETTLE (*Lamium sp.*)

Sclerenchyma (strengthening tissue)

Mesophyll (layer of photosynthetic tissue)

Pith with stellate parenchyma (star-shaped packing tissue)

Vascular bundle

Xylem

Phloem

Epidermis (outer layer of cells) with thick cuticle (waterproof covering)

Sclerenchyma (strengthening tissue)

RUSH (*Juncus sp.*)

Epidermis (outer layer of cells)

Phloem

Xylem

Vascular tissue

Lacuna (air space)

Pith

Cortex (layer between epidermis and vascular tissue)

Endodermis (inner layer of cortex)

MARE'S TAIL (*Hippuris vulgaris*)

Parenchyma (packing tissue) with bundles of sclerenchyma (strengthening tissue)

Vascular bundle (xylem, phloem, and sclerenchyma fibres)

Epidermis (outer layer of cells)

Mesophyll (layer of photosynthetic tissue)

Cortex (layer between epidermis and vascular tissue)

COCONUT PALM (*Cocos nucifera*)

135

Leaves

LEAVES ARE THE MAIN SITES OF PHOTOSYNTHESIS (see pp. 138-139) and transpiration (water loss by evaporation) in plants. A typical leaf consists of a thin, flat lamina (blade) supported by a network of veins; a petiole (leaf stalk); and a leaf base, where the petiole joins the stem. Leaves can be classified as simple, in which the lamina is a single unit, or compound, in which the lamina is divided into separate leaflets. Compound leaves may be pinnate, with pinnae (leaflets) on both sides of a rachis (main axis), or palmate, with leaflets arising from a single point at the tip of the petiole. Leaves can be classified further by the overall shape of the lamina, and by the shape of the lamina's apex, margin, and base.

CHECKERBLOOM
(*Sidalcea malviflora*)

SIMPLE LEAF SHAPES

Subacute apex

Acuminate apex

Entire margin

Entire margin

Cuneate base

Cordate base

PANDURIFORM
Croton
(*Codiaeum variegatum*)

LANCEOLATE
Sea buckthorn
(*Hippophae rhamnoides*)

GENERAL LEAF FEATURES

Apex

Lamina (blade)

Midrib

Margin

Lateral vein

Lamina base

Petiole (leaf stalk)

Leaf base

Sweet chestnut
(*Castanea sativa*)

COMPOUND LEAF SHAPES

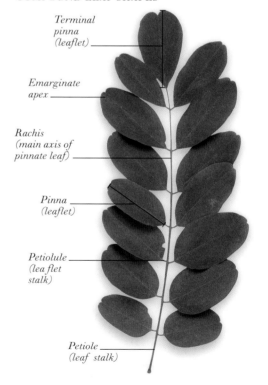

Terminal pinna (leaflet)

Emarginate apex

Rachis (main axis of pinnate leaf)

Pinna (leaflet)

Petiolule (lea flet stalk)

Petiole (leaf stalk)

ODD PINNATE
False acacia
(*Robinia pseudoacacia*)

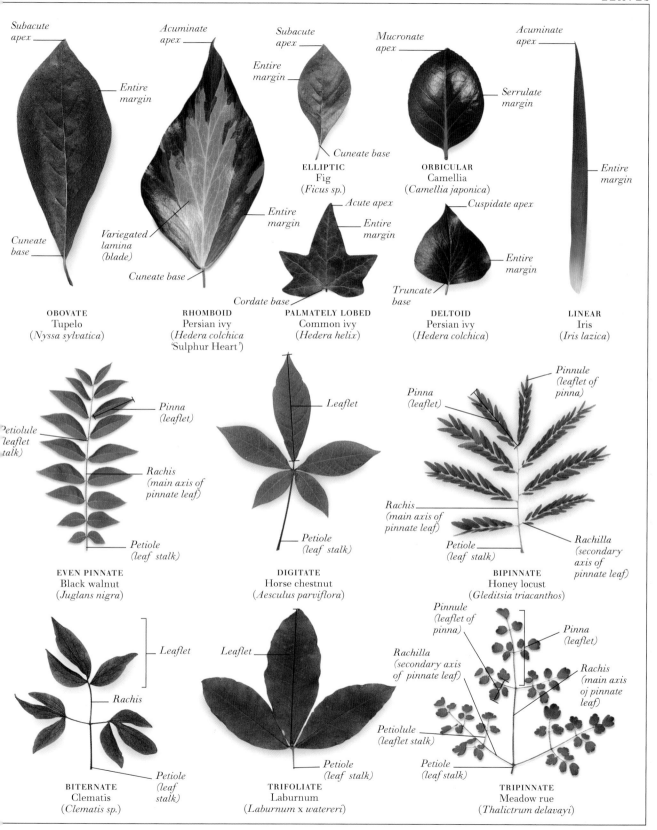

Subacute apex

Entire margin

Cuneate base

OBOVATE
Tupelo
(*Nyssa sylvatica*)

Acuminate apex

Variegated lamina (blade)

Entire margin

Cuneate base

RHOMBOID
Persian ivy
(*Hedera colchica*
'Sulphur Heart')

Subacute apex

Entire margin

Cuneate base

ELLIPTIC
Fig
(*Ficus sp.*)

Acute apex

Entire margin

Cordate base

PALMATELY LOBED
Common ivy
(*Hedera helix*)

Mucronate apex

Serrulate margin

ORBICULAR
Camellia
(*Camellia japonica*)

Cuspidate apex

Entire margin

Truncate base

DELTOID
Persian ivy
(*Hedera colchica*)

Acuminate apex

Entire margin

LINEAR
Iris
(*Iris lazica*)

Pinna (leaflet)

Petiolule (leaflet stalk)

Rachis (main axis of pinnate leaf)

Petiole (leaf stalk)

EVEN PINNATE
Black walnut
(*Juglans nigra*)

Leaflet

Petiole (leaf stalk)

DIGITATE
Horse chestnut
(*Aesculus parviflora*)

Pinnule (leaflet of pinna)

Pinna (leaflet)

Rachis (main axis of pinnate leaf)

Petiole (leaf stalk)

Rachilla (secondary axis of pinnate leaf)

BIPINNATE
Honey locust
(*Gleditsia triacanthos*)

Leaflet

Rachis

Petiole (leaf stalk)

BITERNATE
Clematis
(*Clematis sp.*)

Leaflet

Petiole (leaf stalk)

TRIFOLIATE
Laburnum
(*Laburnum x watereri*)

Pinnule (leaflet of pinna)

Rachilla (secondary axis of pinnate leaf)

Petiolule (leaflet stalk)

Petiole (leaf stalk)

Pinna (leaflet)

Rachis (main axis oj pinnate leaf)

TRIPINNATE
Meadow rue
(*Thalictrum delavayi*)

137

Photosynthesis

PHOTOSYNTHESIS IS THE PROCESS by which plants make their food using sunlight, water, and carbon dioxide. It takes place inside special structures in leaf cells called chloroplasts. The chloroplasts contain chlorophyll, a green pigment that absorbs energy from sunlight. During photosynthesis, the absorbed energy is used to join together carbon dioxide and water to form the sugar glucose, which is the energy source for the whole plant; oxygen, a waste product, is released into the air. Leaves are the main sites of photosynthesis, and have various adaptations for that purpose: flat laminae (blades) provide a large surface for absorbing sunlight; stomata (pores) in the lower surface of the laminae allow gases (carbon dioxide and oxygen) to pass into and out of the leaves; and an extensive network of veins brings water into the leaves and transports the glucose produced by photosynthesis to the rest of the plant.

MICROGRAPH OF LEAF
Lily (*Lilium sp.*)

Stoma (pore)

Guard cell (controls opening and closing of stoma)

Lower surface of lamina (blade)

THE PROCESS OF PHOTOSYNTHESIS

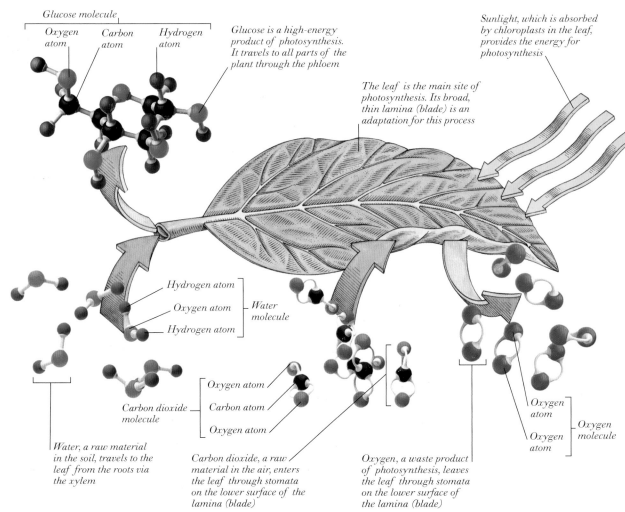

Glucose molecule

Oxygen atom

Carbon atom

Hydrogen atom

Glucose is a high-energy product of photosynthesis. It travels to all parts of the plant through the phloem

Sunlight, which is absorbed by chloroplasts in the leaf, provides the energy for photosynthesis

The leaf is the main site of photosynthesis. Its broad, thin lamina (blade) is an adaptation for this process

Hydrogen atom

Oxygen atom

Hydrogen atom

Water molecule

Carbon dioxide molecule

Oxygen atom

Carbon atom

Oxygen atom

Oxygen atom

Oxygen atom

Oxygen molecule

Water, a raw material in the soil, travels to the leaf from the roots via the xylem

Carbon dioxide, a raw material in the air, enters the leaf through stomata on the lower surface of the lamina (blade)

Oxygen, a waste product of photosynthesis, leaves the leaf through stomata on the lower surface of the lamina (blade)

CROSS-SECTION THROUGH LEAF
Christmas rose
(*Helleborus niger*)

Cuticle (waterproof covering)

Upper (adaxial) epidermis (outer layer of cells)

Cell wall

Cytoplasm

Vacuole

Chloroplast (photosynthetic organelle)

Palisade mesophyll (tightly packed layer of photosynthetic tissue)

Nucleus

Intercellular space

Sclerenchyma (strengthening tissue)

Xylem (tissue that transports water and mineral salts)

Phloem (tissue that transports sugars and other nutrients)

Spongy mesophyll (loosely packed layer of photosynthetic tissue)

Vein

Lower (abaxial) epidermis (outer layer of cells)

Parenchyma (packing tissue)

Guard cell (controls opening and closing of stoma)

Stoma (pore)

Substomatal chamber

INTERNAL VIEW OF CHLOROPLAST

Granum (stack of thylakoids that hold chlorophyll molecules in position)

Lamella (membrane of thylakoid)

Thylakoid (flat sac of granum)

Deoxyribonucleic acid (DNA) strand

Stroma (watery matrix)

Starch grain

Chloroplast envelope

Outer membrane

Inner membrane

Ribosome (site of protein synthesis)

Stroma thylakoid (link between grana)

Flowers 1

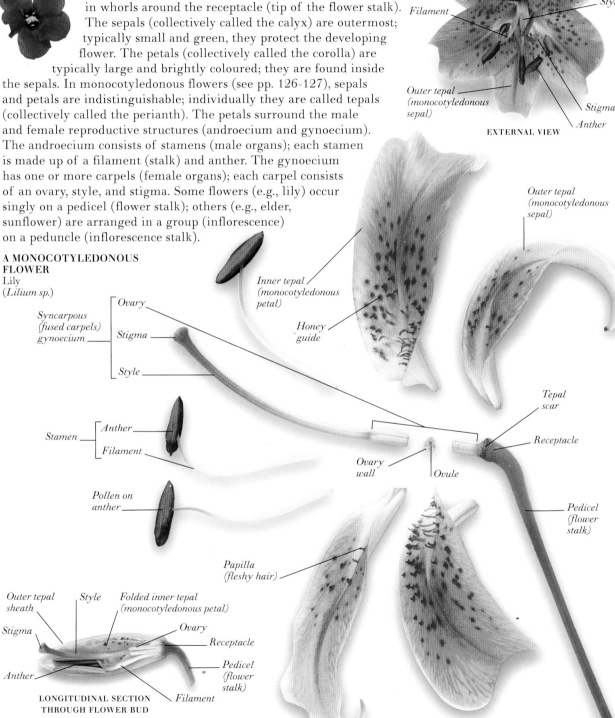

FLOWERS ARE THE SITES OF SEXUAL REPRODUCTION in flowering plants. Their component parts are arranged in whorls around the receptacle (tip of the flower stalk). The sepals (collectively called the calyx) are outermost; typically small and green, they protect the developing flower. The petals (collectively called the corolla) are typically large and brightly coloured; they are found inside the sepals. In monocotyledonous flowers (see pp. 126-127), sepals and petals are indistinguishable; individually they are called tepals (collectively called the perianth). The petals surround the male and female reproductive structures (androecium and gynoecium). The androecium consists of stamens (male organs); each stamen is made up of a filament (stalk) and anther. The gynoecium has one or more carpels (female organs); each carpel consists of an ovary, style, and stigma. Some flowers (e.g., lily) occur singly on a pedicel (flower stalk); others (e.g., elder, sunflower) are arranged in a group (inflorescence) on a peduncle (inflorescence stalk).

A MONOCOTYLEDONOUS FLOWER
Lily
(*Lilium* sp.)

Inner tepal (monocotyledonous petal)

Honey guide

Groove secreting nectar

Filament

Style

Outer tepal (monocotyledonous sepal)

Stigma

Anther

EXTERNAL VIEW

Outer tepal (monocotyledonous sepal)

Inner tepal (monocotyledonous petal)

Honey guide

Tepal scar

Receptacle

Ovary wall

Ovule

Pedicel (flower stalk)

Syncarpous (fused carpels) gynoecium

Ovary

Stigma

Style

Stamen

Anther

Filament

Pollen on anther

Papilla (fleshy hair)

Outer tepal sheath

Style

Folded inner tepal (monocotyledonous petal)

Stigma

Ovary

Receptacle

Anther

Pedicel (flower stalk)

Filament

LONGITUDINAL SECTION THROUGH FLOWER BUD

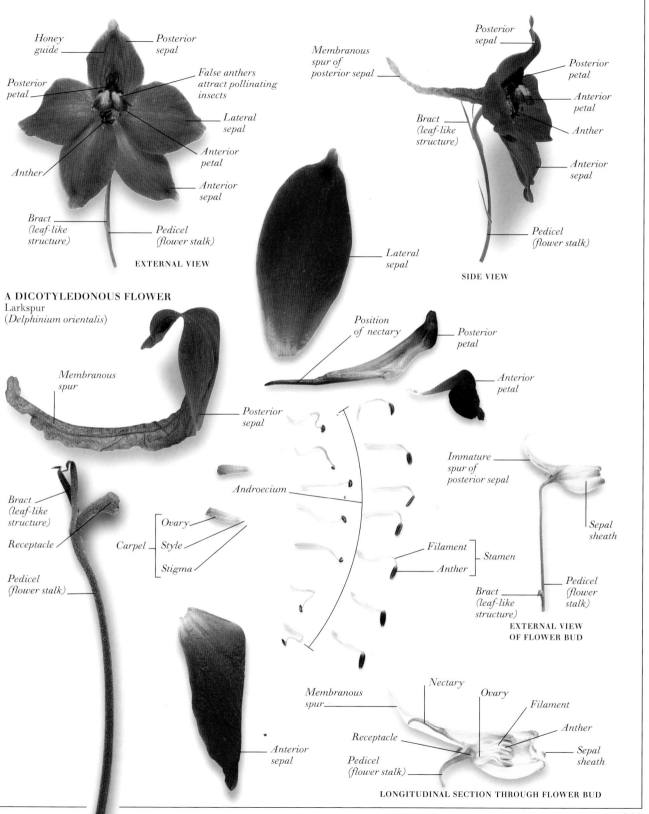

Honey guide

Posterior sepal

Posterior petal

False anthers attract pollinating insects

Lateral sepal

Anterior petal

Anterior sepal

Anther

Bract (leaf-like structure)

Pedicel (flower stalk)

EXTERNAL VIEW

A DICOTYLEDONOUS FLOWER
Larkspur
(*Delphinium orientalis*)

Membranous spur of posterior sepal

Posterior sepal

Posterior petal

Anterior petal

Anther

Bract (leaf-like structure)

Anterior sepal

Pedicel (flower stalk)

SIDE VIEW

Lateral sepal

Membranous spur

Posterior sepal

Position of nectary

Posterior petal

Anterior petal

Bract (leaf-like structure)

Receptacle

Pedicel (flower stalk)

Carpel

Ovary

Style

Stigma

Androecium

Filament

Anther

Stamen

Bract (leaf-like structure)

Immature spur of posterior sepal

Sepal sheath

Pedicel (flower stalk)

EXTERNAL VIEW OF FLOWER BUD

Anterior sepal

Membranous spur

Nectary

Ovary

Filament

Anther

Receptacle

Sepal sheath

Pedicel (flower stalk)

LONGITUDINAL SECTION THROUGH FLOWER BUD

141

Flowers 2

COMPOUND INFLORESCENCE
(CAPITULUM)
Sunflower
(*Helianthus annulus*)

Disc florets

Ray floret

Florets (small flowers) are grouped together to resemble a single large flower

Sterile ray floret to attract pollinating insects

Outer fertilized floret

Two-lobed stigma

Florets with anthers ready to shed pollen

Style

Pollen

Anther

Inner, immature florets

Corolla tube (fused petals)

Pappus (modified sepal)

Ovary

Corolla tube (fused petals)

Ovary

FLORETS FROM SUNFLOWER

Pollen

Anther

Nectar

Disc floret

Ray floret

Stigma

Style

Ovary

Bract (leaf-like structure)

Hair

Pith

Corolla tube (fused petals)

Pappus (modified sepal)

Domed receptacle (flattened top of inflorescence stalk)

LONGITUDINAL SECTION THROUGH SUNFLOWER INFLORESCENCE

Epidermis (outer layer of cells) of peduncle (inflorescence stalk)

Peduncle (inflorescence stalk)

ARRANGEMENT OF FLOWERS ON STEM

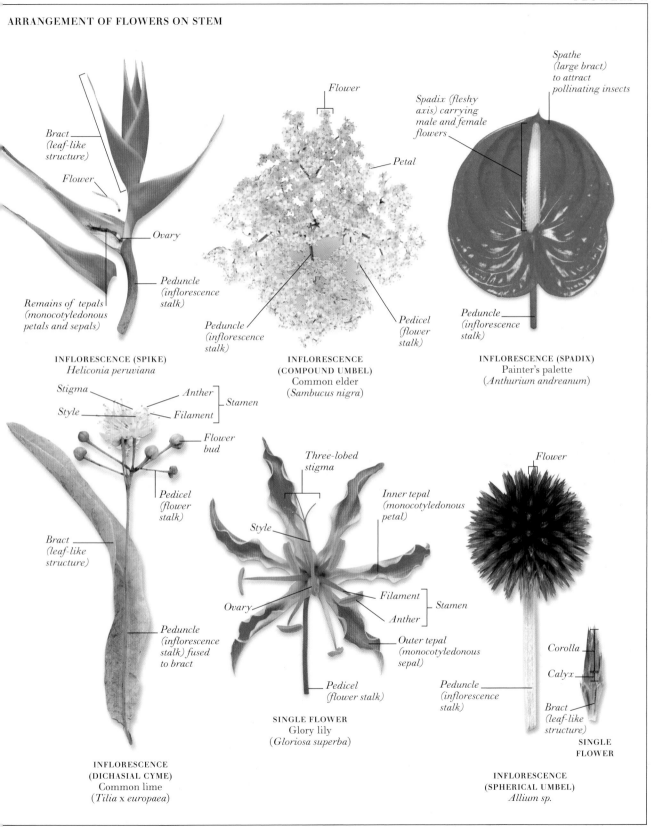

Bract
(leaf-like
structure)

Flower

Ovary

Peduncle
(inflorescence
stalk)

Remains of tepals
(monocotyledonous
petals and sepals)

INFLORESCENCE (SPIKE)
Heliconia peruviana

Flower

Petal

Peduncle
(inflorescence
stalk)

Pedicel
(flower
stalk)

**INFLORESCENCE
(COMPOUND UMBEL)**
Common elder
(*Sambucus nigra*)

Spadix (fleshy
axis) carrying
male and female
flowers

Spathe
(large bract)
to attract
pollinating insects

Peduncle
(inflorescence
stalk)

INFLORESCENCE (SPADIX)
Painter's palette
(*Anthurium andreanum*)

Stigma

Style

Anther

Filament

Stamen

Flower
bud

Pedicel
(flower
stalk)

Bract
(leaf-like
structure)

Peduncle
(inflorescence
stalk) fused
to bract

**INFLORESCENCE
(DICHASIAL CYME)**
Common lime
(*Tilia* x *europaea*)

Three-lobed
stigma

Style

Ovary

Inner tepal
(monocotyledonous
petal)

Filament

Anther

Stamen

Outer tepal
(monocotyledonous
sepal)

Pedicel
(flower stalk)

SINGLE FLOWER
Glory lily
(*Gloriosa superba*)

Flower

Peduncle
(inflorescence
stalk)

Corolla

Calyx

Bract
(leaf-like
structure)

**SINGLE
FLOWER**

**INFLORESCENCE
(SPHERICAL UMBEL)**
Allium sp.

Pollination

POLLINATION IS THE TRANSFER OF POLLEN (which contains the male sex cells) from an anther (part of the male reproductive organ) to a stigma (part of the female reproductive organ). This process precedes fertilization (see pp. 146-147). Pollination may occur within the same flower (self-pollination), or between flowers on separate plants of the same species (cross-pollination). In most plants, pollination is carried out either by insects (entomophilous pollination) or by the wind (anemophilous pollination). Less commonly, birds, bats, or water are the agents of pollination. Insect-pollinated flowers are typically brightly coloured, scented, and produce nectar, on which insects feed. Such flowers also tend to have patterns that are visible only in ultraviolet light, which many insects can see but which humans cannot. These features attract insects, which become covered with the sticky or hooked pollen grains when they visit one flower, and then transfer the pollen to the next flower they visit. Wind-pollinated flowers are generally small, relatively inconspicuous, and unscented. They produce large quantities of light pollen grains that are easily blown by the wind to other flowers.

REPRODUCTIVE STRUCTURES IN WIND-POLLINATED PLANT
Sweet chestnut
(*Castanea saliva*)

Flower bud

Prominent stigma protrudes from flower

Female flower

Petiole (leaf stalk)

Bract (leaf-like structure)

Peduncle (inflorescence stalk)

Part of male catkin (inflorescence adapted for wind pollination)

Male flower

Peduncle (inflorescenc stalk)

Filament

Anther

FEMALE

MALE

REPRODUCTIVE STRUCTURES IN INSECT-POLLINATED PLANTS

Stigma

Style

Dehisced (split open) pollen sac

Boundary between two fused carpels (each carpel consists of a stigma, style, and ovary)

Ovary

Endothecium (pollen sac wall)

Pollen grain

Anther

Filament

Stamen

Calyx (whorl of sepals)

MICROGRAPH OF CARPELS (FEMALE ORGANS)
Yellow-wort
(*Blackstonia perfoliata*)

MICROGRAPH OF STAMENS (MALE ORGANS)
Common centaury
(*Centaurium erythraea*)

MICROGRAPHS OF POLLEN GRAINS

Exine (outer coat of pollen grain)

Pore

EUROPEAN FIELD ELM
(*Ulmus minor*)

Colpus (furrow-shaped aperture)

Exine (outer coat of pollen grain)

JUSTICIA AUREA

Exine (outer coat of pollen grain)

Pore

Baculum (rod-shaped structure)

MEADOW CRANESBILL
(*Geranium pratense*)

Colpus (furrow-shaped aperture)

Exine (outer coat of pollen grain)

Equatoria furrow

BOX-LEAVED MILKWORT
(*Polygala chamaebuxus*)

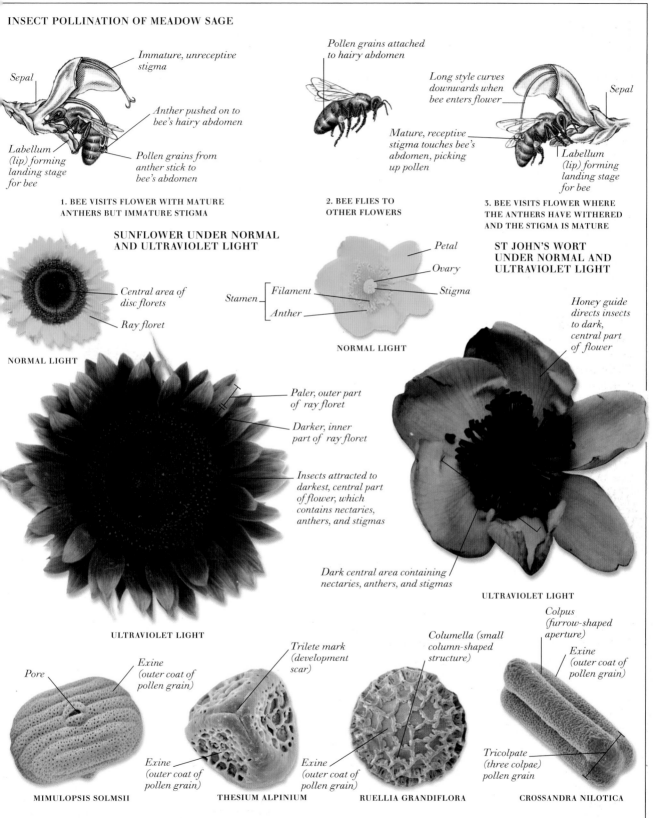

INSECT POLLINATION OF MEADOW SAGE

Immature, unreceptive stigma

Sepal

Anther pushed on to bee's hairy abdomen

Labellum (lip) forming landing stage for bee

Pollen grains from anther stick to bee's abdomen

1. BEE VISITS FLOWER WITH MATURE ANTHERS BUT IMMATURE STIGMA

Pollen grains attached to hairy abdomen

2. BEE FLIES TO OTHER FLOWERS

Long style curves downwards when bee enters flower

Sepal

Mature, receptive stigma touches bee's abdomen, picking up pollen

Labellum (lip) forming landing stage for bee

3. BEE VISITS FLOWER WHERE THE ANTHERS HAVE WITHERED AND THE STIGMA IS MATURE

SUNFLOWER UNDER NORMAL AND ULTRAVIOLET LIGHT

Central area of disc florets

Ray floret

NORMAL LIGHT

Petal

Ovary

Stigma

Stamen — *Filament* / *Anther*

NORMAL LIGHT

ST JOHN'S WORT UNDER NORMAL AND ULTRAVIOLET LIGHT

Honey guide directs insects to dark, central part of flower

Paler, outer part of ray floret

Darker, inner part of ray floret

Insects attracted to darkest, central part of flower, which contains nectaries, anthers, and stigmas

Dark central area containing nectaries, anthers, and stigmas

ULTRAVIOLET LIGHT

ULTRAVIOLET LIGHT

Colpus (furrow-shaped aperture)

Exine (outer coat of pollen grain)

Trilete mark (development scar)

Columella (small column-shaped structure)

Pore

Exine (outer coat of pollen grain)

Exine (outer coat of pollen grain)

Exine (outer coat of pollen grain)

Tricolpate (three colpae) pollen grain

MIMULOPSIS SOLMSII

THESIUM ALPINIUM

RUELLIA GRANDIFLORA

CROSSANDRA NILOTICA

Fertilization

FERTILIZATION IS THE FUSION of male and female gametes (sex cells) to produce a zygote (embryo). Following pollination (see pp. 144-145), the pollen grains that contain the male gametes are on the stigma, some distance from the female gamete (ovum) inside the ovule. To enable the gametes to meet, the pollen grain germinates and produces a pollen tube, which grows down and enters the embryo sac (the inner part of the ovule that contains the ovum). Two male gametes, travelling at the tip of the pollen tube, enter the embryo sac. One gamete fuses with the ovum to produce a zygote that will develop into an embryo plant. The other male gamete fuses with two polar nuclei to produce the endosperm, which acts as a food store for the developing embryo. Fertilization also initiates other changes: the integument (outer part of ovule) forms a testa (seed coat) around the embryo and endosperm; the petals fall off; the stigma and style wither; and the ovary wall forms a layer (called the pericarp) around the seed. Together, the pericarp and seed form the fruit, which may be succulent (see pp. 148-149) or dry (see pp. 150-151). In some species (e.g., blackberry), apomixis can occur: the seed develops without fertilization of the ovum by a male gamete but endosperm formation and fruit development take place as in other species.

BANANA
(*Musa 'lacatan'*)

DEVELOPMENT OF A SUCCULENT FRUIT
Blackberry
(*Rubus fruticosus*)

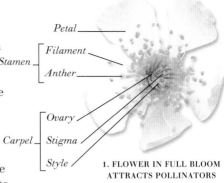

Petal
Stamen { *Filament*
Anther
Carpel { *Ovary*
Stigma
Style

**1. FLOWER IN FULL BLOOM
ATTRACTS POLLINATORS**

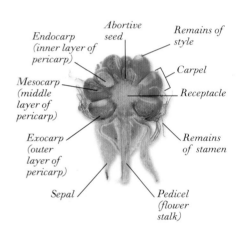

*Endocarp
(inner layer of
pericarp)*
*Abortive
seed*
*Remains of
style*
Carpel
Receptacle
*Mesocarp
(middle
layer of
pericarp)*
*Exocarp
(outer
layer of
pericarp)*
*Remains
of stamen*
Sepal
*Pedicel
(flower
stalk)*

**4. PERICARP FORMS
FLESH, SKIN, AND A HARD INNER
LAYER (SHOWN IN CROSS-SECTION)**

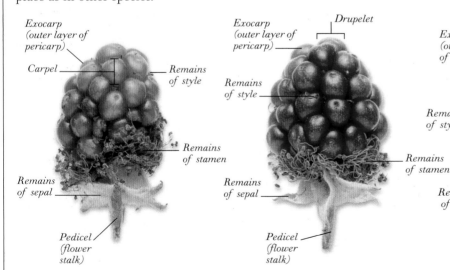

*Exocarp
(outer layer of
pericarp)*
Carpel
*Remains
of style*
*Remains
of stamen*
*Remains
of sepal*
*Pedicel
(flower
stalk)*

**7. MESOCARP (FLESHY PART OF PERICARP)
OF EACH CARPEL STARTS TO
CHANGE COLOUR**

*Exocarp
(outer layer of
pericarp)*
Drupelet
*Remains
of style*
*Remains
of stamen*
*Remains
of sepal*
*Pedicel
(flower
stalk)*

**8. CARPELS MATURE INTO DRUPELETS
(SMALL FLESHY FRUITS WITH SINGLE SEEDS
SURROUNDED BY HARD ENDOCARP)**

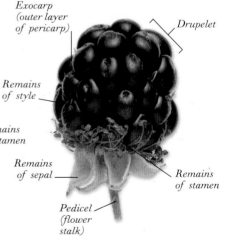

*Exocarp
(outer layer
of pericarp)*
Drupelet
*Remains
of style*
*Remains
of sepal*
*Remains
of stamen*
*Pedicel
(flower
stalk)*

**9. MESOCARP OF DRUPELET BECOMES
DARKER AND SWEETER**

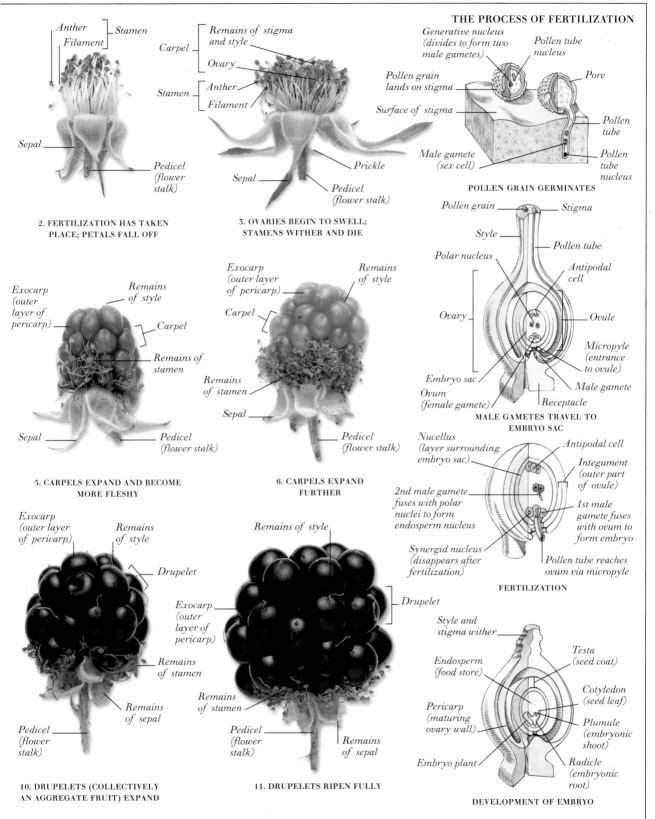

THE PROCESS OF FERTILIZATION

Generative nucleus (divides to form two male gametes)

Pollen tube nucleus

Pollen grain lands on stigma

Pore

Surface of stigma

Male gamete (sex cell)

Pollen tube

Pollen tube nucleus

POLLEN GRAIN GERMINATES

Anther
Filament
} Stamen

Sepal

Pedicel (flower stalk)

2. FERTILIZATION HAS TAKEN PLACE; PETALS FALL OFF

Remains of stigma and style
Carpel
Ovary
Stamen { Anther
Filament

Prickle

Sepal

Pedicel (flower stalk)

3. OVARIES BEGIN TO SWELL; STAMENS WITHER AND DIE

Pollen grain
Stigma
Style
Pollen tube
Polar nucleus
Antipodal cell
Ovary
Ovule
Micropyle (entrance to ovule)
Male gamete
Embryo sac
Ovum (female gamete)
Receptacle

MALE GAMETES TRAVEL TO EMBRYO SAC

Exocarp (outer layer of pericarp)
Remains of style
Carpel
Remains of stamen
Sepal
Pedicel (flower stalk)

5. CARPELS EXPAND AND BECOME MORE FLESHY

Exocarp (outer layer of pericarp)
Remains of style
Carpel
Remains of stamen
Sepal
Pedicel (flower stalk)

6. CARPELS EXPAND FURTHER

Nucellus (layer surrounding embryo sac)
Antipodal cell
Integument (outer part of ovule)
2nd male gamete fuses with polar nuclei to form endosperm nucleus
1st male gamete fuses with ovum to form embryo
Synergid nucleus (disappears after fertilization)
Pollen tube reaches ovum via micropyle

FERTILIZATION

Exocarp (outer layer of pericarp)
Remains of style
Drupelet
Remains of stamen
Remains of sepal
Pedicel (flower stalk)

10. DRUPELETS (COLLECTIVELY AN AGGREGATE FRUIT) EXPAND

Remains of style
Exocarp (outer layer of pericarp)
Drupelet
Remains of stamen
Pedicel (flower stalk)
Remains of sepal

11. DRUPELETS RIPEN FULLY

Style and stigma wither
Endosperm (food store)
Testa (seed coat)
Cotyledon (seed leaf)
Pericarp (maturing ovary wall)
Plumule (embryonic shoot)
Embryo plant
Radicle (embryonic root)

DEVELOPMENT OF EMBRYO

Succulent fruits

A FRUIT IS A FULLY DEVELOPED and ripened ovary (seed-producing part of a plant's female reproductive organs). Fruits may be succulent or dry (see pp. 150-151). Succulent fruits are fleshy and brightly coloured, making them attractive to animals, which eat them and so disperse the seeds away from the parent plant. The wall (pericarp) of a succulent fruit has three layers: an outer exocarp, a middle mesocarp, and an inner endocarp. These three layers vary in thickness and texture in different types of fruits and may blend into each other. Succulent fruits can be classed as simple (derived from one ovary) or compound (derived from several ovaries). Simple succulent fruits include berries, which typically have many seeds, and drupes, which typically have a single stone or pip (e.g., cherry and peach). Compound succulent fruits include aggregate fruits, which are formed from many ovaries in one flower, and multiple fruits, which develop from the ovaries of many flowers. Some fruits, known as false fruits or pseudocarps, develop from parts of the flower in addition to the ovaries. For example, the flesh of the apple is formed from the receptacle (the upper end of the flower stalk).

BERRY
Cocoa
(*Theobroma cacao*)

HESPERIDIUM (A TYPE OF BERRY)
Lemon
(*Citrus limon*)

Pedicel (flower stalk)

Endocarp

Mesocarp

Pedicel (flower stalk)

Exocarp

Leathery exocarp

Seed

Oil gland

Vesicle (juice sac)

Remains of style

Remains of style

Placenta

EXTERNAL VIEW OF FRUIT

LONGITUDINAL SECTION THROUGH FRUIT

Hilum (point of attachment to ovary)

Embryo

Seed

Carpel wall

Carpel

Testa (seed coat)

Placenta

Cotyledon (seed leaf)

EXTERNAL VIEW AND SECTION THROUGH SEED

CROSS-SECTION THROUGH FRUIT

SYCONIUM (A TYPE OF FALSE FRUIT)
Fig
(*Ficus carica*)

Peduncle (inflorescence stalk)

Remains of female flowers

Fleshy infolded receptacle

Pip (seed surrounded by endocarp)

Rema of mo flowe

Skin

Pore closed by scales

EXTERNAL VIEW OF FRUIT

LONGITUDINAL SECTION THROUGH FRUIT

FRUIT WITH FLESHY ARIL
Lychee
(*Litchi chinensis*)

Pedicel (flower stalk)

Pedicel (flower stalk)

Remains of style

Endocarp

EXTERNAL VIEW AND SECTION THROUGH PIP

Seed

Drupelet

Aril (fleshy outgrowth from seed stalk)

Pip

Endocarp

Cotyledon (seed leaf)

Pedicel (flower stalk)

Embryo

Testa (seed coat)

Pericarp (fruit wall)

Pericarp (fruit wall)

EXTERNAL VIEW OF FRUIT

LONGITUDINAL SECTION THROUGH FRUIT

REMAINS OF A SINGLE FEMALE FLOWER

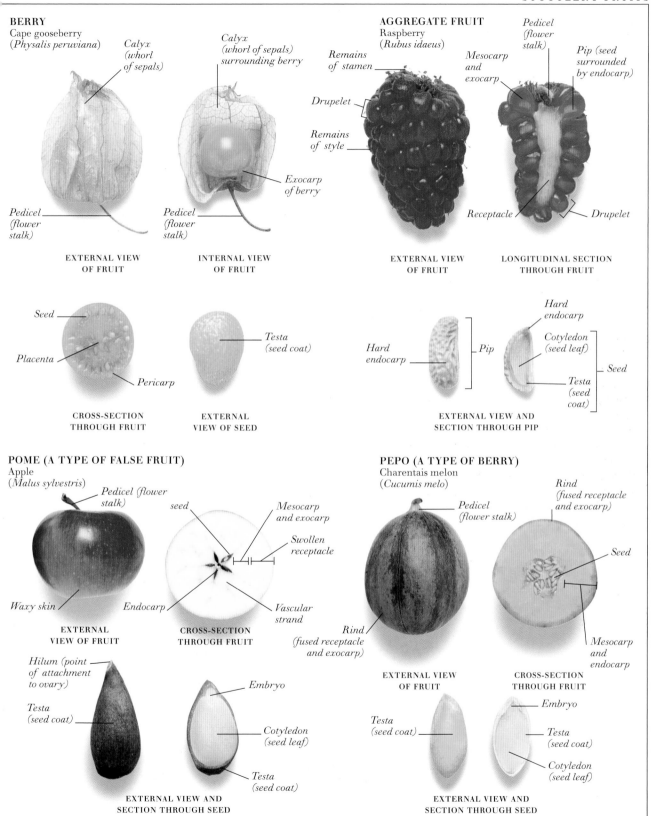

BERRY
Cape gooseberry
(*Physalis peruviana*)

Calyx (whorl of sepals)

Calyx (whorl of sepals) surrounding berry

Pedicel (flower stalk)

Pedicel (flower stalk)

Exocarp of berry

EXTERNAL VIEW
OF FRUIT

INTERNAL VIEW
OF FRUIT

Seed

Placenta

Pericarp

Testa (seed coat)

CROSS-SECTION
THROUGH FRUIT

EXTERNAL
VIEW OF SEED

AGGREGATE FRUIT
Raspberry
(*Rubus idaeus*)

Remains of stamen

Drupelet

Remains of style

Pedicel (flower stalk)

Mesocarp and exocarp

Pip (seed surrounded by endocarp)

Receptacle

Drupelet

EXTERNAL VIEW
OF FRUIT

LONGITUDINAL SECTION
THROUGH FRUIT

Hard endocarp

Hard endocarp

Pip

Cotyledon (seed leaf)

Testa (seed coat)

Seed

EXTERNAL VIEW AND
SECTION THROUGH PIP

POME (A TYPE OF FALSE FRUIT)
Apple
(*Malus sylvestris*)

Pedicel (flower stalk)

seed

Mesocarp and exocarp

Swollen receptacle

Waxy skin

Endocarp

Vascular strand

EXTERNAL
VIEW OF FRUIT

CROSS-SECTION
THROUGH FRUIT

Hilum (point of attachment to ovary)

Testa (seed coat)

Embryo

Cotyledon (seed leaf)

Testa (seed coat)

EXTERNAL VIEW AND
SECTION THROUGH SEED

PEPO (A TYPE OF BERRY)
Charentais melon
(*Cucumis melo*)

Pedicel (flower stalk)

Rind (fused receptacle and exocarp)

Seed

Rind (fused receptacle and exocarp)

Mesocarp and endocarp

EXTERNAL VIEW
OF FRUIT

CROSS-SECTION
THROUGH FRUIT

Testa (seed coat)

Embryo

Testa (seed coat)

Cotyledon (seed leaf)

EXTERNAL VIEW AND
SECTION THROUGH SEED

Dry fruits

DRY FRUITS HAVE A HARD, DRY PERICARP (fruit wall) around their seeds unlike succulent fruits, which have fleshy pericarps (see pp. 148-149). Dry fruits are divided into three types: dehiscent, in which the pericarp splits open to release the seeds; indehiscent, which do not split open; and schizocarpic, in which the fruit splits but the seeds are not exposed. Dehiscent dry fruits include capsules (e.g., love-in-a-mist), follicles (e.g., delphinium), legumes (e.g., pea), and siliquas (e.g., honesty). Typically, the seeds of dehiscent fruits are dispersed by the wind. Indehiscent dry fruits include nuts (e.g., sweet chestnut), nutlets (e.g., goosegrass), achenes (e.g., strawberry), caryopses (e.g., wheat), samaras (e.g., elm), and cypselas (e.g., dandelion). Some indehiscent dry fruits are dispersed by the wind, assisted by "wings" (e.g., elm) or "parachutes" (e.g., dandelion); others (e.g., goosegrass) have hooked pericarps to aid dispersal on animals' fur. Schizocarpic dry fruits include cremocarps (e.g., hogweed), and double samaras (e.g., sycamore); these are dispersed by the wind.

NUTLET
Goosegrass
(*Galium aparine*)

LEGUME
Pea
(*Pisum sativum*)

Pedicel (flower stalk)
Receptacle
Remains of sepal
Remains of stamen
Pericarp (fruit wall)
Remains of style and stigma

EXTERNAL VIEW OF FRUIT

Pedicel (flower stalk)
Receptacle
Remains of sepal
Placenta
Funicle (stalk attaching seed to placenta)
Pericarp (fruit wall)
Seed
Remains of style and stigma

INTERNAL VIEW OF FRUIT

Funicle (stalk attaching seed to placenta)
Micropyle (pore for water absorption)
Testa (seed coat)

Cotyledon (seed leaf)
Radicle (embryonic root)
Testa (seed coat)
Plumule (embryonic shoot)

EXTERIOR VIEW AND SECTION THROUGH SEED

NUT
Sweet chestnut
(*Castanea sativa*)

Line of splitting between valves of cupule
Peduncle (inflorescence stalk)
Remains of male inflorescence
Nut (indehiscent fruit)
Spiky cupule (husk around fruit formed from bracts)

EXTERNAL VIEW OF FRUIT WITH SURROUNDING CUPULE

Remains of stigma
Remains of style
Nut (indehiscent fruit)
Woody pericarp (fruit wall)

Remains of stigma
Remains of style
Embryo
Cotyledon (seed leaf)
Testa (seed coat)
Woody pericarp (fruit wall)

EXTERNAL VIEW AND SECTION THROUGH FRUIT

ACHENE
Strawberry
(*Fragaria x ananassa*)

Sepal
Pedicel (flower stalk)
Swollen receptacle
Remains of stigma and style
Achene (one-seeded dry fruit)

EXTERNAL VIEW OF FRUIT

Sepal
Pedicel (flower stalk)
Swollen fleshy tissues of receptacle

LONGITUDINAL SECTION THROUGH FRUIT

Pericarp (fruit wall)
Cotyledon (seed leaf)
Testa (seed coat)

EXTERNAL VIEW AND SECTION THROUGH SEED

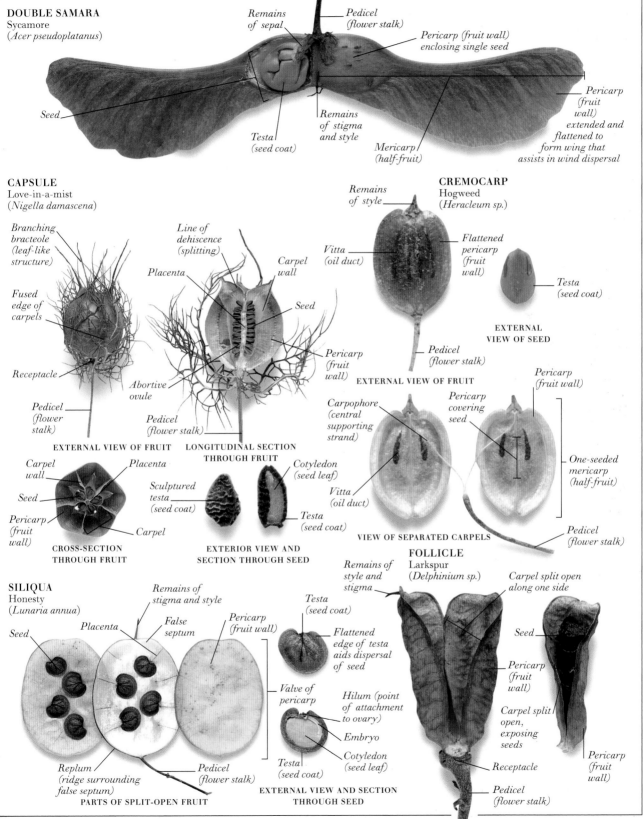

DOUBLE SAMARA
Sycamore
(*Acer pseudoplatanus*)

Remains of sepal

Pedicel (flower stalk)

Pericarp (fruit wall) enclosing single seed

Seed

Remains of stigma and style

Testa (seed coat)

Mericarp (half-fruit)

Pericarp (fruit wall) extended and flattened to form wing that assists in wind dispersal

CAPSULE
Love-in-a-mist
(*Nigella damascena*)

Branching bracteole (leaf-like structure)

Line of dehiscence (splitting)

Placenta

Carpel wall

Fused edge of carpels

Seed

Receptacle

Pericarp (fruit wall)

Abortive ovule

Pedicel (flower stalk)

Pedicel (flower stalk)

EXTERNAL VIEW OF FRUIT

LONGITUDINAL SECTION THROUGH FRUIT

Carpel wall

Placenta

Seed

Cotyledon (seed leaf)

Pericarp (fruit wall)

Sculptured testa (seed coat)

Carpel

Testa (seed coat)

CROSS-SECTION THROUGH FRUIT

EXTERIOR VIEW AND SECTION THROUGH SEED

CREMOCARP
Hogweed
(*Heracleum sp.*)

Remains of style

Flattened pericarp (fruit wall)

Vitta (oil duct)

Testa (seed coat)

EXTERNAL VIEW OF SEED

Pedicel (flower stalk)

EXTERNAL VIEW OF FRUIT

Pericarp (fruit wall)

Carpophore (central supporting strand)

Pericarp covering seed

Vitta (oil duct)

One-seeded mericarp (half-fruit)

VIEW OF SEPARATED CARPELS

Pedicel (flower stalk)

SILIQUA
Honesty
(*Lunaria annua*)

Remains of stigma and style

Seed

False septum

Placenta

Pericarp (fruit wall)

Replum (ridge surrounding false septum)

Pedicel (flower stalk)

PARTS OF SPLIT-OPEN FRUIT

Testa (seed coat)

Flattened edge of testa aids dispersal of seed

Valve of pericarp

Hilum (point of attachment to ovary)

Embryo

Cotyledon (seed leaf)

Testa (seed coat)

EXTERNAL VIEW AND SECTION THROUGH SEED

FOLLICLE
Larkspur
(*Delphinium sp.*)

Remains of style and stigma

Carpel split open along one side

Seed

Pericarp (fruit wall)

Carpel split open, exposing seeds

Receptacle

Pericarp (fruit wall)

Pedicel (flower stalk)

Germination

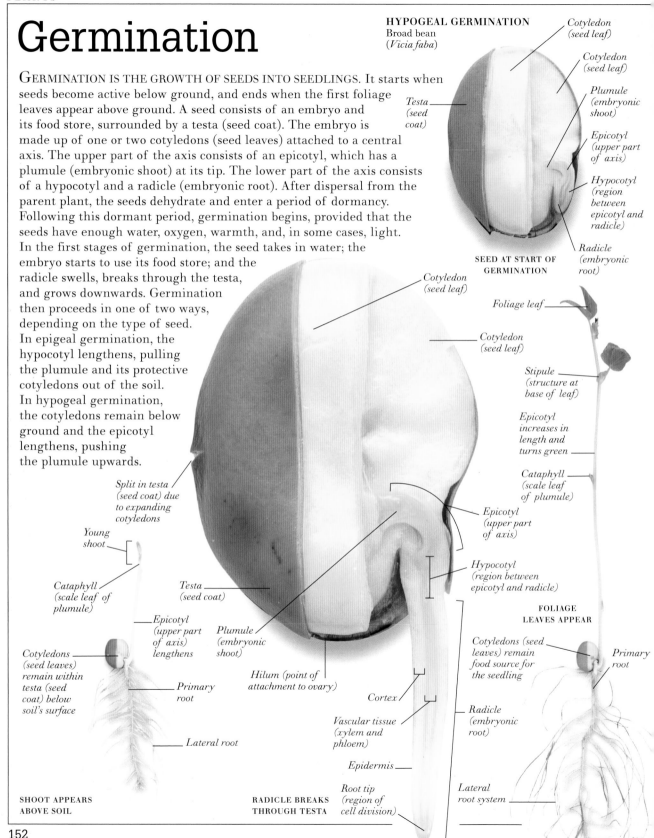

GERMINATION IS THE GROWTH OF SEEDS INTO SEEDLINGS. It starts when seeds become active below ground, and ends when the first foliage leaves appear above ground. A seed consists of an embryo and its food store, surrounded by a testa (seed coat). The embryo is made up of one or two cotyledons (seed leaves) attached to a central axis. The upper part of the axis consists of an epicotyl, which has a plumule (embryonic shoot) at its tip. The lower part of the axis consists of a hypocotyl and a radicle (embryonic root). After dispersal from the parent plant, the seeds dehydrate and enter a period of dormancy. Following this dormant period, germination begins, provided that the seeds have enough water, oxygen, warmth, and, in some cases, light. In the first stages of germination, the seed takes in water; the embryo starts to use its food store; and the radicle swells, breaks through the testa, and grows downwards. Germination then proceeds in one of two ways, depending on the type of seed. In epigeal germination, the hypocotyl lengthens, pulling the plumule and its protective cotyledons out of the soil. In hypogeal germination, the cotyledons remain below ground and the epicotyl lengthens, pushing the plumule upwards.

HYPOGEAL GERMINATION
Broad bean
(*Vicia faba*)

Testa (seed coat)

Cotyledon (seed leaf)

Cotyledon (seed leaf)

Plumule (embryonic shoot)

Epicotyl (upper part of axis)

Hypocotyl (region between epicotyl and radicle)

Radicle (embryonic root)

SEED AT START OF GERMINATION

Cotyledon (seed leaf)

Foliage leaf

Cotyledon (seed leaf)

Stipule (structure at base of leaf)

Epicotyl increases in length and turns green

Cataphyll (scale leaf of plumule)

Epicotyl (upper part of axis)

Hypocotyl (region between epicotyl and radicle)

FOLIAGE LEAVES APPEAR

Cotyledons (seed leaves) remain food source for the seedling

Primary root

Radicle (embryonic root)

Lateral root system

Split in testa (seed coat) due to expanding cotyledons

Young shoot

Cataphyll (scale leaf of plumule)

Testa (seed coat)

Epicotyl (upper part of axis) lengthens

Plumule (embryonic shoot)

Hilum (point of attachment to ovary)

Cortex

Vascular tissue (xylem and phloem)

Epidermis

Cotyledons (seed leaves) remain within testa (seed coat) below soil's surface

Primary root

Lateral root

Root tip (region of cell division)

SHOOT APPEARS ABOVE SOIL

RADICLE BREAKS THROUGH TESTA

EPIGEAL GERMINATION
Black bean
(*Phaseolus sp.*)

*Testa
(seed coat)*

*Raphe
(ridge)*

*Hilum (point
of attachment
to ovary)*

*Micropyle
(pore for
water
absorption)*

**EXTERNAL VIEW OF SEED AT
START OF GERMINATION**

*Epicotyl
(upper part
of axis)*

*Plumule
(embryonic
shoot)*

*Testa
(seed coat)*

*Hypocotyl
(region between
epicotyl and
radicle)*

*Radicle
(embryonic
root)*

*Hilum
(point of
attachment
to ovary)*

*Cotyledon
(seed leaf)*

**LONGITUDINAL SECTION
THROUGH SEED AT START OF
GERMINATION**

*Epicotyl
(upper part
of axis)*

*Testa
(seed coat)*

*Plumule
(embryonic
shoot)*

*Cotyledon
(seed leaf)*

*Hypocotyl
(region between
epicotyl and radicle)*

Lateral root

*Primary root
(elongated
radicle)*

**RADICLE BREAKS THROUGH
TESTA AND LENGTHENS**

*First foliage
leaf fully
grown*

*Petiole
(leaf stalk)*

*Growing
point*

*Cotyledon (seed
leaf) withers*

*First foliage leaf
protected by cotyledons
(seed leaves)*

*Cotyledon
(seed leaf)*

*Hypocotyl (region
between epicotyl
and radicle)
straightens
and lengthens*

*Testa
(seed
coal)
splits*

*Hypocotyl
"hook" pushes
out of soil*

*Hypocotyl (region
between epicotyl and
radicle) elongates*

*Testa (seed
coal) shed*

*Lateral
root*

*Testa (seed
coat) begins to
disintegrate*

Root

Root

*Primary
root*

**HYPOCOTYL
"HOOK" APPEARS
ABOVE SOIL**

**HYPOCOTYL
STRAIGHTENS,
PULLING LEAVES
AND COTYLEDONS
OUT OF SOIL**

**FIRST FOLIAGE
LEAVES FULLY
DEVELOPED**

*Root cap
(protective
covering for
root tip)*

153

Vegetative reproduction

MANY PLANTS CAN PROPAGATE THEMSELVES by vegetative reproduction. In this process, part of a plant separates off, takes root, and grows into a new plant. Vegetative reproduction is a type of asexual reproduction; that is, it involves only one parent, and there is no fusion of gametes (sex cells). Plants use various structures to reproduce vegetatively. Some plants use underground storage organs. Such organs include rhizomes (horizontal, underground stems), the branches of which produce new plants; bulbs (swollen leaf bases) and corms (swollen stems), which produce daughter bulbs or corms that separate off from the parent; and stem tubers (thickened underground stems) and root tubers (swollen adventitious roots), which also separate off from the parent. Other propagative structures include runners and stolons, creeping horizontal stems that take root and produce new plants; bulbils, small bulbs that develop on the stem or in the place of flowers, and then drop off and grow into new plants; and adventitious buds, miniature plants that form on leaf margins before dropping to the ground and growing into mature plants.

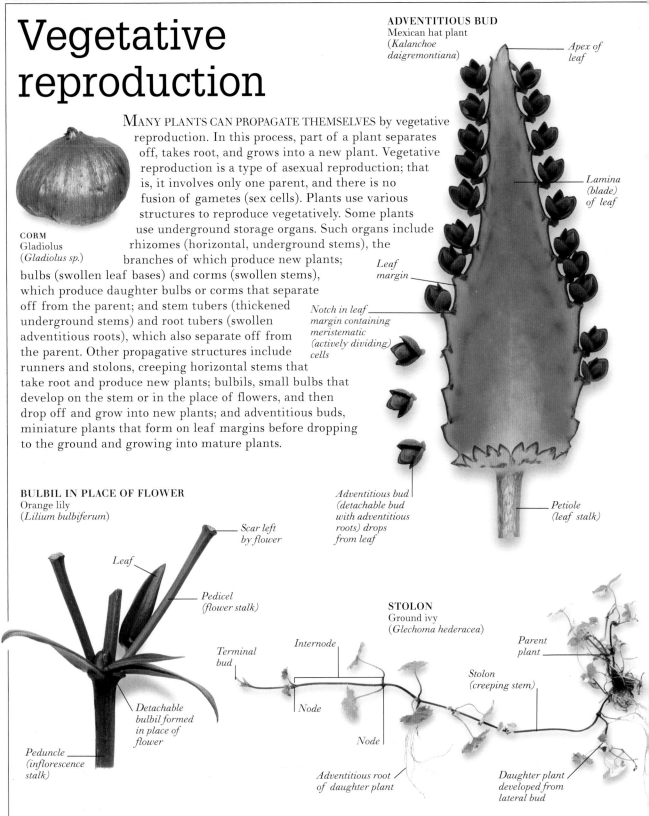

CORM
Gladiolus
(*Gladiolus sp.*)

ADVENTITIOUS BUD
Mexican hat plant
(*Kalanchoe daigremontiana*)

Apex of leaf

Lamina (blade) of leaf

Leaf margin

Notch in leaf margin containing meristematic (actively dividing) cells

Adventitious bud (detachable bud with adventitious roots) drops from leaf

Petiole (leaf stalk)

BULBIL IN PLACE OF FLOWER
Orange lily
(*Lilium bulbiferum*)

Scar left by flower

Leaf

Pedicel (flower stalk)

Detachable bulbil formed in place of flower

Peduncle (inflorescence stalk)

Terminal bud

Internode

Node

Node

Adventitious root of daughter plant

STOLON
Ground ivy
(*Glechoma hederacea*)

Parent plant

Stolon (creeping stem)

Daughter plant developed from lateral bud

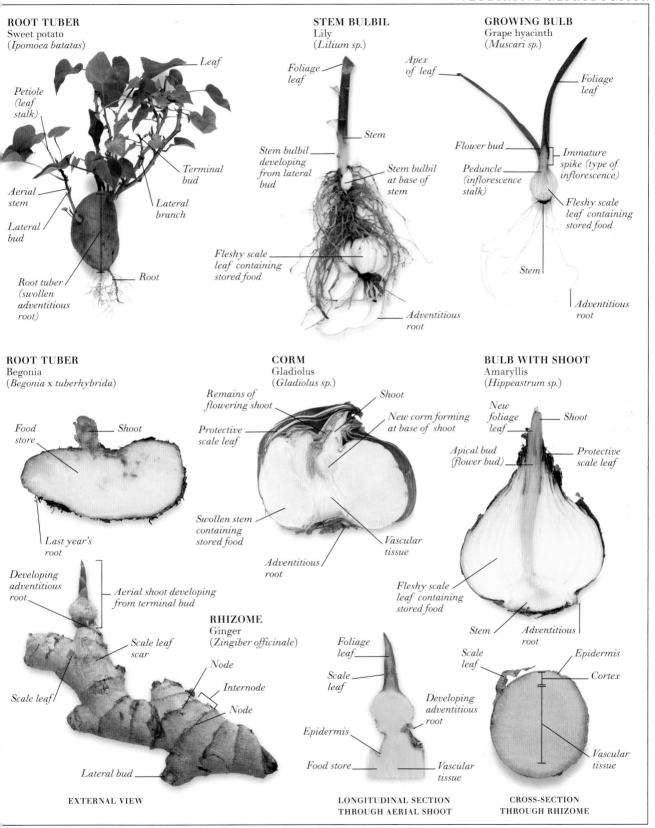

ROOT TUBER
Sweet potato
(*Ipomoea batatas*)

Leaf

Petiole
(leaf
stalk)

Terminal
bud

Aerial
stem

Lateral
branch

Lateral
bud

Root tuber
(swollen
adventitious
root)

Root

STEM BULBIL
Lily
(*Lilium sp.*)

Foliage
leaf

Stem

Stem bulbil
developing
from lateral
bud

Stem bulbil
at base of
stem

Fleshy scale
leaf containing
stored food

Adventitious
root

GROWING BULB
Grape hyacinth
(*Muscari sp.*)

Apex
of leaf

Foliage
leaf

Flower bud

Immature
spike (type of
inflorescence)

Peduncle
(inflorescence
stalk)

Fleshy scale
leaf containing
stored food

Stem

Adventitious
root

ROOT TUBER
Begonia
(*Begonia x tuberhybrida*)

Food
store

Shoot

Last year's
root

Developing
adventitious
root

Aerial shoot developing
from terminal bud

Scale leaf
scar

Scale leaf

Node

Internode

Node

Lateral bud

EXTERNAL VIEW

CORM
Gladiolus
(*Gladiolus sp.*)

Remains of
flowering shoot

Shoot

New corm forming
at base of shoot

Protective
scale leaf

Swollen stem
containing
stored food

Vascular
tissue

Adventitious
root

RHIZOME
Ginger
(*Zingiber officinale*)

Foliage
leaf

Scale
leaf

Developing
adventitious
root

Epidermis

Food store

Vascular
tissue

**LONGITUDINAL SECTION
THROUGH AERIAL SHOOT**

BULB WITH SHOOT
Amaryllis
(*Hippeastrum sp.*)

New
foliage
leaf

Shoot

Apical bud
(flower bud)

Protective
scale leaf

Fleshy scale
leaf containing
stored food

Stem

Adventitious
root

Scale
leaf

Epidermis

Cortex

Vascular
tissue

**CROSS-SECTION
THROUGH RHIZOME**

Dryland plants

DRYLAND PLANTS (XEROPHYTES) are able to survive in unfavourable habitats. All are found in places where little water is available; some live in high temperatures that cause excessive loss of water from the leaves. Xerophytes show a number of adaptations to dry conditions; these include reduced leaf area, rolled leaves, sunken stomata, hairs, spines, and thick cuticles. One group, succulent plants, stores water in specially enlarged spongy tissues found in leaves, roots, or stems. Leaf succulents have enlarged, fleshy, water-storing leaves. Root succulents have a large, underground water-storage organ with short-lived stems and leaves above ground. Stem succulents are represented by the cacti (family Cactaceae). Cacti stems are fleshy, green, and photosynthetic; they are typically ribbed or covered by tubercles in rows, with leaves being reduced to spines or entirely absent.

LEAF SUCCULENT
Lithops sp.

STEM SUCCULENT
Golden barrel cactus
(*Echinocactus grusonii*)

Areole (modified lateral shoot)

Trichome (hair)

Spine (modified leaf)

Waxy cuticle (waterproof covering)

Water-storing parenchyma (packing tissue)

Tubercle (projection from stem surface)

Vascular cylinder (transport tissue)

Root

LONGITUDINAL SECTION THROUGH STEM

Spine (modified leaf)

Tubercle (projection from stem surface)

Root

EXTERNAL VIEW

Sinuous (wavy) cell wall

Stoma (pore) controlling exchange of gases

MICROGRAPH OF STEM SURFACE

Spine (modified leaf)

Areole (modified lateral shoot)

Tubercle (projection from stem surface)

Waxy cuticle (waterproof covering)

DETAIL OF STEM SURFACE

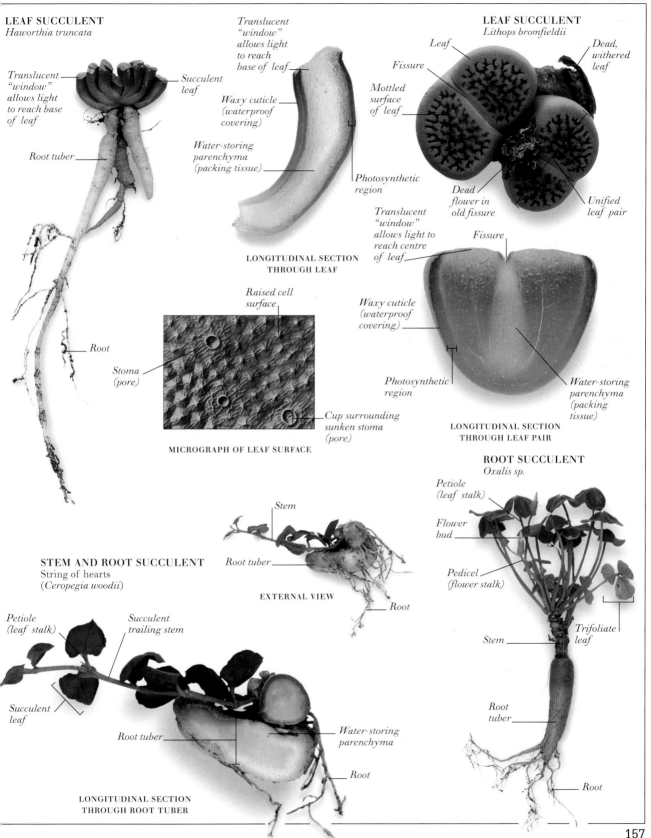

LEAF SUCCULENT
Haworthia truncata

Translucent "window" allows light to reach base of leaf

Succulent leaf

Root tuber

Root

Translucent "window" allows light to reach base of leaf

Waxy cuticle (waterproof covering)

Water-storing parenchyma (packing tissue)

Photosynthetic region

LONGITUDINAL SECTION THROUGH LEAF

Raised cell surface

Stoma (pore)

Cup surrounding sunken stoma (pore)

MICROGRAPH OF LEAF SURFACE

LEAF SUCCULENT
Lithops bromfieldii

Leaf

Fissure

Mottled surface of leaf

Dead, withered leaf

Dead flower in old fissure

Unified leaf pair

Translucent "window" allows light to reach centre of leaf

Fissure

Waxy cuticle (waterproof covering)

Photosynthetic region

Water-storing parenchyma (packing tissue)

LONGITUDINAL SECTION THROUGH LEAF PAIR

ROOT SUCCULENT
Oxalis sp.

Petiole (leaf stalk)

Flower bud

Pedicel (flower stalk)

Trifoliate leaf

Stem

Root tuber

Root

STEM AND ROOT SUCCULENT
String of hearts
(*Ceropegia woodii*)

Stem

Root tuber

Root

EXTERNAL VIEW

Petiole (leaf stalk)

Succulent trailing stem

Succulent leaf

Root tuber

Water-storing parenchyma

Root

LONGITUDINAL SECTION THROUGH ROOT TUBER

Wetland plants

WETLAND PLANTS GROW SUBMERGED IN WATER, either partially (e.g., water hyacinth) or completely (e.g., pond weeds), and show various adaptations to this habitat. Typically, there are numerous air spaces inside the stems, leaves, and roots; these aid gas exchange and buoyancy. Submerged parts generally have no cuticle (waterproof covering), enabling the plants to absorb minerals and gases directly from the water; in addition, being supported by the water, they need little of the supportive tissue found in land plants. Stomata, the gas exchange pores, are absent from plants that are completely submerged; in partially submerged plants with floating leaves (e.g., water lilies), stomata are found on the upper leaf surfaces, where they cannot be flooded.

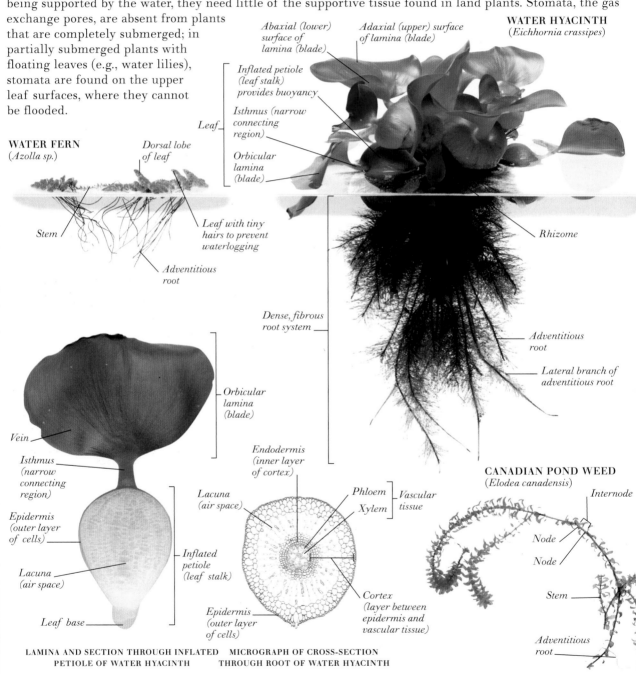

WATER FERN
(*Azolla* sp.)

Dorsal lobe of leaf

Stem

Leaf with tiny hairs to prevent waterlogging

Adventitious root

WATER HYACINTH
(*Eichhornia crassipes*)

Abaxial (lower) surface of lamina (blade)

Adaxial (upper) surface of lamina (blade)

Inflated petiole (leaf stalk) provides buoyancy

Isthmus (narrow connecting region)

Leaf

Orbicular lamina (blade)

Rhizome

Dense, fibrous root system

Adventitious root

Lateral branch of adventitious root

Orbicular lamina (blade)

Vein

Isthmus (narrow connecting region)

Epidermis (outer layer of cells)

Lacuna (air space)

Leaf base

Endodermis (inner layer of cortex)

Lacuna (air space)

Phloem

Xylem

Vascular tissue

Inflated petiole (leaf stalk)

Epidermis (outer layer of cells)

Cortex (layer between epidermis and vascular tissue)

CANADIAN POND WEED
(*Elodea canadensis*)

Internode

Node

Node

Stem

Adventitious root

LAMINA AND SECTION THROUGH INFLATED PETIOLE OF WATER HYACINTH

MICROGRAPH OF CROSS-SECTION THROUGH ROOT OF WATER HYACINTH

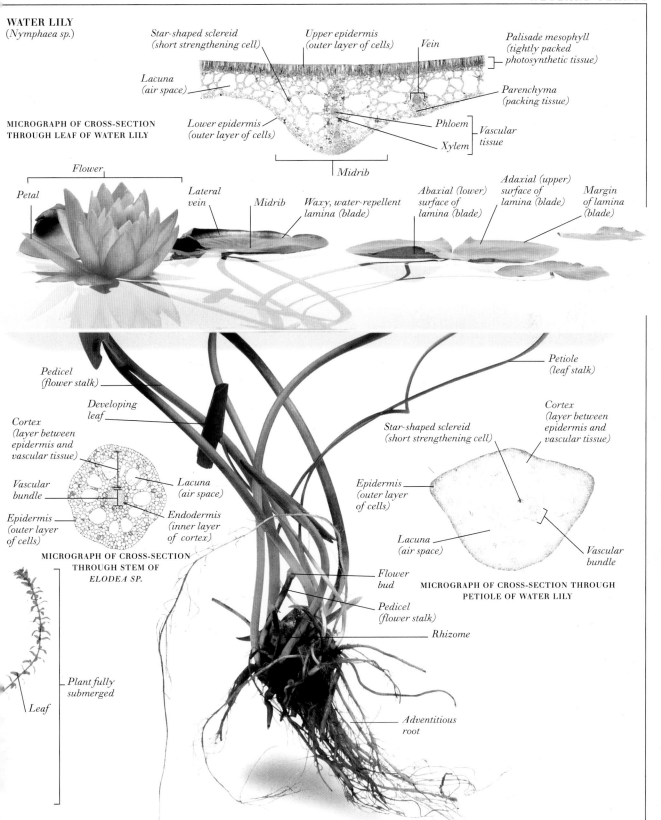

WATER LILY
(Nymphaea sp.)

Star-shaped sclereid (short strengthening cell)

Upper epidermis (outer layer of cells)

Vein

Palisade mesophyll (tightly packed photosynthetic tissue)

Lacuna (air space)

Parenchyma (packing tissue)

MICROGRAPH OF CROSS-SECTION
THROUGH LEAF OF WATER LILY

Lower epidermis (outer layer of cells)

Phloem

Xylem

Vascular tissue

Midrib

Flower

Petal

Lateral vein

Midrib

Waxy, water-repellent lamina (blade)

Abaxial (lower) surface of lamina (blade)

Adaxial (upper) surface of lamina (blade)

Margin of lamina (blade)

Pedicel (flower stalk)

Developing leaf

Petiole (leaf stalk)

Cortex (layer between epidermis and vascular tissue)

Star-shaped sclereid (short strengthening cell)

Cortex (layer between epidermis and vascular tissue)

Vascular bundle

Lacuna (air space)

Epidermis (outer layer of cells)

Epidermis (outer layer of cells)

Endodermis (inner layer of cortex)

MICROGRAPH OF CROSS-SECTION
THROUGH STEM OF
ELODEA SP.

Lacuna (air space)

Vascular bundle

MICROGRAPH OF CROSS-SECTION THROUGH
PETIOLE OF WATER LILY

Flower bud

Pedicel (flower stalk)

Rhizome

Plant fully submerged

Leaf

Adventitious root

Carnivorous plants

*Areola
("window" of
transparent tissue)*

Fishtail nectary

Wing

Hood

Pitcher

*Tubular
petiole
(leaf stalk)*

*Areola
("window" of
transparent
tissue)*

CARNIVOROUS (INSECTIVOROUS) PLANTS FEED ON INSECTS and other small animals, in addition to producing food in their leaves by photosynthesis. The nutrients absorbed from trapped insects enable carnivorous plants to thrive in acid, boggy soils that lack essential minerals, especially nitrates, where most other plants could not survive. All carnivorous plants have some leaves modified as traps; many use bright colours and scented nectar to attract prey; and most use enzymes to digest the prey. There are three types of traps. Pitcher plants, such as the monkey cup and cobra lily, have leaves modified as pitcher-shaped pitfall traps, half-filled with water; once lured inside the mouth of the trap, insects lose their footing on the slippery surface, fall into the liquid, and either decompose or are digested. Venus fly traps use a spring-trap mechanism; when an insect touches trigger hairs on the inner surfaces of the leaves, the two lobes of the trap snap shut. Butterworts and sundews entangle prey by sticky droplets on the leaf surface, while the edges of the leaves slowly curl over to envelop and digest the prey.

Smooth surface

Nectar roll

*Dome-shaped
hood develops*

*Fishtail
nectary
appears*

*Immature
pitcher*

Wing

Mouth

*Downward
pointing hair*

**DEVELOPMENT OF MODIFIED
LEAF IN COBRA LILY**

*Immature
trap*

*Interlocked
teeth*

*Closed
trap*

*Red colour of trap
attracts insects*

VENUS FLY TRAP
(*Dionaea muscipula*)

*Phyllode
(flattened
petiole)*

*Summer petiole
(leaf stalk)*

*Nectary zone
(glands secrete
nectar)*

*Digestive zone
(glands
secrete
digestive
enzymes)*

Tooth

*Lobe
of trap*

*Midrib
(hinge of
trap)*

Trigger hair

*Trap
(twin-lobed
leaf blade)*

*Spring petiole
(leaf stalk)*

*Sensory
hinge*

*Trigger
hair*

*Inner
surface
of trap*

*Digestive
gland*

**MICROGRAPH OF LOBE OF
VENUS FLY TRAP**

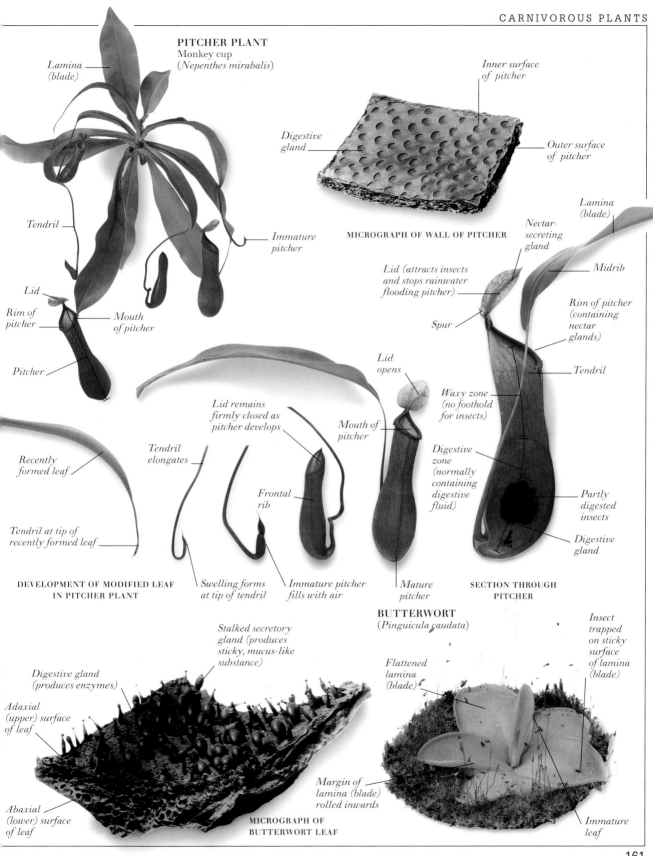

PITCHER PLANT
Monkey cup
(*Nepenthes mirabalis*)

Lamina
(blade)

Tendril

Immature
pitcher

Lid

Rim of
pitcher

Mouth
of pitcher

Pitcher

Digestive
gland

Inner surface
of pitcher

Outer surface
of pitcher

MICROGRAPH OF WALL OF PITCHER

Lamina
(blade)

Nectar-
secreting
gland

Midrib

Lid (attracts insects
and stops rainwater
flooding pitcher)

Rim of pitcher
(containing
nectar
glands)

Spur

Tendril

Lid
opens

Waxy zone
(no foothold
for insects)

Mouth of
pitcher

Digestive
zone
(normally
containing
digestive
fluid)

Partly
digested
insects

Digestive
gland

Recently
formed leaf

Lid remains
firmly closed as
pitcher develops

Tendril
elongates

Frontal
rib

Tendril at tip of
recently formed leaf

**DEVELOPMENT OF MODIFIED LEAF
IN PITCHER PLANT**

Swelling forms
at tip of tendril

Immature pitcher
fills with air

Mature
pitcher

**SECTION THROUGH
PITCHER**

BUTTERWORT
(*Pinguicula caudata*)

Insect
trapped
on sticky
surface
of lamina
(blade)

Stalked secretory
gland (produces
sticky, mucus-like
substance)

Flattened
lamina
(blade)

Digestive gland
(produces enzymes)

Adaxial
(upper) surface
of leaf

Abaxial
(lower) surface
of leaf

Margin of
lamina (blade)
rolled inwards

Immature
leaf

**MICROGRAPH OF
BUTTERWORT LEAF**

Epiphytic and parasitic plants

EPIPHYTIC AND PARASITIC PLANTS GROW ON OTHER LIVING PLANTS. Typically, epiphytic plants are
not rooted in the soil; instead, they live above ground level on the stems and branches of other
plants. Epiphytes obtain water from trapped rainwater and from moisture in the air, and
minerals from organic matter that has accumulated on the surface of the plant on which
they are growing. Like other green plants, epiphytes produce their food by photosynthesis. Epiphytes
include tropical orchids and bromeliads (air plants), and some mosses that live in temperate regions.
Parasitic plants obtain all their nutrient requirements from the host plants on which they grow. The parasites
produce haustoria, root-like organs that penetrate the stem or roots of the host and grow inwards to merge
with the host's vascular tissue, from which the parasite extracts water, minerals, and manufactured nutrients.
As they have no need to produce their own food, parasitic plants
lack chlorophyll, the green photosynthetic pigment, and they
have no foliage leaves. Partial parasitic plants (e.g., mistletoe)
obtain water and minerals from the host plant but have
green leaves and stems and are therefore able to
produce their own food by photosynthesis.

EPIPHYTIC ORCHID
Brassavola nodosa

Peduncle
(inflorescence
stalk)

Pedicel
(flower
stalk)

Flower

Scale
leaf

Aerial
root

Node

Stem

Bark of tree to
which epiphyte
is attached

Inflorescence
(spike)

Peduncle
(inflorescence
stalk)

Flower
bud

Strap-shaped
arching leaf
(part of rosette
of leaves)

Leaf margin
with spines

Overlapping leaf
bases in which
rainwater is trapped

EPIPHYTIC BROMELIAD
Aechmea miniata

Mass of
adventitious roots

Stem

Bark of tree to
which epiphyte
is attached

Leaf

Velamen
(multi-layered epidermis
capable of absorbing
water from rain or
condensation)

Cortex
(layer between
epidermis and
vascular tissue)

Cortex cell
containing
chloroplasts

Vascular
tissue { Xylem
Phloem

Exodermis
(outer layer
of cortex)

Pith

Endoderm
(inner layer
of cortex)

**MICROGRAPH OF CROSS-SECTION THROUGH
AERIAL ROOT OF EPIPHYTIC ORCHID**

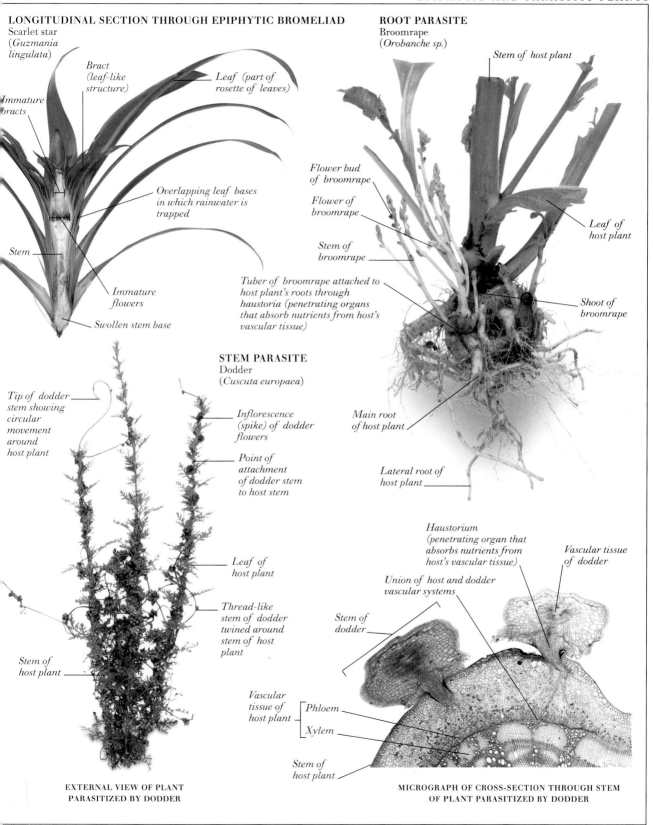

LONGITUDINAL SECTION THROUGH EPIPHYTIC BROMELIAD
Scarlet star
(*Guzmania lingulata*)

Bract (leaf-like structure)

Leaf (part of rosette of leaves)

Immature bracts

Overlapping leaf bases in which rainwater is trapped

Stem

Immature flowers

Swollen stem base

ROOT PARASITE
Broomrape
(*Orobanche sp.*)

Stem of host plant

Flower bud of broomrape

Flower of broomrape

Stem of broomrape

Tuber of broomrape attached to host plant's roots through haustoria (penetrating organs that absorb nutrients from host's vascular tissue)

Leaf of host plant

Shoot of broomrape

Main root of host plant

Lateral root of host plant

STEM PARASITE
Dodder
(*Cuscuta europaea*)

Tip of dodder stem showing circular movement around host plant

Inflorescence (spike) of dodder flowers

Point of attachment of dodder stem to host stem

Leaf of host plant

Thread-like stem of dodder twined around stem of host plant

Stem of host plant

Vascular tissue of host plant

Phloem

Xylem

Stem of host plant

Haustorium (penetrating organ that absorbs nutrients from host's vascular tissue)

Vascular tissue of dodder

Union of host and dodder vascular systems

Stem of dodder

EXTERNAL VIEW OF PLANT PARASITIZED BY DODDER

MICROGRAPH OF CROSS-SECTION THROUGH STEM OF PLANT PARASITIZED BY DODDER

ANIMALS

Sponges, jellyfish, and sea anemones

SPONGES ARE MAINLY MARINE animals that make up the phylum Porifera. They are among the simplest of all animals, having no tissues or organs. Their bodies consist of two layers of cells separated by a jelly-like layer (mesohyal) that is strengthened by mineral spicules or protein fibres. The body is perforated by a system of pores and water channels called the aquiferous system. Special cells (choanocytes) with whip-like structures (flagella) draw water through the aquiferous system, thereby bringing tiny food particles to the sponge's cells. Jellyfish (class Scyphozoa), sea anemones (class Anthozoa), and corals (also class Anthozoa) belong to the phylum Cnidaria, also known as Coelenterata. More complex than sponges, coelenterates have simple tissues, such as nervous tissue; a radially symmetrical body; and a mouth surrounded by tentacles with unique stinging cells (cnidocytes).

INTERNAL ANATOMY OF A SPONGE

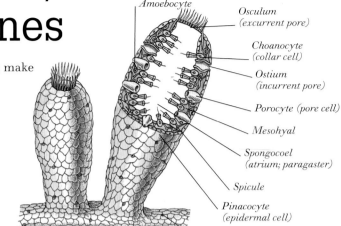

- *Amoebocyte*
- *Osculum (excurrent pore)*
- *Choanocyte (collar cell)*
- *Ostium (incurrent pore)*
- *Porocyte (pore cell)*
- *Mesohyal*
- *Spongocoel (atrium; paragaster)*
- *Spicule*
- *Pinacocyte (epidermal cell)*
- *Ostium (incurrent pore)*

SKELETON OF A SPONGE

- *Protein matrix*
- *Pore*

EXTERNAL FEATURES OF A SEA ANEMONE

- *Tentacle*

EXAMPLES OF SEA ANEMONES

JEWEL ANEMONE
(Corynactis viridis)

PARASITIC ANEMONE
(Calliactis parasitica)

PLUMOSE ANEMONE
(Metridium senile)

MEDITERRANEAN SEA ANEMONE
(Condylactis sp.)

GREEN SNAKELOCK ANEMONE
(Anemonia viridis)

BEADLET ANEMONE
(Actinia equina)

GHOST ANEMONE
(Actinothoe sphyrodeta)

Sagartia elegans

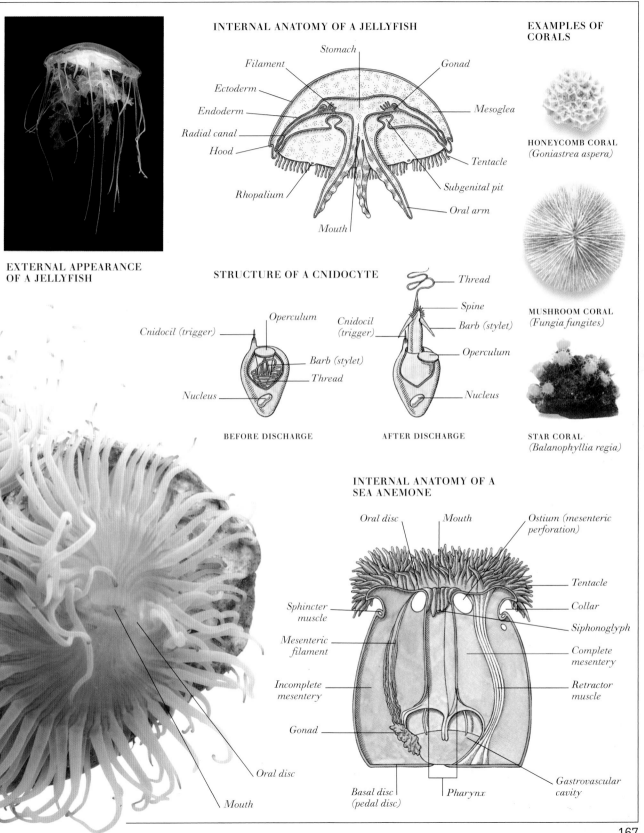

EXTERNAL APPEARANCE OF A JELLYFISH

INTERNAL ANATOMY OF A JELLYFISH

Stomach
Filament
Gonad
Ectoderm
Endoderm
Mesoglea
Radial canal
Hood
Rhopalium
Tentacle
Subgenital pit
Oral arm
Mouth

EXAMPLES OF CORALS

HONEYCOMB CORAL
(Goniastrea aspera)

MUSHROOM CORAL
(Fungia fungites)

STAR CORAL
(Balanophyllia regia)

STRUCTURE OF A CNIDOCYTE

Cnidocil (trigger)
Operculum
Barb (stylet)
Thread
Nucleus

BEFORE DISCHARGE

Thread
Spine
Cnidocil (trigger)
Barb (stylet)
Operculum
Nucleus

AFTER DISCHARGE

INTERNAL ANATOMY OF A SEA ANEMONE

Oral disc
Mouth
Ostium (mesenteric perforation)
Tentacle
Sphincter muscle
Collar
Siphonoglyph
Mesenteric filament
Complete mesentery
Incomplete mesentery
Retractor muscle
Gonad
Gastrovascular cavity
Basal disc (pedal disc)
Pharynx
Oral disc
Mouth

167

Insects

**PUPA
(CHRYSALIS)**

THE WORD INSECT REFERS to small invertebrate creatures, especially those with bodies divided into sections. Insects, including beetles, ants, bees, butterflies, and moths, belong to various orders in the class Insecta, which is a division of the phylum Arthropoda. Features common to all insects are an exoskeleton (external skeleton); three pairs of jointed legs; three body sections (head, thorax, and abdomen); and one pair of sensory antennae. Beetles (order Coleoptera) are the biggest group of insects, with about 300,000 species (about 30 per cent of all known insects). They have a pair of hard elytra (wing cases), which are modified front wings. The principal function of the elytra is to protect the hind wings, which are used for flying. Ants, together with bees and wasps, form the order Hymenoptera, which contains about 200,000 species. This group is characterized by a marked narrowing between the thorax and abdomen. Butterflies and moths form the order Lepidoptera, which has about 150,000 species. They have wings covered with tiny scales, hence the name of their order (Lepidoptera means "scale wings"). The separation of lepidopterans into butterflies and moths is largely artificial as there are no features that categorically distinguish one group from the other. In general, however, most butterflies fly by day, whereas most moths are night-flyers. Some insects, including butterflies and moths, undergo complete metamorphosis (transformation) during their life-cycle. A butterfly metamorphoses from an egg to a larva (caterpillar), then to a pupa (chrysalis), and finally to an imago (adult).

EXAMPLES OF INSECTS

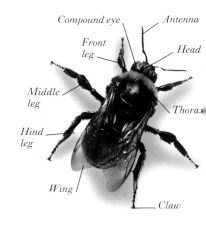

Compound eye
Antenna
Front leg
Head
Middle leg
Thorax
Hind leg
Wing
Claw

BUMBLEBEE

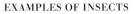

Compound eye
Stigma (spot)
Vein
Abdomen

DAMSELFLY

**EXTERNAL FEATURES
OF A BEETLE**

Elytron
Tarsus
Claw
Tibia
Costal margin
Pedicel
Apex
Femur
Vein
Flagellum
Trochanter
Wing
Mandible
Scape
Coxa
Labrum
Labial palp
Abdomen
Compound eye
Head
Prothorax
Mesothorax
Front leg
Scutellum
Hind leg
Metathorax
Middle leg

CRICKET

ANT

FLY

EARWIG

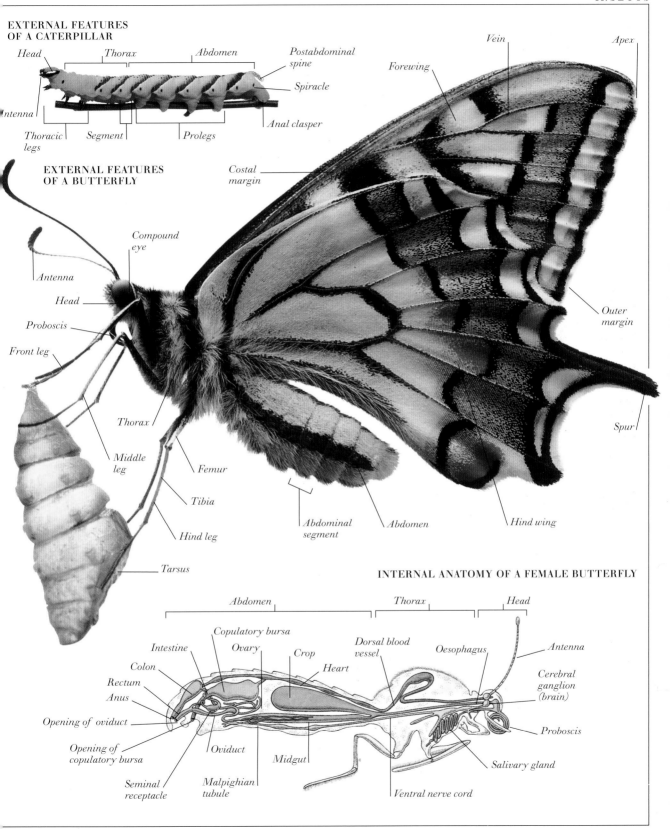

EXTERNAL FEATURES
OF A CATERPILLAR

Head
Thorax
Abdomen
Postabdominal
spine
Spiracle
Antenna
Anal clasper
Thoracic
legs
Segment
Prolegs

Vein
Forewing
Apex
Costal
margin

EXTERNAL FEATURES
OF A BUTTERFLY

Compound
eye
Antenna
Head
Proboscis
Front leg
Thorax
Middle
leg
Femur
Tibia
Hind leg
Tarsus
Abdominal
segment
Abdomen
Hind wing

Outer
margin
Spur

INTERNAL ANATOMY OF A FEMALE BUTTERFLY

Abdomen
Thorax
Head

Copulatory bursa
Intestine
Ovary
Crop
Dorsal blood
vessel
Oesophagus
Antenna
Colon
Heart
Cerebral
ganglion
(brain)
Rectum
Anus
Proboscis
Opening of oviduct
Opening of
copulatory bursa
Oviduct
Midgut
Salivary gland
Seminal
receptacle
Malpighian
tubule
Ventral nerve cord

169

Arachnids

THE CLASS ARACHNIDA INCLUDES SPIDERS (order Araneae) and scorpions (order Scorpiones). The class is part of the phylum Arthropoda, which also includes insects and crustaceans.

Spiders and scorpions are characterized by having four pairs of walking legs; a pair of pincer-like mouthparts called chelicerae; another pair of frontal appendages called pedipalps, which are sensory in spiders but used for grasping in scorpions; and a body divided into two sections (a combined head and thorax called a cephalothorax or prosoma, and an abdomen or opisthosoma). Unlike other arthropods, spiders and scorpions lack antennae. Spiders and scorpions are carnivorous. Spiders poison prey by biting with the fanged chelicerae, scorpions by stinging with the end of the metasoma (tail).

MEXICAN TRUE RED-LEGGED TARANTULA
(Euathlus emilia)

INTERNAL ANATOMY OF A FEMALE SPIDER

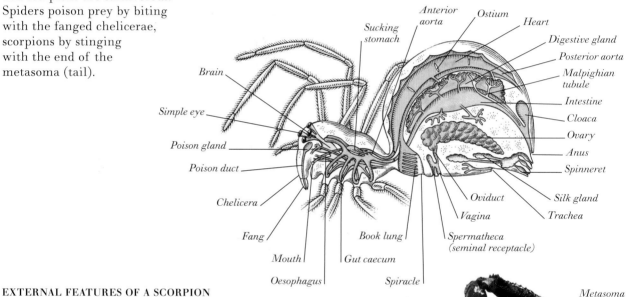

Anterior aorta
Ostium
Heart
Digestive gland
Posterior aorta
Malpighian tubule
Intestine
Cloaca
Ovary
Anus
Spinneret
Silk gland
Trachea
Spermatheca (seminal receptacle)
Oviduct
Vagina
Sucking stomach
Brain
Simple eye
Poison gland
Poison duct
Chelicera
Fang
Mouth
Oesophagus
Gut caecum
Book lung
Spiracle

EXTERNAL FEATURES OF A SCORPION

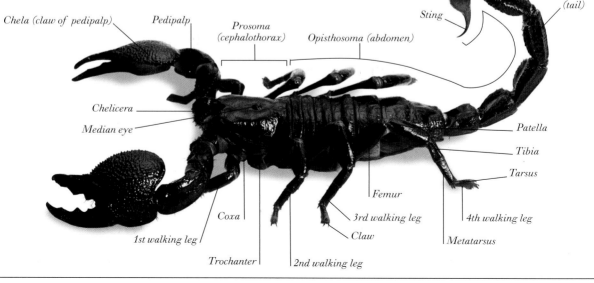

Chela (claw of pedipalp)
Pedipalp
Prosoma (cephalothorax)
Opisthosoma (abdomen)
Sting
Metasoma (tail)
Chelicera
Median eye
Patella
Tibia
Tarsus
Coxa
3rd walking leg
4th walking leg
1st walking leg
Claw
Metatarsus
Femur
Trochanter
2nd walking leg

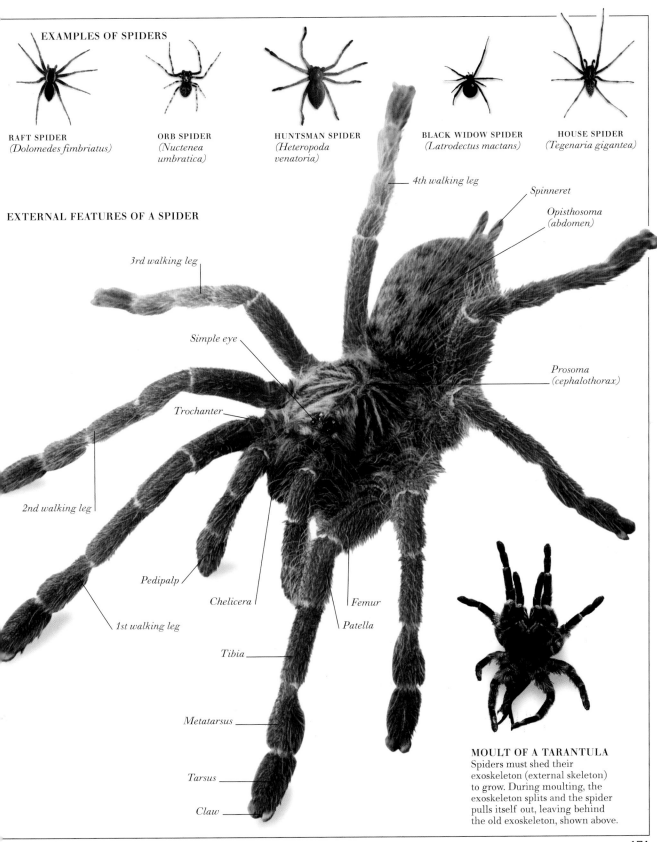

EXAMPLES OF SPIDERS

RAFT SPIDER
(Dolomedes fimbriatus)

ORB SPIDER
(Nuctenea umbratica)

HUNTSMAN SPIDER
(Heteropoda venatoria)

BLACK WIDOW SPIDER
(Latrodectus mactans)

HOUSE SPIDER
(Tegenaria gigantea)

EXTERNAL FEATURES OF A SPIDER

4th walking leg

Spinneret

Opisthosoma (abdomen)

3rd walking leg

Simple eye

Prosoma (cephalothorax)

Trochanter

2nd walking leg

Pedipalp

Chelicera

Femur

1st walking leg

Patella

Tibia

Metatarsus

Tarsus

Claw

MOULT OF A TARANTULA
Spiders must shed their exoskeleton (external skeleton) to grow. During moulting, the exoskeleton splits and the spider pulls itself out, leaving behind the old exoskeleton, shown above.

171

Crustaceans

THE SUBPHYLUM CRUSTACEA is one of the largest groups in the phylum Arthropoda. The subphylum is divided into several classes, the most important of which are Malacostraca and Cirripedia. The class Malacostraca includes crayfish, crabs, lobsters, and shrimps. Typical features of malacostracans include a body divided into two sections (a combined head and thorax called a cephalothorax, and an abdomen); an exoskeleton (external skeleton) with a large plate (carapace) covering the cephalothorax; stalked, compound eyes; and two pairs of antennae. The class Cirripedia includes barnacles, which, unlike other crustaceans, spend their adult lives attached to a surface, such as a rock. Other characteristics of cirripedes include an exoskeleton of overlapping calcareous plates; a body consisting almost entirely of thorax (the abdomen and head are minute); and six pairs of thoracic appendages (cirri) used for filter feeding.

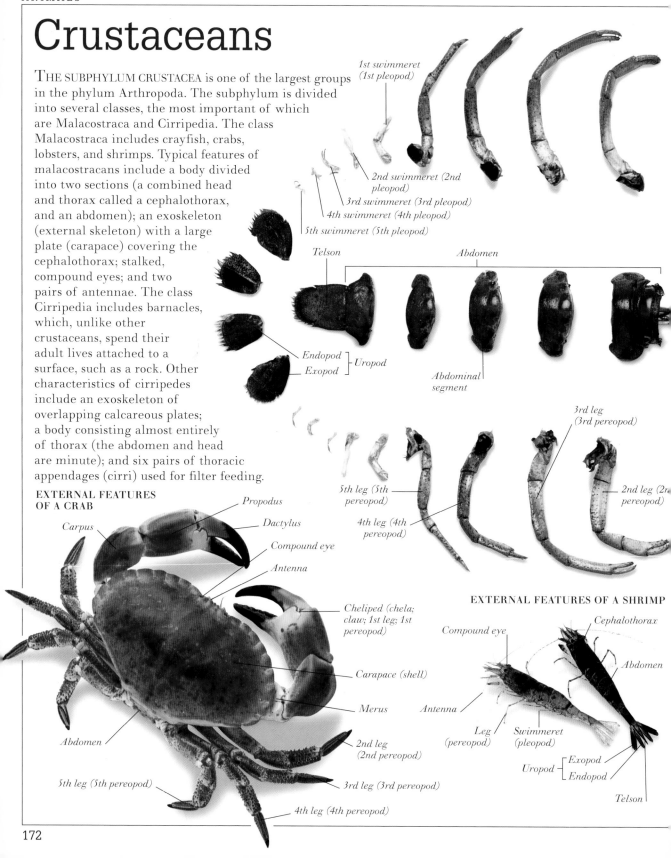

1st swimmeret (1st pleopod)

2nd swimmeret (2nd pleopod)

3rd swimmeret (3rd pleopod)

4th swimmeret (4th pleopod)

5th swimmeret (5th pleopod)

Telson

Abdomen

Endopod

Exopod

Uropod

Abdominal segment

3rd leg (3rd pereopod)

2nd leg (2nd pereopod)

5th leg (5th pereopod)

4th leg (4th pereopod)

EXTERNAL FEATURES OF A CRAB

Propodus

Dactylus

Compound eye

Antenna

Carpus

Cheliped (chela; claw; 1st leg; 1st pereopod)

Carapace (shell)

Merus

Abdomen

2nd leg (2nd pereopod)

5th leg (5th pereopod)

3rd leg (3rd pereopod)

4th leg (4th pereopod)

EXTERNAL FEATURES OF A SHRIMP

Cephalothorax

Abdomen

Compound eye

Antenna

Leg (pereopod)

Swimmeret (pleopod)

Uropod

Exopod

Endopod

Telson

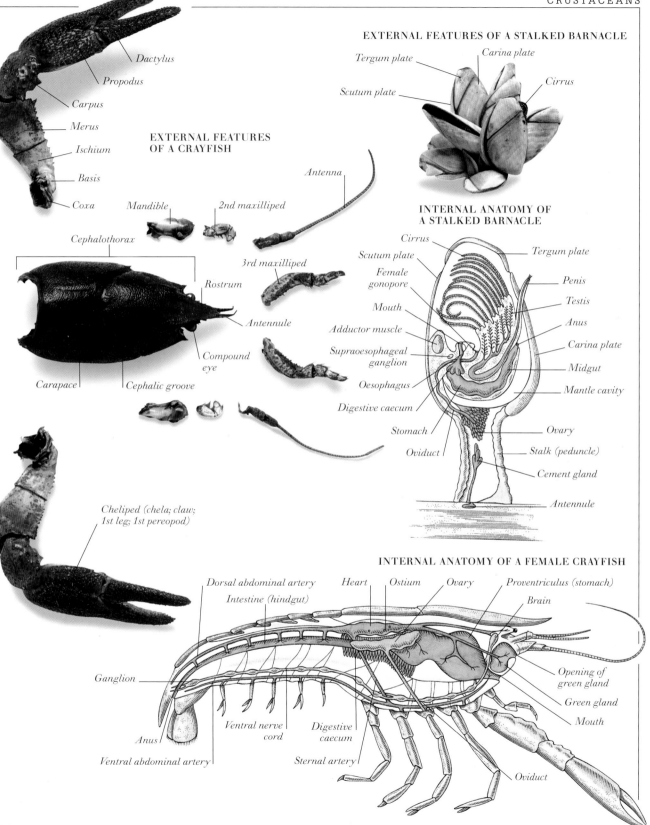

EXTERNAL FEATURES OF A STALKED BARNACLE

Tergum plate
Carina plate
Scutum plate
Cirrus

EXTERNAL FEATURES OF A CRAYFISH

Dactylus
Propodus
Carpus
Merus
Ischium
Basis
Coxa

Antenna

Mandible
2nd maxilliped

Cephalothorax

3rd maxilliped

Rostrum

Antennule

Compound eye

Carapace
Cephalic groove

INTERNAL ANATOMY OF A STALKED BARNACLE

Cirrus
Scutum plate
Female gonopore
Mouth
Adductor muscle
Supraoesophageal ganglion
Oesophagus
Digestive caecum
Stomach
Oviduct

Tergum plate
Penis
Testis
Anus
Carina plate
Midgut
Mantle cavity
Ovary
Stalk (peduncle)
Cement gland
Antennule

Cheliped (chela; claw; 1st leg; 1st pereopod)

INTERNAL ANATOMY OF A FEMALE CRAYFISH

Dorsal abdominal artery
Intestine (hindgut)
Heart
Ostium
Ovary
Proventriculus (stomach)
Brain
Ganglion
Opening of green gland
Green gland
Mouth
Anus
Ventral nerve cord
Digestive caecum
Ventral abdominal artery
Sternal artery
Oviduct

Starfish and sea urchins

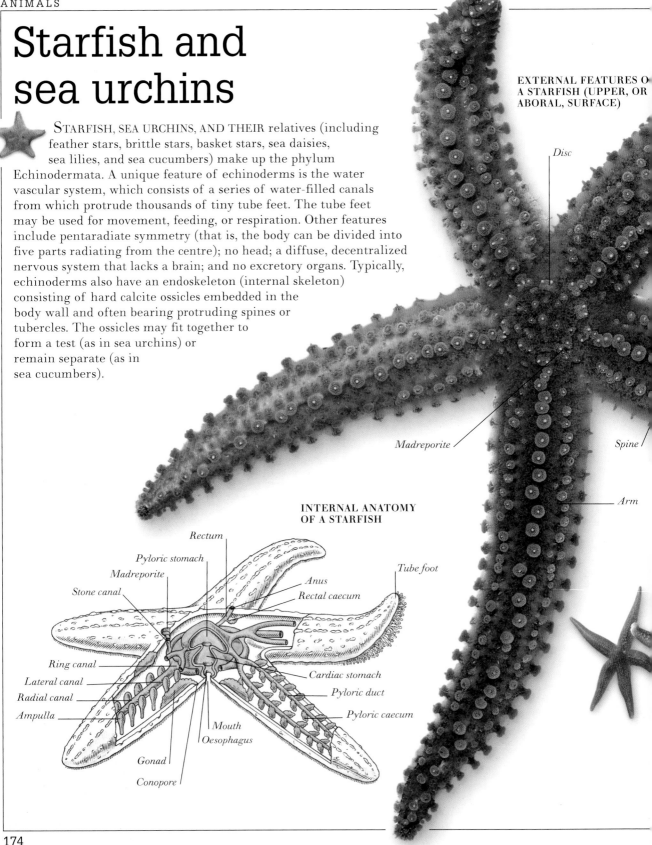

STARFISH, SEA URCHINS, AND THEIR relatives (including feather stars, brittle stars, basket stars, sea daisies, sea lilies, and sea cucumbers) make up the phylum Echinodermata. A unique feature of echinoderms is the water vascular system, which consists of a series of water-filled canals from which protrude thousands of tiny tube feet. The tube feet may be used for movement, feeding, or respiration. Other features include pentaradiate symmetry (that is, the body can be divided into five parts radiating from the centre); no head; a diffuse, decentralized nervous system that lacks a brain; and no excretory organs. Typically, echinoderms also have an endoskeleton (internal skeleton) consisting of hard calcite ossicles embedded in the body wall and often bearing protruding spines or tubercles. The ossicles may fit together to form a test (as in sea urchins) or remain separate (as in sea cucumbers).

**EXTERNAL FEATURES O[F]
A STARFISH (UPPER, OR
ABORAL, SURFACE)**

Disc

Madreporite

Spine

Arm

**INTERNAL ANATOMY
OF A STARFISH**

Rectum

Pyloric stomach

Madreporite

Stone canal

Anus

Rectal caecum

Tube foot

Ring canal

Lateral canal

Radial canal

Ampulla

Cardiac stomach

Pyloric duct

Pyloric caecum

Mouth

Oesophagus

Gonad

Conopore

Tube foot

EXAMPLES OF SEA URCHINS

EDIBLE SEA URCHIN
(*Echinus escelentus*)

**CALIFORNIAN PURPLE
SEA URCHIN**
(*Strongylocentrotus
purpuratus*)

**PENCIL SLATE SEA
URCHIN**
(*Heterocentrotus
mammillatus*)

**INTERNAL ANATOMY
OF A SEA URCHIN**

Gonopore

Anus

Madreporite

Genital plate

Intestine

Gonad

Stone canal

Axial gland

Ring canal

Siphon

Polian vesicle

Test

Pharynx

Spine

Nerve ring

Radial nerve

Mouth

Radial canal

Tube foot

Ampulla

**EXTERNAL FEATURES OF A
SEA URCHIN (UPPER, OR
ABORAL, SURFACE)**

Anus

Spine

Tube foot

CUSHION STAR
(*Asterina gibbosa*)

COMMON BRITTLE STAR
(*Ophiothix fragilis*)

Tube foot

**EXAMPLES OF
STARFISH**

Mouth

Ambulacral groove

COMMON STARFISH
(*Asterias rubens*)

**EXTERNAL FEATURES OF A STARFISH
(LOWER, OR ORAL, SURFACE)**

Molluscs

THE PHYLUM MOLLUSCA (MOLLUSCS) is a large group of animals that includes octopuses, snails, and scallops. Octopuses and their relatives – including squid and cuttlefish – form the class Cephalopoda. Cephalopods typically have a head with a radula (a file-like feeding organ) and beak; a well-developed nervous system; sucker-bearing tentacles; a muscular mantle (part of the body wall) that can expel water through the siphon, enabling movement by jet propulsion; and a small shell or no shell. Snails and their relatives – including slugs, limpets, and abalones – make up the class Gastropoda. Gastropods typically have a coiled external shell, although some, such as slugs, have a small internal shell or no shell; a flat foot; and a head with tentacles and a radula. Scallops and their relatives – including clams, mussels, and oysters – make up the class Bivalvia (also called Pelecypoda). Features of bivalves include a shell with two halves (valves); large gills that are used for breathing and filter feeding; and no radula.

EXTERNAL FEATURES OF A SCALLOP

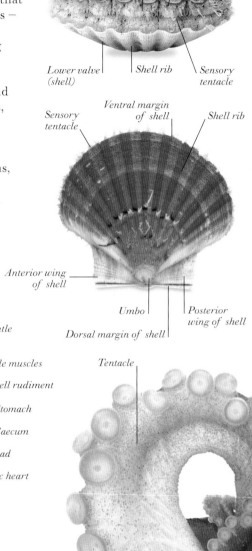

Upper valve (shell) Mantle Ocellus (eye)

Lower valve (shell) Shell rib Sensory tentacle

Sensory tentacle Ventral margin of shell Shell rib

Anterior wing of shell

Umbo

Posterior wing of shell

Dorsal margin of shell

INTERNAL ANATOMY OF AN OCTOPUS

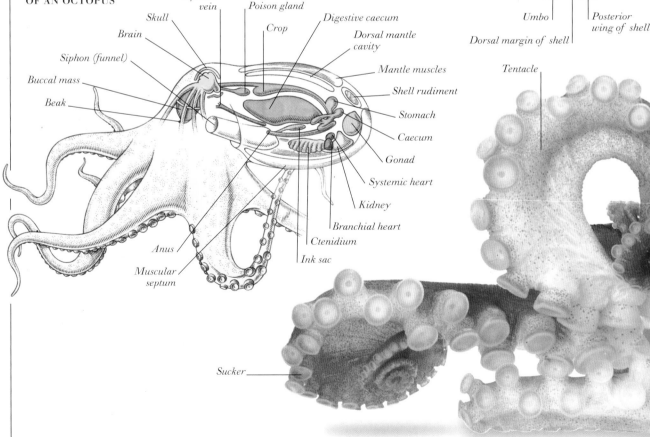

Cephalic vein
Skull
Brain
Siphon (funnel)
Buccal mass
Beak
Poison gland
Crop
Digestive caecum
Dorsal mantle cavity
Mantle muscles
Shell rudiment
Stomach
Caecum
Gonad
Systemic heart
Kidney
Branchial heart
Ctenidium
Ink sac
Anus
Muscular septum
Tentacle
Sucker

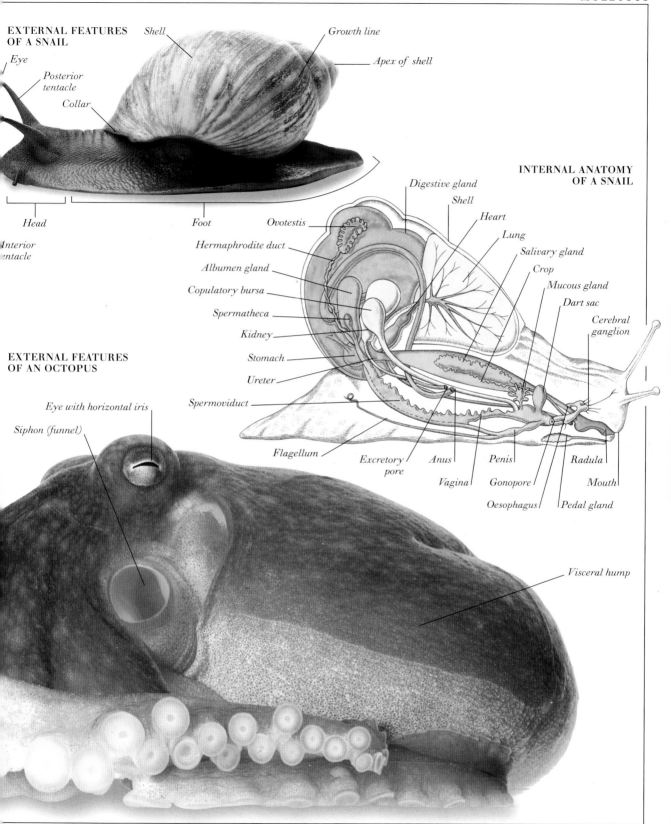

EXTERNAL FEATURES OF A SNAIL

Eye

Posterior tentacle

Collar

Shell

Growth line

Apex of shell

Head

Foot

Anterior tentacle

INTERNAL ANATOMY OF A SNAIL

Digestive gland

Shell

Heart

Lung

Salivary gland

Crop

Mucous gland

Dart sac

Cerebral ganglion

Ovotestis

Hermaphrodite duct

Albumen gland

Copulatory bursa

Spermatheca

Kidney

Stomach

Ureter

Spermoviduct

Flagellum

Excretory pore

Anus

Penis

Radula

Mouth

Vagina

Gonopore

Oesophagus

Pedal gland

EXTERNAL FEATURES OF AN OCTOPUS

Eye with horizontal iris

Siphon (funnel)

Visceral hump

Sharks and jawless fish

SHARKS, DOGFISH (WHICH ARE actually small sharks), skates, and rays belong to a class of fishes called Chondrichthyes, which is a division of the superclass Gnathostomata (meaning "jawed mouths"). Also sometimes known as elasmobranchs, sharks and their relatives have a skeleton made of cartilage (hence their common name, cartilaginous fish), a characteristic that distinguishes them from bony fish (see pp. 180-181). Other important features of cartilaginous fish are extremely tough, tooth-like scales, and lack of a swim bladder. Jawless fish—lampreys and hagfish—are primitive, eel-like fish that make up the order Cyclostomata (meaning "round mouths"), a division of the superclass Agnatha (meaning "without jaws"). In addition to their characteristic round, sucker-like mouths and lack of jaws, cyclostomes also have smooth, slimy skin without scales, and unpaired fins.

SHARKS' JAWS

Jaws of an adult tiger shark

Jaws of a young tiger shark

EXTERNAL FEATURES OF A DOGFISH

Snout

Eye

Gill slit

Pectoral fin

Anterior dorsal fin

Posterior dorsal fin

FEATURES OF A LAMPREY'S HEAD

Outer lip

Mouth

Tongue

Sucker

Eye

Tooth

Fringed inner lip

EXTERNAL FEATURES OF A LAMPREY

Eye

Gill opening

Sucker

Anal fin

Caudal fin

178

EXAMPLES OF CARTILAGINOUS FISH

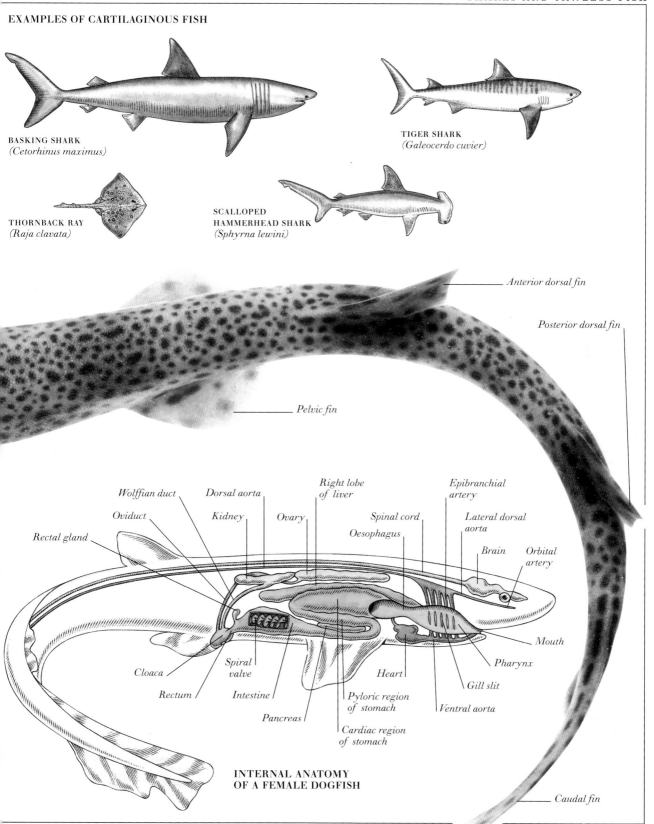

BASKING SHARK
(*Cetorhinus maximus*)

TIGER SHARK
(*Galeocerdo cuvier*)

THORNBACK RAY
(*Raja clavata*)

**SCALLOPED
HAMMERHEAD SHARK**
(*Sphyrna lewini*)

Anterior dorsal fin

Posterior dorsal fin

Pelvic fin

Wolffian duct

Dorsal aorta

Right lobe
of liver

Epibranchial
artery

Oviduct

Kidney

Ovary

Spinal cord

Lateral dorsal
aorta

Rectal gland

Oesophagus

Brain

Orbital
artery

Mouth

Cloaca

Spiral
valve

Pharynx

Rectum

Intestine

Heart

Gill slit

Pancreas

Pyloric region
of stomach

Ventral aorta

Cardiac region
of stomach

**INTERNAL ANATOMY
OF A FEMALE DOGFISH**

Caudal fin

Bony fish

BONY FISH, SUCH AS CARP, TROUT, SALMON, perch, and cod, are by far the best known and largest group of fish, with more than 20,000 species (over 95 per cent of all known fish). As their name suggests, bony fish have skeletons made of bone, in contrast to the cartilaginous skeletons of sharks, jawless fish, and their relatives (see pp. 178-179). Other typical features of bony fish include a swim bladder, which functions as a variable-buoyancy organ, enabling a fish to remain effortlessly at whatever depth it is swimming; relatively thin, bone-like scales; a flap (called an operculum) covering the gills; and paired pelvic and pectoral fins. Scientifically, bony fish belong to the class Osteichthyes, which is a division of the superclass Gnathostomata (meaning "jawed mouths").

HOW FISH BREATHE

Fish "breathe" by extracting oxygen from water through their gills. Water is sucked in through the mouth; simultaneously, the opercula close to prevent the water from escaping. The mouth is then closed, and muscles in the walls of the mouth, pharynx, and opercular cavity contract to pump the water inside over the gills and out through the opercula. Some fish rely on swimming with their mouths open to keep water flowing over the gills.

Pharynx

Gill raker

Water out

Gill sli

Mouth

Water in

Gill filament

Operculum

EXAMPLES OF BONY FISH

MANDARINFISH
(Synchiropus splendidus)

ANGLERFISH
(Caulophryne jordani)

LIONFISH
(Pterois volitans)

OCEANIC SEAHORSE
(Hippocampus kuda)

Vertebra

Neural spine

Hypural

Haemal spine

Caudal fin ray

Anal fin ray

Radial cartilage

STURGEON
(Acipenser sturio)

SNOWFLAKE MORAY EEL
(Echidna nebulosa)

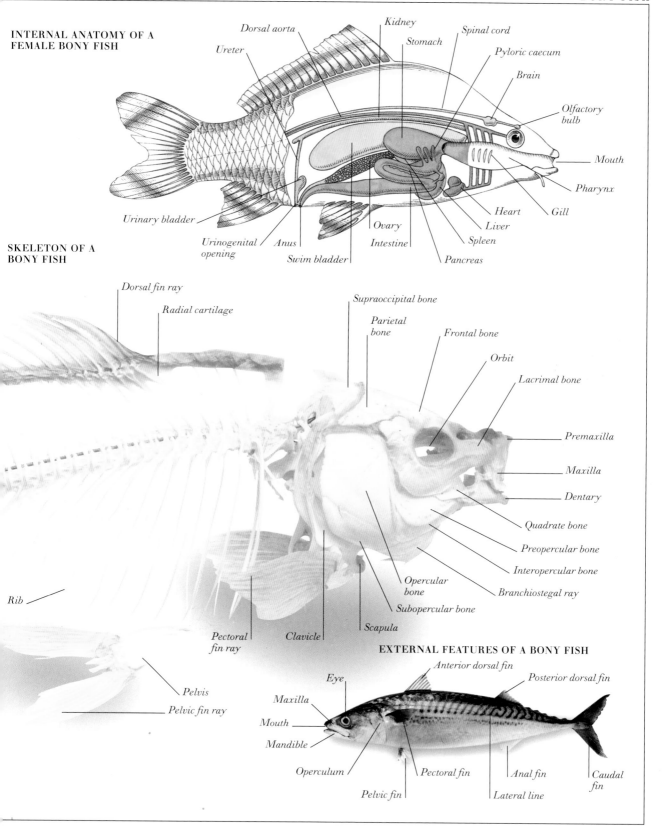

INTERNAL ANATOMY OF A FEMALE BONY FISH

Dorsal aorta

Ureter

Kidney

Stomach

Spinal cord

Pyloric caecum

Brain

Olfactory bulb

Mouth

Pharynx

Gill

Heart

Liver

Spleen

Pancreas

Intestine

Ovary

Swim bladder

Anus

Urinogenital opening

Urinary bladder

SKELETON OF A BONY FISH

Dorsal fin ray

Radial cartilage

Supraoccipital bone

Parietal bone

Frontal bone

Orbit

Lacrimal bone

Premaxilla

Maxilla

Dentary

Quadrate bone

Preopercular bone

Interopercular bone

Branchiostegal ray

Opercular bone

Subopercular bone

Scapula

Clavicle

Pectoral fin ray

Rib

Pelvis

Pelvic fin ray

EXTERNAL FEATURES OF A BONY FISH

Anterior dorsal fin

Posterior dorsal fin

Eye

Maxilla

Mouth

Mandible

Operculum

Pelvic fin

Pectoral fin

Anal fin

Lateral line

Caudal fin

Amphibians

THE CLASS AMPHIBIA INCLUDES FROGS and toads (which make up the order Anura), and newts and salamanders (which make up the order Urodela). Amphibians typically have moist, scaleless, hairless skin; lungs; and are cold-blooded. They also undergo complete metamorphosis, from eggs laid in water through various water-living larval stages (such as tadpoles) to land-living adults. Typical features of adult frogs and toads include a squat body with no tail; long, powerful hind legs; and large, often bulging, eyes. Adult newts and salamanders typically have a long body with a well-developed tail; and relatively short, equal-sized legs. However, newts and salamanders show considerable variation; for example, in some species the adults have minute legs, external gills rather than lungs, and spend their entire lives in water.

INTERNAL ANATOMY OF A FEMALE FROG

Larynx

Right bronchus

Stomach

Right lung

Pulmonary artery

Heart

Left lung

Liver

Pancreas

Posterior vena cava

Duodenum

Right kidney

Spleen

Dorsal aorta

Left kidney

Cloaca

Mesentery

Rectum

Small intestine (ileum)

Left ureter

EXTERNAL FEATURES OF A FROG

Hind limb

Trunk

Head

Forelimb

5 digits

Tympanum (eardrum)

External nostril

Mouth

4 digits

Web

Eye

EXTERNAL FEATURES OF A SALAMANDER

Eye

Tail

Forelimb

Hind limb

Digit

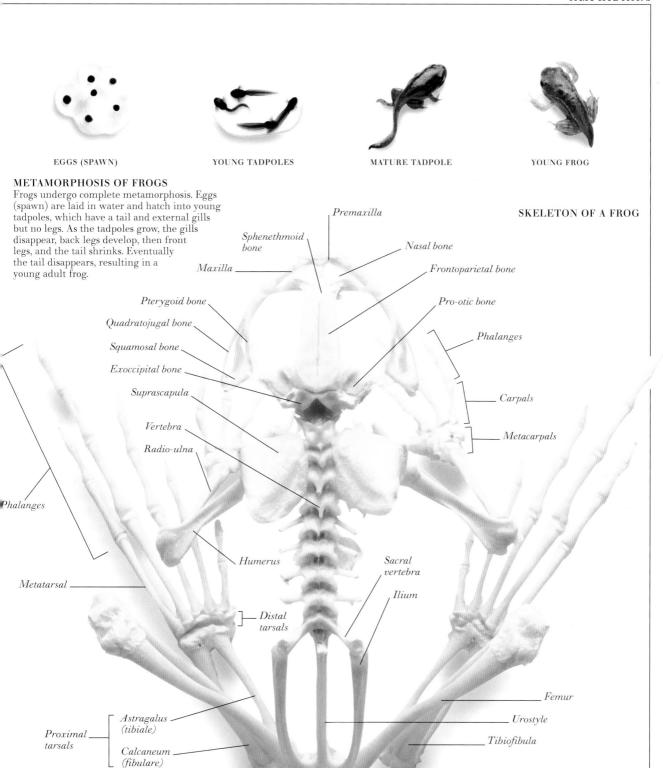

EGGS (SPAWN)   YOUNG TADPOLES   MATURE TADPOLE   YOUNG FROG

METAMORPHOSIS OF FROGS

Frogs undergo complete metamorphosis. Eggs (spawn) are laid in water and hatch into young tadpoles, which have a tail and external gills but no legs. As the tadpoles grow, the gills disappear, back legs develop, then front legs, and the tail shrinks. Eventually the tail disappears, resulting in a young adult frog.

SKELETON OF A FROG

Premaxilla

Sphenethmoid bone

Nasal bone

Maxilla

Frontoparietal bone

Pro-otic bone

Pterygoid bone

Phalanges

Quadratojugal bone

Squamosal bone

Exoccipital bone

Carpals

Suprascapula

Metacarpals

Vertebra

Radio-ulna

Phalanges

Humerus

Metatarsal

Sacral vertebra

Distal tarsals

Ilium

Femur

Astragalus (tibiale)

Urostyle

Proximal tarsals

Tibiofibula

Calcaneum (fibulare)

Ischium

Lizards and snakes

LIZARDS AND SNAKES BELONG to the order Squamata, a division of the class Reptilia. Characteristic reptilian features include scaly skin, lungs, and cold-bloodedness. Most reptiles lay leathery-shelled eggs, although some hatch the eggs inside their bodies and give birth to live young. Lizards belong to the suborder Lacertilia. Typically, they have long tails, and shed their skin in several pieces. Many lizards can regenerate a tail if it is lost; some can change colour; and some are limbless. Snakes make up the suborder Ophidia (also called Serpentes). All snakes have long, limbless bodies; can dislocate their lower jaw to swallow large prey; and have eyelids that are joined together to form a single transparent covering over the front of the eye. Most snakes shed their skin in a single piece. Constrictor snakes kill their prey by squeezing; venomous snakes poison their prey.

EXAMPLES OF SNAKES

MEXICAN MOUNTAIN KING SNAKE
(Lampropeltis triangulum annulata)

BANDED MI
SNA
*(Lamprope
ruthve*

EXTERNAL FEATURES OF A LIZARD

Eye

Mouth

External nostril

Crest

Eardrum

Masseteric scale

Dorsal scale

Dewlap

Foreleg

Belly

Ventral scale

SKELETON OF A LIZARD

Skull

Orbit

Scapula

Cervical vertebrae

Phalanges

Carpals

Metacarpal

Ulna

Humerus

Radius

Rib

Thoracolumbar vertebrae

Pelvis

Sacrum

Femur

Tibia

Fibula

Tarsals

Metatarsal

Caudal vertebrae

Phalanges

Toe

Claw

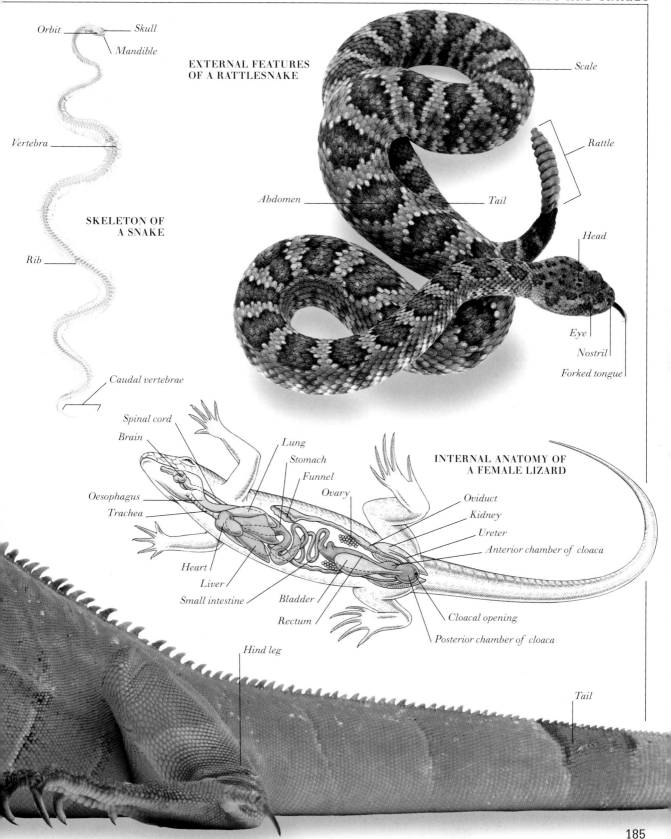

EXTERNAL FEATURES
OF A RATTLESNAKE

Orbit
Skull
Mandible

Scale

Vertebra

Rattle

Abdomen
Tail

SKELETON OF
A SNAKE

Head

Rib

Eye

Nostril

Forked tongue

Caudal vertebrae

INTERNAL ANATOMY OF
A FEMALE LIZARD

Spinal cord
Brain
Lung
Stomach
Funnel
Ovary

Oesophagus
Trachea

Oviduct
Kidney
Ureter
Anterior chamber of cloaca

Heart
Liver
Small intestine
Bladder
Rectum

Cloacal opening
Posterior chamber of cloaca

Hind leg

Tail

185

Crocodilians and turtles

CROCODILIANS AND TURTLES BELONG to different orders in the class Reptilia. The order Crocodilia includes crocodiles, alligators, caimans, and gharials. Typically, crocodilians are carnivores (flesh-eaters), and have a long snout, sharp teeth for gripping prey, and hard, square scales. All crocodilians are adapted to living on land and in water: they have four strong legs for moving on land; a powerful tail for swimming; and their eyes and nostrils are high on the head so that they stay above water while the rest of the body is submerged. The order Chelonia includes marine turtles, terrapins (freshwater turtles), and tortoises (land turtles). Characteristically, chelonians have a short, broad body encased in a bony shell with an outer horny covering, into which the head and limbs can be withdrawn; and a horny beak instead of teeth.

GHARIAL
(Gavialis gangeticus)

NILE CROCODILE
(Crocodylus niloticus)

AMERICAN ALLIGATOR
(Alligator mississippiensis)

SKELETON OF A CROCODILE

Cervical vertebrae

Thoracic vertebrae

Lumbar vertebrae

Sacrum

Caudal vertebrae

Skull

Mandible

Scapula

Humerus

Radius

Ulna

Rib

Femur

Fibula

Phalanges

Metatarsals

Tarsals

Tibia

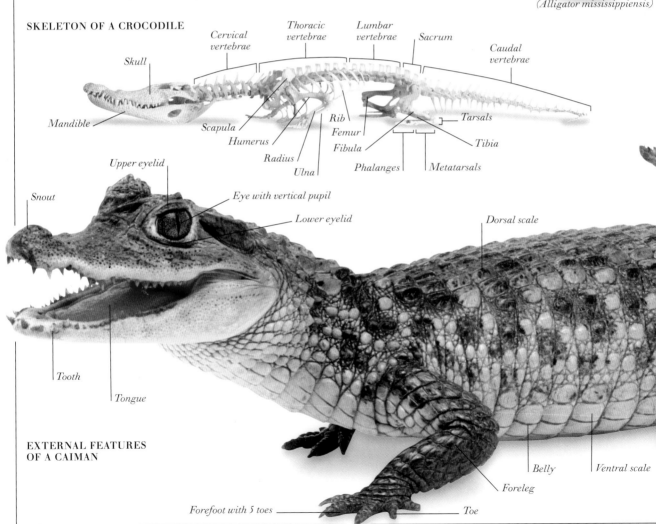

Upper eyelid

Eye with vertical pupil

Lower eyelid

Dorsal scale

Snout

Tooth

Tongue

EXTERNAL FEATURES OF A CAIMAN

Belly

Ventral scale

Foreleg

Forefoot with 5 toes

Toe

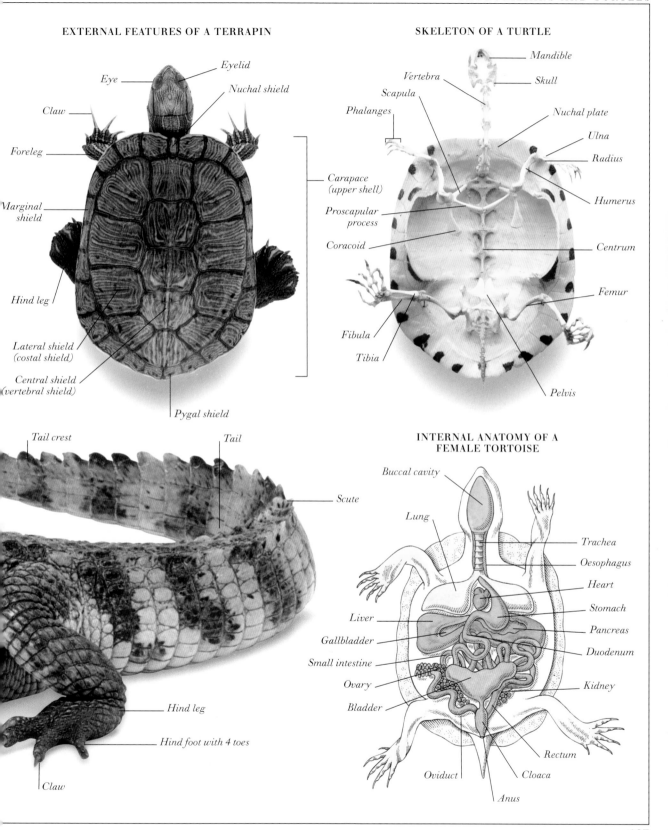

EXTERNAL FEATURES OF A TERRAPIN

Eye
Eyelid
Nuchal shield
Claw
Foreleg
Marginal shield
Hind leg
Lateral shield (costal shield)
Central shield (vertebral shield)
Pygal shield
Carapace (upper shell)

SKELETON OF A TURTLE

Vertebra
Scapula
Phalanges
Mandible
Skull
Nuchal plate
Ulna
Radius
Humerus
Proscapular process
Coracoid
Centrum
Fibula
Tibia
Femur
Pelvis

Tail crest
Tail
Scute
Hind leg
Hind foot with 4 toes
Claw

INTERNAL ANATOMY OF A FEMALE TORTOISE

Buccal cavity
Lung
Liver
Gallbladder
Small intestine
Ovary
Bladder
Trachea
Oesophagus
Heart
Stomach
Pancreas
Duodenum
Kidney
Rectum
Oviduct
Cloaca
Anus

Birds 1

BIRDS MAKE UP THE CLASS AVES. There are more than 9,000 species, almost all of which can fly (the only flightless birds are penguins, ostriches, rheas, cassowaries, and kiwis). The ability to fly is reflected in the typical bird features: forelimbs modified as wings; a streamlined body; and hollow bones to reduce weight. All birds lay hard-shelled eggs, which the parents incubate. Birds' beaks and feet vary according to diet and way of life. Beaks range from general-purpose types suitable for a mixed diet (those of thrushes, for example), to types specialized for particular foods (such as the large, curved, sieving beaks of flamingos). Feet range from the webbed "paddles" of ducks, to the talons of birds of prey. Plumage also varies widely, and in many species the male is brightly coloured for courtship display whereas the female is drab.

EXTERNAL FEATURES OF A BIRD

Forehead
Eye
Crown
Nostril
Nape
Upper mandible
Beak
Lower mandible
Chin
Throat
Breast
Belly
Flank
Thigh
Claw
Toe
Tarsus
Under tail coverts
Tail feathers (retrices)
Primary flight feathers (primaryremiges)
Secondary flight feathers (secondary remiges)
Greater wing coverts (major coverts)
Minor coverts
Lesser wing coverts
Median wing coverts

EXAMPLES OF BIRDS

MALE TUFTED DUCK
(*Aythya fuligula*)

WHITE STORK
(*Ciconia ciconia*)

MALE OSTRICH
(*Struthio camelus*)

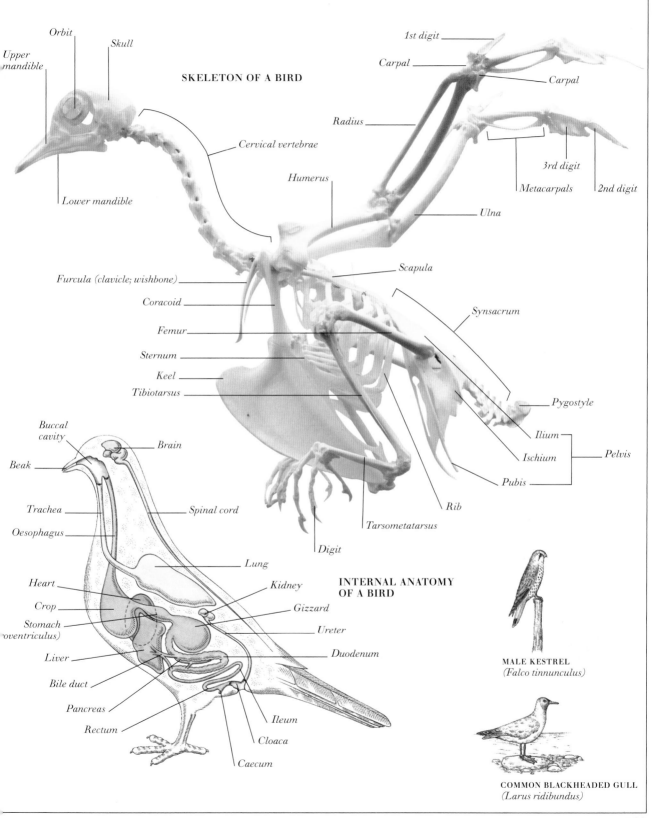

SKELETON OF A BIRD

Orbit

Skull

Upper mandible

1st digit

Carpal

Carpal

Radius

Cervical vertebrae

Humerus

3rd digit

Metacarpals

2nd digit

Lower mandible

Ulna

Furcula (clavicle; wishbone)

Scapula

Coracoid

Synsacrum

Femur

Sternum

Keel

Tibiotarsus

Pygostyle

Ilium

Ischium

Pelvis

Pubis

Rib

Tarsometatarsus

Digit

INTERNAL ANATOMY OF A BIRD

Buccal cavity

Brain

Beak

Trachea

Spinal cord

Oesophagus

Lung

Heart

Kidney

Crop

Gizzard

Stomach (proventriculus)

Ureter

Liver

Duodenum

Bile duct

Pancreas

Rectum

Ileum

Cloaca

Caecum

MALE KESTREL
(*Falco tinnunculus*)

COMMON BLACKHEADED GULL
(*Larus ridibundus*)

Birds 2

EXAMPLES OF BIRDS' FEET

KITTIWAKE
(Rissa tridactyla)
The webbed feet are
adapted for paddling
through water.

LITTLE GREBE
(Tachybaptus ruficollis)
The lobed, flattened feet
are adapted for swimming
underwater.

TAWNY OWL
(Strix aluco)
The clawed feet are adapted
for gripping prey.

EXAMPLES OF BIRDS' BEAKS

KING VULTURE
(Sarcorhamphus papa)
The hooked beak is adapted
for pulling apart flesh.

GREATER FLAMINGO
(Phoenicopterus ruber)
In the living bird, the large,
curved beak contains a
cartilaginous "sieve" for
filtering food particles
from water.

MISTLE THRUSH
(Turdus viscivorus)
The general-purpose beak is
suitable for a wide range of
animal and plant foods.

BLUE-AND-YELLOW MACAW
(Ara ararauna)
The broad, powerful, hooked beak
is adapted for crushing seeds and
eating fruit.

BONES OF A BIRD'S WING

1st digit
Carpal
Radius
3rd digit
Metacarpals
Humerus
2nd digit
Carpal
Ulna

Alula (spurious wing)

FEATHERS OF A BIRD'S WING

Minor coverts

Major coverts

Secondary flight feathers (secondary remiges)

Primary flight feathers (primary remiges)

STRUCTURE OF A FEATHER

Downcurved edge
Rachis (shaft)
Outer vane
Tip
Calamus (quill)
Upcurved edge
Inner vane

Eggs

AN EGG IS A SINGLE CELL, produced by the female, with the capacity to develop into a new individual. Development may take place inside the mother's body (as in most mammals) or outside, in which case the egg has a protective covering such as a shell. Egg yolk nourishes the growing young. Eggs developing inside the mother generally have little yolk, because the young are nourished from her body. Eggs developing outside may also have little yolk if they are produced by animals whose young go through a larval stage (such as a caterpillar) that feeds itself while developing into the adult form. The shelled eggs of birds and reptiles contain enough yolk to sustain the young until it hatches into a juvenile version of the adult.

SECTION THROUGH A CHICKEN'S EGG

Yolk
Yolk sac
Shell
Allantoic fluid
Allantois
Chorioallantoic membrane
Air sac
Albumen (egg white)
Amnion
Amniotic fluid
Developing chick
Developing wing
Shell membrane

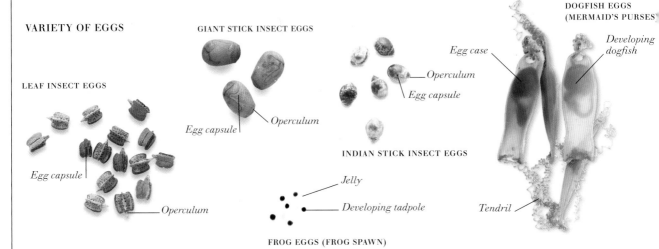

VARIETY OF EGGS

LEAF INSECT EGGS

Egg capsule
Operculum

GIANT STICK INSECT EGGS

Egg capsule
Operculum

INDIAN STICK INSECT EGGS

Operculum
Egg capsule

FROG EGGS (FROG SPAWN)

Jelly
Developing tadpole

DOGFISH EGGS (MERMAID'S PURSES)

Egg case
Developing dogfish
Tendril

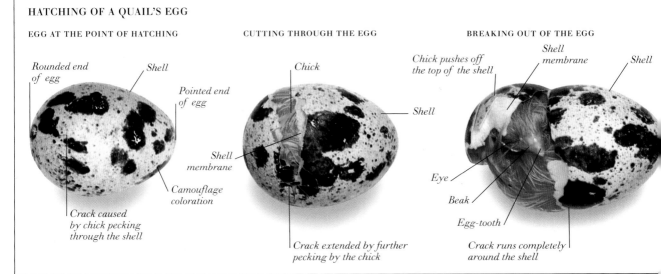

HATCHING OF A QUAIL'S EGG

EGG AT THE POINT OF HATCHING

Rounded end of egg
Shell
Pointed end of egg
Shell membrane
Camouflage coloration
Crack caused by chick pecking through the shell

CUTTING THROUGH THE EGG

Chick
Shell
Shell membrane
Crack extended by further pecking by the chick

BREAKING OUT OF THE EGG

Chick pushes off the top of the shell
Shell membrane
Shell
Eye
Beak
Egg-tooth
Crack runs completely around the shell

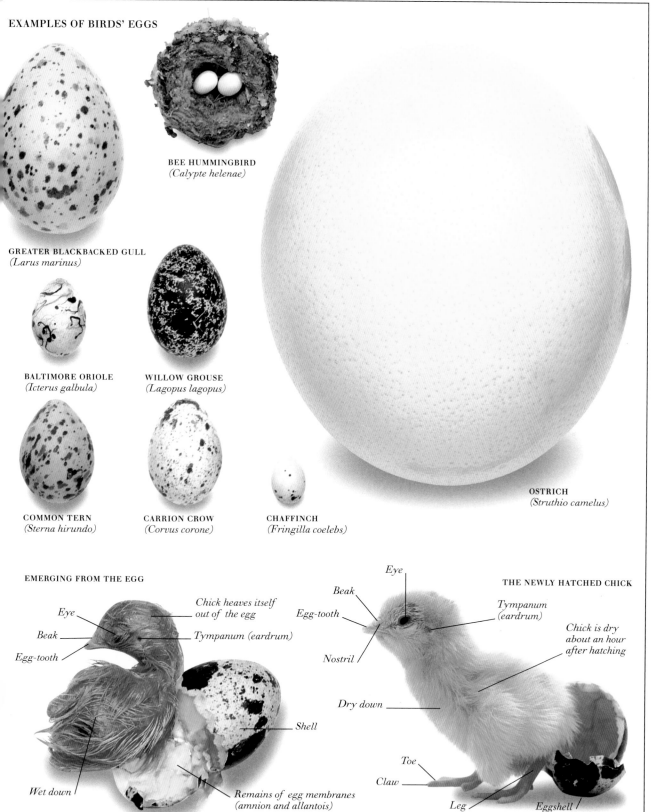

EXAMPLES OF BIRDS' EGGS

BEE HUMMINGBIRD
(Calypte helenae)

GREATER BLACKBACKED GULL
(Larus marinus)

BALTIMORE ORIOLE
(Icterus galbula)

WILLOW GROUSE
(Lagopus lagopus)

COMMON TERN
(Sterna hirundo)

CARRION CROW
(Corvus corone)

CHAFFINCH
(Fringilla coelebs)

OSTRICH
(Struthio camelus)

EMERGING FROM THE EGG

Eye

Beak

Egg-tooth

Chick heaves itself
out of the egg

Tympanum (eardrum)

Shell

Wet down

Remains of egg membranes
(amnion and allantois)

THE NEWLY HATCHED CHICK

Eye

Beak

Egg-tooth

Nostril

Tympanum
(eardrum)

Chick is dry
about an hour
after hatching

Dry down

Toe

Claw

Leg

Eggshell

Carnivores

THE MAMMALIAN ORDER CARNIVORA includes cats, dogs, bears, raccoons, pandas, weasels, badgers, skunks, otters, civets, mongooses, and hyenas. The order's name is derived from the fact that most of its members are carnivores (flesheaters). Typical carnivore features therefore reflect a hunting life-style: speed and agility; sharp claws and well-developed canine teeth for holding and killing prey; carnassial teeth (cheek teeth) for cutting flesh; and forward-facing eyes for good distance judgment. However, some members of the order – bears, badgers, and foxes, for example – have a more mixed diet, and a few are entirely herbivorous (plant-eating), notably pandas. Such animals have no carnassial teeth and tend to be slower-moving than pure flesh-eaters.

EXTERNAL FEATURES OF A MALE LION

Nose

Eye

Mane

Nostril

Vibrissa (whisker)

Tongue

Canine tooth

Incisor tooth

Chest

Elbow

Lower arm

Toe

SKULL OF A LION

Coronoid process

Zygomatic arch

Sagittal crest

Orbit

Nasal bone

Maxilla

Upper premolars

Upper canine

Lower canine

Mandible

Lower premolars

Occipital condyle

Tympanic bulla

Condyle

Angular process

Upper carnassial tooth (4th upper premolar)

SKULL OF A BEAR

Sagittal crest

Occipital condyle

Zygomatic arch

Orbit

Upper molars

Nasal bone

Upper premolars

Maxilla

Upper canine

Upper incisor

Lower incisor

Lower canine

Mandible

Tympanic bulla

Angular process

Condyle

Lower molars

Lower premolars

CARNIVORES

EXAMPLES OF CARNIVORES

ALSATIAN DOG
(Canis familiaris)

MANED WOLF
(Chrysocyon brachyurus)

RACCOON
(Procyon lotor)

AMERICAN BLACK BEAR
(Ursus americanus)

SKELETON OF A DOMESTIC CAT

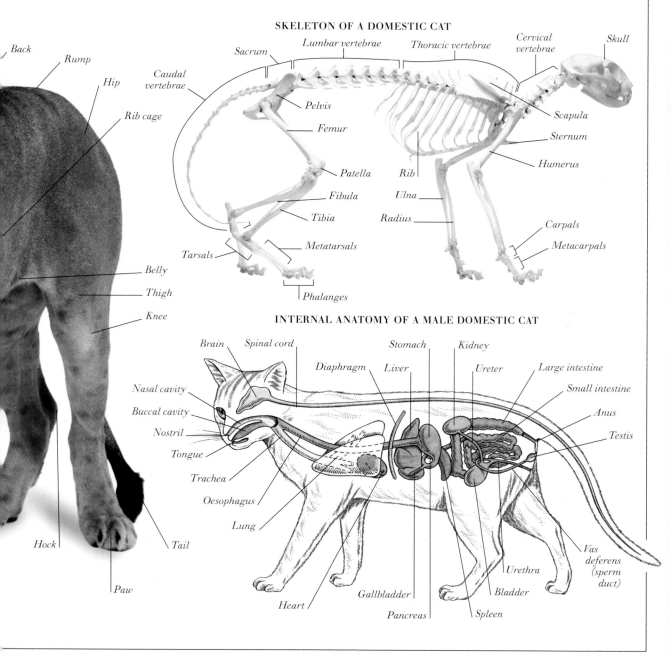

Back

Rump

Hip

Rib cage

Sacrum

Lumbar vertebrae

Thoracic vertebrae

Cervical vertebrae

Skull

Caudal vertebrae

Pelvis

Femur

Scapula

Sternum

Humerus

Patella

Rib

Fibula

Ulna

Tibia

Radius

Carpals

Metacarpals

Tarsals

Metatarsals

Belly

Thigh

Knee

Phalanges

INTERNAL ANATOMY OF A MALE DOMESTIC CAT

Brain

Spinal cord

Stomach

Kidney

Diaphragm

Liver

Ureter

Large intestine

Nasal cavity

Small intestine

Buccal cavity

Anus

Nostril

Testis

Tongue

Trachea

Oesophagus

Lung

Vas deferens (sperm duct)

Hock

Tail

Heart

Gallbladder

Pancreas

Spleen

Bladder

Urethra

Paw

195

Rabbits and rodents

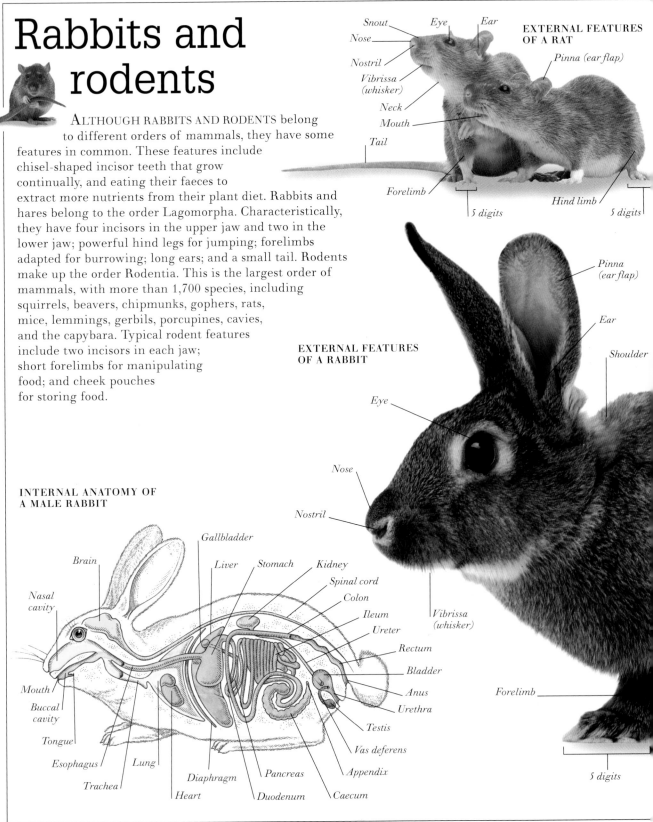

ALTHOUGH RABBITS AND RODENTS belong to different orders of mammals, they have some features in common. These features include chisel-shaped incisor teeth that grow continually, and eating their faeces to extract more nutrients from their plant diet. Rabbits and hares belong to the order Lagomorpha. Characteristically, they have four incisors in the upper jaw and two in the lower jaw; powerful hind legs for jumping; forelimbs adapted for burrowing; long ears; and a small tail. Rodents make up the order Rodentia. This is the largest order of mammals, with more than 1,700 species, including squirrels, beavers, chipmunks, gophers, rats, mice, lemmings, gerbils, porcupines, cavies, and the capybara. Typical rodent features include two incisors in each jaw; short forelimbs for manipulating food; and cheek pouches for storing food.

EXTERNAL FEATURES OF A RAT

Snout
Eye
Ear
Nose
Pinna (ear flap)
Nostril
Vibrissa (whisker)
Neck
Mouth
Tail
Forelimb
5 digits
Hind limb
5 digits

EXTERNAL FEATURES OF A RABBIT

Pinna (ear flap)
Ear
Shoulder
Eye
Nose
Nostril
Vibrissa (whisker)
Forelimb
5 digits

INTERNAL ANATOMY OF A MALE RABBIT

Brain
Gallbladder
Liver
Stomach
Kidney
Spinal cord
Colon
Ileum
Ureter
Rectum
Bladder
Anus
Urethra
Testis
Vas deferens
Appendix
Caecum
Duodenum
Pancreas
Diaphragm
Heart
Lung
Trachea
Esophagus
Tongue
Buccal cavity
Mouth
Nasal cavity

SKELETON OF A HARE

Skull

Cervical vertebrae

Thoracic vertebrae

Mandible

Scapula

Lumbar
vertebrae

Sternum

Rib

Humerus

Femur

Radius

Pelvis

Ulna

Patella

Sacrum

Fibula

Carpals

Tibia

Metacarpals

Caudal
vertebrae

Phalanges

Phalanges

Tarsals

Metatarsals

Tail

Knee

Hind limb

4 digits

EXAMPLES OF RODENTS

GREY SQUIRREL
(Sciuris carolinensis)

PLAINS VISCACHA
(Lagostomus maximus)

CRESTED PORCUPINE
(Hystrix africaeaustralis)

AMERICAN BEAVER
(Castor canadensis)

CAPYBARA
(Hydrochoerus hydrochaeris)

Ungulates

UNGULATES IS A GENERAL TERM FOR a large, varied group of mammals that includes horses, cattle, and their relatives. The ungulates are divided into two orders on the basis of the number of toes. Members of the order Perissodactyla (odd-toed ungulates) have one or three toes. Perissodactyls include horses, asses, and zebras (all of which are one-toed), and rhinoceroses and tapirs (which are three-toed). Members of the order Artiodactyla (even-toed ungulates) have two or four toes. Most artiodactyls have two toes, which are typically encased in hooves to give the so-called cloven hoof. Two-toed, cloven-hoofed artiodactyls include cows and other cattle, sheep, goats, antelopes, deer, and giraffes. The other main two-toed artiodactyls are camels and llamas. Most two-toed artiodactyls are ruminants; that is, they have a four-chambered stomach and chew the cud. The principal four-toed artiodactyls are pigs, peccaries, and hippopotamuses.

Chambers of stomach

Rumen   Omasum   Abomasum   Reticulum

Colon

Anus

Rectum

Caecum

Small intestine

Duodenum

Mou

Tongue

Oesophagus

DIGESTIVE SYSTEM OF A COW

Croup

Loin

Ba

Root of tail

Buttock

Tail

Thigh

Flank

Belly

Stifle

Gaskin

Hock

Chestnut

Shannon bone
(cannon bone)

Coronet

Heel

Hoof

Pastern

**COMPARISON OF THE FRONT FEET
OF A HORSE AND A COW**

**SKELETON OF THE LEFT
FRONT FOOT OF A HORSE**

**SKELETON OF THE RIGHT
FRONT FOOT OF A COW**

2nd metacarpal
(splint bone)

3rd metacarpal
(cannon bone)

Fused 3rd and
4th metacarpals

Sesamoid
bone

Sesamoid
bone

Phalanges of
3rd digit

Phalanges of
3rd digit

Hoof bone

Phalanges
of 4th digit

Hoof bone of 3rd digit

Hoof bone of
4th digit

EXAMPLES OF UNGULATES

MALE RED DEER
(Cervus elephas)
An even-toed ungulate
(order Artiodactyla)

BACTRIAN CAMEL
(Camelus ferus)
An even-toed ungulate
(order Artiodactyla)

GIRAFFE
(Giraffa camelopardalis)
An even-toed ungulate
(order Artiodactyla)

BLACK RHINOCEROS
(Diceros bicornis)
An odd-toed ungulate
(order Perissodactyla)

EXTERNAL FEATURES OF A HORSE

Mane
Poll
Crest
Ear
Forelock
Withers
Forehead
Eye
Muzzle
Nose
Nostril
Cheek
Mouth
Neck
Chin groove
Shoulder
Breast
bow
Forearm
Knee
Cannon bone
Fetlock
Pastern

SKELETON OF A HORSE

Lumbar vertebrae
Thoracic vertebrae
Orbit
Atlas
Axis
Skull
Sacrum
Caudal vertebrae
Cervical vertebrae
Pelvis
Scapula
Femur
Mandible
Fibula
Sternum
Tibia
Patella
Humerus
Calcaneum
Rib
Radius
Tarsals
2nd metatarsal
Ulna
Carpals
4th metatarsal
3rd metatarsal
3rd metacarpal (cannon bone)
Phalanges of 3rd digit
Phalanges of 3rd digit

199

Elephants

THE TWO SPECIES OF elephants – African and Asian – are the only members of the mammalian order Proboscidea. The bigger African elephant is the largest land animal: a fully grown male may be up to 4 m (13 ft) tall and weigh as much as 7 tonnes (6.9 tons). A fully grown male Asian elephant may be 3.3 m (11 ft) tall and weigh 5.4 tonnes (5.3 tons). The trunk – an extension of the nose and upper lip – is the elephant's other most obvious feature. It is used for manipulating and lifting, feeding, drinking and spraying water, smelling, touching, and producing trumpeting sounds. Other characteristic features include a pair of tusks, used for defence and for crushing vegetation; thick, pillar-like legs and broad feet to support the massive body; and large ear flaps that act as radiators to keep the elephant cool.

DIFFERENCES BETWEEN AFRICAN AND ASIAN ELEPHANTS

Flat forehead

Very large ears

2 "lips" at the end of the trunk

Concave back

4 toenails

AFRICAN ELEPHANT
(Loxodonta africana)

3 toenails

Twin-domed forehead

Smaller ears

1 "lip" at the end of the trunk

Arched back

5 toenails

4 toenails

ASIAN ELEPHANT
(Elephas maximus)

Rump

INTERNAL ANATOMY OF A FEMALE ELEPHANT

Spinal cord

Heart

Duodenum

Stomach

Kidney

Ureter

Uterus

Rectum

Bladder

Anal flap

Anus

Vagina

Brain

Nasal cavity

Buccal cavity

Mouth

Tongue

Tusk

Epiglottis

Oesophagus

Trachea

Lung

Diaphragm

Nasal passage

Nostril

Spleen

Vulva

Small intestine

Hind leg

Toenail

EXTERNAL FEATURES OF A FEMALE AFRICAN ELEPHANT (TUSKS REMOVED)

Flat forehead

Eye

Pinna (ear flap)

SKULL OF AN ASIAN ELEPHANT

Orbit

Cranium

Maxilla

Jugal bar

Premaxilla

Tusk (upper incisor)

Upper molars

Lower molars

Mandible

Annulus (ring) of trunk

SKELETON OF AN AFRICAN ELEPHANT (TUSKS REMOVED)

Cervical vertebrae

Thoracolumbar vertebrae

Skull

Sacrum

Belly

Caudal vertebrae

Foreleg

Mandible

Trunk (proboscis)

Scapula

Pelvis

Sternum

Upper "lip" of trunk

Rib

Femur

Humerus

Lower "lip" of trunk

Patella

Radius

Tibia

Ulna

Carpals

Fibula

Metacarpals

Tarsals

Phalanx

Phalanx

Metatarsals

201

Primates

THE MAMMALIAN ORDER PRIMATES consists of monkeys, apes, and their relatives (including humans). There are two suborders of primates: Prosimii, the primitive primates, which include lemurs, tarsiers, and lorises; and Anthropoidea, the advanced primates, which include monkeys, apes, and humans. The anthropoids are divided into New World monkeys, Old World monkeys, and hominids. New World monkeys typically have wide-apart nostrils that open to the side; and long tails, which are prehensile (grasping) in some species. This group of monkeys lives in South America, and includes marmosets, tamarins, and howler monkeys. Old World monkeys typically have close-set nostrils that open forwards or downwards; and non-prehensile tails. This group of monkeys lives in Africa and Asia, and includes langurs, mandrills, macaques, and baboons. Hominids typically have large brains, and no tail. This group includes the apes – chimpanzees, gibbons, gorillas, and orangutans – and humans.

INTERNAL ANATOMY OF A FEMALE CHIMPANZEE

Buccal cavity
Tongue
Trachea
Lung
Liver
Pancreas
Small intestine
Caecum
Appendix
Ovary
Uterus
Vagina
Brain
Nasal cavity
Spinal cord
Oesophagus
Heart
Diaphragm
Stomach
Spleen
Large intestine
Rectum
Bladder
Urethra

SKELETON OF A RHESUS MONKEY

Skull
Orbit
Cervical vertebrae
Mandible
Thoracic vertebrae
Clavicle
Scapula
Rib
Humerus
Lumbar vertebrae
Femur
Radius
Ulna
Sacrum
Carpals
Patella
Tibia
Metacarpals
Fibula
Pelvis
Phalanges
Caudal vertebrae
Tarsals
Metatarsals
Phalanges

SKULL OF A CHIMPANZEE

Temporal bone
Suture
Frontal bone
Parietal bone
Supraorbital ridge
Orbit
Occipital bone
Maxilla
Premaxilla
Auditory meatus
Zygomatic arch
Incisor tooth
Mandible
Molar tooth
Premolar tooth
Canine tooth

EXAMPLES OF PRIMATES

RING-TAILED LEMUR
(Lemur catta)
A prosimian

MALE RED HOWLER MONKEY
(Alouatta seniculus)
A New World monkey

MALE MANDRILL
(Mandrillus sphinx)
An Old World monkey

CHIMPANZEE
(Pan troglodytes)
An ape

EXTERNAL FEATURES OF
A YOUNG GORILLA

GOLDEN LION TAMARIN
(Leontopithecus rosalia)
A New World monkey

Pinna (ear flap)

Brow ridge

Eye

Shoulder

Nostril

Mouth

Upper arm

Thigh

Forearm

Chest

Elbow

Knee

Lower leg

Hand

Foot

Toe

Finger

Toenail

203

Dolphins, whales, and seals

DOLPHINS, WHALES, AND SEALS belong
to two orders of mammals adapted to living
in water. Dolphins and whales make up the
order Cetacea. Typical cetacean features include
a streamlined, fish-like shape; forelimbs in the form
of flippers; no visible hind limbs; a horizontally flattened
tail; and thick blubber under the skin. There are two groups
of cetaceans: toothed whales, including sperm whales, white whales,
beaked whales, dolphins, and porpoises; and the larger whalebone (baleen)
whales, including rorquals, grey whales, and right whales. The blue whale – a
rorqual – is the largest living animal: an adult may be up to 30 m (100 ft) long
and weigh 130 tonnes (128 tons). Seals and their relatives – sea lions and
walruses – make up the order Pinnipedia. Characteristically, they have a
streamlined, torpedo-shaped body; forelimbs and hind limbs modified as
flippers; thick blubber; and no external ears.

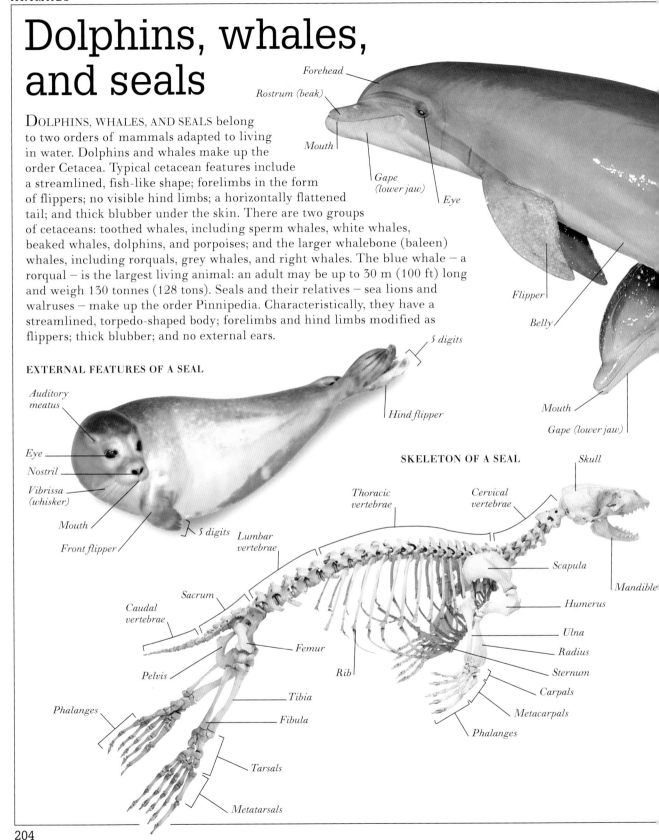

Forehead

Rostrum (beak)

Mouth

Gape
(lower jaw)

Eye

Flipper

Belly

Mouth

Gape (lower jaw)

5 digits

Hind flipper

EXTERNAL FEATURES OF A SEAL

Auditory
meatus

Eye

Nostril

Vibrissa
(whisker)

Mouth

Front flipper

5 digits

SKELETON OF A SEAL

Skull

Thoracic
vertebrae

Cervical
vertebrae

Scapula

Mandible

Humerus

Ulna

Radius

Sternum

Carpals

Metacarpals

Phalanges

Lumbar
vertebrae

Sacrum

Caudal
vertebrae

Femur

Rib

Pelvis

Tibia

Fibula

Phalanges

Tarsals

Metatarsals

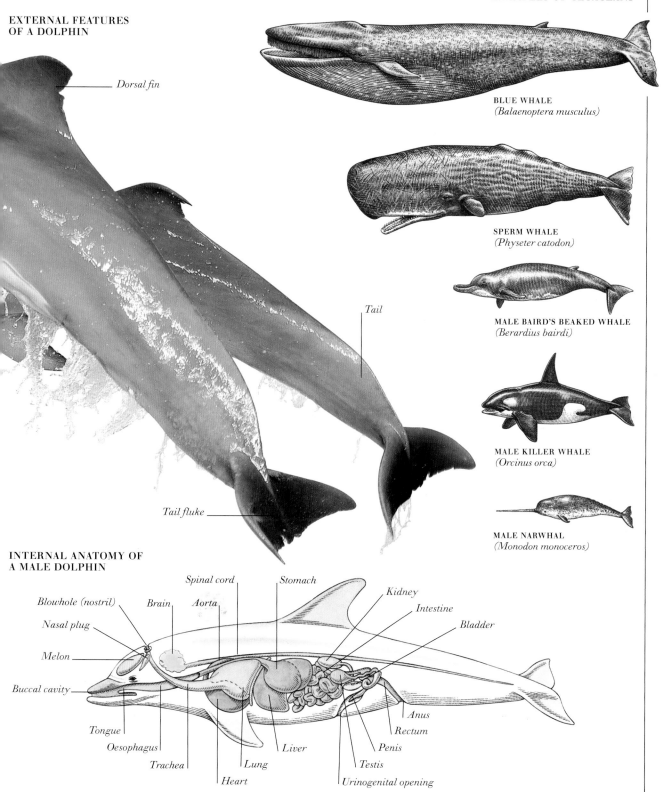

EXAMPLES OF CETACEANS

EXTERNAL FEATURES
OF A DOLPHIN

Dorsal fin

Tail

Tail fluke

BLUE WHALE
(*Balaenoptera musculus*)

SPERM WHALE
(*Physeter catodon*)

MALE BAIRD'S BEAKED WHALE
(*Berardius bairdi*)

MALE KILLER WHALE
(*Orcinus orca*)

MALE NARWHAL
(*Monodon monoceros*)

INTERNAL ANATOMY OF
A MALE DOLPHIN

Spinal cord

Stomach

Kidney

Blowhole (nostril)   *Brain*   *Aorta*

Intestine

Nasal plug

Bladder

Melon

Buccal cavity

Anus

Rectum

Tongue

Penis

Oesophagus

Testis

Trachea

Liver

Urinogenital opening

Heart

Lung

Marsupials and Monotremes

MARSUPIALS AND MONOTREMES are two orders of
mammals that differ from other mammalian groups
in the ways that their young develop. The order
Marsupalia, the pouched mammals, is made up
of kangaroos and their relatives. Typically,
marsupials give birth to their young at a
very early stage of development. The
young then crawls to the mother's
pouch (which is on the outside of
her abdomen), where it attaches
itself to a nipple and remains until
fully developed. Most marsupials live in
Australia, although the opossums – which
are classified as marsupials despite not
having a pouch – live in the Americas.
The order Monotremata is made up of
the platypus and its relatives (the echidnas,
or spiny anteaters). The monotremes are
primitive mammals that lay eggs, which the
mother incubates. The monotremes are found
only in Australia and New Guinea.

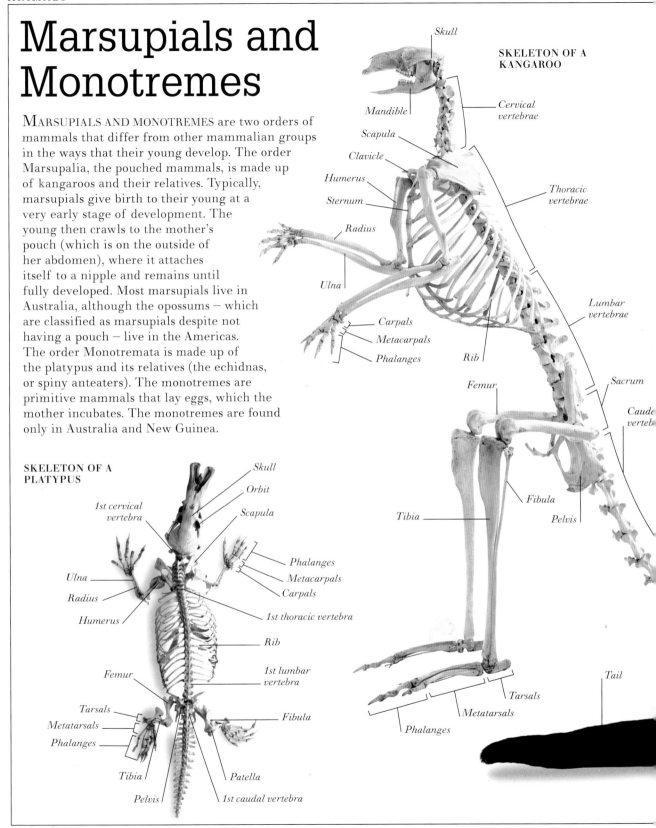

SKELETON OF A KANGAROO

Skull
Mandible
Scapula
Clavicle
Humerus
Sternum
Radius
Ulna
Cervical vertebrae
Thoracic vertebrae
Lumbar vertebrae
Carpals
Metacarpals
Phalanges
Rib
Femur
Sacrum
Caude verteb
Fibula
Pelvis
Tibia
Tail
Tarsals
Metatarsals
Phalanges

SKELETON OF A PLATYPUS

Skull
Orbit
Scapula
1st cervical vertebra
Ulna
Radius
Humerus
Phalanges
Metacarpals
Carpals
1st thoracic vertebra
Rib
Femur
1st lumbar vertebra
Fibula
Tarsals
Metatarsals
Phalanges
Tibia
Patella
Pelvis
1st caudal vertebra

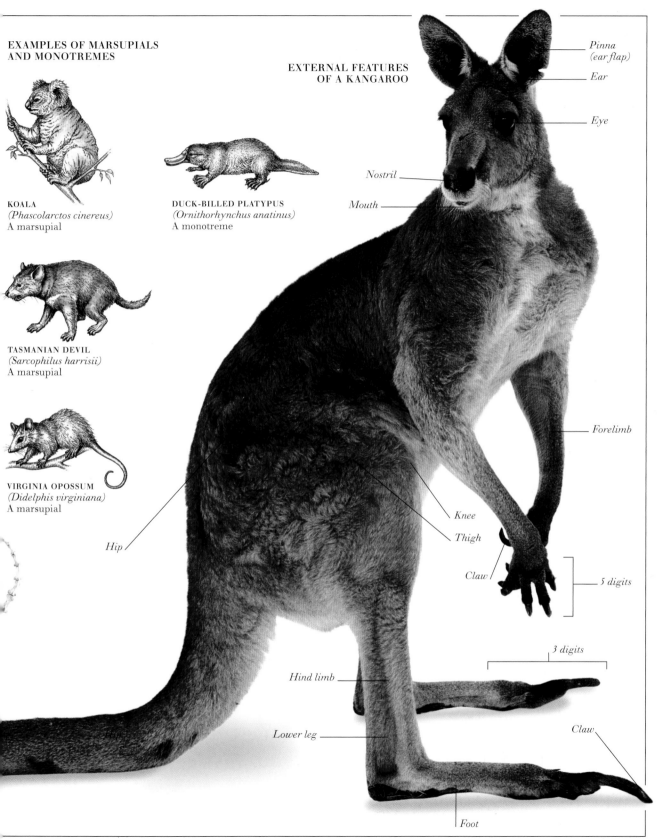

EXAMPLES OF MARSUPIALS AND MONOTREMES

KOALA
(Phascolarctos cinereus)
A marsupial

DUCK-BILLED PLATYPUS
(Ornithorhynchus anatinus)
A monotreme

TASMANIAN DEVIL
(Sarcophilus harrisii)
A marsupial

VIRGINIA OPOSSUM
(Didelphis virginiana)
A marsupial

EXTERNAL FEATURES OF A KANGAROO

Pinna (ear flap)

Ear

Eye

Nostril

Mouth

Forelimb

Knee

Thigh

Claw

5 digits

Hip

3 digits

Hind limb

Lower leg

Claw

Foot

207

THE HUMAN BODY

Body features

ALTHOUGH THERE IS enormous variation between the external appearances of humans, all bodies contain the same basic features. The outward form of the human body depends on the size of the skeleton, the shape of the muscles, the thickness of the fat layer beneath the skin, the elasticity or sagginess of the skin, and the person's age and sex. Males tend to be taller than females, with broader shoulders, more body hair, and a different pattern of fat deposits under the skin; the female body tends to be less muscular and has a shallower and wider pelvis to allow for childbirth.

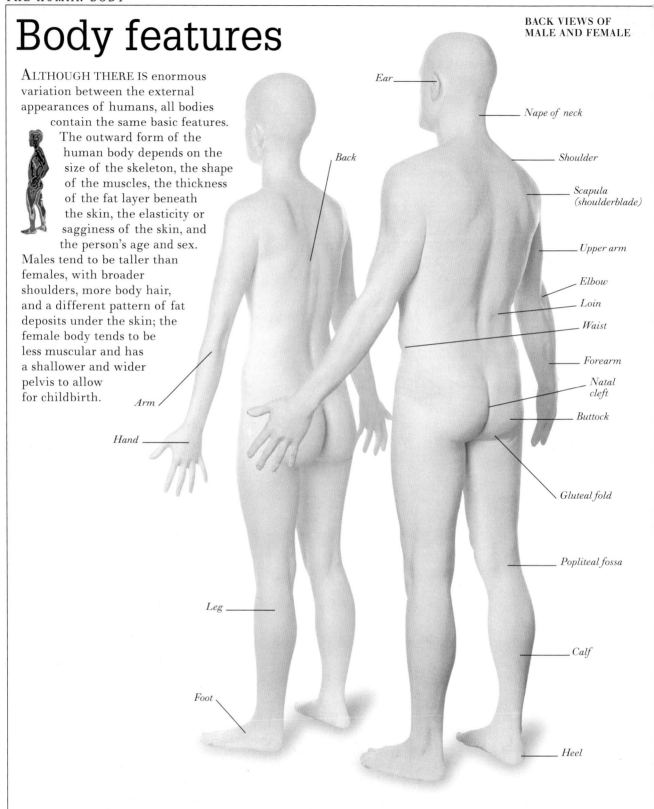

Ear

Nape of neck

Shoulder

Scapula (shoulderblade)

Upper arm

Elbow

Loin

Waist

Forearm

Natal cleft

Buttock

Gluteal fold

Popliteal fossa

Back

Arm

Hand

Leg

Foot

Calf

Heel

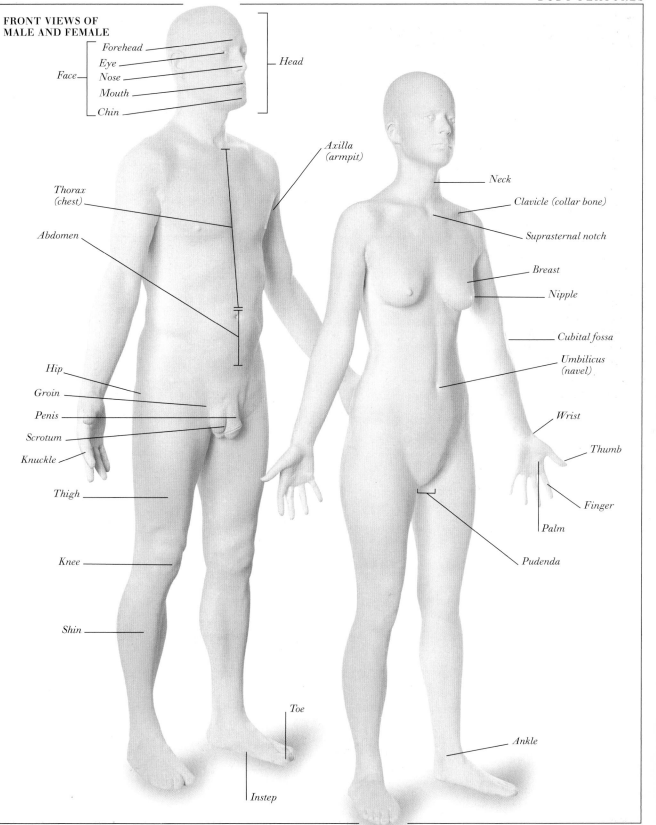

FRONT VIEWS OF MALE AND FEMALE

Forehead

Eye

Face — Nose

Mouth

Chin

Head

Axilla (armpit)

Thorax (chest)

Abdomen

Neck

Clavicle (collar bone)

Suprasternal notch

Breast

Nipple

Cubital fossa

Umbilicus (navel)

Hip

Groin

Penis

Scrotum

Knuckle

Thigh

Wrist

Thumb

Finger

Palm

Knee

Pudenda

Shin

Toe

Ankle

Instep

Head

IN A NEWBORN BABY, the head accounts for one-quarter of the total body length; by adulthood, the proportion has reduced to one-eighth. Contained in the head are the body's main sense organs: eyes, ears, olfactory nerves that detect smells, and the taste buds of the tongue. Signals from these organs pass to the body's great coordination centre: the brain, housed in the protective, bony dome of the skull. Hair on the head insulates against heat loss, and adult males also grow thick facial hair. The face has three important openings: two nostrils through which air passes, and the mouth, which takes in nourishment and helps form speech. Although all heads are basically similar, differences in the size, shape, and colour of features produce an infinite variety of appearances.

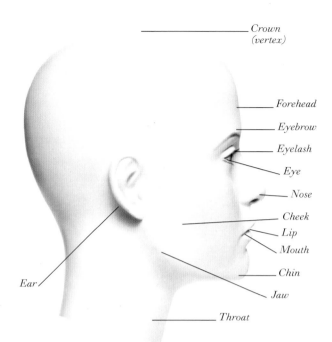

Crown (vertex)
Forehead
Eyebrow
Eyelash
Eye
Nose
Cheek
Lip
Mouth
Chin
Jaw
Throat
Ear

SECTION THROUGH HEAD

Superior sagittal sinus
Cerebrum
Frontal sinus
Sphenoidal sinus
Superior concha
Middle concha
Inferior concha
Vestibule
Maxilla (upper jaw)
Hard palate
Soft palate
Tongue
Uvula
Mandible (lower jaw)
Palatine tonsil
Epiglottis
Trachea
Oesophagus

Skull
Pineal body
Pituitary gland
Cerebellum
Pons
Medulla oblongata
Pharynx
Cervical vertebra
Spinal cord
Intervertebral disc

**FRONT VIEW OF EXTERNAL
FEATURES OF HEAD**

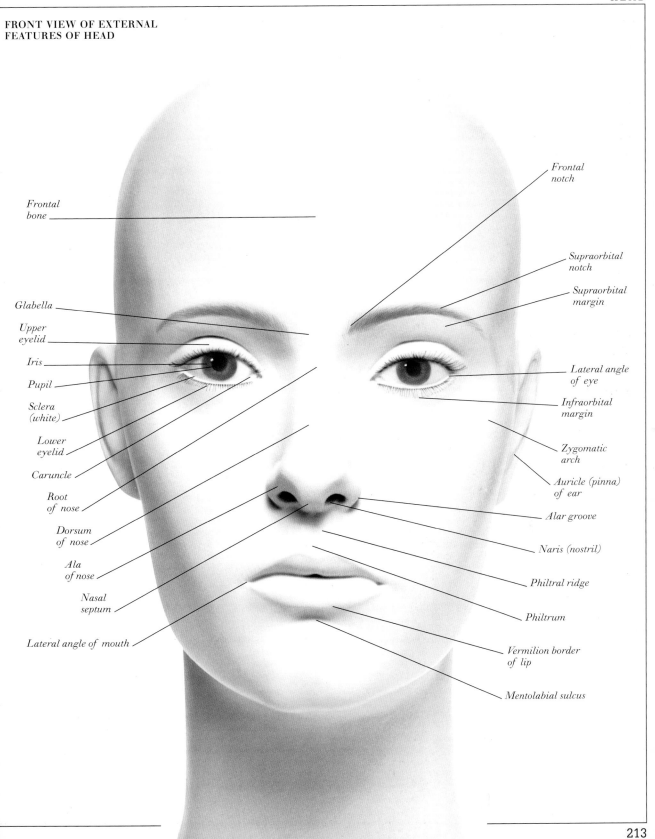

Frontal
notch

Frontal
bone

Supraorbital
notch

Supraorbital
margin

Glabella

Upper
eyelid

Iris

Lateral angle
of eye

Pupil

Infraorbital
margin

Sclera
(white)

Lower
eyelid

Zygomatic
arch

Caruncle

Auricle (pinna)
of ear

Root
of nose

Alar groove

Dorsum
of nose

Naris (nostril)

Ala
of nose

Philtral ridge

Nasal
septum

Philtrum

Lateral angle of mouth

Vermilion border
of lip

Mentolabial sulcus

Body organs

ALL THE VITAL BODY ORGANS except for the brain are enclosed within the trunk or torso (the body apart from the head and limbs). The trunk contains two large cavities separated by a muscular sheet called the diaphragm. The upper cavity, known as the thorax or chest cavity, contains the heart and lungs. The lower cavity, called the abdominal cavity, contains the stomach, intestines, liver, and pancreas, which all play a role in digesting food. Also within the trunk are the kidneys and bladder, which are part of the urinary system, and the reproductive organs, which hold the seeds of new human life. Modern imaging techniques, such as contrast X-rays and different types of scans, make it possible to see and study body organs without the need to cut through their protective coverings of skin, fat, muscle, and bone.

MAJOR INTERNAL STRUCTURES

Thyroid gland

Larynx

Heart

Right lung

Left lung

Diaphragm

Liver

Stomach

Large intestine

Small intestine

Greater omentum

IMAGING THE BODY

SCINTIGRAM OF
HEART CHAMBERS

ANGIOGRAM OF
RIGHT LUNG

CONTRAST X-RAY OF
GALLBLADDER

SCINTIGRAM OF
NERVOUS SYSTEM

DOUBLE CONTRAST
X-RAY OF COLON

ULTRASOUND SCAN
OF TWINS IN UTERUS

ANGIOGRAM OF
KIDNEYS

ANGIOGRAM OF
ARTERIES OF HEAD

CT SCAN THROUGH
FEMALE CHEST

THERMOGRAM OF
CHEST REGION

ANGIOGRAM OF
ARTERIES OF HEART

MRI SCAN THROUGH
HEAD AT EYE LEVEL

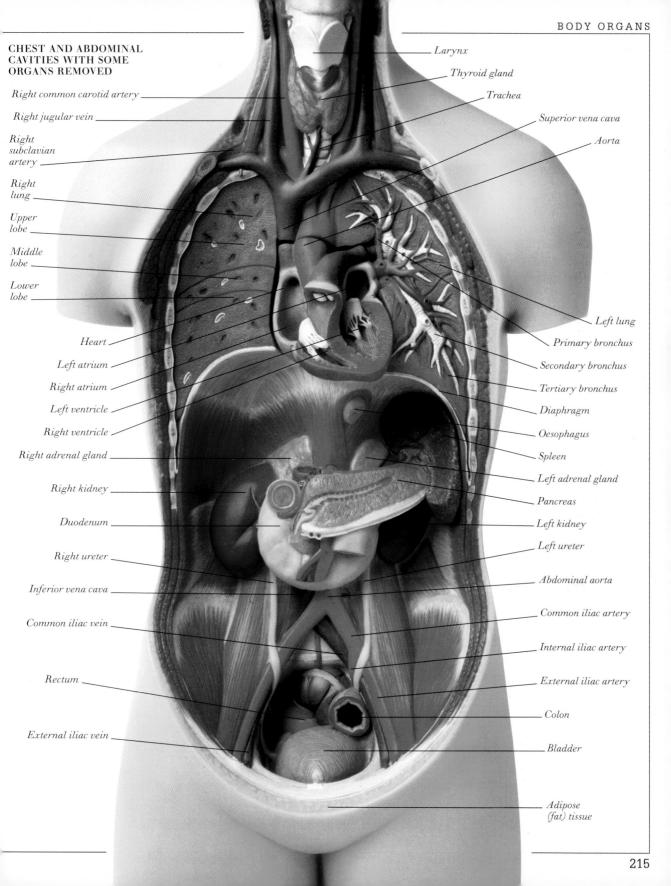

CHEST AND ABDOMINAL CAVITIES WITH SOME ORGANS REMOVED

Right common carotid artery

Right jugular vein

Right subclavian artery

Right lung

Upper lobe

Middle lobe

Lower lobe

Heart

Left atrium

Right atrium

Left ventricle

Right ventricle

Right adrenal gland

Right kidney

Duodenum

Right ureter

Inferior vena cava

Common iliac vein

Rectum

External iliac vein

Larynx

Thyroid gland

Trachea

Superior vena cava

Aorta

Left lung

Primary bronchus

Secondary bronchus

Tertiary bronchus

Diaphragm

Oesophagus

Spleen

Left adrenal gland

Pancreas

Left kidney

Left ureter

Abdominal aorta

Common iliac artery

Internal iliac artery

External iliac artery

Colon

Bladder

Adipose (fat) tissue

Body cells

EVERYONE IS MADE UP OF BILLIONS OF CELLS, which are the basic structural units
of the body. Bones, muscles, nerves, skin, blood, and all other body tissues are
formed from different types of cells. Each cell has a specific function but
works with other types of cells to perform the enormous number of tasks
needed to sustain life. Most body cells have a similar basic structure.
Each cell has an outer layer (called the cell membrane) and
contains a fluid material (cytoplasm). Within the cytoplasm are
many specialized structures (organelles). The most important
organelle is the nucleus, which contains
vital genetic material and acts
as the cell's control centre.

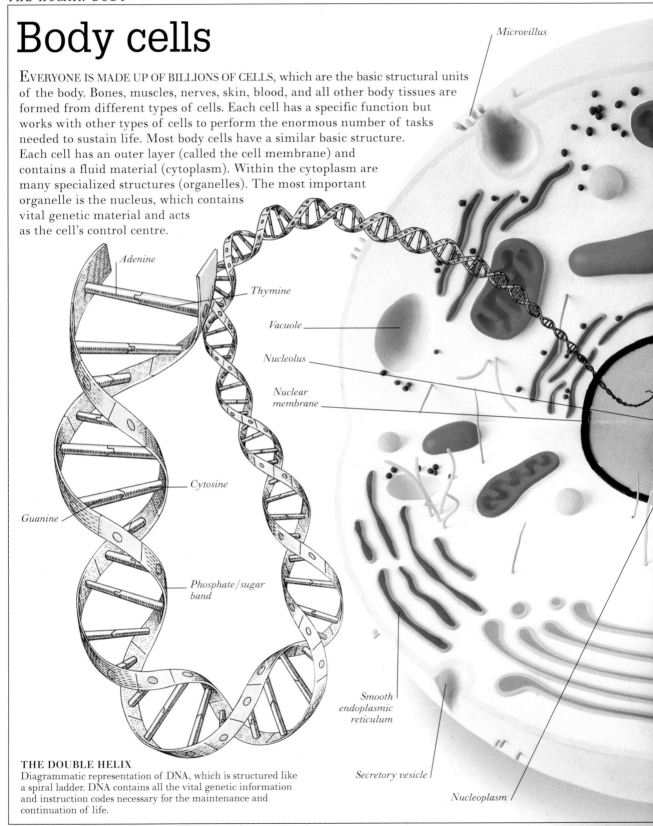

Microvillus

Adenine

Thymine

Vacuole

Nucleolus

*Nuclear
membrane*

Cytosine

Guanine

*Phosphate/sugar
band*

*Smooth
endoplasmic
reticulum*

Secretory vesicle

Nucleoplasm

THE DOUBLE HELIX
Diagrammatic representation of DNA, which is structured like
a spiral ladder. DNA contains all the vital genetic information
and instruction codes necessary for the maintenance and
continuation of life.

GENERALIZED HUMAN CELL

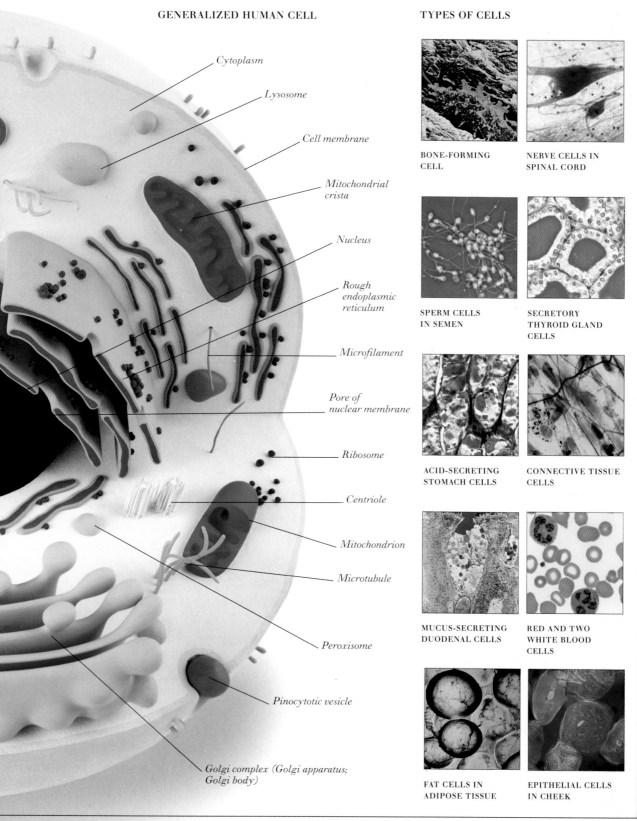

Cytoplasm

Lysosome

Cell membrane

Mitochondrial crista

Nucleus

Rough endoplasmic reticulum

Microfilament

Pore of nuclear membrane

Ribosome

Centriole

Mitochondrion

Microtubule

Peroxisome

Pinocytotic vesicle

Golgi complex (Golgi apparatus; Golgi body)

TYPES OF CELLS

BONE-FORMING CELL

NERVE CELLS IN SPINAL CORD

SPERM CELLS IN SEMEN

SECRETORY THYROID GLAND CELLS

ACID-SECRETING STOMACH CELLS

CONNECTIVE TISSUE CELLS

MUCUS-SECRETING DUODENAL CELLS

RED AND TWO WHITE BLOOD CELLS

FAT CELLS IN ADIPOSE TISSUE

EPITHELIAL CELLS IN CHEEK

Skeleton

THE SKELETON IS A MOBILE FRAMEWORK made up of 206 bones, approximately half of which are in the hands and feet. Although individual bones are rigid, the skeleton as a whole is remarkably flexible and allows the human body a huge range of movement. The skeleton serves as an anchorage for the skeletal muscles, and as a protective cage for the body's internal organs. Female bones are usually smaller and lighter than male bones, and the female pelvis is shallower and has a wider cavity.

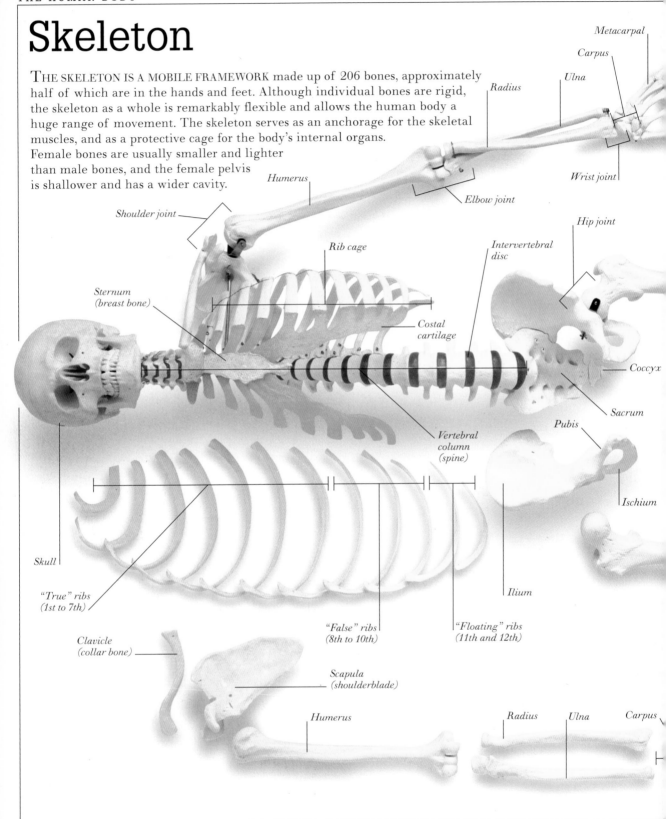

Metacarpal

Carpus

Ulna

Radius

Wrist joint

Humerus

Elbow joint

Shoulder joint

Hip joint

Rib cage

Intervertebral disc

Sternum (breast bone)

Costal cartilage

Coccyx

Sacrum

Pubis

Vertebral column (spine)

Ischium

Skull

Ilium

"True" ribs (1st to 7th)

"False" ribs (8th to 10th)

"Floating" ribs (11th and 12th)

Clavicle (collar bone)

Scapula (shoulderblade)

Humerus

Radius

Ulna

Carpus

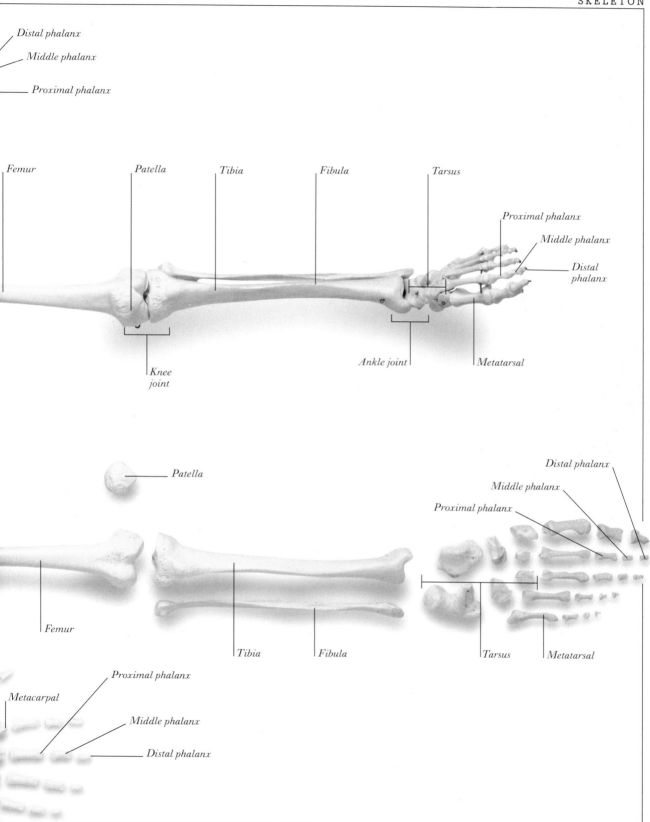

Distal phalanx

Middle phalanx

Proximal phalanx

Femur

Patella

Tibia

Fibula

Tarsus

Proximal phalanx

Middle phalanx

Distal phalanx

Knee joint

Ankle joint

Metatarsal

Patella

Distal phalanx

Middle phalanx

Proximal phalanx

Femur

Tibia

Fibula

Tarsus

Metatarsal

Metacarpal

Proximal phalanx

Middle phalanx

Distal phalanx

Skull

THE SKULL is the most complicated bony structure of the body but every feature serves a purpose. Internally, the main hollow chamber of the skull has three levels that support the brain, with every bump and hollow corresponding to the shape of the brain. Underneath and towards the back of the skull is a large round hole, the foramen magnum, through which the spinal cord passes. To the front of this are many smaller openings through which nerves, arteries, and veins pass to and from the brain. The roof of the skull is formed from four thin, curved bones that are firmly fixed together from the age of about two years. At the front of the skull are the two orbits, which contain the eyeballs, and a central hole for the airway of the nose. The jaw bone hinges on either side at ear level.

RIGHT SIDE VIEW OF A FETAL SKULL

Anterior fontanelle

Parietal bone

Coronal suture

Frontal bone

Nasal bone

Mental symphysis

Lambdoid suture

Occipital bone

Mastoid fontanelle

External auditory meatus

Sphenoidal fontanelle

RIGHT SIDE VIEW OF SKULL

Greater wing of sphenoid bone

Coronal suture

Frontal bone

Frontozygomatic suture

Parietal bone

Supraorbital margin

Squamous suture

Orbital cavity

Nasal bone

Anterior nasal spine

Maxilla (upper jaw)

Lambdoid suture

Mandible (lower jaw)

Occipital bone

Temporal bone

External auditory meatus

Mastoid process

Condyle

Coronoid process

Zygomatic bone

Mental foramen

VIEW OF SKULL FROM BELOW

External occipital crest

Foramen magnum

Occipital condyle

Carotid canal

Mastoid process

Pharyngeal tubercle

Styloid process

Zygomatic arch

Posterior border of vomer

Concha

Mandible (lower jaw)

Pterygoid plate

Pterygoid hamulus

Greater palatine foramen

Posterior nasal aperture

FRONT VIEW OF SKULL

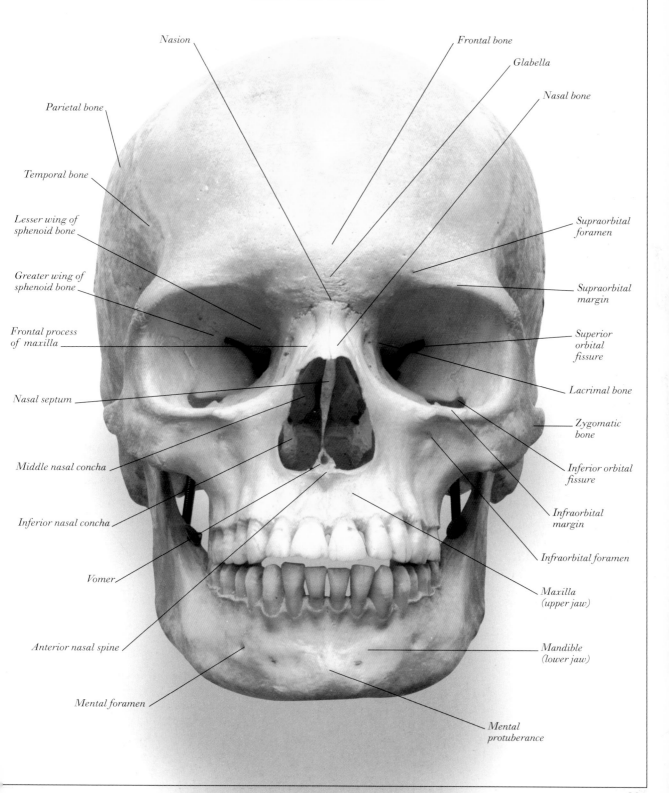

Nasion

Frontal bone

Glabella

Nasal bone

Parietal bone

Temporal bone

Lesser wing of
sphenoid bone

Greater wing of
sphenoid bone

Frontal process
of maxilla

Nasal septum

Middle nasal concha

Inferior nasal concha

Vomer

Anterior nasal spine

Mental foramen

Supraorbital
foramen

Supraorbital
margin

Superior
orbital
fissure

Lacrimal bone

Zygomatic
bone

Inferior orbital
fissure

Infraorbital
margin

Infraorbital foramen

Maxilla
(upper jaw)

Mandible
(lower jaw)

Mental
protuberance

Spine

THE SPINE (OR VERTEBRAL COLUMN) has two main functions: it serves as a protective surrounding for the delicate spinal cord and forms the supporting back bone of the skeleton. The spine consists of 24 separate differently shaped bones (vertebrae) with a curved, triangular bone (the sacrum) at the bottom. The sacrum is made up of fused vertebrae; at its lower end is a small tail-like structure made up of tiny bones collectively called the coccyx. Between each pair of vertebrae is a disc of cartilage that cushions the bones during movement. The top two vertebrae differ in appearance from the others and work as a pair: the first, called the atlas, rotates around a stout vertical peg on the second, the axis. This arrangement allows the skull to move freely up and down, and from side to side.

SPINE DIVIDED INTO VERTEBRAL SECTIONS

FRONT

Cervical vertebrae

Thoracic vertebrae

Lumbar vertebrae

Sacral vertebrae

Coccygeal vertebrae

TYPES OF VERTEBRAE (VIEWED FROM ABOVE)

ATLAS

Anterior arch

Anterior tubercle

Vertebral foramen

Transverse process

Lateral mass with superior articular facet

Posterior arch

Posterior tubercle

Transverse foramen

AXIS

Facet

Dens

Vertebral foramen

Spinous process

Lamina

Transverse process and foramen

CERVICAL VERTEBRA

Body

Anterior tubercle

Posterior tubercle

Superior articular process

Spinous process

Vertebral foramen

Transverse foramen

SKULL AND SPINE

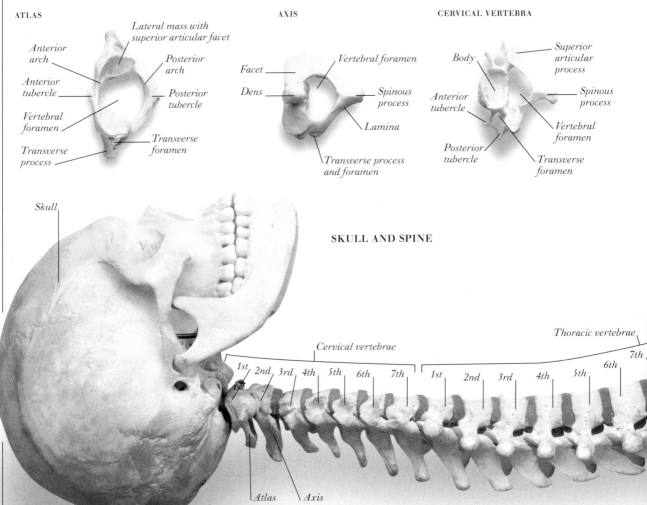

Skull

Cervical vertebrae

Thoracic vertebrae

1st 2nd 3rd 4th 5th 6th 7th

1st 2nd 3rd 4th 5th 6th 7th

Atlas

Axis

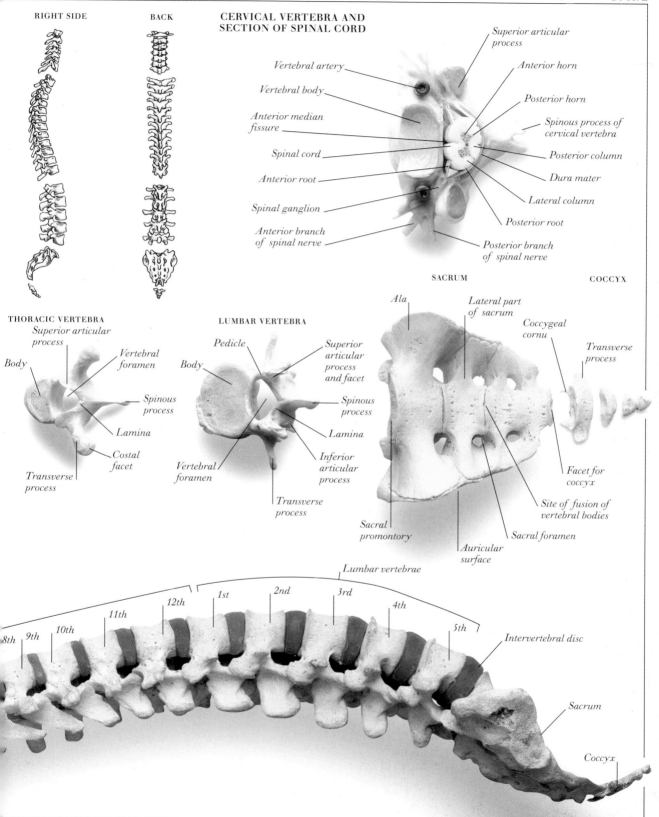

RIGHT SIDE

BACK

CERVICAL VERTEBRA AND SECTION OF SPINAL CORD

Superior articular process

Vertebral artery

Vertebral body

Anterior median fissure

Spinal cord

Anterior root

Spinal ganglion

Anterior branch of spinal nerve

Anterior horn

Posterior horn

Spinous process of cervical vertebra

Posterior column

Dura mater

Lateral column

Posterior root

Posterior branch of spinal nerve

SACRUM

COCCYX

THORACIC VERTEBRA

Superior articular process

Body

Vertebral foramen

Spinous process

Lamina

Costal facet

Transverse process

LUMBAR VERTEBRA

Pedicle

Body

Superior articular process and facet

Spinous process

Lamina

Inferior articular process

Vertebral foramen

Transverse process

Ala

Lateral part of sacrum

Sacral promontory

Auricular surface

Sacral foramen

Site of fusion of vertebral bodies

Facet for coccyx

Coccygeal cornu

Transverse process

Lumbar vertebrae

1st

2nd

3rd

4th

5th

8th

9th

10th

11th

12th

Intervertebral disc

Sacrum

Coccyx

Bones and joints

BONES FORM the body's hard, strong skeletal framework. Each bone has a hard, compact exterior surrounding a spongy, lighter interior. The long bones of the arms and legs, such as the femur (thigh bone), have a central cavity containing bone marrow. Bones are composed chiefly of calcium, phosphorus, and a fibrous substance known as collagen. Bones meet at joints, which are of several different types. For example, the hip is a ball-and-socket joint that allows the femur a wide range of movement, whereas finger joints are simple hinge joints that allow only bending and straightening. Joints are held in place by bands of tissue called ligaments. Movement of joints is facilitated by the smooth hyaline cartilage that covers the bone ends and by the synovial membrane that lines and lubricates the joint.

LIGAMENTS SURROUNDING HIP JOINT

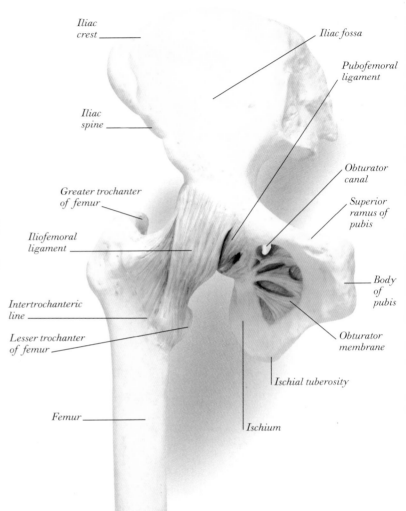

Iliac crest

Iliac fossa

Pubofemoral ligament

Iliac spine

Obturator canal

Superior ramus of pubis

Greater trochanter of femur

Iliofemoral ligament

Body of pubis

Intertrochanteric line

Obturator membrane

Lesser trochanter of femur

Ischial tuberosity

Femur

Ischium

SECTION THROUGH LEFT FEMUR

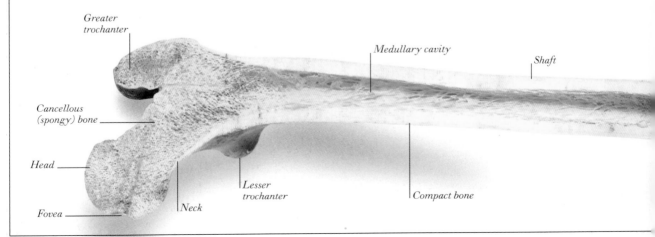

Greater trochanter

Medullary cavity

Shaft

Cancellous (spongy) bone

Head

Lesser trochanter

Compact bone

Fovea

Neck

SECTION THROUGH HIP JOINT

Psoas major muscle

Iliacus muscle

Iliac crest

External
iliac artery

Hyaline cartilage
of acetabulum

Hyaline cartilage
of head of femur

Ligament of
head of femur

Femoral
artery

Articular
cavity

Gluteus
minimus muscle

Gluteus
medius muscle

Acetabular
labrum

Head
of femur

Greater
trochanter
of femur

Neck of
femur

Vastus
lateralis
muscle

Shaft
of femur

Pectineus
muscle

Adductor
longus muscle

Iliacus
muscle

Vastus
medialis muscle

**SECTION OF
COMPACT BONE**

Parallel rows of concentric
bony layers make up this
strong material.

BONE MARROW SMEAR

Composed mainly of red and
white blood cells, marrow fills
the cavities of bones.

Lateral
epicondyle

Patellar
surface

Adductor tubercle

Medial
epicondyle

SECTION THROUGH LONG BONE

Osteon
(haversian system)

Osteocyte
(bone cell)

Intermediate
lamella

Endosteum

Haversian lamella

Outer lamella

Sharpey's
fibre

Periosteum

Haversian canal

Lacuna

Volkmann's vessel

Muscles 1

THERE ARE THREE MAIN TYPES OF MUSCLE: skeletal muscle (also called voluntary muscle because it can be consciously controlled); smooth muscle (also called involuntary muscle because it is not under voluntary control); and the specialized muscle tissue of the heart. Humans have more than 600 skeletal muscles, which differ in size and shape according to the jobs they do. Skeletal muscles are attached either directly or indirectly (via tendons) to bones, and work in opposing pairs (one muscle in the pair contracts while the other relaxes) to produce body movements as diverse as walking, threading a needle, and an array of facial expressions. Smooth muscles occur in the walls of internal body organs and perform actions such as forcing food through the intestines, contracting the uterus (womb) in childbirth, and pumping blood through the blood vessels.

SOME OTHER MUSCLES IN THE BODY

Iris

Pupil

IRIS
The muscle fibres contract and dilate (expand) to alter pupil size.

TONGUE
Interlacing layers of muscle allow great mobility.

ILEUM
Opposing muscle layers transport semi-digested food.

SUPERFICIAL SKELETAL MUSCLES

FRONT VIEW

Brachioradialis

Flexors of forearm

Brachialis

Frontalis

Orbicularis oculi

Temporalis

Sternocleidomastoid

Trapezius

Pectoralis major

Deltoid

Serratus anterior

Biceps brachii

Rectus abdominis

Linea alba

External oblique

Tensor fasciae latae

Iliopsoas

Pectineus

Vastus lateralis

Gracilis

Adductor longus

Rectus femoris

Sartorius

Vastus medialis

Gastrocnemius

Tibialis anterior

BACK VIEW

Extensors
of hand

Flexors
of hand

Temporalis

Sternocleidomastoid

Trapezius

Deltoid

Triceps
brachii

Teres minor

Teres major

Infraspinatus

Rhomboideus major

Latissimus dorsi

Gluteus
maximus

Adductor
magnus

Gracilis

Biceps femoris

Semitendinosus

Gastrocnemius

Soleus

Peroneus
brevis

MOVEMENT OF THE FOREARM
Controlled movement of the limbs relies
on coordinated relaxation and contraction
of opposing muscles. To raise the forearm,
the biceps (two-rooted muscle) contracts
and shortens while the triceps (three-
rooted muscle) relaxes; the reverse
occurs when the forearm is lowered.

Triceps in
resting phase

Biceps in
resting phase

Forearm
at rest

Triceps
relaxes

Biceps
contracts

Forearm
half raised

Triceps fully
relaxed

Biceps fully
contracted

Forearm
fully raised

Triceps
contracts

Biceps
relaxes

Forearm
half lowered

Triceps back in
resting phase

Biceps back in
resting phase

Forearm
back at rest

Muscles 2

SKELETAL MUSCLE FIBRE

Myofibril

Sarcomere

*Motor
end plate*

Nucleus

*Synaptic
knob*

*Sarcoplasmic
reticulum*

Sarcolemma

*Schwann
cell*

Endomysium

*Motor
neuron*

*Node of
Ranvier*

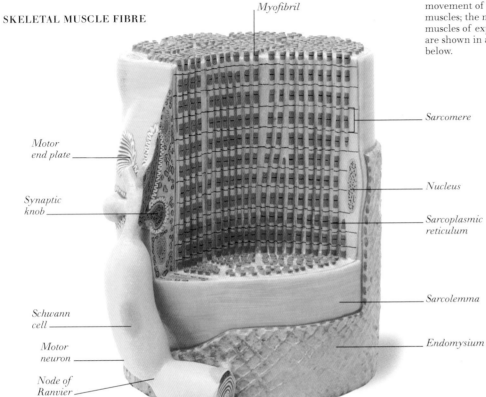

MUSCLES OF FACIAL EXPRESSION

A single expression is the result of movement of many muscles; the main muscles of expression are shown in action below.

FRONTALIS

CORRUGATOR SUPERCILII

ORBICULARIS ORIS

ZYGOMATICUS MAJOR

DEPRESSOR ANGULI ORIS

TYPES OF MUSCLE

CARDIAC MUSCLE

SKELETAL MUSCLE

SMOOTH MUSCLE

CONTRACTION OF SKELETAL MUSCLE

RELAXED STATE

CONTRACTED STATE

**MUSCLES OF
HEAD AND NECK**

Frontalis

Procerus

Temporalis

Corrugator
supercilii

Orbicularis
oculi

Levator labii
superioris

Zygomaticus
major

Nasalis

Orbicularis oris

Buccinator

Masseter

Risorius

Levator anguli oris

Platysma

Depressor labii
inferioris

Mentalis

Depressor anguli oris

Thyrohyoid

Scalenus medius

Sternocleidomastoid

Sternohyoid

Omohyoid

Cricothyroid

Trapezius

Hands

THE HUMAN HAND is an extremely versatile tool, capable of delicate manipulation as well as powerful gripping actions. The arrangement of its 27 small bones, moved by 37 skeletal muscles that are connected to the bones by tendons, allows a wide range of movements. Our ability to bring the tips of our thumbs and fingers together, combined with the extraordinary sensitivity of our fingertips due to their rich supply of nerve endings, makes our hands uniquely dextrous.

X-RAY OF LEFT HAND OF A YOUNG CHILD

Area of ossification in phalanx

Area of ossification in metacarpal

Area of ossification in wrist

Epiphysis of ulna

Epiphysis of radius

Areas of cartilage in the wrist and at the ends of the finger bones are the sites of growth and have still to ossify.

BONES OF HAND

Ring finger

Middle finger

Index finger

Little finger

Distal phalanx

Middle phalanx

Proximal phalanx

2nd metacarpal

3rd metacarpal

4th metacarpal

5th metacarpal

Hamate

Pisiform

Capitate

Triquetral

Lunate

Ulna

Head

Shaft

Base

Distal phalanx of thumb

Proximal phalanx of thumb

1st metacarpal

Trapezium

Trapezoid

Scaphoid

Radius

STRUCTURES UNDERLYING SKIN OF PALM OF HAND

Flexor pollicis brevis muscle

Opponens pollicis muscle

Abductor pollicis brevis muscle

Flexor retinaculum

Radial artery

Adductor pollicis muscle

2nd lumbrical muscle

Digital artery

Digital nerve

Flexor digitorum tendon

Opponens digiti minimi muscle

Abductor digiti minimi muscle

Ulnar nerve

Ulnar artery

Palmaris longus tendon

EXTERNAL FEATURES OF BACK OF HAND

Little finger

Distal interphalangeal joint

Proximal interphalangeal joint

Extensor digitorum tendon

Head of ulna

Ring finger

Middle finger

Cuticle

Lunule

Index finger

Nail

Metacarpophalangeal joint

Wrist

Distal end of radius

Thumb

Feet

THE FEET AND TOES are essential elements
in body movement. They bear and propel the
weight of the body during walking and
running, and also help to maintain balance
during changes of body position. Each foot
has 26 bones, more than 100 ligaments,
and 33 muscles, some of which are
attached to the lower leg. The heel
pad and the arch of the foot act
as shock absorbers, providing
a cushion against the jolts that
occur with every step.

LIGAMENTS OF FOOT

2nd toe

*Hallux
(big toe)*

3rd toe

*Distal
phalanx of
hallux*

4th toe

*5th
(little) toe*

*Distal
phalanx*

*Proximal
phalanx of
hallux*

*Middle
phalanx*

*Proximal
phalanx*

*1st
metatarsal*

*2nd
metatarsal*

*3rd
metatarsal*

*1st
cuneiform*

*4th
metatarsal*

*2nd
cuneiform*

*5th
metatarsal*

*3rd
cuneiform*

Navicular

Cuboid

Talus

Calcaneus

*Posterior
cuneonavicular
ligament*

*Articular
capsule of
interphalangeal
joint*

*Plantar
calcaneonavicular
ligament*

*Articular capsule of
metatarsophalangeal
joint*

*Posterior
tarsometatarsal
ligament*

*Talonavicular
ligament*

*Bifurcate
ligament*

*Deltoid
ligament*

Fibula

Tibia

*Calcanean
(Achilles)
tendon*

*Interosseous
ligament*

STRUCTURES UNDERLYING SKIN OF FOOT

Extensor hallucis
longus tendon

1st dorsal
interosseous muscle

Medial
malleolus

Flexor hallucis
longus muscle

Calcanean
(Achilles)
tendon

Flexor digitorum
longus muscle

Soleus
muscle

Inferior extensor
retinaculum

Tibialis
anterior muscle

Tibia

Extensor
digitorum
longus tendon

Abductor digiti
minimi muscle

Lateral
malleolus

Tibialis
posterior muscle

Fibula

Peroneus
brevis muscle

Extensor hallucis
brevis muscle

Extensor digitorum
brevis muscle

Peroneus brevis tendon

Peroneus
longus muscle

EXTERNAL FEATURES OF FOOT

Toenail

Hallux
(big toe)

Interphalangeal
joint

Extensor hallucis
longus tendon

Extensor digitorum
longus tendon

Medial malleolus

2nd toe

3rd toe

4th toe

5th
(little) toe

Lateral malleolus

233

Skin and hair

SKIN IS THE BODY'S LARGEST ORGAN, a waterproof barrier that protects the internal organs against infection, injury, and harmful sun rays. The skin is also an important sensory organ and helps to control body temperature. The outer layer of the skin, known as the epidermis, is coated with keratin, a tough, horny protein that is also the chief constituent of hair and nails. Dead cells are shed from the skin's surface and are replaced by new cells from the base of the epidermis, the region that also produces the skin pigment, melanin. The dermis contains most of the skin's living structures, and includes nerve endings, blood vessels, elastic fibres, sweat glands that cool the skin, and sebaceous glands that produce oil to keep the skin supple. Beneath the dermis lies the subcutaneous tissue (hypodermis), which is rich in fat and blood vessels. Hair shafts grow from hair follicles situated in the dermis and subcutaneous tissue. Hair grows on every part of the skin apart from the palms of the hands and soles of the feet.

SECTION OF HAIR

Medulla

Cortex

Melanin granule

Cell nucleus residue

Macrofibril

Cuticle

SECTIONS OF DIFFERENT TYPES OF SKIN

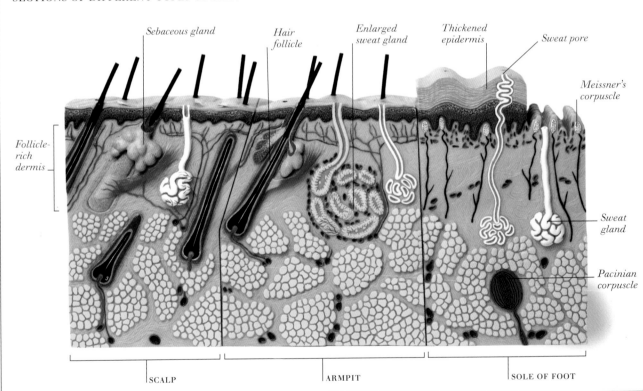

Sebaceous gland

Hair follicle

Enlarged sweat gland

Thickened epidermis

Sweat pore

Meissner's corpuscle

Follicle-rich dermis

Sweat gland

Pacinian corpuscle

SCALP

ARMPIT

SOLE OF FOOT

SECTION OF SKIN

Stratum granulosum

Stratum spinosum

Stratum corneum

Sweat pore

Hair shaft

Sweat duct

Stratum basale

Merkel's disc

Dermal papilla

Epidermis

Free nerve ending

Meissner's corpuscle

Vascular plexus

Dermis

Nerve fibre

Sebaceous gland

Arrector pili muscle

Hair bulb

Papilla

Hypodermis

Pacinian corpuscle

Adipose (fat) tissue

Ruffini corpuscle

Artery

Vein

Sweat gland

Hair follicle

PHOTOMICROGRAPHS OF SKIN AND HAIR

SECTION OF SKIN
The flaky cells at the skin's surface are shed continuously.

SWEAT PORE
This allows loss of fluid as part of temperature control.

SKIN HAIR
Two hairs pushing through the outer layer of skin.

HEAD HAIR
The root and part of the shaft of a hair from the scalp.

Brain

THE BRAIN IS THE MAJOR ORGAN of the central nervous
system and the control centre for all the body's voluntary
and involuntary activities. It is also responsible for the
complexities of thought, memory, emotion, and language.
In adults, this complex organ is a mere 1.4 kg (3 lb) in weight,
containing over 10 thousand million nerve cells. Three distinct
regions can easily be seen – the brainstem, the cerebellum,
and the large cerebrum. The brainstem controls vital body
functions, such as breathing and digestion. The cerebellum's
main functions are the maintenance of posture and the
coordination of body movements. The cerebrum, which
consists of the right and left cerebral hemispheres joined
by the corpus callosum, is the site of most conscious and
intelligent activities.

**MRI SCAN OF TRANSVERSE
SECTION THROUGH BRAIN**

*White
matter*

Skull

Scalp

*Grey
matter*

*Lateral
ventricle*

*Longitudinal
fissure*

*Coronal
section*

*Sagittal
section*

**SAGITTAL SECTION
THROUGH BRAIN**

Central sulcus

Fornix

Cerebrum

Parietal lobe

*Corpus
callosum*

*Parieto-occipital
sulucs*

Thalamus

*Pineal
body*

*Occipital
lobe*

*Frontal
lobe*

Aqueduct

Hypothalamus

Cerebellum

*Optic
chiasma*

4th ventricle

Pituitary gland

*Mesencephalon
(midbrain)*

Pons

Brainstem

Spinal cord

*Medulla
oblongata*

SECTION THROUGH SKULL AND BRAIN

Scalp

Epicranial aponeurosis

Arachnoid granulation

Pericranium

Skull

Lateral lacuna

Dura mater

Arachnoid mater

Superior sagittal sinus

Pia mater

Falx cerebri

Subarachnoid space

Cerebrum — Grey matter, White matter

Cerebral vessel

EXTERNAL ANATOMY OF BRAIN

Parietal lobe

Parieto-occipital sulcus

Precentral gyrus

Postcentral gyrus

Central sulcus

Frontal lobe

Lateral sulcus

Temporal lobe

Occipital lobe

Cerebellum

SPECIFIC ROLES OF AREAS OF CEREBRUM

Skilled movements

Basic movements

Sensation

Visual recognition

Behaviour and emotion

Speech

Hearing

Vision

Balance and muscle coordination

CORONAL SECTION THROUGH BRAIN

Corpus callosum

Longitudinal fissure

Grey matter, White matter — Cerebrum

Caudate nucleus

Lateral ventricle

Fornix

Lentiform nucleus

Internal capsule

Thalamus

Crus cerebri of midbrain

3rd ventricle

Pons

Medulla oblongata

Cerebellum

NERVE CELLS IN BRAIN

The dark cells are Purkinje's cells, which are among the largest nerve cells in the body.

237

Nervous system

THE NERVOUS SYSTEM IS THE BODY'S internal, electrochemical, communications network. Its main parts are the brain, spinal cord, and nerves. The brain and spinal cord form the central nervous system (CNS), the body's chief controlling and coordinating centres. Billions of long neurons, many grouped as nerves, make up the peripheral nervous system, transmitting nerve impulses between the CNS and other regions of the body. Each neuron has three parts: a cell body, branching dendrites that receive chemical signals from other neurons, and a tube-like axon that conveys these signals as electrical impulses.

CENTRAL AND PERIPHERAL NERVOUS SYSTEMS

Cranial nerves
Cerebrum
Cerebellum
Cervical nerves
Brachial plexus
Spinal cord
Thoracic nerves
Radial nerve
Median nerve
Ulnar nerve
Lumbar nerves
Sacral nerves
Sacral plexus
Femoral nerve
Pudendal nerve
Sciatic nerve
Cutaneous nerve
Common peroneal nerve
Posterior tibial nerve
Superficial peroneal nerve
Deep peroneal nerve

SECTION THROUGH SPINAL CORD

Spinal ganglion
Grey matter
Central canal
Posterior root of spinal nerve
Spinal nerve
White matter
Anterior median fissure
Anterior root of spinal nerve

STRUCTURE OF A MOTOR NEURON

Cell body

Nucleus

Synaptic knob

Axon hillock

Axon

Dendrite

Nucleolus

Nissl body

Schwann cell

Node of Ranvier

Mitochondrion

Myelin sheath

TYPES OF NERVE ENDING

FREE NERVE ENDING

MEISSNER'S CORPUSCLE

MERKEL'S DISC

RUFFINI CORPUSCLE

PACINIAN CORPUSCLE

STRUCTURE OF A SYNAPTIC KNOB

Presynaptic axon

Microtubule

Neurofilament

Endoplasmic reticulum

Mitochondrion

Synaptic vesicle

Neurotransmitter

Presynaptic membrane

Myelin sheath

Axon

Cell body

Nucleus

Dendrite

TYPES OF NEURON

MULTIPOLAR

Motor end plate

Node of Ranvier

Schwann cell

UNIPOLAR

Dendrite

Axon

Cell body

Nucleus

Receptor

BIPOLAR

Dendrite

Axon

Cell body

Nucleus

Dendrite

Eye

THE EYE IS THE ORGAN OF SIGHT. The two eyeballs, protected
within bony sockets called orbits and on the outside by the
eyelids, eyebrows, and tear film, are directly connected
to the brain by the optic nerves. Each eye is moved by
six muscles, which are attached around the eyeball.
Light rays entering the eye through the pupil
are focused by the cornea and lens to form
an image on the retina. The retina contains
millions of light-sensitive cells, called
rods and cones, which convert the image
into a pattern of nerve impulses. These
impulses are transmitted along the optic
nerve to the brain. Information from
the two optic nerves is processed
in the brain to produce a
single coordinated image.

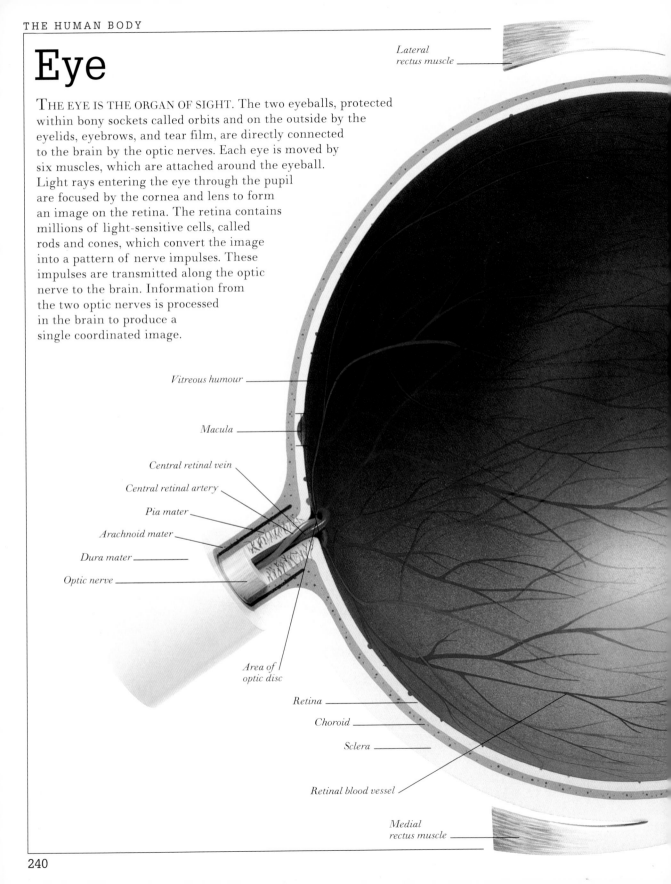

Lateral
rectus muscle

Vitreous humour

Macula

Central retinal vein

Central retinal artery

Pia mater

Arachnoid mater

Dura mater

Optic nerve

Area of
optic disc

Retina

Choroid

Sclera

Retinal blood vessel

Medial
rectus muscle

SECTION THROUGH LEFT EYE

LACRIMAL (TEAR-PRODUCING) APPARATUS

Lacrimal sac

Lacrimal canaliculus

Lacrimal gland

Middle meatus

Middle nasal concha

Nasal septum

Inferior nasal concha

Nasolacrimal duct

Lacrimal punctum

Iris

Anterior chamber

Posterior chamber

Aqueous humour

Conjunctiva

Pupil

Cornea

Lens

Sphincter muscle

Dilator muscle

Zonular ligament

Sinus venosus sclerae

Iridocorneal angle

Ciliary body

Ora serrata

OPHTHALMOSCOPIC VIEW OF RETINA

Retinal blood vessel

Macula

Optic disc

The blind spot, where the optic nerve leaves the eye, can be clearly seen as a light circular area towards the centre of the image.

MUSCLES SURROUNDING RIGHT EYE

Medial rectus

Superior oblique

Levator palpebrae superioris

Trochlea

Superior rectus

Annular tendon

Inferior rectus

Lateral rectus

Inferior oblique

Ear

THE EAR IS THE ORGAN OF HEARING AND BALANCE. The outer ear consists of a flap called the auricle or pinna and the auditory canal. The main functional parts – the middle and inner ears – are enclosed within the skull. The middle ear consists of three tiny bones, known as auditory ossicles, and the eustachian tube, which links the ear to the back of the nose. The inner ear consists of the spiral-shaped cochlea, and also the semicircular canals and the vestibule, which are the organs of balance. Sound waves entering the ear travel through the auditory canal to the tympanic membrane (eardrum), where they are converted to vibrations that are transmitted via the ossicles to the cochlea. Here, the vibrations are converted by millions of microscopic hairs into electrical nerve signals to be interpreted by the brain.

RIGHT AURICLE (PINNA)

Scaphoid fossa

Upper crux of antihelix

Triangular fossa

Auricle (pinna)

Lower crux of antihelix

Concha

Helix

Auditory canal

Antihelix

Antitragus

Tragus

Intertragic notch

External auditory meatus

Cartilaginous part of meatus

Lobule

Temporal bone

Cartilage of auricle

Mastoid process

Lobule

OSSICLES OF MIDDLE EAR

MALLEUS (HAMMER)   INCUS (ANVIL)   STAPES (STIRRUP)

These three tiny bones connect to form a bridge between the tympanic membrane and the oval window. With a system of membranes they convey sound vibrations to the inner ear.

INTERNAL STRUCTURE OF AMPULLA

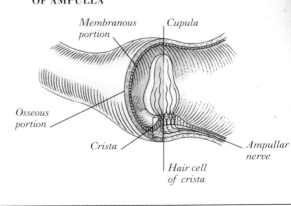

Membranous portion

Cupula

Osseous portion

Crista

Hair cell of crista

Ampullar nerve

LABYRINTH

Utricle

Saccule

Vestibular nerve

Common crus

Tympanic canal

Anterior semicircular canal

Median canal

Vestibular canal

Lateral semicircular canal

Ampulla

Cochlea

Osseous (bony) part of meatus

Tympanic membrane (eardrum)

Semicircular canal

Vestibulocochlear nerve

Cochlea

Tensor tympani muscle

Cochlear nerve

Oval window

Posterior semicircular canal

Internal carotid artery

SECTION THROUGH COCHLEA

Organ of Corti

Median canal

Vestibular canal

Vestibular membrane

Spiral ganglion

Eustachian tube

Cochlear nerve

Hair cells

Styloid process

Tympanic canal

Basilar membrane

243

Nose, mouth, and throat

WITH EVERY BREATH, air passes through the nasal cavity down the pharynx (throat), larynx ("voice box"), and trachea (windpipe) to the lungs. The nasal cavity warms and moistens air, and the tiny layers in its lining protect the airway against damage by foreign bodies. During swallowing, the tongue moves up and back, the larynx rises, the epiglottis closes off the entrance to the trachea, and the soft palate separates the nasal cavity from the pharynx. Saliva, secreted from three pairs of salivary glands, lubricates food to make swallowing easier; it also begins the chemical breakdown of food, and helps to produce taste. The senses of taste and smell are closely linked. Both depend on the detection of dissolved molecules by sensory receptors in the olfactory nerve endings of the nose and in the taste buds of the tongue.

STRUCTURE OF TONGUE

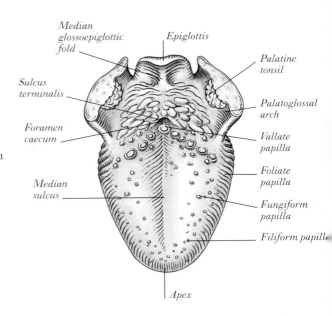

- Median glossoepiglottic fold
- Epiglottis
- Palatine tonsil
- Sulcus terminalis
- Palatoglossal arch
- Foramen caecum
- Vallate papilla
- Foliate papilla
- Median sulcus
- Fungiform papilla
- Filiform papilla
- Apex

STRUCTURES SURROUNDING PHARYNX

- Lingual nerve
- Tongue
- Styloglossus muscle
- Hyoglossus muscle
- Sublingual gland
- Hypoglossal nerve
- Mandible (lower jaw)
- Superior laryngeal nerve
- Submandibular gland
- Superior thyroid artery
- Hyoid bone
- Laryngeal prominence (Adam's apple)
- Thyrohyoid muscle
- Thyrohyoid membrane
- Cricothyroid muscle
- Cricothyroid ligament
- Thyroid gland
- Trachea

TASTE AREAS ON TONGUE

- Bitter
- Sour
- Salt
- Sweet

TYPES OF PAPILLAE

FILIFORM PAPILLAE   FUNGIFORM PAPILLAE   VALLATE PAPILLAE

SECTION THROUGH NOSE, MOUTH, AND THROAT

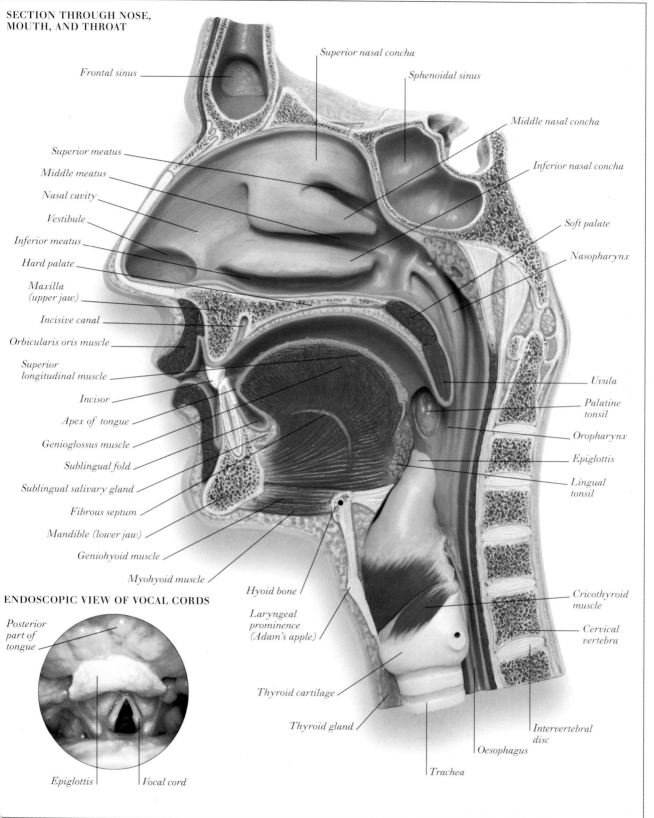

Frontal sinus

Superior nasal concha

Sphenoidal sinus

Middle nasal concha

Inferior nasal concha

Superior meatus

Middle meatus

Nasal cavity

Vestibule

Inferior meatus

Hard palate

Soft palate

Nasopharynx

Maxilla (upper jaw)

Incisive canal

Orbicularis oris muscle

Superior longitudinal muscle

Incisor

Apex of tongue

Genioglossus muscle

Sublingual fold

Sublingual salivary gland

Fibrous septum

Mandible (lower jaw)

Geniohyoid muscle

Myohyoid muscle

Uvula

Palatine tonsil

Oropharynx

Epiglottis

Lingual tonsil

Cricothyroid muscle

Cervical vertebra

Hyoid bone

Laryngeal prominence (Adam's apple)

Thyroid cartilage

Thyroid gland

Intervertebral disc

Oesophagus

Trachea

ENDOSCOPIC VIEW OF VOCAL CORDS

Posterior part of tongue

Epiglottis

Vocal cord

Teeth

THE 20 PRIMARY TEETH (also called deciduous or milk teeth) usually begin to erupt when a baby is about six months old. They start to be replaced by the permanent teeth when the child is about six years old. By the age of 20, most adults have a full set of 32 teeth although the third molars (commonly called wisdom teeth) may never erupt. While teeth help people to speak clearly and give shape to the face, their main function is the chewing of food. Incisors and canines shear and tear the food into pieces; premolars and molars crush and grind it further. Although tooth enamel is the hardest substance in the body, it tends to be eroded and destroyed by acid produced in the mouth during the breakdown of food.

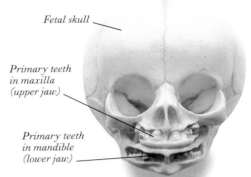

Fetal skull

Primary teeth in maxilla (upper jaw)

Primary teeth in mandible (lower jaw)

FETAL JAWS
By the sixth week of embryonic development areas of thickening occur in each jaw; these areas give rise to tooth buds. By the time the fetus is six months old, enamel has formed on the tooth buds.

DEVELOPMENT OF JAW AND TEETH

Maxilla (upper jaw)

Mandible (lower jaw)

A NEWBORN BABY'S JAWS
The primary teeth can be seen developing in the jaw bones; they begin to erupt around the age of six months.

A FIVE-YEAR-OLD CHILD'S TEETH
There is a full set of 20 erupted primary teeth; the permanent teeth can be seen developing in the upper and lower jaws.

A NINE-YEAR-OLD CHILD'S TEETH
Most of the teeth are primary teeth but the permanent incisors and first molars have now emerged.

AN ADULT'S TEETH
By the age of 20, the full set of 32 permanent teeth (including the wisdom teeth) should be in position.

THE PERMANENT TEETH

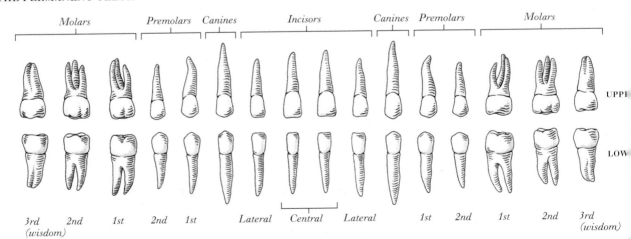

Molars — *Premolars* — *Canines* — *Incisors* — *Canines* — *Premolars* — *Molars*

UPPE

LOW

3rd (wisdom) — *2nd* — *1st* — *2nd* — *1st* — *Lateral* — *Central* — *Lateral* — *1st* — *2nd* — *1st* — *2nd* — *3rd (wisdom)*

STRUCTURE OF A TOOTH

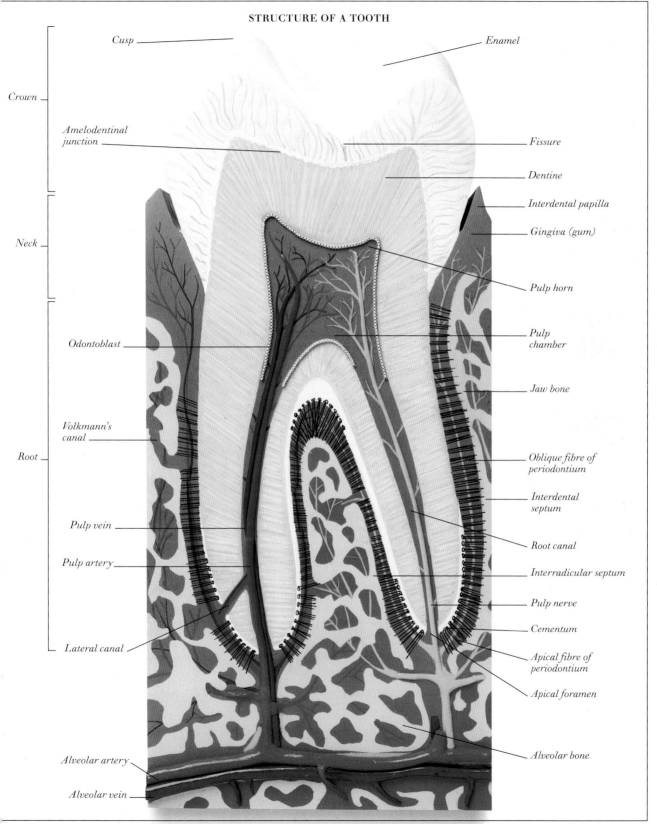

Cusp

Enamel

Crown

Amelodentinal
junction

Fissure

Dentine

Interdental papilla

Gingiva (gum)

Neck

Pulp horn

Odontoblast

Pulp
chamber

Jaw bone

Volkmann's
canal

Oblique fibre of
periodontium

Root

Interdental
septum

Pulp vein

Root canal

Pulp artery

Interradicular septum

Pulp nerve

Cementum

Lateral canal

Apical fibre of
periodontium

Apical foramen

Alveolar bone

Alveolar artery

Alveolar vein

Digestive system

THE DIGESTIVE SYSTEM BREAKS DOWN FOOD into particles so tiny that blood can take nourishment to all parts of the body. The system's main part is a 9 m (30 ft) tube from mouth to rectum; muscles in this alimentary canal force food along. Chewed food first travels through the oesophagus to the stomach, which churns and liquidizes food before it passes through the duodenum, jejunum, and ileum – the three parts of the long, convoluted small intestine. Here, digestive juices from the gallbladder and pancreas break down food particles; many filter out into the blood through tiny fingerlike villi that line the small intestine's inner wall. Undigested food in the colon forms faeces that leave the body through the anus.

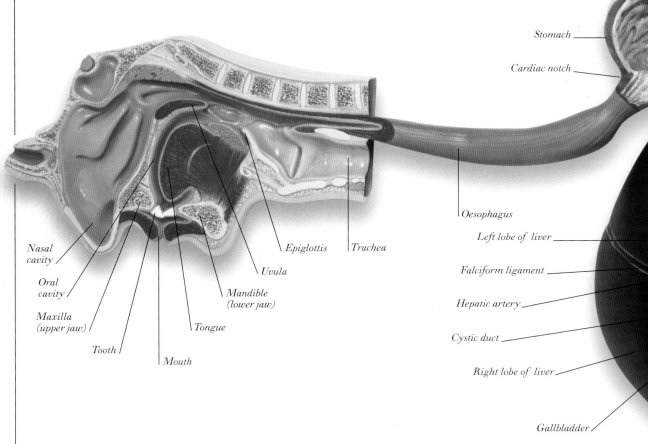

Stomach

Cardiac notch

Nasal cavity

Oral cavity

Maxilla (upper jaw)

Tooth

Mouth

Tongue

Mandible (lower jaw)

Uvula

Epiglottis

Trachea

Oesophagus

Left lobe of liver

Falciform ligament

Hepatic artery

Cystic duct

Right lobe of liver

Gallbladder

ENDOSCOPIC VIEWS INSIDE ALIMENTARY CANAL

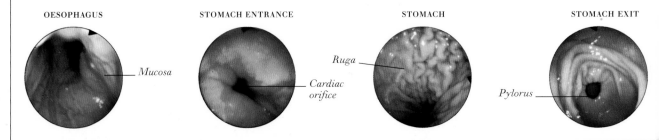

OESOPHAGUS

Mucosa

STOMACH ENTRANCE

Cardiac orifice

STOMACH

Ruga

STOMACH EXIT

Pylorus

ALIMENTARY CANAL

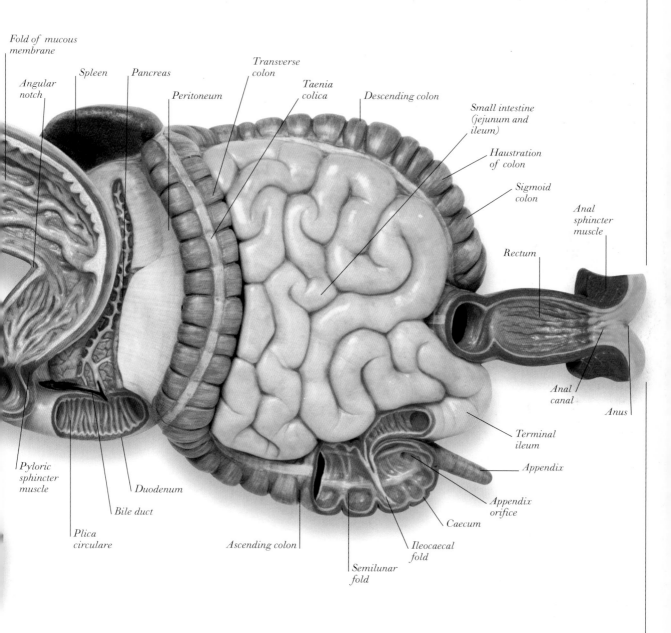

Fold of mucous membrane

Angular notch

Spleen

Pancreas

Peritoneum

Transverse colon

Taenia colica

Descending colon

Small intestine (jejunum and ileum)

Haustration of colon

Sigmoid colon

Anal sphincter muscle

Rectum

Anal canal

Anus

Terminal ileum

Appendix

Appendix orifice

Caecum

Ileocaecal fold

Semilunar fold

Ascending colon

Plica circulare

Bile duct

Duodenum

Pyloric sphincter muscle

DUODENUM

Plica circulare

ILEUM

Villi of mucosa

COLON

Semilunar fold

Blood vessel

RECTUM

Mucosa

Heart

THE HEART IS A HOLLOW MUSCLE in the middle of the chest that pumps blood around the body, supplying cells with oxygen and nutrients. A muscular wall, called the septum, divides the heart lengthways into left and right sides. A valve divides each side into two chambers: an upper atrium and a lower ventricle. When the heart muscle contracts, it squeezes blood through the atria and then through the ventricles. Oxygenated blood from the lungs flows from the pulmonary veins into the left atrium, through the left ventricle, and then out via the aorta to all parts of the body. Deoxygenated blood returning from the body flows from the vena cava into the right atrium, through the right ventricle, and then out via the pulmonary artery to the lungs for reoxygenation. At rest the heart beats between 60 and 80 times a minute; during exercise or at times of stress or excitement the rate may increase to 200 beats a minute.

ARTERIES AND VEINS SURROUNDING HEART

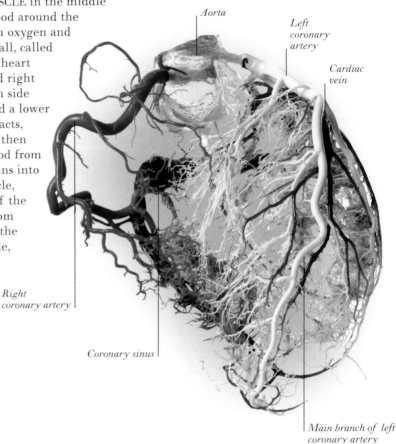

Aorta

Left coronary artery

Cardiac vein

Right coronary artery

Coronary sinus

Main branch of left coronary artery

SECTION THROUGH HEART WALL

Pericardial cavity

Trabecula

Endocardium

Myocardium

Epicardium (visceral pericardium)

Serous pericardium

Fibrous pericardium

HEARTBEAT SEQUENCE

ATRIAL DIASTOLE

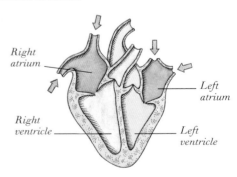

Right atrium

Left atrium

Right ventricle

Left ventricle

Deoxygenated blood enters the right atrium while the left atrium receives oxygenated blood.

STRUCTURE OF HEART

Brachiocephalic trunk

Left subclavian artery

Left common carotid artery

Superior vena cava

Ascending aorta

Left pulmonary vein

Right pulmonary artery

Pulmonary trunk

Fossa ovalis

Pulmonary semilunar valve

Coronary artery

Right pulmonary vein

Right atrium

Chordae tendineae

Opening of inferior vena cava

Muscular part of interventricular septum

Branch of coronary artery

Left ventricle

Papillary muscle

Tricuspid valve

Chordae tendineae

Myocardium of left ventricle

Right ventricle

Trabecula

ATRIAL SYSTOLE (VENTRICULAR DIASTOLE)

Right atrium contracts

Left atrium contracts

Tricuspid valve opens

Mitral valve opens

Right ventricle dilates

Left ventricle dilates

Left and right atria contract, forcing blood into the relaxed ventricles.

VENTRICULAR SYSTOLE

Pulmonary artery

Aorta

Pulmonary valve opens

Aortic valve opens

Tricuspid valve closes

Mitral valve closes

Right ventricle contracts

Left ventricle contracts

Ventricles contract and force blood to the lungs for oxygenation and via the aorta to the rest of the body.

Circulatory system

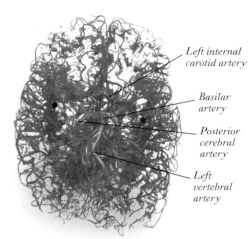

THE CIRCULATORY SYSTEM consists of the heart and
blood vessels, which together maintain a continuous
flow of blood around the body. The heart pumps
oxygen-rich blood from the lungs to all parts of the
body through a network of tubes called arteries, and
smaller branches called arterioles. Blood returns to the heart via
small vessels called venules, which lead in turn into larger tubes
called veins. Arterioles and venules are linked by a network of
tiny vessels called capillaries, where the exchange of oxygen
and carbon dioxide between blood and body cells takes place.
Blood has four main components: red blood cells, white
blood cells, platelets, and liquid plasma.

ARTERIAL SYSTEM OF BRAIN

Left internal
carotid artery

Basilar
artery

Posterior
cerebral
artery

Left
vertebral
artery

CIRCULATORY SYSTEM OF HEART AND LUNGS

Superior vena cava

Aorta

Right ventricle

Left ventricle

CIRCULATORY SYSTEM OF LIVER

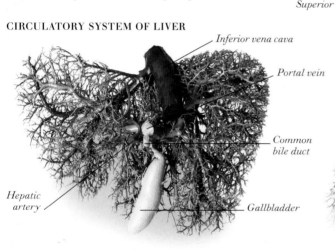

Inferior vena cava

Portal vein

Common
bile duct

Hepatic
artery

Gallbladder

SECTION OF MAIN ARTERY

Tunica
media

Collagen and elastic fibres

External elastic lamina

Tunica
adventitia

Internal
elastic lamina

Tunica intima

Endothelium

Arteriole

SECTION OF MAIN VEIN

Tunica media

Collagen and elastic fibres

External elastic lamina

Tunica
adventitia

Valve cusp

Internal
elastic lamina

Tunica intima

Endothelium

PRINCIPAL ARTERIES AND VEINS OF CIRCULATORY SYSTEM

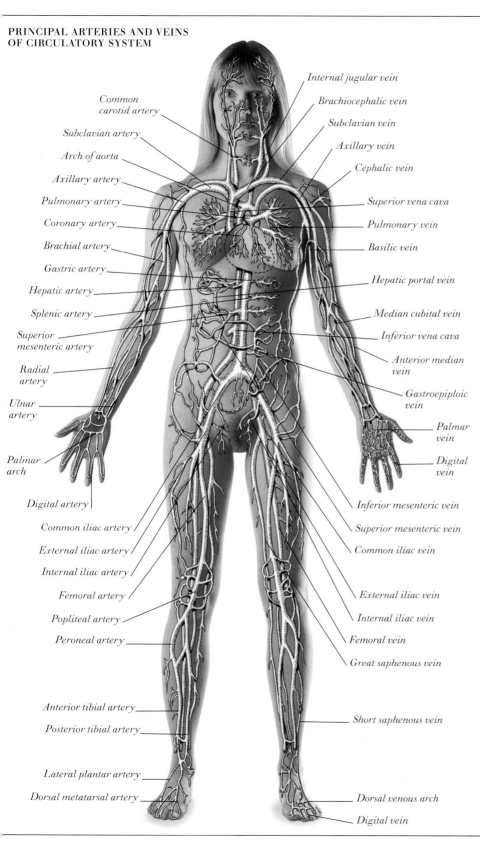

Common carotid artery
Subclavian artery
Arch of aorta
Axillary artery
Pulmonary artery
Coronary artery
Brachial artery
Gastric artery
Hepatic artery
Splenic artery
Superior mesenteric artery
Radial artery
Ulnar artery
Palmar arch
Digital artery
Common iliac artery
External iliac artery
Internal iliac artery
Femoral artery
Popliteal artery
Peroneal artery
Anterior tibial artery
Posterior tibial artery
Lateral plantar artery
Dorsal metatarsal artery

Internal jugular vein
Brachiocephalic vein
Subclavian vein
Axillary vein
Cephalic vein
Superior vena cava
Pulmonary vein
Basilic vein
Hepatic portal vein
Median cubital vein
Inferior vena cava
Anterior median vein
Gastroepiploic vein
Palmar vein
Digital vein
Inferior mesenteric vein
Superior mesenteric vein
Common iliac vein
External iliac vein
Internal iliac vein
Femoral vein
Great saphenous vein
Short saphenous vein
Dorsal venous arch
Digital vein

TYPES OF BLOOD CELLS

RED BLOOD CELLS
These cells are biconcave in shape to maximize their oxygen-carrying capacity.

WHITE BLOOD CELLS
Lymphocytes are the smallest white blood cells; they form antibodies against disease.

PLATELETS
Tiny cells that are activated whenever blood clotting or repair to vessels is necessary.

BLOOD CLOTTING

Filaments of fibrin enmesh red blood cells as part of the process of blood clotting.

Respiratory system

THE RESPIRATORY SYSTEM supplies the oxygen needed by body cells and carries off their carbon dioxide waste. Inhaled air passes via the trachea (windpipe) through two narrower tubes, the bronchi, to the lungs. Each lung comprises many fine, branching tubes called bronchioles that end in tiny clustered chambers called alveoli. Gases cross the thin alveolar walls to and from a network of tiny blood vessels. Intercostal (rib) muscles and the muscular diaphragm below the lungs operate the lungs like bellows, drawing air in and forcing it out at regular intervals.

BRONCHIOLE AND ALVEOLI

- Bronchial nerve
- Visceral cartilage
- Branch of pulmonary vein
- Mucosal gland
- Terminal bronchiole
- Bronchial vein
- Branch of pulmonary artery
- Elastic fibres
- Interalveolar septum
- Alveolus
- Connective tissue
- Capillary network
- Epithelium

SEGMENTS OF BRONCHIAL TREE

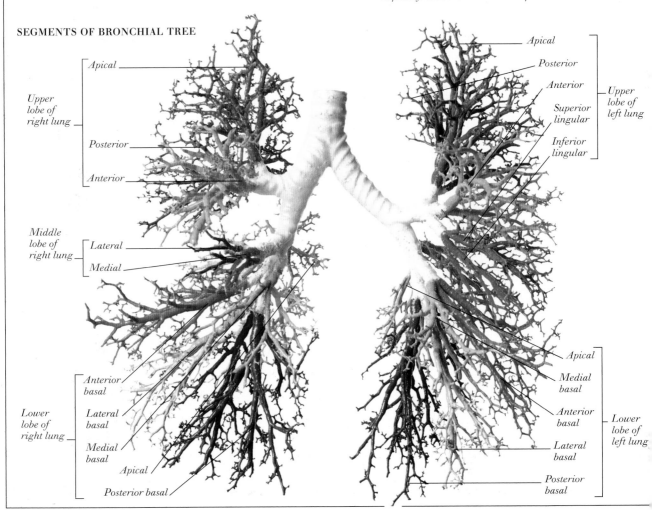

Upper lobe of right lung
- Apical
- Posterior
- Anterior

Middle lobe of right lung
- Lateral
- Medial

Lower lobe of right lung
- Anterior basal
- Lateral basal
- Medial basal
- Apical
- Posterior basal

Upper lobe of left lung
- Apical
- Posterior
- Anterior
- Superior lingular
- Inferior lingular

Lower lobe of left lung
- Apical
- Medial basal
- Anterior basal
- Lateral basal
- Posterior basal

STRUCTURES OF THORACIC CAVITY

GASEOUS EXCHANGE IN ALVEOLUS

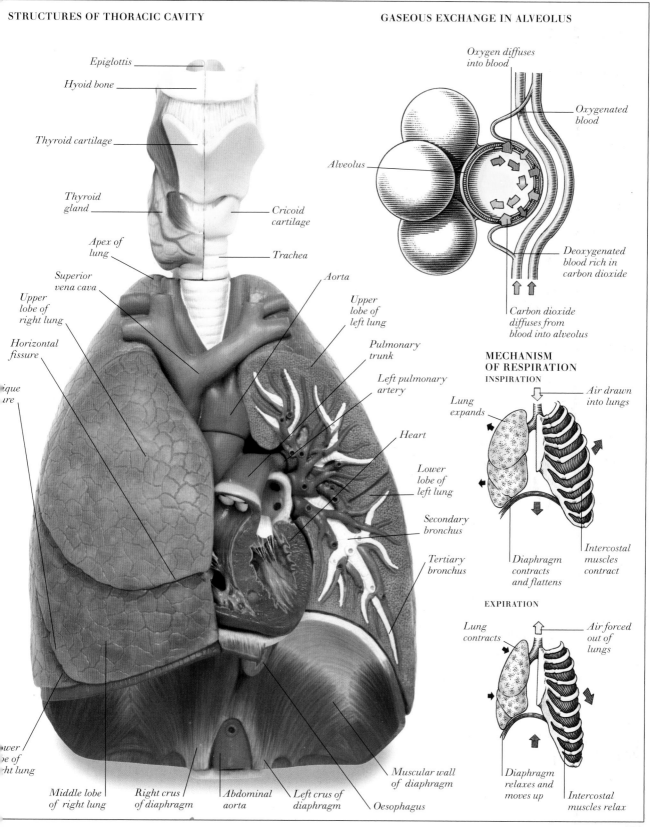

Epiglottis

Hyoid bone

Thyroid cartilage

Thyroid gland

Cricoid cartilage

Apex of lung

Trachea

Superior vena cava

Aorta

Upper lobe of right lung

Upper lobe of left lung

Horizontal fissure

Pulmonary trunk

...ique ...re

Left pulmonary artery

Heart

Lower lobe of left lung

Secondary bronchus

Tertiary bronchus

...wer ...e of ...ht lung

Middle lobe of right lung

Right crus of diaphragm

Abdominal aorta

Left crus of diaphragm

Oesophagus

Muscular wall of diaphragm

Oxygen diffuses into blood

Oxygenated blood

Alveolus

Deoxygenated blood rich in carbon dioxide

Carbon dioxide diffuses from blood into alveolus

MECHANISM OF RESPIRATION
INSPIRATION

Lung expands

Air drawn into lungs

Diaphragm contracts and flattens

Intercostal muscles contract

EXPIRATION

Lung contracts

Air forced out of lungs

Diaphragm relaxes and moves up

Intercostal muscles relax

255

Urinary system

THE URINARY SYSTEM FILTERS WASTE PRODUCTS from the blood and removes them from the body via a system of tubes. Blood is filtered in the two kidneys, which are fist-sized, bean-shaped organs. The renal arteries carry blood to the kidneys; the renal veins remove blood after filtering. Each kidney contains about one million tiny units called nephrons. Each nephron is made up of a tubule and a filtering unit called a glomerulus, which consists of a collection of tiny blood vessels surrounded by the hollow Bowman's capsule. The filtering process produces a watery fluid that leaves the kidney as urine. The urine is carried via two tubes called ureters to the bladder, where it is stored until its release from the body through another tube called the urethra.

ARTERIAL SYSTEM OF KIDNEYS

Aorta

Coeliac trunk

Superior mesenteric artery

Right renal artery

Left renal artery

Right ureter

Left ureter

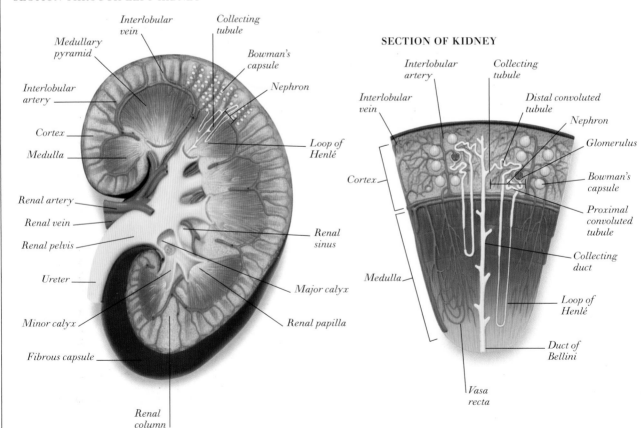

SECTION THROUGH LEFT KIDNEY

Interlobular vein

Collecting tubule

Medullary pyramid

Bowman's capsule

Interlobular artery

Nephron

Cortex

Medulla

Loop of Henlé

Renal artery

Renal vein

Renal pelvis

Renal sinus

Ureter

Major calyx

Minor calyx

Renal papilla

Fibrous capsule

Renal column

SECTION OF KIDNEY

Interlobular artery

Collecting tubule

Interlobular vein

Distal convoluted tubule

Nephron

Cortex

Glomerulus

Bowman's capsule

Proximal convoluted tubule

Medulla

Collecting duct

Loop of Henlé

Duct of Bellini

Vasa recta

MALE URINARY TRACT

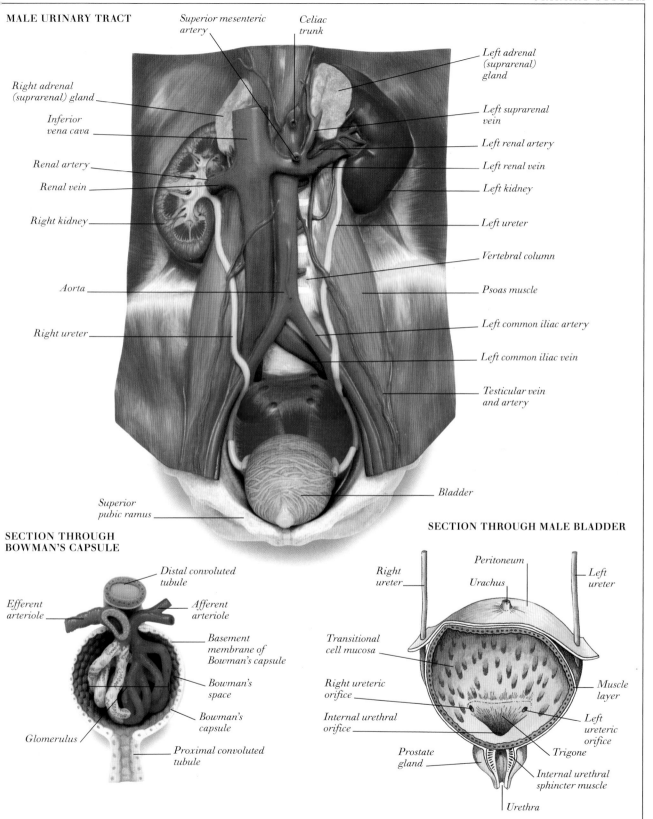

Superior mesenteric artery

Celiac trunk

Left adrenal (suprarenal) gland

Right adrenal (suprarenal) gland

Inferior vena cava

Left suprarenal vein

Left renal artery

Renal artery

Left renal vein

Renal vein

Left kidney

Right kidney

Left ureter

Vertebral column

Aorta

Psoas muscle

Left common iliac artery

Right ureter

Left common iliac vein

Testicular vein and artery

Bladder

Superior pubic ramus

SECTION THROUGH BOWMAN'S CAPSULE

Distal convoluted tubule

Efferent arteriole

Afferent arteriole

Basement membrane of Bowman's capsule

Bowman's space

Bowman's capsule

Glomerulus

Proximal convoluted tubule

SECTION THROUGH MALE BLADDER

Right ureter

Peritoneum

Urachus

Left ureter

Transitional cell mucosa

Right ureteric orifice

Muscle layer

Left ureteric orifice

Internal urethral orifice

Trigone

Prostate gland

Internal urethral sphincter muscle

Urethra

Reproductive system

SEX ORGANS LOCATED IN THE PELVIS create new human lives. Each month a ripe egg is released from one of the female's ovaries into a fallopian tube leading to the uterus (womb), a muscular pear-sized organ. A male produces minute tadpole-like sperm in two oval glands called testes. When the male is ready to release sperm into the female's vagina, many millions pass into his urethra and leave his body through the fleshy penis. The sperm travel up through the vagina into the uterus and fallopian tubes, and one sperm may enter and fertilize an egg. The fertilized egg becomes embedded in the uterus wall and starts to grow into a new human being.

SECTION THROUGH OVARY

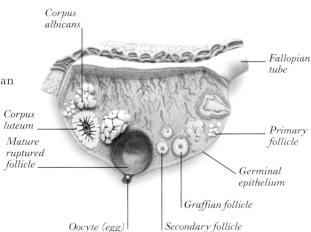

Corpus albicans

Fallopian tube

Corpus luteum

Mature ruptured follicle

Primary follicle

Germinal epithelium

Oocyte (egg)

Graffian follicle

Secondary follicle

SECTION THROUGH FEMALE PELVIC REGION

Ureter

Ampulla of fallopian tube

Fimbria of fallopian tube

Ovary

Isthmus of fallopian tube

Fundus of uterus

Uterus (womb)

Cervix (neck of uterus)

Bladder

Pubic symphysis

Os

Urethra

Rectum

Clitoris

Vagina

External urinary meatus

Anus

Perineum

Labia minora

Labia majora

Introitus (vaginal opening)

FEMALE REPRODUCTIVE ORGANS

Fallopian tube

Fundus of uterus

Isthmus of fallopian tube

Ampulla of fallopian tube

Ovarian ligament

Ovary

Body of uterus (womb)

Os

Vagina

Fimbria of fallopian tube

Cervix (neck of uterus)

MALE REPRODUCTIVE ORGANS

External spermatic fascia

Prostate gland

Ductus (vas) deferens

Seminal vesicle

Cremasteric fascia

Bulbourethral gland

Internal spermatic fascia

Urethra

Epididymis

Corpus spongiosum

Testis (testicle)

Corpus cavernosum

Scrotum

Prepuce (foreskin)

Glans penis

Urethral opening

SECTION THROUGH MALE PELVIC REGION

Intervertebral disc

Ureter

Colon

Sacrum

Seminal vesicle

Ejaculatory duct

Bladder

Pubis of pelvis

Prostate gland

Penis

Corpus cavernosum

Corpus spongiosum

Urethra

Epididymis

Glans penis

Testis (testicle)

Scrotum

EXTERNAL STRUCTURE OF SPERM

Acrosomal cap

Head

Mitochondrial sheath

Terminal ring

Tailpiece

Flagellum

Development of a baby

A FERTILIZED EGG IS NOURISHED AND PROTECTED as it develops into an embryo and then a fetus during the 40 weeks of pregnancy. The placenta, a mass of blood vessels implanted in the uterus lining, delivers nourishment and oxygen, and removes waste through the umbilical cord. Meanwhile, the fetus lies snugly in its amniotic sac, a bag of fluid that protects it against any sudden jolts. In the last weeks of the pregnancy, the rapidly growing fetus turns head-down: a baby ready to be born.

EMBRYO AT FIVE WEEKS

Rudimentary ear

Rudimentary eye

Rudimentary mouth

Heart bulge

Arm bud

Rudimentary liver

Tail bud

Leg bud

Rudimentary vertebra

Amniotic fluid

Umbilicus (navel)

Uterine wall

Fetus

SECTION THROUGH PLACENTA

Umbilical cord

Umbilical vein

Umbilical artery

Amnion

Fetal blood vessels

Chorionic plate

Chorion

Trophoblast

Chorionic villus

Pool of maternal blood

Septum

Decidual plate

Maternal blood vessel

Myometrium

SECTION THROUGH PELVIS IN NINTH MONTH OF PREGNANCY

THE DEVELOPING FETUS

Uterine wall

Placenta

Fallopian tube

SECOND MONTH
All the internal organs have developed by this stage.

Fetus

Intervertebral disc

Vertebra

Spinal cord

Umbilical cord

THIRD MONTH
The fetus is fully formed and now begins a period of rapid growth.

FIFTH MONTH
Although the fetus is here in breech (bottom down) position, it will probably turn by 180° before birth. By the fifth month the baby is moving actively and responds to sound.

Cervix

Bladder

Cervix

Rectum

Anus

Pubic bone

SEVENTH MONTH
The internal organs are maturing in preparation for life outside the uterus. The baby has grown to such a size that there is less room for movement within the uterus.

Vagina

Placenta

Urethra

GEOLOGY, GEOGRAPHY, AND METEOROLOGY

Earth's physical features

MOST OF THE EARTH'S SURFACE (about 70 per cent) is covered with water. The largest single body of water, the Pacific Ocean, alone covers about 30 per cent of the surface. Most of the land is distributed as seven continents; these are (from largest to smallest) Asia, Africa, North America, South America, Antarctica, Europe, and Australasia. The physical features of the land are remarkably varied. Among the most notable are mountain ranges, rivers, and deserts. The largest mountain ranges – the Himalayas in Asia and the Andes in South America – extend for thousands of kilometres. The Himalayas include the world's highest mountain, Mount Everest (8,848 metres). The longest rivers are the River Nile in Africa (6,695 kilometres) and the Amazon River in South America (6,437 kilometres). Deserts cover about 20 per cent of the total land area. The largest is the Sahara, which covers nearly a third of Africa. The Earth's surface features can be represented in various ways. Only a globe can correctly represent areas, shapes, sizes, and directions, because there is always distortion when a spherical surface – the Earth's, for example – is projected on to the flat surface of a map. Each map projection is therefore a compromise: it shows some features accurately but distorts others. Even satellite mapping does not produce completely accurate maps, although they can show physical features with great clarity.

EXAMPLES OF MAP PROJECTIONS

CYLINDRICAL PROJECTION

CYLINDRICAL-PROJECTION MAP

SATELLITE MAPPING OF THE EARTH

Satellite takes photographs of the Earth

Solar panel

Earth's rotation

Antenna

Earth

Polar orbit of satellite

Area of Earth's surface on each photograph

Composite picture of Earth created from thousands of separate images

180° 160° 120° 80°

Great Slave Lake

Great Bear Lake

Lake Superior

Greenland

Mackenzie-Peace River

Baffin Island

Bering Sea

NORTH AMERICA

Hudson Bay

Rocky Mountains

Sonoran Desert

Lake Huron

Lake Ontario

Lake Erie

Lake Michigan

Sierra Madre

Chihuahuan Desert

Appalachian Mountains

Gulf of Mexico

ATLANTIC OCEAN

Mississippi-Missouri River

Caribbean Sea

Guiana Highlands

Am River

PACIFIC OCEAN

Bra Hig

Andes

Atacama Desert

Gran Chaco

Parana River

Pampas

Patagonia

180° 160° 120° 80°

CONICAL
PROJECTION

CONICAL-
PROJECTION MAP

AZIMUTHAL
PROJECTION

AZIMUTHAL-
PROJECTION MAP

MODIFIED
AZIMUTHAL-PROJECTION MAP

SATELLITE MAP OF THE EARTH

160°   180°

120°

80°

40°

0°

*ARCTIC
OCEAN*

*Ural
Mountains*

*Kara
Kum*

*River
Ob-Irtysh*

*River
Lena*

ARCTIC CIRCLE
(66° 32'N)

Sea of Azov

Caucasus

Carpathians

Alps

*River
Amur*

renees

EUROPE

Black Sea

ASIA

Lake Baikal

ns

*Mediterranean
Sea*

*Sea of
Japan*

Honshu

TROPIC OF
CANCER
(23° 30 N)

*Red
Sea*

Gobi Desert

*Yellow River
(Huang He)*

PACIFIC
OCEAN

AFRICA

Pamirs

*Caspian
Sea*

Himalayas

*South
China
Sea*

*Yangtze River
(Chang Jiang)*

*Thar
Desert*

*Arabian
Desert*

River Mekong

Borneo

New Guinea

EQUATOR
(0°)

*River Congo
(Zaire)*

River Nile

Lake Victoria

*Takla Makan
Desert*

Sumatra

*Lake
Tanganyika*

INDIAN
OCEAN

*Australian
Desert*

AUSTRALASIA

*Namib
Desert*

Madagascar

Lake Nyasa

TROPIC OF
CAPRICORN
(23° 30'S)

*Kalahari
Desert*

Drakensberg

New Zealand

ANTARCTIC CIRCLE
(66° 32'S)

ANTARCTICA

0°

40°

80°

120°

160°   180°

GREENWICH
MERIDIAN

EAST OF GREENWICH
MERIDIAN

The rock cycle

THE ROCK CYCLE IS A CONTINUOUS PROCESS through which old rocks are transformed into new ones. Rocks can be divided into three main groups: igneous, sedimentary, and metamorphic. Igneous rocks are formed when magma (molten rock) from the Earth's interior cools and solidifies (see pp. 274-275). Sedimentary rocks are formed when sediment (rock particles, for example) becomes compressed and cemented together in a process known as lithification (see pp. 276-277). Metamorphic rocks are formed when igneous, sedimentary, or other metamorphic rocks are changed by heat or pressure (see pp. 274-275). Rocks are added to the Earth's surface by crustal movements and volcanic activity. Once exposed on the surface, the rocks are broken down into rock particles by weathering (see pp. 282-283). The particles are then transported by glaciers, rivers, and wind, and deposited as sediment in lakes, deltas, deserts, and on the ocean floor. Some of this sediment undergoes lithification and forms sedimentary rock. This rock may be thrust back to the surface by crustal movements or forced deeper into the Earth's interior, where heat and pressure transform it into metamorphic rock. The metamorphic rock in turn may be pushed up to the surface or may be melted to form magma. Eventually, the magma cools and solidifies - below or on the surface -forming igneous rock. When the sedimentary, igneous, and metamorphic rocks are exposed once more on the Earth's surface, the cycle begins again.

HEXAGONAL BASALT
COLUMNS, ICELAND

THE ROCK CYCLE

Igneous rock

Cooling and solidification (crystallization)

Weathering, transport, and deposition

Sediment

Magma

Heat and pressure (metamorphism)

Weathering, transport, and deposition

Weathering, transport, and deposition

Compression and cementation (lithification)

Melting

Heat and pressure (metamorphism)

Metamorphic rock

Sedimentary rock

STAGES IN THE ROCK CYCLE

Magma extruded as lava, which solidifies to form igneous rock

Lava flow

Vent

Main conduit

Secondary conduit

Lava

Ash

Rock surrounding magma changed by heat to form metamorphic rock

Intense heat of rising magma melts some of the surrounding rock

Sedimentary rock crushed and folded to form metamorphic rock

IGNEOUS ROCK

Pyroxene
crystal

Olivine
crystal

Plagioclase
feldspar

Coarse-
grained
texture

Dark
pyroxene
crystal

PHOTOMICROGRAPH
OF GABBRO

PIECE OF
GABBRO

SEDIMENTARY ROCK

Mud
groundmass
(matrix)

Brown colouring
from iron oxides

Fine-
grained
texture

Ammonite
shell embedded
in rock

Ammonite
shell

PHOTOMICROGRAPH OF
SHELLY LIMESTONE

PIECE OF SHELLY
LIMESTONE

METAMORPHIC ROCK

Garnet crystal
(pink)

Quartz and
feldspar crystals
(grey)

Red garnet
crystal

Wavy
foliation

PHOTOMICROGRAPH OF
GARNET-MICA SCHIST

PIECE OF GARNET-
MICA SCHIST

Mountain

Glacier erodes rocks
and carries rock
particles to river

Waterfall
erodes rock

River erodes valley
floor and carries rock
particles downstream

Rock particles deposited
as sediment in lake

Rock particles deposited by
wind to form sand dunes

Rock particles
deposited in delta

Heavier rock
particles deposited
on continental shelf

Continental
shelf

Continental
slope

Lighter rock particles
collect on ocean floor to
form layers of sediment

Layers of sediment compressed and
cemented to form sedimentary rock

Minerals

A MINERAL IS A NATURALLY OCCURRING SUBSTANCE that has a characteristic chemical composition and specific physical properties, such as habit and streak (see pp. 270-271). A rock, by comparison, is an aggregate of minerals and need not have a specific chemical composition. Minerals are made up of elements (substances that cannot be broken down chemically into simpler substances), each of which can be represented by a chemical symbol. Minerals can be divided into two main groups: native elements and compounds. Native elements are made up of a pure element. Examples include gold (chemical symbol Au), silver (Ag), copper (Cu), and carbon (C); carbon occurs as a native element in two forms, diamond and graphite. Compounds are combinations of two or more elements. For example, sulphides are compounds of sulphur (S) and one or more other elements, such as lead (Pb) in the mineral galena, or antimony (Sb) in the mineral stibnite.

NATIVE ELEMENTS

Dendritic (branching) copper

Limonite groundmass (matrix)

COPPER
(Cu)

SULPHIDES

Cubic galena crystal

GALENA
(PbS)

Prismatic stibnite crystal

Quartz groundmass (matrix)

STIBNITE
(Sb_2S_3)

Perfect octahedral pyrites crystal

Quartz crystal

PYRITES
(FeS_2)

Dendritic (branching) gold

Quartz vein

GOLD
(Au)

White diamond

Kimberlite groundmass (matrix)

DIAMOND
(C)

Hexagonal graphite crystal

GRAPHITE
(C)

OXIDES/HYDROXIDES

Milky quartz groundmass (matrix)

Smoky quartz crystal

SMOKY QUARTZ
(SiO_2)

Rounded bauxite grains in groundmass (matrix)

Mass of specular haematite crystals

BAUXITE
(FeO(OH) and $Al_2O_3.2H_2O$)

SPECULAR HAEMATITE
(Fe_2O_5)

Parallel bands of onyx

ONYX
(SiO_2)

Specular crystals of haematite

Kidney ore haematite

KIDNEY ORE HAEMATITE
(Fe_2O_5)

PHOSPHATES

Limonite groundmass (matrix)

Prismatic pyromorphite crystals

PYROMORPHITE
(Pb$_5$(PO$_4$)$_5$Cl)

Rock groundmass (matrix)

Radiating wavellite crystals

WAVELLITE
(Al$_5$(PO$_4$)$_2$(OH,F)$_5$.5H$_2$O)

CARBONATES

Striated cerussite crystal

CERUSSITE
(PbCO$_3$)

Dog tooth calcite crystal

CALCITE
(CaCO$_3$)

SULPHATES

Rock groundmass (matrix)

Radiating cyanotrichite crystals

CYANOTRICHITE
Cu$_4$Al$_2$(SO$_4$)(OH)$_{12}$.2H$_2$O)

Radiating crystal mass of daisy gypsum

DAISY GYPSUM
(CaSO$_4$.2H$_2$O)

MOLYBDATE

Tabular wulfenite crystal

Dark rock groundmass (matrix)

WULFENITE
(PbMoO$_4$)

SILICATES

Feldspar groundmass (matrix)

Dodecahedral sodalite crystal

SODALITE
(Na$_8$Al$_6$Si$_6$O$_{24}$Cl$_2$)

Transparent bicolored tourmaline crystal

TOURMALINE
(Na(Mg,Fe,Li,Mn,Al)$_3$Al$_6$(BO$_3$)$_5$Si$_6$.O$_{18}$(OH,F)$_4$)

Striated surface of olivine crystal

OLIVINE
(Fe$_2$SiO$_4$ - Mg$_2$SiO$_4$)

Striated prismatic epidote crystal

EPIDOTE
(Ca$_2$(Al,Fe)$_3$(SiO$_4$)$_3$(OH))

Tabular muscovite crystal

MUSCOVITE
(KAl$_2$(Si$_3$Al)O$_{10}$(OH,F)$_2$)

Orthoclase crystal

ORTHOCLASE
(KAlSi$_3$O$_8$)

HALIDES

Cubic fluorite crystal

GREEN FLUORITE
(CaF$_2$)

Cubic rock salt crystal

ORANGE HALITE (ROCK SALT)
(NaCl)

Mineral features

MINERALS CAN BE IDENTIFIED BY STUDYING features such as fracture, cleavage, crystal system, habit, hardness, colour, and streak. Minerals can break in different ways. If a mineral breaks in an irregular way, leaving rough surfaces, it possesses fracture. If a mineral breaks along well-defined planes of weakness, it possesses cleavage. Specific minerals have distinctive patterns of cleavage; for example, mica cleaves along one plane. Most minerals form crystals, which can be categorized into crystal systems according to their symmetry and number of faces. Within each system, several different but related forms of crystal are possible; for example, a cubic crystal can have six, eight, or twelve sides. A mineral's habit is the typical form taken by an aggregate of its crystals. Examples of habit include botryoidal (like a bunch of grapes) and massive (no definite form). The relative hardness of a mineral may be assessed by testing its resistance to scratching. This property is usually measured using Mohs scale, which increases in hardness from 1 (talc) to 10 (diamond). The colour of a mineral is not a dependable guide to its identity as some minerals have a range of colours. Streak (the colour the powdered mineral makes when rubbed across an unglazed tile) is a more reliable indicator.

CLEAVAGE

Cleavage in one direction

CLEAVAGE ALONG ONE PLANE

Cleavage in three directions, forming a block cube

CLEAVAGE ALONG THREE PLANES

Horizontal cleavage

Vertical cleavage

CLEAVAGE ALONG TWO PLANES

Cleavage in four directions, forming a double-pyramid crystal

CLEAVAGE ALONG FOUR PLANES

CRYSTAL SYSTEMS

Cubic iron pyrites crystal

Tetragonal idocrase crystal

Representation of tetragonal system

TETRAGONAL SYSTEM

CUBIC SYSTEM

Representation of cubic system

Hexagonal beryl crystal

Representation of hexagonal/trigonal system

Orthorhombic barytes crystal

Representation of orthorhombic system

HEXAGONAL/TRIGONAL SYSTEM

ORTHORHOMBIC SYSTEM

FRACTURE

Fire opal with conchoidal (shell-like) fracture

Nickel-iron with hackly (jagged) fracture

CONCHOIDAL FRACTURE

HACKLY FRACTURE

Orpiment with uneven fracture

Garnierite with splintery fracture

UNEVEN FRACTURE

SPLINTERY FRACTURE

Monoclinic selenite crystal

Representation of monoclinic system

Triclinic axinite crystal

Representation of triclinic system

MONOCLINIC SYSTEM

TRICLINIC SYSTEM

HABIT

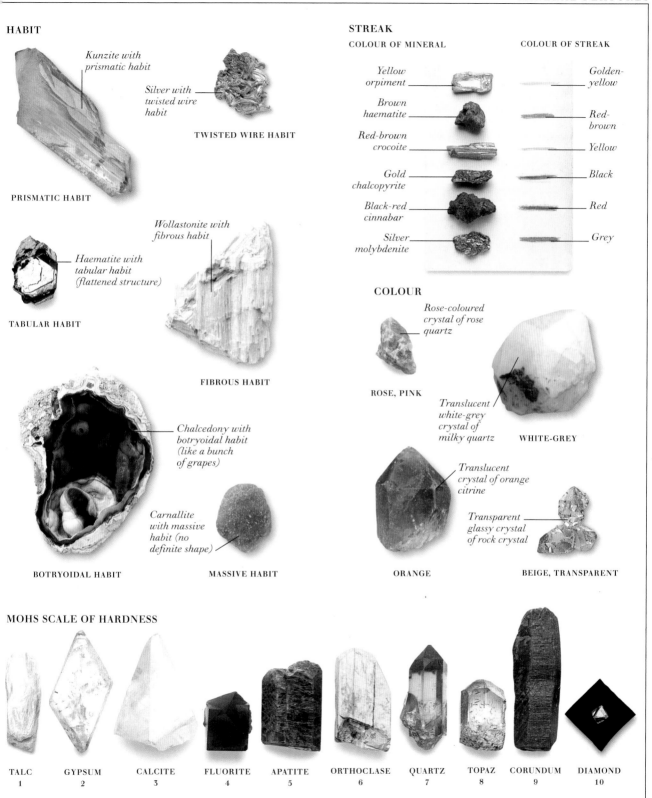

Kunzite with prismatic habit

Silver with twisted wire habit

TWISTED WIRE HABIT

PRISMATIC HABIT

Wollastonite with fibrous habit

Haematite with tabular habit (flattened structure)

TABULAR HABIT

FIBROUS HABIT

Chalcedony with botryoidal habit (like a bunch of grapes)

Carnallite with massive habit (no definite shape)

BOTRYOIDAL HABIT

MASSIVE HABIT

STREAK

COLOUR OF MINERAL	COLOUR OF STREAK
Yellow orpiment	Golden-yellow
Brown haematite	Red-brown
Red-brown crocoite	Yellow
Gold chalcopyrite	Black
Black-red cinnabar	Red
Silver molybdenite	Grey

COLOUR

Rose-coloured crystal of rose quartz

ROSE, PINK

Translucent white-grey crystal of milky quartz

WHITE-GREY

Translucent crystal of orange citrine

Transparent glassy crystal of rock crystal

ORANGE

BEIGE, TRANSPARENT

MOHS SCALE OF HARDNESS

TALC	GYPSUM	CALCITE	FLUORITE	APATITE	ORTHOCLASE	QUARTZ	TOPAZ	CORUNDUM	DIAMOND
1	2	3	4	5	6	7	8	9	10

Volcanoes

VOLCANOES ARE VENTS OR FISSURES in the Earth's crust through which magma (molten rock that originates from deep beneath the crust) is forced on to the surface as lava. They occur most commonly along the boundaries of crustal plates; most volcanoes lie in a belt called the "Ring of Fire", which runs along the edge of the Pacific Ocean. Volcanoes can be classified according to the violence and frequency of their eruptions.

Non-explosive volcanic eruptions generally occur where crustal plates pull apart. These eruptions produce runny basaltic lava that spreads quickly over a wide area to form relatively flat cones. The most violent eruptions take place where plates collide. Such eruptions produce thick rhyolitic lava and may also blast out clouds of dust and pyroclasts (lava fragments). The lava does not flow far before cooling and therefore builds up steep-sided, conical volcanoes. Some volcanoes produce lava and ash eruptions, which build up composite volcanic cones. Volcanoes that erupt frequently are described as active; those that erupt rarely are termed dormant; and those that have stopped erupting altogether are termed extinct. As well as the volcanoes themselves, other features associated with volcanic regions include geysers, hot mineral springs, solfataras, fumaroles, and bubbling mud pools.

HORU GEYSER,
NEW ZEALAND

Folded, rope-like surface

PAHOEHOE
(ROPY LAVA)

VOLCANO TYPES

Basaltic lava plateau
Fissure created by plates moving apart
Gentle slope

FISSURE VOLCANO

Vent
Gentle slope built up by numerous basaltic lava flows

BASIC SHIELD VOLCANO

Vent
Steep, convex sides caused by thick lava cooling quickly

DOME VOLCANO

Slightly concave sides
Vent
Cinder
Fine ash

ASH-CINDER VOLCANO

Lava
Vent
Ash
Steep conical shape
Secondary conduit

COMPOSITE VOLCANO

Caldera (volcanic crater)
New cone
Old cone
Ash

CALDERA VOLCANO

Layers of sedimentary rocks

Metamorphic rocks (rocks altered by heat and pressure)

HOW VOLCANIC PLUGS BECOME EXPOSED

Extinct volcano
Solidified lava forms plug

PLUG FORMATION

Plug exposed
Volcanic cone slowly eroded away

INITIAL EROSION AROUND PLUG

Resistant lava plug remains
Volcanic cone completely eroded away

COMPLETE DENUDATION OF PLUG

LAPILLI
(LAVA FRAGMENT

Small piece of solidified lava

TYPES OF LAVA

Scoria (sharp, angular chunks)

Driblets of lava from roof of tunnel

AA (BLOCKY LAVA)

REMELTED LAVA

LOCATION OF VOLCANOES

▲ Volcano

⊢┼┼┼ Plate boundary

STRUCTURE OF A VOLCANO

Vent

Plug (solidified lava)

Main conduit

Volcanic ash

Cinder cone

Mineral spring

Steeply sloping cone consisting of numerous layers of ash and lava

Laccolith

Secondary conduit

Magma reservoir

Lava flow

Groundwater

VOLCANIC FEATURES

Sulphurous gases

Jet of hot water and steam

Water heated by hot rocks

Steam pressure builds up

Hot water

Mud and surface deposits mixed with hot water

Superheated water

Steam

SOLFATARA

GEYSER

MUD POOL

FUMAROLE

Igneous and metamorphic rocks

IGNEOUS ROCKS ARE FORMED WHEN MAGMA (molten rock that originates from deep beneath the Earth's crust) cools and solidifies. There are two main types of igneous rock: intrusive and extrusive. Intrusive rocks are formed deep underground where magma is forced into cracks or between rock layers to form structures such as sills, dykes, and batholiths. The magma cools slowly to form coarse-grained rocks such as gabbro and pegmatite. Extrusive rocks are formed above the Earth's surface from lava (magma that has been ejected in a volcanic eruption). The molten lava cools quickly, producing fine-grained rocks such as rhyolite and basalt. Metamorphic rocks are those that have been altered by intense heat (contact metamorphism) or extreme pressure (regional metamorphism). Contact metamorphism occurs when rocks are changed by heat from, for example, an igneous intrusion or lava flow. Regional metamorphism occurs when rock is crushed in the middle of a folding mountain range. Metamorphic rocks can be formed from igneous rocks, sedimentary rocks, or even from other metamorphic rocks.

BASALT COLUMNS

IGNEOUS ROCK STRUCTURES

Cinder cone
Large eroded lava flow
Cedar-tree laccolith
Butte
Plug
Cone sheet
Ring dyke
Batholith
Dyke
Sill
Dyke swarm
Lopolith

CONTACT METAMORPHISM

Metamorphic aureole (region where contact metamorphism occurs)

Hot igneous intrusion
Limestone
Shale
Marble (metamorphosed limestone)
Slate (metamorphosed shale)

REGIONAL METAMORPHISM

Mountain range
Slate, formed under low pressure and temperature
Compression
Compression
Schist, formed under medium pressure and temperature
Crust
Gneiss, formed under high pressure and temperature
Mantle
Magma

EXAMPLES OF METAMORPHIC ROCKS

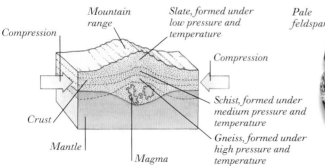

Pale feldspar
Dark mica
Dark mineral band
Pale calcite

GNEISS

FOLDED SCHIST

SKARN

EXAMPLES OF EXTRUSIVE IGNEOUS ROCKS

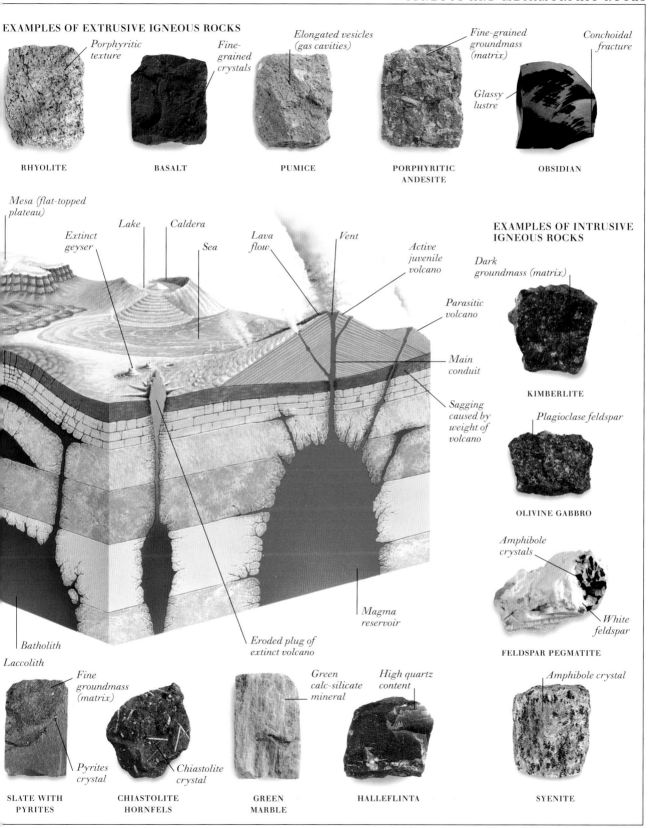

Porphyritic texture

RHYOLITE

Fine-grained crystals

BASALT

Elongated vesicles (gas cavities)

PUMICE

Fine-grained groundmass (matrix)

Glassy lustre

PORPHYRITIC ANDESITE

Conchoidal fracture

OBSIDIAN

Mesa (flat-topped plateau)

Extinct geyser

Lake

Caldera

Sea

Lava flow

Vent

Active juvenile volcano

Parasitic volcano

Main conduit

Sagging caused by weight of volcano

Magma reservoir

Eroded plug of extinct volcano

Batholith

Laccolith

EXAMPLES OF INTRUSIVE IGNEOUS ROCKS

Dark groundmass (matrix)

KIMBERLITE

Plagioclase feldspar

OLIVINE GABBRO

Amphibole crystals

White feldspar

FELDSPAR PEGMATITE

Amphibole crystal

SYENITE

Fine groundmass (matrix)

Pyrites crystal

SLATE WITH PYRITES

Chiastolite crystal

CHIASTOLITE HORNFELS

Green calc-silicate mineral

GREEN MARBLE

High quartz content

HALLEFLINTA

275

Sedimentary rocks

SEDIMENTARY ROCKS ARE FORMED BY THE ACCUMULATION and consolidation of sediments (see pp. 266-267). There are three main types of sedimentary rock. Clastic sedimentary rocks, such as breccia or sandstone, are formed from other rocks that have been broken down into fragments by weathering (see pp. 282-283), which have then been transported and deposited elsewhere. Organic sedimentary rocks – for example, coal (see pp. 280-281) – are derived from plant and animal remains. Chemical sedimentary rocks are formed by chemical processes. For example, rock salt is formed when salt dissolved in water is deposited as the water evaporates. Sedimentary rocks are laid down in layers, called beds or strata. Each new layer is laid down horizontally over older ones. There are usually some gaps in the sequence, called unconformities. These represent periods in which no new sediments were being laid down, or when earlier sedimentary layers were raised above sea level and eroded away.

THE GRAND CANYON, USA

EXAMPLES OF UNCONFORMITIES

Early beds tilted and eroded   *Later beds horizontal*

ANGULAR UNCONFORMITY

No bedding in early rocks   *Later beds horizontal*

NONCONFORMITY

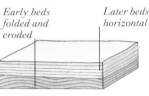

Early beds folded and eroded   *Later beds horizontal*

DISCONFORMITY

SEDIMENTARY LAYERS OF THE GRAND CANYON REGION

Wasatch formation
Kaiparowits formation
Tropic formation
Wahweap sandstone
Dakota sandstone
Carmel formation
Pink Cliffs
Bryce Canyon
Zion Canyon
Gray Cliffs
Sevier fault
White Cliffs
Pipe Spring

Temple Cap sandstone   *Navajo sandstone*   *Kayenta formation*   *Moenave formation*   *Chinle formation*   *Shinarump member*   *Moenkopi formation*   *Kaibab limestone*   *Toroweap formation*   *Coconino sandstone*   *Her shale*

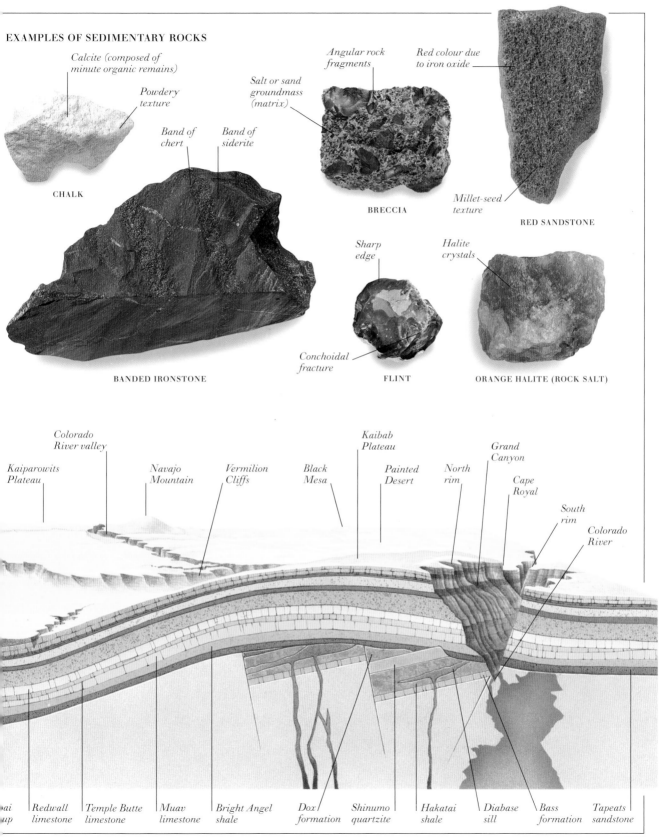

EXAMPLES OF SEDIMENTARY ROCKS

Calcite (composed of minute organic remains)

Powdery texture

CHALK

Band of chert

Band of siderite

BANDED IRONSTONE

Angular rock fragments

Salt or sand groundmass (matrix)

BRECCIA

Red colour due to iron oxide

Millet-seed texture

RED SANDSTONE

Sharp edge

Conchoidal fracture

FLINT

Halite crystals

ORANGE HALITE (ROCK SALT)

Kaiparowits Plateau

Colorado River valley

Navajo Mountain

Vermilion Cliffs

Black Mesa

Kaibab Plateau

Painted Desert

North rim

Grand Canyon

Cape Royal

South rim

Colorado River

ai up

Redwall limestone

Temple Butte limestone

Muav limestone

Bright Angel shale

Dox formation

Shinumo quartzite

Hakatai shale

Diabase sill

Bass formation

Tapeats sandstone

Fossils

FOSSILS ARE THE REMAINS of plants and animals that have been preserved in rock. A fossil may be the preserved remains of an organism itself, an impression of it in rock, or preserved traces (known as trace fossils) left by an organism while it was alive, such as organic carbon outlines, fossilized footprints, or droppings. Most dead organisms soon rot away or are eaten by scavengers. For fossilization to occur, rapid burial by sediment is necessary. The organism decays, but the harder parts – bones, teeth, and shells, for example – may be preserved and hardened by minerals from the surrounding sediment. Fossilization may also occur even when the hard parts of an organism are dissolved away to leave an impression called a mould. The mould is filled by minerals, thereby creating a cast of the organism. The study of fossils (palaeontology) can not only show how living things have evolved, but can also help to reveal the Earth's geological history – for example, by aiding in the dating of rock strata.

PROCESS OF FOSSILIZATION

ANIMAL DIES

Sea
Ammonite
Seabed

SOFT PARTS ROT

Sea
Shell
Seabed

SHELL BURIED

Sea
Shell
Sediment
Seabed

SHELL FOSSILIZED

Shell dissolved away and replaced by minerals
Sea
Sediment
Sediment
Seabed

EXAMPLES OF FOSSILS

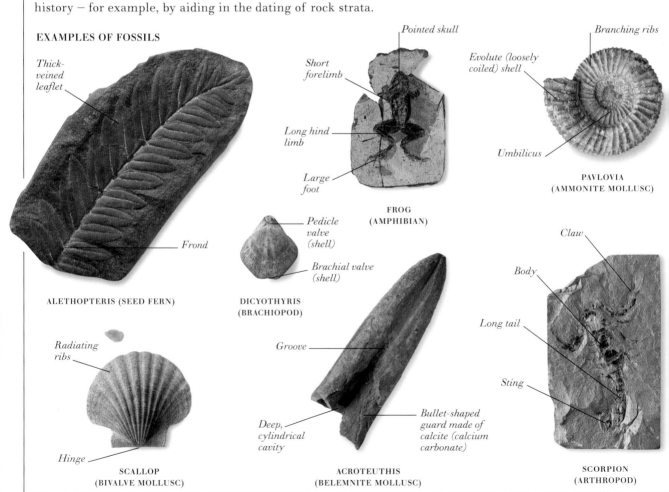

Thick-veined leaflet
Frond

ALETHOPTERIS (SEED FERN)

Pointed skull
Short forelimb
Long hind limb
Large foot

FROG (AMPHIBIAN)

Branching ribs
Evolute (loosely coiled) shell
Umbilicus

PAVLOVIA (AMMONITE MOLLUSC)

Pedicle valve (shell)
Brachial valve (shell)

DICYOTHYRIS (BRACHIOPOD)

Radiating ribs
Hinge

SCALLOP (BIVALVE MOLLUSC)

Groove
Deep, cylindrical cavity
Bullet-shaped guard made of calcite (calcium carbonate)

ACROTEUTHIS (BELEMNITE MOLLUSC)

Claw
Body
Long tail
Sting

SCORPION (ARTHROPOD)

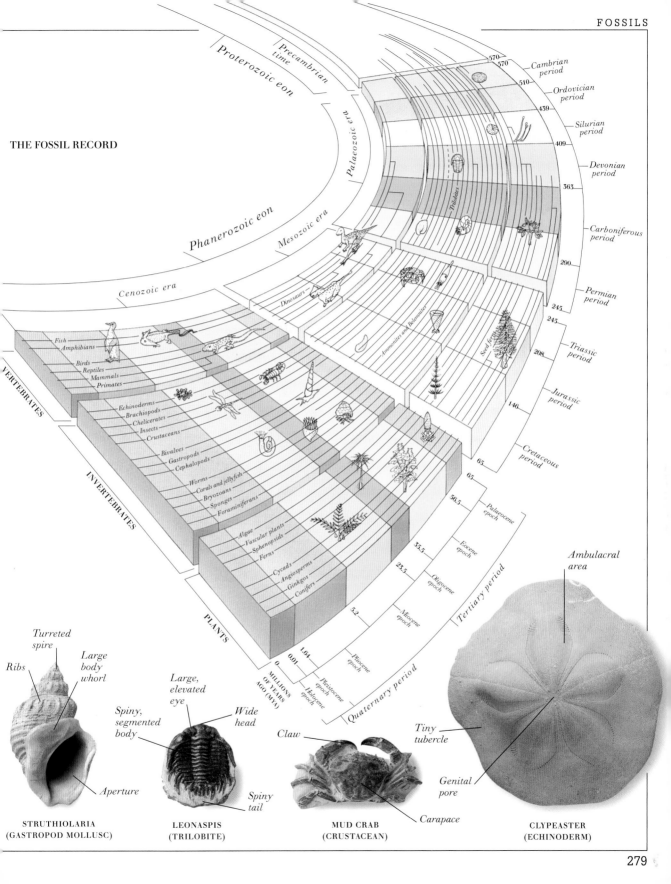

THE FOSSIL RECORD

Precambrian time

Proterozoic eon

Phanerozoic eon

Palaeozoic era

Mesozoic era

Cenozoic era

570

570 — Cambrian period

510 — Ordovician period

439 — Silurian period

409 — Devonian period

363 — Carboniferous period

290 — Permian period

245 — Permian period

245 — Triassic period

208 — Jurassic period

146 — Cretaceous period

65 — Cretaceous period

65

56.5 — Palaeocene epoch

35.5 — Eocene epoch

23.5 — Oligocene epoch

5.2 — Miocene epoch

1.64 — Pliocene epoch

0.01 — Pleistocene epoch

Holocene epoch

Tertiary period

Quaternary period

Trilobites

Dinosaurs

Ammonites and Belemnites

Seed ferns

VERTEBRATES

Fish
Amphibians
Birds
Reptiles
Mammals
Primates

INVERTEBRATES

Echinoderms
Brachiopods
Chelicerates
Insects
Crustaceans
Bivalves
Gastropods
Cephalopods
Worms
Corals and jellyfish
Bryozoans
Sponges
Foraminiferans

PLANTS

Algae
Vascular plants
Sphenopsids
Ferns
Cycads
Angiosperms
Ginkgos
Conifers

MILLIONS OF YEARS AGO (MYA)

0

Turreted spire

Ribs

Large body whorl

Aperture

STRUTHIOLARIA
(GASTROPOD MOLLUSC)

Large, elevated eye

Spiny, segmented body

Wide head

Spiny tail

LEONASPIS
(TRILOBITE)

Claw

Carapace

MUD CRAB
(CRUSTACEAN)

Ambulacral area

Tiny tubercle

Genital pore

CLYPEASTER
(ECHINODERM)

279

Mineral resources

Stalk

Leaf

PLANT MATTER

MINERAL RESOURCES CAN BE DEFINED AS naturally occurring substances that can be extracted from the Earth and are useful as fuels and raw materials. Coal, oil, and gas — collectively called fossil fuels — are commonly included in this group, but are not strictly minerals, because they are of organic origin. Coal formation begins when vegetation is buried and partly decomposed to form peat. Overlying sediments compress the peat and transform it into lignite (soft brown coal). As the overlying sediments accumulate, increasing pressure and temperature eventually transform the lignite into bituminous and hard anthracite coals. Oil and gas are usually formed from organic matter that was deposited in marine sediments. Under the effects of heat and pressure, the compressed organic matter undergoes complex chemical changes to form oil and gas. The oil and gas percolate upwards through water-saturated, permeable rocks and they may rise to the Earth's surface or accumulate below an impermeable layer of rock that has been folded or faulted to form a trap — an anticline (upfold) trap, for example. Minerals are inorganic substances that may consist of a single chemical element, such as gold, silver, or copper, or combinations of elements (see pp. 268-269). Some minerals are concentrated in mineralization zones in rock associated with crustal movements or volcanic activity. Others may be found in sediments as placer deposits — accumulations of high-density minerals that have been weathered out of rocks, transported, and deposited (on river-beds, for example).

OIL RIG, NORTH SEA

Decayed plant matter

About 60% carbon

PEAT

About 70% carbon

Crumbly texture

LIGNITE (BROWN COAL)

Powdery texture

About 80% carbon

BITUMINOUS COAL

Shiny surface

About 95% carbon

ANTHRACITE COAL

HOW COAL IS FORMED

Vegetation

Increasing pressure and temperature

Increasing layers of overlying sediment

Increasing pressure and temperature

Increasing layers of overlying sediment

Increasing pressure and temperature

Peat (about 60% carbon)

PEAT

Lignite (about 70% carbon)

LIGNITE (BROWN COAL)

Bituminous coal (about 80% carbon)

BITUMINOUS COAL

EXAMPLES OF OIL AND GAS TRAPS

Impermeable rock
Oil
Folded impermeable rock
Water-saturated permeable rock

FAULT TRAP

Pinch-out
Fault
Gas
Oil

PINCH-OUT TRAP

Anticline
Folded impermeable rock
Water-saturated permeable rock
Gas
Oil

ANTICLINE TRAP

Folded impermeable rock
Water-saturated permeable rock
Oil
Impermeable salt dome

SALT-DOME TRAP

MAJOR COAL, OIL, AND GAS DEPOSITS

● Coal   ● Oil and gas

HOW AN ANTICLINE TRAP IS FORMED

Layer of sediment containing decayed plant and animal matter
Sea
Old seabed

DEPOSITION OF ORGANIC MATERIAL

Increasing layers of overlying sediment
Sea
Oil and gas formed by chemical reactions, heat, and pressure

FORMATION OF OIL AND GAS

Land
Sea
Anticline
Impermeable rock layer folded to form oil and gas trap
Gas
Oil
Water-saturated permeable rock

COLLECTION OF OIL AND GAS IN ANTICLINE TRAP

MINERALIZATION ZONES

Continental crust
Volcano
Subduction zone
Oceanic crust
Mid-ocean ridge

n, tungsten, muth, and copper

Copper, zinc, gold, and chromium

Copper, gold, silver, tin, lead, and mercury

Lead, zinc, and copper

Chromium

Manganese, cobalt, and nickel

Copper and zinc

281

Weathering and erosion

WEATHERING IS THE BREAKING DOWN of rocks on the Earth's surface. There are two main types: physical (or mechanical) and chemical. Physical weathering may be caused by temperature changes, such as freezing and thawing, or by abrasion from material carried by winds, rivers, or glaciers. Rocks may also be broken down by the actions of animals and plants, such as the burrowing of animals and the growth of roots. Chemical weathering causes rocks to decompose by changing their chemical composition – for example, rainwater may dissolve certain minerals in a rock. Erosion is the wearing away and removal of land surfaces by water, wind, or ice. It is greatest in areas of little or no surface vegetation, such as deserts, where sand dunes may form.

FORMATION OF A HAMADA (ROCK PAVEMENT)

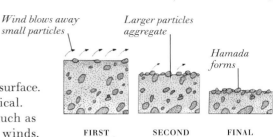

Wind blows away small particles

Larger particles aggregate

Hamada forms

FIRST STAGE

SECOND STAGE

FINAL STAGE

FEATURES OF WEATHERING AND EROSION

Mesa (flat-topped plateau)

Canyon

Zeugen

Joint

Hard rock

Soft rock

Shelf formed of hard rock

Talus (scree)

Alluvial fan (alluvial cone)

Bahada (gentle slope covered with loose rock)

Bolson (alluvium-filled basin)

FEATURES PRODUCED BY WIND ACTION

Wind-blown sand

Mushroom-shaped rock

Neck

Rock base eroded by wind-blown sand

ROCK PEDESTAL

Wind-blown sand

Widened joint

Soft rock

Hard rock

ZEUGEN

Wind-blown sand

Furrow

Hard rock

Soft rock eroded by wind-blown sand

YARDANG

EXAMPLES OF PHYSICAL WEATHERING PROCESSES

Heated rock surface expands

Exfoliation dome

Flaking rock

Fallen debris

EXFOLIATION (ONION-SKIN WEATHERING)

Joint expands and contracts due to temperature changes

Block of fallen rock

BLOCK DISINTEGRATION

Talus (scree)

Joint widened by frozen water

FROST WEDGING

Trunk

Crack widened by tree root

TREE ROOT ACTION

SECTION THROUGH A BARKHAN DUNE

Strong wind

Weak wind

Windward face

Direction of wind-blown sand

Direction of sand movement

Slip face

Foreset strata

Cross-bed set

Topset strata

Bottomset strata

EXAMPLES OF SAND DUNES

Wind direction

Crescent-shaped dune

BARKHAN DUNE

Wind direction

Dune at right angle to wind

TRANSVERSE DUNE

Wind direction

Point where sand ridges meet

STAR DUNE

Wind direction

Parallel dunes

SEIF (LINEAR) DUNE

Canyon

Wadi (dry wash)

Mesa (flat-topped plateau)

Talus (scree)

Butte (flat-topped mesa remnant)

Eroded arch

Residual hill on pediment

Hamada (rock pavement)

Rock pedestal

Barkhan dune

Parabolic dune

Transverse dune

Seif (linear) dune

Inselberg (isolated, steep-sided hill)

Playa (dry lake bed of salt or desiccated clay)

Faultline

Freshwater lake

Fertile oasis

Deflation hollow created by wind erosion

Hard granite

Cuesta (asymmetric ridge)

Faultline

Hard sandstone

Hog's-back (steep ridge)

Caves

CAVES COMMONLY FORM in areas of limestone, although on coastlines they also occur in other rocks. Limestone is made of calcite (calcium carbonate), which dissolves in the carbonic acid naturally present in rainwater, and in humic acids from the decay of vegetation. The acidic water trickles down through cracks and joints in the limestone and between rock layers, breaking up the surface terrain into clints (blocks of rock), separated by grikes (deep cracks), and punctuated by sink-holes (also called swallow-holes or potholes) into which surface streams may disappear. Underground, the acidic water dissolves the rock around crevices, opening up a network of passages and caves, which can become large caverns if the roofs collapse. Various features are formed when the dissolved calcite is redeposited; for example, it may be redeposited along an underground stream to form a gour (series of calcite ridges), or in caves and passages to form stalactites and stalagmites. Stalactites develop where calcite is left behind as water drips from the roof; where the drops land, stalagmites build up.

STALACTITE WITH
RING MARKS

Ring
mark

MERGED
STALACTITES

SURFACE TOPOGRAPHY OF A CAVE SYSTEM

Doline
(depression
caused by
collapse of
cave roof)

Sink-hole

Gorge where
cave roof has
fallen in

Porous
limestone

Resurgence

Limestone terrain
with clints and grikes

Impermeable
rock

STALAGMITE FORMATIONS

Calcite (calcium
carbonate)
crystallized
under water

Thin encrustations
of calcite (calcium
carbonate)

Scar of
bare rock

Former
water table

CALCAREOUS
TUFA

Permeable
limestone

CRYSTALLINE
STALAGMITIC FLOOR

Encrustations
on dead stems
of small plants

Calcite
(calcium
carbonate)

Calcite
(calcium
carbonate)

Encrustations
with fungoid
structure

Resurgence

STALAGMITIC
FLOOR

STALAGMITIC
BOSS

Layer of
impermeable
rock

Present
water table

DEVELOPMENT OF A CAVE SYSTEM

STRUCTURE OF LIMESTONE STRATA

Impermeable rock
Joint
Bedding plane
Permeable limestone
Impermeable rock

INITIAL CAVE

Water seeps through cracks in rock
Calcite (calcium carbonate) deposits begin to form
Stream enters permeable rock
Resurgence
Tunnel
Underground stream

EXTENDED CAVE SYSTEM

Doline caused by collapse of cave roof
Sink-hole
Stalactite
Stalagmite
Gorge
Resurgence
Cave
Dry gallery

INTERCONNECTED CAVE SYSTEM

Stalactite
Pillar (column)
Gorge
Stalactite
Dry gallery (former course of underground stream)
Gour (series of calcite ridges) deposited by running water
Stalagmite
Joint in rock enlarged by water
Bedding plane
Curtain of deposited calcite (calcium carbonate)
Tunnel
Cave
Passage
Cavern
Gour (series of calcite ridges)

Glaciers

GLACIER BAY, ALASKA

A VALLEY GLACIER IS A LARGE MASS OF ICE that forms on land and moves slowly downhill under its own weight. It is formed from snow that collects in cirques (mountain hollows also known as corries) and compresses into ice as more and more snow accumulates. The cirque is deepened by frost wedging and abrasion (see pp. 282-283), and arêtes (sharp ridges) develop between adjacent cirques. Eventually, so much ice builds up that the glacier begins to move downhill. As the glacier moves it collects moraine (debris), which may range in size from particles of dust to large boulders. The rocks at the base of the glacier erode the glacial valley, giving it a U-shaped cross-section. Under the glacier, *roches moutonnées* (eroded outcrops of hard rock) and drumlins (rounded mounds of rock and clay) are left behind on the valley floor. The glacier ends at a terminus (the snout), where the ice melts as fast as it arrives. If the temperature increases, the ice melts faster than it arrives, and the glacier retreats. The retreating glacier leaves behind its moraine and also erratics (isolated single boulders). Glacial streams from the melting glacier deposit eskers and kames (ridges and mounds of sand and gravel), but carry away the finer sediment to form a stratified outwash plain. Lumps of ice carried on to this plain melt, creating holes called kettles.

VALLEY GLACIER

Lateral moraine
Meltwater pool
Medial moraine
Suspended erratic
Horn
Arête (ridge)
Cave
Englacial stream
Hanging valley
Melting glacier
Stream
Ice margin lake
Terminal moraine
Waterfall
Braided stream
Steep side of U-shaped valley
Boulder clay
Terminal lake
Meltwater stream
Roche moutonnée
Lake

Medial moraine
Suspended erratic
Snout
Push moraine
Terminal moraine
Roche moutonnée

POST-GLACIAL VALLEY

Collapsed sediment
Drumlin
Exposed valley floor
Roche moutonnée
Horn of mountain
Kame terrace
Esker
Erratic
Arête (ridge)
Lacustrine terrace
Post-glacial stream
Kame delta
Kettle
Terminal moraine
Kettle lake
Outwash terrace
Boulder clay
Kame
Roche moutonnée
Outwash fan
Steep side of U-shaped valley

286

Cirque
(corrie)

Firn (compressed
snow)

Tributary glacier

Arête
(ridge)

Moving ice

U-shaped
valley

Medial
moraine

ATURES OF A GLACIER

Lateral
moraine

Tributary
moraine joins
medial moraine

Subglacial
stream

Rock being
eroded by ice

ICE-FALL

Gentle
slope

Smooth
surface

Steep
slope

Slope
flattens

Brittle
surface ice

Rougher
surface

Crevasse
deepens and
widens

Viscous
flowing ice

Englacial
moraine

Ice recompresses

Ice block
tilts and twists

Ice breaks
into blocks

Crevasse

Ribbon
lake

CIRQUE FORMATION

**U-SHAPED VALLEY
FORMATION**

Horn

Firn
(compressed
snow)

Material
loosened
by frost
wedging

Arête
(ridge)

Glacier

Cirque
overspills

Fresh
snowfall

Outwash
plain

Sediment
deposited by
meltwater

Meltwater

Stream

EARLY STAGE

DURING GLACIATION

Steep
back wall

Deepened
cirque

Deep U-shaped
valley

Moraine pulled
from ground

Hanging
valley

Glacier

Base of cirque eroded by
glacier's pivoting action

Tarn

Rock lip

LATER STAGE

AFTER GLACIATION

Rivers

RIVERS FORM PART of the water cycle – the continuous circulation of water between the land, sea, and atmosphere. The source of a river may be a mountain spring or lake, or a melting glacier. The course that the river subsequently takes depends on the slope of the terrain and on the rock types and formations over which it flows. In its early, upland stages, a river tumbles steeply over rocks and boulders and cuts a steep-sided V-shaped valley. Farther downstream, it flows smoothly over sediments and forms winding meanders, eroding sideways to create broad valleys and plains. On reaching the coast, the river may deposit sediment to form an estuary or delta (see pp. 290-291).

RIVER CAPTURE

Tributary erodes headwards
River
River

EARLY STAGE

Dry valley
River captured by tributary
River flow decreases
River flow increases

LATER STAGE

THE WATER CYCLE

Precipitation falls on high ground
Wind
Water carried downstream by river
Water vapour released into atmosphere by trees and other plants
Wind
Water vapour forms clouds
Water evaporates from sea
Water stored in sea
River flows into sea
Water seeps underground and flows to sea
Water evaporates from lake

SATELLITE IMAGE OF GANGES RIVER DELTA, BANGLADESH

Ganges River
Ganges delta
Large volume of sediment
Infertile swampland
Distributary

RIVER DRAINAGE PATTERNS

RADIAL CENTRIPETAL PARALLEL DENDRITIC

DERANGED TRELLISED ANNULAR RECTANGULAR

Seabed
Sea
Sediment layers

STAGES IN A RIVER'S DEVELOPMENT

Watershed (divide between drainage systems)

Medial moraine

Gully

Valley head

Glacier

Mountain of impermeable rock

Glacier snout

Interlocking spur

Terminal moraine

V-shaped valley

Meltwater

Tributary stream

Lake

Rapids

Waterfall

River cliff

Eroded boulders

Plunge pool

Low inside bank

ep side bank

Meander

lood-lain

Bluff

Oxbow lake

Point bar

Levee

Distributary

Cliff   Beach   Delta   Larger sedimentary particles deposited close to shore   Smaller sedimentary particles carried farther from river mouth

River features

RIVERS ARE ONE OF THE MAJOR FORCES that shape the landscape. Near its source, a river is steep (see pp. 288-289). It erodes downwards, carving out V-shaped valleys and deep gorges. Waterfalls and rapids are formed where the river flows from hard rock to softer, more easily eroded rock. Farther downstream, meanders may form and there is greater sideways erosion, resulting in a broad river valley. The river sometimes erodes through the neck of a meander to form an oxbow lake. Sediment deposited on the valley floor by meandering rivers and during floods helps to create a flood-plain. Floods may also deposit sediment on the banks of the river to form levees. As a river spills into the sea or a lake, it deposits large amounts of sediment, and may form a delta. A delta is an area of sand-bars, swamps, and lagoons through which the river flows in several channels called distributaries — the Mississippi delta, for example. Often, a rise in sea level may have flooded the river-mouth to form a broad estuary, a tidal section where seawater mixes with fresh water.

HOW WATERFALLS AND RAPIDS ARE FORMED

Hard rock

Plunge pool

Softer rock

WATERFALL

Hard rock

River erodes softer rocks to form rapids

Softer rock

Gently sloping rock strata

RAPIDS

A RIVER VALLEY DRAINAGE SYSTEM

Headward erosion

Waterfall

Gorge

Steep gorge cut by river

Mountain

GORGE

Flood-plain

Sediment bar

Stream

BRAIDING

Entrenched meander

Braiding

Lake

River terrace

Levee

River erodes headwards

HEADWARD EROSION

River erodes downwards

Meander

Natural bridge

Steep cliffs

ENTRENCHED MEANDER

Old meander

Bridge

River

NATURAL BRIDGE

Oxbow lake

Lake

River-mouth

Sediment deposited on seabed

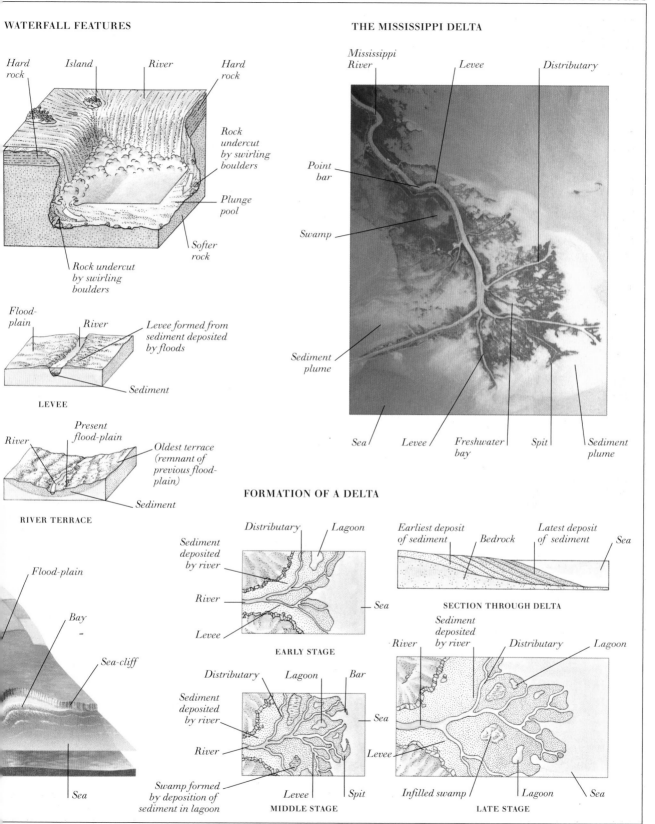

WATERFALL FEATURES

Hard rock
Island
River
Hard rock
Rock undercut by swirling boulders
Plunge pool
Softer rock
Rock undercut by swirling boulders

Flood-plain
River
Levee formed from sediment deposited by floods
Sediment

LEVEE

River
Present flood-plain
Oldest terrace (remnant of previous flood-plain)
Sediment

RIVER TERRACE

Flood-plain
Bay
Sea-cliff
Sea

THE MISSISSIPPI DELTA

Mississippi River
Levee
Distributary
Point bar
Swamp
Sediment plume
Sea
Levee
Freshwater bay
Spit
Sediment plume

FORMATION OF A DELTA

Distributary
Lagoon
Sediment deposited by river
River
Levee
Sea

EARLY STAGE

Earliest deposit of sediment
Bedrock
Latest deposit of sediment
Sea

SECTION THROUGH DELTA

Distributary
Lagoon
Bar
Sediment deposited by river
River
Sea
Swamp formed by deposition of sediment in lagoon
Levee
Spit

MIDDLE STAGE

Sediment deposited by river
River
Distributary
Lagoon
Levee
Infilled swamp
Lagoon
Sea

LATE STAGE

Lakes and groundwater

NATURAL LAKE OCCUR WHERE a large quantity of water collects in a hollow in impermeable rock, or is prevented from draining away by a barrier, such as moraine (glacial deposits) or solidified lava. Lakes are often relatively short-lived landscape features, as they tend to become silted up by sediment from the streams and rivers that feed them. Some of the more long-lasting lakes are found in deep rift valleys formed by vertical movements of the Earth's crust (see pp. 58-59) – for example, Lake Baikal in Russia, the world's largest freshwater lake, and the Dead Sea in the Middle East, one of the world's saltiest lakes. Where water is able to drain away, it sinks into the ground until it reaches a layer of impermeable rock, then accumulates in the permeable rock above it; this water-saturated permeable rock is called an aquifer. The saturated zone varies in depth according to seasonal and climatic changes. In wet conditions, the water stored underground builds up, while in dry periods it becomes depleted. Where the upper edge of the saturated zone – the water table – meets the ground surface, water emerges as springs. In an artesian basin, where the aquifer is below an aquiclude (layer of impermeable rock), the water table throughout the basin is determined by its height at the rim. In the centre of such a basin, the water table is above ground level. The water in the basin is thus trapped below the water table and can rise under its own pressure along faultlines or well shafts.

LAKE BAIKAL, RUSSIA

LIMESTONE SPRING

COASTAL (VALLEY) SPRING

FAULT SPRING

LAVA SPRING

STRUCTURE OF AN ARTESIAN BASIN

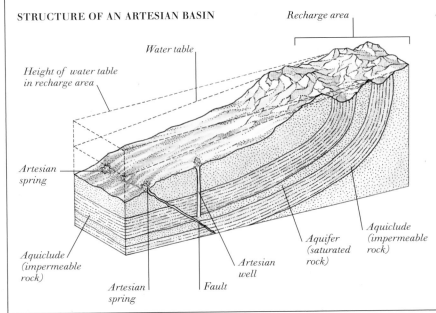

FEATURES OF A GROUNDWATER SYSTEM

Lake

Stream

Zone of aeration

Marsh

Layer of soil moisture

Zone of aeration

Capillary fringe

Water table

Saturated zone

CLOSE-UP OF SURFACE LAYER

Dry-season water table

Present water table (wet season)

Temporarily saturated zone (saturated only in wet season)

Permanently saturated zone (saturated in wet and dry seasons)

EXAMPLES OF LAKES

Glacial deposits

Lake in kettle (former site of ice block)

Oxbow lake (cut-off river meander)

River

KETTLE LAKE

OXBOW LAKE

Caldera (collapsed crater)

Volcanic lake

Movement along strike-slip (lateral) fault

Strike-slip (lateral) fault

Lake in elongated hollow

VOLCANIC LAKE

STRIKE-SLIP (LATERAL) FAULT LAKE

Rift valley

Steep back wall eroded by frost and ice

Moraine or rock lip damming lake

High valley walls

Sinking graben (block fault)

Tarn (circular mountain lake)

GRABEN (BLOCK-FAULT) LAKE

TARN

THE DEAD SEA, ISRAEL/JORDAN

River Jordan

Dead Sea

Steep rift-valley walls

Salt left by evaporation

Israel

Shallow flats

Jordan

293

Coastlines

COASTLINES ARE AMONG THE MOST RAPIDLY changing landscape
features. Some are eroded by waves, wind, and rain, causing
cliffs to be undercut and caves to be hollowed out of solid rock.
Others are built up by waves transporting sand and small rocks in a
process known as longshore drift, and by rivers depositing sediment in
deltas. Additional influences include the activities of living organisms
such as coral, crustal movements, and sea-level variations due to
climatic changes. Rising land or a drop in sea level creates an emergent
coastline, with cliffs and beaches stranded above the new shoreline.
Sinking land or a rise in sea level produces a drowned coastline, typified
by fjords (submerged glacial valleys) or submerged river valleys.

FEATURES OF A SEA-CLIFF

Cliff-top

Cliff-face

High tide
level

Low tide
level

Offshore
deposits

Wave-cut
platform

Undercut
area of cliff

FEATURES OF WAVES

Wave
height

Crest Wavelength Trough

Shorter wavelength
near beach

Circular orbit of water
and suspended particles

Orbit deformed into ellipse
as water gets shallower

Mature river

Headland

Bedding
plane

Sea-cliff

Remnants of
former headland

Estuary

LONGSHORE DRIFT

Pebble

Backwash

Movement of
material
along beach

Build-up
of material
against groyne

Beach

Groyne

Waves approaching
shore at an
oblique angle

Swash
zone

Swash

DEPOSITIONAL FEATURES OF COASTLINES

Bay-head
beach

Wave
direction

Headland

Wave
direction

Tombolo

Island

Wave
direction

Cuspate
foreland

Wave
direction

Barrier
beach

Lagoon

BAY HEAD BEACH

TOMBOLO

CUSPATE FORELAND

BARRIER BEACH

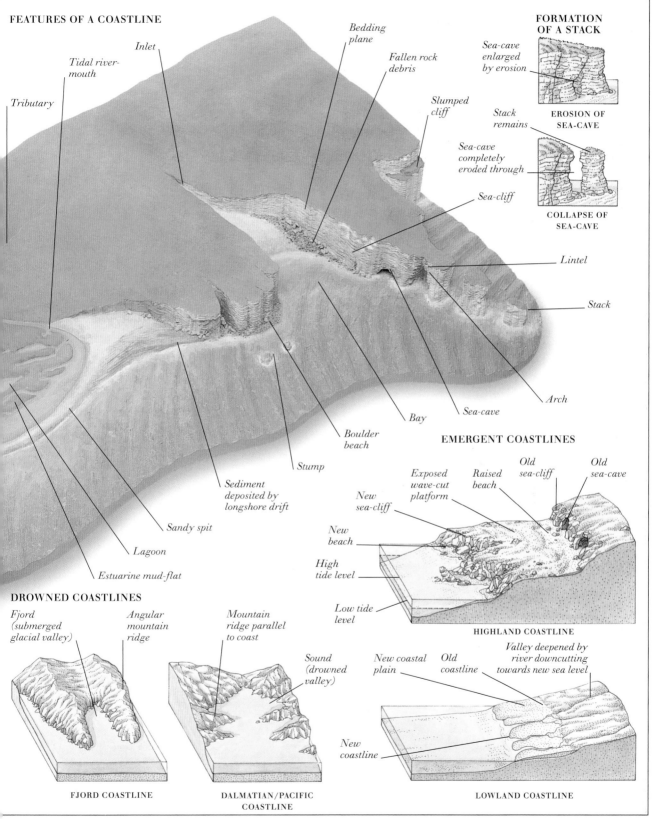

FEATURES OF A COASTLINE

Tributary

Tidal river-mouth

Inlet

Bedding plane

Fallen rock debris

Slumped cliff

Sea-cliff

FORMATION OF A STACK

Sea-cave enlarged by erosion

EROSION OF SEA-CAVE

Stack remains

Sea-cave completely eroded through

COLLAPSE OF SEA-CAVE

Lintel

Stack

Arch

Sea-cave

Bay

Boulder beach

Stump

Sediment deposited by longshore drift

Sandy spit

Lagoon

Estuarine mud-flat

EMERGENT COASTLINES

Exposed wave-cut platform

Raised beach

Old sea-cliff

Old sea-cave

New sea-cliff

New beach

High tide level

Low tide level

HIGHLAND COASTLINE

DROWNED COASTLINES

Fjord (submerged glacial valley)

Angular mountain ridge

Mountain ridge parallel to coast

Sound (drowned valley)

New coastal plain

Old coastline

Valley deepened by river downcutting towards new sea level

New coastline

FJORD COASTLINE

DALMATIAN/PACIFIC COASTLINE

LOWLAND COASTLINE

295

Oceans and seas

OCEANS AND SEAS COVER ABOUT 70 PER CENT of the Earth's surface and account for about 97 per cent of its total water. These oceans and seas play a crucial role in regulating temperature variations and determining climate. Their waters absorb heat from the Sun, especially in tropical regions, and the surface currents distribute it around the Earth, warming overlying air masses and neighbouring land in winter and cooling them in summer. The oceans are never still. Differences in temperature and salinity drive deep current systems, while surface currents are generated by winds blowing over the oceans. All currents are deflected – to the right in the Northern Hemisphere, to the left in the Southern Hemisphere – as a result of the Earth's rotation. This deflective factor is known as the Coriolis force. A current that begins on the surface is immediately deflected. This current in turn generates a current in the layer of water beneath, which is also deflected. As the movement is transmitted downwards, the deflections form an Ekman spiral. The waters of the oceans and seas are also moved by the constant ebb and flow of tides. These are caused by the gravitational pull of the Moon and Sun. The highest tides (Spring tides) occur at full and new Moon; the lowest tides (neap tides) occur at first and last quarter.

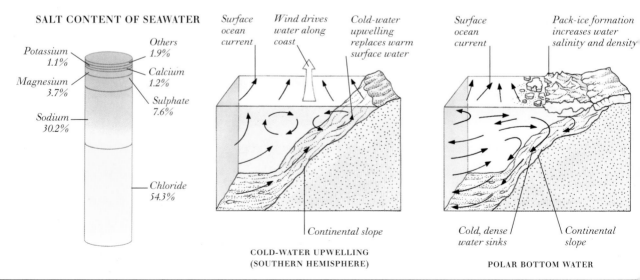

SALT CONTENT OF SEAWATER

Potassium 1.1%
Others 1.9%
Magnesium 3.7%
Calcium 1.2%
Sodium 30.2%
Sulphate 7.6%
Chloride 54.3%

Surface ocean current
Wind drives water along coast
Cold-water upwelling replaces warm surface water
Continental slope

COLD-WATER UPWELLING
(SOUTHERN HEMISPHERE)

Surface ocean current
Pack-ice formation increases water salinity and density
Cold, dense water sinks
Continental slope

POLAR BOTTOM WATER

ARCTIC CIRCLE
(66° 32'N)

TROPIC OF
CANCER
(23° 30'N)

EQUATOR
(0°)

TROPIC OF
CAPRICORN
(23° 30'S)

SOUTH
INDIAN
GYRE

ANTARCTIC
CIRCLE
(66° 32'S)

Oyashio Current

Kuroshio Current

North Equatorial Current

Equatorial Countercurrent

South Equatorial Current

Northeast Monsoon Drift

North Equatorial Current

Equatorial Countercurrent

South Equatorial Current

West Australian Current

East Australian Current

EFFECT OF CORIOLIS FORCE

North Pole

Coriolis force

Equator

Original direction of wind or current

Actual direction of wind or current

South Pole

Winds and currents deflected to right in Northern Hemisphere

Winds and currents deflected to left in Southern Hemisphere

EKMAN SPIRAL (NORTHERN HEMISPHERE)

Wind

Surface current caused by wind

Subsurface current slightly deflected by Coriolis force

Deep current at 180° to surface current

Midwater current further deflected by Coriolis force

HOW TIDES ARE CAUSED

HIGH
SPRING TIDE

New Moon

LOW
NEAP TIDE

Last quarter

Moon's gravitational pull

HIGH
SPRING TIDE

Full Moon

Equal and opposite tidal bulge produced by centrifugal effect due to Earth's spin

LOW
NEAP TIDE

First quarter

Earth's orbit

Earth

Tidal bulge caused by Sun's gravitational pull

Tidal bulge caused by Moon's gravitational pull

Sun's gravitational pull

Sun

Sun's gravitational pull reinforces centrifugal effect, producing large tidal bulge

Sun's gravitational pull diminishes Moon's effect

Moon's orbit

Moon

Tidal bulge where Moon's gravitational pull is strongest

The ocean floor

THE OCEAN FLOOR COMPRISES TWO SECTIONS: the continental
shelf and slope, and the deep-ocean floor. The continental shelf and
slope are part of the continental crust, but may extend far into the ocean.
Sloping quite gently to a depth of about 140 metres, the continental shelf
is covered in sandy deposits shaped by waves and tidal currents. At the
edge of the continental shelf, the seabed slopes down to the abyssal plain,
which lies at an average depth of about 3,800 metres. On this deep-
ocean floor is a layer of sediment made up of clays, fine oozes formed
from the remains of tiny sea creatures, and occasional mineral-rich
deposits. Echo-sounding and remote sensing from satellites has revealed
that the abyssal plain is divided by a system of mountain ranges, far
bigger than any on land – the mid-ocean ridge. Here, magma (molten
rock) wells up from the Earth's interior and solidifies, widening the
ocean floor (see pp. 58-59). As the ocean floor spreads, volcanoes that
have formed over hot spots in the crust move away from their magma
source; they become extinct and are increasingly submerged and
eroded. Volcanoes eroded below sea level remain as seamounts
(underwater mountains). In warm waters, a volcano that projects
above the ocean surface often acquires a fringing coral reef, which
may develop into an atoll as the volcano becomes submerged.

CONTINENTAL-SHELF FLOOR

Bedrock
exposed by
tidal scour

Shoreline

Parallel strips
of coarse
material left
by strong
tidal currents

Sand
deposited
in wavy
pattern by
weaker
currents

Irregular patches of
fine sand deposited
by weakest currents

FEATURES OF THE OCEAN FLOOR

Sediment

Submarine
canyon

Continental
shelf

Course of
mud river

Continental
rise

Continental
slope

Guyot (flat-topped
seamount)

Seamount
(underwater
mountain)

Abyssal
plain

Continental
crust

Ooze (sediment
consisting of remains
of tiny sea creatures)

Layer of
volcanic
rock

Pillow
lava

Volcanic
crystalline
rock

Oceanic
crust

DEEP-OCEAN FLOOR SEDIMENTS

KEY

- Calcareous ooze
- Pelagic clay
- Glacial sediments
- Siliceous ooze
- Terrigenous sediments
- Continental margin sediments
- Metalliferous muds
- Major nodule fields

ECHO-SOUND PROFILE OF OCEAN FLOOR

Sand wave

Event mark indicates synchronization of survey equipment

Sand wave

Seabed profile

Minor oscillations caused by ship's movement

Velocity of sound in water (1,493 m/sec)

Reference code

Mid-ocean ridge

Ocean trench

Magma (molten rock)

Sediment

DEVELOPMENT OF AN ATOLL

Volcanic island

Sea level

Coral grows on shoreline

Lagoon

FRINGING REEF

Eroded volcanic island subsides

Coral continues to grow, forming barrier reef

BARRIER REEF

Lagoon

Coral continues to grow where waves bring food

Dead coral

Volcanic island becomes submerged

ATOLL

Coral submerged too deeply to grow

Volcanic island is submerged further

SUBMERGED ATOLL

299

The atmosphere

JET STREAM

THE EARTH IS SURROUNDED BY ITS ATMOSPHERE, a blanket of gases that enables life to exist on the planet. This layer has no definite outer edge, gradually becoming thinner until it merges into space, but over 80 per cent of atmospheric gases are held by gravity within about 20 kilometres of the Earth's surface. The atmosphere blocks out much harmful ultraviolet solar radiation, and insulates the Earth against extremes of temperature by limiting both incoming solar radiation and the escape of re-radiated heat into space. This natural balance may be distorted by the greenhouse effect, as gases such as carbon dioxide have built up in the atmosphere, trapping more heat. Close to the Earth's surface, differences in air temperature and pressure cause air to circulate between the equator and poles. This circulation, together with the Coriolis force, gives rise to the prevailing surface winds and the high-level jet streams.

ATMOSPHERIC CIRCULATION AND WINDS

North Pole (high pressure)
Rotation of Earth
Polar cell
Polar easterlies
Ferrel cell
Low-pressure zone
Polar jet stream
Westerlies
Subtropical jet stream
High-pressure zone
Hadley cell
North-east trade winds
Equator
Intertropical convergence zone (low pressure)
Warm equatorial air rises and flows towards pole
South-east trade winds
High-pressure zone
Air cools and sinks
Westerlies
South Pole (high pressure)
Low-pressure zone
Polar easterlies

Exosphere (altitude above about 500 km)
Corona
Thermosphere (altitude about 100–500 km)
Ozone layer absorbs ultraviolet radiation from Sun
Mesosphere (altitude about 50–100 km)
Stratosphere (altitude about 10–50 km)
Troposphere (altitude up to about 10 km)

FORMATION OF ROSSBY WAVES IN THE JET STREAM

Long Rossby wave develops in polar jet stream
Cold air
Rossby wave becomes more pronounced
Fully developed Rossby wave
Warm air

INITIAL UNDULATION

DEEPENING WAVE

DEVELOPED WAVE

STRUCTURE OF THE ATMOSPHERE

GLOBAL WARMING

Solar radiation
re-radiated as heat

Some re-radiated
heat escapes
into space

Sun

Some re-radiated
heat reflected back
to Earth

Incoming solar
radiation

Earth

Atmosphere

**NATURALLY MODERATED
GREENHOUSE EFFECT**

Meteor (shooting star)
burns up as it passes
through atmosphere

Less re-radiated
heat escapes

Solar radiation
re-radiated as heat

More re-radiated
heat reflected
back to Earth

Surface
temperature
rises

Aurora

"Greenhouse
gases" accumulate
in atmosphere

Incoming solar
radiation

**UNBALANCED GREENHOUSE
EFFECT**

14% of incoming solar
radiation absorbed
by atmosphere

7% of incoming solar
radiation reflected
by atmosphere

COMPOSITION OF THE LOWER ATMOSPHERE

24% of incoming
solar radiation
reflected by clouds

Other elements less
than 0.1%

Argon 0.93%

Cosmic rays (high-energy
particles from space)
penetrate to stratosphere

Oxygen 21%

Some absorbed
heat re-radiated
by atmosphere

4% of incoming solar
radiation reflected by
oceans and land

Nitrogen 78%

51% of incoming solar
radiation absorbed by
Earth's surface

Some absorbed heat
re-radiated by clouds

Weather

WEATHER IS DEFINED AS THE ATMOSPHERIC CONDITIONS at a particular time and place; climate is the average weather conditions for a given region over time. Weather is assessed in terms of temperature, wind, cloud cover, and precipitation, such as rain or snow. Fine weather is associated with high-pressure areas, where air is sinking. Cloudy, wet, changeable weather is common in low-pressure zones with rising, unstable air. Such conditions occur at temperate latitudes, where warm air meets cool air along the polar fronts. Here, spiralling low-pressure cells known as depressions (mid-latitude cyclones) often form. A depression usually contains a sector of warmer air, beginning at a warm front and ending at a cold front. If the two fronts merge, forming an occluded front, the warm air is pushed upwards. An extreme form of low-pressure cell is a hurricane (also called a typhoon or tropical cyclone), which brings torrential rain and exceptionally strong winds.

TYPES OF OCCLUDED FRONT

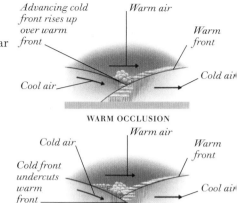

Advancing cold front rises up over warm front

Warm air

Warm front

Cool air

Cold air

WARM OCCLUSION

Cold air

Warm air

Warm front

Cold front undercuts warm front

Cool air

COLD OCCLUSION

FORMS OF PRECIPITATION

Water droplets less than 0.5 mm in diameter fall as drizzle

Water droplets coalesce to form raindrops 0.5–5.0 mm in diameter

Rising air

RAIN FROM CLOUDS NOT REACHING FREEZING LEVEL

Coalesced water droplets fall as rain

Ice crystal

Snowflakes grown from ice crystals fall as snow

Rising air

Snowflakes melt to fall as rain

RAIN AND SNOW FROM CLOUDS REACHING FREEZING LEVEL

Vertical air currents toss frozen water droplets up and down

Alternate freezing and melting builds up layers of ice

Rising air

Ice falls as hailstones

HAIL

TYPES OF CLOUD

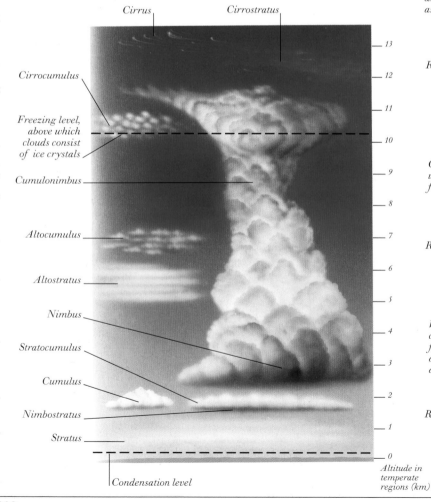

Cirrus

Cirrostratus

Cirrocumulus

Freezing level, above which clouds consist of ice crystals

Cumulonimbus

Altocumulus

Altostratus

Nimbus

Stratocumulus

Cumulus

Nimbostratus

Stratus

Condensation level

Altitude in temperate regions (km)

13
12
11
10
9
8
7
6
5
4
3
2
1
0

STRUCTURE OF A HURRICANE

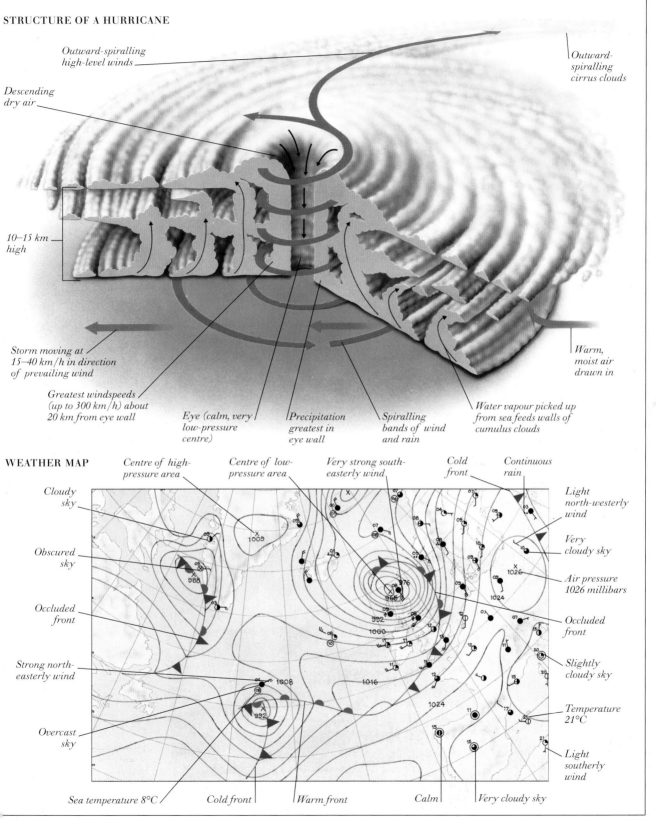

Outward-spiralling high-level winds

Outward-spiralling cirrus clouds

Descending dry air

10–15 km high

Storm moving at 15–40 km/h in direction of prevailing wind

Greatest windspeeds (up to 300 km/h) about 20 km from eye wall

Eye (calm, very low-pressure centre)

Precipitation greatest in eye wall

Spiralling bands of wind and rain

Water vapour picked up from sea feeds walls of cumulus clouds

Warm, moist air drawn in

WEATHER MAP

Centre of high-pressure area

Centre of low-pressure area

Very strong south-easterly wind

Cold front

Continuous rain

Cloudy sky

Light north-westerly wind

Obscured sky

Very cloudy sky

Occluded front

Air pressure 1026 millibars

Strong north-easterly wind

Occluded front

Slightly cloudy sky

Overcast sky

Temperature 21°C

Light southerly wind

Sea temperature 8°C

Cold front

Warm front

Calm

Very cloudy sky

303

PHYSICS AND CHEMISTRY

The variety of matter

PLANT AND INSECT (LIVING MATTER)

MATTER IS ANYTHING THAT HAS A MASS. It includes everything from natural substances, such as minerals or living organisms, to synthetic materials. Matter can exist in three distinct states – solid, liquid, and gas. A solid is rigid and retains its shape. A liquid is fluid, has a definite volume, and will take the shape of its container. A gas (also fluid) fills a space, so its volume will be the same as the volume of its container. Most substances can exist as a solid, a liquid, or a gas: the state is determined by temperature. At very high temperatures, matter becomes plasma, often considered to be a fourth state of matter. All matter is composed of microscopic particles, such as atoms and molecules (see pp. 308-309). The arrangement and interactions of these particles give a substance its physical and chemical properties, by which matter can be identified. There is a huge variety of matter because particles can arrange themselves in countless ways, in one substance or by mixing with others. Natural glass, for example, seems to be a solid but is, in fact, a supercool liquid: the atoms are not locked into a pattern and can flow. Pure substances known as elements (see p. 310) combine to form compounds or mixtures. Mixtures called colloids are made up of larger particles of matter suspended in a solid, liquid, or gas, while a solution is one substance dissolved in another.

TYPES OF COLLOID

HAIR GEL (SOLID IN LIQUID)

SHAVING FOAM (AIR IN LIQUID)

MIST (LIQUID IN GAS)

EXAMPLES OF MATTER

The element silicon in pure crystalline form

Polythene is made by combining natural materials in new ways

Low pressure gases

Streaks of plasma (mixture of electrons and charged atoms)

Voltage tears electrons from atoms of low pressure gases inside

Central electrode

POLYTHENE (SYNTHETIC POLYMER)

PURE SILICON (SEMICONDUCTOR)

BALL CONTAINING HIGH-TEMPERATURE GAS (PLASMA)

Obsidian is molten volcanic rock that cools quickly, so atoms cannot form a regular pattern

Solid crystals dissolve in liquid water

Water

Potassium permanganate crystals

Azurite is found naturally with deposits of copper ore

OBSIDIAN (NATURAL GLASS)

AZURITE (CRYSTALLINE MINERAL)

POTASSIUM PERMANGANATE AND WATER (SOLUTION)

STATES OF MATTER

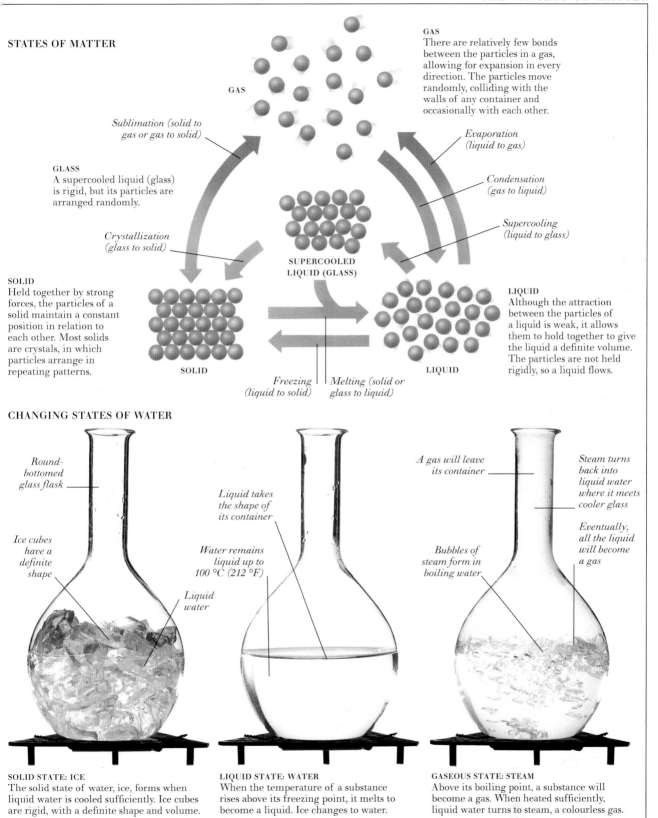

GAS
There are relatively few bonds between the particles in a gas, allowing for expansion in every direction. The particles move randomly, colliding with the walls of any container and occasionally with each other.

GAS

Sublimation (solid to gas or gas to solid)

Evaporation (liquid to gas)

GLASS
A supercooled liquid (glass) is rigid, but its particles are arranged randomly.

Condensation (gas to liquid)

Crystallization (glass to solid)

Supercooling (liquid to glass)

SUPERCOOLED LIQUID (GLASS)

SOLID
Held together by strong forces, the particles of a solid maintain a constant position in relation to each other. Most solids are crystals, in which particles arrange in repeating patterns.

LIQUID
Although the attraction between the particles of a liquid is weak, it allows them to hold together to give the liquid a definite volume. The particles are not held rigidly, so a liquid flows.

SOLID

LIQUID

Freezing (liquid to solid)

Melting (solid or glass to liquid)

CHANGING STATES OF WATER

Round-bottomed glass flask

A gas will leave its container

Steam turns back into liquid water where it meets cooler glass

Liquid takes the shape of its container

Ice cubes have a definite shape

Water remains liquid up to 100 °C (212 °F)

Eventually, all the liquid will become a gas

Liquid water

Bubbles of steam form in boiling water

SOLID STATE: ICE
The solid state of water, ice, forms when liquid water is cooled sufficiently. Ice cubes are rigid, with a definite shape and volume.

LIQUID STATE: WATER
When the temperature of a substance rises above its freezing point, it melts to become a liquid. Ice changes to water.

GASEOUS STATE: STEAM
Above its boiling point, a substance will become a gas. When heated sufficiently, liquid water turns to steam, a colourless gas.

Atoms and molecules

FALSE-COLOUR
IMAGE OF ACTUAL
GOLD ATOMS

ATOMS ARE THE smallest individual parts of an element (see pp. 310-311). They are tiny, with diameters in the order of one ten-thousand-millionth of a metre (10^{-10} m). Two or more atoms join together (bond) to form a molecule of a substance known as a compound. For example, when atoms of the elements hydrogen and fluorine join together, they form a molecule of the compound hydrogen fluoride. So molecules are the smallest individual parts of a compound. Atoms themselves are not indivisible – they possess an internal structure. At their centre is a dense nucleus, consisting of protons, which have a positive electric charge (see p. 316), and neutrons, which are uncharged. Around the nucleus are the negatively charged electrons. It is the electrons that give a substance most of its physical and chemical properties. They do not follow definite paths around the nucleus. Instead, electrons are said to be found within certain regions, called orbitals. These are arranged around the nucleus in "shells", each containing electrons of a particular energy. For example, the first shell (1) can hold up to two electrons, in a so-called s-orbital (1s). The second shell (2) can hold up to eight electrons, in s-orbitals (2s) and p-orbitals (2p). If an atom loses an electron, it becomes a positive ion (cation). If an electron is gained, an atom becomes a negative ion (anion). Ions of opposite charges will attract and join together, in a type of bonding known as ionic bonding. In covalent bonding, the atoms bond by sharing their electrons in what become molecular orbitals.

ATOMIC ORBITALS

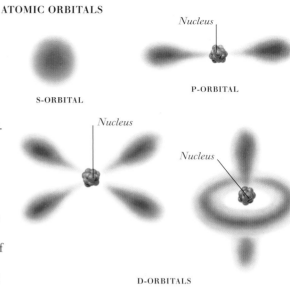

Nucleus

S-ORBITAL

Nucleus

P-ORBITAL

Nucleus

Nucleus

D-ORBITALS

MOLECULAR ORBITALS

Nucleus

Nucleus

π- (PI) ORBITAL

Nucleus

Nucleus

Σ- (SIGMA) ORBITAL

Nucleus

SP³-HYBRID ORBITAL

EXAMPLE OF IONIC BONDING

1s-orbital

1s-orbital

1s-orbital

Second shell holds seven electrons

Second shell now holds eight electrons, and is "filled"

Charged atoms (ions) held together by electrostatic forces

Electron transfer

Li^+ ion

F^- ion

2s-orbital

2p-orbital

2p-orbital

2s-orbital

2p-orbital

Lithium atom loses 2s electron and becomes positively charged (Li^+ ion)

Fluorine atom gains electron and becomes negatively charged (F^- ion)

1. NEUTRAL LITHIUM ATOM (Li)

NEUTRAL FLUORINE ATOM (F)

2. ELECTRON TRANSFER

3. IONIC BONDING: LITHIUM FLUORIDE MOLECULE (LiF)

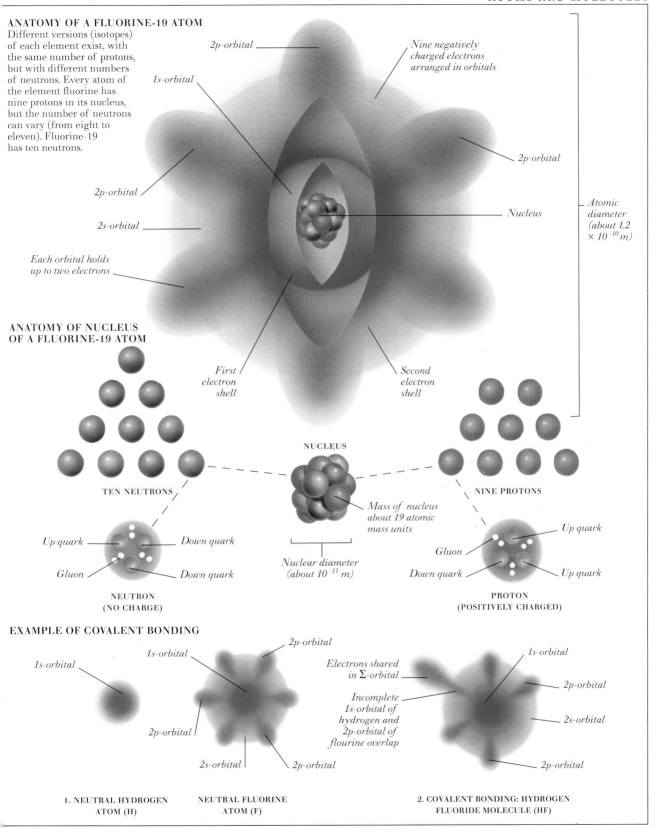

ANATOMY OF A FLUORINE-19 ATOM
Different versions (isotopes) of each element exist, with the same number of protons, but with different numbers of neutrons. Every atom of the element fluorine has nine protons in its nucleus, but the number of neutrons can vary (from eight to eleven). Fluorine-19 has ten neutrons.

2p-orbital

1s-orbital

2p-orbital

2s-orbital

Each orbital holds up to two electrons

Nine negatively charged electrons arranged in orbitals

2p-orbital

Nucleus

Atomic diameter (about 1.2 × 10^{-10} m)

First electron shell

Second electron shell

ANATOMY OF NUCLEUS OF A FLUORINE-19 ATOM

NUCLEUS

TEN NEUTRONS

NINE PROTONS

Mass of nucleus about 19 atomic mass units

Nuclear diameter (about 10^{-15} m)

Up quark

Down quark

Gluon

Down quark

Up quark

Gluon

Down quark

Up quark

NEUTRON (NO CHARGE)

PROTON (POSITIVELY CHARGED)

EXAMPLE OF COVALENT BONDING

1s-orbital

1s-orbital

2p-orbital

2p-orbital

2s-orbital

2p-orbital

Electrons shared in Σ-orbital

Incomplete 1s-orbital of hydrogen and 2p-orbital of flourine overlap

1s-orbital

2p-orbital

2s-orbital

2p-orbital

1. NEUTRAL HYDROGEN ATOM (H)

NEUTRAL FLUORINE ATOM (F)

2. COVALENT BONDING: HYDROGEN FLUORIDE MOLECULE (HF)

The periodic table

AN ELEMENT is a substance that consists of atoms of one type only. The 92 elements that occur naturally, and the 17 elements created artificially, are often arranged into a chart called the periodic table. Each element is defined by its atomic number – the number of protons in the nucleus of each of its atoms (it is also the number of electrons present). Atomic number increases along each row (period) and down each column (group). The shape of the table is determined by the way in which electrons arrange themselves around the nucleus: the positioning of elements in order of increasing atomic number brings together atoms with a similar pattern of orbiting electrons (orbitals). These appear in blocks. Electrons occupy shells of a certain energy (see pp. 308–309). Periods are ordered according to the filling of successive shells with electrons, while groups reflect the number of electrons in the outer shell (valency electrons). These outer electrons are important – they decide the chemical properties of the atom. Elements that appear in the same group have similar properties because they have the same number of electrons in their outer shell. Elements in Group 0 have "filled shells", where the outer shell holds its maximum number of electrons, and are stable. Atoms of Group I elements have just one electron in their outer shell. This makes them unstable – and ready to react with other substances.

METALS AND NON-METALS

Elements at the left-hand side of each period are metals. Metals easily lose electrons and form positive ions. Non-metals, on the right of a period, tend to become negative ions. Semi-metals, which have properties of both metals and non-metals, are between the two.

TYPES OF ELEMENT KEY:

- Alkali metals
- Alkaline earth metals
- Transition metals
- Lanthanides
- Actinides
- Poor metals
- Semi-metals
- Non-metals
- Noble gases
- Unknown chemical properties

Atomic number is number of protons in each nucleus

Atomic number goes up by one along each period

1st transition metals

Two series always separated out from the table to give it a coherent shape

s-block

d-block

RELATIVE ATOMIC MASS

Atomic number
Chemical symbol
Chemical name
Relative atomic mass

Atomic mass (formerly atomic weight) is the mass of each atom of an element. It is equal to the number of protons plus the number of neutrons (electrons have negligible mass). The figures given are the averages for all the different versions (isotopes) of each element, measured relative to the mass of carbon-12.

| 1 | H | Hydrogen | 1.0 |

Soft, silvery, and highly reactive metal

SODIUM: GROUP 1 METAL

Silvery, reactive metal

MAGNESIUM: GROUP 2 METAL

Hard, silvery metal

CHROMIUM: 1ST TRANSITION METAL

Radioactive metal

PLUTONIUM: ACTINIDE SERIES METAL

| 57 La Lanthanum 138.9 | 58 Ce Cerium 140.1 | 59 Pr Praseodymium 140.9 | 60 Nd Neodymium 144.2 |
| 89 Ac Actinium (227) | 90 Th Thorium 252.0 | 91 Pa Protactinium 231.0 | 92 U Uranium 258.0 |

Bright yellow crystal

SULPHUR:
GROUP 6 SOLID NON-METAL

IODINE:
GROUP 7
SOLID NON-METAL

Purple-black solid turns to gas easily

ALLOTROPES OF CARBON
Some elements exist in more than one form — these are known as allotropes. Carbon powder, graphite, and diamond are allotropes of carbon. They all consist of carbon atoms, but have very different physical properties.

DIAMOND

GRAPHITE   CARBON POWDER

Boron and carbon groups   *Nitrogen and oxygen groups*   *Halogens*   *Group 0*

| | | | | | 2
He
Helium
4.0 | ⎤ *Period* |
| *Group III* | *Group IV* | *Group V* | *Group VI* | *Group VII* | | |

| 5
B
Boron
10.8 | 6
C
Carbon
12.0 | 7
N
Nitrogen
14.0 | 8
O
Oxygen
16.0 | 9
F
Fluorine
19.0 | 10
Ne
Neon
20.2 | *Short period* |
| 13
Al
Aluminium
27.0 | 14
Si
Silicon
28.1 | 15
P
Phosphorus
31.0 | 16
S
Sulphur
32.1 | 17
Cl
Chlorine
35.5 | 18
Ar
Argon
40.0 | |

2nd transition metals   *3rd transition metals*

26 **Fe** Iron 55.8	27 **Co** Cobalt 58.9	28 **Ni** Nickel 58.7	29 **Cu** Copper 63.5	30 **Zn** Zinc 65.4	31 **Ga** Gallium 69.7	32 **Ge** Germanium 72.6	33 **As** Arsenic 74.9	34 **Se** Selenium 79.0	35 **Br** Bromine 79.9	36 **Kr** Krypton 83.8	⎤ *Long period*
44 **Ru** Ruthenium 101.1	45 **Rh** Rhodium 102.9	46 **Pd** Palladium 106.4	47 **Ag** Silver 107.9	48 **Cd** Cadmium 112.4	49 **In** Indium 114.8	50 **Sn** Tin 118.7	51 **Sb** Antimony 121.8	52 **Te** Tellurium 127.6	53 **I** Iodine 126.9	54 **Xe** Xenon 131.3	
76 **Os** Osmium 190.2	77 **Ir** Iridium 192.2	78 **Pt** Platinum 195.1	79 **Au** Gold 197.0	80 **Hg** Mercury 200.6	81 **Tl** Thallium 204.4	82 **Pb** Lead 207.2	83 **Bi** Bismuth 209.0	84 **Po** Polonium (209)	85 **At** Astatine (210)	86 **Rn** Radon (222)	
108 **Hs** Hassium (269)	109 **Mt** Meitnerium (278)	110 **Ds** Darmstadtium (281)	111 **Rg** Roentgenium (281)	112 **Cn** Copernicium (285)	113 **Uut** Ununtrium (286)	114 **Uuq** Ununquadium (289)	115 **Uup** Ununpentium (289)	116 **Uuh** Ununhexium (293)	117 **Uus** Ununseptium (294)	118 **Uuo** Ununoctium (294)	

Unreactive, colourless gas glows red in discharge tube

d-block   *p-block*

Yellow, unreactive precious metal

Soft, shiny, reactive metal

Shiny semi-metal

NOBLE GASES
Group 0 contains elements that have a filled (complete) outer shell of electrons, which means the atoms do not need to lose or gain electrons by bonding with other atoms. This makes them stable and they do not easily form ions or react with other elements. Noble gases are also called rare or inert gases.

NEON:
GROUP 0
COLOURLESS GAS

GOLD:
3RD TRANSITION METAL

TIN:
GROUP 4 POOR METAL

ANTIMONY:
GROUP 5 SEMI-METAL

| 61
Pm
Promethium
(145) | 62
Sm
Samarium
150.4 | 63
Eu
Europium
152.0 | 64
Gd
Gadolinium
157.3 | 65
Tb
Terbium
158.9 | 66
Dy
Dysprosium
162.5 | 67
Ho
Holmium
164.9 | 68
Er
Erbium
167.3 | 69
Tm
Thulium
168.9 | 70
Yb
Ytterbium
173.0 | 71
Lu
Lutetium
175.0 |
| 93
Np
Neptunium
(237) | 94
Pu
Plutonium
(244) | 95
Am
Americium
(243) | 96
Cm
Curium
(247) | 97
Bk
Berkelium
(247) | 98
Cf
Californium
(251) | 99
Es
Einsteinium
(252) | 100
Fm
Fermium
(257) | 101
Md
Mendelevium
(258) | 102
No
Nobelium
(259) | 103
Lr
Lawrencium
(262) |

f-block

Chemical reactions

A CHEMICAL REACTION TAKES PLACE whenever bonds between atoms are broken or made. In each case, atoms or groups of atoms rearrange, making new substances (products) from the original ones (reactants). Reactions happen naturally, or can be made to happen; they may take years, or only an instant. Some of the main types are shown here. A reaction usually involves a change in energy (see pp. 314-315). In a burning reaction, for example, the making of new bonds between atoms releases energy as heat and light. This type of reaction, in which heat is given off, is an exothermic reaction. Many reactions, like burning, are irreversible, but some can take place in either direction, and are said to be reversible. Reactions can be used to form solids from solutions: in a double decomposition reaction, two compounds in solution break down and re-form into two new substances, often creating a precipitate (insoluble solid); in displacement, an element (eg. copper) displaces another element (eg. silver) from a solution. The rate (speed) of a reaction is determined by many different factors, such as temperature, and the size and shape of the reactants. To describe and keep track of reactions, internationally recognized chemical symbols and equations are used. Reactions are also used in the laboratory to identify matter. An experiment with candle wax, for example, demonstrates that it contains carbon and hydrogen.

SALT FORMATION (ACID ON METAL)

Glass beaker

Hydrogen gas (H_2) given off

Zinc (Zn) replaces hydrogen in acid (HCl) to form zinc chloride solution ($ZnCl_2$)

Hydrogen in acid driven off when acid meets a reactive metal

Hydrochloric acid (HCl)

Effervescence

Zinc metal chippings (Zn)

Zinc metal chippings (Zn)

THE REACTION
Hydrochloric acid added to zinc produces zinc chloride and hydrogen.
$$Zn + 2HCl \rightarrow ZnCl_2 + H_2$$

DISPLACEMENT

Copper metal (Cu)

Copper (Cu) displaces silver ions (Ag^{2+}) from silver nitrate solution ($AgNO_3$)

Silver nitrate solution ($AgNO_3$)

Blue solution of copper nitrate ($Cu(NO_3)_2$) forms

Two metals compete for nitrate ions

Glass flask

Needles of silver metal (Ag) form

THE REACTION
Copper metal added to silver nitrate solution produces copper nitrate and silver metal.
$$Cu + 2AgNO_3 \rightarrow Cu(NO_3)_2 + 2Ag$$

BURNING MATTER

Ammonium dichromate (($NH_4)_2Cr_2O_7$)

In this burning reaction, atoms form simpler substances and give off heat and light

Flame

Ammonium dichromate (($NH_4)_2Cr_2O_7$) converts to chromium oxide (Cr_2O_3)

Nitrogen monoxide (NO) and water vapour (H_2O) given off as colourless gases

THE REACTION
When lit, ammonium dichromate combines with oxygen from air.
$$(NH_4)_2Cr_2O_7 + O_2 \rightarrow Cr_2O_3 + 4H_2O + 2NO$$

A REVERSIBLE REACTION

Flat-bottomed glass flask

Potassium Chromate solution (K_2CrO_4)

Bright yellow solution contains potassium and chromate ions

Pipette

Hydrochloric acid (HCl) added in drops

Acid causes reaction to take place

Chromate ions converted to orange dichromate ions

Potassium dichromate (KCr_2O_7) forms

Pipette

Sodium hydroxide (NaOH) added in drops

Sodium hydroxide (NaOH) neutralizes the acid

Solution turns to bright orange of potassium dichromate

Potassium dichromate (KCr_2O_7) re-forms to potassium chromate (K_2CrO_4)

Solution returns to original bright yellow colour

1. THE REACTANT
Potassium chromate dissolves in water to form potassium ions and chromate ions.
$$K_2CrO_4 \rightarrow 2K^+ + CrO_4^{2-}$$

2. THE REACTION
Addition of hydrochloric acid changes chromate ions into dichromate ions.
$$2CrO_4^{2-} \rightarrow Cr_2O_7^{2-}$$

3. REVERSING
Addition of sodium hydroxide changes dichromate ions back into chromate ions.
$$Cr_2O_7^{2-} \rightarrow 2CrO_4^{2-}$$

FERMENTATION

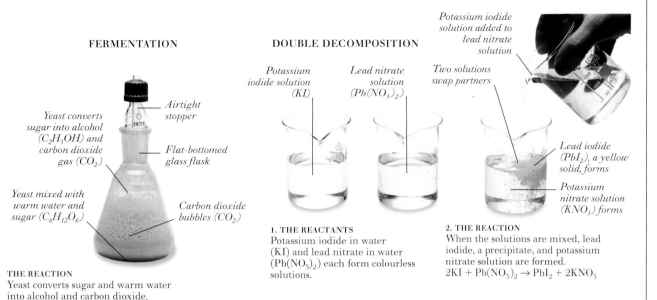

Yeast converts sugar into alcohol (C_2H_5OH) and carbon dioxide gas (CO_2)

Airtight stopper

Flat-bottomed glass flask

Yeast mixed with warm water and sugar ($C_6H_{12}O_6$)

Carbon dioxide bubbles (CO_2)

THE REACTION
Yeast converts sugar and warm water into alcohol and carbon dioxide.
$$C_6H_{12}O_6 \rightarrow 2C_2H_5OH + 2CO_2$$

DOUBLE DECOMPOSITION

Potassium iodide solution (KI)

Lead nitrate solution ($Pb(NO_3)_2$)

Two solutions swap partners

Potassium iodide solution added to lead nitrate solution

Lead iodide (PbI_2), a yellow solid, forms

Potassium nitrate solution (KNO_3) forms

1. THE REACTANTS
Potassium iodide in water (KI) and lead nitrate in water ($Pb(NO_3)_2$) each form colourless solutions.

2. THE REACTION
When the solutions are mixed, lead iodide, a precipitate, and potassium nitrate solution are formed.
$$2KI + Pb(NO_3)_2 \rightarrow PbI_2 + 2KNO_3$$

TESTING CANDLE WAX, AN ORGANIC COMPOUND

Burning produces carbon dioxide gas (CO_2) and water vapour (H_2O)

Delivery tube

Clamp stand

Unburned carbon forms soot particles

Gases are trapped in funnel

Bung

Delivery tube

Bung

Flame

Thistle funnel

U-tube

Bung

Tube connection to pump that sucks gases through

Burning candle wax

Water vapour condenses to form liquid water (H_2O)

Clamp

Carbon dioxide gas (CO_2) given off

Test tube

Candle wax ($C_{18}H_{38}$), a hydrocarbon, contains the elements carbon and hydrogen

Water vapour trapped by solid drying agent, anhydrous copper sulphate ($CuSO_4$)

Anhydrous copper sulphate ($CuSO_4$)

Calcium hydroxide ($Ca(OH)_2$) and carbon dioxide (CO_2) form insoluble calcium carbonate ($CaCO_3$): lime water becomes milky

Calcium hydroxide solution (lime water, $Ca(OH)_2$)

Anhydrous copper sulphate crystals ($CuSO_4$) combine with water vapour (H_2O) to form darker blue hydrated copper sulphate ($CuSO_4$. $10H_2O$)

1. THE BURNING REACTION
Burning wax produces carbon dioxide gas and water vapour.
$$2C_{18}H_{38} + 55O_2 \rightarrow 36CO_2 + 38H_2O$$

2. TESTING FOR WATER VAPOUR
A solid drying agent traps water vapour, proving the presence of hydrogen in the candle wax.
$$CuSO_4 + 10H_2O \rightarrow CuSO_4 . 10H_2O$$

3. TESTING FOR CARBON DIOXIDE
Calcium hydroxide in solution reacts with carbon dioxide, forming a carbonate and turning milky.
$$Ca(OH)_2 + CO_2 \rightarrow CaCO_3 + H_2O$$

Energy

ANYTHING THAT HAPPENS – from a pin-drop to an explosion – requires energy. Energy is the capacity for "doing work" (making something happen). Various forms of energy exist, including light, heat, sound, electrical, chemical, nuclear, kinetic, and potential energies. The Law of Conservation of Energy states that the total amount of energy in the Universe is fixed – energy cannot be created or destroyed. It means that energy can only change from one form to another (energy transfer). For example, potential energy is energy that is "stored", and can be used in the future. An object gains potential energy when it is lifted; as the object is released, potential energy changes into the energy of motion (kinetic energy). During transference, some of the energy converts into heat. A combined heat and power station can put some of the otherwise "waste" heat to useful effect in local schools and housing. Most of the Earth's energy is provided by the Sun, in the form of electromagnetic radiation (see pp. 316-317). Some of this energy transfers to plant and animal life, and ultimately to fossil fuels, where it is stored in chemical form. Our bodies obtain energy from the food we eat, while energy needed for other tasks, such as heating and transport, can be obtained by burning fossil fuels – or by harnessing natural forces like wind or moving water – to generate electricity. Another source is nuclear power, where energy is released by reactions in the nucleus of an atom. All energy is measured by the international unit, the joule (J). As a guide, one joule is about equal to the amount of energy needed to lift an apple one metre.

SANKEY DIAGRAM SHOWING ENERGY FLOW IN A COAL-FIRED COMBINED HEAT AND POWER STATION

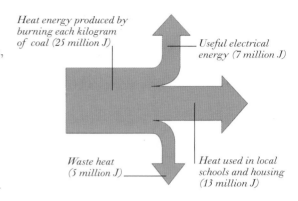

Heat energy produced by burning each kilogram of coal (25 million J)

Useful electrical energy (7 million J)

Waste heat (5 million J)

Heat used in local schools and housing (13 million J)

CROSS-SECTION OF HYDROELECTRIC POWER STATION WITH FRANCIS TURBINE

Transformer

Insulator

High voltage cable

Switch gear including circuit braker

Bushing

Rotor house

Generator unit

Gate

Generator rotor turned by turbine

Shaft

Francis turbine

Curved blade

Gate

Afterbay

Screen

Water in reservoir

Potential energy of water intake turns turbine

Penstock

Draft tube

Tailrace

Water that flows out has lost some energy

CROSS-SECTION OF NUCLEAR POWER STATION WITH PRESSURIZED WATER REACTOR

Steam generator

Concrete shielding

Water pressurizer

Steel girder framework

Control rod

Reactor core

Pump

Moderator (water)

Enriched uranium fuel

Coolant (water) takes heat from reactor core to heat exchanger

Water pumped back into steam generator

Heat exchanger

Water in heat exchanger turns to steam

Steam drives turbine

Pump

Turbine shaft turns generator

Generator produces electric current at 25,000 volts

Water cools used steam

Steam loses energy to turbine and condenses back to water

Transformer increases voltage to 300,000 volts

High voltage cable

Pylon carries high voltage electricity

Hot water to cooling tower

Cold water from cooling tower

ENERGY SYSTEMS

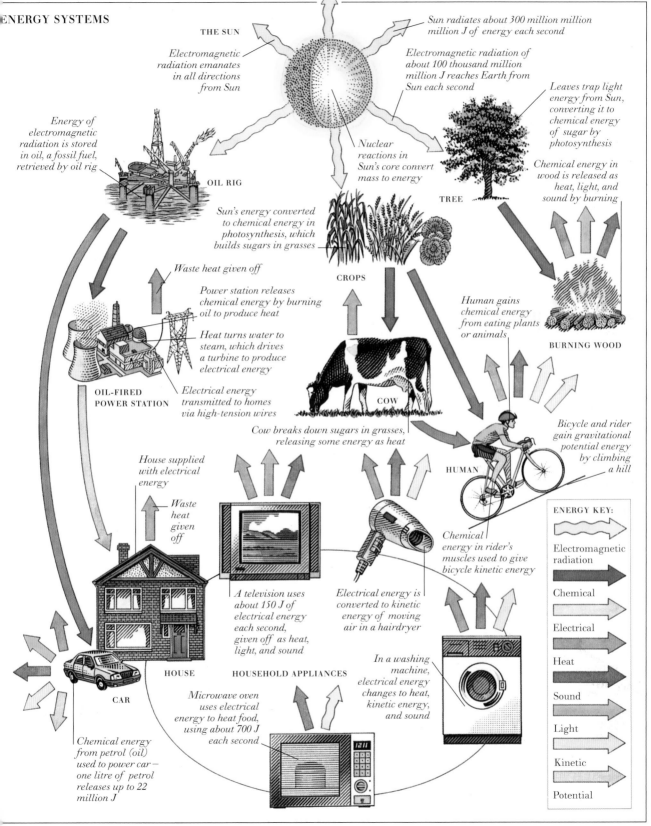

THE SUN

Electromagnetic radiation emanates in all directions from Sun

Sun radiates about 300 million million million J of energy each second

Electromagnetic radiation of about 100 thousand million million J reaches Earth from Sun each second

Energy of electromagnetic radiation is stored in oil, a fossil fuel, retrieved by oil rig

OIL RIG

Nuclear reactions in Sun's core convert mass to energy

Leaves trap light energy from Sun, converting it to chemical energy of sugar by photosynthesis

Chemical energy in wood is released as heat, light, and sound by burning

TREE

Sun's energy converted to chemical energy in photosynthesis, which builds sugars in grasses

Waste heat given off

Power station releases chemical energy by burning oil to produce heat

Heat turns water to steam, which drives a turbine to produce electrical energy

Electrical energy transmitted to homes via high-tension wires

OIL-FIRED POWER STATION

CROPS

Human gains chemical energy from eating plants or animals

BURNING WOOD

COW

Cow breaks down sugars in grasses, releasing some energy as heat

Bicycle and rider gain gravitational potential energy by climbing a hill

HUMAN

House supplied with electrical energy

Waste heat given off

A television uses about 150 J of electrical energy each second, given off as heat, light, and sound

Electrical energy is converted to kinetic energy of moving air in a hairdryer

Chemical energy in rider's muscles used to give bicycle kinetic energy

HOUSE

HOUSEHOLD APPLIANCES

In a washing machine, electrical energy changes to heat, kinetic energy, and sound

CAR

Microwave oven uses electrical energy to heat food, using about 700 J each second

Chemical energy from petrol (oil) used to power car — one litre of petrol releases up to 22 million J

ENERGY KEY:

Electromagnetic radiation

Chemical

Electrical

Heat

Sound

Light

Kinetic

Potential

Electricity and magnetism

ELECTRICAL EFFECTS result from an imbalance of electric charge. There are two types of electric charge, named positive (carried by protons) and negative (carried by electrons). If charges are opposite (unlike), they attract one another, while like charges repel. Forces of attraction and repulsion (electrostatic forces) exist between any two charged particles. Matter is normally uncharged, but if electrons are gained, an object will gain an overall negative charge; if they are removed, it becomes positive. Objects with an overall negative or positive charge are said to have an imbalance of charge, and exert the same forces as individual negative and positive charges. On this larger scale, the forces will always act to regain the balance of charge. This causes static electricity. Lightning, for example, is produced by clouds discharging a huge excess of negative electrons. If charges are "free" – in a wire or material that allows electrons to pass through it – the forces cause a flow of charge called an electric current. Some substances exhibit the strange phenomenon of magnetism – which also produces attractive and repulsive forces. Magnetic substances consist of small regions called domains. Normally unmagnetized, they can be magnetized by being placed in a magnetic field. Magnetism and electricity are inextricably linked, a fact put to use in motors and generators.

LIGHTNING

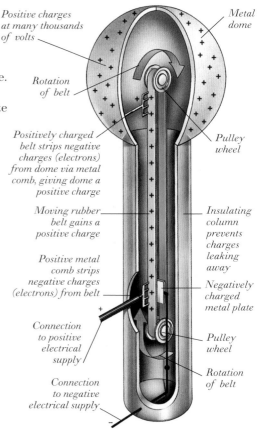

Positive charges at many thousands of volts

Metal dome

Rotation of belt

Positively charged belt strips negative charges (electrons) from dome via metal comb, giving dome a positive charge

Moving rubber belt gains a positive charge

Positive metal comb strips negative charges (electrons) from belt

Connection to positive electrical supply

Connection to negative electrical supply

Pulley wheel

Insulating column prevents charges leaking away

Negatively charged metal plate

Pulley wheel

Rotation of belt

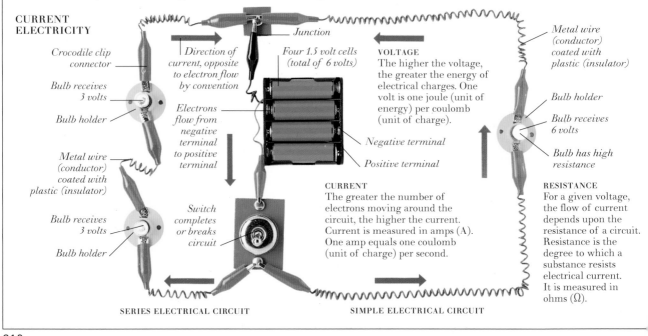

CURRENT ELECTRICITY

Crocodile clip connector

Bulb receives 3 volts

Bulb holder

Metal wire (conductor) coated with plastic (insulator)

Bulb receives 3 volts

Bulb holder

Direction of current, opposite to electron flow by convention

Electrons flow from negative terminal to positive terminal

Switch completes or breaks circuit

Junction

Four 1.5 volt cells (total of 6 volts)

Negative terminal

Positive terminal

VOLTAGE
The higher the voltage, the greater the energy of electrical charges. One volt is one joule (unit of energy) per coulomb (unit of charge).

CURRENT
The greater the number of electrons moving around the circuit, the higher the current. Current is measured in amps (A). One amp equals one coulomb (unit of charge) per second.

Metal wire (conductor) coated with plastic (insulator)

Bulb holder

Bulb receives 6 volts

Bulb has high resistance

RESISTANCE
For a given voltage, the flow of current depends upon the resistance of a circuit. Resistance is the degree to which a substance resists electrical current. It is measured in ohms (Ω).

SERIES ELECTRICAL CIRCUIT

SIMPLE ELECTRICAL CIRCUIT

MAGNETIC FIELDS AND FORCES

Iron filings

Profile of magnetic field

Bar magnet

North-seeking pole

Like poles repel

North-seeking pole

North-seeking pole

Unlike poles attract

North-seeking pole

South-seeking pole of electromagnet

North-seeking pole

South-seeking pole

Unlike poles attract

South-seeking pole

Direction of force

South-seeking pole

South-seeking pole

Like poles repel

Electromagnet

Wire to battery

MAGNETIC DOMAINS

Domain

Direction of magnetization within domain is random

Direction of magnetization within domain has aligned

Domain aligned with magnetization has grown

Domain boundary

Domain not aligned with magnetization has shrunk

Direction of overall magnetization

UNMAGNETIZED IRON

MAGNETIZED IRON IN A MAGNETIC FIELD

GENERATING MAGNETISM FROM ELECTRICITY

Direction of magnetic field (from north pole to south pole)

Electric current produces magnetic field

Magnetic field

Coil carries electric current

Direction of current

Metal wire (conductor) coated with plastic (insulator)

Negative terminal

Positive terminal

Four 1.5 volt cells (total of 6 volts)

CIRCUIT WITH ELECTROMAGNET

GENERATING ELECTRICITY FROM MAGNETISM

Terminal box

Coil of wire

Permanent magnet

Bearing

Non-drive end

Coil of wire

Terminal

Stator

Main rotor turns in magnetic field produced by coil of wire in stator

Fan

Drive end

Coil of wire

Shaft

Secondary (exciter) rotor

Coil of wire rotates within magnetic field of permanent magnet

Coated copper winding

Permanent magnet

Iron core

Steel casing

Commutator

Terminal

Spindle

End of shaft

Terminal

ELECTRIC GENERATOR
In a generator, the rotor rotates within the magnetic field of the stator to produce an electric current.

ELECTRIC MOTOR
In a motor, magnetic forces between the winding and permanent magnet produce a rotary motion.

Light

INFRA-RED IMAGE
OF A HOUSE

LIGHT IS A FORM OF ENERGY. It is a type of electromagnetic radiation, like X-rays or radio waves. All electromagnetic radiation is produced by electric charges (see pp. 316-317): it is caused by the effects of oscillating electric and magnetic fields as they travel through space. Electromagnetic radiation is considered to have both wave and particle properties. It can be thought of as a wave of electricity and magnetism. In that case, the difference between the various forms of radiation is their wavelength. Radiation can also be said to consist of particles, or packets of energy, called photons. The difference between light and X-rays, for instance, is the amount of energy that each photon carries. The complete range of radiation is referred to as the electromagnetic spectrum, extending from low energy, long wavelength radio waves to high energy, short wavelength gamma rays. Light is the only part of the electromagnetic spectrum that is visible. White light from the Sun is made up of all the visible wavelengths of radiation, which can be seen when it is separated by using a prism. Light, like all forms of electromagnetic radiation, can be reflected (bounced back) and refracted (bent). Different parts of the electromagnetic spectrum are produced in different ways. Sometimes visible light – and infra-red radiation – is generated by the vibrating particles of warm or hot objects. The emission of light in this way is called incandescence. Light can also be produced by fluorescence, a phenomenon in which electrons gain and lose energy within atoms.

MAXWELLIAN DIAGRAM OF ELECTROMAGNETIC RADIATION AS WAVES

Oscillating electric field

Wavelength

Oscillating magnetic field

Two fields at right angles

Direction of travel

ELECTROMAGNETIC RADIATION AS PARTICLES

Photon thought of as wave packet of energy

Blue light has about twice the energy of red light

Red light has long wavelength

Blue light has shorter wavelength: waves are more tightly packed

PHOTON OF RED LIGHT

PHOTON OF BLUE LIGHT

SPLITTING WHITE LIGHT INTO THE SPECTRUM

Prism forms spectrum by bending wavelengths at different angles

Glass prism

White light

Red light (wavelength: $6.2–7.7 \times 10^{-7}m$)

Orange light (wavelength: $5.9–6.2 \times 10^{-7}m$)

Yellow light (wavelength: $5.7–5.9 \times 10^{-7}m$)

Green light (wavelength: $4.9–5.7 \times 10^{-7}m$)

Blue light (wavelength: $4.5–4.9 \times 10^{-7}m$)

Violet light (wavelength: $3.9–4.5 \times 10^{-7}m$)

THE ELECTROMAGNETIC SPECTRUM

ENERGY (JOULES)

10^{-28} | 10^{-27} | 10^{-26} | 10^{-25} | 10^{-24} | 10^{-23} | 10^{-22} | 10^{-21} | 10^{-20}

WAVELENGTH (METERS)

10^{4} | 10^{3} | 10^{2} | 10 | 1 | 10^{-1} | 10^{-2} | 10^{-3} | 10^{-4} | 10

Long-wave radio

Medium-wave radio

Short-wave radio

Very high-frequency (VHF) radio

Microwaves

Infra-red radiation

Radio waves

ARTIFICIAL LIGHT SOURCES

FLUORESCENT TUBE

Glass tube filled with mercury vapour

Coiled tungsten filament

Ceramic end-piece

Electrical contact

Glass support

Filament heated and negatively charged electrons emitted

Electrons accelerate from one coil to the other

Electrons collide with mercury atoms

Mercury atom

Energy from collision produces ultraviolet light (short-wave radiation)

Action of ultraviolet light on phosphor produces visible light (long-wave radiation)

Free electron

Phosphor coating

Glass

SECTION OF PHOSPHOR COATING OF FLUORESCENT TUBE: HOW FLUORESCENT LIGHT IS PRODUCED

INCANDESCENT LIGHT BULB

SECTION OF FILAMENT OF INCANDESCENT LIGHT BULB: HOW INCANDESCENT LIGHT IS PRODUCED

Moving electrons collide with metal atoms

Hot filament gives out light

Vibration of metal atoms increases temperature

Lead-in wire

Glass bulb

Seal

Glass support

Screw fitting

Electrical contact

Coiled tungsten filament

Mixture of unreactive gases at low pressure

Electrical contact

REFLECTION OF LIGHT

Incident laser light

Mirror

Mirror support

Light strikes smooth surface at an angle, which reflects it at the same angle

Reflected light

REFRACTION OF LIGHT

Glass (transparent substance)

Incident laser light

Light enters substance

Light slows down and bends as passes from air to glass

Light speeds up as leaves glass

Refracted (bent) light

10^{-18} 10^{-17} 10^{-16} 10^{-15} 10^{-14} 10^{-13} 10^{-12} 10^{-11} 10^{-10} 10^{-9} 10^{-8}

10^{-7} 10^{-8} 10^{-9} 10^{-10} 10^{-11} 10^{-12} 10^{-13} 10^{-14} 10^{-15} 10^{-16} 10^{-17}

Visible light

Ultraviolet radiation

X-rays

Gamma rays

Force and motion

FORCES ARE PUSHES OR PULLS that change the motion of objects. To make a stationary object move, or a moving object stop, a force is needed. A force is also required to change the speed or direction of an object. This change in speed or direction is known as acceleration. Acceleration depends on the size (magnitude) of the force, and on the mass of the object. The effects of forces were first summarized by Isaac Newton in his three laws of motion. The international unit of force, named after him, is the newton (N), which is approximately equal to the weight of one apple. Gravity – the force of attraction between any two masses – can be measured using a newton meter (spring balance). Forces are put to useful effect in machines. A simple machine, such as a wheel and axle, is a device that changes the size or direction of an applied force. It allows an applied force (the effort) to produce another force (the load). A lever uses a bar that turns on a fulcrum to exert force. In all simple machines, there is a relationship between force and distance. A small force (in a compound pulley, for instance) moves through a large distance to lift a heavy object a small distance. This is called the Law of Simple Machines.

SIMPLE MACHINES

Single-pulley system (simple pulley)

Pulley wheel

Simple pulley only changes direction of a force

Effort is the same size as the load (10 N) and is pulled the same distance

One rope attached to load

Load of 10 N

Two-pulley system (simple pulley)

Pulley wheel

Effort is half the load (5 N), but the rope must be pulled twice the distance

Two ropes share the force and distance

Pulley wheel

Load of 10 N

Four-pulley system (compound pulley)

Two pulley wheels

Effort is one quarter of the load (2.5 N), but the rope must be pulled four times the distance

Four ropes share the force and distance

Two pulley wheels

Load of 10 N

SIMPLE AND COMPOUND PULLEYS

NEWTON METERS (SPRING BALANCES)

Weight is measured using a spring

When weight pulls downwards, pointer moves along scale and measures force

Weight is 10 N

Weight is 20 N

Mass of 1 kg

Mass of 2 kg

WEIGHT AND MASS
The "mass" of an object is a measure of the quantity of matter that it possesses. Mass is usually measured in grams (g) or kilograms (kg). The "weight" of an object is the force exerted on the object's mass by gravity. Since weight is a force, its unit is the newton (N).

Wheel and axle multiplies the effort

Force is transmitted to the wheels by the chain

Pedal

Crank

Effort, provided by cyclist's muscles, is smaller than the load, but moves through a greater distance

A larger force, the load, is produced at the axle

WHEEL AND AXLE

A screw, acting like a wedge wrapped around a shaft, multiplies the effort

Effort, a turning force supplied through a screwdriver

Pitch (the angle of the screw thread)

The smaller the angle of pitch, the less force is required, but more turns are needed to move it through a greater distance

A larger force, the load, pulls the screw into wood

SCREW

Effort pushes axe into wood

Axe blade has wedge shape

Wedge multiplies effort

A larger force, the load, moves through a smaller distance to push wood apart

WEDGE

NEWTON'S THREE LAWS OF MOTION

NEWTON'S FIRST LAW

When no force acts on a body, it will
continue in a state of rest or uniform motion.

Mass of 1 kg

*Newton meter shows
no applied force*

*Mass of trolley
is negligible*

*Trolley is not in motion, and will
remain at rest until a force acts*

NO FORCE, NO ACCELERATION: STATE OF REST

*Constant
speed*

Mass of 1 kg

*Newton meter
shows no
applied force*

*Trolley is in motion, and will continue at a
constant speed in a straight line until a force acts*

NO FORCE, NO ACCELERATION: UNIFORM MOTION

NEWTON'S SECOND LAW

When a force acts on a body, the motion of the body will change. The size of the change
will depend upon the mass of the object and the magnitude of the applied force.

*Acceleration
is 2 ms^{-2}*

*Trolley and mass (1 kg) gain
2 metres per second of speed
each second (2 ms^{-2})*

*Newton meter registers
force of 2 N*

Mass of 1 kg

*Acceleration is
1 ms^{-2}*

*Trolley and mass (2 kg)
gain 1 metre per second of
speed each second (1 ms^{-2})*

*Newton meter
registers force of 2 N*

Mass of 2 kg

*With the same applied force, an object with 2 kg mass
accelerates at half the rate of object with 1 kg mass*

FORCE AND ACCELERATION: SMALL MASS, LARGE ACCELERATION   **FORCE AND ACCELERATION: LARGE MASS, SMALL ACCELERATION**

NEWTON'S THIRD LAW

If one object exerts a force on another, an equal and opposite force,
called the reaction force, is applied by the second object on the first.

*Newton meters pull on each other with
equal and opposite forces*

*Acceleration: the trolley and
mass accelerate at 2 ms^{-2}*

*Newton meter registers
force of 2 N to the left*

*Newton meter registers
force of 2 N to the right*

Mass of 1 kg

*Person experiences
a reaction force*

ACTION AND REACTION

THREE CLASSES OF LEVER

*Fulcrum,
between effort
and load*

Effort

*d is
ter than
t, but moves
ugh smaller
nce*

CLASS 1 LEVER
Pliers consist of two class 1 levers.

Fulcrum

*Load,
between effort
and fulcrum*

*Effort is smaller than load, but
moves through greater distance*

CLASS 2 LEVER
Nutcrackers consist of two class 2 levers.

*Load is applied
at open end*

*Effort forces
tongs together*

*Load is smaller
than effort, but
moves through
greater distance*

*Effort, between
fulcrum and load*

Fulcrum

CLASS 3 LEVER
Tongs consist of two class 3 levers.

RAIL AND ROAD

Steam locomotives

WAGONS THAT ARE PULLED along tracks have been used to transport material since the 16th century, but these trains were drawn by men or horses until the invention of the steam locomotive. Steam locomotives enabled the basic railway system to realize its true potential. In 1804, Richard Trevithick built the world's first working steam locomotive in South Wales. It was not entirely successful, but it encouraged others to develop new designs. By 1829, the British engineer Robert Stephenson had built the "Rocket", considered to be the forerunner of the modern locomotive. The "Rocket" was a self-sufficient unit, carrying coal to heat the boiler and a water supply for generating steam. Steam passed from the boiler to force the pistons back and forth, and this movement turned the driving wheels, propelling the train forwards. Used steam was then expelled in characteristic "chuffs". Later steam locomotives, like "Ellerman Lines" and the "Mallard", worked in a similar way, but on a much larger scale. The simple design and reliability of steam locomotives ensured that they changed very little in 120 years of use, before being replaced from the 1950s by more efficient diesel and electric power (see pp. 326-329).

"ROCKET" STEAM LOCOMOTIVE, 1829

Chimney
Pipe takes steam from boiler to cylinder
Smokebox
Remains of firebox
Leaf spring
Regulator (throttle)
Valve chest
"Rocked" nameplate
Wrought iron boiler
Valve setting control
Wooden buffer beam
Wooden driving wheel
Metal tyre
Ballast
Rail chair
Wooden sleeper
Piston rod
Carrying wheel
Axle
Wrought iron rail
Cylinder
Drive platfor

"ELLERMAN LINES", 1949 (CUTAWAY VIEW)

S.

Vacuum reservoir
Panel brace
Water tank
Coal space
Tender hand brake
Cab
Firebox
Brick arch
Water filler
Panel sheeting
Hand rail
Buffer
Footplate
Brake vacuum pipe
Wheel guard
Axle
Axle box
Tender wheel
Brake rigging
Water float to indicate water level
Water float lever
Step
Coupling
Grate
Axle box cover
Coil spring
Trailing wheel
Fire drawn into fire tubes

TENDER

CAB INTERIOR OF "MALLARD" EXPRESS STEAM LOCOMOTIVE, 1938

Steam sanding control
Blower isolator valve
Pressure gauge isolator valve

Vacuum brake isolator valve
Steam chest pressure gauge
Vacuum brake pressure gauge
Blower control
Regulator controls flow of steam to cylinders
Cab side-window
Vacuum brake lever
Live steam water injector control
Manual sanding lever
Reverser handle
Driver's seat
Steam-operated reversing shaft lock control

Steam heating isolator valve
Sliding roof vent
Boiler pressure gauge
Gauge glass to show level of water in boiler
Exhaust steam water injector control
Steam heating pressure gauge
Glass deflector
Whistle lever
Cylinder drain cock lever
Control valve for hot water hose
Fireman's seat
Steam heat safety valve

Oil can warming tray
Firebox
Firehole
Firebox door

Fire tube
Thermal siphon
Steam dome
Regulator valve
Mechanical lubricator
Superheater tube inside flue tube
Boiler
Pipe takes steam from boiler to cylinder
Chimney
Blast-pipe
Smokebox
Smokebox door
Lubricating pipe
Piston valve
Buffer
Screw coupling
Leading wheel
Cylinder
Bogie frame
Piston, linked to connecting rod
Slide bar
Combination lever
Connecting rod
Expansion lever
Crank
Driving wheel
Coupling rod
Brake rigging
Brake shoe

STEAM LOCOMOTIVE

Diesel trains

RUDOLF DIESEL FIRST DEMONSTRATED the diesel engine
in Germany in 1898, but it was not until the 1940s that diesel
locomotives were successfully established on both passenger
and freight services, in the US. Early diesel locomotives like
the "Union Pacific" were more expensive to build than steam
locomotives, but were more efficient and cheaper to operate,
especially where oil was plentiful. One feature of diesel engines
is that the power output cannot be coupled directly to the wheels.
To convert the mechanical energy produced by diesel engines,
a transmission system is needed. Almost all diesel locomotives
have electric transmissions, and are known as "diesel-electric"
locomotives. The diesel engine works by drawing air into the
cylinders and compressing it to increase its temperature; a small
quantity of diesel fuel is then injected into it. The resulting
combustion drives the generator (more recently an alternator)
to produce electricity, which is fed to electric motors connected
to the wheels. Diesel-electric locomotives are essentially
electric locomotives that carry their own power plants,
and are used worldwide today. The "Deltic" diesel-electric
locomotive, similar to the one shown here, replaced
classic express steam locomotives, and ran
at speeds up to 160 kph (100 mph).

**FRONT VIEW OF "UNION PACIFIC"
DIESEL-ELECTRIC LOCOMOTIVE, 1950s**

Exhaust vent · Windscreen wiper · Horn · Cab front window · Head-light · Cab door · Name of operating railroad · Illuminated locomotive unit number · Railroad crest · Cab step · Step · Motor-driven bogie axle · Air-brake coupling hose · Centre buck-eye coupler

PROTOTYPE "DELTIC" DIESEL-ELECTRIC LOCOMOTIVE, 1956

Engine room vent · Inspection hatch · Engine exhaust port · Radiator fan · Engine room window · Engine room vent

DELTIC

Fuel tank · Water for heating boiler · Inspection socket · Folding step · Drain for radiator coolant · Radiator coolant · Sand box · Telescopic damper · Drain for control reservoir

DIESEL ENGINE OF BRITISH RAIL CLASS 20 DIESEL-ELECTRIC LOCOMOTIVE

EXAMPLES OF FREIGHT CARS

Exhaust vent

Cylinder head (V-four configuration)

Turbo-charged diesel engine drives generator

Generator cooling fan

Generator compartment vent

Auxiliary generator

Main generator produces electricity that drives wheels

Main chassis member

Innermost wheel set on cab-end bogie

Air brake pipe

Brake rigging

Battery box

Engine crankcase

Air reservoir and isolator valves

Lubricating oil primary pump and fuel supply pump

BOX CAR

HOPPER CAR

REFRIGERATOR CAR

LIVESTOCK CAR

FLAT CAR WITH BULKHEADS

Cab door

Driver's seat

Cab

Warning horn

Windscreen

Windscreen wiper

Cab window

Manufacturer's logo

Cab vent

Indicator light

Sand box

Buffer

Brake cylinder

Roller-bearing axle box

Brake shoe

Brake actuating chain

Transverse leaf spring secondary suspension

Coil spring primary suspension

AUTOMOBILE CAR

Electric and high-speed trains

THE FIRST ELECTRIC LOCOMOTIVE ran in 1879 in Berlin, Germany. In Europe, electric trains developed as a more efficient alternative to the steam locomotive and diesel-electric power. Like diesels, electric trains employ electric motors to drive the wheels but, unlike diesels, the electricity is generated externally at a power station. Electric current is picked up either from a catenary (overhead cable) via a pantograph, or from a third rail. Since it does not carry its own power-generating equipment, an electric locomotive has a better power-to-weight ratio and greater acceleration than its diesel-electric equivalent. This makes electric trains suitable for urban routes with many stops. They are also faster, quieter, and less polluting. The latest electric French TGV (Train à Grande Vitesse) reaches 300 kph (186 mph); other trains, like the London to Paris and Brussels "Eurostar", can run at several voltages and operate between different countries. Simpler electric trains perform special duties – the "People Mover" at Gatwick Airport in Britain runs between terminals.

HOW ALTERNATING CURRENT (AC) ELECTRIC TRAINS WORK

Running rail for return current

Feeder station provides current

Catenary

Vacuum circuit breaker

Pantograph collects current

Thyristor converter converts current (ac) to direct current (dc)

Traction motor turns wheel

Control circuit

Transformer steps down voltage

Axle brush

FRONT VIEW OF PARIS METRO

Route number

Windscreen wiper

Unit number

Operator's initials (Régie Autonome des Transports Parisien)

Rubber running wheel

Guard for rubber wheel

Door open/shut indicator light

Driver's seat

Handle

Front light (white)

Rear light (red)

Buffing pad

Rubber guide wheel

FRONT VIEW OF ITALIAN STATE RAILWAYS CLASS 402 ELECTRIC LOCOMOTIVE

Collector strip for electric current

Double-arm pantograph

Head-light

Windscreen wiper

Italian State Railways crest

Number of electric (E) locomotive (class 402 No. 5)

Buffer

"Jumper" cable

Conventional hook-screw coupling

Front light (white)

Rear light (red)

SIDE VIEW OF SHANGHAI MAGLEV TRAIN

Automatic door

On-board levitation magnet

Driver compartment

Guideu

"EUROSTAR" MULTI-VOLTAGE ELECTRIC TRAIN

Cab window

Rear light (red)

Fibre glass reinforced plastic cover

Aerofoil wheel guard

Grille over warning horn

Head-light (white)

Fibreglass reinforced plastic cover

Aerofoil wheel guard

Sanding pipe

FRONT VIEW

Cab side-window

Cab front window

Electric equipment compartment

Cab door

Side vent

3002

Leading driven axle

Horizontal telescopic damper

Third (electric) rail collector shoe

Coil spring suspension

SIDE VIEW

TGV ELECTRIC HIGH-SPEED TRAIN

Luggage rack

Reading light

Double-glazed and tinted side-window

Sliding curtain

Seat

Main overhead lighting

Automatic electric carriage end door

Antimacassar

Headrest

Armrest

Centre gangway

INTERIOR OF TGV

Cab side-window

Cab front window

Windscreen wiper

Emergency exit door

Access panel for servicing

Nose air deflector dam

Cab door

Hand rail

Side vent

Roof vent

306

SNCF

Vertical damper

Horizontal damper

SIDE VIEW OF TGV

Train equipment

MODERN RAILWAY TRACK consists of two parallel steel rails clipped on to a support called a sleeper. Sleepers are usually made of reinforced concrete, although wood and steel are still used. The distance between the inside edges of the rails is the track gauge. It evolved in Britain, which uses a gauge of 1,435 mm (4 ft 8½ in), known as the standard gauge. As engineering grew more sophisticated, narrower gauges were adopted because they cost less to build. The loading gauge, which is equally important, determines the size of the largest loaded vehicle that may pass through tunnels and under bridges with adequate clearance. Safe train operation relies on following a signalling system. At first, signalling was based on a simple time interval between trains, but it now depends on maintaining a safe distance between successive trains travelling in the same direction. Most modern signals are colour lights, but older mechanical semaphore signals are still used. On the latest high-speed lines, train drivers receive control instructions by electronic means. Signalling depends on reliable control of the train by effective braking. For fast, modern trains, which have considerable momentum, it is essential that each vehicle in the train can be braked by the driver or by a train control system, such as Automatic Train Protection (ATP). Braking is achieved by the brake shoe acting on the wheel rim (rim brakes), by disc brakes, or, increasingly, by electrical braking.

MECHANICAL SEMAPHORE SIGNAL

Red, square-ended arm in raised position means "all clear"

Red glass

Green glass

Actuating lever system

Motor operating "home" stop signal

Green glass

Yellow glass

Yellow, "distant" warning arm in horizontal position means "caution"

Tubular steel post

Ladder

Electrical relay box

FOUR-ASPECT COLOUR LIGHT SIGNAL

Glass (yellow)

Glass (green)

Yellow glass (lit)

Glass (red)

Lamp shield

Lifting lug

Clip

Base

FRONT VIEW

SIDE VIEW

HOW A MODERN MAIN-LINE SIGNALLING SYSTEM WORKS

Red "stop" light instructs next train not to enter this section of track

Green "all clear" light instructs train B to proceed into this section of track

Green "all clear" light instructs train B to proceed into this section of track

Green "all clear" light instructs train B to proceed into this section of track

Pantograph

Catenary

Train B

Track

EXAMPLES OF INTERNATIONAL TRACK GAUGES

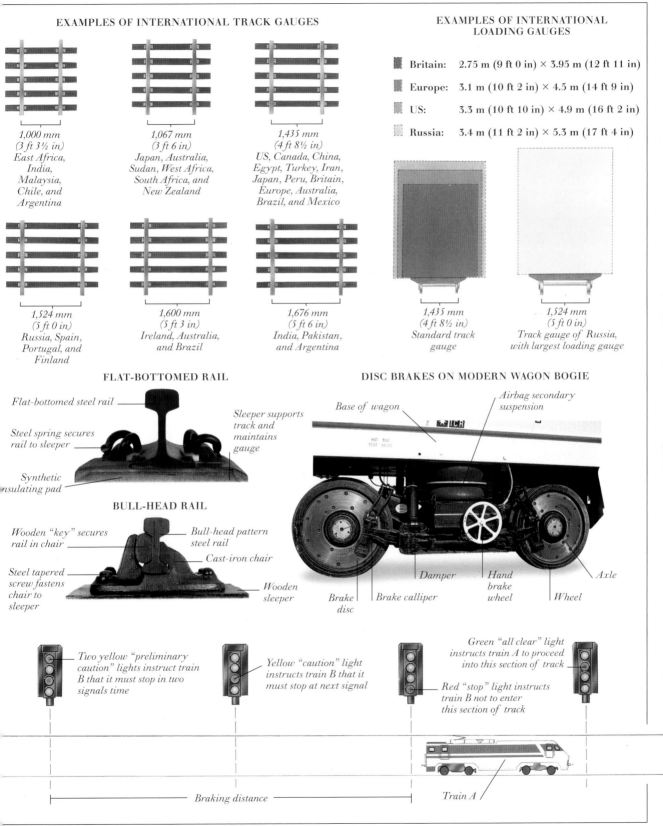

1,000 mm
(3 ft 3½ in)
East Africa,
India,
Malaysia,
Chile, and
Argentina

1,067 mm
(3 ft 6 in)
Japan, Australia,
Sudan, West Africa,
South Africa, and
New Zealand

1,435 mm
(4 ft 8½ in)
US, Canada, China,
Egypt, Turkey, Iran,
Japan, Peru, Britain,
Europe, Australia,
Brazil, and Mexico

1,524 mm
(5 ft 0 in)
Russia, Spain,
Portugal, and
Finland

1,600 mm
(5 ft 3 in)
Ireland, Australia,
and Brazil

1,676 mm
(5 ft 6 in)
India, Pakistan,
and Argentina

EXAMPLES OF INTERNATIONAL LOADING GAUGES

Britain: 2.75 m (9 ft 0 in) × 3.95 m (12 ft 11 in)

Europe: 3.1 m (10 ft 2 in) × 4.5 m (14 ft 9 in)

US: 3.3 m (10 ft 10 in) × 4.9 m (16 ft 2 in)

Russia: 3.4 m (11 ft 2 in) × 5.3 m (17 ft 4 in)

1,435 mm
(4 ft 8½ in)
Standard track
gauge

1,524 mm
(5 ft 0 in)
Track gauge of Russia,
with largest loading gauge

FLAT-BOTTOMED RAIL

Flat-bottomed steel rail

Steel spring secures rail to sleeper

Synthetic insulating pad

Sleeper supports track and maintains gauge

BULL-HEAD RAIL

Wooden "key" secures rail in chair

Steel tapered screw fastens chair to sleeper

Bull-head pattern steel rail

Cast-iron chair

Wooden sleeper

DISC BRAKES ON MODERN WAGON BOGIE

Base of wagon

Airbag secondary suspension

Brake disc

Brake calliper

Damper

Hand brake wheel

Wheel

Axle

Two yellow "preliminary caution" lights instruct train B that it must stop in two signals time

Yellow "caution" light instructs train B that it must stop at next signal

Green "all clear" light instructs train A to proceed into this section of track

Red "stop" light instructs train B not to enter this section of track

Braking distance

Train A

Trams and buses

METROLINK TRAM,
MANCHESTER,
BRITAIN

AS CITY POPULATIONS exploded in the 1800s, there was an urgent need for mass transportation. Trams were an early solution. The first trams, like buses, were horse-drawn, but in 1881, electric street tramways appeared in Berlin, Germany. Electric trams soon became widespread throughout Europe and North America. Trams run on rails along a fixed route, using electric motors that receive power from overhead cables. As road networks developed, motorized buses offered a flexible alternative to trams. By the 1930s, they had replaced tram systems in many cities. City buses typically have doors at both front and rear to make loading and unloading easier. Double-decker designs are popular, occupying the same amount of street space as single-decker buses but able to transport twice the number of people. Buses are also commonly used for inter-city travel and touring. Tour buses have reclining seats, large windows, luggage space, and toilets. Recently, as city traffic has become increasingly congested, many city planners have designed new tram routes to run alongside bus routes as part of an integrated transport system.

EARLY TRAM, c.1900

Trolley boom

Trolley head

Trolley base

Drop window

Upper deck

Quarter light

Brake

Stair

Lower deck

Platform

Controller

Truck

Lifeguard

MCW METROBUS, LONDON, BRITAIN

Upper deck air intake

Window vent

Upper deck windscreen

Route information

Destination screen

Offside mirror

Asymmetric windscreen

Windscreen wiper

Sidelight

Head-light

Grille

Fog light

Number plate

Manufacturer's badge

Route number

Nearside mirror

Licence holder

Turning indicator

Square roof dome

Mirror for driver to see upstairs

Operator's logo

Destination screen

Nearside mirror

Front bumper

Entrance door

Emergency door control

Turning indicator

FRONT VIEW

SINGLE-DECKER BUS, NEW YORK, US

Wheelchair access
Sliding window
Sloped roof dome
Tinted glass
Air intake
Tyre
Axle
Exit door
Access panel
Sidelight
Entrance door
Bumper

SIDE VIEW

Marker light
Repeater indicator
Entrance door
Side mirror
Route number
Head-light
Turning indicator
Number plate
Bumper

FRONT VIEW

DOUBLE-DECKER TOUR BUS, PARIS, FRANCE

Tinted glass
Air intake
Access panel
Skirt
Access door
Twin rear axle
Side entrance
Single front axle
Tyre
Raked windscreen
Panoramic window
Turning indicator
Bumper
Plug-style entrance door

Paris Vision

Sliding window vent
Upper saloon window
Advertising panel
Air intake
Lower saloon window
Fleet number
Engine access panel
Rear bumper
Emergency door control
Two-leaf style exit door
Legal lettering
London Buses logo
Tyre
Axle
Skirt

SIDE VIEW

LONDON BUSES

The first cars

THE EARLIEST ROAD VEHICLE powered by an engine, the Cugnot steam traction engine, was built in 1770. More practical steam carriages, such as the Bordino, were available in the early 19th century, but they were heavy and cumbersome. Restrictive laws and the introduction of railways, faster and able to carry more passengers, saw the decline of "cars" powered by steam. It was not until 1860 that the first practical power unit for road vehicles was developed, with the invention of the internal combustion engine by the Belgian Etienne Lenoir. By around 1890, Karl Benz and Gottlieb Daimler in Germany, and Albert de Dion and Armand Peugeot in France were building cars for sale to the public. These early cars, despite being primitive, expensive, and produced in limited numbers, heralded the age of the motor car.

STEAM-POWERED CUGNOT "FARDIER", 1770

Chimney

Steam pipe

Twin cylinder engine

Rocking beam

Steering tiller

Brake pedal

Seat

Wooden frame

Wooden wheel (artillery wheel)

Load space

Haystack boiler

Carrying fork

Piston rod

Ratchet wheel

Single front driving wheel

Step

Log basket

Broad, rough tyre

BORDINO STEAM CARRIAGE, 1854

Chimney

Hood iron (landau iron)

Landau body

Drop-down window

Leather hood

Fire-tube boiler

Sprung chassis

Water tank

Safety valve

Safety valve weight

Coke hopper

Chauffeur's seat (stoker's seat; spider seat; tiger seat)

Step

Tie bar

Full-elliptic leaf spring

Iron tyre

Wooden spoke

Wooden wheel (artillery wheel)

Hub

Tie rod

Connecting rod

Steam chest

Twin-cylinder steam engine

Unsprung chassis

Steam distributor valve

SIDE VIEW OF PETROL-DRIVEN BENZ MOTORWAGEN, 1886

Steering tiller

Brake quadrant

Brake lever

Cooling water tank

Steering column

Full-elliptic leaf spring

Steering rack

Bevel gear

Steering link

Final drive sprocket

Steering head

Seat spring

Driven pulley

Wheel fork

Tubular chassis

Driving chain

Driving sprocket

Hub

Solid rubber tyre

Tangent-spoked wire wheel

REAR VIEW OF BENZ MOTORWAGEN, 1886

Pinion

Lubricator

Cooling tank

Crown wheel

Driving pulley

Fuel tank

Drive belt

Big-end bearing

Groove for rope starter

Crankshaft

Flywheel

Seat squab

OVERHEAD VIEW OF BENZ MOTORWAGEN, 1886

Candle lamp

Driver's seat

Steering tiller

Brake lever

Dashboard

Headlamp

Round pin

Splinter bar

Towing hook

Forecarriage

Steam pipe

Spoke

Frame

Steering link

Footboard

Steering tiller

Brake lever

Tool and battery box

Trembler coil box

Intake pipe

Single cylinder

Fuel tank

Cooling water tank

Oil-filled lubricator

Flywheel

Crown wheel

Crankshaft

Drive belt

Driving pulley

Elegance and utility

DURING THE FIRST DECADE OF THE 20TH CENTURY, the motorist who could afford it had a choice of some of the finest cars ever made. These handbuilt cars were powerful and luxurious, using the finest woods, leathers, and cloths, and bodywork made to the customer's individual requirements; some had six-cylinder engines as big as 15 litres. The price of such cars was several times that of an average house, and their yearly running costs were also very high. As a result, basic, utilitarian cars became popular. Costing perhaps one-tenth of the price of a luxury car, these cars had very little trim and often had only single-cylinder engines.

1904 OLDSMOBILE SINGLE-CYLINDER ENGINE

Oil bottle dripfeed

Crankcase

Exhaust pipe

Starting handle bracket

Cylinder head

Carburettor

Cylinder

Starter cog

Engine timing gear

Crankshaft

Gear band

Flywheel

FRONT VIEW OF 1906 RENAULT

Canopy

Mahogany framed windscreen

Cast aluminium wheel spider

Rear window

British Automobile Association badge

Bedford cord upholstery

Window blind

British Royal Automobile Club badge

Blind pull

Window lift strap

Rear-view mirror

Broad lace trim

Lamp bracket

Oil side lamp

Windscreen support

Dashboard radiator

Mudguard (wing)

Brass bevel

Access panel

Bonnet catch

Bail handle

Lifting handle

Mirror reflector

Acetylene headlamp

X 825

Steering spindle

Elliott steering knuckle

Chevron-tread tyre

Dumb iron

Screwdown greaser

Front axle

Starting handle

Track rod

SIDE VIEW OF 1906 RENAULT

Luggage grid

Button-quilted upholstery

Mahogany-framed plate glass window

Round-corner single limousine coachwork

Rear oil lamp

Shock absorber

Hub

Hub cap

Beaded edge tyre

Tyre security bolt

1904 OLDSMOBILE TRIM AND BODYWORK

Reflector

Rear lamp

Engine cover handle

Engine cover

Mudguard

Seat back rest frame

Dashboard

Tiller

Brake pedal

Throttle pedal

Mirror

Mudguard stay

Ignition switch

Seat squab

1904 OLDSMOBILE CHASSIS

Front steering track-rod

Front spring

Brake rod

Full-elliptic steering spring

Steering wiffletree

Rear spring

Starting handle bracket

Front axle

Combined spring and chassis unit

Non-skid tyre

Brass scrollwork

Blind pull

Canopy

Openable windscreen

Brass bevel

Division

Dashboard

Oil side lamp

Bonnet

Broad lace trim

Leather upholstery

Handbrake

Steering wheel

Water pipe

Gear lever

Plug lead conduit

Acetylene headlamp

Fuel/air intake pipe

Bi-block engine

Bulb horn

Spare tyre

Dashboard radiator

Jump seat (opera seat; strapontin)

Rim clamp

Tyre carrier

Running board

Leather valance

Tyre strap

Bonnet stay

Exhaust manifold

Starting handle

Wooden artillery wheel

Mass-production

THE FIRST CARS WERE HAND-ASSEMBLED from individually built parts, a time-consuming procedure that required skilled mechanics and made cars very expensive. This problem was solved, in America, by a Detroit car manufacturer named Henry Ford; he introduced mass-production by using standardized parts, and later combined these with a moving production line. The work was brought to the workers, each of whom performed one simple task in the construction process as the chassis moved along the line. The first mass-produced car, the Ford Model T, was launched in 1908 and was available in a limited range of body styles and colours. However, when the production line was introduced in 1914, the colour range was cut back; the Model T became available, as Henry Ford said, in "any colour you like, so long as it's black". Ford cut the production time for a car from several days to about 12 hours, and eventually to minutes, making cars much cheaper than before. As a result, by 1920 half the cars in the world were Model T Fords.

FRONT VIEW OF 1913 FORD MODEL T

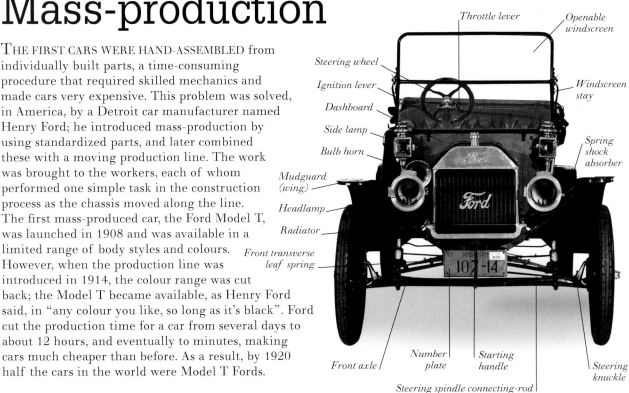

Throttle lever
Openable windscreen
Steering wheel
Ignition lever
Windscreen stay
Dashboard
Side lamp
Spring shock absorber
Bulb horn
Mudguard (wing)
Headlamp
Radiator
Front transverse leaf spring
Front axle
Number plate
Starting handle
Steering knuckle
Steering spindle connecting-rod

STAGES OF FORD MODEL T PRODUCTION

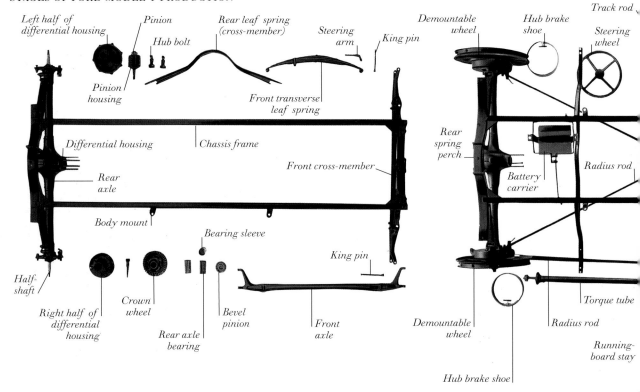

Left half of differential housing
Pinion
Rear leaf spring (cross-member)
Steering arm
King pin
Demountable wheel
Hub brake shoe
Track rod
Hub bolt
Steering wheel
Pinion housing
Front transverse leaf spring
Differential housing
Chassis frame
Rear spring perch
Radius rod
Front cross-member
Rear axle
Battery carrier
Body mount
Bearing sleeve
King pin
Half-shaft
Crown wheel
Bevel pinion
Front axle
Demountable wheel
Radius rod
Right half of differential housing
Rear axle bearing
Torque tube
Running-board stay
Hub brake shoe

SIDE VIEW OF 1913 FORD MODEL T

Hood

Rear seat

Hood frame

Rear door

Front seat

Steering wheel

Horn bulb

Steering column

Windscreen

Side lamp

Bonnet

Radiator filler cap

Radiator filler neck

Front mudguard

Spring shock absorber

Rear mudguard (rear wing)

Tyre valve

Drain plug

Horn

Wooden-spoked wheel

Running board

Spare tyre

Dummy front door

Radius rod

Hub cap

Valance

Steering column

Drag link

Demountable wheel

Bun lamp burner

Fuel sediment bowl

Running-board bracket

Light switch

Starter switch

Radiator shell

Headlamp rim

Headlamp

Starter

Track rod

Ruckstell axle

Rear cross-member

Bonnet clip

Brake drum

Steering gearbox

Handbrake

Radiator hose

Drop arm

Drag link

Crank handle

Cylinder block

Torque tube

Greaser

Transmission casing

Radiator apron

Brake rod

Tank support

Front wing stay

Carburettor

Radiator

Steering arm

Demountable wheel

Clincher wheel

Battery strap

Reflector

Bonnet clip

Fender eye bolt

Handbrake quadrant

Running-board support

Detachable rim

Headlamp shell

Running board

The "people's car"

THE MOST POPULAR CAR in the history of car manufacture is the Volkswagen Beetle, originally called the KdF Wagen. The car was developed in Germany in the 1930s by Dr. Ferdinand Porsche. At that time, Germany had only half the number of cars of Britain or France, and Adolf Hitler took a personal interest in the development of the Volkswagen ("people's car"). The intention was to provide a new industry, new jobs, and a car so cheap that anyone in work could afford it. Dr. Porsche designed a car that was cheap to build and run; its rear-mounted, air-cooled engine cut down the number of parts needed and also reduced weight. However, few civilians managed to obtain the Beetle before the outbreak of the Second World War in 1939. After the war, the Beetle proved so popular that eventually more than 20 million were sold.

CUSTOMIZED VOLKSWAGEN BEETLE

FLAT-FOUR CYLINDER ARRANGEMENT

WORKING PARTS OF VOLKSWAGEN BEETLE

Fuel tank
Steering tie-rod
Fuel tank sender unit
Fuel filler neck
Windscreen-wiper motor assembly
Steering box assembly
Steering idler
Frame head
Anti-roll bar
Suspension strut
Brake back plate
Track control arm
Pedal cluster
Dust shroud
Strut insert (shock absorber)
Front suspension top mount
Gear lever knob
Front road spring
Seat mount
Front suspension top mount
Handbrake
Floor pan (platform chassis)
Torsion bar cover
Rear brake drum
Trailing arm
Rear lamp
Air scoop
Quarter light
Bonnet
Indicator
Tail pipe
Pressed steel wheel
Fuel filler cap
Tyre
Sports wheel
Rear shock absorber
Drive shaft
Heat exchanger
Transaxle (gearbox and final drive)
Starter motor
Clutch and flywheel
Counterweight
Piston
Flat-four engine
Crankshaft
Air filter
Tail pipe
Big end
Connecting rod (con-rod)

BODY SHELL OF VOLKSWAGEN BEETLE

Front bumper

Bonnet release handle

Nearside headlamp unit

Offside headlamp unit

Nearside front indicator lens

Chrome trim strip

Bonnet

Offside front indicator lens

Nearside front mudguard (front wing)

Offside front mudguard (front wing)

Front wing piping

Spare-wheel well

Front wing piping

Bonnet hinge

Blade

Offside running board

Quarter light

Arm

Mirror

Nearside running board

Door catch

Windscreen wiper

Steering column

Wind deflector (baffle)

Sun roof

Quarter light

Door handle

Window winder handle

Passenger door

Body shell

Window winder regulator

Rear wing piping

Drop glass

Rear wing piping

Air intake vents

Rear valance

Engine lid (engine cover)

Nearside rear mudguard (rear wing)

Air intake vents

Offside rear mudguard (rear wing)

Number plate light

Number plate

Offside rear lamp cluster (rear lamp unit)

Nearside rear lamp cluster (rear lamp unit)

WRV 408L

Rear bumper

341

Early engines

STEAM AND ELECTRICITY were used to power cars until early this century, but neither power source was ideal. Electric cars had to stop frequently to recharge their heavy batteries, and steam cars gave smooth power delivery but were too complicated for the average motorist to use. A rival power source, the internal combustion engine, was invented in 1860 by Etienne Lenoir (see pp. 334-335). This engine converted the force of a controlled explosion into rotary motion, to turn the wheels of a vehicle. Early variations on this basic model included sleeve valves, separately cast cylinders, and the two-stroke combustion cycle. Today, many internal combustion engines, including the Wankel rotary and diesels (see pp. 346-347), use the four-stroke cycle, first demonstrated by Nikolaus Otto in 1876. The Otto cycle, often described as "suck, squeeze, bang, blow", has proved the best method of ensuring that the engine turns over smoothly and that exhaust emissions are controllable.

TROJAN TWO-STROKE ENGINE, 1927

Port linking combustion chambers of upper and lower cylinders

Water connection

Upper paired cylinder

Spark plug

Wide piston-ring

Transfer port

Wire gauze pad

Upper piston

Flywheel

Flexible, forked connecting-rod

Counterweight

Big end

Crankcase

BERSEY ELECTRIC CAB, 1896

Mounting for tray of 40 batteries

Housing for electric motors

SECTIONED WHITE STEAM CAR, 1903

Steering wheel

Throttle wheel

Brake lever

Reverse lever

Automatic cylinder lubricator

Flash steam generator

Lamp bracket

High-pressure cylinder

Rocking lever

Exhaust pipe

Water pump

Condenser

Low-pressure cylinder

Fuel tank

Semi-elliptic spring

Brake drum

Spiral tubes

Flitch-plated wooden chassis

Drop arm

Water tank

Drag link

Dumb iron

CYCLE OF A FOUR-STROKE INTERNAL COMBUSTION ENGINE

INDUCTION STROKE ("SUCK")

Exhaust port closed
Inlet valve
Inlet port opens
Fuel and air (the "charge") sucked into cylinder
Piston moves downwards
Counterweight
Crankshaft
Crankpin

COMPRESSION STROKE ("SQUEEZE")

Exhaust port closed
Charge compressed by piston
Inlet port closed
Connecting rod (con-rod)
Piston moves upwards

POWER STROKE ("BANG")

Spark plug
Inlet port closed
Exhaust port closed
Charge ignited by spark plug
Explosion pushes piston downwards
Big end

EXHAUST STROKE ("BLOW")

Exhaust valve
Inlet port closed
Exhaust port opens
Burned gases forced out of cylinder
Piston moves upwards

16-HORSEPOWER HUMBER ENGINE, 1911

Brass housing for ignition cable
Inlet port
Water pipe
Valve cap
Spark plug
Side valve (inlet valve)
Pair-cast cylinder
Water jacket
Fan bracket
Tappet
Valve spring
Timing chain
Timing chest
Flywheel
Camshaft
Oil pump
Oil sump
Crankcase
Starting handle

DAIMLER DOUBLE-SLEEVE VALVE ENGINE, 1910

Spark plug socket
Junk ring
Cylinder head
Inlet port
Exhaust port
Inlet manifold
Outer sleeve valve
Water jacket
Cylinder wall
Inner sleeve valve
Piston
Carburettor
Engine bearer
Flywheel

OUTER SLEEVE VALVE

Oil groove

INNER SLEEVE VALVE

Sleeve port
Eye for connecting con-rods to secondary crankshaft

343

Modern engines

TODAY'S PETROL ENGINE WORKS on the same basic principles as the first car engines of a century ago, although it has been greatly refined. Modern engines, often made from special metal alloys, are much lighter than earlier engines. Computerized ignition systems, fuel injectors, and multi-valve cylinder heads achieve a more efficient combustion of the fuel/air mixture (the charge) so that less fuel is wasted. As a result of this greater efficiency, the power and performance of a modern engine are increased, and the level of pollution in the exhaust gases is reduced. Exhaust pollution levels today are also lowered by the increasing use of special filters called catalytic converters, which absorb many exhaust pollutants. The need to produce ever more efficient engines means that it can take up to seven years to develop a new engine for a family car, at a cost of many millions of pounds.

FRONT VIEW OF A FORD COSWORTH V6 12-VALVE

Idle control valve
Plenum chamber
Valve rocker
Power steering pump reservoir
Oil dipstick
Steering pump pulley
High-tension ignition lead (spark plug lead)
Cogged drive belt
Fan
Alternator
Crankshaft pulley
Viscous coupling
Oil sump

FRONT VIEW OF A FORD COSWORTH V6 24-VALVE

Idle control valve
Plenum chamber
Exhaust gas recirculation valve
Camshaft timing gear
Steering pump drive pulley
Camshaft chain
Belt tensioner
Air conditioning pump
Alternator cooling fan
Oil sump
Drive belt
Crankshaft pulley

SECTIONED VIEW OF A JAGUAR STRAIGHT 6

Cam follower (bucket tappet)
Valve spring
Cam lobe
Cam
Combustion chamber
Compression ring
Cam cover
Camshaft
Distributor
Cylinder head
Fan
Valve stem
Air conditioning refrigerant pipe
Exhaust valve
Suspension self-levelling pump
Cylinder liner
Power steering pump
Water jacket
Piston
Swash plate
Connecting rod (con-rod)
Drive belt
Main bearing housing
Big end
Compressor piston
Transmission adaptor plate
Air conditioning compressor
Crankshaft counterweight
Oil sump
Oil pick-up pipe
Anti-surge baffle
Crankcase
Oil-control ring (scraper ring)

FRONT VIEW OF A JAGUAR V12

Air cleaner

Camshaft sprocket

Distributor

Fuel injector nozzle

Inlet manifold tract

Plenum chamber

Camshaft

Cam follower

Coolant outlet

Cam cover

Piston ring land

Piston ring groove

Exhaust manifold

Piston skirt

Viscous coupling

Gudgeon pin

Cooling fan

Fan drive shaft

Alternator

Belt pulley

Alternator pulley

Piston

Crankshaft

STRAIGHT 4 CYLINDER ARRANGEMENT

Counterweight

Connecting rod (con-rod)

V12 CYLINDER ARRANGEMENT

SECTIONED VIEW OF A JAGUAR V12

Distributor drive shaft

Fuel pipe

Throttle butterfly

Inlet manifold

Ignition amplifier

Throttle linkage

Air inlet

Exhaust valve

Cam cover

Inlet valve

Oil feed pipe

Timing chain

Cylinder head

Piston crown

Coolant rail (water rail)

Piston ring land

Exhaust heat shield

Water pump

Exhaust manifold

Piston

Oil pipe banjo

Ancillary drive pulley

Drive plate

Timing chain drive sprocket

Starter ring

Connecting rod (con-rod)

Counterweight (balance weight)

Main bearing

Crankcase

Pipe to oil cooler

Sump

Oil filter

Alternative engines

THE MOST COMMON TYPE OF ALTERNATIVE ENGINE is the diesel engine, which, instead of igniting the compressed fuel/air mixture with a spark, uses compression alone, heating the mixture to the point where it explodes. A diesel engine's fuel consumption is low in comparison with similarly sized piston engines, despite its heavier, reinforced moving parts and cylinder block. Another type of engine is the rotary-combustion, first successfully developed by Felix Wankel in the 1950s. Its two trilobate (three-sided) rotors revolve in housings shaped in a fat figure-of-eight. The four sequences of the four-stroke cycle, which occur consecutively in a piston engine, occur simultaneously in a rotary engine, producing power in a continuous stream.

ROTARY-ENGINED MAZDA RX-7

Aerodynamic windscreen

Headrest

Hood bag

Front spoiler (chin spoiler)

Side marker lamp

Rubbing strake

Cast alloy wheel

WANKEL ROTARY ENGINE

OIL-PUMP HOUSING

Distributor fixing point (drive point)

FRONT SIDE HOUSING

Intake port

FRONT ROTOR CHAMBER

Trailing spark-plug hole

Dipstick tube

INTERMEDIATE HOUSING

Oil filler

Intake port

REAR ROTOR CHAMBER

Aluminium alloy backing

Oil-pump drive

Coolant passage

Exhaust port

Leading spark-plug hole

Water drain bolt

Trailing spark-plug hole

Leading spark-plug hole

THE WANKEL ROTARY CYCLE

Exhaust port

Intake port

Fuel/air mixture being compressed

Water passage

Burning gas expands

Trilobate rotor

Exhaust port closed

Gas continues to expand

Stationary gear (fixed gear)

Compression continues

Vacuum sucks in fuel/air mixture

Burnt gas exhausts

Rotor gear

Compressed gas ignites

Fuel/air mixture continues to enter

Burnt gas begins to expand

Burnt gas continues to exhaust

Output shaft turns

Compression begins

FORD TURBOCHARGED DIESEL ENGINE

Engine lifting eye

Rocker cover

Baffle plate

Inlet track

Turbo impeller (inlet rotor)

Turbo propeller (exhaust rotor)

Exhaust

Bell housing

Oil filler cap

Cam follower

Valve return spring

Water jacket

Water pump pulley

Compression ring

Oil-control ring

Piston

Ancillary drive belt

Water jacket

Oil cooler

Oil cooler matrix

Oil filter

Engine block

Oil sump pan

Oil return pipe for turbocharger

REAR SIDE HOUSING

Chrome plating

Exhaust port

ROTOR AND SEALS

Outer oil seal

Inner oil seal spring

Inner oil seal

Corner seal spring

Rotor bearing

Corner seal insert

Rotor gear

Corner seal

Side gear

Rotor

Balancing drilling

Apex seal

Apex seal spring

Inner oil seal groove

Outer oil seal groove

Outer oil seal spring

Hole for output shaft

Side seal spring

Side seal

Side seal groove

Apex seal groove

OUTPUT SHAFT

Front counterweight

Front eccentric rotor journal

Oil hole

Rear stationary gear (fixed gear)

V-belt pulley

Front stationary gear (fixed gear)

Main journal

Eccentric shaft

Rear eccentric rotor journal

Oil jet

Flywheel with balance weight

Bodywork

THE BODY OF A MODERN mass-produced car is built on the monocoque (single-shell) principle, in which the roof, side panels, and floor are welded into a single integral unit. This bodyshell protects and supports the car's internal parts. Steel and glass are used to construct the bodyshell, creating a unit that is both light and strong. Its lightness helps to conserve energy, while its strength protects the occupants. Modern bodywork is designed with the aid of computers, which are used to predict factors such as aerodynamic efficiency and impact-resistance. High-technology is also employed on the production line, where robots are used to assemble, weld, and paint the body.

RENAULT LOGO

Door handle

Door lock

Left-hand door glass

Left-hand quarter glass

Tail-gate support

Window washer jet

Rear window glass

Heating element contact

Tail-gate support

Tail-gate

Rear bumper

Bodyshell

Fuel cap

Right-hand quarter glass

Zinc phosphating

Degreased bare metal

Right-hand door glass

Primer

Base coat colour

Cataphoresic coating

Varnish

Chrome passivation

Door key and lock

Door handle

Left-hand door

Left-hand mirror assembly

Door hinge

Electric window motor

Rear hatch

Aerial

Side marker lamp

SIDE VIEW OF A RENAULT CLIO

Spoiler bumper

Bonnet-release cable

Bonnet

Bonnet catch

Bonnet hinge

Front bumper

Windscreen glass

Window winder cable

Window winder handle

Door hinge

Right-hand door

Right-hand mirror assembly

Bonnet

Headrest

Headlamp

Spoiler bumper

Fog-lamp

FRONT VIEW OF A RENAULT CLIO

Mechanical components

A TYPICAL MODERN CAR has several thousand individual mechanical components. These are assembled to form the car's various mechanical systems: engine and exhaust, transmission, steering, suspension, and brakes. To ensure that each system functions properly, components are manufactured to extremely fine tolerances – to within a five-hundredth of a millimetre (about one ten-thousandth of an inch) in some cases.

Alloy wheel

Hub cap

Hub nut

Hub seal

Exhaust downpipe

Silencer

Catalytic converter

Suspension spring

Torsion bar

Handbrake

Nearside rear suspension arm

Anti-roll bar

Gear lever

Rear silencer

Fuel tank

Steering wheel

Steering rack

Offside rear suspension arm

Steering column

Vent pipe

Shock absorber

Clutch pedal

Hub and brake drum

Electric fuel pump

Brake cylinder

Brake shoe

Brake pedal

Hub seal

Brake backplate

Throttle pedal

Fuel tank filler neck

Hub nut

Clutch cable

Hub cap

Throttle cable

Wheel trim

Steel wheel

MECHANICAL COMPONENTS
OF A RENAULT CLIO, 1991

Brake shield

Alloy wheel

Clutch release
bearing

Brake
disc

Hub

Nearside
drive shaft

Clutch pressure
plate

Track-rod
end

Upper
suspension
arm

Brake hose

Top hose

Track
rod

Brake
pad

Power
steering
pump

Clutch
centre
plate

Gearbox
(transmission)

Bottom
hose

Gear-
change rod

Lower
suspension
arm

Anti-roll
bar

Starter
motor

Flywheel

Fan
motor

Electronic
ignition unit

Power steering
belt

Exhaust
Manifold

Subframe

Intake
manifold

Brake
cylinder

Water
pump

Fan motor support

Brake
servo

Alternator
belt

Alternator

Engine

Brake caliper
fixing bolt

Distributor

Suspension
strut

Brake caliper
locking plate

Air cleaner

Brake
caliper

Radiator

Hub
carrier

Offside
drive shaft

Brake
hose

Lock nut and washer

Brake disc

Front hub
bearing

Brake shield

Steel wheel

Wheel trim

Car trim

A MODERN CAR HAS TWO TYPES OF TRIM, according to the materials used: hard (chrome and plastics) and soft (upholstery materials). Safety and comfort are priorities in the trim's design: seats help the occupants to maintain a comfortable posture, rubber seals keep out dirt and moisture, and headlamps light the way. Older cars had interior or leather panelling cut and fitted by craftsmen; modern cars use precisely moulded plastics and seat fabrics cut by robot-controlled lasers to reduce costs and production time. Doors are now trimmed off the production line so that complex wiring can be built in.

TRIM OF A RENAULT CLIO, 1991

Rear quarter trim panel

Inner roof trim

Roof seal

Quarter trim panel

Quarter panel moulding

Rear seat belt

Rear tyre

Split, folding rear seat assembly

Centre seat belt

Rear seat belt stalk (catch)

Rear shelf

Rear shelf radio speaker

Tail-gate trim

Rear wiper blade

Tail-gate seal

Rear wiper arm

Rear shelf radio speaker

Gear lever surrou

Number plate lamp

Rear indicator and stop lamp assembly

Rear wheel embellisher (wheel trim)

Untrimmed headrest

Rear seat belt

Quarter panel moulding

HALOGEN HEADLAMP BULB

Rear tyre

Rear quarter trim panel

Roof seal

Quarter trim panel

SPOTLAMP BULB

Filament

MARKER LAMP BULB

Filament

Inner roof trim

FESTOON BULB

Contact

Bayonet fixing

Contact

Contact

Roof moulding

Window winder handle

Door seal

Front tyre

Front wheel embellisher (wheel trim)

Door lock handle

Door pull handle

Indicator lamp

Fog-lamp

Inner sill trim

Door moulding (rubbing strip)

Inner windscreen moulding

Front seat belt

Front door radio speaker

Dash radio speaker

Headlamp

Front seat assembly

Sun visor

Dash panel (instrument panel)

Windscreen wiper bracket and spindles

Windscreen wiper blade

Interior light

Radio

Heater unit

Washer jet

Fan blade

Rear-view mirror

Centre console

Steering wheel

Windscreen seal

Fascia (dash)

Headlamp

Sun visor

Windscreen wiper arm

Front seat frame

Dash radio speaker

Front seat belt

Control stalk

Front door radio speaker

Inner windscreen moulding

Door trim panel

Inner sill trim

Door moulding (rubbing strip)

Fog-lamp

Door seal

Door pull handle

Window winder handle

Front tyre

Front wheel embellisher (wheel trim)

Indicator lamp

Door lock handle

Hybrid car

THERE HAVE BEEN SEVERAL proposed alternatives to conventional petrol- or diesel-powered cars, including cars that use solar or battery power. The object is to lower harmful emissions and conserve natural resources. One of the alternatives already in production is the hybrid car. A hybrid vehicle uses two or more fuels. Examples include diesel-electric trains and mopeds. The latter combine the power of a petrol engine with pedal power. In a hybrid car, petrol consumption is reduced by the provision of additional power by an electric motor during acceleration. The motor is driven by power from on-board batteries that are recharged by an engine-driven generator when the car is decelerating or cruising. Some hybrid cars transfer energy from the wheels to a flywheel during braking. The flywheel drives the generator, which recharges the batteries.

HONDA INSIGHT

Aerial

Windscreen

Aerodynamic roof

Wing mirror

Plastic front wings

Front air dam

Plastic bumper

Aerodynamic underside components

Cooling intake

Aluminium bonnet

SIDE VIEW OF 1-LITRE VTEC ENGINE

Motor power cables

Air-intake duct

Ignition coils

Coolant pipe

Electric motor housing

Lightweight plastic intake manifold

Lightweight magnesium alloy oil sump pan

Oil filter

Air conditioning compressor

Engine drive belt

FRONT VIEW OF 1-LITRE VTEC ENGINE

Dipstick

Rocker cover

Ignition coils

Water pump

Belt tensioner

Air conditioning compressor

Crankshaft pulley

Drive belt

HOW HYBRID POWER WORKS

Petrol engine provides power for acceleration and to generator

Inverter

Battery

Inverter controls direction of electrical current

Electric motor

Power from generator recharges battery during deceleration

Power from battery to motor during acceleration

Inverter cooling fan

Motor electronic control module (ECM)

Battery electronic control module (ECM)

Battery cooling fan

REAR VIEW

INVERTER AND BATTERY

High-voltage cables

High-voltage connector

DC converter

Inverter housing

Motor electronic control module (ECM)

Battery electronic control module (ECM)

⚠ **DANGER**
HIGH VOLTAGE
You can be killed or hurt.
Before servicing:
- Shut off main switch and remove ignition key.
- Check voltage at junction board terminal.
- Always wear insulated gloves and use insulated tools.
- Carefully read and follow service manual instruction.

INVERTER ASSEMBLY

BATTERY ASSEMBLY

Inverter cooling fan connector

Magnesium housing for air intake

DC converter connection

Junction board

Cover mounting bracket

Battery cooling fan

Manifold connector

O₂ sensor

Catalyst

Rear exhaust section connector

EXHAUST WITH CATALYTIC CONVERTER

Racing cars

SINCE MOTORING BEGAN, racing cars have been a major
focus of innovation in car design. Features that are now
commonplace, such as disc brakes, turbochargers, and even
safety belts, were used first on competition cars. Research into
racing cars has contributed to a new understanding of engine
performance, aerodynamics, and tyre adhesion, and has led
to the development of ultra-light materials such as carbon-
fibre for car bodies. A modern McLaren Formula One car has
a low, streamlined body and an open cockpit but, unlike its
forerunner, it also has front and rear wings that push the
wheels firmly on to the track, huge tyres for extra grip, and
electronic sensors that continually relay information to the
pits about the car's performance.

72° V10 ENGINE

Fuel injection trumpet guard

Cam cover

Gearbox fixing stud

Water and oil pump assembly

Mercedes-Benz

Harmonically-tuned exhaust system

Cylinder head

Stressed cylinder block

Cylinder head

Stressed cylinder block

BACK VIEW OF MCLAREN MERCEDES MP4-13

Upper flap

Grooved racing tyre

Warning light

Half-shaft

Rear wing end-plate

One-piece side pod and engine cover

Side pod air outlet

Diffuser

Exhaust pipe

Differential

SIDE VIEW OF MCLAREN MERCEDES MP4-13

Head rest

Engine air intake

On-board TV mini-camera

Engine cover

Winglet

Rear wing end-plate

Alloy wheel

Wheel nut

Side pod

LOCTITE
CAMOZZI
WARSTEIN
BRIDGESTONE
POTENZA

Hakkinen
BOSS
HUGO BOSS
Mobil 1
Mercedes-Benz
West
We

OVERHEAD VIEW OF MCLAREN MERCEDES MP4-13

Front wing end-plate

Front wing

Nose cover

Lower wishbone

Front brake duct

Grooved racing tyre

Driver's radio aerial

Rear-view mirror

One-piece side pod and engine cover

Radius arm

Rear wing endplate

Slot

Upper flap

Rear wing upper mainplane

Upper wishbone

Turning vane

Safety harness

Driver protection

Grooved racing tyre

FRONT VIEW OF MCLAREN MERCEDES MP4-13

Rear wing upper mainplane

Engine air intake

Rear-view mirror

Driver's radio aerial

Radiator air intake

Front brake duct

Upper wishbone

Grooved racing tyre

Lower wishbone

End-plate

Steering link

Wing supports

Front wing

Rear-view mirror

Forward rollover structure

Driver's radio aerial

Alloy wheel

High nose

Turning vane

Wheel nut

Front wing end-plate

Bicycle anatomy

THE BICYCLE IS A TWO-WHEELED, light-weight machine, which is propelled by human power. It is efficient, cheap, easily manufactured, and one of the world's most popular forms of transport. The first pedal-driven bicycle was built in Scotland in 1839. Since then the basic design – of a frame, wheels, brakes, handlebars, and saddle – has been gradually improved, with the addition of a chain, gear system, and pneumatic tyres (tyres inflated with air). The recent invention of the mountain bike (all-terrain bike) has been an important development. With its strong, rugged frame, wide tyres, and 21 gears, a mountain bike enables riders to reach rough and hilly areas that were previously inaccessible to cyclists.

REAR WHEEL

Tyre

Spoke

Rim

Hub

Saddle

Seat post

Seat post quick-release bolt

Cable guide

Straddle wire

Seat tube

Rear cantilever brake

Seat stay

Front derailleur

Rear drop-outs

Rear hub quick-release spindle

Bottom bracket shell

Bottom bracket axle

Crank bolt

Washer

17-tooth sprocket

13-tooth sprocket

Adjustable cup

Fixed cup

Bottom bracket sleeve

Caged ball bearings

Lock washer

Freewheel locknut

Lock ring

Jockey wheel

Chain

Lock washer

23-tooth sprocket

Rear derailleur

Derailleur cage plate

Jockey wheel

46-tooth chain ring

Toe clip

30-tooth sprocket

Sprocket spacer

Spoke guard

GEAR SYSTEM

Toe strap

Pedal

Spider

FREEWHEEL SPROCKETS

Gear cable

Gearshift

Handlebar
stem

Gearshift

Handlebar

Handlebar
grip

Expander
bolt

Lock
nut

Rear brake
cable

Top tube

Lock
washer

Brake
lever

Brake lever

Top race

Front brake
cable

Hub

Cable guide

Head
tube

Top cup

Caged ball
bearings

Spoke

**BICYCLE
FRAME**

Bottom
cup

Rubber
bearing
seal

Down
tube

Steerer
tube

Straddle wire

Bottom
race

Toe clip

Front
cantilever
brake

Toe
strap

Cantilever
brake boss

Rim

Inner tube

Pedal

Left crank
arm

Fork blade

24-tooth
chain ring

Front hub
quick-release
spindle

36-tooth
chain ring

Handlebar

Dust cap

Saddle

Frame

Brake lever
and gearshift

Valve

Pedal

Tyre

Chain

FRONT WHEEL

Bicycles

ALTHOUGH ALL BICYCLES are made up of the same basic components, they can vary greatly in design. A racing bike, such as the Eddy Merckx model, with its light frame and steep head- and seat-angles, is built for speed. Its design forces the rider to adopt the "aerotuck", a crouched, aerodynamic position. While a touring bike resembles the racing bike in many respects, it is designed for comfort and stability on long-distance journeys. Touring bikes are characterized by more relaxed frame angles, heavy chain stays that support the rear panniers, and a long wheelbase (the distance between the wheel axles) for reliable handling. All-round bicycles, known as "hybrids", combine the light weight and speed of sports bikes with the rugged durability of mountain bikes (see pp. 358-359). Bicycles that are not designed for conventional road use include time-trial bikes, which have a short head tube, sloping top tube, "aero" handlebars, and aerodynamic tubing. Most Human Powered Vehicles (HPVs) are recumbents – the rider has a recumbent position – which maximize power output and minimize drag (resistance). Essential to the safety of all riders are helmets, and both front and rear lights; locks protect against theft.

FRONT AND REAR LIGHTS

HELMET

Hard outer shell

Red rear light

Air vent

White front light

Polystyrene padding

Quick-release strap

EDDY MERCKX RACING BICYCLE

Saddle

Seat post

Cable guide

Saddle clamp

Seat-post bolt

Rear brake cable

Brake-block bolt

Brake block

Top tube (crossbar)

Steel frame

Seat stay

Seat tube

Down tube

Tyre

Water-bottle cage

Tyre tread

Front derailleur

Tyre wall

Wheel rim

Freewheel sprocket

STEEL LOCK

Key

Hardened steel

Pick-proof lock

Rear derailleur

Pulley bolt

Tension pulley

Chain

Chain ring

Crank

Spider

Crank bolt

Pedal

Chain stay

Toe clip

CANNONDALE SH600 HYBRID BICYCLE

Gel-filled saddle

Light-weight frame

Straight handlebar

Brake bridge

Cantilever brake

All-surface tyre

CANNONDALE ST1000 TOURING BICYCLE

Rear mudguard

Water bottle

Drop handlebar

Front mudguard

Rear pannier

Front pannier

Long chain stay

Large diameter aluminium tubing

Headset

Stem

Binder bolt

Handlebar

Front brake cable

Brake lever

Head tube

Brake pivot bolt

Brake pad

Fork

Hub quick-release lever

Spoke

Spoke nipple

Presta valve

Hub

ROSSIN ITALIAN TIME-TRIAL BICYCLE

Aero handlebar

Sloping top tube

Steep seat tube

Hollow disc wheel

Short head tube

Clipless pedal

Narrow tyre

Tri-spoke wheel

WINDCHEETAH SL MARK VI "SPEEDY" RACING HPV BICYCLE

Fleecy headrest

Fibreglass bucket seat

Joystick

Brake lever

53-tooth chain ring

Clipless pedal

7-speed freewheel

Aluminium tubing

Drum brake

Extended racing chain

The motorcycle

THE MOTORCYCLE HAS EVOLVED from a motorized cycle – a basic bicycle with an engine – into a sophisticated, high-performance machine. In 1901, the Werner brothers established the most viable location for the engine by positioning it low in the centre of the chassis (see pp. 364-365): the new Werner became the basis for the modern motorcycle. Motorcycles are used for many purposes – for commuting, delivering messages, touring, and racing – and different machines have been developed according to the demands of different types of riders. The Vespa scooter, for instance, which is small-wheeled, economical, and easy-to-ride, was designed to meet the needs of the commuter. Sidecars provided transport for the family until the arrival of cheap cars caused their popularity to decline. Enthusiast riders generally favour larger capacity machines that are capable of greater performance and offer more comfort. Four-cylinder machines have been common since the Honda CB750 appeared in 1969. Despite advances in motorcycle technology, many riders are attracted to the traditional looks of motorcycles like the twin-cylinder Harley-Davidson. The Harley-Davidson Glides exploit the style of the classic American V-twin engine, where the cylinders are placed in a V-formation.

1901 WERNER MOTORCYCLE

Vacuum-operated inlet valve
Fuel tank
Bicycle-type saddle
Electric ignition control
Pulley rim rear brake
Inlet-over-exhaust (IOE) engine
A 220
Alloy crankcase
Twisted rawhide drive belt
Cast iron cylinder barrel

1988 HARLEY-DAVIDSON FLHS ELECTRA GLIDE

1965 BMW R/60 WITH 1952 STEIB CHAIR

Handlebar
Head-light
Mirror
Windscreen
Adjustable link
Sidecar
Sidelight
Mudguard
Sidecar chassis rail
Sidecar wheel
Sidecar lower link
Exhaust pipe
Fuel tank
Horizontally opposed engine
Indicator
Square-section tyre
Side reflector

FRONT VIEW

Backrest
Passenger seat
Passenger grab rail
Pannier
Luggage rack
Licence plate
Tail-light

Mudguard
Canvas shroud
Speedometer
Ignition lock
Tail-light
Grab handle
Tool tray
Lockable luggage boot
Mudguard stay
Silencer
Silencer bracket
Suspension linkage
Bullet-shaped sidecar body
Drum brake
Disc brake
Knock-off wheel nut
SIDE VIEW
Long leading-link fork (Earles fork)
Crash bar
Exhaust clamp

1969 HONDA CB750

Tail-light
Shock absorber
Seat
Seat strap
Mirror
Oil tank
Front brake lever
Indicator
Telescopic fork
Mudguard stay
Disc brake
Clutch cover
Single overhead camshaft engine
Heat shield
Passenger footrest
Exhaust pipe

1963 VESPA GRAND SPORT 160 MARK 1

Monocoque chassis
Engine cover
Cooling grille
Tail-light
Seat strap
Throttle
Seat
Twist grip gear change
Front brake lever
Clutch lever
Head-light
Horn
Shock absorber
Choke
Petrol tap
Kick-starter
Centre stand
Silencer
Foot brake
Rubber foot mat
Drum brake
Single-sided trailing-link fork
Windscreen

Mirror
Brake master cylinder
Handgrip
Front brake lever
Light switch
Clutch cable
Throttle cable
Windscreen adjustor
Head-light
Fog-lamp
Indicator
Telescopic fork
Side reflector
Mudguard

Padded seat
Oil tank filler cap
Oil tank
Manufacturer's logo
Fuel tank
HARLEY-DAVIDSON
Gearbox
Air filter
45° V-twin engine
Exhaust pipe
Footrest
Passenger footrest
Brake pedal
Crash bar
Duplex tubular cradle frame
Brake calliper
Disc brake
Cast alloy wheel

The motorcycle chassis

THE MOTORCYCLE CHASSIS is the main "body" of the motorcycle, to which the engine is attached. Consisting of the frame, wheels, suspension, and brakes, the chassis performs various functions. The frame, which is built from steel or alloy, keeps the wheels in line to maintain the handling of the motorcycle, and serves as a structure for mounting other components. The engine and gearbox unit is bolted into place, while items such as the seat, the mudguards, and the fairing are more easily removable. Suspension cushions the rider from irregularities in the road surface. In most suspension systems, coil springs controlled by an oil damper separate the main mass of the motorcycle from the wheels. At the front, the spring and damper are usually incorporated in a telescopic fork; the rear employs a pivoted swingarm. The suspension also helps to retain maximum contact between the tyres and the road, necessary to effective braking and steering. Drum brakes were common until the 1970s, but modern motorcycles use disc brakes, which are more powerful.

1985 HONDA VF750 WITH BODYWORK

Racing number plate · Dual seat · Fuel tank · Frame-mounted fairing · Telescopic fork · HRC · Mudguard · Disc brake · Box-section swingarm · V4 engine unit · Box-section tubular cradle frame · Floating disc brake

1985 HONDA VF750 WITH BODYWORK REMOVED

Brake master cylinder · Headstock · Bracing tube · Square-section steel tubing · Rear sub-frame · Bodywork mounting point · Shock absorber top mounting · Engine mounting plate · Exhaust mounting strap · Shock absorber · Exhaust pipe · Light alloy wheel · Axle adjustor · Disc brake · Disc brake calliper · Box-section swingarm · Brake torque arm · Brake master cylinder · Footrest hanger · Brake pedal · Swingarm pivot · Multiplate clutch · Oil level window · Oil sump · Engine cover · Engine mounting bolt · V4 engine unit · Radiator · Oil cooler · Radiator pipe

DRUM BRAKE

OPERATING PARTS OF DISC BRAKE SYSTEM

Brake fluid reservoir

Master cylinder

Push-rod

Piston

Hydraulic brake fluid

Wheel disc

Calliper assembly

Piston

Brake pad

EXTERIOR OF DRUM BRAKE

Bolt hole

Torque arm

Air cooling scoop

Axle hole

Cooling fin

Speedometer drive

Cable stop

Brake plate

Operating arm

INTERIOR OF DRUM BRAKE

Torque arm

Bolt hole

Brake shoe

Pivot

Brake shoe return spring

Operating cam

Axle hole

Brake shoe return spring

High-friction material

Clutch cable

Hydraulic brake hose

Telescopic fork leg

Fork slide

Light alloy wheel

Axle

Floating disc brake

Brake calliper

SPRING/DAMPER UNIT

Rubber mounting bush

Twin rate spring

Damper rod

Damper body

Pre-load adjustor

Rubber mounting bush

HOW A SPRING/DAMPER UNIT WORKS

Rubber mounting bush

Spring

Damper rod

Non-return valve

Hydraulic fluid

Compressible gas

Hydraulic fluid chamber

Rubber mounting bush

TYPES OF TYRE

RACING SLICK TYRE

No tread pattern

TUBELESS SPORTS TYRE

Radial groove

TRIALS TYRE

Knobbly tread pattern

GENERAL-USE TYRE

Hard-wearing rubber compound

Motorcycle engines

MOTORCYCLE ENGINES must be light-weight and compact, and have a good power output. They have between one and six cylinders, can be cooled by air or water, and the capacity of the combustion chamber varies from 49cc (cubic centimetres) to 1500cc. Two types of internal combustion engine are common: the four-stroke, which is used in cars (see pp. 342-343), and the two-stroke. A basic two-stroke engine has only three moving parts – the crankshaft, the connecting rod, and the piston – but the power output is high. The engine fires every two strokes (rather than every four), giving a "power stroke" every revolution (see p. 343). Power is conveyed from the engine to the rear wheel by the transmission system. This usually consists of a clutch, a gearbox, and a final drive system. Clutches are multiplate devices, which run in oil. Gearboxes have five or six speeds and are operated by foot pedal. Shaft and belt drive systems are used in some cases, but chain drive to the rear wheel is most common.

EXTERIOR OF STANDARD TWO-STROKE ENGINE

Spark plug cap
Fuel tap
Carburettor mounting
Kick-starter
Carburettor
Cylinder head
Cooling fin
Exhaust port
Case screw
Clutch activating arm
Engine cover
Gear lever

TRANSMISSION SYSTEM

GEARBOX

1st gear
6th gear
4th gear
3rd gear
5th gear
2nd gear
Gear lever selector shaft
Input shaft
Splines for mounting gear lever
Bearing
Output shaft
Splines for mounting final drive sprocket
Gear tooth
Selector fork
Copper oil feed pipe
Aluminium outer casing

MULTIPLATE CLUTCH

Fibre plate
Key locks fibre plate to outer drum
Outer clutch drum, connected to engine
Pressure plate, connected to inner clutch drum
Springs force plates together
Straight-cut primary-drive gear
Metal plate

MODERN "O RING" DRIVE CHAIN

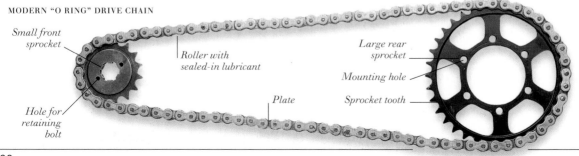

Small front sprocket
Roller with sealed-in lubricant
Large rear sprocket
Mounting hole
Plate
Sprocket tooth
Hole for retaining bolt

VELOCETTE OVERHEAD VALVE (OHV) ENGINE

Screw and lock nut tappet adjustor

Oil feed pipe

Inlet port

Spark plug lead

Cam follower

Magneto drive

Camshaft gear

Engine mounting bolt hole

Oil passageway

Crankcase

Oil pump

Mounting lug

Rocker arm

Rocker cover retaining bolt

Cylinder head

Exhaust port

Cylinder head

Combustion chamber

Cooling fin

Piston

Push rod

Valve lifter

Timing gear

Engine mounting bolt hole

Crankshaft

Non-return valve

Oil sump

Competition motorcycles

THERE ARE MANY TYPES of motorcycle sport
and in each, a specialist machine has evolved
to perform to specific requirements. Races take
place on roads or tracks or "off-road", in fields,
dirt tracks, and even the desert. "Grand Prix"
world championships in road-racing are
contested by three classes: 125cc, 250cc two-
strokes; the top class of 500cc two-strokes; and
900cc four-stroke machines. The latest racing
sidecars have more in common with racing
cars than motorcycles. The rider and
passenger operate within an all-enclosing,
aerodynamic fairing. The Suzuki RGV500
shown here, like other Grand Prix machines,
carries advertising, which helps to cover the
cost of developing motorcycle technology. In
Speedway, which originated in the US in
1902, motorcycles operate without brakes or a
gearbox. Off-road competition motorcycles
have less emphasis on high power output.
In Motocross, for example, which is held on
rough terrain, they must have high ground
clearance, flexible long-travel suspension, and
tyres with a chunky tread pattern.

1992 HUSQVARNA MOTOCROSS TC610

Throttle cable
Handlebar brace
Long seat
Racing number
Hand protector
Radiator air vent
Flexible plastic mudguard
Light-weight exhaust system
Telescopic fork
Plastic guard
Axle
Overhead camshaft engine
Gear lever
Shock absorber
Disc brake
Knobbly tyre
Disc brake
Brake calliper
Alloy swingarm
Shock absorber linkage

1992 SUZUKI RGV500
SIDE VIEW

Exhaust pipe
Racing number
Air vent
One-piece seat and tail unit
Shock absorber
Minimal seat padding
Arched alloy swingarm

Exhaust pipe
Vent
Exhaust pipe
Silencer
Handlebar
Shock absorber mounting
Footrest
Three-spoke alloy wheel
Rear brake pedal
Drive chain
Exhaust pipe
Wide, slick tyre
Axle adjustor
Brake pedal
Disc brake master cylinder
Disc brake
Rear brake calliper
Slick racing tyre
Drive chain
Footrest
Light-weight alloy frame

REAR VIEW

1981 WESLAKE SPEEDWAY

Throttle

Carburettor cover

Fuel tank filler cap

Throttle cable

Oil filler cap

Mudguard

Seat

Fuel tank

Mudguard

Wheel cover

Telescopic fork

Narrow tyre

Wide tyre

Brakeless wheel hub

Silencer

Footrest

Oil pump

Overhead valve engine

Tubular open cradle frame

Fairing stay

Throttle cable

Fuel tank breather

Fuel tank

Throttle

Front brake lever

Telescopic fork

Mudguard

Sponsor's logo

Air vent

Braided steel hydraulic hose

Brake calliper

Carbon-fibre disc brake

Three-spoke alloy wheel

Slick tyre

Quickly detachable (QD) fairing

1968 KIRBY BSA RACING SIDECAR

FRONT VIEW

Rev counter

Windscreen

All-enclosing fairing

Fuel tank

Battery

Wheel guard

Square-section tyre

Passenger windscreen

Passenger grab rail

SIDE VIEW

Throttle cable

Exhaust pipe

Rev counter

All-enclosing fairing

Sidecar chassis

Engine

Fuel cap

Fibreglass wheel guard

Windscreen

Racing number

Clutch lever

Fairing

Front brake lever

Radiator

Mudguard

Hydraulic brake hose

Axle

Slick tyre

FRONT VIEW

Sea and Air

Ships of Greece and Rome

ROMAN ANCHOR

Stock

Shank

Palm

Acutely angled arm

Ring

Crown

IN THE EXPANSIVE EMPIRES OF GREECE AND ROME, powerful fleets were needed for battl trade, and communication. Greek galleys were powered by a sail and many oars. A new armament, the embolos (ram), was fitted on to the galley bow. As ramming duels required fast and manoeuvrable boats, extra rows of oarsmen were added, culminating in the trireme. During the fifth and fourth centuries B.C., the trireme dominated the Mediterranean. It was powered by 170 oarsmen, rowing with one oar each. The oarsmen were ranged on three levels, as the model opposite shows. The trireme also carried archers and soldiers for boarding. Galleys were pulled out of the water when not in use, and were kept in dockyard ship-sheds. The merchant ships of the Greeks and Romans were mighty vessels too. The full-bodied Roman corbita, for example, could hold up to 400 tons and carried a cargo of spices, gems, silk, and animals. The construction of these boats was based on a stout hull with planking secured by mortice and tenon. Some of these ships embarked on long voyages, sailing even as far as India. To make them easier to steer, corbitas set a fore sail called an "artemon". It flew from a forward-leaning mast that was a forerunner of the long bowsprits carried by the great clipper ships of the 19th century.

ATTIC VASE SHOWING A GALLEY

Bronze mast truck

Keraia (yard)

Kalos (brailing rope)

Mast

Embolos (ram; beak)

Ophthalmos (eye)

Kope (oar)

Kubernetes (helmsman)

Sternpost

Pedalia (twin rudder)

Oar port sleeve

ROMAN CORBITA

Double halyard

Bullseye

Antenna (yard)

Artemon (fore sail)

Oculus (eye)

Tabling

Bolt rope

Prow

Windlass

Fore mast

Buntline

Brace

Roband (rope band)

Ceruchi (lift)

Heraldic device

Ring

Ruden (brail line)

Fore stay

Anchor

Sheet

Scala (ladder)

Catena (riding bitt)

Ancorale (anchor rope; anchor rode)

Hatch board

Deck beam

Zosteres (rubbing strake)

Cargo hold

Masthead

Single clump block

Malus (mast)

Rope parrel

Bullet block

Antenna (yard)

Brace block

Timber fairlead

Shroud

Leather reinforcing strip

Scala (ladder)

Velum (main sail)

Sheer pole

Deadeye

Lanyard

Poop break

Poop deck

Clew

Midships fence

Constratum (deck)

Bitt

ROWING POSITIONS ON A GREEK TRIREME (TRIERE)
The katastroma (deck) has been removed from this model to show the positions taken by oarsmen on a trireme.

Deck rail

Tropeter (leather grommet)

Paraxeiresia (outrigger)

Kope (oar)

Stanchion

Zugon (thwart; seat)

Thranite (upper level oarsman)

Zygian (middle level oarsman)

Thalamian (lower level oarsman)

Hyperesion (oarsman's cushion)

Pine hull

Main double halyard

Main brace

Main sheet

Hole and peg joint

Poop deck house

Clavus (tiller)

Swan neck ornament

Stern balustrade

Ring bolt

Sternpost

Gubernator (helmsman)

Wale

Planking

Shaft

Oar lanyard

Blade

Gubernacula (rudders)

MORTICE-AND-TENON FASTENINGS FOR HULL PLANKS

Mortice

Gomphoi (dowel)

Tenon

Hull plank

Viking ships

IN THE DARK AGES and early medieval times, the longships of Scandinavia were one of the most feared sights for people of northern Europe. The Vikings launched raids from Scandinavia every summer in longships equipped with a single steering oar on the right, or "steerboard", side (hence "starboard"). A longship had one row of oars on each side and a single sail. The hull had clinker (overlapping) planks. Prowheads adorned fighting ships during campaigns of war. The sailing longship was also used for local coastal travel. The karv below was probably built as transport for an important family, while the smaller faering (top right) was a rowing boat only. The fleet of William of Normandy that invaded England in 1066 owed much to the Viking boatbuilding tradition, and has been depicted in the Bayeux Tapestry (above). Seals used by port towns and royal courts through the ages provide an excellent record of contemporary ship design. The seal opposite shows how ships changed from the Viking period to the end of the Middle Ages. The introduction of the fighting platform – the castle – and the addition of extra masts and sails changed the character of the medieval ship. Note also that the steering oar has been replaced by a centred rudder.

BOATBUILDERS' TOOLS

Shave

Broad axe

Sheer

Breast auger

Master shipwright

Stempost

Hood end

Keel

T-handle auger

Axe

Strake

Tree cut for planking

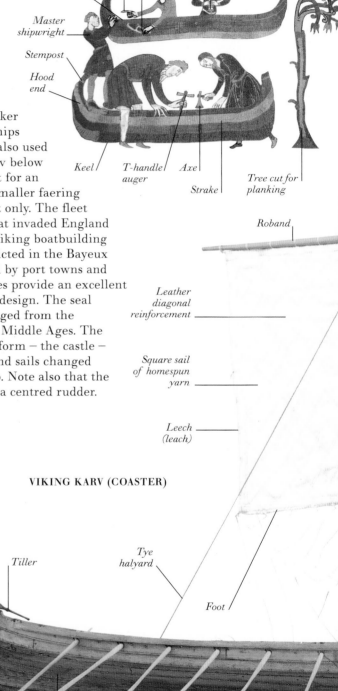

Zoomorphic head

Eye

Tooth

Braiding

Serpentine neck

Lozenge-shaped recess

Rectangular cross-band

DRAGON PROWHEAD

Snake-tail ornament

VIKING KARV (COASTER)

Roband

Leather diagonal reinforcement

Square sail of homespun yarn

Leech (leach)

Tye halyard

Foot

Tiller

Sternpost

Boss (rudder pivot)

Steering oar (side rudder)

Oar

Starboard (steerboard) side

Keel

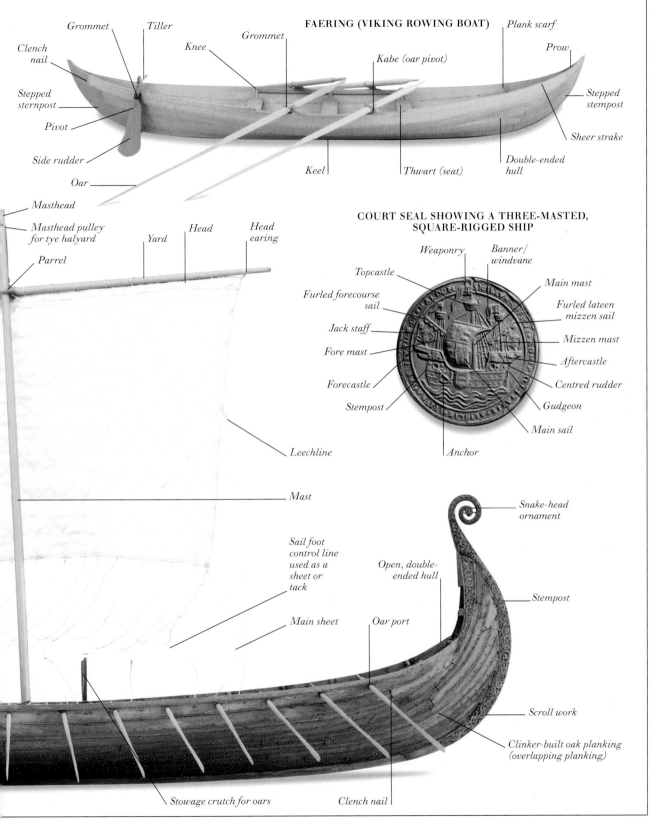

FAERING (VIKING ROWING BOAT)

Grommet

Tiller

Knee

Grommet

Kabe (oar pivot)

Plank scarf

Prow

Clench nail

Stepped sternpost

Pivot

Side rudder

Oar

Keel

Thwart (seat)

Stepped stempost

Sheer strake

Double-ended hull

Masthead

Masthead pulley for tye halyard

Parrel

Yard

Head

Head earing

COURT SEAL SHOWING A THREE-MASTED, SQUARE-RIGGED SHIP

Weaponry

Banner/ windvane

Topcastle

Main mast

Furled forecourse sail

Furled lateen mizzen sail

Jack staff

Mizzen mast

Fore mast

Aftercastle

Forecastle

Centred rudder

Stempost

Gudgeon

Anchor

Main sail

Leechline

Mast

Snake-head ornament

Sail foot control line used as a sheet or tack

Open, double-ended hull

Stempost

Main sheet

Oar port

Scroll work

Clinker-built oak planking (overlapping planking)

Stowage crutch for oars

Clench nail

375

Medieval warships and traders

FROM THE 16TH CENTURY, SHIPS WERE BUILT WITH A NEW FORM OF HULL, constructed from carvel (edge-to-edge) planking. Warships of the time, like King Henry VIII of England's Mary Rose, boasted awesome fire power. The ship carried both long-range cannon in bronze, and short-range, anti-personnel guns in iron. Elsewhere, ships took on a multiformity of shapes. Dhows transported slaves from East Africa to Arabia, their fore-and-aft rigged lateen sails allowing them to sail close to the wind around the lands of the Indian Ocean. The Chinese sailed to East Africa and Arabia in junks, trading goods that were carried in watertight compartments. New astronomical tools helped medieval sailors to find their way. Cross-staves and astrolabes were used to measure the altitude of the sun or stars. One of a choice of four cross-pieces was slid up or down the staff of the cross-stave – which was graduated in degrees of altitude – until its top aligned with the celestial body and its base with the horizon. The sighting rule of the astrolabe was simply lined up with a known body, and its altitude read from marks on the metal disc. With sundials, the sailor could use the shadow of the sun to show the time of day.

DHOW

Main yard
Furled lateen main sail
Mizzen yard
Parrel
Furled lateen mizzen sail
Main mast
Shroud
Mizzen mast
Parrel tackle
Tiller
Stem head
Rudder
Eye
Raking stempost

JUNK

Su-wei (fourth mast)
Topsail
Chung-ta-wei (main mast)
Wei-wei (mizzen mast)
Halyard
Erh-wei (second mast)
Sail batten
T'on-wei (port fore-mast)
Rudder head
Lug sail
Transom
Grapnel-type anchor
Rudder
Quarterdeck house
Cargo hatch
Oar

SAILING WARSHIP

Fore top yard
Fore topmast
Fore topcastle
Lift
Fore yard
Fore stay
Fore topmast stay
Bowsprit
Sprit yard
Fore mast
Ratline
Shroud
Woolding
Forecastle
Forecastle castle-deck gunport
Beakhead
Rigging rail
Chain wale (channel)
Hawse hole
Anchor cable
Stempost

Main topgallant mast

Main topgallant yard

Main topmast topcastle

Main top yard

Main topmast stay

Mizzen topmast

Main topmast

Mizzen top yard

Mizzen topcastle

Main topcastle

Lift

Lift

Main yard

Bonaventure top yard

Parrel

Tye

Bonaventure topmast

Jeer

Mizzen topcastle

Brace

30 degree cross-piece

Main stay

Bonaventure topcastle

Mizzen mast

Bonaventure yard

Mizzen yard

Bonaventure mast

Main mast

Aftercastle

Swifting tackle

Aftercastle castle-deck gunport

Upper deck gunport

Chain wale (channel)

Lid

Deadeye

Gangway

Gun carriage

Transom

Rudder

Sternpost

Keel

Blindage (removable archery screen)

Wale

Main deck gunport

Carvel planking

Port bower anchor

CROSS-STAVE (CROSS-STAFF)

90 degree cross-piece (transversary)

Clamp

Boxwood staff

60 degree cross-piece

30 degree cross-piece

Altitude scale in degrees and minutes

10 degree cross-piece (dutch shoe)

Ocular end

SUNDIAL

Style of the gnomon (edge)

Needle

Gnomon

Hour line

Outrigger

Pivot

Dial

ASTROLABE

Swivel suspension ring

Graduated ring

Scale of degrees

Pivot

Alidade (sighting rule)

Bottom ballast

Scribed arc decoration

The expansion of sail

BY THE 18TH CENTURY, SAILING SHIPS had become fast and effective floating fortresses. The navies of the north European powers competed with each other by building heavily-armed fighting ships called "men-of-war". The distinctive round stern of the ship below, with its open gallery, balcony, and elaborate wood carving is typical of the period. Hulls around this time were semicircular in cross section, although many boat designers were soon to return to the V-shaped hulls used by the Vikings. Ships of the period carried more sail than ever before. A labyrinth of rigging supported the masts and yards from which the profusion of square sails were set. Ships grew higher, as extra masts were fitted above the lower mast, and the bowsprit became longer to allow the ship to carry staysails, spritsails, and jibsails. Ships went into battle in single file, so that broadsides from the multiple decks of guns would have maximum effect. Ships were classified by rates, the rating of a vessel depending on how many guns it had. A first rate ship had more than 100 guns. The guns fired solid round shot, usually made of iron.

WOODEN SAILING SHIP

Gilded truck

Main topgallant mast

Main topgallant shroud

Bolster

Trestle trees

Main topmast

Main topmast backstay

Main topmast shroud

Cap

Main top

Mast-head

Main top rail

Hounds

Futtock shroud

Mizzen topmast

Mizzen topmast stay

Mizzen topmast shroud

Mizzen top

Lift

Mizzen yard

Mizzen backstay

Vang

Fiddle block

Mizzen shroud

Mizzen mast

Mizzen stay

Taffrail

Poop rail

Main shroud

Main mast

BOW

Brace

Lift

Foot rope

Studding sail boom

Main top rail

Studding sail yard (stuns'l yard)

Wash cant

Knee of the head

Hawse hole

Jacob's ladder

Rope preventer

Rudder chain

Rudder

Sternpost

Pintle strap

Gudgeon strap

Ship's wheel

Binnacle box

Keel

Channel

Chain

Step

Boat slide

SAIL PATTERN OF A 74-GUN SHIP

Main topgallant stay

Gilded truck

Fore topgallant mast

Fore topgallant stay

Fore topgallant backstay

Mizzen topgallant sail

Main topgallant sail

Fore mast topgallant sail

Fore mast topsail

Mizzen topsail

Mizzen topgallant sail

Fore topsail

Jibsail

Mouse and collar

Mizzen course

Main topmast stay

Fore topmast shroud

Main topmast preventer stay

Ratline

Fore topmast

Fore top

Fore topmast stay

Fore topmast preventer stay

Main course

Fore mast course

Sprit topsail

Main topsail

Spritsail course

Fore topmast backstay

Fore shroud

Main stay

Mainstay tackle

Fore hatch tackle

Fore mast

Cap

Bee

Rope woolding

Fore stay

Fish davit

Mainrail head

Anchor buoy

Jib boom

Truck

Jack staff

Outer spritsail yard

Spritsail yard

Foot rope

Bowsprit

Bobstay

Figurehead

Rail

Trailboard

Draught (draft) mark

Bower anchor

Tallow coating

Capstan   Clewline   Gunport   Gun   Gripe

STERN

Main topgallant yard

Fore topgallant yard

Main topsail yard

Yardarm

Fore topsail yard

Main yard

Fore yard

Mizzen topmast yard

Stern lantern

Captain's cabin (great cabin)

Balcony

Upper gallery

Stern quarter gallery

Port

Fore staysail

Fore

A ship of the line

THE 74-GUN WOODEN SHIP WAS A MAINSTAY of British and French battlefleets in the late 18th and early 19th centuries. This "ship of the line" was heavy enough to fight with the most potent of rivals, yet nimble too. The length of such a ship was determined by the number of guns required for each deck, allowing enough room for crews to man them. The gun deck was about 52 m (170 ft) long. The decks had to be very strong to carry the weight of the guns. The deck planks have been removed on the vessel pictured below, to show just how close together the beams had to be to make the hull strong enough. Only timber with a perfect grain was used. The upper deck was open at the waist, but afore and abaft were officers' cabins. The forecastle and quarterdeck carried light guns and acted as platforms for working rigging and for reconnaissance. The ship's longboats (launches) were carried on booms between the gangways.

LONGBOAT

Truck
Mast
Jib halyard
Fore stay halyard
Shroud
Fore sail halyard
Parrel
Bowsprit
Traveller
Stempost
Waterline
Deadeye
Oar
Side bench
Flag halyard
Backstay
Topping lift
Peak halyard
Main sheet
Gaff
Boom

Thole pin
Planking
Rabbit line
Sheerplank
Windlass bar
Frame
Floor
Transom
Keel
Thwart (seat)
Tiller
Rudder

UPPER DECK OF A 74-GUN SHIP

Stock
Hoop
Cathead
Ring
Knighthead
Heads (privy)
Head beam
Figurehead
Head rail
Roundhouse
Boomkin
Anchor cable
Sheave for cat tackle
Fluke
Hoop
Stock
Arm
Deck beam
Foremast hole
Timber head
Fore bitt
Steam grating
Galley stove chimney
Belfry
Deadeye
Waterway
Gangway
Capstan
Breastwork
Carling (carline)
Forked beam
Bulwark
Pawl
Main companion way
Skid beam

Head
Forecastle (fo'c'sle)
Waist

BOW

Figurehead
Headboard
Head rail
Main rail
Middle rail
Lower rail
Supporter
Cat block
Ekeing
Cheek
Catted anchor
Riband
Hawse piece
Side step
Stempost
Deadwood
Hawse hole
Frame
Main wale

STERN

Cove
Taffrail
Screen bulkhead
Balcony
Side counter timber
Counter timber
Tuck
Upper counter rail
Drop
Lower counter rail
Gunport lid
Filling transom
Wing transom
Timber under transom
Cant frame
After fashion piece
Tuck rail

Eye bolt
Main bitt
Ledge
Hatch coaming / shot garland
Spirketting
Backstay stool
Companion ladder
Master's sea cabin
Mizzen mast hole
Channel
Great cabin (captain's cabin)
Coaming
Pilaster
Ledge (batten)
Screen bulkhead
Standard knee
Poop rail
Necking
Stern carving
Wardroom
Upper finishing
Taffrail
Gunport drip (eyebrow; rigol)
Mizzen bitt
Clerk's cabin
Quarter gallery
Main mast hole
Mast partner
Grating
Lodging knee
Gunport lid
Rail at break of poop deck
Quarterdeck
Poop deck

381

Rigging

MOST SAILING SHIPS HAVE TWO TYPES OF RIGGING. Standing rigging – kept taut by rigging screws or old-fashioned lanyards and deadeyes – refers to the ropes, wires, and chains that support the masts and yards (horizontal spars). Running rigging, which includes types of block and tackle, halyards, and sheets, is used to hoist, lower, or trim sails.

BOWSPRIT AND JIB BOOM

Outer jib stay

Inner jib stay

Inner jib tack

Bowsprit cap

Fore topmast staysail tack

Bowsprit

Foot rope

Boom guy block

Spear

Martingale (dolphin striker)

Martingale backrope

Lizard

Chain bobstay

Fore stay

Jib boom

Whisker boom

Upper deadeye

Lower deadeye

Chain plate

Butterfly plate

OTHER RIGGING FITTINGS

Handle

Eye plate lug

Parallel shaft

BELAYING PIN

MAST BAND

STANDING BLOCK

Arse (tail)

Running part

Shoulder

Lug

Eye

Crown

SHACKLE

Crown

Clear

Jaw

Screw thread

Shank

Shoulder

Eye

SHACKLE PIN

Swivel becket

Hauling part (fall)

Shell

Lug

Soft eye

Served eye splice

Standing part

RIGGING TOOLS

Sailmaker's whipping

BLOCK AND TACKLE (PURCHASE; HANDY BILLY)

RIGGER'S GAUGE FOR MEASURING THE DIAMETER OF ROPE OR WIRE

Cheese (cheesing)

Fore royal stay

Flying jib tack

Outer jib tack

Outer martingale stay

Middle martingale stay

Inner martingale stay

Eye

SCORED BULLSEYE FAIRLEAD

Eye

Strap

SHEET LEAD

Base

RUNNING BLOCK

Double rope becket

DUTCH TRIPLE FIDDLE BLOCK

Flat seizing

Swallow

Strop

LANYARD AND DEADEYES

Leather pointing

Turk's head

Hitched hauling end

UPPER DEADEYE

Swallow

Sheave (shiver; shiv)

Standing part

LANYARD

LOWER DEADEYE

Grooving

Binding

Bolt

Shoulder   Back   Shank

HOOK

Crown

Clear

Jaw

Fixed   Bill
lug

Cheek

Penny washer (pin cover plate)

SPLICING FID

ROPE SERVING MALLET

HEAVER FOR WIRE SERVING

PRICKERS

HOLLOW SPIKE FOR WIRE

MARLINSPIKE

RIGGING SCREW (TURNBUCKLE)

Shroud

Spun yarn serving

Flat wire seizing

Solid heart thimble

Cotter pin

Fork end

Tail

Right hand screw

Open body

Left hand screw

Safe working load mark

Seizing

Swallow

Shoulder

Face

Eye

Nut

Crown

Sails

THERE ARE TWO MAIN TYPES OF SAIL, often used in combination. Square sails are driving sails. They are usually attached by parrels to yards, square to the mast to catch the following wind. On fore-and-aft sails, such as lateen and lug sails, the luff (leading edge) usually abuts a mast or a stay. The head of the sail may abut a gaff, and the foot a boom. Around the world, a great range of rigs (sail patterns), such as the ketch, lugger, and schooner, have evolved to suit local needs. Sails are made from strips of cloth, cut to give the sail a belly and strong enough to resist the most violent of winds. Cotton and flax are the traditional sail materials, but synthetic fabrics are now commonly used.

SECTION OF A SAIL

Seizing LUFF (LEADING EDGE) *Luff slide* *Bolt rope* *Head*

Round thimble

Rope strand

Grommet

Head cringle

LEECH
(LEACH)

Sharp point

Flat seam

SERVING MALLET

Groove for spunyarn rope

Flatboard

NEEDLES AND SEAMING TWINE

Synthetic flax (duradon)

Handle

Tabling

Seaming twine

Luff cloth

Needle packet

Grip

Rat's tail

Needle SAILMAKER'S FID

SAILCLOTHS

KEVLAR
ON FLEX
FILM

HEAVYWEIGHT
NYLON CLOTH

SAIL HOOK

SAILMAKER'S PALM

Strap *Thumbhole*

Cowhide face

Crown

MYLAR

NYLON
AND
SILICON
CLOTH

Bill *Shank*

Metal needle pad

BEESWAX

Handle SAILMAKER'S MALLET *Cheek*

SYNTHETIC
FLAX
(DURADON)

WOVEN
DACRON

Whipping *Hide grip* *Seizing*

Groove made by thread

SAILMAKING TOOLS

Copper face

Mizzen gaff topsail

Main sail

Main gaff topsail

Fore staysail

Jibsail

Mizzen sail

KETCH

Mizzen yard topsail

Dipping lug foresail

Standing lug mizzen

LUGGER

SAILS AND RUNNING RIGGING OF A DOUBLE TOPSAIL SCHOONER

Upper topsail lift

Lower topsail brace

Main topsail halyard

Flying jib halyard

Fore upper topsail

Triatic stay

Foot rope

Upper topsail brace

Outer jib halyard

Fore peak halyard

Lower topsail clewline

Fore yard lift

Fore lower topsail

Inner jib halyard

Fore throat halyard

Fore staysail halyard

Fore sail

Mast hoop

Yard

Head

Gaff

Fore topmast staysail

Main gaff topsail

Fore sail

Main sail

Fore staysail

Jibsail

SAILING RIGS

FISHERMAN'S SCHOONER (FORE-AND-AFT SCHOONER)

Inner jib downhaul

Outer jib downhaul

Outer jib sheet

Flying jib sheet

Inner jib sheet

Flying jib downhaul

Flying jib

Outer jib

Reef point

Inner jib

Fore staysail

Fore staysail sheet

Luff

Boom

Foot

Mooring and anchoring

FOR LARGE VESSELS IN OPEN WATER, ANCHORAGE IS ESSENTIAL. By holding a ship securely to the seabed, an anchor prevents the vessel from being at the mercy of wave, tide, and current. The earliest anchors were nothing more than stones. In later years, many anchors had a standard design, much like the Admiralty pattern anchor shown on this page. The Danforth anchor is somewhat different. It has particularly deep flukes to give it great holding power. On large sailing ships, anchors were worked by teams of sailors. They turned the drum of a capstan by pushing on bars slotted into the revolving cylinder. This, in turn, lifted or lowered the anchor chain. In calm harbours and estuaries, ships can moor (make fast) without using anchors. Berthing ropes can be attached to bollards both inboard and on the quayside. Berthing ropes are joined to each other by bends, like those opposite.

STONE ANCHOR (KILLICK)

Rope hole

TYPES OF ANCHOR

CLOSE-STOWING ANCHOR

CQR ANCHOR (SECURE ANCHOR; PLOUGH ANCHOR)

ADMIRALTY ANCHOR TYPE ACII

ADMIRALTY PATTERN ANCHOR

STOCKLESS ANCHOR

MUSHROOM ANCHOR (PERMANENT MOORING ANCHOR)

ANCHOR CHAIN

End link | Common link | Patent link

SHACKLE, SWIVELS, AND LINK

Crown

Bolt | Lug

GALVANIZED "D" SHACKLE

MOORING SWIVEL

CHAIN SWIVEL

Screw thread

MAILLOT (SCREW LINK)

DANFORTH ANCHOR

Shank

Pea (bill)

Fluke

Stock

Tripping palm | Crown

Throat

Blade

TWIN BOLLARDS WITH RAKED PILLARS AND A HAWSER (HEAVY ROPE)

Flat

Rim

Base

BERTHING ROPES (HAWSERS)

Ship
Twin bollards
Stern rope
Head rope
Quayside
After breast rope
After spring rope
Fore spring rope
Fore breast rope
Bollard

MOORING ROPE BENDS

HAWSER BEND (TWO DOUBLE ROUND TURNS AND DOUBLE HALF HITCHES)

Standing part
Seizing

CARRICK BEND

Seizing

SINGLE SHEET BEND (SWAB HITCH)

Bare end (fag end)
Standing part
Thin rope
Thick rope

Three-strand hawser belayed with figure of eight turns
Outboard end
Pillar
Foundry plug
Horn
Bolt hole
Cross piece
Bitter end (inboard end)

Bar hole (pigeon hole)
Cap
Upper head (drumhead)
Strengthening chock
Barrel
Trenail (treenail)
Strengthening chock
Pawl slot
Lignum vitae bearing
Whelp

WOOD CAPSTAN WITH A VERTICAL SPINDLE

Tapered spindle
Spigot
Pin

387

Ropes and knots

ALL KINDS OF ROPES ARE USED AT SEA, from thin twines and yarns to thick hawsers. Synthetic fibres have been developed specifically for use at sea. Nylon ropes stretch, and so are ideal for anchoring; polypropylene has little stretch, so is ideal for halyards and sheets. Different types of knots are used for different purposes. Knots that join two ropes are called bends; hitches join a rope to another object; and bowlines produce an eye (loop) in the end of a rope. Ropes can be joined by splicing (unravelling the ends and weaving them together) or seizing (lashing the ropes together side by side).

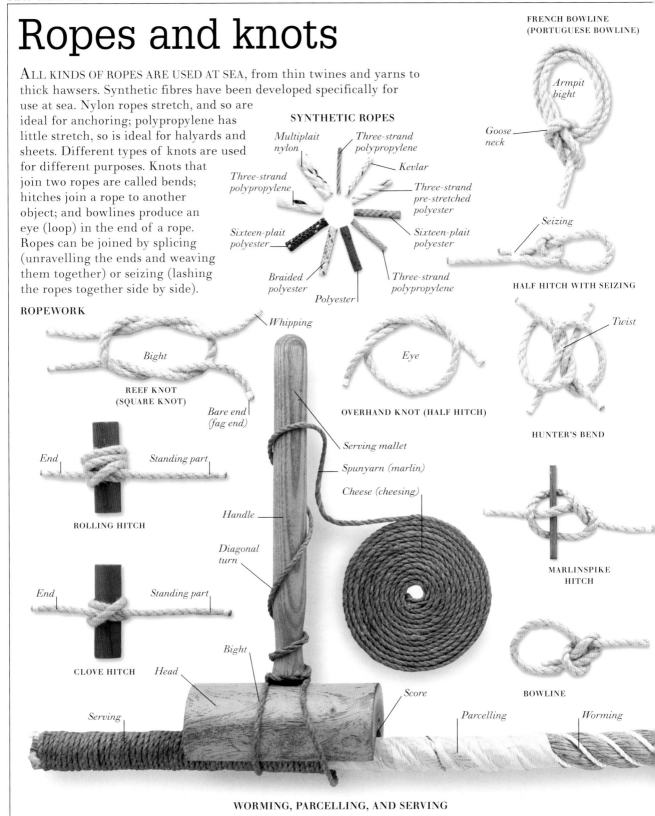

FRENCH BOWLINE (PORTUGUESE BOWLINE)

Armpit bight

Goose neck

Seizing

HALF HITCH WITH SEIZING

SYNTHETIC ROPES

Multiplait nylon

Three-strand polypropylene

Kevlar

Three-strand polypropylene

Three-strand pre-stretched polyester

Sixteen-plait polyester

Sixteen-plait polyester

Braided polyester

Three-strand polypropylene

Polyester

ROPEWORK

Whipping

Bight

REEF KNOT (SQUARE KNOT)

Bare end (fag end)

Eye

OVERHAND KNOT (HALF HITCH)

Twist

HUNTER'S BEND

End

Standing part

ROLLING HITCH

Serving mallet

Spunyarn (marlin)

Cheese (cheesing)

Handle

Diagonal turn

MARLINSPIKE HITCH

End

Standing part

CLOVE HITCH

Head

Bight

Score

BOWLINE

Serving

Parcelling

Worming

WORMING, PARCELLING, AND SERVING

THUMB KNOT

SPANISH BOWLINE

FLAT SEIZING
(ROUND SEIZING)

DOUBLE CARRICK BEND

End

Frapped turn

Heaving line knot

LIGHTERMAN'S HITCH

HEAVING LINE BEND

Standing part

JURY MAST KNOT
(MAST HEAD BEND)

SHEET BEND (SWAB HITCH)

MANHARNESS KNOT
(BUTTERFLY KNOT;
ARTILLERY LOOP)

Cheese (cheesing)

Marlinspike

HEAVING LINE

PINNED SHEEPSHANK

Jaw

Rat tail

Hawser laid three-strand manilla rope with right-handed lay

Paddle wheels and propellers

THE INVENTION OF THE STEAM ENGINE IN THE 18TH CENTURY made mechanically driven ships fitted with paddle wheels or propellers a viable alternative to sails. Paddle wheels have fixed or feathered floats, and the model shown below features both types. Feathered floats give more propulsive power than fixed floats because they are almost upright at all times in the water. Paddle wheels were superseded by the propeller on ocean-going vessels in the mid-19th century. Propellers are more efficient, work better in rough water, and are less vulnerable in collisions. The first propellers were two-bladed but later three- and four-bladed versions are more powerful; the shape and pitch of blades have also been refined over the years. At the beginning of the 18th century, tillers were superseded on many larger ships by the ship's wheel as a means of steering.

SHIP'S WHEEL

King spoke handle

Handle

Spoke

Rim plate

Felloe (rim section)

Maker's name

Nave plate

Nave

THREE-BLADED PROPELLER

Blade

Tapered shaft hole

Hub

Keyway

Propeller blade tip trace

Blade

Pitch

Propeller diameter

Hub

Propeller hub trace

PROPELLER ACTION

PADDLE WHEEL WITH FIXED FLOATS

Wrist pin

Limb

Fixed float

Hub

Deck beam

OSCILLATING STEAM ENGINE

Slip eccentric for slide valve

Ahead/astern controls

Main crank

Slide valve

Strut

Frame

Piston rod (tail rod)

Stuffing box

Oscillating cylinder

Bottom plate (bedplate)

Slide valve rod

Control platform

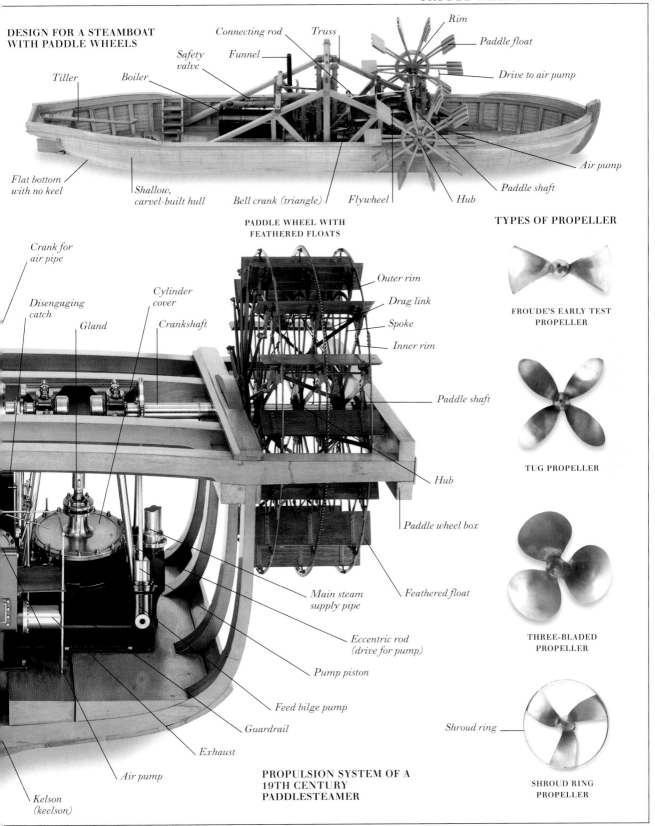

DESIGN FOR A STEAMBOAT WITH PADDLE WHEELS

Connecting rod

Truss

Rim

Paddle float

Safety valve

Funnel

Drive to air pump

Tiller

Boiler

Air pump

Flat bottom with no keel

Shallow, carvel-built hull

Bell crank (triangle)

Flywheel

Hub

Paddle shaft

Paddle shaft

PADDLE WHEEL WITH FEATHERED FLOATS

TYPES OF PROPELLER

Crank for air pipe

Outer rim

Disengaging catch

Cylinder cover

Drag link

Gland

Spoke

Crankshaft

Inner rim

FROUDE'S EARLY TEST PROPELLER

Paddle shaft

Hub

TUG PROPELLER

Paddle wheel box

Main steam supply pipe

Feathered float

THREE-BLADED PROPELLER

Eccentric rod (drive for pump)

Pump piston

Feed bilge pump

Guardrail

Shroud ring

Exhaust

Air pump

PROPULSION SYSTEM OF A 19TH CENTURY PADDLESTEAMER

SHROUD RING PROPELLER

Kelson (keelson)

Anatomy of an iron ship

IRON PARTS WERE USED IN THE HULLS OF WOODEN SHIPS AS EARLY AS 1675, often in the same form as the wooden parts that they replaced. Eventually, as on the tea clipper Cutty Sark (below), iron rigging was found to be stronger than the traditional rope. The first "ironclads" were warships whose wooden hulls were protected by iron armour plates. Later ironclads actually had iron hulls. The model opposite is based on the British warship HMS Warrior, launched in 1860, the first battleship built entirely of iron. The plan of the iron paddlesteamer (bottom), built somewhat later, shows that this vessel was a sailing ship; but it also boasted a steam propulsion plant amidships that turned two side paddlewheels. Early iron hulls were made from plates that were painstakingly rivetted together (as below), but by the 20th century vessels began to be welded together, whole sections at a time. The Second World War "liberty ship" was one of the first of these "production-line vessels".

TEA CLIPPER

Steel yard

Iron wire stay

Steel lower mast

Steel bowsprit

Wooden planking with copper sheathing

Forged iron anchor

RIVETTED PLATES

Pan head rivet

Plate

Button head rivet (snap head)

Seam

LIBERTY SHIP

Gun section

Accommodation section

Cargo derrick

Weld line

Stern section

Midships section

Cargo hold

Bow section

PLAN OF AN IRON PADDLESTEAMER

Mizzen mast

Poop deck

Lounge

Deck lantern

Main mast

Steam whistle

Crankshaft

Paddle wheel

Steering position

Guardrail

Binnacle

State room

After funnel

Guardrail

Eccentric

Connecting rod

Steering gear

Skylight

Stern

Vertical frame ladder

Mast step

Rudder

Rudder post

Heel of rudder post

Bar keel

Afterpeak

Tank

Cabin

Main mast step

Donkey boiler

Box boiler

Foundation

Reversing wheel

Bottom plate

Side lever

Cylinder

Stern framing

CUTAWAY SECTION OF AN IRONCLAD

Bulwark cap

Waterway

Deck planking

Upper deck stringer (tie) plate

Bulwark

Scupper

Upper deck beam

Upper sheer strake

Upper deck pillar (stanchion)

Teak backing

Topside strake

Main deck beam

Wrought iron armour plate

Main sheer strake

Main deck pillar (stanchion)

Main deck tie plate

Lower deck beam

Lower deck tie plate

Lighting hole

Angle bar (I bar)

Box sister keelson

Hold pillar (stanchion)

Frame

Centre line keelson

Bilge stringer

Bilge strake

Bilge keelson

Limber hole

Side keelson

Floor

Bottom plating

Garboard strake

Keel

Forward funnel

Ventilator cowl

Capstan

Bowsprit

Fore mast

Skylight

Chimney

Hatch

Main deck

Hawse pipe

Stem

Beam

Chain locker

Bulkhead stiffener

Deep floor

Smoke box

'Tween decks ladder

Lower deck

Forepeak

Forefoot

Combustion chamber

Cabin

Centre girder

Deck beam

The battleship

IN THE EARLY YEARS OF THE 20TH CENTURY, sea warfare – attacking enemy vessels or defending a ship – was revolutionized by the introduction of Dreadnought-type battleships like the Brazilian vessel below. These new ships combined the latest advances in steam propulsion, gunnery, and armour plating. The gun turret was designed to fire shells over huge distances. It was protected by armour 30 cm (12 in) thick. The measurements given for the guns of this ship refer to the bore diameter. Where "weight" is quoted, this is the weight of the shell that the gun fires. Torpedoes – as portrayed on the upper cigarette card (right) – were self-propelled underwater missiles, often steered by gyro-control. Depth charges were designed in the First World War for use against submerged U-boats. They are canisters filled with explosives that are detonated by depth-sensitive pistols. The lower cigarette card shows depth charges being fired by a "thrower", fired from a torpedo tube, and rolled from the stern. Ship's shields were fitted to warships from the late 19th century onwards. The shield shown opposite depicts a traditional ship's cannon.

20TH CENTURY WEAPONRY

Torpedo tube

Sight

Warhead

TORPEDOES

DEPTH CHARGES

Side-thrown canister

Stern-rolled canister

Torpedo-fired canister

Boat handling derrick

BRAZILIAN BATTLESHIP

Rangefinder

Forward funnel

Light screen

Lifeboat

Compass

Gunnery spotting top

Purchase wire

Searchlight

Searchlight platform

Compass and rangefinder platform

Ship's wheel

Leading block

Tripod mast

Navigating bridge

Boat winch

Conning tower

Captain's shelter/ chart house

Weather shutter for gun

"F" turret

Arms of Brazil

Jack staff

30 cm (12 in) gun

Skylight

Stem (false ram bow)

Porthole

Belt armour

Forward accommodation ladder

Sighting hood

"A" turret

Turret barbette

Open gun mounting

12 cm (4.7 in) gun

Steam launch

Guest boat boom

SHIP'S SHIELD

Rope moulding

Muzzle moulding

Swell of muzzle

Chase

Reinforce

Ogee

Astragal

Trunnion

Lion crest

Radio antenna

Upper wireless and telegraphy yard (Upper W/T yard)

Topgallant mast

Wireless and telegraphy yard (W/T yard)

Lower yard

Signal gear

Ladder way

Brake slip

Davit

Clump cathead

Guardrail

Hawser fairlead

Sheet anchor

Starboard bower anchor

Lifeboat davit

Breakwater

Cable holder

Anchor chain

Bollard

Hawse pipe

Boat boom

Towing fairlead

Port bower anchor

Exhaust pipe

Searchlight

Searchlight platform

After compass platform

After bridge

1.3 kg (3 pound) gun ("three pounder")

"X" turret

"Y" turret

Officer's accommodation ladder

Whaler

Davit for whaler

Flagmast

Vedette boat

Gig

After funnel

Funnel stay

"P" turret

Ash chute

Hen coop

Bilge keel

Gun battery

Torpedo net boom

Turret roof rail

Propeller shaft boss

Torpedo net

Propeller

Propeller shaft

Rudder

Stern walk

Scarph

Aft anchor

Life buoy

Frigates and submarines

FROM THE MID-19TH CENTURY, ARMOURED SHIPS provided a new challenge to enemy craft. In response, huge revolving gun turrets were developed. These could fire in any direction, could be loaded from the breech very rapidly, and, instead of cannonballs, they discharged exploding shells. Modern fighting ships, like the frigate, combine heavy ship-borne armament with light helicopter weaponry. Submarines function below the surface of the sea. Their speed and ability to fire missiles from under water are their major assets. The nuclear submarine can stay under water for several years without refuelling.

Stabilizer fin

Aft hydroplane

Propeller

Lower rudder

Rangefinder

Look out periscope

Local control cabinet

Breech wheel

Breech block

Loading arm

Slide locking lever

Slide

Sighting hood

Recoil cylinder

Elevating wheel

Guide for gun loading cage

Blast bag (breeches)

Rammer lever

Gun loading cage

Floor of gun house

Turret roller

Training rack gearing

Roller path

Working chamber

GUN TURRET
In this turret for two 37 cm (15 in) guns, shells are carried in a hoisting cage. The shell is rammed into the gun, followed by the propellant (charge). Once the breech is closed, the gun is ready for firing. The whole operation requires around 70 sailors.

Training gear

Rammer

Waiting position

Roller path support

Floor

"Walking pipe" (water supply)

Barbette (armour)

Main hoisting cage

Turret trunk

Cordite handling room

Cordite supply shuttle

Cordite case

FRIGATE

Ensign staff

Lynx helicopter

SONAR torpedo decoy

Rudder

Practice projectile

High-explosive projectile

Shell bogie

Shell room

Hydraulic grab

Shell-handling gear

Variable pitch propeller

Ladder way

Steam pipework
Machinery raft
Main turbine
Conning tower
Machinery control room
Switchboard room

Snort mast
Electronic warfare mast
Periscope
Control room
Sonar room
Galley
Officers' mess

NUCLEAR "HUNTER-KILLER" SUBMARINE

SONAR transducer array

Main engine steam condenser
Distiller
Diesel motor compartment
Reactor space
Carbon dioxide scrubber compartment
Wireless office
Junior ratings' mess
Torpedo compartment
Senior ratings' mess
Junior ratings' bunk space
Torpedo tube
Forward hydroplane

Muzzle

Barrel

15 cm (6 in) SHELL
This shell is designed to burst in the air above its target.

Driving band

SHELL CASE

Bursting charge (explosive)
Flash tube
Body
Wooden packing

Expelling plate

CROSS-SECTION OF THE SHELL

Transit plug
Bullet

Surveillance RADAR
Navigation/helicopter control RADAR antenna
Motor whaler
Mast
RADAR for gunnery and missile control
Signalling lamp
Jack staff
Seacat missile launcher
Vent
Aerial rig
Oerlikon gun position
Stern gallery
Funnel
Enclosed bridge
Aerial
Exocet missile launcher
Gun turret
11 cm (4.5 in) gun

F174

RADAR for gunnery and missile control
Stabilizer
Liferaft cylinder
Signal flag compartment
Reel
Fairlead
Anchor
Anti-submarine torpedo tube
Triple "chaff" rocket launcher
Bilge keel
Pennant number
SONAR bulge
Porthole
Bollard
Breakwater
Draught (draft) mark

Pioneers of flight

FLIGHT HAS FASCINATED MANKIND for centuries, and countless unsuccessful flying machines have been designed. The first successful flight was made by the French Montgolfier brothers in 1783, when they flew a balloon over Paris. The next major advance was the development of gliders, notably by the Englishman Sir George Cayley, who in 1845 designed the first glider to make a sustained flight, and by the German Otto Lil ienthal, who became known as the world's first pilot because he managed to achieve controlled flights. However, powered flight did not become a practical possibility until the invention of lightweight, petrol-driven internal combustion engines at the end of the 19th century. Then, in 1903, the American brothers Orville and Wilbur Wright made the first powered flight in their Wright Flyer biplane, which used a four-cylinder, petrol-driven engine. Aircraft design advanced rapidly, and in 1909 the Frenchman Louis Blériot made his pioneering flight across the English Channel (see pp. 400-401). The American Glenn Curtiss also achieved several "firsts" in his Model-D Pusher and its variants, most notably winning the world's first competition for airspeed at Reims in 1909.

FRONT VIEW OF WRIGHT FLYER, 1903

Biplane elevator

Chain drive to starboard propeller

Pusher propeller (rear-mounted propeller)

Fuel tank

Propeller-shaft bracing strut

Take-off and landing skid

Offset pilot's cradle

Side-mounted engine to balance pilot's weight

SIDE VIEW OF CURTISS MODEL-D PUSHER, 1911

Nine-cylinder Salmson radial engine

Pusher propeller (rear-mounted propeller)

Aileron operating arm

Wing strut

Body cradle that pivots to control ailerons

Fuel filler cap

Oil filler cap

Fuel and oil tank

Rudder control wheel

Elevator wire for diving

Lap strap

Control column

Throttle

Nose-wheel brake

Footrest

Aileron

Turnbuckle

Fuel pipe

Pneumatic tyre

Rubber-tyred nose-wheel

Seat support strut

Pilot's seat

Elevator wire for climbing

Wing-protecting skid

Thin, cambered lower wing

Engine and propeller thrust frame

Starboard main landing gear

SIDE VIEW OF WRIGHT FLYER, 1903

Wing warping wire

Pusher propeller (rear-mounted propeller)

Water-filled radiator

Chain drive

Front diagonal strut

Plain cotton fabric

Rigid leading edge

Elevator drive wheel

Steel hub

Steel propeller shaft

Water pipe

Interplane strut

Rudder

Front-mounted biplane elevator

Bracing wire

Braced rudder strut

Landing skid

Elevator control cable

Pilot's cradle

Magneto

Rudder control cable

Warping connection strut

Four-cylinder 12-HP engine

Propeller-shaft bracing strut

Softwood strut

Tailplane

Elevator control wire

Laminated wooden boom

Rudder bracing wire

Rudder

Elevator operating arm

Elevator

FRONT VIEW OF CURTISS MODEL-D PUSHER, 1911

Rudder control wheel

Fuel and oil tank

Nine-cylinder Salmson radial engine

Elevator operating arm

Anti-lift wire

Aileron operating arm

Starboard aileron

Port aileron

Carved interplane strut

Wing-protecting skid

Wing-protecting skid

Lift wire

Control column

Tubular steel leg

Interplane strut pin-jointed to front spar

Seat beam

Main landing gear lateral brace

Footrest

Axle

Early monoplanes

RUMPLER MONOPLANE, 1908

MONOPLANES HAVE ONE WING on each side of the fuselage. The principal disadvantage of this arrangement in early, wooden-framed aircraft was that single wings were weak and required strong wires to brace them to king-posts above and below the fuselage. However, single wings also had advantages: they experienced less drag than multiple wings, allowing greater speed; they also made aircraft more manoeuvrable because single wings were easier to warp (twist) than double wings, and warping the wings was how pilots controlled the roll of early aircraft. By 1912, the French pilot Louis Blériot had used a monoplane to make the first flight across the English Channel, and the Briton Robert Blackburn and the Frenchman Armand Deperdussin had proved the greater speed of monoplanes. However, a spate of crashes caused by broken wings discouraged monoplane production, except in Germany, where all-metal monoplanes were developed in 1917. The wings of all-metal monoplanes did not need strengthening by struts or bracing wires, but despite this, such planes were not widely adopted until the 1930s.

RUMPLER MONOPLANE, 1908

FRONT VIEW OF BLACKBURN MONOPLANE, 1912

Taut fabric

Carved wooden propeller

King-post

Hub bolted to propeller

Nose-ring

Pilot's viewing aperture

Exhaust valve push-rod

Gnome seven-cylinder rotary engine

Elevator hinge

Elevator

Landing gear rear cross-member

Wheel fairing

Tailskid

Rubber-sprung wheel

Landing gear front strut

Axle

Landing skid

Landing gear rear strut

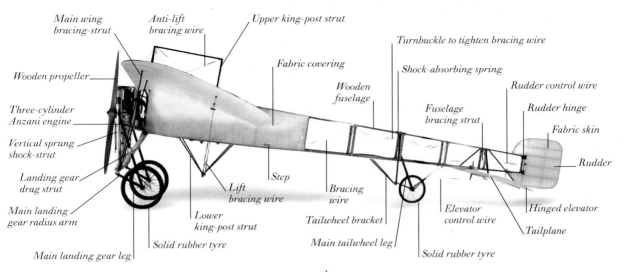

Main wing bracing-strut

Anti-lift bracing wire

Upper king-post strut

Wooden propeller

Three-cylinder Anzani engine

Vertical sprung shock-strut

Landing gear drag strut

Main landing gear radius arm

Main landing gear leg

Solid rubber tyre

Lower king-post strut

Lift bracing wire

Step

Fabric covering

Wooden fuselage

Bracing wire

Tailwheel bracket

Main tailwheel leg

Turnbuckle to tighten bracing wire

Shock-absorbing spring

Fuselage bracing strut

Elevator control wire

Solid rubber tyre

Rudder control wire

Rudder hinge

Fabric skin

Rudder

Hinged elevator

Tailplane

SIDE VIEW OF BLÉRIOT XI, 1909

Anti-lift bracing wire

Leading edge

Rib

Bracing wire anchor bolt

Turnbuckle to tighten bracing wire

Concave undersurface

Lift bracing wire

Warped wing

King-post

Anti-lift bracing wire

Lateral control wheel

Aluminium cowl

Carved wooden propeller

Rudder post

Large fin

Tailplane

Domed topdeck

Rudder

Hub

Engine mount

Elevator

Diagonal bracing

Triangular-section rear fuselage

Lift bracing wire

Landing gear rear strut

Braced landing gear structure

Rubber-sprung wheel

Landing skid

Forward fuselage structure

Elevator-operating bracket

Tailskid

SIDE VIEW OF BLACKBURN MONOPLANE, 1912

Biplanes and triplanes

BIPLANES DOMINATED AIRCRAFT DESIGN until the 1930s, largely because some early monoplanes (see pp. 400-401) were too fragile to withstand the stresses of flight. The struts between biplanes' wings made the wings strong compared with those of early monoplanes, although the greater surface area of biplanes' wings increased drag and reduced speed. Many aircraft designers also developed triplanes, which had a particular advantage over biplanes: more wings meant a shorter wingspan to achieve the same lifting power, and a shorter wingspan gave greater manoeuvrability. Triplanes were most successful as fighters during World War I, the German Fokker triplane being a notable example. However, the greater manoeuvrability of triplanes was no advantage for normal flying and so most manufacturers continued to make biplanes. Many other aircraft designs were attempted. Some were quadruplanes, with four pairs of wings. Some had tandem wings (two pairs of monoplane wings, one behind the other). One of the most bizarre designs was by the Englishman Horatio Phillips: it had 20 sets of narrow wings and looked rather like a Venetian blind.

LAMINATED
PROPELLER

Rudder hinge

RAF Central
Flying School
badge

Rudder

Fin

Navigation
light

K
3215

Elevator

Rudder
cable

Tailplane

Tailwheel

Bracing
strut

Valve rocker

Air cooling
baffle

Magneto

Wing strut

Fuel tank

Throttle

Harness

Pilot's
seat

**SIDE VIEW OF AVRO
TRIPLANE IV, 1910**

Crankcase
breather pipe

Directly
driven
propeller

AVRO

Main front strut
to engine mount

Limit of
fuselage
skin

Skid upper
bracing strut

Ash skid

Rubber cord
suspension

Axle

Turnbuckle

Skid rear strut

Lateral bracing strut

Rubber tyre

Wire wheel

Wheel rim

AVRO TUTOR BIPLANE, 1931

Pin joint

Aileron hinge strut

Navigation light

Slat-arm fairing

Aileron control wire

Lift bracing wire

Instructor's cockpit

Engine cowling

Wooden-domed deck

Padded coaming

Nose-ring

Pupil's cockpit

Propeller hub

RAF roundel

Laminated-wood, fixed-pitch propeller

Metal leading edge

Exhaust pipe

Exhaust collector ring

Main landing gear leg

Aircraft registration code

Inspection cover

Radius rod

Manufacturer's logo

Inflation valve

Fabric-covered steel-tube fuselage

Fabric-covered aluminium and steel wing

Recessed nose of aileron

FRONT VIEW OF AVRO TRIPLANE IV, 1910

Unpainted, varnished fabric

Leading edge

Fuel filler and vent

Fixed-pitch wooden propeller

Anti-lift bracing wire

Top wing

Wing strut

Middle wing

Rib

Bottom wing

Landing skid

Axle

Elevator

Tailplane

Lift bracing wire

Triangular-section fuselage

Triangular-section fuselage

Fuselage bracing wire

Rudder control cable

Lateral bracing strut

Tailplane

Rudder

Metal plate anchorage

Elevator control cable

Longeron

Rudder control cable

Rubber cord suspension

Tailskid pivot

Tailskid

Elevator

World War I aircraft

WHEN WORLD WAR I STARTED in 1914, the main purpose of military aircraft was reconnaissance. The British-built BE 2, of which the BE 2B was a variant, was well-suited to this duty; it was very stable in flight, allowing the occupants to study the terrain, take photographs, and make notes. The BE 2 was also one of the first aircraft to drop bombs. One of the biggest problems for aircraft designers during the war was mounting machine-guns. On aircraft that had front-mounted propellers, the field of fire was restricted by the propeller and other parts of the aircraft. The problem was solved in 1915 by the Dutchman Anthony Fokker, who designed an interrupter gear that prevented a machine-gun from firing when a propeller blade passed in front of the barrel. The German LVG CVI had a forward-firing gun to the right of the engine, as well as a rear-cockpit gun, and a bombing capability. It was one of the most versatile aircraft of the war.

FLYING HELMET

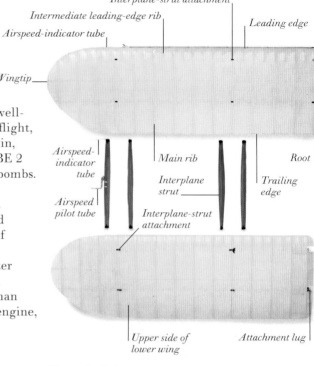

PORT WINGS FROM A BE 2B

Interplane-strut attachment
Intermediate leading-edge rib
Airspeed-indicator tube
Leading edge
Wingtip
Airspeed-indicator tube
Main rib
Root
Interplane strut
Trailing edge
Airspeed pilot tube
Interplane-strut attachment
Upper side of lower wing
Attachment lug

Cabane strut fairing
Observer's windscreen
BE 2B, 1914
Engine air intake (ram scoop)
Top-wing centre section
Cabane strut
Wooden propeller
Lift bracing wire
Pilot's windscreen
Air-cooled V8 engine
Plywood skin
Crankcase
Control column
Padded coaming
Buffed metal cowling
Silencing heat exchanger
Exhaust pipe
Landing gear front strut
Elevator rocking arm
Ash skid
Step
Step
Lateral control wire
Reconnaissance camera bracket
Pneumatic rubber tyre
Bomb rack
Wheel cover
V-strut
Lower-wing attachment
112 lb (51 kg) bomb

SIDE VIEW OF LVG CVI, 1917

Pilot's cockpit

Observer's cockpit

Cold-water pipe

Exhaust pipe

Starboard aileron

7.92-mm Parabellum machine-gun

230-HP Benz six-cylinder water-cooled engine

Fin

Rudder

Rudder control wire

Laminated wooden propeller

Elevator

Steel drive bracket

Air ventilator inlet

Pitot head

Pivoted, sprung tailskid

Aircraft registration code

Interplane strut

Pneumatic rubber tyre

Elevator control wire

Aircraft type

Aileron control cable

Axle

Bracing wire

Tyre inflation aperture

FRONT VIEW OF LVG CVI, 1917

230-HP Benz six-cylinder water-cooled engine

Lozenge-patterned fabric

Forward-firing machine-gun

Exhaust stack

Wooden propeller

Pitot head

Interplane strut

Anti-lift bracing wire

Lift bracing wire

Main fuel tank

Turnbuckle

Gravity-feed fuel tank

Pneumatic rubber tyre

Axle

Tailskid

Landing gear strut

Multiple rubber-cord suspension

Fixed tailplane

Rib

Rudder

Fabric covering

Elevator

Fabric lacing

Tailplane attachment

Rudder post

Steel lug

Elevator hinge

Aircraft registration code

Spar

Shock-absorbing spring

Steel V-strut

Trailing edge

Pivoted tailskid

National marking

Leading edge

Rib

HORIZONTAL TAIL OF A BE 2B

Early passenger aircraft

Green starboard navigation light

Flush-riveted metal-skinned wing

Leading edge

Fuel-jettison valve

Static discharge wick

Split flap in landing position

UNTIL THE 1930s, most passenger aircraft were biplanes, with two pairs of wings and a wooden or metal framework covered with fabric or, sometimes, plywood. Such aircraft were restricted to low speeds and low altitudes because of the drag on their wings. Many had an open cockpit, situated behind or in front of an enclosed – but unpressurized – cabin that carried a maximum of ten people. The passengers usually sat in wicker chairs that were not bolted to the floor, and the journey could be bumpy when flying through turbulence. Warm clothing, and ear plugs to reduce the effects of prolonged noise, were often required. During the 1930s, powerful, streamlined, all-metal monoplanes, such as the Lockheed Electra shown here, became widespread. By 1939, the advent of pressurized cabins allowed fast flights at high altitudes, where there is less turbulence. Flying boats were still necessary on many routes until 1945 because of inadequate runways and the frequency of emergency sea-landings. World War II, however, resulted in enough good runways being built for land-planes to become standard on all major airline routes.

PASSENGER CABIN TRIM

Roof trim panel

Forward bulkhead upper panel

Passenger service-panel aperture

Ash-tray

Starboard wall forward panel

Cockpit door panel

Forward bulkhead lower panel

Starboard wall mid-forward panel

SIDE VIEW OF LOCKHEED ELECTRA, 1934

Cockpit windscreen

Sliding window

Emergency escape hatch

Oil tank

Steel firewall

Passenger window

Air intake

Ventilator exit

Nose

Propeller pitch-change cylinder

Blade counterweight

Spinner mounting disc

Variable-pitch propeller

Pratt & Whitney nine-cylinder radial engine

Exhaust collector ring

Red port navigation light

Landing gear door

Exhaust pipe

Brake pipe

Electrically driven split flap

Passenger door

Static discharge wick

Aileron

Main landing gear

Aluminium wheel

Mudguard

Metal-skinned wing

Cockpit windscreen

High-visibility tip

Variable-pitch propeller

Cylinder-cooling gills

Valve push-rod tube

Pratt & Whitney nine-cylinder radial engine

Inner wing containing fuel tank

Streamlined spinner

Fixed landing light

Red filter signal light

Exhaust pipe

Single-leg main landing gear

Pilot mast

Tank drain tap

Landing gear door

Landing gear fork

Battery compartment

Electrical service compartment

Single-leg main landing gear

Brake pipe

Axle

Pneumatic rubber tyre

Axle

Inspection cover

Tailwheel

Brake pipe

Landing gear fork

Disc brake

Pneumatic rubber tyre

PASSENGER SEAT

Roof trim

Backrest

Seat button

Starboard wall aft panel

Bulkhead starboard trim

Document panel

Lap strap

Armrest

Bulkhead port trim

Starboard wall mid-aft panel

Seat anchor bolthole

Wall anchor

Floor anchor

Interior cabin trim for aft bulkhead between cabin and luggage hold

Seat cushion

PORT ENGINE COWLINGS

Rotating beacon

Starboard rudder

Inspection door

Starboard trimtab

Fixed tailplane

Tailplane

Port fin

120° nose-ring segment

Aluminium flush-riveted skin

Propeller-hub spinner

Port trimtab

Ventilator exit

Port trimtab

NC5171N

Tailplane tip

Aircraft registration code

120° cowling panel

Joining latch

Swivelling rubber-tyred tailwheel

World War II aircraft

WHEN WORLD WAR II began in 1939, air forces had already replaced most of their fabric-skinned biplanes with all-metal, stressed-skin monoplanes. Aircraft played a far greater role in military operations during World War II than ever before. The wide range of aircraft duties, and the introduction of radar tracking and guidance systems, put pressure on designers to improve aircraft performance. The main areas of improvement were speed, range, and engine power. Bombers became larger and more powerful − converting from two to four engines − in order to carry a heavier bomb load; the US B-17 Flying Fortress could carry up to 6.2 tonnes (6.1 tons) of bombs over a distance of about 3,200 km (2,000 miles). Some aircraft increased their range by using drop tanks (fuel tanks that were jettisoned when empty to reduce drag). Fighters needed speed and manoeuvrability: the Hawker Tempest shown here had a maximum speed of 700 kph (435 mph), and was one of the few Allied aircraft capable of catching the German jet-powered V1 "flying bomb". By 1944, Britain had introduced its first turbojet-powered aircraft, the Gloster Meteor fighter, and Germany had introduced the fastest fighter in the world, the turbojet-powered Me 262, which had a maximum speed of 868 kph (540 mph).

PROPELLER

High-visibility yellow tip

Light-alloy propeller spinner

Variable-pitch aluminium-alloy blade

COMPONENTS OF A HAWKER TEMPEST MARK V, c.1943

STARBOARD ENGINE COWLINGS

Radiator-access cowling

Lower side-cowling

Upper side-cowling

Cowling fastener

2,400-HP Napier Sabre 24-cylinder engine

Cartridge starter

Propeller governor

Radiator header tank

Propeller drive shaft

Distributor

Ejector exhaust

Magneto

Starter motor

Engine top cowling

Cowling fastener

Upper side-cowling

Lower side-cowling

Radiator-access cowling

PORT ENGINE COWLINGS

SECTIONED B-17G FLYING FORTRESS BOMBER, c.1943

Astronavigation dome

First pilot's seat

Oxygen bottle

Upper gun turret

1,000 lb (454 kg) bomb

Radio operator's seat

Ammunition belt

Ammunition box

Waist gun

Dorsal fin

Ammunition feed

Fin

VHF aerial

Rudder

"Cheyenne-type" tail-gun turret

Hand-held gun

Plastic nose

Bomb aimer's viewing panel

Chin gun turret

HF radio aerial

Bomb door

Direction-finding-aerial fairing

Navigator's seat

Sperry ball gun turret

Ammunition feed

Entrance door

Oxygen bottle

Retracted tailwheel

Tail gunner's compartment

Ammunition feed

PORT WING UNDERSIDE

Flap

Landing gear door

Wing front fillet panel

Wing fillet panel

Cockpit starboard access panel

Wing rear fillet panel

Starboard tailplane

Elevator hinge

Starboard elevator

Leading edge

Elevator control rod

Canopy rail

Seat pan

Harness strap

FUSELAGE

Canopy rail

VHF radio whip aerial

Fin

Tail fairing

Trimtab operating rod

Rudder

Flat, bulletproof windscreen

Armoured seat back

RAF C1-type roundel

Dorsal fin

Tailplane root

Gyroscopic gunsight

Plastic cockpit canopy

Cockpit front belly panel

Cockpit centre belly panel

Tail band

Tailplane front attachment bracket

Tailplane rear attachment bracket

Rear spar trunnion

Cockpit rear belly panel

Port elevator trimtab

Wing fillet panel

Trailing edge

Wing front fillet panel

Wing rear fillet panel

Camouflage

Port tailplane

TAIL

Outboard ammunition-feed blister

Cockpit port access panel

Trailing edge

Wing upper surface

HAWKER TEMPEST MARK V FIGHTER, c.1943

Aileron

Hispano Mark V 20-mm cannon

Headrest

Armour-plated seat back

Squadron code

Rudder

Dorsal fin

Exhaust pipe

Gyroscopic gunsight

RAF C1-type roundel

RAF B-type roundel

Propeller spinner

Engine air intake

Radiator

Radiator outlet

Pitot head

Instant-identification "invasion" stripes

Retracted tailwheel

Rudder trimtab

NV7□B

SA

Yellow-painted leading edge

Wingtip

PORT WING

Modern piston aero-engines

MID WEST TWO-STROKE,
THREE-CYLNDER ENGINE

PISTON ENGINES today are used mainly to power the vast numbers of light aircraft and microlights, as well as crop-sprayers and crop-dusters, small helicopters, and fire-bombers (which dump water on large fires). Virtually all heavier aircraft are now powered by jet engines. Modern piston aero-engines work on the same basic principles as the engine used by the Wright brothers in the first powered flight in 1903. However, today's engines are more sophisticated than earlier engines. For example, modern aero-engines may use a two-stroke or a four-stroke combustion cycle; they may have from one to nine air- or water-cooled cylinders, which may be arranged horizontally, in-line, in V formation, or radially; and they may drive the aircraft's propeller either directly or through a reduction gearbox. One of the more unconventional types of modern aero-engine is the rotary engine shown here, which has a trilobate (three-sided) rotor spinning in a chamber shaped like a fat figure-of-eight.

MID WEST 75-HP TWO-STROKE, THREE-CYLINDER ENGINE

- Spark plug
- Coolant outlet
- Cylinder head
- Piston
- Cylinder barrel
- Exhaust manifold
- Exhaust port
- Cylinder liner
- Upper crankcase
- Coolant pump
- Pump drive belt
- Reduction gearbox
- Driven gear
- Gearbox drive splines
- Connecting rod (con-rod)
- Small end
- Propeller drive flange
- Big end
- Counterweight
- Generator rotor
- Torsional vibration damper
- Crankshaft
- Sprag clutch
- Gearbox mounting plate
- Lower crankcase
- Stator
- Ignition trigger housing
- Engine mounting plate

ROTOR AND HOUSINGS OF A MID WEST SINGLE-ROTOR ENGINE

- Propeller bolt hole
- Propeller drive flange
- Dowel
- Stud
- Coolant jacket
- Inlet tract
- Roller
- Eccentric-shaft bearing
- Stud hole
- Stud hole
- Propeller shaft rear bearing
- Coolant jacket
- Dowel
- Dowel hole
- Rotor chamber
- Exhaust tract

GEARBOX CASE   FRONT HOUSING (FRONT END-PLATE)   TROCHOID HOUSING

MID WEST 90-HP TWIN-ROTOR ENGINE

Propeller-bolt collar

Propeller drive flange

Reduction gearbox

Lubricating oil feed

Engine front mounting plate

Blanking plate over air inlet

Carburettor

Rotor-cooling air duct

Pipe clamp joint

Rotor-cooling air pump

Upper rubber anti-vibration engine mount

Upper rotor-cooling air duct

Generator housing

Electric cable

Front bearing mount

Oil pump drive shaft cover

Torsional vibration damper

Fuel pipe inlet connection

Fuel drip tray

Blanking plate over exhaust port

Exhaust pipe flange

Lower rubber anti-vibration engine mount

Starter motor

Flywheel

Engine rear mounting plate

OUTPUT SHAFT OF A MID WEST ROTARY ENGINE

Balance weight

Drive gear

Front bearing

Drive gear spline

Starterring teeth

Oil seal spacer ring

Flywheel retaining thread

Eccentric shaft

Rotor bearing

Rear bearing

Flywheel

Corner bolt

Rotor tip seal

Tip seal groove

Rotor gear teeth

Rotor bearing

Cooling fins

Rotor tip spring

Balancing drilling

Rotor side seal

Side seal spring

Side seal groove

Fixed gear (stationary gear)

Engine mounting

Stud hole

Dowel hole

Coolant jacket

Outlet manifold

Pump drive shaft

Fixing stud

Bolt hole

Inlet manifold

Water pump cover and oil pump housing

Thermostat

Oil pump

ROTOR AND SEALS

REAR HOUSING (REAR END-PLATE)

WATER PUMP HOUSING

Modern jetliners 1

BAE-146 JETLINER

MODERN JETLINERS HAVE ENABLED ordinary people to travel to places where once only the wealthy could afford to go. Compared with the first jetliners (which were introduced in the 1940s), modern ones are much quieter, burn fuel more efficiently, and produce less air pollution. These advances are largely due to the replacement of turbojet engines with turbofan engines (see pp. 418-419). The greater power of turbofan engines at low speeds enables modern jetliners to carry more fuel and passengers than turbojet aircraft; a model Boeing 747-400 (popularly known as a "jumbo jet") can fly 400 people for 13,700 km (8,500 miles) without needing to refuel. Jetliners fly at high altitudes, typically cruising at 8,000-11,000 m (26,000-36,000 ft), where they can use fuel efficiently and usually avoid bad weather. The pilot always controls the aircraft during take-off and landing, but at other times the aircraft is usually controlled by an autopilot. Autopilots are complex on-board mechanisms that detect deviations from an aircraft's route and make appropriate adjustments to the flight controls. Flight decks are also equipped with radars that warn pilots of approaching hazards, such as mountain ranges, bad weather, and other aircraft.

Shoulder cowling

Engine pylon

Hinged cowling panel

Nose cowling

Fan duct nozzle

Core-engine jet pipe

Fire-extinguisher discharge indicator

Oil-filler door

Push-in door for hand-held fire-extinguisher

Drain mast

TURBOFAN ENGINE COWLING

STRUCTURAL COMPONENTS OF A BAE-146 JETLINER

Oil-filler door for integrated-drive generator

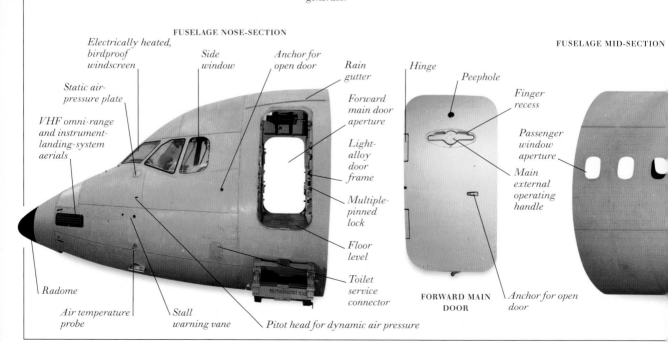

FUSELAGE NOSE-SECTION

FUSELAGE MID-SECTION

Electrically heated, birdproof windscreen

Side window

Anchor for open door

Rain gutter

Hinge

Peephole

Finger recess

Static air-pressure plate

Forward main door aperture

Passenger window aperture

VHF omni-range and instrument-landing-system aerials

Light-alloy door frame

Main external operating handle

Multiple-pinned lock

Floor level

Radome

Toilet service connector

Air temperature probe

Stall warning vane

Pitot head for dynamic air pressure

FORWARD MAIN DOOR

Anchor for open door

Overwing
fuel-filler cap

Systems
connector

Overwing fuel-
filler cap

Fuel contents
indicator

STARBOARD
WING
ASSEMBLY

Centre-line (spine)
of aircraft

Single-piece skin
over inboard wing

Rubber sealing strip

Rubber sealing strip

Trailing edge

Trailing edge
of fixed wing

Spoiler anchorage

Hydraulic actuator
attachment

Pivot point

Flap-track fairing

Screw
joint

Aft section

Hinge

INBOARD LIFT
SPOILERS

Stainless-steel
flap seal

MOVABLE FLAP TRACK AND FAIRING

Track roller

Upper carriage
attached to flap

FOWLER FLAP

Anchor
bearing

Track

Tab-hinge line

Leading edge

Gearbox
mount

Bellcrank
lever

Root

Gearbox unit

Carriage
drive nut

Flap drive
screw

Lower carriage

Skin lap-
joint

Leading
edge

Main spar
bridge

Root rib

Wing-root mount
containing central
fuel tank

Inboard
tab

Attachment structure for
wing-to-fuselage fairing

Cabin air-pressure
discharge valve

Floor
level

Fairing of
landing gear bay

Fairing of landing
gear pivot

Yellow anti-
corrosion paint

413

Modern jetliners 2

Landing and taxiing light

Heated de-icing
leading edge

Roll-spoiler hinge

Roll-spoiler hydraulic actuator attachment

STARBOARD WING

Fixed trailing edge

Aileron hinge

Starboard
navigation
light

Hinge

Hydraulic actuator attachment

Spoiler arm

Aerodynamic
balance

Horn
balance

Recessed hinge

Hinge
bracket

INTERMEDIATE
LIFT SPOILER

Flap
seal

OUTBOARD ROLL SPOILER

AILERON

Trimtab

Servo-tab

MAIN FOWLER FLAP

Leading edge

Flap tip

Static discharge wick attachment

Outboard tab

Tab-hinge line

FUSELAGE SPINE FAIRING

Landing gear
door

Hydraulic brake pipe

Main pivot

Finger
recess

Peephole

Hot-air de-icing duct

Electrical harness

Oleo
lock-jack

Skin lap-joint

Passenger
window
aperture

Light-
alloy beam

Direction
bar

Main
external
operating
handle

Hinge

Brake
pipe

Shock-strut bearing

Pneumatic
tyre

Outer
wheel
axle

Side brace
and retraction
jack trunnions

Hinge

Wheel hub

Pivoted
trailing-
link arm

Hydraulic
brake pipe

Lower pivot

Anchor for open door

Cabin air-
discharge aperture

STARBOARD TWIN-WHEEL MAIN LANDING GEAR

AFT MAIN DOOR

BAE-146 MODERN JETLINER

Tailplane

Logo

Rudder

Fin

Starboard aft
service door

Flap-track
fairing

Core-engine
jet pipe

Main landing
gear fairing

Landing light

Starboard inboard
engine

VHF
aerial

Water-drain
mast

VHF radio aerial

Forward door for
crew and service

Radome

**STARBOARD
ELEVATOR**

Horn
balance

Tab
hinge

Aerodynamic
balance

Recessed
hinge

Root

Trimtab

Servo-tab

**TAILPLANE
FAIRINGS**

Intermediate
fairing (fin tip)

Aft fairing

Fin trailing edge

Forward
fairing

Side
fairing

Elevator
chassis
box

Tailplane attachment
bracket

Heated de-icing
leading edge

FIN

Forward
spar

Fairing panel

Fin-attachment
skin

Aft spar

Access to yaw dampers
and rudder trim jack

Centre-line
(spine)

TAILPLANE

Heated de-icing
leading edge

Elevator
hinge

Rain gutter

Fin leading-edge
attachment

Auxiliary power
unit (APU)
inlet

Operating arm

Hinge

Skin lap-
joint

Trailing
edge

STARBOARD AIR-BRAKE

Tailplane
tip

Auxiliary power unit
(APU) vent

Oil-
cooler
duct

Aft main door aperture

Heated drain mast

FUSELAGE TAIL-SECTION

Supersonic jetliners

COMPUTER-DESIGNED SST

SUPERSONIC AIRCRAFT FLY FASTER than the speed of sound (Mach 1). There are many supersonic military aircraft, but only two supersonic passenger-carrying aircraft (also called SSTs, or supersonic transports) have been produced: the Russian Tu-144, and Concorde, produced jointly by Britain and France. The Tu-144 was withdrawn in 1978, after only seven months in service. The concorde remained in service from 1976 until 2003, with a break for modifications from July 2000 until October 2001. Its features included a droop nose, which lowered during take-off and landing to aid visibility from the cockpit; the pumping of fuel between forward and aft trim tanks helped stabilize the aircraft. The concorde had a narrow fuselage and shortspan wings to reduce drag during supersonic flight. Its noisy turbojet engines with afterburners enabled it to carry 100 passengers at a cruising speed of Mach 2 at 15,000-18,000 m (50,000-60,000 ft). Once an aircraft is flying faster than Mach 1, it produces a continuous air-pressure wave, which is heard as a "sonic boom".

Strake
Fin
Standby pitot head
Starboard outboard engine air-intake
Inboard elevon-jack fairing
Nose-gear leg

FRONT VIEW OF CONCORDE

Toilets
Electrothermal de-icing panel
Starboard forward trim tank
Overhead hand-baggage bin
Passenger accommodation
Seat attachment rail

OVERHEAD VIEW OF THE CONCORDE

Variable nozzle
Leading edge
Underfloor air-conditioning duct
Life-raft
Wardrobe
VHF aerial
Forward galley
Additional crew's seat
Aluminium-alloy layers and insulation
Third pilot's seat
Erosion-resistant radome
Cockpit windscreen
Retractable visor
"A" frame
Lateral bracing strut
Telescopic strut
Port forward trim tank
Nose-gear leg
Steering actuator
Machined skin panel
Weather radar
Standby flight-control hydraulic jack
Plug-type passenger door
Nose-gear door
Multi-ply high-pressure tyre
Visor jack
Captain's seat
Droop-nose hinge
Cockpit air-conditioning duct
Upper rudder
Fin
Dorsal fin
Emergency exit
Pivoted retractable frame
Tail cone
Aft door
G-BOAG
Elevon (combined elevator and aileron)
Hot-section steel and titanium skin
Engine cowling
Landing gear door
Bogie main landing gear

SECTIONED VIEW OF THE CONCORDE

Fire-suppression bottle access panel

Pressurized keel box

Fuel tank

Main air duct

Emergency exit

Cold-air unit

Static discharge wick

Elevon (combined elevator and aileron)

Cabin air duct

Inspection panel

Flight-control mixing unit

HF radio aerials fairing

Emergency oxygen cylinders

Upper rudder

Auxiliary power unit

Tail cone

Lower-rudder power control unit

Servo control-unit fairing

Fuel-jettison pipe

Air-conditioning duct

Rear bulkhead

Aft galley unit

Rear emergency door

Tank inspection access

Inboard elevon (combined elevator and aileron)

Landing gear hydraulics

Port main landing-gear leg well

Variable nozzle

Nozzle actuator

Heat-exchanger exhaust

Elevon power control unit

Honeycomb elevon structure

Fuel tank

Heat exchanger

Rolls-Royce Olympus Mark 610 turbojet

Engine front support link

Spar

Rib

Leading edge

Middle passenger door

Fuel pipe

VHF aerial

Port engine fuel pumps

Four-wheel bogie

Port main landing gear leg

Forward ramp drive

Main landing gear cross-beam

Upper lip of port engine air intakes

Retraction jack

SIDE VIEW OF THE CONCORDE

VHF aerial

Emergency exit

Passenger window

Flight deck windscreen

Retracted visor

Nose in drooped position

Standby pitot head

Nose-gear leg

Aerodynamic strake

Radome

Nose-leg telescopic strut

Starboard forward door

Steerable twin-wheel nose-gear

Jet engines

JET ENGINES ARE USED BY MOST MILITARY and heavy aircraft, and by many helicopters. The simplest type of jet engine, or gas turbine, is the turbojet. It works by continuously burning a mixture of fuel and air in a combustion chamber to produce a jet of hot exhaust gas that is expelled through a nozzle to produce thrust. The hot gas also spins turbine blades, which, in turn, spin the blades of an air compressor; the compressor forces air into the combustion chamber. Many of the fastest aircraft use turbojets, with additional booster units called afterburners, but their use is restricted by their high noise emission. Most jetliners use turbofan jet engines, which are quieter. An enormous fan, driven by a low-pressure turbine, feeds some air into the compressor but feeds most of it through bypass ducts to join the exhaust jetstream in the tail cone. The bypass stream produces most of the thrust. Many smaller, propeller-driven aircraft use turboprop jet engines, in which the engine powers a propeller.

NPT 301 MODERN TURBOJET

Fuel sprayer
Turbine rotor
Reverse-flow combustion chamber
Radial diffuser
Centrifugal compressor
Exhaust diffuser
Inducer
Air intake
Tail cone
Jet pipe
Exhaust nozzle
Nose cone
Igniter
Alternator
Nozzle guide vane
Air impingement starter
Combustion chamber casing

Plenum ring for hot anti-icing air
Flow splitter
Gearbox bevel drive
Integral oil tank
High-pressure compressor
Combustion chamber
Fuel manifold
High-pressure turbine
Centrifugal compressor
Fuel nozzle
Temperature and pressure sensor
Low-pressure fan
Inlet cone (rotating spinner)
Pressure line
Fan case with special structure to contain broken fan
Electronic engine control and airframe interface connector
Fan duct
Electronic engine control (EEC) unit
Compressor front bearing
Engine front mount
Electrical wiring harness
Fuel and oil heat exchanger
Oil filter
Compressor air-bleed connection

PRATT & WHITNEY CANADA PW120 SERIES MODERN TURBOPROP

Alternator mount pad
Propeller speed probe
Reduction gearbox
Propeller hub flange
Propeller brake pad
Engine front mount
Torquemeter mount
Gearbox oil scavenge line
Autofeather unit
Electronic engine control (EEC) unit
Air intake
Oil filter
Oil tank
Oil-pressure regulating valve
Accessory drive pad
Throttle lever
Fuel-cooled oil cooler
Fuel filter
Fuel heater
Fuel manifold
Intercompressor bleed valve
Intercompressor diffuser pipe
High-pressure bleed venturi connector
Turbine support case
Jet pipe connection
Oil pipe
Thermocouple bus-bar
Fuel nozzle
Igniter plug
Engine rear mount

HOW JET ENGINES WORK

TURBOFAN

Fan sucks air in
Fan blade
Rotating blades compress air
Fuel inlet
Inner drive shaft
Outer drive shaft
Exhaust gases provide extra thrust
Bypass air provides main thrust
High-pressure turbine spins outer drive shaft to drive compressor
Fuel/air mixture ignites

TURBOPROP

Compressor sucks air in
Propeller spins to provide main thrust
Reduction gearbox
Fuel inlet
Rotating blades compress air
Combustion chamber
Three-stage turbine driven by hot gas
Exhaust gases add a little thrust
Turbine shaft drives propeller and compressor

TURBOJET

Compressor sucks air in
Rotating blades compress air
Fuel inlet
Fuel/air mixture ignites
Combustion chamber
Turbine blades driven by hot gas
Exhaust gases provide all the thrust
Turbine drives compressor via drive shaft

Low-pressure turbine
Heat shield
Blade tip sealing shroud
Exhaust cone
Core jet pipe (exhaust fairing)
Scavenge oil line
Inter-module bolted joint
Fuel shut-off valve cable

SECTIONED PRATT & WHITNEY CANADA PW305 MODERN TURBOFAN

Modern military aircraft

MODERN MILITARY AIRCRAFT ARE AMONG THE MOST SOPHISTICATED and expensive products of the 21st century. Fighters need computer-operated controls for manoeuvrability, powerful engines, and effective air-to-air weapons. Most modern fighters also have guided missiles, radar, and passive, infra-red sensors. These developments enable today's fighters to engage in combat with adversaries that are outside visual range. Bombers carry a large weapon load and enough fuel for long-range flights. A few military aircraft, such as the Tornado and the F-14 Tomcat, have variable-sweep ("swing") wings. During take-off and landing their wings are fully extended, but for high-speed flight and low-level attacks the wings are pivoted fully back. A recent development is the "stealth" bomber, which is designed to absorb or deflect enemy radar in order to remain undetected. Earlier bombers, such as the Tornado, use terrain-following radars to fly so close to the ground that they avoid enemy radar detection.

FRONT VIEW OF A PANAVIA TORNADO

Instrument landing system aerial

Birdproof windscreen

Air data probe

Port variable-incidence air intake

Wing-root glove fairing

Starboard inboard stores pylon

Taileron

Starboard main landing gear door

Main landing gear leg

Laser ranger and marked-target seeker

Starboard nose-gear door

Steerable twin-wheel nose-gear

Radome containing ground-mapping, attack, and terrain-following radars

Taxiing light

Wing extended for take-off and landing

Wing pivoted back for high-speed flight

SWING-WING F-14 TOMCAT FIGHTER

SIDE VIEW OF A PANAVIA TORNADO GR1A (RECONNAISSANCE VERSION), 1986

Pilot's cockpit

Navigator's instrument console

Navigator's cockpit

Single canopy over both cockpits

Engine air intake

Navigation light

Flat, birdproof windscreen

High-velocity air duct to disperse rain

Upper "request identification" aerial

Air data probe

Radome containing ground-mapping, attack, and terrain-following radars

UHF aerial

Angle-of-attack probe

Tacan (tactical air navigation) aerial

Emergency canopy release handle

Nose-gear door

Steerable nose-gear leg

Pitot head

Twin nose-wheel

Window covering infra-red reconnaissance camera

Hinged auxiliary air intake

Cold air intake (ram scoop)

Heat exchanger exhaust duct

NORTHROP B-2 ("STEALTH" BOMBER), 1989

Starboard split rudder

Inboard elevons (combined elevators and ailerons)

Refractory (heat-resistant) skin behind exhaust outlet

Variable-incidence gust-alleviator

Wing leading edge coated with radar-absorbent material

Port wingtip rudder

Outboard elevon (combined elevator and aileron)

Leading-edge aerial

Engine aft bulkhead

Wing containing fuel tank

Weapon-bay rear bulkhead

Flight refuelling receptacle

Auxiliary air intake

Weapon-bay front bulkhead

Air intake coated with radar-absorbent material

Space for extra crew member

Ejector-seat roof hatches

Port outboard stores pylon

Port navigation light

Two-seater cockpit

Fin-tip aerial fairing

Radar warning receiver looking forwards

Instrument landing system aerial

Fin

Radar warning receiver looking rearwards

Heat exchanger air intake (ram scoop)

Extended port air-brake

Rudder

Wing-root glove fairing

Heat exchanger hot-air exhaust

Wing-root pneumatic seal

Air-brake jack

Fin-root aerial fairing

Spine end fairing

Thrust-reverser (closed)

Port fully-variable afterburner nozzle

Port flap

Port taileron (combined tailplane and aileron)

Port inboard stores pylon

Wingtip aerial fairing

Hydraulic hand-pump

Port navigation light

Lower "request identification" aerial

Powered leading-edge slat

Main-gear door

Port main landing gear

Port outboard stores pylon

Helicopters

HELICOPTERS USE ROTATING BLADES for lift, propulsion, and steering. The first machine to achieve sustained, controlled flight using rotating blades was the autogiro built in the 1920s by the Spaniard Juan de la Cierva. His machine had unpowered blades above the fuselage that relied on the flow of air to rotate them and provide lift as the autogiro was driven forwards by a conventional propeller. Then, in 1939, the Russian-born American Igor Sikorsky produced his VS-300, the forerunner of modern helicopters. Its engine-driven blades provided lift, propulsion, and steering. It could take off vertically, hover, and fly in any direction, and had a tail rotor to prevent the helicopter body from spinning. The introduction of gas turbine jet engines to helicopters in 1955 produced quieter, safer, and more powerful machines. Because of their versatility in flight, helicopters are today used for many purposes, including crop-spraying, traffic surveillance, and transporting crews to deep-sea oil rigs, as well as acting as gunships, air ambulances, and air taxis.

BELL 47G-3B1

BELL 47G-3B1

Droop stop
Blade counterweight
Main rotor hub
Blade-root attachment
Stabilizer-bar weight
Direct-vision panel
Main rotor mast
Tail-rotor drive shaft
Fuel vent pipe
Frameless plastic canopy
Fuel tank
Protective gaiter
Fuel tank cradle
Exhaust pipe
Radio
Air intake pipe
Instrument panel
Electric fuel pump
Cyclic-pitch lever
Battery
Battery overspill
Electrical inverter
Pitot head
Breather pipe
Oil tank
Anti-collision beacon
Carburettor hot-air intake pipe
Landing light
Air filter
Landing skid
VHF omni-range aerial
Navigation light
Ground handling wheel
Valve-rocker cover
Ventilator
Electric power socket
Lycoming six-cylinder engine
Collective-pitch lever
Riveted light-alloy forward fuselage section

SCHWEIZER 300C

Blade-root attachment

Three-blade main rotor

Outside air-temperature gauge

Ventilator

Flight-control rod

Anti-collision beacon

Anti-torque tail rotor

Magnetic compass

Main rotor mast

Automatic direction-finding aerial

Plastic canopy

Navigation aerial

Cyclic-pitch lever

Fuel tank

G-SAND

Tail boom

Vertical tail

Tail rotor guard

Engine air intake

Tubular bracing strut

Pitot head

Tail-rotor drive shaft

Anti-collision beacon

Tail-boom support strut

Exhaust silencer

Landing skid

Landing gear damper

Transponder aerial

Transmission drive-pulley cover

Landing light

Lycoming four-cylinder engine

High-visibility tip

Anti-torque tail rotor

Twin-blade main rotor

Tail rotor hub

Anti-collision beacon

Triangular-section, unskinned rear fuselage

Elevator upper control wire

Synchronized elevator

Tail rotor gearbox

G-BGID

Tubular tail rotor guard

Elevator lower control wire

Tail-rotor pitch control wire

Small fixed fin

Main rotor blade

Droop stop

Main rotor hub

Allison 250-C20J turboshaft engine

Anti-collision beacon

Blade-root attachment

Jet pipe

VHF aerial

Horizontal stabilizer

Upper fin

Main rotor mast

Anti-torque tail rotor

Air temperature probe

G-HUMT

Forward-hinged door

Lower fin

Transponder aerial

Flush-riveted aluminium fuselage

Tail boom

Boarding step

Baggage compartment door

Landing skid

Rear cross-tube

BELL 206 JETRANGER

Light aircraft

LIGHT AIRCRAFT, SUCH AS THE ARV SUPER 2 shown here, are small, lightweight, and of simple construction. More than a million have been built since World War I, mainly for recreational use by private owners. Virtually all light aircraft have piston engines, most of which are air-cooled, although some are liquid-cooled. Open cockpits, almost universal in the 1920s, have today been replaced by enclosed cabins. The cabins of high-wing aircraft have one or two doors, whereas those of low-wing aircraft usually have a sliding or hinged canopy. Most modern light aircraft are made of aluminium alloy, although some are made of wood or of fibre-reinforced materials. Light aircraft today also usually have navigational instruments, an electrical system, cabin heating, wheel brakes, and a two-way radio.

Port wingtip

Aileron mass balance

Aileron torque tube

Port aileron

PORT MAIN LANDING GEAR

Inner tube

Tyre

Hub

Brake disc

Stub axle

Landing gear leg

Brake mount

Brake pipe

Hydraulic brake calliper

TAILPLANE AND RUDDER

Elevator

Rudder tip fairing

Rudder mass balance

Fin tip fairing

Rudder

Fin

Dorsal fin

Rear fuselage top skin

Rear attachment-bracket for wing

Elevator trimtab

Drive pillar

Attachment plate

REAR FUSELAGE

Longeron

Frame

Battery box

Diaphragm

Side skin

Coolant outlet

Aluminium radiator

Air scoop

Coolant inlet

Rear fuselage bottom skin

"Skin-grip" pin

Tailplane

Elevator push-rod

Elevator push-rod

Rocking elevator arm

CONTROL RODS AND CABLES

Flap torque tube

Aileron rod

Aileron torque tube

Rudder cable

Flap drive-rod

Flap drive-rod

STARBOARD MAIN LANDING GEAR

Brake calliper

Brake pipe

Landing gear leg

Brake disc

Stub axle

Inner tube

Tyre

Hub

SIDE VIEW OF ARV SUPER 2

Spinner

Canopy

Wing

Communications aerial

Navigational aerial

Fin

Dorsal fin

Rudder

Engine cowling

Elevator

Tailplane

Tailskid

Nose-gear

Radiator

Wing strut

Step

Main landing gear

Aircraft registration code

Venturi for instruments

G-BNHB

Tyre

PORT WING

Port top-wing fairing

Port underwing fairing

Headrest

Wing strut

Port flap

Pitot head

Airspeed-indicator tube

SEAT ASSEMBLY

Seat cushion

Backrest

Lap strap

Quick-release mechanism

Lap-strap length adjuster

Bolted anchor

CANOPY

Direct-vision panel

Pressurized strut

Hinge

Leading-edge fairing

Moulded plastic

Canopy latch

Outside air-temperature gauge

COCKPIT

Fibreglass canopy frame

Fuel tank top skin

Rudder pedal

Cockpit coaming

Forward attachment bracket for wing

Control-column aperture

Semi-bulkhead

Nose-leg upper mount

Firewall

Fibreglass fuel tank

Bulkhead

Lap-strap attachment bracket

"Skin-grip" pin

THREE-CYLINDER ENGINE

Port engine cowling

Air intake box

Water outlet

Carburettor

Backplate

Engine mount

Cylinder head

Exhaust manifold

Gearbox

Fuel hose

Propeller drive flange

PROPELLER

Spinner

Flanged plate

Starboard engine cowling

CONTROL COLUMN AND FLAP LEVER

Elevator arm

Torque tube assembly

Control column

Flap lever

Elevator push-rod

Flap lever detent box

Release button

Throttle lever

Brake lever

Elevator trimtab lever

Carburettor hot air lever

Bearing assembly

Pilot's handgrip

INSTRUMENT PANEL

Flight instruments

Engine instruments

Glove box

Radio plugs

NOSE-GEAR

Steering stop

Nose-leg down tube

Rubber bungee (elasticated cord) shock absorber

Damper unit

Pivoted fork

Hoop

Axle bolt

Nose-wheel

STARBOARD WING

Wing strut

Starboard underwing fairing

Starboard top-wing fairing

Gliders, hang-gliders, and microlights

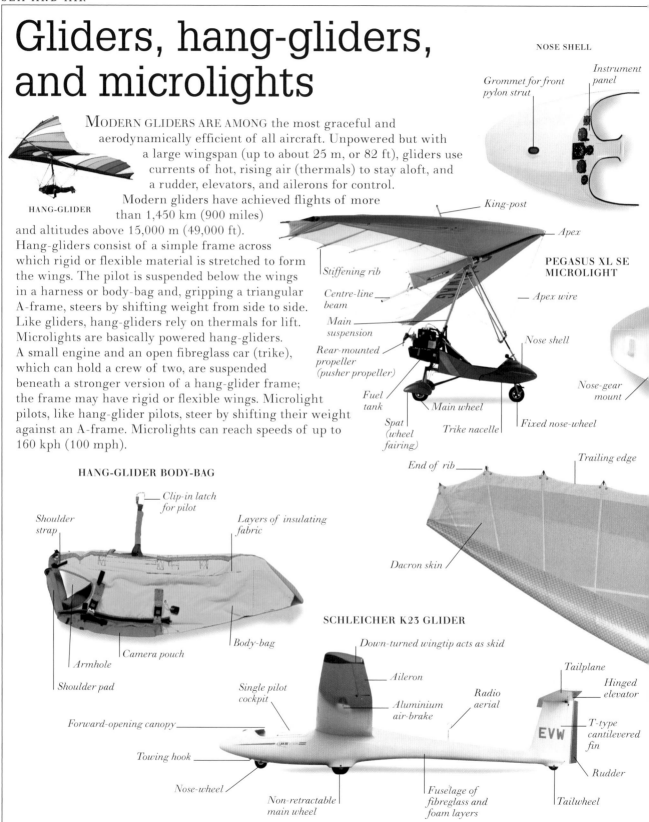

MODERN GLIDERS ARE AMONG the most graceful and aerodynamically efficient of all aircraft. Unpowered but with a large wingspan (up to about 25 m, or 82 ft), gliders use currents of hot, rising air (thermals) to stay aloft, and a rudder, elevators, and ailerons for control. Modern gliders have achieved flights of more than 1,450 km (900 miles) and altitudes above 15,000 m (49,000 ft). Hang-gliders consist of a simple frame across which rigid or flexible material is stretched to form the wings. The pilot is suspended below the wings in a harness or body-bag and, gripping a triangular A-frame, steers by shifting weight from side to side. Like gliders, hang-gliders rely on thermals for lift. Microlights are basically powered hang-gliders. A small engine and an open fibreglass car (trike), which can hold a crew of two, are suspended beneath a stronger version of a hang-glider frame; the frame may have rigid or flexible wings. Microlight pilots, like hang-glider pilots, steer by shifting their weight against an A-frame. Microlights can reach speeds of up to 160 kph (100 mph).

HANG-GLIDER

NOSE SHELL

Grommet for front pylon strut

Instrument panel

King-post

Apex

Stiffening rib

Centre-line beam

Main suspension

Rear-mounted propeller (pusher propeller)

Fuel tank

Spat (wheel fairing)

Main wheel

Trike nacelle

Fixed nose-wheel

PEGASUS XL SE MICROLIGHT

Apex wire

Nose shell

Nose-gear mount

End of rib

Trailing edge

Dacron skin

HANG-GLIDER BODY-BAG

Clip-in latch for pilot

Shoulder strap

Layers of insulating fabric

Camera pouch

Armhole

Shoulder pad

Body-bag

SCHLEICHER K23 GLIDER

Down-turned wingtip acts as skid

Single pilot cockpit

Aileron

Aluminium air-brake

Radio aerial

Tailplane

Hinged elevator

Forward-opening canopy

T-type cantilevered fin

Towing hook

EVW

Rudder

Nose-wheel

Non-retractable main wheel

Fuselage of fibreglass and foam layers

Tailwheel

SOLAR WINGS PEGASUS QUASAR MICROLIGHT

Foot throttle

Pilot's steering bar

Passenger's steering bar and footrest

Lap strap

Fuel tank filler nozzle

Spat (wheel fairing)

Engine mount

Pylon fairing

Aircraft name

Air outlet

Rear engine cowling

Pylon strut

Footbrake

Pilot's seat

Hand throttle

Pylon-strut strap

Passenger's seat

Main wing-strut

TRIKE UNIT

Trailing edge

Leading edge

TWIN-CYLINDER ENGINE

Propeller drive gearbox

Twin carburettors

Air filter

Dual ignition plug

Air cooling fan

Exhaust connection

Engine rear mount

Metal hub

Sealed lid

Waterproof stowage box

TRIKE NACELLE

EXHAUST PIPE

After silencer

Main exhaust silencer

PROPELLER

WINGFRAME

Centre-line beam

Eyelet tensioning trailing edge to rib

Bracing cable

Rib

Single spar

King-post

Leading edge

Semi-rigid fibreglass skin

Lift bracing wire

THE VISUAL ARTS

Drawing

DRAWINGS CAN BE FINISHED WORKS OF ART, or preparatory studies for paintings and other visual arts. They can be made using a wide variety of drawing instruments such as pencils, graphite sticks, chalks, charcoal, pens and inks, and silver wires. The most common drawing instrument is the graphite pencil. A graphite pencil consists of a thin rod of graphite mixed with clay, encased in wood. Charcoal is one of the oldest drawing instruments. It is produced by firing twigs of willow, vine, or other woods at high temperatures in airtight containers. Erasers can be used to rub out marks made by drawing materials such as graphite pencils or charcoal, or to achieve a particular effect – such as smudging. Fixative is often applied – using a mouth diffuser or aerosol spray fixative – to prevent smudging once a drawing is finished. Silver lines can be produced by drawing silver wire across specially prepared paper – a technique known as silverpoint. The lines are permanent and cannot be erased. In time the silver lines oxidize and turn brown.

FIXATIVE AND MOUTH DIFFUSER

Hinge

Liquid fixative consisting of dissolved resin

Fixative is sucked into tube and sprayed on to drawing

CHALK, CRAYON, AND CHARCOAL

Calcite (calcium carbonate) mixed with pigment

BLUE CHALK

Iron oxide mixed with chalk

SANGUINE CRAYON

Carbonized wood

WILLOW CHARCOAL

ERASERS

Hard texture

Medium-soft, light line

PLASTIC ERASER

Soft texture

Very soft, dark line

PUTTY ERASER

DRAWING INSTRUMENTS

2B GRAPHITE PENCIL

8B GRAPHITE PENCIL

SILVER WIRE IN A METAL HOLDER

DRAWING MATERIALS

Graphite stick

Coloured pencil

Bulldog clip

Dip pen

DRAWING BOARD

Drawing board

Paper

Drawing clip

Pencil sharpener

Sketch book

Ink bottle

Silver lines oxidize to a light brown colour

Figures drawn in ink on top of lines

Line drawn in silverpoint using a rule

Vanishing point located on head of man riding rearing horse

Lines of squared pavement slabs recede toward a single vanishing point

Complex perspective drawing done as a preparatory study for a painting

Paper prepared with size (glue) and pigment

EXAMPLE OF A SILVERPOINT DRAWING
The Adoration of the Magi, Leonardo da Vinci, 1481
Pen and ink over silverpoint on paper
16.5 × 29.2 cm (6½ × 11½ in)

One of a series of drawings recording London during 1944–1945

Charcoal lines softened by rubbing and smudging

Charcoal gives strong, expressive lines

Handmade, tinted paper

Broad charcoal mark

Lines rapidly drawn on site

EXAMPLE OF A CHARCOAL DRAWING
St. Paul's and the River, David Bomberg, 1945
Charcoal on paper
50.8 × 65.8 cm (20 × 25⅛ in)

Tempera

THE TERM TEMPERA is applied to any paint in which pigment is tempered (mixed) with a water-based binding medium – usually egg yolk. Egg tempera is applied to a smooth surface such as vellum (for illuminated manuscripts) or more commonly to hardwood panels prepared with gesso – a mixture of chalk and size (glue). Hog hair brushes are used to apply the gesso. A layer of gesso grosso (coarse gesso) is followed by successive layers of gesso sotile (fine gesso) that are sanded between coats to provide a smooth, yet absorbent ground. The paint is applied with fine sable brushes in thin layers, using light brushstrokes. Tempera dries quickly to form a tough skin with a satin sheen. The luminous white surface of the gesso combined with the overlaid paint produces the brilliant crispness and rich colours particular to this medium. Egg tempera paintings are frequently gilded with gold. Leaves of finely beaten gold are applied to a bole (reddish-brown clay) base and polished by burnishing.

MATERIALS FOR GILDING

Parchment for protecting gold leaf from draughts

Brush

Bowl containing diluted bole

Gold leaf

Gilder's knife

Gilder's tip for picking up gold leaf

Gilder's cushion

Gold leaf smoothed and polished with a burnisher

Surface prepared with gesso

Gold leaf applied in overlapping layers

Bole brushed on to gesso

Burnisher

Agate tip

MATERIALS FOR TEMPERA PANEL PAINTING

Yolk

EGG

White

SIZE (GLUE)

GESSO

Mortar

Lip

MORTAR AND PESTLE

Pestle for crushing and grinding pigments

EGG YOLK BINDING MEDIUM

EXAMPLES OF BRUSHES

FLAT HOG HAIR BRUSH

SABLE BRUSH SIZE 6

SABLE BRUSH SIZE 1

EXAMPLE OF A TEMPERA PAINTING
Presentation in the Temple, Ambrogio Lorenzetti, 1342
Tempera on wood, 257 × 168 cm (8 ft 5⅛ in × 5 ft 6 ⅛in)

Altarpiece commissioned for Siena Cathedral, Italy

Textured gold ornament made by punching motifs into the gilded surface

The red tinge of the bole is just visible beneath the gold

Edge of a sheet of gold leaf

Crisp edge characteristic of tempera painting

Vine black used to create the dim cathedral interior

Highlights on the beard made by applying thin layers of white over dried paint

Red drapery painted in vermilion

Raised right hand and pointing finger is the gesture of prophecy

Receding floor tiles create the impression of depth

Patch of discoloured varnish, left from last cleaning

VERDACCIO

**VERMILION AND
LEAD WHITE**

VERMILION

**RED EARTH
(IRON OXIDE)**

EXAMPLES OF PIGMENTS

MALACHITE

**ULTRAMARINE
LAPIS LAZULI**

VINE BLACK

LEAD TIN YELLOW

Warm flesh tones achieved by layering vermilion and white over an undercoat of verdaccio

Ultramarine lapis lazuli, as costly as gold, was reserved for significant figures such as the Virgin Mary

Patterned gold halo glitters in candlelight

Craquelure (pattern of cracks in the paint)

**DETAIL FROM "PRESENTATION
IN THE TEMPLE"**

Fresco

FRESCO IS A METHOD OF WALL PAINTING. In buon fresco (true fresco), pigments are mixed with water and applied to an intonaco (layer of fresh, damp lime-plaster). The intonaco absorbs and binds the pigments as it dries making the picture a permanent part of the wall surface. The intonaco is applied in sections called giornate (daily sections). The size of each giornata depends on the artist's estimate of how much can be painted before the plaster sets. The junctions between giornate are sometimes visible on a finished fresco. The range of colours used in buon fresco are limited to lime-resistant pigments such as earth colours (below). Slaked lime (burnt lime mixed with water), bianco di San Giovanni (slaked lime that has been partly exposed to air), and chalk can be used to produce fresco whites. In fresco secco (dry fresco), pigments are mixed with a binding medium and applied to dry plaster. The pigments are not completely absorbed into the plaster and may flake off over time.

CROSS-SECTION SHOWING FRESCO LAYERS

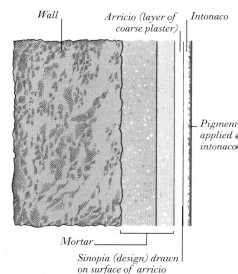

Wall

Arricio (layer of coarse plaster)

Intonaco

Pigment applied intonaco

Mortar

Sinopia (design) drawn on surface of arricio

EXAMPLES OF EARTH COLOUR PIGMENTS

RAW UMBER

RED EARTH (IRON OXIDE)

GREEN EARTH

RAW SIENNA

EXAMPLES OF FRESCO BRUSHES

Round hog hair brush

Rust-resistant twine binding

Dome-shaped hog hair brush

Pointed hog hair brush

INGREDIENTS FOR FRESCO WHITES

Marble slab for mixing ingredients

Bianco di San Giovanni

Slaked lime

Chalk

TONDO

MUCCINI

RIGA

EXAMPLE OF A FRESCO
The Expulsion of the Merchants from the Temple, Giotto, c.1306
Fresco, 200 × 185 cm (78 × 72 in)

One of a series of frescoes in the Arena Chapel, Padua, Italy

Temple acts as a backdrop for the action

Patches of azurite blue have turned green due to reaction with carbon dioxide

Bianco di San Giovanni often used for fresco whites

Gold leaf applied to apostle's halo

Hairline junction between giornate is visible

Green earth pigment applied to robe

Child painted on top of apostle's robe

Red earth pigment applied in buon fresco has retained rich hue

Azurite blue applied in fresco secco has flaked off to reveal the plaster beneath

Dry, matt surface characteristic of buon fresco

Paint applied in buon fresco to child's face

White dove represents the Holy Ghost

Paint applied in fresco secco to child's body has flaked off

Sinopia (design) sketched in red earth

Artist has to finish giornata before plaster dries

Junction between giornate

A fresco was generally worked in zones from the top down

Area with little detail can be painted quickly, allowing a larger giornata to be completed

Highly detailed area takes a longer time to paint, restricting the size of the giornata

DETAIL FROM "THE EXPULSION"

GIORNATE (DAILY SECTIONS) IN "THE EXPULSION"

Oils

OIL PAINTS ARE MADE BY MIXING and grinding pigment with a drying vegetable oil such as linseed oil. The paint can be applied to many different surfaces and textures – the most common being canvas. Before painting, the canvas is stretched on a wooden frame and its surface is prepared with layers of size (glue) and primer. The two main types of brushes used in oil painting are stiff hog hair bristle brushes – generally used for covering large areas; and soft hair brushes made from sable or synthetic material – generally used for fine detail. Other tools, including painting knives, can also be used to achieve different effects. Oil paint can be applied thickly (a technique known as impasto), or can be thinned down using a solvent – such as turpentine or white spirit. Varnishes are sometimes applied to finished paintings to protect their surface and to give them a matt or gloss finish.

KIDNEY-SHAPED PALETTE

DAMMAR RESIN VARNISH

Crystals are dissolved and applied to painting to protect its surface

COMMERCIAL OIL PAINTS

CADMIUM RED

Lightfast opaque colour

ULTRAMARINE

Transparent colour

LINSEED OIL

Oil derived from seeds of flax plant

EQUIPMENT FOR MAKING OIL PAINT

EXAMPLES OF PIGMENTS

CADMIUM RED

CERULEAN BLUE

DOUBLE DIPPER (PALETTE ATTACHMENT)

Screw-top lid

Container for storing solvent or drying oil

EXAMPLES OF BRUSHES

SYNTHETIC BRUSH

SABLE BRUSH

HOG HAIR BRISTLE BRUSHES

Flat hog hair brush

Filbert hog hair brush

Flat hog hair brush

Filbert hog hair brush

Round hog hair brush

Long, wooden handle

Protective, plastic case

Airtight jar for storing paint

Palette knife for mixing drying oil and pigment

PAINTING KNIVES

TROWEL-SHAPED PAINTING KNIFE

DIAMOND-SHAPED PAINTING KNIFE

Blade

Blade

Glass muller for grinding drying oil and pigment

Glass slab with abrasive surface

Cranked, steel shank

Cranked, steel shank

EXAMPLE OF AN OIL PAINTING
Fritillarias, Vincent van Gogh, 1886
Oil on canvas, 73.5 × 60.5 cm (29 × 24 in)

Artist's signature scratched in wet paint with the end of the brush

Each leaf painted in a single, rapid stroke

Impasto (deep ridges of paint applied in thick strokes)

Strong directional brushstrokes on table draw attention to the vase

Background enlivened by dabs of white and green

Orange and blue (complementary colours) placed together to give maximum contrast and enhance one another to appear brighter

Features of vase highlighted by generous touches of yellow

RADIAL STUDIO EASEL

Top sliding-block adjusts to canvas height

Canvas support

Height adjustment key

Angle adjustment key

Tripod

CANVAS STRETCHED ON WOODEN FRAME (VIEWED FROM THE BACK)

Staple

Canvas prepared with glue (size) and primer

Wooden frame

Unprimed canvas

EXAMPLES OF CANVASES

COTTON DUCK

FINE LINEN

COARSE LINEN

Watercolour

WATERCOLOUR PAINT IS MADE OF GROUND PIGMENT mixed with a water-soluble binding medium, usually gum arabic. It is usually applied to paper using soft hair brushes such as sable, goat hair, squirrel, and synthetic brushes. Watercolours are often diluted and applied as overlaying washes (thin, transparent layers) to build up depth of colour. Washes can be laid in a variety of ways to create a range of different effects. For example, a wet-in-wet wash can be achieved by laying a wash on top of another wet wash. The two washes blend together to give a fused effect. Sponges are used to modify washes by soaking up paint so that areas of pigment are lightened or removed from the paper. Watercolours can also be applied undiluted – a technique known as dry brush – to create a broken-colour effect. Watercolours are generally transparent and allow light to reflect from the surface of the paper through the layers of paint to give a luminous effect. They can be thickened and made opaque by adding body colour (Chinese white).

GUM ARABIC

Natural sap from acacia tree

NATURAL SPONGE

ANATOMY OF A SABLE BRUSH

Soft red sable hair

Toe (tip)

Wooden handle

SOFT HAIR BRUSHES

Hair trimmed and cemented into ferrule

ROUND SABLE BRUSH (SIZE 6)

Round ferrule

Hair tied with clove hitch knot

ROUND SABLE BRUSH (SIZE 1)

TUBES OF WATERCOLOUR PAINT

SYNTHETIC WASH BRUSH

WINSOR GREEN

SQUIRREL MOP WASH BRUSH

CADMIUM YELLOW

PORTABLE BOX OF WATERCOLOUR PAINTS

Painted colour swatch

Chinese white

Pan of watercolour paint

Lid can be used for mixing colours

LARGE GOAT HAKE WASH BRUSH

EXAMPLE OF A WATERCOLOUR
Burning of the Houses of Parliament, Turner, 1834
Watercolour on paper, 29.2 × 44.5 cm (11½ × 17½ in)

*Transparent
washes laid
on top of
each other
to create
tonal depth*

*Transparent
washes allow
light to reflect
off the surface
of the paper
to give a
luminous
effect*

*Highlight
scratched
out with
a scalpel*

*Paper shows
through thin
wash to
give flames
added
highlight*

*Crowd
painted with
thin strokes
laid over a
pale wash*

*Undiluted paint applied, then partly
washed out, to create the impression of water*

**EXAMPLES OF
WATERCOLOUR PAPERS**

EXAMPLES OF WASHES

SMOOTH-
TEXTURED
PAPER

MEDIUM-
TEXTURED
PAPER

WASH OVER DRY BRUSH
Wash laid over paint
applied with dry brush
gives two-tone effect

GRADED WASH
Strong wash applied
to tilted paper gives
graded effect

DRY BRUSH
Undiluted paint dragged
across surface of paper
gives broken effect

ROUGH-
TEXTURED
PAPER

COLOUR WHEEL OF WATERCOLOUR PAINTS

Yellow (primary colour)

*Secondary colours
made by mixing
yellow and blue*

*Secondary colours
made by mixing
red and yellow*

Blue (primary colour)

WET-IN-WET
Two diluted washes
left to run together
to give fused effect

Red (primary colour)

*Secondary colours made
by mixing blue and red*

Pastels

PASTELS ARE STICKS OF PIGMENT made by mixing ground pigment with chalk and a binding medium, such as gum arabic. They vary in hardness depending on the proportion of the binding medium to the chalk. Soft pastel – the most common form of pastel – contains just enough binding medium to hold the pigment in stick form. Pastels can be applied directly to any support (surface) with sufficient tooth (texture). When a pastel is drawn over a textured surface, the pigment crumbles and lodges in the fibres of the support. Pastel marks have a particular soft, matt quality and are suitable for techniques such as blending, scumbling, and feathering. Blending is a technique of rubbing and fusing two or more colours on the support using fingers or various tools such as tortillons (paper stumps), soft hair brushes, putty erasers, and soft bread. Scumbling is a technique of building up layers of pastel colours. The side or blunted tip of a soft pastel is lightly drawn over an underpainted area so that patches of the colour beneath show through. Feathering is a technique of applying parallel strokes of colour with the point of a pastel, usually over an existing layer of pastel colour. A thin spray of fixative can be applied – using a mouth diffuser (see pp. 430-431) or aerosol spray fixative – to a finished pastel painting, or in between layers of colour, to prevent smudging.

EQUIPMENT FOR MAKING PASTELS

Glass muller

Chalk

Glass slab with abrasive surface

Gum arabic

Ivory-black pigment

Cobalt-blue pigment

EXAMPLES OF SOFT PASTELS

COBALT-BLUE HALF PASTEL

VERMILION HALF PASTEL

OLIVE-GREEN FULL PASTEL

MAUVE FULL PASTEL

EQUIPMENT USED WITH PASTELS

BOXED PASTEL SET

Boxed set containing a mixture of portrait and landscape colours

Foam compartments protect the pastels

Soft pastel

Wooden tray

PUTTY ERASER

AEROSOL SPRAY FIXATIVE

SOFT HAIR BRUSH

BREAD

Soft bread suitable for erasing and blending

TORTILLONS (PAPER STUMPS)

Soft point used for blending

Tight roll of paper

EXAMPLE OF A PASTEL PAINTING
Woman Drying her Neck, Edgar Degas, c.1898
Pastel on cardboard, 62.5 x 65.5 cm (24½ x 25½in)

Pastels applied directly to support

Colours are blended together using fingers or tools such as tortillons

Built up layers of pastel

Rich colour of fabric created by overlaying yellows and oranges

Broken colours, characteristic of scumbling technique

Toned colour of paper visible beneath thinly applied pastels

Pure bright colours laid side by side produce strong contrasts

DETAIL FROM "WOMAN DRYING HER NECK"

Feathering technique used to produce skin tones

EXAMPLES OF TEXTURED PAPERS AND PASTEL BOARDS

WATERCOLOUR PAPER(ROUGH TEXTURE)

GLASS PAPER

WATERCOLOUR PAPER (MEDIUM TEXTURE)

INGRES PAPER

FLOCKED PASTEL BOARD

CANSON PAPER

EXAMPLES OF COLOURED AND TINTED PAPERS

Acrylics

ACRYLIC PAINT IS MADE BY MIXING PIGMENT with a synthetic resin. It can be thinned with water but dries to become water insoluble. Acrylics are applied to many surfaces, such as paper and acrylic-primed board and canvas. A variety of brushes, painting knives, rollers, air-brushes, plastic scrapers, and other tools are used in acrylic painting. The versatility of acrylics makes them suitable for a wide range of techniques. They can be used opaquely or – by adding water – in a transparent, watercolour style. Acrylic mediums can be added to the paint to adjust its consistency for special effects such as glazing and impasto (ridges of paint applied in thick strokes) or to make it more matt or glossy. Acrylics are quick-drying, which allows layers of paint to be applied on top of each other almost immediately.

EXAMPLES OF BRUSHES

Sable brush

Hog hair sash brush

Synthetic hog hair brush

Synthetic sable brush

Hog hair brush

Goat hair brush

Synthetic wash brush

Ox hair brush

EXAMPLES OF PAINTS USED IN ACRYLICS

Azo yellow

Phthalo green

Cerulean blue

Phthalo blue

Quinacridone red

Titanium white

Yellow ochre

Burnt sienna

Burnt umber

Pad of disposable paper palettes

Credit card

Paint spread evenly

PAINTING TOOLS

Flexible, plastic blade

Stippled effect achieved using thick paint

Striated effect

Glue spreader

PLASTIC PAINTING KNIFE

PLASTIC SCRAPERS

Paint cup

Main lever

Blended tones

Nozzle

Plastic handle

Uniform tone

AIR-BRUSH

Air hose

SPONGE ROLLER

EXAMPLE OF AN ACRYLIC PAINTING
A Bigger Splash, David Hockney, 1967
Acrylic on canvas, 242.5 x 243.8 cm (95½ x 96 in)

Paint applied evenly using a roller

Cotton duck canvas support (surface)

Flatness of rollered areas enhanced by adding gel medium to the paint

Masking tape stuck on to canvas to define main shapes, and paint applied within these areas using a roller

Thin strip of pool edge left unpainted

Splash painted using thicker paint and small brush

Imprecise edge on end of spring board where paint has seeped under masking tape

EXAMPLES OF ACRYLIC PAINTS AND TECHNIQUES

Opaque effect

Extruded (squeezed) effect

Paint applied using painting knife

PURPLE ACRYLIC PAINT

YELLOW ACRYLIC PAINT

ORANGE ACRYLIC PAINT

Transparent, watercolour effect

Translucent, impasto glaze

Thick impasto with coarse texture

BLUE ACRYLIC PAINT DILUTED WITH WATER

GREEN ACRYLIC PAINT MIXED WITH GEL MEDIUM

RED ACRYLIC PAINT MIXED WITH TEXTURE PASTE

Calligraphy

CALLIGRAPHY IS BEAUTIFULLY FORMED LETTERING. The term applies to written text and illumination (the decoration of manuscripts using gold leaf and colour). The essential materials needed to practise calligraphy are a writing tool, ink, and a writing surface. Quills are among the oldest writing tools. They are usually made from goose or turkey feathers, and are noted for their flexibility and ability to produce fine lines. A quill point, however, is not very durable and constant recutting and trimming is required. The most commonly used writing instrument in western calligraphy is a detachable, metal nib held in a penholder. The metal nib is very durable, and there are a wide range of different types. Particular types of nibs – such as copperplate, speedball, and roundhand nibs – are used for specific styles of lettering. Some nibs have integral ink reservoirs and others have reservoirs that are detachable. Brushes are also used for writing, and for filling in outlined letters and painting decoration. Other writing tools used in calligraphy are fountain pens, felt-tip pens, rotring pens, and reed pens. Calligraphy inks may come in liquid form, or as a solid ink stick. Ink sticks are ground down in distilled water to form a liquid ink. The most common writing surfaces for calligraphy are good quality, smooth -surfaced papers. To achieve the best writing position, the calligrapher places the paper on a drawing board set at an angle.

EQUIPMENT USED IN BRUSH LETTERING

Brush rest

Wolf hair brush

Goat hair brush

BRUSHES AND BRUSH REST

Liquid ink made by grinding down ink stick in distilled water

Solid carbon ink stick

Ink stone

INK STICK AND STONE

PENS, NIBS, AND BRUSHES USED IN CALLIGRAPHY

PENHOLDER

FELT-TIP PEN

AUTOMATIC PEN

REED PEN

SQUARE SABLE BRUSH

POINTED SABLE BRUSH

COPPERPLATE NIB

SPEEDBALL NIB

ROUNDHAND NIB AND DETACHABLE INK RESERVOIR

Feather

Feather stripped for better handling

Barrel

Hand-cut point

GOOSE-FEATHER QUILL

GOAT HAIR BRUSH

WOLF HAIR BRUSH

FOUNTAIN PEN AND INK

Bottle of permanent black ink

Barrel

Clip

Nib

Outer cap

EXAMPLES OF LETTERING STYLES

Apex

Bowl

Curved stroke

Stem

Inner counter

Stem

Stem

Arm

Counter

A B C D E

Crossbar

Inner counter

Counter

Inner counter

ROMAN CAPITALS

CHINESE LETTERING

Rice paper

Broad brush stroke

Chinese character meaning long life

Artist's stamped signature

Cap line

Ascender

Curved stroke

Ear

Arch

X line

Base line

Abcgmpt

Crossbar

Descender line

Serif

Neck

Descender

Height of letter determined by adder of nib widths

ITALIC ROMAN

ARTIST'S STAMP

Stamp

Stamped signature of the artist

Ink pad

Slightly pinched (curved) vertical stroke

Letter filled in using brush

Inner counter

O R S W

Tail

Spine

Pointed apex

VERSAL

DRAWING BOARD

Adjustable set square

Blade with parallel motion

AN ILLUMINATED MANUSCRIPT

Style of lettering called Gothic book script

Large decorative letter used to mark the opening of a chapter

Words written carefully by hand

Gold leaf

Grid lines provide guide to position of words and pictures

EXAMPLES OF CALLIGRAPHY PAPERS

Standard European paper

Indian handmade paper

Flecked, tinted paper

Imitation parchment paper

Printmaking 1

PRINTS ARE MADE BY FOUR BASIC printing processes – intaglio, lithographic, relief, and screen. In intaglio printing, lines are engraved or etched into the surface of a metal plate. Lines are engraved by hand using sharp metal tools. They are etched by corroding the metal plate with acid, using acid-resistant ground to protect the areas not to be etched. The plate is then inked and wiped, leaving the grooves filled with ink and the surface clean. Dampened paper is laid over the plate, and both paper and plate are passed through the rollers of an etching press. The pressure of the rollers forces the paper into the grooves, so that it takes up the ink, leaving an impression on the paper. Lithographic printing is based on the antipathy between grease and water. An image is drawn on a surface – usually a stone or metal plate – with a greasy medium, such as tusche (lihographic ink). The greasy drawing is fixed on to the plate by applying an acidic solution, such as gum arabic. The surface is then dampened and rolled with ink. The ink adheres only to the greasy areas and is repelled by the water. Paper is laid on the plate and pressure is applied by means of a press. In relief printing, the non-printing areas of a wood or linoleum block are cut away using gouges, knives, and other tools. The printing areas are left raised in relief and are rolled with ink. Paper is laid on the inked block and pressure is applied by means of a press or by burnishing (rubbing) the back of the paper. The most common forms of relief printing are woodcut, wood engraving, and linocut. In screen printing, the printing surface is a mesh stretched across a wooden frame. A stencil is applied to the mesh to seal the nonprinting areas and ink is scraped through the mesh to produce an image.

THE FOUR MAIN PRINTING PROCESSES

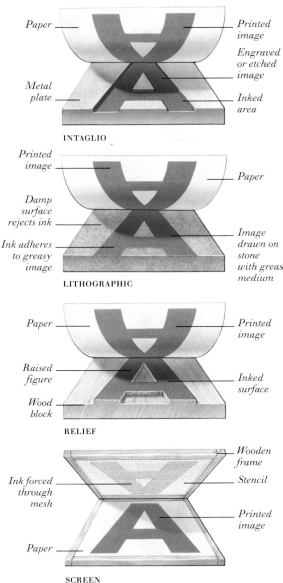

Paper — Printed image
Metal plate — Engraved or etched image
Inked area

INTAGLIO

Printed image — Paper
Damp surface rejects ink
Ink adheres to greasy image — Image drawn on stone with greasy medium

LITHOGRAPHIC

Paper — Printed image
Raised figure
Wood block — Inked surface

RELIEF

Wooden frame
Ink forced through mesh — Stencil
Printed image
Paper

SCREEN

LEATHER INK DABBER

EQUIPMENT USED IN INTAGLIO PRINTING

ROCKER SCRIBER ROULETTE SCRAPER BURNISHER CLAMP

ETCHING PRESS USED FOR INTAGLIO PRINTMAKING

Flywheel

Paper

Felt blanket cushions and distributes pressure exerted by rollers

Spoke

Screw pressure adjustor

Handle

Top roller

Position guide

Printed image

Inked-up copper plate

Sliding bed (plank) is wound between steel rollers

GROUND

Acid-resistant ground rolled on to metal plate before etching

GROUND ROLLER

Gelatine roller

Wooden handle

EXAMPLE OF AN INTAGLIO PRINT
Annie with a Sun Hat, Jock McFadyen, 1993
Etched copper plate, 41 × 40 cm (16 × 15¾ in)

EXAMPLES OF PRINTING PAPERS

Printmaking 2

EXAMPLE OF A LITHOGRAPHIC STONE AND PRINT

Crown Gateway 2, Mandy Bonnell, 1987
Lithograph, 50 × 40 cm (19½ × 15¾ in)

IMAGE DRAWN ON STONE   LITHOGRAPIC PRINT

EXAMPLE OF A SCREEN PRINT

Sea Change, Patrick Hughes, 1992
Screen print, 77 × 94.5 cm (30 × 37 in)

SCREEN AND SQUEEGEE

Squeegee

Rubber blade

Mesh

Wooden frame

EQUIPMENT USED IN LITHOGRAPHIC PRINTING

CRAYON AND HOLDER

LITHOGRAPHIC PENCIL

TUSCHE (LITHOGRAPHIC INK) PEN

ERASING STICK

EXPANDABLE SPONGE

TUSCHE (LITHOGRAPHIC INK) STICK

RUBBING INK

INK ROLLER

MILD ACIDIC SOLUTION   GUM ARABIC SOLUTION

WATER-BASED SCREEN PRINTING INKS

BLUE ACRYLIC INK   RED ACRYLIC INK   BROWN TEXTILE INK

EQUIPMENT USED IN RELIEF PRINTING

V-SHAPED GOUGE

INK ROLLER

Rubber roller

LINOLEUM AND WOODCUT BLOCK

U-SHAPED GOUGE

GRAVER

Linoleum

KNIFE

SCORPER

WOOD ENGRAVING

Side-grain wood block

END-GRAIN WOOD BLOCK

INKED-UP ENGRAVED BLOCK

WOOD ENGRAVING PRINT

RELIEF-PRINTING PRESS

Spiral spring

Crown

Tympan lowered on to printing block

Piston

Printed image

Staple (frame)

Bar (pressure handle)

Printing block

Bed is rolled under platen

Drum handle

Platen

Counterweight

Rail

Drum (rounce)

Leg

Pillar (post)

Foot

Mosaic

MOSAIC IS THE ART OF MAKING patterns and pictures from tesserae (small, coloured pieces of glass, marble, and other materials). Different materials are cut into tesserae using different tools. Smalti (glass enamel) and marble are cut into pieces using a hammer and a hardy (a pointed blade) embedded in a log. Vitreous glass is cut into pieces using a pair of nippers. Mosaics can be made using a direct or indirect method. In the direct method, the tesserae are laid directly into a bed of cement–based adhesive. In the indirect method, the design is drawn in reverse on paper or cloth. The tesserae are then stuck face-down on the paper or cloth using water-soluble glue. Adhesive is spread with a trowel on to a solid surface – such as a wall – and the back of the mosaic is laid into the adhesive. Finally, the paper or cloth is soaked off to reveal the mosaic. Gaps between tesserae can be filled with grout. Grout is forced into gaps by dragging a grouting squeegee across the face of the mosaic. Mosaics are usually used to decorate walls and floors, but they can also be applied to smaller objects.

EQUIPMENT FOR BREAKING MARBLE

Sawn strip of marble, ready for breaking into cubes

Mosaic hammer

Alicante (red marble) pieces

Hardy (pointed blade) embedded in a log

NIPPERS *Hardwearing, tungsten carbide tip*

Handle with rubber grip

SMALTI (GLASS ENAMEL)

RED SMALTI

EXAMPLE OF A MOSAIC (DIRECT METHOD)
Seascape, Tessa Hunkin, 1993
Smalti mosaic on board
80 cm (31½ in) diameter

Gold-leaf smalti

YELLOW SMALTI

BLUE SMALTI

MOSAIC TOOLS

CEMENT-BASED ADHESIVE

GROUT

TROWEL *Notch*

Steel blade

Wooden handle

GROUTING SQUEEGEE

Wooden handle

Rubb blade

Nicobond

STAGES IN THE CREATION OF A MOSAIC (INDIRECT METHOD)

COLOUR SKETCH
A colour sketch is drawn
in oil pastel to give a clear
impression of how the finished
mosaic will look.

REVERSE IMAGE
Tesserae are glued face-down
on reverse image on paper.
Mosaic is then attached to solid
surface and paper is removed.

MOSAIC POT

Geometric design

Grout

MOSAIC MOSQUE DESIGN

Floral design

Geometric border

Andamenti (line along which tesserae are laid)

Grout fills the gaps between the tesserae

Mosaic mounted on board

Vitreous glass cut into triangular shape with nippers

Gold tessera with ripple finish

Gold tessera placed upside-down

VITREOUS GLASS

GREEN VITREOUS GLASS WITH GOLD LEAF

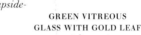

Plain finish

Ripple finish

RED VITREOUS GLASS

SHEETS OF VITREOUS GLASS

BLUE VITREOUS GLASS

FINISHED MOSAIC
Goldfish, Tessa Hunkin, 1993
Vitreous glass mosaic on board
35.5 × 25.5 cm (14 × 10 in)

Border of square vitreous glass

Sculpture 1

THE TWO TRADITIONAL METHODS OF MAKING SCULPTURE are carving and modelling. A carved sculpture is made by cutting away the surplus from a block of hard material such as stone, marble, or wood. The tools used for carving vary according to the material being carved. Heavy steel points, claws, and chisels that are struck with a lump hammer are generally used for stone and marble. Sharp gouges and chisels that are struck with a wooden mallet are used for wood. Sculptures formed from hard materials are generally finished by filing with rasps, rifflers, and other abrasive implements. Modelling is a process by which shapes are built up, using malleable materials such as clay, plaster, and wax. The material is cut with wire-ended tools and modelled with the fingers or a variety of hardwood and metal implements. For large or intricate modelled sculptures an armature (frame), made from metal or wood, is used to provide internal support. Sculptures formed in soft materials may harden naturally or can be made more durable by firing in a kiln. Modelled sculptures are often first designed in wax or another material to be cast later in a metal (see pp. 454-455) such as bronze. The development of many new materials in the 20th century has enabled sculptors to experiment with new techniques such as construction (joining preformed pieces of material such as machine components, mirrors, and furniture) and kinetic (mobile) sculpture.

EXAMPLES OF MARBLE CARVING TOOLS

1.1 kg (2½ lb) iron head

Ash handle

LUMP HAMMER

EXAMPLES OF WOODCARVING TOOLS

CABINET RASP

STRAIGHT GOUGE

SALMON BEND GOUGE

CHISEL

Stone for sharpening woodcarving tools

Cedar box

ARKANSAS HONE-STONE

CALLIPERS

Curved leg

Gap measures distance between two points on a sculpture

Wing nut

WIDE MARBLE CLAW

NARROW MARBLE CLAW

POINT

FLAT CHISEL

BULLNOSE CHISEL

EXAMPLES OF RIFFLERS (FOR STONE, MARBLE, AND WOOD)

30 CM (12 IN) RIFFLER

15 CM (6 IN) RIFFLER

Surface for sharpening stonecarving tools

DIAMOND WHETSTONE

CARVING MALLET

EXAMPLE OF A CARVED WOOD SCULPTURE
Mary Magdalene, Donatello, 1454-1455
Poplar wood, height 188 cm (6 ft 2 in)

*Tiny holes along
the hairline made
with a point*

*Soft skin texture tooled
with a fine-toothed
marble claw*

**DETAIL OF
SLAVE'S HEAD**

EXAMPLE OF A CARVED MARBLE SCULPTURE
The Rebel Slave, Michelangelo, 1513-1516
Marble, height 213 cm (7 ft)

*Hair worked
with a narrow
claw*

*Translucent white
marble, quarried at
Carrara, Italy*

*Surface rubbed
smooth with
rifflers and
pumice*

*Strut gives added
support to long
slender limb*

*Base scored with
jagged parallel
cuts made with
point and lump
hammer*

*Series of tiny
punch holes,
made with
a fine point,
outline the
form*

*The dimensions of the marble block
determine the size of the sculpture*

*Delicately
modelled
hand carved
with a chisel*

*Hair
highlighted
with gold
leaf*

*Figure cut
from single
length of
poplar*

*Deep
ridges of
hair cut
with a
gouge*

*Wood prepared
with gesso
(chalk and glue)
and painted*

*Foot carved in
deep relief*

*Rough surface
made by driving
a point into the
marble at an
oblique angle*

DETAIL OF SLAVE'S FOOT

Sculpture 2

EXAMPLES OF MODELLING TOOLS

WIRE-ENDED CUTTING TOOL

CURVED MOULDING TOOL

SPATULA-ENDED WAX MODELLING TOOL

ROUNDED WAX MODELLING TOOL

EXAMPLES OF BRONZE FINISHING TOOLS

HOOKED RIFFLER

POINTED RIFFLER

SPIRIT LAMP (FOR HEATING WAX MODELLING TOOLS)

Wick

Brass holder

Glass bowl

Methylated spirit

STAGES IN THE LOST-WAX METHOD OF CASTING
Based on Mars, Giambologna, c.1546

Wax-covered wire armature

ORIGINAL MODEL
An original, solid wax model is made and preserved so that numerous replicas can be cast.

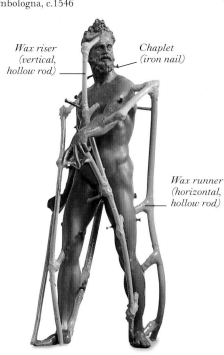

Wax riser (vertical, hollow rod)

Chaplet (iron nail)

Wax runner (horizontal, hollow rod)

HOLLOW WAX FIGURE IS CAST
A new, hollow wax model is cast from the original model. It is filled with a plaster core that is held in place with nails. Wax runners and risers are attached.

Fire-resistant clay

FIGURE IS BAKED IN CASTING MOULD
The model is encased in clay and baked. The wax melts away (through the channels made by the wax rods) and is replaced by molten bronze.

MODELLING STAND AND ARMATURE

Aluminium wire figure

Fixed iron armature support

Screw-hole for fastening the iron to modelling board

Marine ply modelling board

Aluminium table stand

Rotating table top

Height adjustor

Tripod

EXAMPLE OF A CLAY MODEL
Madonna and Child, Henry Moore, 1943
Terracotta, height 18.4 cm (7¼ in)

Clay smoothed to create the effect of soft skin

Incision made with serrated tool

Maquette (small sketch) modelled from a solid lump of clay

Terracotta clay, fires at 1,000°C to 1,050°C (1,832°F to 1,922°F)

Model for a much larger bronze sculpture

Roughly worked clay

Strips of clay, added to the model, give the effect of folded drapery

Metal riser

Metal runner

Golden brown colour of untreated bronze

Stump left by rod will be filed down

Dark brown patina

Hole left by nail will be plugged with bronze

STATUE IS STRIPPED OF CLAY
When the bronze has cooled, the clay mould is broken open to reveal the bronze statue with solid metal runners and risers.

STATUE IS FINISHED
The nails are pulled out and a large hole is made to remove the plaster core. When the metal rods have been sawn off, the sculpture is filed to refine the surface.

STATUE IS CLEANED
Finally the work is cleaned and polished. An artificial patina (colouring) is achieved by treating the surface with chemicals.

ARCHITECTURE

Ancient Egypt

THE CIVILIZATION OF THE ANCIENT EGYPTIANS (which lasted from about 3100 BC until it was finally absorbed into the Roman empire in 30 BC) is famous for its temples and tombs. Egyptian temples were often huge and geometric, like the Temple of Amon-Re (below and right). They were usually decorated with hieroglyphs (sacred characters used for picture-writing) and painted reliefs depicting gods, Pharaohs (kings), and queens. Tombs were particularly important to the Egyptians, who believed that the dead were resurrected in the after-life. The tombs were often decorated – as, for example, the surround of the false door opposite – in order to give comfort to the dead. The best-known ancient Egyptian tombs are the pyramids, which were designed to symbolize the rays of the sun. Many of the architectural forms used by the ancient Egyptians were later adopted by other civilizations; for example, columns and capitals were later used by the ancient Greeks (see pp. 460-461) and ancient Romans (see pp. 462-465).

FRONT VIEW OF HYPOSTYLE HALL, TEMPLE OF AMON-RE

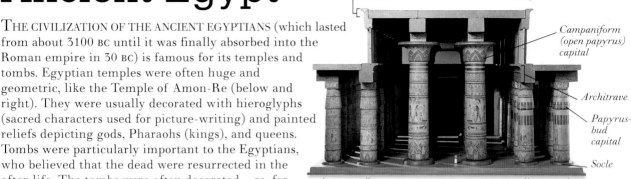

Cornice decorated with cavetto moulding

Campaniform (open papyrus) capital

Architrave

Papyrus-bud capital

Socle

Side aisle *Central nave* *Side aisle*

SIDE VIEW OF HYPOSTYLE HALL, TEMPLE OF AMON-RE, KARNAK, EGYPT, c.1290 BC

Horus, the sun-god   *Architrave*   *Stone slab forming flat roof of side aisle*

Kepresh crown with disc

Chons, the moon-god   *Amon-Re, king of the gods*   *Hathor, the sky-goddess*   *Papyrus motif*   *Cartouche (oval border) containing the titles of the Pharaoh (king)*   *Socle*   *Aisle running north-south*

LIMESTONE FALSE DOOR WITH HIEROGLYPHS, TOMB OF KING TJETJI, GIZA, EGYPT, c.2400 BC

Lintel

Hieroglyph representing a house

Disc representing sun or light

Eroded image of Tjetji

Hoe-shaped hieroglyph representing "mr" sound

Head of false door

Image of Tjetji's wife

Limestone stela (slab)

Image of Tjetji's daughter

PLANT CAPITAL OF THE PTOLEMAIC-ROMAN PERIOD, EGYPT, 332-30 BC

Palm leaf

Papyrus flower

Papyrus leaf

Papyrus stem

Lotus bud

Lotus stem

Cornice decorated with cavetto moulding

Bead moulding

Trellis window

Rectangular pier decorated with hieroglyphs

Elevated roof of central nave

Clerestory

Disc representing sun or light

Architrave

Square abacus

Papyrus-bud capital

Papyriform column

Shaft

Scene depicting a Pharaoh (king) paying homage to the god Amon-Re

Central nave

ANCIENT EGYPTIAN BUILDING DECORATION

DECORATED WINDOW, MEDINET HABU, EGYPT, C.1198BC

ROPE AND PATERAE DECORATION

CAPITAL WITH THE HEAD OF THE SKY-GODDESS HATHOR, TEMPLE OF ISIS, PHILAE, EGYPT, 283-47 BC

LOTUS AND PAPYRUS FRIEZE DECORATION

Ancient Greece

THE CLASSICAL TEMPLES OF ANCIENT GREECE were built according to the belief that certain forms and proportions were pleasing to the gods. There were three main ancient Greek architectural orders (styles), which can be distinguished by the decoration and proportions of their columns, capitals (column tops), and entablatures (structures resting on the capitals). The oldest is the Doric order, which dates from the seventh century BC and was used mainly on the Greek mainland and in the western colonies, such as Sicily and southern Italy. The Temple of Neptune, shown here, is a classic example of this order. It is hypaethral (roofless) and peripteral (surrounded by a single row of columns). About a century later, the more decorative Ionic order developed on the Aegean Islands. Features of this order include volutes (spiral scrolls) on capitals and acroteria (pediment ornaments). The Corinthian order was invented in Athens in the fifth century BC and is typically identified by an acanthus leaf on the capitals. This order was later widely used in ancient Roman architecture.

CAPITALS OF THE THREE ORDERS OF ANCIENT GREEK ARCHITECTURE

DORIC CAPITAL, THE PROPYLAEUM (GATEWAY), THE ACROPOLIS, ATHENS, GREECE, 449 BC

- Abacus
- Echinus
- Annulet
- Trachelion (neck)

IONIC CAPITAL, THE PROPYLAEUM (GATEWAY), TEMPLE OF ATHENA POLIAS, PRIENE, GREECE, c.334 BC

- Abacus
- Lesbian leaf pattern
- Coussinet (cushion)
- Cyma reversa profile
- Volute
- Echinus with egg and dart decoration
- Eye
- Palmette

CORINTHIAN CAPITAL FROM A STOA (PORTICO), PROBABLY FROM ASIA MINOR

- Mask
- Abacus
- Volute
- Cauliculus
- Bell-shaped core
- Acanthus leaf

TEMPLE OF NEPTUNE, PAESTUM, ITALY, c.460 BC

- Pediment
- Doric entablature
- Pteron (external colonnade)
- Raking cornice
- Trachelion (neck)
- Taenia
- Triglyph
- Metope
- Glyph (channel)
- Euthynteria
- Drum
- Stylobate
- Column of the Doric order

PLAN OF THE TEMPLE OF NEPTUNE, PAESTUM

ANCIENT GREEK BUILDING DECORATION

Pronaos (vestibule)

Naos wall

Anta (pilaster terminating naos wall)

Naos (cella)

Peristyle

Opisthodomos (rear portico)

Pteron (external colonnade)

Hexastyle pteron (colonnade of six columns)

Volute

FACADE, TREASURY OF ATREUS, MYCENAE, GREECE, 1350-1250 BC

Meander

FRETWORK, PARTHENON, ATHENS, GREECE, 447-436 BC

ACROTERION, TEMPLE OF APHAIA, AEGINA, GREECE, 490 BC

Griffon (gryphon)

Raking cornice

ANTEFIXA, TEMPLE OF APHAIA, AEGINA, GREECE, 490 BC

Palmette

Volute

Regula (short fillet beneath taenia)

Eaves

Cornice

Frieze

Architrave

Capital

Shaft

Crepidoma (stepped base)

Entasis (slight curve of a column)

Intercolumniation

Fluting

Ancient Rome 1

IN THE EARLY PERIOD OF THE ROMAN EMPIRE extensive use
was made of ancient Greek architectural ideas, particularly
those of the Corinthian order (see pp. 460-461). As a result,
many early Roman buildings – such as the Temple of Vesta
(opposite) – closely resemble ancient Greek buildings. A
distinctive Roman style began to evolve in the first century
AD. This style developed the interiors of buildings (the Greeks
had concentrated on the exterior) by using arches, vaults, and
domes inside the buildings, and by ornamenting internal walls.
Many of these features can be seen in the Pantheon. Exterior
columns were often used for decorative, rather than structural,
purposes, as in the Colosseum and the Porta Nigra (see
pp. 464-465). Smaller buildings had timber frames with
wattle-and-daub walls, as in the mill (see pp. 464-465).
Roman architecture remained influential for many centuries,
with some of its principles being used in the 11th century in
Romanesque buildings (see pp. 468-469) and also in the 15th
and 16th centuries in Renaissance buildings (see pp. 474-477).

ANCIENT ROMAN BUILDING DECORATION

FESTOON, TEMPLE OF VESTA,
TIVOLI, ITALY, C.80 BC

RICHLY DECORATED
ROMAN OVUM

INTERIOR OF THE PANTHEON, ROME, ITALY, 118-c.128

Inner dome,
following the
curve of a
depressed arch

Outer
saucer
dome

Entablature

Curved
cornice

Lesene

Cornice

Triangular
pediment

Concave
niche

Marble veneer   Segmental pediment   Pedestal

FRONT VIEW OF THE PANTHEON

Series of concentric,
step-like rings

Oculus

Outer saucer dome

Intermediate
block

Dentil ornament

Engaged
pediment

Entablature
with
inscription

Raking
cornice

Pediment

Rotunda

Octastyle portico
(eight-column portico)

SIDE VIEW OF THE PANTHEON

Entablature

Pitched roof

Eaves

Intermediate
block

Upper
cornice

Relieving
arch

Opening for
ventilation

Cornice

Colonnade

Ornamental
band decorated
with festoons

Attached
fluted pilaster

TEMPLE OF VESTA, TIVOLI, ITALY, c.80 BC

Circular naos (cella)

Architrave

Ceiling

Fascia

Corinthian entablature

Corinthian capital

Pteron (colonnade)

Naos (cella) window

Opus incertum (concrete wall faced with irregularly shaped stones)

Egg and dart decoration

Upper torus

Scotia

Lower torus

Jamb with corrugated surface

Naos (cella) door

Cornice

Podium

Threshold

FRIEZE, FORUM OF TRAJAN, ROME, ITALY, 98-113

KEYSTONE, ARCH OF TITUS, ROME, ITALY, 81

Oculus illuminating interior of rotunda

Coffer

Stepped side of coffer

Frieze decorated with arabesques, urns, and winged horses

Step-like ring

Barrel vault

Passageway

Coffer

Engaged pediment

Monolithic shaft (shaft made from a single stone)

Barrel vault

Raking cornice

Pediment

Entablature

Corinthian column

Entablature

Aedicule (tabernacle)

Festoon

Fluting

Corinthian pilaster

Base

Corinthian capital

Rotunda

Portico

Ancient Rome 2

SIDE VIEW OF A ROMAN MILL

Principal rafter
Wall-plate
Wall-post
Top-plate
Floorboard
Intermediate
floor-joist
Sill
Stud
Foundation

Lath
Pantile

Verge
Eaves
Plain
fascia
Plaster
coating

Grille · Joist · Boarding

Half-round ridge tile · King-strut
Pitched roof · Lath
Ashlar post · Principal rafter
Tie-beam
Plain fascia
Wall-plate
Flat soffit
Intermediate
floor-joist
Top-plate
Mill
wheel
Wall-post
Sill
Binder

Wattle-and-daub wall
with plaster coating · Supporting
post · Floor-
joist · Foundation
post

THE COLOSSEUM (FLAVIAN AMPHITHEATRE), ROME, ITALY, 70-82

Bracket for
velarium
(awning)

Third floor
Corinthian
pilaster

Round arch
Second floor
Corinthian
half-column

Entablature

Ionic
half-column

First floor

Doric
half-column

Ground floor

Crowning
cornice

Barrel vault

Horizontal gangway

Arcade

External travertine shell

Intermediate shell

Inner shell

PORTA NIGRA, TRIER, GERMANY, c.240-260

Crowning cornice

Impost

Semicircular tower

Parapet

Keystone

Round-arched window

Arcaded passageway

Lesene

Voussoir

Semicircular tower

Cornice

Entablature

Frieze

Relieving arch

Architrave

Arcading

Apse (added in Middle Ages)

Attached column

Courtyard

Round arch

Entrance to town

Capital

Shaft

Base

Facade

Opening to staircase

Maenianum summum (gallery)

Rectangular window

String course

Cuneus (wedge of seating)

Opus quadratum (square masonry)

Arched opening to staircase

Radiating, wedge-shaped chamber

ROMAN WATTLE-AND-DAUB WALL, 1ST CENTURY BC

Hazel twig framework

Clay mixture

Plaster

Paintwork

Radial wall

Opus incertum (concrete wall faced with irregularly shaped stones)

Cornice

Ambulatory corridor

Attached rectangular pier

Keystone

Impost

Tuscan capital

Voussoir

Tuscan pilaster

Medieval castles and houses

WARFARE WAS COMMON IN EUROPE in the Middle Ages, and many monarchs and nobles built castles as a form of defence. Typical medieval castles have outer walls surrounding a moat. Inside the moat is a bailey (courtyard), protected by a chemise (jacket-wall). The innermost and strongest part of a medieval castle is the keep. There are two main types of keep: towers called donjons, such as the Tour de César and Coucy-le-Château, and rectangular keeps ("hall-keeps"), such as the Tower of London. Castles were often guarded by salients (projecting fortifications), like those of the Bastille. Medieval houses typically had timber cruck (tent-like) frames, wattle-and-daub walls, and pitched roofs, like those on medieval London Bridge (opposite).

DONJON, TOUR DE CESAR, PROVINS, FRANCE, 12TH CENTURY

Oculus — Battlements (crenellations) — Loophole — Hemispherical cupola — Conical spire — Gallery — Flying buttress — Squinch — Hexahedral hall — Vaulted room — Semicircular turret — Main entrance — Fireplace — Bailey — Staircase to chemise (jacket-wall) — Embrasure — Chemise (jacket-wall) — Plain impost — Depressed cupola — Vaulted staircase — Motte

SALIENT, CAERNARVON CASTLE, BRITAIN, 1283-1323

Loophole

CRUCK-FRAMED HOUSE, BRITAIN, c.1200

Timber cruck frame

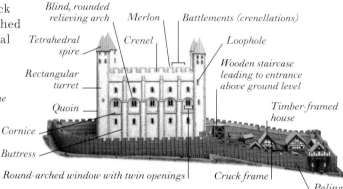

TOWER OF LONDON, BRITAIN, FROM 1070

Blind, rounded relieving arch — Merlon — Battlements (crenellations) — Tetrahedral spire — Crenel — Loophole — Rectangular turret — Wooden staircase leading to entrance above ground level — Quoin — Timber-framed house — Cornice — Buttress — Round-arched window with twin openings — Cruck frame — Paling

Curtain wall — Pointed relieving arch — Semicircular relieving arch — Plain string course — Bracket decorated with scroll moulding

Rectangular window — Sunken rectangular panel — Round-arched window — Semicircular salient — Loophole — Lateral circular salient

THE BASTILLE, PARIS, FRANCE, 14TH CENTURY

MEDIEVAL LONDON BRIDGE, BRITAIN, 1176 (WITH 14TH-CENTURY BATTLEMENTED BUILDING, NONESUCH HOUSE, AND TWO-TOWERED GATE)

Gate-house

Battlemented building

Chapel pier

Railing

Onion-shaped dome

Pitched roof

Shaped gable

Nonesuch House

Crypt of Becket Chapel

Starling

Two-towered gate

Oriel window

Timber framing with ornamental woodwork

Pier

Pointed Gothic stone arch

Timber framing

DONJON, COUCY-LE-CHATEAU, AISNE, FRANCE, 1225-1245

Cornice

Pointed arch

Loophole

Round arch

Parapet

Gallery

Passageway

Pointed arch

Inner hall

Tribune (elevated platform)

Dodecahedral second floor

Springing point of rib vault

Projecting rectangular pier

Engaged colonette

Window opening

Chimney-shaft

Dodecahedral first floor

Rectangular opening

Fireplace

Archivolt decorated with torus and fascia

Embrasure

Bridge to castle entrance

Steps

Mezzanine (entresol) housing drawbridge windlass

Dodecahedral ground floor

Entrance

Moat

Passageway inside structure of outer wall

Four-centred relieving arch

Niche

Corbel with sculptural decoration

Capital

String course

Ruin of segmental ramp leading to chemise (jacket-wall)

Medieval churches

DURING THE MIDDLE AGES, large numbers of churches were built in Europe. European churches of this period typically have high vaults supported by massive piers and columns. In the 10th century, the Romanesque style developed. Romanesque architects adopted many Roman or early Christian architectural ideas, such as cross-shaped ground-plans – like that of Angoulême Cathedral (opposite) – and the basilican system of a nave with a central vessel and side aisles. In the mid-12th century, flying buttresses and pointed vaults appeared. These features later became widely used in Gothic architecture (see pp. 470-471). Bagneux Church (opposite) has both styles: a Romanesque tower, and a Gothic nave and choir.

CHURCH-ROOF BOSS, BRITAIN

ROMANESQUE CAPITALS

"THE FLIGHT INTO EGYPT" CAPITAL, CATHEDRAL OF ST. LAZARE, AUTUN, FRANCE, 1120-1130

"CHRIST IN MAJESTY" CAPITAL, BASILICA OF ST. MADELEINE, VEZELAY, FRANCE, 1120-1140

Finial

Octahedral spire

Incline

Circular staircase-turret

Loophole

Octahedral crossing tower

Round-arched window

Series of archivolts decorated with tori

Series of jambs decorated with colonettes

Pitched roof

Barrel vault

Lean-to roof

Transept

Semicircular transverse arch

Tribune (elevated platform)

Vaulting shaft

Quadrant arch

Attached half-column

Colonette

Round arcade arch

Romanesque capital

Round stilted arch

Twin opening of gallery bays

Arcade

Square central shaft

Compound pier

Attached half-column

Side aisle

Main vessel

Side aisle

GROUND-PLAN OF ANGOULEME CATHEDRAL, FRANCE, FROM c.1105

Heavily moulded transverse arch

Crossing

Transept chapel

Chevet (choir with round apse and chapels)

Transept

Engaged column

Dome

Buttress

Nave

Transverse arch with plain fascia

Nave bay

Clustered column

Vestibule

CHOIR, CHURCH OF ST. SERGE, ANGERS, FRANCE, c.1215-1220

Historiated boss

Diagonal rib with torus moulding

Longitudinal ridge-rib

Loophole

Cell

Gable

Transverse arch

Domed rib-vault

Lierne

Formeret

Round-arched window

Cubic abacus

Attached colonette

Embrasure

Cornice

Vaulting shaft

Rectangular side-chapel

Impost with foliated frieze

Arcade column

Bay of main vessel

Historiated keystone

Tas-de-charge

Polyhedral abacus

Foliated capital

Rectangular apse

Octahedral socle

BAGNEUX CHURCH, FRANCE, 1170-1190

Moulded rib with an arris between two tori

Flying buttress

Roof space

Lean-to roof

Cell

Polyhedral abacus

Transverse arch

Oculus

Tower vault

Square-roofed pinnacle

Triforium

Foliated capital

Triple vaulting-shaft

Quadripartite vault

Formeret

Attached compound pier

Corbel

Pier buttress

Embrasure

Weathering

Attached half-column

Base

Square socle

Intrados of arch with flat band between two tori

Nave column

Compound pier

Arcade

Nave

Choir

Octahedral socle

Bay

Attached colonette

Exterior wall

Tower

Pointed arch

Torus moulding

Colonette

Tower-vault oculus

Recessed panel

Round arch

Impost

Pier supporting tower

Side aisle

Gothic 1

GOTHIC STAINED
GLASS WITH FOLIATED
SCROLL MOTIF, ON
WOODEN FORM

GOTHIC BUILDINGS are characterized by rib vaults, pointed or lancet arches, flying buttresses, decorative tracery and gables, and stained-glass windows. Typical Gothic buildings include the Cathedrals of Salisbury and old St. Paul's in England, and Notre Dame de Paris in France (see pp. 472-473). The Gothic style developed out of Romanesque architecture in France (see pp. 468-469) in the mid-12th century, and then spread throughout Europe. The decorative elements of Gothic architecture became highly developed in buildings of the English Decorated style (late 13th-14th century) and the French Flamboyant style (15th-16th century). These styles are exemplified by the tower of Salisbury Cathedral and the staircase in the Church of St. Maclou (see pp. 472-473), respectively. In both of these styles, embellishments such as ballflowers and curvilinear (flowing) tracery were used liberally. The English Perpendicular style (late 14th-15th century), which followed the Decorated style, emphasized the vertical and horizontal elements of a building. A notable feature of this style is the hammer-beam roof.

GROUND-PLAN OF SALISBURY CATHEDRAL

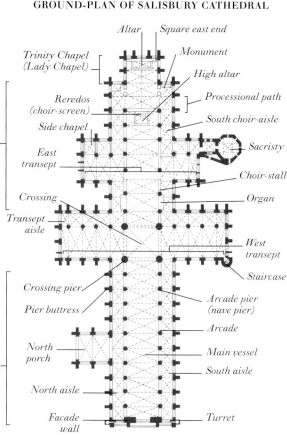

Altar
Square east end
Trinity Chapel (Lady Chapel)
Monument
High altar
Reredos (choir-screen)
Processional path
Side chapel
South choir-aisle
Choir
East transept
Sacristy
Crossing
Choir-stall
Transept aisle
Organ
West transept
Crossing pier
Staircase
Pier buttress
Arcade pier (nave pier)
Arcade
North porch
Main vessel
South aisle
Nave
North aisle
Facade wall
Turret

GOTHIC TORUS WITH BALLFLOWERS

Limestone block
Block members carved into rolls
Block members cut polygonally
Pencil guideline
Early stage of ballflower carving

BLOCK AFTER INITIAL CUTTING

BLOCK WITH MEMBERS CUT INTO ROLLS

Torus
Ballflower
Fillet
Mason's mark

FINISHED BLOCK

Trinity Chapel (Lady Chapel)
Choir
Finial
Octahedral pinnacle with small spire
Blind semi-arch
Staggered triple lancet windows
Turret-like pinnacle
Parapet decorated with blind arches filled with trefoils
Mullion
Stained glass
Base
Cornice
Lean-to roof
East transept facade
Buttress

Weather-vane

Orb

NORTH SIDE, SALISBURY
CATHEDRAL, BRITAIN, 1220-1280
(STEEPLE AND SPIRE ADDED
DURING 14TH CENTURY)

WEST FACADE,
SALISBURY CATHEDRAL

Spire

Band with
lozenge
decoration

Trefoil in a
spandrel

Aureole

Gable

Staggered triple
lancet window

Semi-attached
gable with
small pilasters

Blind rhombus tracery
filled with a quatrefoil

Spire

Parapet

Turret-like
pinnacle

Pitched roof

Finial

Row of blind
trefoil arches

Ballflower
decoration

Staggered
triple lancet
window

Blind pointed
arches filled
with twin
lancets and
quatrefoils

Spire-like
pinnacle

Parapet

Tracertied parapet
with lozenge
decoration

Small
gable
crowning
buttress

Projecting
turret

Blind
gabled
arch

Octahedral
turret

Angle
buttress

Row of gabled
niches under
trefoil arches

Row of blind
arches filled
with trefoils

North porch

Niche under small
gabled roof

Gable

Battlemented
cornice

Blind semi-arch

Lateral
porch

Crocket

Nave

Main porch

Octafoil

Cinquefoil moulding

Blind lancet

Flying buttress

Spire

Moulded side
of gable

Spire-like
pinnacle

Pitched roof

Flying buttress

Lateral turret

Small gable
crowning
buttress

Crocket

Buttress

Angle
buttress

West transept
facade

Weathering

Pier buttress

Trefoil
decoration

North
porch

Archivolt

Twin lancet window under pointed
arch, crowned by a quatrefoil

Gothic 2

CURVILINEAR (FLOWING) TRACERY FROM A BALUSTRADE, 14TH OR 15TH CENTURY

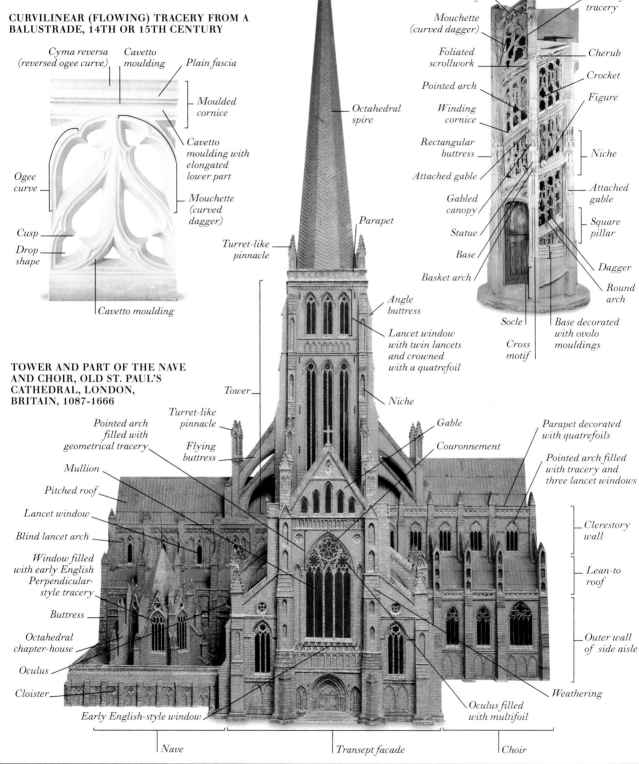

Cyma reversa (reversed ogee curve)

Cavetto moulding

Plain fascia

Moulded cornice

Cavetto moulding with elongated lower part

Mouchette (curved dagger)

Ogee curve

Cusp

Drop shape

Cavetto moulding

SPIRAL STAIRCASE TO ORGAN, CHURCH OF ST. MACLOU, ROUEN, FRANCE, c.1519

Trefoil

Mouchette (curved dagger)

Flamboyant tracery

Foliated scrollwork

Cherub

Pointed arch

Crocket

Winding cornice

Figure

Rectangular buttress

Niche

Attached gable

Attached gable

Gabled canopy

Square pillar

Statue

Base

Dagger

Basket arch

Round arch

Socle

Base decorated with ovolo mouldings

Cross motif

Octahedral spire

Parapet

Turret-like pinnacle

Angle buttress

Lancet window with twin lancets and crowned with a quatrefoil

TOWER AND PART OF THE NAVE AND CHOIR, OLD ST. PAUL'S CATHEDRAL, LONDON, BRITAIN, 1087-1666

Tower

Niche

Pointed arch filled with geometrical tracery

Turret-like pinnacle

Gable

Couronnement

Parapet decorated with quatrefoils

Flying buttress

Mullion

Pitched roof

Pointed arch filled with tracery and three lancet windows

Lancet window

Clerestory wall

Blind lancet arch

Lean-to roof

Window filled with early English Perpendicular-style tracery

Buttress

Octahedral chapter-house

Outer wall of side aisle

Oculus

Cloister

Weathering

Oculus filled with multifoil

Early English-style window

Nave

Transept facade

Choir

SPIRE AND TRANSEPT ROOF, CATHEDRAL OF NOTRE DAME DE PARIS, FRANCE, c.1163-1250

Ridge

Common rafter

Architrave of window zone, also acting as collar-beam

Principal

Attached baluster

Attached column

Strut

Raised surface

Hammer-post

Bevelled edge

Arched brace

Wooden panel

Hammer-beam

Gothic window tracery

Collar-beam decorated with pearl motif

Gothic window

Arched brace

Bracket

Brace

Impost

TRUSS OF HAMMER-BEAM ROOF, THE UPPER FRATER (LATER BLACKFRIARS' PLAYHOUSE), LONDON, BRITAIN, PROBABLY 14TH CENTURY

TYPICAL GOTHIC FEATURES

FLYING BUTTRESS OVER SIDE AISLES, MILAN CATHEDRAL, ITALY, C.1385-1485

GARGOYLE, HORSLEY CHURCH, DERBYSHIRE, BRITAIN, C.1450

HAMMER-BEAM ROOF, CHURCH OF ST. BOTOLPH, TRUNCH, NORFOLK, BRITAIN, 1360-1380

Rafter

Straight brace

Beam

Gable

Round arch

Pinnacle

Oculus

Blind trefoil

Lancet arch

Trefoil arch

Cusp

Quatrefoil

Colonette

Pointed arch

Lesene

Lancet arch

Balustrade

Mullion

Triangular cornice

Cornice with chamfered edge

Geometrical tracery

Trefoil arch

Balustrade

Stud

Upper collar

Scissor brace

Ridge-board

Principal rafter

Common rafter

Vertical strut

Intermediate collar

Raised valley-rafter

Beam

Jack-rafter

Clasped purlin

Queen-post

Lower collar

King-post

Scissor-beam

Tie-beam

Passing brace

Octahedral spire

Roof truss of nave and transept

Renaissance 1

THE RENAISSANCE was a European movement – lasting roughly from the 14th century to the mid-17th century – in which the arts and sciences underwent great changes. In architecture, these changes were marked by a return to the classical forms and proportions of ancient Roman buildings. The Renaissance originated in Italy, and the buildings most characteristic of its style can be found there, such as the Palazzo Strozzi shown here. Mannerism is a branch of the Renaissance style that distorts the classical forms; an example is the Laurentian Library staircase. As the Renaissance style spread to other European countries, many of its features were incorporated into the local architecture; for example, the Château de Montal in France (see pp. 476-477) incorporates aedicules (tabernacles).

FACADE ON TO PIAZZA, PALAZZO STROZZI

Crowning cornice

Arch window

Round arch

Light

Rustication

Arched doorway

Rectangular window

SIDE VIEW OF PALAZZO STROZZI, FLORENCE, ITALY, 1489 (BY G. DA SANGALLO, B. DA MAIANO, AND CRONACA)

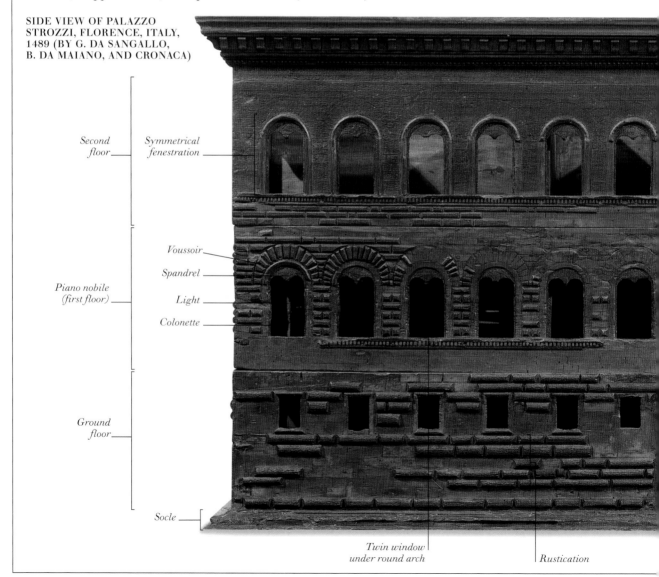

Second floor

Symmetrical fenestration

Piano nobile (first floor)

Voussoir

Spandrel

Light

Colonette

Ground floor

Socle

Twin window under round arch

Rustication

DETAILS FROM ITALIAN RENAISSANCE BUILDINGS

PANEL FROM DRUM OF DOME,
FLORENCE CATHEDRAL, 1420-1436

COFFERING IN DOME,
PAZZI CHAPEL,
FLORENCE, 1429-1461

STAIRCASE,
LAURENTIAN LIBRARY,
FLORENCE, 1559

PORTICO, VILLA ROTUNDA,
VICENZA, 1567-1569

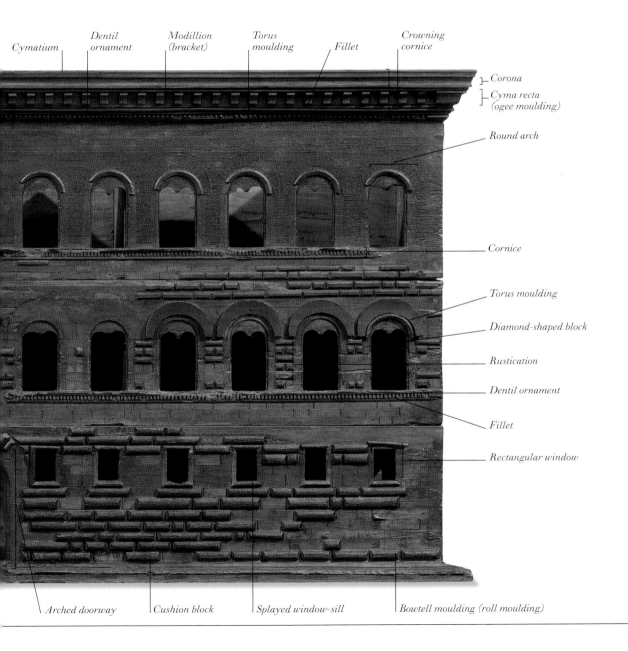

Cymatium

Dentil ornament

Modillion (bracket)

Torus moulding

Fillet

Crowning cornice

Corona

Cyma recta (ogee moulding)

Round arch

Cornice

Torus moulding

Diamond-shaped block

Rustication

Dentil ornament

Fillet

Rectangular window

Arched doorway

Cushion block

Splayed window-sill

Bowtell moulding (roll moulding)

Renaissance 2

**DETAILS FROM
EUROPEAN
RENAISSANCE
BUILDINGS**

STONE WALL, QUOINS,
AND SHELL DECORATION,
CASA DE LAS CONCHAS,
SALAMANCA, SPAIN, 1475-1483

SPIRAL-STAIRCASE
TOWER, CHATEAU DE
BLOIS, FRANCE, 1514-1530

CONICAL DOME, CHATEAU
DE CHAMBORD, FRANCE,
1519-1547

PAIR OF CHIMNEY-STACKS, PALAIS
DE FONTAINEBLEAU, FRANCE, FROM 1528

Chimney-stack

Ridge of
half-round tiles

Pitched roof

Finial

Medallion

Pinnacle

Foliated volute with
dolphin head

Gable

Head-shaped
keystone

Dormer window

Frieze with
shell-pattern
decoration

Finial

Ionic capital with
head-shaped
decoration

Putto holding
candelabrum

Blind pediment

Grotesque
figure

Medallion with
bust of Robert
de Montal

Lesene decorated
with paterae

Frieze decorated
with sculptural
wreaths, tendrils, and
grotesque figures

Lesene

Pedestal

Dado

Plinth   Cornice   Architrave   Portal   Pilaster

Hipped roof

Conical spire
of turret

Fish-scale tile

Belvedere

Keystone
decorated
with scroll
ornament

Cornice
decorated with
fascias and an
ogee moulding

Rectangular
window

Transom

Aedicule
(tabernacle)

Double pilaster

Mullion

Shell

Concave,
arched niche

Small pier
decorated
with
statuette in
concave
niche

Cornice

Frieze with
scroll motif

Pseudo-Corinthian
capital

NORTH-WING STAIRCASE, CHATEAU DE MONTAL

Hipped roof
Conical spire
Eaves with oversailing fascias and fillets
Turret
Loophole
Cornice with fascias and ogee mouldings
Rib vault
Column
Conical corbel
Second-floor landing
First-floor landing
Flight of stairs
Lesene
Pier supporting flight of stairs
Handrail
Pier supporting first-floor landing
Riser
Tread

CAMPANILE, CHURCH OF ST. EUSTACHE, PARIS, FRANCE, 1532-1640

Weather-vane
Orb
Fish-scale tile
Hemispherical dome
Semicircular torus moulding
Weathering
Fillet
Ogee moulding
Plain fascia
Small architrave
Archivolt
Plain fascia
Volute
Cavetto moulding
Emphasized keystone
Capital
Cincture
Fillet
Zinc plating
Square pillar

GLOBE THEATRE, LONDON, BRITAIN, 1599

Balustrade
Thatched roof
Loft used as storage room
Window stage
Outer wall
Railing
Post supporting bay window
Upper-gallery support
Stage-door
Standing room
Bench
Round pillar (stage-post)
Square, carved base
Balcony stage
Stage cover
Ornamental panelling
Hipped roof
Turret
Pitched roof
Timber-framed hut, housing windlass
Music gallery
Light curtain
Ornamental panelling with concave brace decoration
Door to dressing-rooms
Box (gentlemen's room)
Upper gallery (twopenny gallery)
Middle gallery
Lower gallery
Partition separating galleries from boxes
Study (inner stage) with traverse (crossing)
Platform stage
Low balustrade
Paling
Door to tiring-house

Baroque and neoclassical 1

THE BAROQUE STYLE EVOLVED IN THE EARLY 17TH CENTURY in Rome. It is characterized by curved outlines and ostentatious decoration, as can be seen in the Italian church details (right). The baroque style was particularly widely favoured in Italy, Spain, and Germany. It was also adopted in Britain and France, but with adaptations. The British architects Sir Christopher Wren and Nicholas Hawksmoor, for example, used baroque features – such as the concave walls of St. Paul's Cathedral and the curved buttresses of the Church of St. George in the East (see pp. 480-481) – but they did so with restraint. Similarly, the curved buttresses and volutes of the Parisian Church of St. Paul-St. Louis are relatively plain. In the second half of the 17th century, a distinct classical style (known as neoclassicism) developed in northern Europe as a reaction to the excesses of baroque. Typical of this new style were churches such as the Madeleine (a proposed facade is shown below), as well as secular buildings such as the Cirque Napoleon (opposite) and the buildings of the British architect Sir John Soane (see pp. 482-483). In early 18th-century France, an extremely lavish form of baroque developed, known as rococo. The balcony from Nantes (see pp. 482-483) with its twisted ironwork and head-shaped corbels is typical of this style.

DETAILS FROM ITALIAN BAROQUE CHURCHES

SCROLLED BUTTRESS, CHURCH OF ST. MARIA DELLA SALUTE, VENICE, 1631-1682

STATUE OF THE ECSTASY OF ST. THERESA, CHURCH OF ST. MARIA DELLA VITTORIA, ROME, 1645-1652

PROPOSED FACADE, THE MADELEINE (NEOCLASSICAL), PARIS, FRANCE, 1764 (BY P. CONTANT D'IVRY)

CIRQUE NAPOLEON (NEOCLASSICAL), PARIS, FRANCE, 1852 (BY J.I. HITTORFF)

EXTERIOR

Rectangular panel

Small polyhedral roof

Attached colonette

Polyhedral iron roof

Projecting entablature

Palmette

Sculpted frieze

Cornice

Pedestal

Smooth, vertical rustication

Projecting pedestal

Statue of Amazon on horseback

Hanging wreath

Eagle carrying festoons

Dado (die)

Plinth

Smooth rustication

INTERIOR

King-post

Statue of Minerva

Tie-beam

Orb

Brace

Polyhedral lantern

Painted inner roof

Strut

Straight brace

Roll moulding

Projecting entablature

Crest

Projecting socle

Outer wall

Attached Corinthian column

Frieze painted with scenes from classical mythology

Circle (auditorium)

Finial with cavetto moulding

Foliated panel

Transverse arch

Window hood-mould

Crowning cornice

Fascia

Volute

Dentil

Barrel vault

Raised window jamb

Clerestory level

Rectangular door leading to roofed space

Groin vault

Curved buttress

Gallery level

Semi-parabolic curve

Short pilaster

Modillion (bracket)

Semicircular arched window

Pier-shaped pinnacle

Cornice

Corinthian capital

Architrave decorated with oversailing fascias

Gallery

Cornice

Depressed arch

Foliated frieze

Small cupola

Balustrade

Pendentive

Oeil-de-boeuf ("ox-eye") window

Keystone decorated with scroll ornament

Archivolt

Cornice

Archivolt decorated with plain fascias

Formeret (wall rib)

Window jamb

Arcade level

Arcade

Round arch

Window-sill

Outer wall

Buttress

Round arch

Re-entrant corner

Base

Doorway connecting chapels

Socle

Side chapels

Main vessel

Side chapels

NAVE, CHURCH OF ST. PAUL-ST. LOUIS (FRENCH BAROQUE), PARIS, FRANCE, FROM 1627 (BY E. MARTELLANGE)

Baroque and neoclassical 2

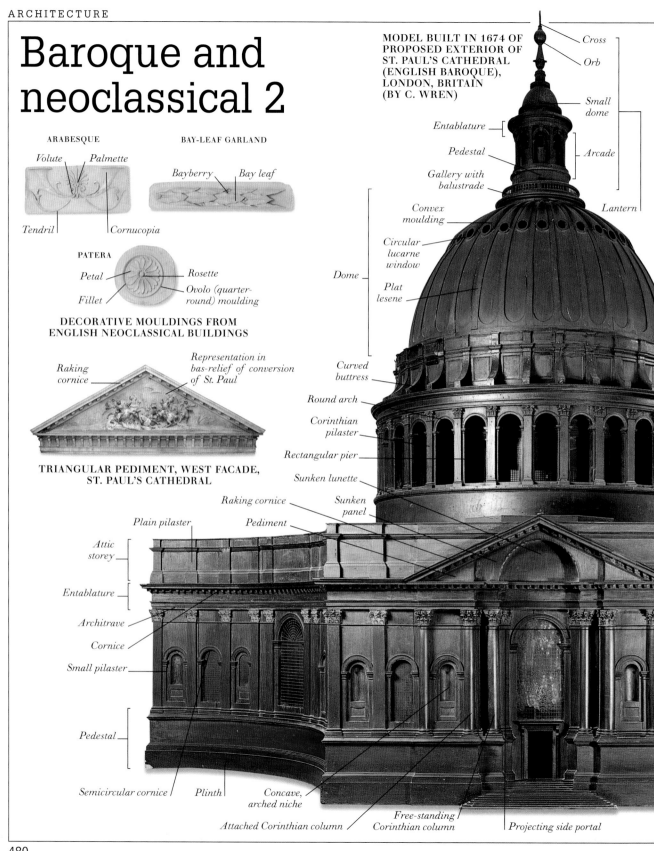

ARABESQUE

Volute
Palmette
Tendril
Cornucopia

BAY-LEAF GARLAND

Bayberry
Bay leaf

PATERA

Petal
Rosette
Fillet
Ovolo (quarter-round) moulding

DECORATIVE MOULDINGS FROM ENGLISH NEOCLASSICAL BUILDINGS

Raking cornice
Representation in bas-relief of conversion of St. Paul

TRIANGULAR PEDIMENT, WEST FACADE, ST. PAUL'S CATHEDRAL

MODEL BUILT IN 1674 OF PROPOSED EXTERIOR OF ST. PAUL'S CATHEDRAL (ENGLISH BAROQUE), LONDON, BRITAIN (BY C. WREN)

Cross
Orb
Small dome
Entablature
Pedestal
Gallery with balustrade
Arcade
Lantern
Convex moulding
Circular lucarne window
Dome
Plat lesene
Curved buttress
Round arch
Corinthian pilaster
Rectangular pier
Sunken lunette
Sunken panel
Raking cornice
Pediment
Plain pilaster
Attic storey
Entablature
Architrave
Cornice
Small pilaster
Pedestal
Semicircular cornice
Plinth
Concave, arched niche
Attached Corinthian column
Free-standing Corinthian column
Projecting side portal

CHURCH OF ST. GEORGE IN THE EAST (ENGLISH BAROQUE), LONDON, BRITAIN, 1714-1734 (BY N. HAWKSMOOR)

SOUTH SIDE

WEST FACADE

Fluted, circular pinnacle

Fluted capital

Plain buttress

Urn

Sunken panel

Round-arched window

Oeil-de-boeuf ("ox-eye") window

Lateral pilaster-strip

Semicircular crypt-window

Pierced parapet

Semicircular window

Platband

Octahedral dome

Triple keystone

Cornice

Plain pedestal

Square post

Label mould

Octahedral turret

Plain frieze

East pediment

Semicircular apse

Emphasized keystone

Emphasized quoin

Side entrance

Steeple

Cornice

Octahedral lantern

Square stone block

Three-tier belfry

Pepper-pot lantern

Broken pediment

Ionic capital

Stepped archivolt

Parapet

Set-back buttress

Cornice decorated with ogee moulding and fascias

Finial

Volute

Raking cornice

Continuous hood-mould

Triple band

Platband

Curved buttress

Dog-leg staircase set in oval stone walls

Ionic twin columns

Attic of drum

Drum

Arcade

Pedestal

Stepped tetrahedral roof

Urn

Entablature

Rectangular window

Statuette

Twin columns

Cruciform pedestal

Circular lucarne window

Triangular lesene

Stepped cornice

Lantern

Dome

Cornice

Raking cornice of facade pediment

Dentil ornament

Frieze

Corinthian capital

Corinthian twin pilasters

Dado

Round-arched window

Concave wall

Re-entrant

Doorway

Emphasized keystone

Architrave

Crepidoma (stepped base)

Rectangular vestibule

Corinthian capital

Baroque and neoclassical 3

DETAILS FROM BAROQUE, NEOCLASSICAL, AND ROCOCO BUILDINGS

PORTICO, THE VYNE, HAMPSHIRE, BRITAIN, 1654 (NEOCLASSICAL)

GILT IRONWORK FROM SCREEN, PALAIS DE VERSAILLES, FRANCE, 1669-1674 (FRENCH BAROQUE)

WINDOW, PALAZZO STANGA, CREMONA, ITALY, EARLY 18TH CENTURY (ROCOCO)

ATLAS (MALE CARYATID), UPPER BELVEDERE, VIENNA, AUSTRIA, 1721 (GERMAN-STYLE BAROQUE)

BALCONY, NANTES, FRANCE, 1730-1740 (ROCOCO)

MASONRY OF A NICHE IN THE ROTUNDA (NEOCLASSICAL), BANK OF ENGLAND, LONDON, BRITAIN, 1794 (BY J. SOANE)

Scoop-pattern concave moulding

Keystone

Frieze

Spandrel

Semi-dome

Voussoir

Rotunda wall

Flat, rectangular niche

Rounded niche

Flat, square niche

CORNER OF THE NEW STATE PAPER OFFICE (NEOCLASSICAL), LONDON, BRITAIN, 1830-1831 (BY J. SOANE)

Classical-style entablature

Cornice

Frieze

Architrave

Pantile (S-shaped roofing tile)

Fascia

Eaves

Curved corbel

Scroll-shaped corbel

Second-floor window

Smooth rustication

Cornice

Drip-cap

Cornice

Frieze

Window architrave

Window jamb

First-floor window

Window-sill in the form of a frieze

Ground-floor window

Splayed window-sill

Vermiculated rustication

TYRINGHAM HOUSE (NEOCLASSICAL), BUCKINGHAMSHIRE, BRITAIN, 1793-1797 (BY J. SOANE)

ROOF LEVEL (ATTIC LEVEL)

Space for illumination above unroofed central hall

Chimney-stack

Space above unroofed main staircase

Oculus illuminating secondary staircase

Flat roof

Parapet rail

Balustrade

Baluster

Cornice

Attic storey of convex portico

Cornice

FIRST-FLOOR LEVEL (CHAMRER FLOOR)

Upper level of central hall, open to floor below

Main staircase

Secondary staircase

Abacus

Pilaster capital

Attached Tuscan twin pilasters

Window-sill

Triangular pilaster

First-floor storey of convex portico

Bow front

GROUND-FLOOR LEVEL (PRINCIPAL FLOOR)

Withdrawing-room

Central hall

Library and breakfast-room

Main staircase

Water-closet (toilet)

Secondary staircase

Eating-room

Segmented lintel course

Band incised with Greek-style fret ornament

Window-sill

Window architrave

Window jamb

Base

Basement

Plinth

Horizontal rustication

Vestibule (entrance hall)

Ground-floor storey of convex portico

FACADE OF TYRINGHAM HOUSE

Chimney-stack

Voussoir

Basement window

Entrance door

Circular entrance steps

Rail

Baluster

Parapet

Balustrade

Cornice

Entablature

Capital

Shaft

Ionic column

Base

PROSTYLE COLONNADE

483

Arches and vaults

ARCHES ARE CURVED STRUCTURES used to bridge spans and to support the weight of upper parts of buildings, such as domes, as in St. Paul's Cathedral (below) and the antique temple (opposite). The voussoirs (wedge-shaped blocks) that form an arch (right) support each other and convert the downward force of the weight of the building into an outward force. This outward force is in turn transferred to buttresses, piers, or abutments. A vault is an arched roof or ceiling. There are four main types of vault (opposite). A barrel vault is a single vault, semicircular in cross-section; a groin vault consists of two barrel vaults intersecting at right-angles; a rib vault is a groin vault reinforced by ribs; and a fan vault is a rib vault in which the ribs radiate from the springing point (where the arch begins) like a fan.

PARTS OF AN ARCH

Voussoir · Keystone · Crown · Abutment
Keystone
Abutment
Extrados
Haunch
Abutment · Intrados (soffit) · Springing point · Span
Intrados (soffit)
Impost
Abutment

FRONT · **SIDE**

ARCHES AND BASE OF DOME, ST. PAUL'S CATHEDRAL, LONDON, BRITAIN, 1675-1710 (BY C. WREN)

Inner dome
Pilaster
Base
Colonnade
Passageway
Cornice
Pendentive
Opening to passageway
Pedestal of outer dome
"Whispering Gallery"
Upper arch (concealing difference in heights between main arch and minor arches)
Triangular buttress
Moulded bracket
Round arch
Extrados
Intrados (soffit)
Springing point
Impost
Semi-dome
Upper barrel-vaulted passage opening on to side aisle
Barrel vault
Abutment
Passage leading to side aisle
Strut built into masonry to strengthen pier (added in the 20th century)
Minor arch leading to side aisle
Main arch leading to nave
Pier
Minor arch

TYPES OF ARCH

HORSESHOE ARCH (MOORISH ARCH), GREAT MOSQUE, CORDORA, SPAIN, 785

BASKET ARCH (SEMI-ELLIPTICAL ARCH), PALATINE CHAPEL, AIX-LA-CHAPELLE, FRANCE, 790-798

TUDOR ARCH, TOWER OF LONDON, BRITAIN, C.1086-1097

LANCET ARCH, WESTMINSTER ABBEY, LONDON, BRITAIN, 1503-1519

TREFOIL ARCH, BEVERLI MINSTER, YORKSHIRE, BRITAIN, C.1300

TYPES OF VAULT

Transverse rib

Temporary brace

Horizontal abutment

Temporary structure used to centre vault

BARREL VAULT (TUNNEL VAULT; WAGON VAULT)

Barrel vault

Voussoir

Right-angled intersection

Groin

GROIN VAULT

Transverse ridge-rib

Longitudinal ridge-rib

Transverse arch

Diagonal rib

RIB VAULT

Tierceron (secondary rib)

Ridge-rib

Springing point

Concave-sided lozenge

Panel

FAN VAULT

ENGLISH BOND BRICKWORK OF GROIN VAULT AND RIB VAULT

Right-angled intersection

Groin

Header

Stretcher

Cell of barrel vault

Springing point

EXTRADOS OF GROIN VAULT

Stretcher

Header

Cell

Extrados of diagonal rib

Springing point

EXTRADOS OF RIB VAULT

INTERIOR DECORATION OF COFFERED VAULT

Compass

Square

Hammer

Coffer (square sunken panel)

Chamfered edge

Arris moulding

Mason's tools

COMPOSITE MODEL OF ANTIQUE FRENCH TEMPLE

Coved dome

Lesene

Series of plain fascias

Re-entrant angle

Cavetto moulding

Fillet

Cornice

Plain frieze

Architrave

Ionic capital

Chamfered corner

Keystone decorated with scroll

Plain Ionic column

Shaft

Scotia

Plinth

Dado

Base

Pedestal of lantern

Archivolt decorated with plain fascias

Abutment

Dentil

Round arch

Cornice

Horizontal band

Twisted vertical band

Naos (celia)

Intercolumniation

Lantern

Coved dome

Pedestal of dome

Entablature

Fluted Ionic column

Pedestal of column

Ionic column with twisted vertical bands (wreaths) and horizontal bands

Domes

A DOME IS A CONVEX ROOF. Domes are categorized according to the shapes of both the base and the section through the centre of the dome. The base may be circular, square, or polygonal (many-sided), depending on the plan of the drum (the walls on which the dome rests). The section of a dome may be the same shape as any arch (see pp. 484-485). Various types of dome are illustrated here: a hemispherical dome, which has a circular base and a semicircular section; a saucer dome, which has a circular base and a segmental (less than a semicircle) section; a polyhedral dome, which is a dome on a polygonal base whose sides meet at the top of the dome; and an onion dome, which has a circular or polygonal base and an ogee-shaped section. Many domes have a lantern (a turret with windows) to provide light inside.

LANTERN AND UPPER DOME TIMBERING, ST. PAUL'S CATHEDRAL

DOME TIMBERING, CHURCH OF THE SORBONNE, PARIS, FRANCE, 1635-1642 (BY J. LEMERCIER)

Ogee-curved dome

Window zone

Pedestal

Floorboard

Ashlar piece

Pin

Short strut

Mortise-and-tenon joint

Principal rafter

Straight brace

Vertical post

Tie-beam

Circular baseplate

Common rafter

Straight brace

Deeply projecting pier buttress

Cornice

Depressedhood-mould

Circular lucarne window

Floor-joist

Hood-mould

Waisted-oval lucarne window

Ogee-curved window-frame

Shaft connecting lantern and church interior

ROOF WITH LANTERN AND ONION DOME

Weathercock

Ellipsoid orb

Keeled lesene

Fish-scaletile

Octahedral base

Sloping roof

Round arch

Attached pillar

Vertical band

Oversailing fascia

Octahedral base of lantern

Onion dome

Oversailing fascia

Tetrahedral capital

Return

Window

Torus

Fillet

Lantern

Tetrahedral roof

REPRESENTATION OF DOME METALLING, CHURCH OF THE SORBONNE

Cross

Orb

Square rib

Inverted ovolo (quarter-round)

Fillet

Plain fascia

Round-arched window

Ovolo (quarter-round)

Fillet

Astragal

Volute

Roll moulding

Buttress

Volute

Cornice

Projecting pier buttress

Inverted demi-heart torus moulding

Waisted-oval lucarne window

Small volute

Gutter

Semicircular torus moulding

Triple lesene

Plain fascia

Fillet

Small roll

Parapet

Lantern

Dome on a circular base

Fish-scale tile

Hood-mould

486

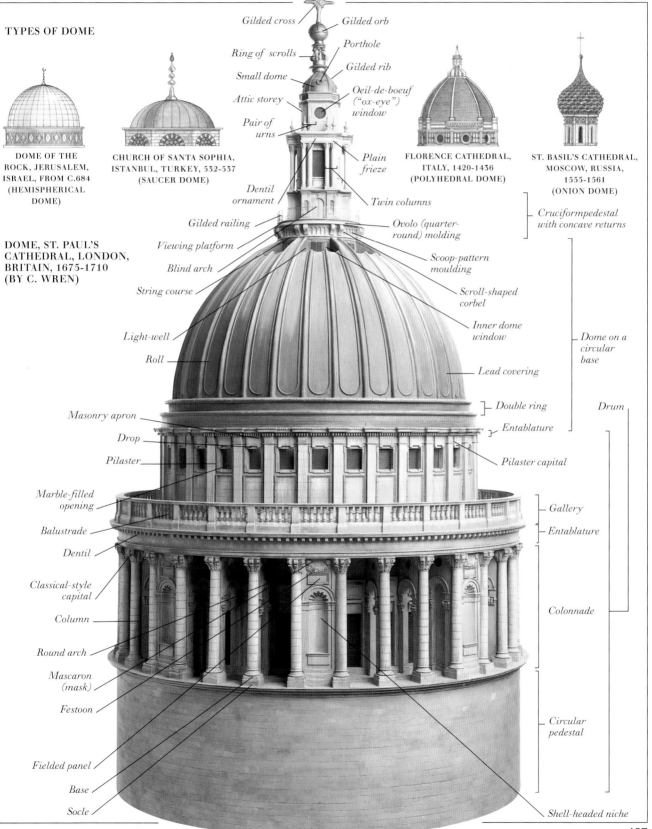

TYPES OF DOME

DOME OF THE
ROCK, JERUSALEM,
ISRAEL, FROM C.684
(HEMISPHERICAL
DOME)

CHURCH OF SANTA SOPHIA,
ISTANBUL, TURKEY, 532-537
(SAUCER DOME)

FLORENCE CATHEDRAL,
ITALY, 1420-1436
(POLYHEDRAL DOME)

ST. BASIL'S CATHEDRAL,
MOSCOW, RUSSIA,
1555-1561
(ONION DOME)

DOME, ST. PAUL'S
CATHEDRAL,
LONDON,
BRITAIN, 1675-1710
(BY C. WREN)

Gilded cross

Gilded orb

Ring of scrolls

Porthole

Small dome

Gilded rib

Attic storey

Oeil-de-boeuf
("ox-eye")
window

Pair of
urns

Plain
frieze

Dentil
ornament

Twin columns

Gilded railing

Ovolo (quarter-
round) molding

Viewing platform

Scoop-pattern
moulding

Blind arch

String course

Scroll-shaped
corbel

Light-well

Inner dome
window

Roll

Lead covering

Masonry apron

Double ring

Drop

Entablature

Pilaster

Pilaster capital

Marble-filled
opening

Gallery

Balustrade

Entablature

Dentil

Classical-style
capital

Column

Colonnade

Round arch

Mascaron
(mask)

Festoon

Circular
pedestal

Fielded panel

Base

Socle

Shell-headed niche

Cruciform pedestal
with concave returns

Dome on a
circular
base

Drum

Islamic buildings

OPUS SECTILE MOSAIC DESIGN

THE ISLAMIC RELIGION was founded by the prophet Mohammed, who was born in Mecca (in present-day Saudi Arabia) about 570 AD. In the following three centuries, Islam spread from Arabia to North Africa and Spain, as well as to India and much of the rest of Asia. The worldwide influence of Islam remains strong today. Common characteristics of Islamic buildings include ogee arches and roofs, onion domes, and walls decorated with carved stone, paintings, inlays, or mosaics. The most important type of Islamic building is the mosque – the place of worship – which generally has a minaret (tower) from which the muezzin (official crier) calls Muslims to prayer. Most mosques have a mihrab (decorative niche) that indicates the direction of Mecca. As figurative art is not allowed in Islam, buildings are ornamented with geometric and arabesque motifs, and inscriptions (frequently Koranic verses).

Bud-like onion dome
Depressed arch surrounding mihrab
Painted roof pavilion
Turkish-crescent finial
Lotus-flower pendentive
Crest
Arabic inscription
Painted minaret with censer (incense burner)
Spandrel
Series of recessed arches
Semi-dome
Arched niche within a niche
Mural resembling tomb
Polyhedral niche
Recessed colonettes

MIHRAB, JAMI MASJID (PRINCIPAL OR CONGREGATIONAL MOSQUE), BIJAPUR, INDIA, c.1636

Shield
Herring-bone pattern
Tablet flower
Spandrel with floral design
Ogee arch
Carved stone
Undulating band
Cusp
Volute
Impost
Capital with stylized floral design
Panel with fret pattern
Jali (latticed screen) with geometrical patterns
Band with Arabic inscriptions praising Allah (God)
Attached colonette

ARCH, THE ALHAMBRA, GRANADA, SPAIN, 1333-1354

Enamelled turquoise earthenware tile
Trigon
Column shaft
Cube with chamfered corners
Polygonal capital
Niche
Enamelled white earthenware tile
Arabesques of stylized plants
Enamelled lapis blue earthenware tile

MIHRAB WITH COLUMN, EL-AINYI MOSQUE, CAIRO, EGYPT, 15TH CENTURY

EXAMPLES OF ISLAMIC MOSAICS, EGYPT AND SYRIA

Star-shaped motif
Triangle of yellow marble
Greek cross of red marble
Rhombus of black marble
Stone band

STAR AND GREEK-CROSS MOSAIC

Mosaic tessellation
Stone
Black marble
Turquoise glass
Tessera (small mosaic piece)

FRET-PATTERN MOSAIC

Greek cross of black and yellow marble
Star-shaped motif
Stone band
Rhombus of red marble

STAR AND GREEK-CROSS MOSAIC

Parallelogram of black marble
Triangle of yellow marble
Rhombus of red marble
Symmetrical quadrilateral of stone
Star-shaped motif

MOSAIC OF HEXAGONS, TRIANGLES, AND SYMMETRICAL QUADRILATERALS

Hexagonal design
Band of black marble
Band of stone

HEXAGON AND BAND MOSAIC

Triangle of turquoise glass
Parallelogram of mother-of-pearl

DANCETTE-PATTERN MOSAIC

Symmetrical quadrilateral of black marble
Triangle of stone
Hexagon of red marble

MOSAIC OF HEXAGONS, TRIANGLES, AND SYMMETRICAL QUADRILATERALS

MARBLE TOMB OF ITIMAD-UD-DAULA, AGRA, INDIA, c.1622-1628

Kalasa finial (finial with orbs)
Padmakosa (lotus petal)
Ogee-curved roof
Chajya (deep eaves)
Domed roof
Parapet decorated with lattice-work
Balcony
Roof pavilion
Cusped arch
Circular top of minaret
Pietra dura inlay (slices of semi-precious stone laid in sockets)
Cornice
Bracket
Spandrel decorated with arabesque
Octahedral base of minaret
Star-pattern inlay
Sandstone plinth
Sandstone parapet decorated with lattice-work
Jali (latticed screen) with geometrical patterns
Depressed entrance arch
Sandstone stairway
Opus sectile mosaic (geometric mosaic) of stone, tile, glass, and enamel

South and east Asia

THE TRADITIONAL ARCHITECTURE of south and east Asia has been
profoundly influenced by the spread from India of Buddhism and Hinduism.
This influence is shown both by the abundance and by the architectural
styles of temples and shrines in the region. Many early Hindu temples
consist of rooms carved from solid rock-faces. However, free-standing
structures began to be built in southern India from about the eighth
century AD. Many were built in the Dravidian style, like the Temple of
Virupaksha (opposite) with its characteristic antarala (terraced tower),
perforated windows, and numerous arches, pilasters, and carvings.
The earliest Buddhist religious monuments were Indian stupas,
which consisted of a single hemispherical dome surmounted by a
chattravali (shaft) and surrounded by railings with ornate gates.
Later Indian stupas and those built elsewhere were sometimes
modified; for example, in Sri Lanka, the dome became bell-shaped,
and was called a dagoba. Buddhist pagodas, such as the Burmese
example (right), are multistoreyed temples, each storey having a
projecting roof. The form of these buildings probably derived from
the yasti (pointed spire) of the stupa. Another feature of many
traditional Asian buildings is their imaginative roof-forms, such
as gambrel (mansard) roofs, and roofs with angle-rafters (below).

DETAILS FROM EAST ASIAN BUILDINGS

**KASUGA-STYLE ROOF WITH
SUMIGI (ANGLE-RAFTERS),
KASUGADO SHRINE OF
ENJOJI, NARA, JAPAN,
12TH-14TH CENTURY**

**TERRACES, TEMPLE OF
HEAVEN, BEIJING, CHINA,
15TH CENTURY**

**GAMBREL (MANSARD) ROOF
WITH UPSWEPT EAVES AND
UNDULATING GABLES,
HIMEJI CASTLE, HIMEJI,
JAPAN, 1608-1609**

**CORNER CAPITAL WITH
ROOF BEAMS, POPCHU-SA
TEMPLE, POPCHU-SA, SOUTH
KOREA, 17TH CENTURY**

**SEVEN-STOREYED
PAGODA IN
BURMESE STYLE,
c.9TH-10TH
CENTURY**

*Gilded
band*

*Gilded iron
hti (crown)*

Dubika (mast)

*Arrow
motif*

*Torus moulding
with spiral
carving*

*Decorative
eaves board*

*Ogee-arched
motif with
decorative
carvings*

*Ogee-arched
motif forming
horn*

Hip-rafter

Pentroof

*Undulating
moulding*

*Engaged
pillar*

*Baluster
finial*

*Arched
entrance*

Balustrade

*Rectangular
window*

Baluster

Pillar

*Straight
brace*

PERFORATED STONE WINDOWS, TEMPLES OF VIRUPAKSHA AND MALLIKARJUNA, PATTADAKAL, INDIA, 8TH CENTURY

Tablet flower

Fret motif

Chain motif

Floral pattern

Leaf

Scroll motif

Sickle motif

Semicircle

DAGOBA STUPA, KANDY, SRI LANKA, c.2ND CENTURY BC- 7TH CENTURY AD

Chattra (umbrella)

Hanging ornament

Chattravali (shaft)

Ring with indentations symbolizing chattras

Ornamental metalwork

Yasti (tee; pointed spire)

Harmika (stylized square railing)

Auda (bell-shaped dome)

Trimala (series of three circular courses)

Circular base

SIDE VIEW AND PLAN VIEW, TEMPLE OF VIRUPAKSHA, PATTADAKAL, INDIA, c.746

Stupica (small stupa) of the Dravidian order

Dravidian finial

Blind chataya arch

Antarala (terraced tower)

Perforated window

Gopuram finial (wagon-like finial)

Bracketed capital

Small gopuram (gate-head)

Parapet

Roll cornice

Niche with statue

Gate

Plan view

Panel with bas-relief carving

Twin pilasters

Pillar

Pradakshina (circumambulatory passage around shrine)

Shrine

Shrine chamber

Niche

Gate

Mandapa (pillared hall)

491

The 19th century

BUILDINGS OF THE 19TH CENTURY are characterized by the use of new materials and by a great diversity of architectural styles. From the end of the 18th century, iron and steel became widely used as alternatives to wood for the framework of buildings, as in the flax-spinning mill shown here. Built in Britain in 1796, this mill exemplifies an architectural style that became common throughout the industrialized world for more than a century. The Industrial Revolution also brought mass-production of building parts – a development that enabled the British architect Sir Joseph Paxton to erect London's Crystal Palace (a building made entirely of iron and glass) in only nine months, ready for the Great Exhibition of 1851. The 19th century saw a widespread revival of older architectural styles. For example, in the USA and Germany, Neo-Greek architecture was fashionable; in Britain and France, Neo-Baroque, Neo-Byzantine, and Neo-Gothic styles (as seen in the Palace of Westminster and Tower Bridge) were dominant.

Cast-iron wall-plate
Machinery space
Cast-iron mortise-and-tenon joint
Inverted T-section cast-iron beam
Segmentally arched brick vault
Paved ground floor
Pitched roof
Ridge
Verge
Gutter
Anchor-joint
Drain-pipe
End flange
Concrete floor
Tapering part of column
Strengthened central column

**FLAX-SPINNING MILL,
SHREWSBURY, BRITAIN,
1796 (BY C. BAGE)**

Multi-gabled roof (ridge and furrow roof)
Ridge
Furrow
Verge
Timber rafter
Cast-iron wall-plate
Gable
Tapering part of column
Segmentally arched brick vault
Cast-iron mortise-and-tenon joint
Tie-rod
Cast-iron cruciform column
Inverted T-section cast-iron beam
Bonded brick wall
Gutter
Drain-pipe
Three courses of stretchers
Course of headers
Course of decorative headers
Cast-iron lattice window
Cast-iron tenon
Anchor-joint
Strengthened central column
Stone foundation
Quoin
Jamb
Gauged arch (segmental arch of tapered bricks)

CLOCK TOWER ("BIG BEN"), PALACE OF WESTMINSTER, LONDON, BRITAIN, 1836-1868 (BY C.BARRY AND A.W.N. PUGIN)

- Finial
- Spire
- Skylight
- Cornice decorated with shields
- Iron railing
- Small orb
- Orb
- Iron tracery
- Dormer window
- Round arch filled with open tracery
- Tetrahedral spire
- Bell chamber
- Balustrade
- Ogee tracery arch filled with trefoil
- Flying buttress
- Pinnacle
- Spandrel
- Octahedral shaft with billet decoration
- Dial
- Cornice
- Moulded corbel
- Star-shaped corner buttress
- Panelled field filled with tracery
- Slender diagonal buttress
- Narrow window
- String course
- Carved panel
- Stepped storeys

DETAILS FROM BUILDINGS IN REVIVALIST STYLES

CUPOLA, MERCHANTS' EXCHANGE, PHILADELPHIA, USA, 1832-1834 (NEO-GREEK)

SCULPTURE AND PEDIMENT, OPERA HOUSE, PARIS, FRANCE, 1861-1874 (NEO-BAROQUE)

DOMED TURRET, WESTMINSTER CATHEDRAL, LONDON, BRITAIN, 1894-1903 (NEO-BYZANTINE)

TOWER BRIDGE, LONDON, BRITAIN, 1886-1894 (BY H. JONES)

- Tetrahedral spire
- Finial
- Spire
- Cornice
- Finial
- High-level footbridge
- Dormer head (gable) filled with blind tracery
- Parapet
- Parapet of balcony
- Octahedral upper turret
- Lattice-work
- Heraldic shield
- Cast-iron tracery
- Cast-iron panelling
- Wedge-shaped corbel
- Archway
- Moulded corbel
- String course
- Drawbridge (bascule)
- Steel brace
- Stone panel
- Circular turret/buttress
- Archway
- Pier

CRYSTAL PALACE EXHIBITION HALL, LONDON, BRITAIN, 1851 (BY J. PAXTON)

- Longitudinal girder
- Window
- Cast-iron ornamental arch-plate
- Arched facade
- Ridge and furrow glass roof-windows
- Crest
- Semicircular barrel vault
- Cast-iron trapezium
- Octahedral column
- Side exit
- Sheet-iron louvre
- Strengthened support
- Entrance

The early 20th century

ARCHITECTURE OF THE EARLY 20TH CENTURY is notable for radical new types of steel-and-glass buildings – particularly skyscrapers – and the widespread use of steel-reinforced concrete. The steel-framed skyscraper was pioneered in Chicago in the 1880s, but did not become widespread until the first decades of the 20th century. As construction techniques were refined, skyscrapers became higher and higher; for example, the Empire State Building (right) of 1929-1931 has 102 storeys. Many buildings of this period were constructed from lightweight concrete slabs, which could be supported by cantilever beams or by pilotis (stilts), as in the Villa Savoye (below). The early 20th century also produced a great variety of architectural styles, some of which are illustrated opposite. Despite their diversity, the styles of this period generally had one thing in common: they were completely new, with few links to past architectural styles. This originality is in marked contrast to 19th-century architecture (see pp. 492-493), much of which was revivalist.

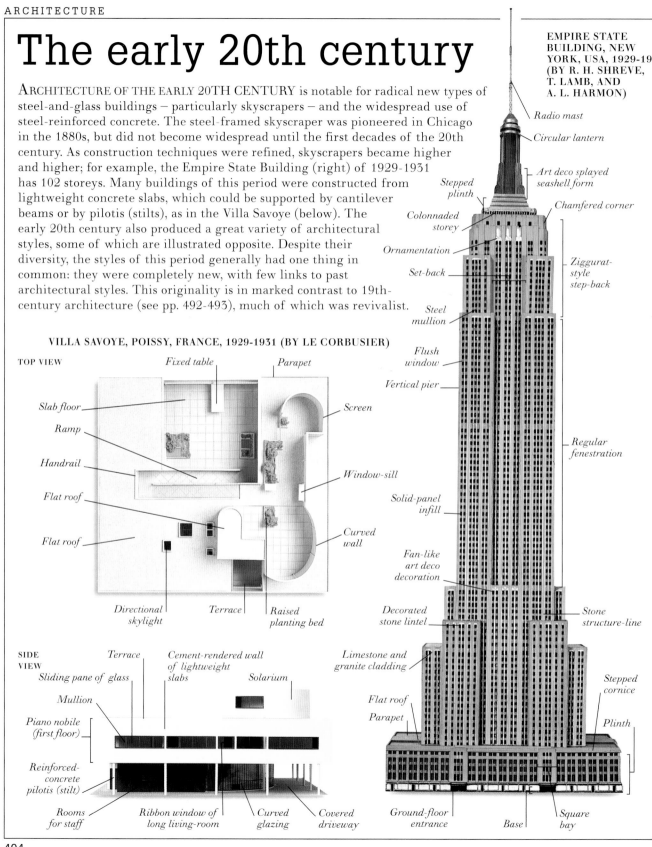

EMPIRE STATE BUILDING, NEW YORK, USA, 1929-19 (BY R. H. SHREVE, T. LAMB, AND A. L. HARMON)

Radio mast

Circular lantern

Art deco splayed seashell form

Stepped plinth

Chamfered corner

Colonnaded storey

Ornamentation

Ziggurat-style step-back

Set-back

Steel mullion

Flush window

Vertical pier

Regular fenestration

Solid-panel infill

Fan-like art deco decoration

Decorated stone lintel

Stone structure-line

Limestone and granite cladding

Flat roof

Parapet

Stepped cornice

Plinth

Ground-floor entrance

Base

Square bay

VILLA SAVOYE, POISSY, FRANCE, 1929-1931 (BY LE CORBUSIER)

TOP VIEW

Fixed table

Parapet

Slab floor

Screen

Ramp

Handrail

Window-sill

Flat roof

Curved wall

Flat roof

Directional skylight

Terrace

Raised planting bed

SIDE VIEW

Terrace

Cement-rendered wall of lightweight slabs

Solarium

Sliding pane of glass

Mullion

Piano nobile (first floor)

Reinforced-concrete pilotis (stilt)

Rooms for staff

Ribbon window of long living-room

Curved glazing

Covered driveway

MIDWAY GARDENS, CHICAGO, USA, 1914 (BY F. L. WRIGHT)

Flagpole

Plain coping-stone

Main floor

Decorated cement frieze

Terrace

Steps

Stage

Orchestra shell

Tiled, shallow pitched roof

Projecting balustrade

Ridge

Ornamental light

Hip

Main pavilion

Arcade

Terrace

Octagonal window

Ornamental sculpture

Flat roof

Stone plinth

Cantilevered, latticed shade

Tiled frieze

Deep-set window

Planting bed

Brick pier

Slit window

Stepped flat-roofs

Terrace

Ornamented coping-stone

EAST SIDE

NORTH SIDE

EARLY 20TH-CENTURY ARCHITECTURAL STYLES

DORMER WINDOW, STUDIO ELVIRA, MUNICH, GERMANY, 1902 (ART NOUVEAU)

AEG TURBINE HALL, BERLIN, GERMANY, 1909 (DEUTSCHER WERKBUND)

ROBIE HOUSE, CHICAGO, USA, 1909-1910 (PRAIRIE STYLE)

GRUNDTVIG CHURCH, COPENHAGEN, DENMARK, 1920 (EXPRESSIONIST)

VERTEX, CHRYSLER BUILDING, NEW YORK, USA, 1928-1930 (ART DECO)

TOWER, TOWN HALL, HILVERSUM, NETHERLANDS, 1930 (DUTCH CUBIST)

CASA DEL FASCIO, COMO, ITALY, 1932-1936 (GRUPPO SEVEN CUBIST)

MOTIF ABOVE DOORWAY, HOOVER FACTORY, LONDON, BRITAIN, 1933 (ART DECO)

495

Modern buildings 1

KAWANA HOUSE, JAPAN, FROM 1987 (BY N. FOSTER)

ARCHITECTURE SINCE ABOUT THE 1950s is generally known as modern architecture. One of its main influences has been functionalism – a belief that a building's function should be apparent in its design. Both the Centre Georges Pompidou (below and opposite) and the Hong Kong and Shanghai Bank (see pp. 498-499) are functionalist buildings: on each, elements of engineering and the building's services are clearly visible on the outside. In the 1980s, some architects rejected functionalism in favour of post-modernism, in which historical styles – particularly neoclassicism – were revived, using modern building materials and techniques. In many modern buildings, walls are made of glass or concrete hung from a frame, as in the Kawana House (right); this type of wall construction is known as curtain walling. Other modern construction techniques include the intricate interlocking of concrete vaults – as in the Sydney Opera House (see pp. 498-499) – and the use of high-tension beams to create complex roof shapes, such as the paraboloid roof of the Church of St. Pierre de Libreville (see pp. 498-499).

Solar panel
Concrete frame
Pile foundation
Raft   *Composite cladding-panel*

SIDE VIEW

Rocker-beam
Curtain walling
Lattice-beam
Floor-beam connection   *Floor*

FRONT VIEW

SERVICES FACADE, CENTRE GEORGES POMPIDOU, PARIS, FRANCE, 1977 (BY R. PIANO AND R. ROGERS)

Metal-faced, fire-resistant panel
Air-conditioning duct
Cooling tower
Water-pipe

Grand gallery level
Main gallery levels
Library level
Administrative level
Mezzanine gallery level
Reception level

Staircase to grand hall   *Electrical plant*   *Water-cooled, fire-resistant column*   *Continuous glazing*   *Tinted glass*   *Services entrance*

PRINCIPAL FACADE, CENTRE GEORGES POMPIDOU

Steel lattice-beam

Main truss

Gerberette (cast-steel rocker-beam)

Suspended fire-resistant glass curtain

Gallery space

External walkway

Electronically operated roller-blind

Cooling tower

Continuous glazing

Terrace

Cradle support for escalator

Cross-bracing

Double fire-escape staircase

Reinforced-concrete and steel floor-plate

Double floor-height

Main entrance

Glazed escalator tube

Node

Water-cooled, fire-resistant steel column

Exposed "plug-in" services

Steel lattice-beam

Dual air-conditioning unit for roof

Elevator

Elevator-motor room

Vertical-duct distribution zone

Metal sandwich-panel (insulating panel)

Gerberette (cast-steel rocker-beam)

Rose connection

Outer tension-column

External steel-lattice mullion

Water-cooled, fire-resistant cross-beam

Double fire-escape staircase

Water storage tank

Cross-bracing

Open gallery floor

Water-pipe

Steel-framed services column

Double cross-bracing

Modern buildings 2

HONG KONG AND SHANGHAI BANK, HONG KONG, 1981-1985 (BY N. FOSTER)

Inverted top-truss

Soffit

Mast

Illuminated fascia

Curved glazing

External maintenance crane

Cockpit

Counterweight

Boom

Circular access platform

Steel column

Sun-shade louvre

Face panel

Mullion

Hanger

Handrail

Composite cladding-panel

Top beam

Outer diagonal beam

Escalator

Outer bottom boom

Inner diagonal beam

Fire-escape staircase

Inner bottom boom

External staircase

Pin joint

Refuge terrace

Double floor-height

Hanger

Full-height glazing

Two-storey stability truss (coathanger truss)

Sun scoop

Flange

Glazed curtain wall

Lightweight, column-free, steel and concrete floor

Vertical, glazed typhoon screen

Glazed soffit

Entrance lobby

Plaza

SOUTH FACADE

Soffit

Helicopter landing-pad

Navigation light

Stepped elevation

Face panel

Horizontal window

Vertical window

External maintenance crane

Cross-bracing

Service shaft

Double floor-height

Sun scoop

10-floor-high atrium

Internal bridge

EAST SIDE

498

CHURCH OF ST. PIERRE, LIBREVILLE, GABON, 1990

Lattice-truss

Cross-bracing

Paraboloid roof

Rafter

Concave curve

Convex curve

Tension member

Mullion

Plate connector

Eaves

Rendered, splayed outer wall

Entrance

Full-height glazing

Bolt

Tinted glass

Circular steps

Reinforced plinth

Concrete shoe

Inner diagonal beam

Beam housing

Pin joint

Glulam wall-plate (glued and laminated wall-plate)

Secondary hall

Main hall

OPERA HOUSE, SYDNEY, AUSTRALIA, 1959-1973 (BY J. UTZON)

Vaults with curved ribs

Precast concrete rib

Glass wall

Mullion

Bronze glazing bar

Main hall

Precast concrete rib-segment

Ridge

Continuous glazing

Solid podium

Ribbon window

HARBOUR FACADE

Vault roof constructed of chevron-shaped, precast tiles

Vault over restaurant

Staircase

Solid podium

Pink cladding

Pink granite-aggregate paving slab

Main line of support

Awning

Staircase

Terrace

WEST SIDE

MUSIC

Musical notation

MUSICAL NOTATION IS ANY METHOD by which sounds are written down so that they can be read and performed by others. The present-day conventional system of notation uses a five-line stave (staff) – divided by vertical lines into sections known as bars – on which notes, rests, clefs, key signatures, time signatures, accidentals, and other symbols are written. A note indicates the duration of a sound and, according to its position on the stave, its pitch. Notes can be arranged on the stave in order of pitch to form a scale. A silence in the music is indicated by a rest. The clef, which is placed at the begininng of a stave, fixes the pitch. The key signature, which is placed after the clef, indicates the key. The time signature, placed after the key signature, shows the number of beats in a bar. Accidentals are used to indicate the raising or lowering of the pitch of a note.

ELEMENTS OF MUSICAL NOTATION

CLEFS

Treble (or G) clef

Alto (or C) clef

Bass (or F) clef

TIME SIGNATURES

Six-eight time

Three-four time

Stave (staff)

NOTES

Breve

Minim

Quaver

Semibreve

Crotchet

Semiquaver

RESTS

Breve rest

Minim rest

Quaver rest

Semibreve rest

Crotchet rest

Semiquaver rest

SCALE

C D E F G A B C

ACCIDENTALS

Sharp

Natural

Double sharp

Flat

Double flat

Key signature

Moderately fast and quiet

Tie (bind)

Repeat the previous bar

Treble clef

Bass clef

Four-four time (common time)

Key signature

Alto clef

Treble voice

Alto voice

Tenor voice

Bass voice

Organ part for right hand

Organ part for left hand

Organ pedal line

Instruments of the orchestra written in Italian

Bar line

Bass clef

Bar

Crotchet

FLUTES

OBOES

CLARINETS IN A

BASSOONS

Accidental sharp

Tie (bind)

Accidental natural

Unison (both clarinets play the same note)

Semibreve

Crotchet

HORNS IN D

TRUMPETS IN D

TIMPANI IN D AND A

FIRST AND SECOND VIOLINS

VIOLAS

VOICES

CELLOS

Semibreve rest

Accidental sharp

Slur

Piano (play softly)

Pianissimo (play very softly)

Crotchet rest

ORGAN

DOUBLE BASSES

Orchestras

AN ORCHESTRA IS A GROUP of musicians that plays music written for a specific combination of instruments. The number and type of instruments included in the orchestra depends on the style of music being played. The modern orchestra (also known as a symphony orchestra) is made up of four sections of instruments – stringed, woodwind, brass, and percussion. The stringed section consists of violins, violas, cellos (violoncellos), double basses, and sometimes a harp (see pp. 510-511). The main instruments of the woodwind section are flutes, oboes, clarinets, and bassoons – the piccolo, cor anglais, bass clarinet, saxophone, and double bassoon (contrabassoon) can also be included if the music requires them (see pp. 508-509). The brass section usually consists of horns, trumpets, trombones, and the tuba (see pp. 506-507). The main instruments of the percussion section are the timpani (see pp. 518-519). The side drum, bass drum, cymbals, tambourine, triangle, tubular bells, xylophone, vibraphone, tam-tam (gong), castanets, and maracas can also be included in the percussion section (see pp. 516-517). The musicians are usually arranged in a semi-circle – strings spread along the front, woodwind and brass in the centre, and percussion at the back. A conductor stands in front of the musicians and controls the tempo (speed) of the music and the overall balance of the sound, ensuring that no instruments are too loud or too soft in relation to the others.

TUBULAR BELLS

TAM-TAM (GONG)

VIBRAPHONE

XYLOPHONE

CASTANETS

TAMBOURINE

MARACAS

TRIANGLE

TRUMPETS

HORNS

CLARINETS

BASS CLARINET

SAXOPHONE

PICCOLO

HARP

SECOND VIOLINS

FIRST VIOLINS

CYMBALS

SIDE DRUM

BASS DRUM

TIMPANI

EXAMPLE OF A LAYOUT OF THE
INSTRUMENTS FOR A MODERN
(SYMPHONY) ORCHESTRA

TROMBONES

TUBA

BASSOONS

DOUBLE BASSOON

DOUBLE BASSES

FLUTES

OBOES

COR ANGLAIS

VIOLAS

Score

CONDUCTOR'S
STAND

CELLOS

Brass instruments

BRASS INSTRUMENTS ARE WIND INSTRUMENTS that are made of metal, usually brass. Although they appear in many different shapes and sizes, all brass instruments have a mouthpiece, a length of hollow tube, and a flared bell. The mouthpiece of a brass instrument may be cup-shaped, as in the cornet, or cone-shaped, as in the horn. The tube may be wide or narrow, mainly conical, as in the horn and tuba, or mainly cylindrical, as in the trumpet and trombone. The sound of a brass instrument is made by the player's lips vibrating against the mouthpiece, so that the air vibrates in the tube. By changing lip tension, the player can vary the vibrations and produce notes of different pitches. The range of notes produced by a brass instrument can be extended by means of a valve system. Most brass instruments, such as the trumpet, have piston valves that divert the air in the instrument along an extra piece of tubing (known as a valve slide) when pressed down. The total length of the tube is increased and the pitch of the note produced is lowered. Instead of valves, the trombone has a movable slide that can be pushed away from or drawn toward the player. The sound of a brass instrument can also be changed by inserting a mute into the bell of the instrument.

BUGLE

Brace

Tuning slide

Counterbalancing weight

SIMPLIFIED DIAGRAM SHOWING HOW A PISTON VALVE SYSTEM WORKS

Piston valves at rest

Air bypasses piston valves

PISTON VALVES AT REST

First piston valve pressed down

Second and third piston valves at rest

Air diverted through first valve slide

PISTON VALVE PRESSED DOWN

TRUMPET

Finger button

First piston valve

Spring returns piston valve to rest position

Second piston valve

Third piston valve

Holes divert air into valve slides

Little finger support

Music stand holder

Narrow, cylindrical tube

Flared bell

Cup-shaped mouthpiece

Mouthpiece receiver

Tuning slide

First valve slide

Tuning slide water key

First valve slide thumb hook

Second valve slide

Third valve slide finger ring

Third valve slide

Third valve slide water key

SECTIONS OF A TROMBONE

Flared bell

EXAMPLES OF MUTES

CUP MUTE

TENOR MUTE

ALTO MUTE

Inner tube

Outer tube of slide

Cup-shaped mouthpiece

Mouthpiece brace held by the left hand

Slide brace held by the right hand

Narrow, cylindrical tube

Water key

TROMBONE

Flared bell

Outer tube of slide

Cup-shaped mouthpiece

FLUGELHORN

Piston valves

Little finger support

Flared bell

Cup-shaped mouthpiece

Valve slide

Conical tube

HORN

Cone-shaped mouthpiece

Finger key

Rotary valves

Narrow, conical bore

Large, flared bell

CORNET

Piston valves

Little finger support

Flared bell

Cup-shaped mouthpiece

Bore widens after valves

Valve slide

TUBA

Large, flared bell

Piston valves

Cup-shaped mouthpiece

Valve slide

Wide, conical tube

Woodwind instruments

WOODWIND INSTRUMENTS ARE wind instruments that are generally made of wood, although some are made of metal or plastic. The sound of a woodwind instrument is produced by the vibration of air in a hollow tube. The air is made to vibrate by blowing across a blow hole – as in the flute and piccolo – or by blowing through a single reed – as in the clarinet and saxophone – or a double reed – as in the bassoon, cor anglais, and oboe. The pitch of a woodwind instrument can be changed by opening or closing holes cut into the tube of the instrument.

Bell

Double reed

Bell joint

Curved crook

Cylindrical, metal tube

Conical, wooden tube

Tenor joint

Double reed

Key

Body joint

Conical, wooden tube

Upper joint

Crook

Blow hole

Head joint

Bass joint

Key

Lip plate

PICCOLO

Double reed

Foot joint

Key

Right-hand rest

Cork

Finger hole

Butt

Key

Key

Upper joint

Mouthpiece with single reed

Middle joint

Key

Ligature

Middle joint

Body joint

Barrel joint

BASSOON

Finger hole

Cylindrical, metal tube

Cylindrical, wooden tube

Bell joint

Conical, wooden tube

Lip plate

Head joint

Key

Upper joint

Bulb-shaped bell

COR ANGLAIS

Blow hole

Bell joint

FLUTE

Flared bell

OBOE

Middle joint

Bell joint

Flared bell

CLARINET

TENOR SAXOPHONE

Mouthpiece with single reed

Conical, metal tube

Upturned, flared bell

SECTIONS OF A TENOR SAXOPHONE

Mouthpiece with single reed

Ligature

Neck

Upper octave key

Key rod

KEYS FOR THE LEFT THUMB

Lower octave key

Key

Key

KEYS FOR THE LEFT HAND

Key rod

Key

Mother-of-pearl touchpiece (button)

KEYS FOR THE RIGHT HAND

Key

Key rod

MAIN BODY OF SAXOPHONE

Conical, metal tube

Key rod

KEYS FOR THE LEFT PALM

KEYS FOR THE RIGHT PALM

Tonehole

Upturned, flared bell

Mother-of-pearl touchpiece (button)

Pad made up of layers of felt and cork

Roller

Key guard

Tonehole

Cup

Key rod

Key

Metal centre of pad reflects sound

Key guard

KEYS FOR THE RIGHT LITTLE FINGER

Padded key

KEYS FOR THE LEFT LITTLE FINGER

Key guard

Stringed instruments

STRINGED INSTRUMENTS PRODUCE SOUND by the vibration of stretched strings. This may be done by drawing a bow across the strings, as in the violin; or by plucking the strings, as in the harp and guitar (see pp. 512-513). The four modern members of the bowed string family are the violin, viola, cello (violoncello), and double bass. Each consists of a hollow, wooden body, a long neck, and four strings. The bow is a wooden stick with horsehair stretched across its length. The vibrations made by drawing the bow across the strings are transmitted to the hollow body, and this itself vibrates, amplifying and enriching the sound produced. The harp consists of a set of strings of different lengths stretched across a wooden frame. The strings are plucked by the player's thumbs and fingers — except the little finger of each hand — which produces vibrations that are amplified by the harp's soundboard. The pitch of the note produced by any stringed instrument depends on the length, weight, and tension of the string. A shorter, lighter, or tighter string gives a higher note.

Scroll eye

Scroll

Peg-hole

Ebony tuning-pegs

Neck made of maple wood

Strings

Fingerboard

Rounded shoulder

Belly (soundboard)

Waist

Bridge

Sound-hole

Rib

Purfling

Tailpiece

Tailpiece loop fits around end-pin

Chin rest

End-pin (tail-pin)

SECTIONS OF A VIOLIN

Head

Point

Stick

Horsehair

Scroll

Scroll eye

Peg-box

Tuning-peg

Nut

String

Fingerboard

Rounded shoulder

Purfling

Belly (soundboard)

Waist

Sound-hole

Bridge

Tuning adjustor

Frog

Tailpiece

Screw

Chin rest

VIOLIN BOW

VIOLIN

HARP

Crown

Tuning-peg

Neck (string arm)

Shoulder

String

Soundboard

Pillar

Pedestal

Foot

Pedal

DOUBLE BASS BOW

Head

Point

Inward-curving stick

Horsehair

Frog

Screw

Scroll

Scroll eye

Tuning-pegs at back of peg-box

Nut

Fingerboard

String

Sloping shoulder

Belly (soundboard)

Purfling

Waist

Bridge

Rib

Sound-hole

Sound-hole

Bridge

Tailpiece

Spike

DOUBLE BASS

Scroll

Scroll eye

Peg-box

Tuning-peg

Nut

Fingerboard

String

Rounded shoulder

Belly (soundboard)

Waist

Sound-hole

Bridge

Purfling

Tuning adjustor

Tailpiece

Spike

CELLO (VIOLONCELLO)

Scroll

Tuning-peg

Scroll eye

Peg-box

Nut

Fingerboard

String

Belly (soundboard)

Rounded shoulder

Purfling

Waist

Sound-hole

Bridge

Tuning adjustor

Tailpiece

Chin rest

VIOLA

Guitars

THE GUITAR IS A PLUCKED stringed instrument
(see pp. 510-511). There are two types of guitar –
acoustic and electric. Acoustic guitars have hollow
bodies and six or twelve strings. Plucking the strings
produces vibrations that are amplified by their hollow
bodies. Electric guitars usually have solid bodies and
six strings. Pick-ups placed under the strings convert
their vibrations into electronic signals that are magnified
by an amplifier, and sent to a loudspeaker where they are
converted into sounds (see pp. 520-521). Electric bass
guitars are very similar in structure to electric guitars,
and produce sound in the same way, but have four
strings and play bass notes.

ACOUSTIC GUITAR

Hollow body

String

Fret

Machine head

Neck

Headstock

Sound-hole

B string

Bridge

G string

D string

A string

Maker's label

Low E string

Lining glued along top and bottom edge of rib

Rib

End block

Strap peg

Saddle

Bridge pin

Joint

Transverse (crosswise) strut strengthens back

Back made of two pieces of cherry wood joined together

Bridge

Binding

COMPONENTS OF AN ACOUSTIC GUITAR

Top E string

Nut

Truss rod cover

Screws

Machine heads

Headstock

Machine head

Truss rod slot

Truss rod

Position dots

Fingerboard

Fretwire slot

Fretwire

Bracing

Sound-hole

Soundboard made of two pieces of spruce joined together

EXAMPLES OF ACOUSTIC GUITARS

Rose

Sound-hole

Hollow body

String

Machine head

Bridge

Neck

Headstock

Scratchplate

WASHBURN TWELVE-STRING

Hollow, metal body

Sound-hole

Tailpiece

String

Machine head

Neck

Headstock

Resonator

DOBRO RESONATOR

EXAMPLES OF ELECTRIC GUITARS

Solid body

Pick-up

Scratchplate

String

Machine head

Bridge

Neck

Headstock

Output socket

Vibrato arm

FENDER STRATOCASTER

Solid body

Pick-up

Toggle switch

String

Machine head

Bridge

Neck

Headstock

Scratchplate

GIBSON LES PAUL

Solid body

Pick-up

String

Machine head

Bridge

Neck

Headstock

Output socket

Scratchplate

FENDER JAZZ BASS

Keyboard instruments

KEYBOARD INSTRUMENTS are instruments that are sounded by means of a keyboard. The organ and piano are two of the principal members of the keyboard family. The organ consists of pipes which are operated by one or more manuals (keyboards) and a pedal board. The pipes are lined up in rows (known as ranks or registers) on top of a wind chest. The sound of the organ is made when air is admitted into a pipe by pressing a key or pedal. The piano consists of wire strings stretched over a metal frame, and a keyboard and pedals that operate hammers and dampers. The piano frame is either vertical – as in the upright piano – or horizontal – as in the grand piano. When a key is at rest, a damper lies against the string to stop it vibrating. When a key is pressed down, the damper moves away from the string as the hammer strikes it, causing the string to vibrate and sound a note.

ORGAN PIPE

UPRIGHT PIANO

Muffler felt

Pressure bar

Tuning pin

Pin block

Hammer

Hammer rail

88–note keyboard

Wooden case

Keybed

Metal frame

Soundboard

String

Hitch pin

Treble bridge

Bass bridge

Una corda (soft) pedal

Sostenuto pedal

Damper (sustaining) pedal

ORGAN CONSOLE

Pipe

Pedal stop

Swell stop

Swell manual (keyboard)

Great manual (keyboard)

Choir manual (keyboard)

Music stand

Choir stop

Great stop

Thumb piston

Toe piston

Pedal board

Foot pedal

Swell pedal

UPRIGHT PIANO ACTION

KEY AT REST

String

Hammer

Damper lies against string, and stops it vibrating

Hammer rest

Back check

Damper lever

Action lever

Jack

Capstan screw

Key released

KEY PRESSED DOWN

String

Hammer strikes string

Damper moves away from string, allowing it to vibrate

Hammer rest

Back check

Damper lever

Action lever

Jack

Capstan screw

Key pressed down

CONCERT GRAND PIANO (VIEWED FROM ABOVE)

Soundboard

Bass bridge

Hitch pin

Metal frame

Single bass note string

Long bridge

CONCERT GRAND PIANO (FRONT VIEW)

Lid

String

Wooden case

Keyboard

Una corda (soft) pedal

Sostenuto pedal

Damper (sustaining) pedal

Tenor note strings (two strings for each note)

Treble note strings (three strings for each note)

Wooden case

Hammer

Tuning pin

Wrest plank

Keyboard lid

88-note keyboard

STEINWAY & SONS NEW YORK HAMBURG

STEINWAY

Percussion instruments

TEMPLE BLOCKS

PERCUSSION INSTRUMENTS are a large group of instruments that produce sound by being struck, shaken, scraped, or clashed together. Most percussion instruments – such as the tam-tam (gong), cymbals, and maracas – do not have a definite pitch and are used for rhythm and impact, and the distinctive timbre (colour) of their sound. Other percussion instruments – such as the xylophone, vibraphone, and tubular bells – are tuned to a definite pitch and can play melody, harmony, and rhythms. The xylophone and vibraphone each have two rows of bars that are arranged in a similar way to the black and white keys of a piano. Metal tubes are suspended below the bars to amplify the sound. The vibraphone has electrically operated fans that rotate in the tubes and produce a vibrato (wavering pitch) effect.

TUBULAR BELLS

Tube struck with mallet

Hollow, metal tube

Damper bar

Metal frame

Mechanism linking pedal and damper bar

Row of tubes graduated in length and pitch

Damper pedal

EXAMPLES OF BEATERS

SOFT-HEADED BEATER

Fell-covered head

HARD-HEADED BEATER

Rosewood head

MALLET

Leather-covered head

XYLOPHONE

Row of bars graduated in length and pitch

Wooden bar struck with hard-headed beater

Hollow, metal tube

Metal stand

TAM-TAM (GONG)

Tam-tam struck in centre with soft-headed beater

Cord

Metal frame

Rim

Large, metal disc

CYMBALS

Leather strap fits around player's hand

Pad protects hands from vibrations

Thin, convex disc of copper and tin alloy

SECTIONS OF A MARACA

Wooden handle

Lead shot

Hollow, wooden head

TRIANGLE

Steel rod bent into triangular shape

Steel beater

CLAVES

Hardwood sticks clashed together to give a sharp crack

CASTANETS

Cord

Hollowed wood

VIBRAPHONE

Row of bars graduated in length and pitch

Metal bar struck with soft-headed beater

Metal frame

Damper pedal

Metal tube containing electrically operated fan that produces vibrato (wavering pitch) effect

Electric cable

Drums

A DRUM IS A percussion instrument that consists of a drumhead, made of skin or plastic, stretched over one or both ends of a hollow vessel (the body-shell). Drums are played in most parts of the world and are made in a number of different shapes and sizes. They can be divided into three groups according to the shape of the body-shell: frame drums (e.g., tambourines), bowl-shaped drums (e.g., timpani), and tubular drums (e.g., congas). Drums are usually sounded by striking the drumhead with the hands or with beaters, such as a hard-headed stick. The drumhead vibrates, and its vibrations are amplified by the hollow body-shell. The snare drum has wires – known as snares – stretched across the lower drumhead; the snares vibrate against the lower drumhead when the drum is played. Most drums, such as congas, do not have a definite pitch and can play only rhythms (see pp. 516-517). Other drums, such as timpani, have a definite pitch and can play melody, harmony, and rhythms. They can be tuned by adjusting the tension of the drumhead. Different types of drum can be combined together with other percussion instruments to form a drum kit. The basic components of the drum kit are bass drum, tom-toms, floor tom (tenor drum), snare drum, and cymbals.

TAMBOURINE

DRUM KIT

Crash cymbal

Tension key

Tension rod

Tom-tom

Lug

Hi-hat cymbal

Snare drum

Tripod stand

SNARE DRUM (VIEWED FROM BELOW)

Snare mounting

Adjustable damper

Lug

Transparent lower drumhead

Upper drumhead

Snare

Stick

Snare release lever

Chain

Tension screw

Felt-covered beater

Pedal

Pedal

EXAMPLES OF BEATERS

Acorn

HARD-HEADED STICK

Taper

SOFT-HEADED STICK

Felt-covered head

WIRE BRUSH

Wire bristles

Ride cymbal

Tension key

Tom-tom

Height adjustment key

Tension rod

Lug

Floor tom (tenor drum)

Tension rod

Lug

Wooden body-shell

Height adjustment key

Leg

Bass drum

Rubber foot

CONGAS

Metal hoop

Drumhead

Tension rod

Wooden body-shell

Tripod stand

Leg

TIMPANUM (KETTLE DRUM)

Drumhead

Tension rod

Tuning gauge

Metal hoop

Copper body-shell

Strut

Crown

Tension rod

Tuning pedal

Castor

Electronic instruments

ELECTRONIC INSTRUMENTS generate electronic signals
that are magnified by an amplifier, and sent to a loudspeaker
where they are converted into sounds. Synthesizers, and other
electronic instruments, simulate the characteristic sounds of
conventional instruments, and also create entirely new sounds.
Most electronic instruments are keyboard instruments, but electronic
wind and percussion instruments are also popular. A digital sampler
records and stores sounds from musical instruments or other sources.
When the sound is played back, the pitch of the original sound can be
altered. A keyboard can be connected to the sampler so that a tune can
be played using the sampled sounds. With a MIDI (Musical Instrument
Digital Interface) system, a computer can be linked with other electronic
instruments, such as keyboards and electronic drums, to make sounds
together or in sequence. It is also possible, using music software, to
compose and play music on a home computer.

ELECTRONIC DRUMS

Drum pad

Height
adjustment key

Tripod

HOME KEYBOARD

Power
button

Volume
control

Function
display

Memory record
button

Tone editor
control

Demonstration
tune button

Pitch
modulator

Multi-accompaniment
system control

Tone and rhythm
pattern selector

Key

SYNTHESIZER

Memory
card slot

Joystick

Function
display

Edit control

Data entry
key pad

Sound structure
guide

Volume
control

Pitch
modulator

Sound selection control

Key

DIGITAL SAMPLER

External input

Volume knob

Display illumination

D beam

External mic

Effect knobs

Effect buttons

Roland SP-555

Sample

Bank buttons

Loop capture

Pads 1–16

WIND SYNTHESIZER

Mouthpiece

Keys for right hand

WIND CONTROLLER

Keys for left hand

POWER PACK

MIDI (Musical Instrument Digital Interface) cable

SOUND MODULE

Connecting cable

YAMAHA WT 11

Store button

Data entry key pad

Input connector socket

Volume control

Edit control

Play button

Function display

Effect balance control

Second optical drive

Optical drive

Audio clock settings

COMPUTER DISPLAY

Surround sound special effect plug-in

Start and stop controls

MOTU

Software effect plug-in

Power button

Recorded information

Headset jack

Status light

USB ports (2)

FireWire 800 ports (2)

Virtual mixing board

SYSTEM UNIT

KEYBOARD

MOUSE

COMPUTER WITH MIDI AND AUDIO SOFTWARE SEQUENCER

SPORTS

Soccer

GAMES INVOLVING KICKING A BALL have a long history and were recorded in China as early as 300 BC; in medieval Europe, street football was banned as a menace to the public; only in 1863 were the rules established, specifically banning carrying the ball for all players except the goalkeeper, and separating rugby from soccer. Soccer, officially termed association football, is a team sport in which players attempt to score goals by passing and dribbling the ball down the field past opposing defenders, and kicking or heading the ball into the goal net, outwitting the defending goalkeeper. Each team consists of ten outfield players (defenders, midfielders, and strikers) and a goalkeeper. Players from the opposing team may challenge the player in possession of the ball, but an illegal or foul tackle results in a penalty if a foul occurs inside the penalty area or a free kick if outside the penalty area. The round ball used in soccer is more easily controlled than the oval balls used in American, Canadian, and Australian rules football and in rugby. The result is a more "open" or flowing game which is played and watched by millions of people worldwide.

ASSISTANT REFEREE'S FLAG

Lightweight, brightly coloured fabric

Handle with rubber grip

REFEREE'S EQUIPMENT

Red card

Yellow card

Referee's whistle

Stop-watch

PITCH MARKINGS

Halfway line

1.5 m (5 ft)

HALFWAY-LINE FLAG

Corner arc

CORNER FLAG

7.3 m (24 ft)

Goal-line

GOAL

SOCCER PITCH

46–91 m (150–300 ft)

- Corner flag
- Corner arc
- Penalty area
- Penalty mark
- Referee
- Halfway-line flag
- Striker
- Striker
- Left midfielder
- Central midfielder
- Left back
- Touch-line
- Central defender
- Goal
- Goalkeeper
- Goal-line
- Penalty arc
- Assistant referee
- Centre circle
- Centre spot
- Halfway line
- Striker
- Right midfielder
- Right back
- Central defender
- Goal area

GOALKEEPER

Goalkeeper's shirt

Glove

Shin guard

Shorts

Sock

Soccer boot

SOCCER STRIP

Open-neck collar

Lightweight, man-made fabric team shirt

Team logo

Manufacturer's logo

Ribbed welt

Sponsor's logo

Ball size number

Manufacturer's name

Edge cut to fit perfectly

MAKING A SOCCER BALL

Hole punched in panel for stitching

Mitre

F.I.F.A. APPROVED

MULTIPLEX

Waxed thread

Bladder valve

Needle

Bladder made from latex rubber

Laminated panel

Panels sewn together with ball inside out

22–23 cm (8½–9 in)

Long cotton sock

Club crest

Team shorts

Synthetic bootlace

Interchangeable nylon stud

SOCCER BOOT

American football

IN AMERICAN AND CANADIAN FOOTBALL, the object of the game is to get the ball across the opponent's goal line, either by passing or carrying it across (a touch-down), or by kicking it between their goalposts (a field goal). An American football team has 11 players on the field at a time, although up to 40 players can appear for each side in a single game. The agile "offence" tries to score points, and the heavy hitting "defence" holds back the opposition. When in possession of the ball, a team has four chances ("downs"), to move it at least ten yards (nine metres) up the field to make a "first down". The opposition gains possession if they fail, or by tackling and intercepting the ball. Canadian football is played on a larger field, with 12 men on each side. A team has only three chances to achieve a first down. Otherwise, the game is very similar to American football. Helmets, face masks, and layers of body padding are worn by the players for protection.

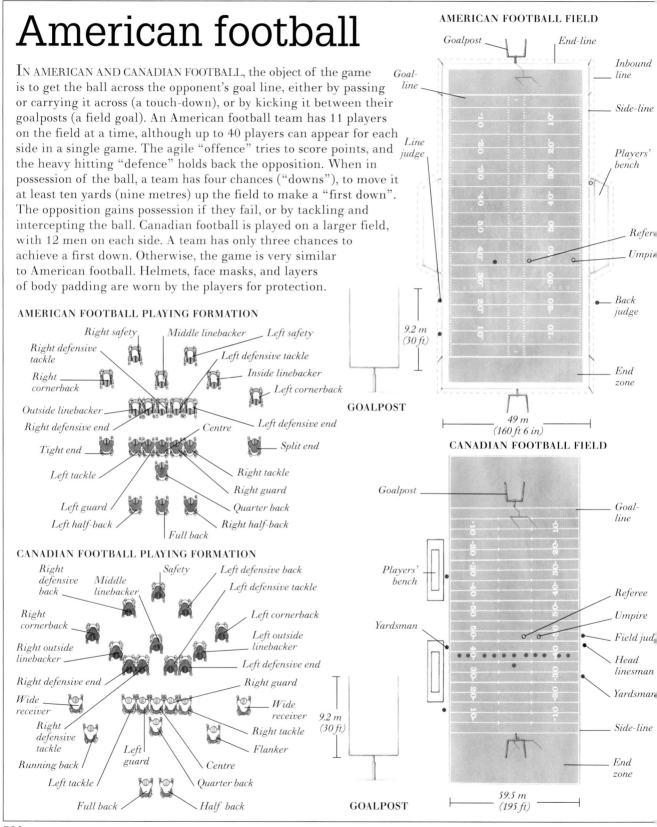

AMERICAN FOOTBALL FIELD

Goalpost
End-line
Goal-line
Inbound line
Side-line
Line judge
Players' bench
Referee
Umpire
Back judge
9.2 m (30 ft)
End zone
49 m (160 ft 6 in)

GOALPOST

CANADIAN FOOTBALL FIELD

Goalpost
Goal-line
Players' bench
Referee
Umpire
Yardsman
Field judge
Head linesman
Yardsman
Side-line
9.2 m (30 ft)
End zone
59.5 m (195 ft)

GOALPOST

AMERICAN FOOTBALL PLAYING FORMATION

Right safety
Middle linebacker
Left safety
Right defensive tackle
Left defensive tackle
Right cornerback
Inside linebacker
Left cornerback
Outside linebacker
Right defensive end
Centre
Left defensive end
Tight end
Split end
Left tackle
Right tackle
Right guard
Left guard
Quarter back
Left half-back
Right half-back
Full back

CANADIAN FOOTBALL PLAYING FORMATION

Right defensive back
Middle linebacker
Safety
Left defensive back
Left defensive tackle
Right cornerback
Left cornerback
Left outside linebacker
Right outside linebacker
Left defensive end
Right defensive end
Right guard
Wide receiver
Wide receiver
Right defensive tackle
Right tackle
Left guard
Flanker
Running back
Centre
Left tackle
Quarter back
Full back
Half back

PLAYER

Team logo

Helmet

Wrist pad

Player's number

Thigh pad

Pants

Studded shoe

PROTECTIVE EQUIPMENT

28 cm (11 in)

Painted white ring

Lace

Brown pebbled leather

FOOTBALL

Tie to shoulder pads

HELMET

Non-breakable plastic

Rubber-coated plastic

Shock absorber

Riddell

SHOULDER PAD

BIKE

BIKE

AIR·LITE

BLUE LASER 40-42

Chest protector weight up to 2.5 kg (5 lb 8 oz)

REFEREE'S SIGNALS

TIME OUT

TOUCH-DOWN OR FIELD GOAL

PERSONAL FOUL

OFFSIDE OR ENCROACHMENT

HOLDING

ILLEGAL MOTION

FIRST DOWN

PASS INTERFERENCE

BIKE

UPPER ARM PAD

BIKE

ELBOW PAD

FINGERLESS GLOVE

Screw-in stud

PONY

BOOT

Fold-over leather tongue

RIB PADS

Strap ties on to shoulder pad

Foam-sponge filling

Tail bone pad

BIKE AL60

BIKE AL60

HIP PAD

Rigid plastic covering

BIKE AL82

BIKE AL82

THIGH PAD

PANTS

KNEE PAD

Australian rules and Gaelic football

VARIETIES OF FOOTBALL have developed all over the world and Australian rules football is considered to be one of the roughest versions, allowing full body tackles although participants wear no protective padding. The game is played on a large, oval pitch by two sides, each of 18 players. Players can kick or punch the ball, which is shaped like a rugby ball, but cannot throw it. Running with the ball is permitted, as long as the ball touches the ground at least once every ten metres. The full backs defend two sets of posts. Teams try to score "goals" (six points) between the inner posts or "behinds" (one point) inside the outer posts. Each game has four quarters of 25 minutes, and the team with the most points at the end of the allotted time is the winner. In Gaelic football, an Irish version of soccer (see pp. 524–525), a size 5 soccer ball is used. Each team can have 15 players on the field at a time. Players are allowed to catch, fist, and kick the ball, or dribble it using their hands or feet, but cannot throw it. Teams are awarded three points for getting the ball into the net, and one point for getting it through the posts above the crossbar. Gaelic football is rarely played outside of Ireland.

START OF PLAY

Field umpire

Centre circle

SCORING

GOAL (6 POINTS)

BEHIND (1 POINT)

AUSTRALIAN RULES FOOTBALL FIELD

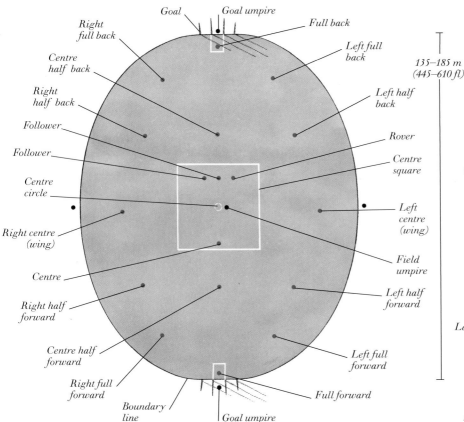

Goal

Goal umpire

Full back

Right full back

Left full back

Centre half back

Left half back

Right half back

Follower

Rover

Follower

Centre square

Centre circle

Left centre (wing)

Right centre (wing)

Centre

Field umpire

Right half forward

Left half forward

Centre half forward

Left full forward

Right full forward

Boundary line

Full forward

Goal umpire

135–185 m (445–610 ft)

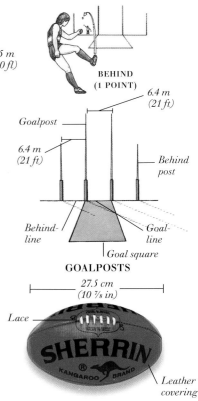

6.4 m (21 ft)

Goalpost

6.4 m (21 ft)

Behind post

Behind-line

Goal-line

Goal square

GOALPOSTS

27.5 cm (10 ⅞ in)

Lace

SHERRIN
KANGAROO BRAND

Leather covering

AUSTRALIAN RULES FOOTBALL

AUSTRALIAN RULES FOOTBALL SKILLS

RUNNING WITH THE BALL

KICKING

TACKLING

TAKING A MARK

PASSING THE BALL

AUSTRALIAN RULES FOOTBALL DRESS

Australian Football League logo

Team colours

Sleeveless team guernsey

Sock

Shorts

GAELIC FOOTBALL PITCH

Corner flag

Goalkeeper

Goal umpire

Goal area

Right full back

Left full back

Full back

Right half-back

Left half-back

Centre half-back

Centre flag

Linesman

Linesman

Left midfielder

Right midfielder

Midfield line

Referee

Left half-forward

Right half-forward

Centre half-forward

Right full-forward

Full forward

Left full-forward

80–90 m
260–295 ft)

CONTROLLING THE BALL

SCORING IN GAELIC FOOTBALL

GOAL (3 POINTS)

POINT (1 POINT)

22–23 cm
(8½–9 in)

6.4 m
(21ft)

Goalpost

Crossbar

Parallelogram

GOAL

oneills all-ireland

GAELIC FOOTBALL

529

Rugby

Rugby is played with an oval ball, which may be carried, thrown, or kicked. There are two codes of rugby, both played at amateur and professional levels. Rugby Union is played by two teams of 15 players. They can score points in two ways: by placing the ball by hand over the opponents' goal-line (a try, scoring four points) or by kicking it over the crossbar of the opponent's goal (a conversion of a try, scoring two points; a penalty kick, scoring three points; or a drop-kick, scoring three points). Rugby League developed from the Union game but is played by 13 players. In League games, a try scores four points; a conversion scores two points; a drop goal scores one point, and a penalty kick scores two points. Scrummages occur in both codes when play stops following an infringement.

RUGBY UNION PITCH

Goal — Dead-ball line

Touch in-goal line

Goal-line

5 m line

Scrum-half

10 m line

Loose-head prop

Flanker

Lock forward

Centre

Left wing

Centre

Full back

Touch-line

Referee

Hooker

Tight-head prop

Touch judge

Flanker

Lock forward

Right wing

Number

Fly-half

In-goal area

68 m (225 ft) maximum

RUGBY UNION SCRUMMAGE

Loose-head prop

Hooker

Tight-head prop

Scrum-half

Flanker

Flanker

Lock forward

Lock forward

Number 8

5.5 m (18 ft)

Upright

Crossbar

Protective padding

3 m (9 ft 10 in)

RUGBY UNION GOALPOST

RUGBY LEAGUE PITCH

Goal — Dead-ball line

Touch in-goal

Goal-line

10 m line

Referee

Touch judge

Blind-side prop

Second-row forward

Loose forward

Left wing

Full back

Touch in-goal line

Touch-line

Hooker

Open-side prop

Touch judge

Second-row forward

Scrum-half

Stand-off half

Centre

Centre

Right wing

68m (225 ft) maximum

RUGBY LEAGUE SCRUMMAGE

Blind-side prop

Hooker

Open-side prop

Scrum-half

Second-row forward

Second-row forward

Loose forward

5.5 m (18 ft)

Upright

Crossbar

Protective padding

RUGBY LEAGUE GOALPOST

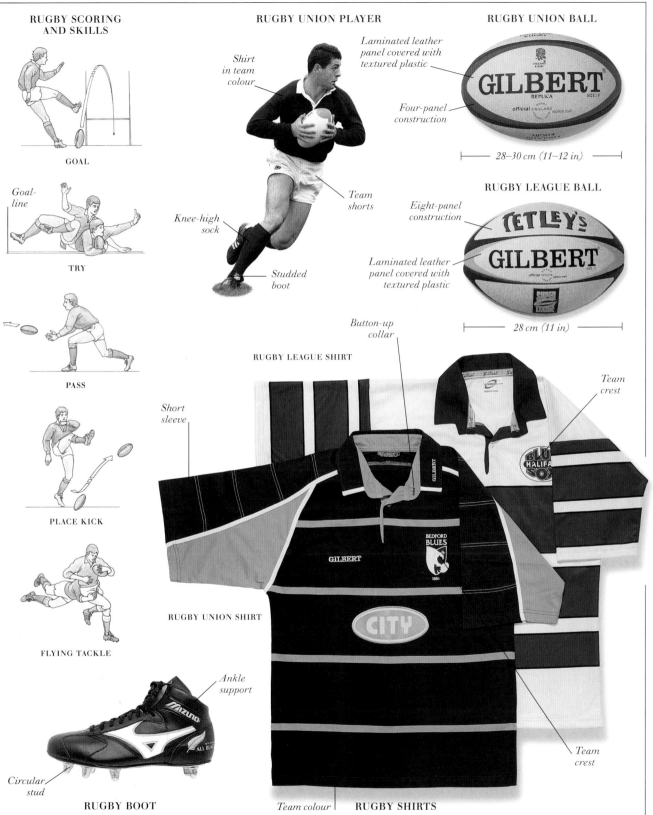

RUGBY SCORING AND SKILLS

GOAL

Goal-line

TRY

PASS

PLACE KICK

FLYING TACKLE

Ankle support

Circular stud

RUGBY BOOT

RUGBY UNION PLAYER

Shirt in team colour

Knee-high sock

Studded boot

Team shorts

RUGBY UNION BALL

Laminated leather panel covered with textured plastic

GILBERT
REPLICA
official ENGLAND replica ball

Four-panel construction

28–30 cm (11–12 in)

RUGBY LEAGUE BALL

Eight-panel construction

TETLEY'S
GILBERT
official TETLEY replica ball

Laminated leather panel covered with textured plastic

28 cm (11 in)

RUGBY LEAGUE SHIRT

Button-up collar

Short sleeve

RUGBY UNION SHIRT

GILBERT

BEDFORD BLUES 1886

CITY

BLUE HALIFAX SOX

Team crest

Team crest

Team colour

RUGBY SHIRTS

531

Basketball

BASKETBALL IS A BALL GAME for two teams of five players, originally devised in 1890 by James Naismath for the Y.M.C.A. in Springfield, Massachusetts, U.S.A. The object of the game is to take possession of the ball and score points by throwing the ball into the opposing team's basket. A player moves the ball up and down the court by bouncing it along the ground or "dribbling"; the ball may be passed between players by throwing, bouncing, or rolling. Players may not run with or kick the ball, although pivoting on one foot is allowed. The game begins with the referee throwing the ball into the air and a player from each team jumping up to try and "tip" the ball to a team-mate. The length of the game and the number of periods played varies at different levels. There are amateur, professional, and international rules. No game ends in a draw. An extra period of five minutes is played, plus as many extra periods as are necessary to break the tie. In addition to the five players on court, each team has up to seven substitutes, but players may only leave the court with the permission of the referee. Basketball is a non-contact sport and fouls on other players are penalized by a throw-in awarded against the offending team; a free throw at the basket is awarded when a player is fouled in the act of shooting. Basketball is a fast-moving game, requiring both physical and mental coordination. Skilful tactical play matters more than simple physical strength and the agility of the players makes the game an excellent spectator sport.

BASKETBALL SKILLS

CHEST PASS

DRIBBLE

OVERHEAD PASS

LAY-UP SHOT

JUMP SHOT

LONG PASS

INTERNATIONAL BASKETBALL COUBT

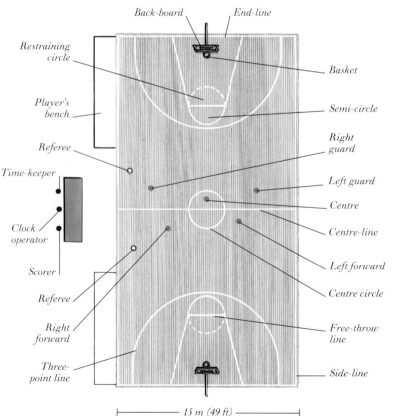

Back-board

End-line

Restraining circle

Player's bench

Referee

Time-keeper

Clock operator

Scorer

Referee

Right forward

Three-point line

Basket

Semi-circle

Right guard

Left guard

Centre

Centre-line

Left forward

Centre circle

Free-throw line

Side-line

15 m (49 ft)

BASKET AND BACK-BOARD

Back-board

Metal rim

Cord net

1.8 m (6 ft)

BASKET AND BACK-BOARD STRUCTURE

3.05 m (10 ft)

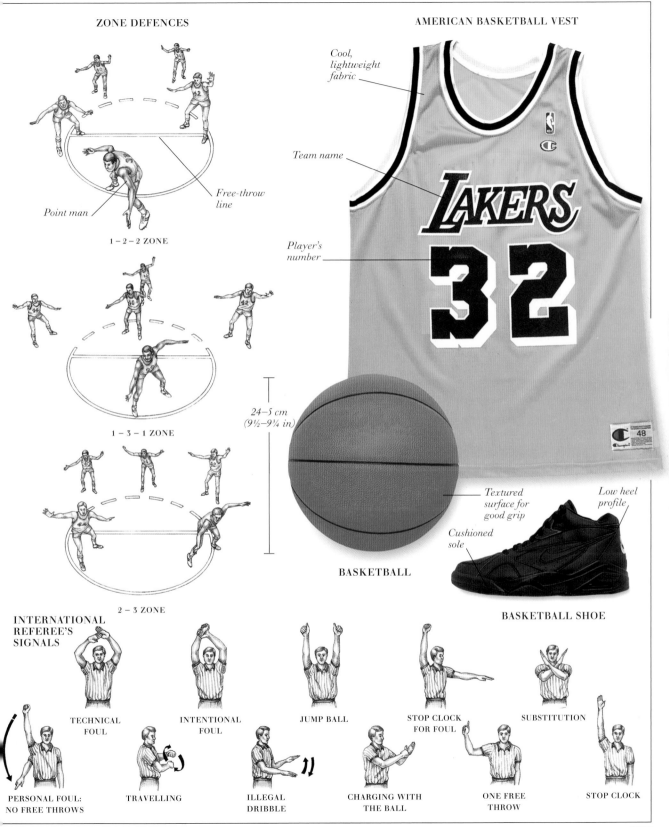

ZONE DEFENCES

Point man

Free-throw line

1 – 2 – 2 ZONE

1 – 3 – 1 ZONE

2 – 3 ZONE

AMERICAN BASKETBALL VEST

Cool, lightweight fabric

Team name

Player's number

LAKERS 32

24–5 cm
(9½–9¼ in)

Textured surface for good grip

Cushioned sole

BASKETBALL

Low heel profile

BASKETBALL SHOE

INTERNATIONAL REFEREE'S SIGNALS

TECHNICAL FOUL

INTENTIONAL FOUL

JUMP BALL

STOP CLOCK FOR FOUL

SUBSTITUTION

PERSONAL FOUL: NO FREE THROWS

TRAVELLING

ILLEGAL DRIBBLE

CHARGING WITH THE BALL

ONE FREE THROW

STOP CLOCK

Volleyball, netball, and handball

VOLLEYBALL, NETBALL, AND HANDBALL are fast-moving team sports played with balls on courts with a hard surface. In volleyball, the object of the game is to hit the ball over a net strung across the centre of the court so that it touches the ground on the opponent's side. The team of six players can take three hits to direct the ball over the net, although the same player cannot hit the ball twice in a row. Players can hit the ball with their arms, hands or any other part of their upper body. Teams score points only while serving. The first team to score 15 points, with a two-point margin over their opponent, wins the game. Netball is one of the few sports played exclusively by women. Similar to basketball (see pp.532–533), it is played on a slightly larger court with seven players instead of five. A team moves the ball towards the goal by throwing, passing, and catching it with the aim of throwing the ball through the opponents' goal net. Players are confined by their playing position to specific areas of the court. Team handball is one of the world's fastest games. Each side has seven players. A team moves the ball by dribbling, passing, or bouncing it as they run. Players may stop, catch, throw, bounce, or strike the ball with any part of the body above the knees. Each team tries to score goals by directing the ball past the opposition's goalkeeper into the net, which is similar to a soccer net.

VOLLEYBALL SHOTS

OVERHAND SERVE SPIKE (SMASH)

UNDERHAND SERVE FOREARM PASS (DIG)

VOLLEYBALL KIT

Team colours

Ribbed cuff

Cotton-knit jersey

Elasticated waist

Mizuno

Shorts

Elasticated knit fabric

Injected moulded padding

VOLLEYBALL COURT

- End-line
- Linesman
- Clear space
- Linesman
- Side-line
- Players' bench
- Referee
- Scorer
- Net
- Left forward
- Back zone
- Left back
- Linesman
- Attack zone
- Attack line
- Umpire
- Centre forward
- Right forward
- Centre back
- Linesman
- Service area
- Server

9 m
(29 ft 6 in)

VOLLEYBALL

Leather covering

21 cm
(8¼ in)

VOLLEYBALL NET

Tape Net Antenna

Men's:
2.4 m (8 ft)
Women's:
2.2 m
(7 ft 4 in)

Post

KNEE PADS

NETBALL COURT

Mineral surface with non-slip tarmacadam coating

Goalpost

Back-line

Goalkeeper

Goal circle

Defence third

Goal defence

Wing defence

Umpire

Scorer

keeper

Scorer

Centre

Central third

Central circle

Goal attack

Wing attack

Transverse line

Goal third

Goal shooter

Side-line

15.2 m (50 ft)

NETBALL

Rubber or leather covering

22.4 cm (8¼ in)

NETBALL GOALPOST AND NET

Ring

Net

Goalpost

3.05 m (10 ft)

NETBALL PASSES

CHEST PASS

UNDERARM PASS

SHOULDER PASS

BOUNCE PASS

HANDBALL COURT

Goal area

Goal

Net

Goal area line

Guide mark

Goal-line

Penalty line

Free-throw line

Players' bench

Side-line

Secretary

Centre line

Court referee

Time-keeper

Left wing

Right wing

Centre back

Centre forward

Left back

Right back

Goalkeeper

Goal-line referee

20m (65 ft 6in)

HANDBALL

Leather covering

MEN'S: 18.8 CM (7½ IN)
WOMEN'S: 17.5 CM (7 IN)

HANDBALL SHOE

HANDBALL NET

Crossbar

Post

Goal-line

2 m (6 ft 6 in)

HANDBALL SKILLS

OVERARM PASS

DRIBBLE

BOUNCE PASS

JUMP SHOT

Baseball

BASEBALL IS A BALL GAME for two teams of nine players. The batter hits the ball thrown by the opposing team's pitcher, into the area between the foul lines. He then runs round all four fixed bases in order to score a run, touching or "tagging" each base in turn. The pitcher must throw the ball at a height between the batter's armpits and knees, a height which is called the "strike zone". A ball pitched in this area that crosses over the "home plate" is called a "strike" and the batter has three strikes in which to try and hit the ball (otherwise he is "struck out"). The fielding team tries to get the batting team out by catching the ball before it bounces, tagging a player of the batting team with the ball who is running between bases, or by tagging a base before the player has reached it. Members of the batting team may stop safely at a base as long as it is not occupied by another member of their team. When the batter runs to first base, his team-mate at first base must run on to second – this is called "force play". A game consists of nine innings and each team will bat once during an inning. When three members of the batting team are out, the teams swap roles. The team with the greatest number of runs wins the game.

BATTER'S HELMET

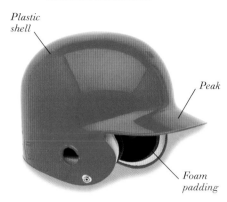

Plastic shell

Peak

Foam padding

CATCHER'S MASK

Wire coated in strong nylon

Plastic-coated foam padding

BASEBALL PITCH

Centre field

Centre fielder

Warning track

Left fielder

Right fielder

Left field

Second baseman

Right field

Foul line

Outfield

PITCHER'S MOUND

Pitcher

Pitcher's rubber

Shortstop

First baseman

Umpire

First base

Third baseman

Infield

Third base

Home run

Coach's box

100 m (325 ft) minimum

Second base

Dugout

On-deck circle

Pitcher's mound

HOME PLATE

Batter

Home plate

Catcher

Home-plate umpire

MAKING A BASEBALL

Woollen yarn

Rubber inner casing

Horsehide strip

Cork centre

Cotton thread outer casing

Woollen strand

Red outer stitching

THE PITCHING SEQUENCE

THE WIND-UP 1

THE WIND-UP 2

THE WIND-UP 3

THE WIND-UP 4

THE RELEASE

THE FOLLOW-THROUGH

UMPIRING SIGNALS

BALL

INFIELD

STRIKE

FAIR BALL

RUNNER IS SAFE

FOUL TIP

BASEBALL EQUIPMENT

Webbed pocket

Fingers laced together

Strap

Thumb

Palm

Leather stitching

Heel

STEERHIDE LEATHER

FIELDER'S GLOVE AND BALL

PONY

Metal heel plate

AMERICAN BASEBALL BOOT

Metal toe plate

Batter's helmet

Bat

Batting glove

Team shirt

Undershirt

Pants

Spiked shoe

BATTER

Hitting area

Official Baseball

Crest

1.1 m (3 ft 6 in) maximum

Handle

Knob

BAT

537

Cricket

CRICKET IS A BALL GAME PLAYED by two teams of eleven players on a pitch with two sets of three stumps (wickets). The bowler bowls the ball down the pitch to the batsman of the opposing team, who must defend the wicket in front of which he stands. The object of the game is to score as many runs as possible. Runs can be scored individually by running the length of the playing strip, or by hitting a ball which lands outside the boundary ("six"), or which lands inside the boundary but bounces or rolls outside ("four"); the opposing team will bowl and field, attempting to dismiss the batsmen. A batsman can be dismissed in one of several ways: by the bowler hitting the wicket with the ball ("bowled"); by a fielder catching the ball hit by the batsman before it touches the ground ("caught"); by the wicket-keeper or another fielder breaking the wicket while the batsman is attempting a run and is therefore out of his ground ("stumped" or "run out"); by the batsman breaking the wicket with his own bat or body ("hit wicket"); by a part of the batsman's body being hit by a ball that would otherwise have hit the wicket ("leg before wicket" ["lbw"]). A match consists of one or two innings and each innings ends when the tenth batsman of the batting team is out, when a certain number of overs (a series of six balls bowled) have been played, or when the captain of the batting team "declares" ending the innings voluntarily.

CRICKET STROKES

FORWARD DEFENSIVE STROKE

BACKWARD DEFENSIVE STROKE

ON-DRIVE

OFF-DRIVE

PULL

HOOK

SQUARE CUT

LEG GLANCE

CRICKET BALL AND WICKE[T]

Leather skin

Seam

BALL

Bail

WICKET

Stump

CRICKET PITCH

Wicket-keeper

Batsman

Wicket

Bowling crease

20 m (66 ft)

Bowler

Return crease

Umpire

Non-striking batsman

POSSIBLE FIELD POSITIONS FOR AN AWAY SWING BOWLER TO A RIGHT-HANDED BATSMAN (IN RED) AND OTHER FIELD POSITIONS

Long on

Long off

Umpire

Bowler

Boundary line

Non-striking batsman

Deep mid-wicket

Extra cover

Mid-on

Silly mid-on

Mid-off

Forward short leg

Silly mid-off

Square leg

Cover

Deep square leg

Point

Square-leg umpire

Gulley

Batsman

Third man

Long leg

Bowler

Leg slip

Second slip

Wicket-keeper

First slip

Fine leg

Sight screen

MAKING A BAT HANDLE

Sarawak cane

Twine wrapped around handle

Rubber strip

LAMINATING THE WOOD

BINDING THE HANDLE

PROTECTIVE CLOTHING

Slit in leather for greater flexibility

Padding protects knuckles from injury

Dimpled rubber improves grip

Polycarbonate shell with cloth covering

Mesh covering for ventilation

Wrist strap

Foam cheek-piece for comfort and good fit

Peak

Protective plastic ear piece

BATTING GLOVE

WICKET-KEEPER'S GLOVES

HELMET

ADDING THE HANDLE TO THE BAT

Rubber grip

V-shaped splice

Grip rolled onto handle

Shoulder of bat

Handle glued into splice

Scoop

Bat

BATSMAN

Padded glove

Cap

Wristband

White shirt

White sweater

Stripes in team colours

MAKING A BAT BLADE

Blade planed by hand

Toe of the bat shaped

Sanded and polished bat

Kiln-dried willow

SEASONING THE TIMBER

CUTTING THE SPLICE

FITTING THE HANDLE

FINISHING TOUCHES

Thigh pad under white trousers

Knee roll

Cricket shoe

Leg pad

Dimpled rubber sole

Hockey, lacrosse, and hurling

ALL OVER THE WORLD, TEAM GAMES have evolved which require that a ball be struck or carried, and tossed at the end of a stick. Early forms of these games include hurling, shinty, bandy, and pelota. Hockey is played by men and women: two teams of eleven players try to gain and keep possession of the ball and score goals by using the hockey stick to propel the ball into their opponents' goal net. Skills such as passing, pushing, or hitting the ball by slapping or lifting it in a flicking movement, and shooting at goal are crucial. Hockey is played indoors and outdoors on grass or synthetic pitches. Lacrosse is played internationally as a 12-a-side game for women and as 10-a-side game for men. The women's pitch has no absolute boundaries but the men's pitch has clearly defined side-lines and end-lines. The ball is kept in play by being carried, thrown or batted with the crosse, and rolled or kicked in any direction. In men's and women's lacrosse, play can continue behind the marked goal areas. Similar skills are required in hurling – a Gaelic field game played on the same pitch as Gaelic football (see pp. 528–529), using the same goalposts and net. In hurling, the ball may be struck with or carried on the hurley and, when off the ground, may be struck with the hand or kicked. Goals (three points) are scored when the ball passes between the posts and under the crossbar; one point is scored when it passes between the posts and over the crossbar.

GOALKEEPER'S EQUIPMENT

Air vent

Hard shell

Face mask

HELMET

Strap

Rigid palm

Padded wrist

GAUNTLET

HOCKEY STICK AND BALL

STICK

Handle

Tape

Slazenger FLEX

Steam-bent ash head

Blade

91 cm (3 ft)

Stitched seam

7–7.5 cm (2¼–3 in)

BALL

HOCKEY FIELD

Centre forward

Inside right

Right wing

Right half

Right back

Side-line

Corner flag

Shooting circle

Goal

Penalty spot

Five yard mark

Goal-line

Inside left

Left wing

Umpire

Centre half

Left half

Left back

Goalkeeper

55 m (180 ft)

Protective overshoe

Padding protects toes against the hard ball

Strap

GOALKEEPER'S KICKER

2.1 m (7 ft)

HOCKEY GOAL

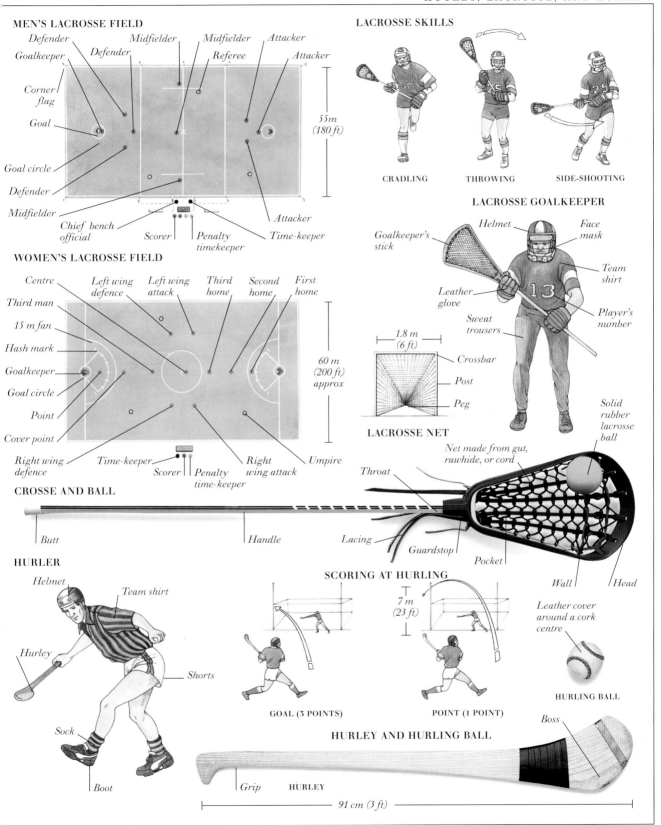

MEN'S LACROSSE FIELD

Defender
Goalkeeper
Defender
Midfielder
Midfielder
Referee
Attacker
Attacker

Corner flag

Goal

Goal circle

Defender

Midfielder

Chief bench official
Scorer
Penalty timekeeper
Time-keeper
Attacker

55m (180 ft)

WOMEN'S LACROSSE FIELD

Centre
Third man
15 m fan
Hash mark
Goalkeeper
Goal circle
Point
Cover point
Left wing defence
Left wing attack
Third home
Second home
First home

Right wing defence
Time-keeper
Scorer
Penalty time-keeper
Right wing attack
Umpire

60 m (200 ft) approx

CROSSE AND BALL

Butt
Handle

HURLER

Helmet
Team shirt
Hurley
Shorts
Sock
Boot

LACROSSE SKILLS

CRADLING
THROWING
SIDE-SHOOTING

LACROSSE GOALKEEPER

Goalkeeper's stick
Helmet
Face mask
Team shirt
Leather glove
Sweat trousers
Player's number
13
Solid rubber lacrosse ball

1.8 m (6 ft)
Crossbar
Post
Peg

LACROSSE NET

Net made from gut, rawhide, or cord
Throat
Lacing
Guardstop
Pocket
Wall
Head

SCORING AT HURLING

7 m (23 ft)

GOAL (3 POINTS)
POINT (1 POINT)

Leather cover around a cork centre

HURLING BALL

HURLEY AND HURLING BALL

Boss
Grip
HURLEY
91 cm (3 ft)

Athletics

THE SPORTS that make up athletics are divided into two main groups: track events – which include sprinting, middle, and long distance running, relay running, hurdling, and walking – and field events which require jumping and throwing skills. Contests designed to test the speed, strength, agility, and stamina of athletes were held by the ancient Greeks over 4,000 years ago. However, the abolition of the Olympic Games in 393 AD meant that athletics were neglected until the revival of large-scale competitions in the mid-nineteenth century. Modern stadia offer areas reserved for the long jump, triple jump, and pole vault usually situated outside the running track. The javelin, shot, hammer, and discus are thrown within the track area. Most athletes specialize in one or two events but, in the heptathlon, women compete in seven events, held over two days: 200 m and 800 m races, 100 m hurdles, javelin, shot put, high jump, and long jump. In the decathlon, men compete in ten events over two days: 100 m, 400 m, and 1,500 m races, 110 m hurdles, javelin, discus, shot put, pole vault, high jump, and long jump.

FIELD EVENT EQUIPMENT

Steel wire

Head

Body

Swivel

HAMMER
7 KG (16 LB)

Metal rim

Centre weight

DISCUS
MEN: 2 KG (4 LB 7 OZ)
WOMEN: 1 KG (2 LB 3 OZ)

Hammer handle

Rubber coating

Shot-pellet filling

12.7 cm (5 in)

10 cm (4 in)

MEN'S SHOT
7 KG (16 LB)

WOMEN'S SHOT
4 KG (8 LB 12 OZ)

JAVELIN   Cord grip   Shaft   Tip

Men: 2.6 m (8 ft 6 in)
Women: 2.3 m (7 ft 6 in)

ATHLETICS TRACK AND FIELD

Finishing post

Pole-vault mat

Pole-vault runway

100 m starting line

Finishing line

Javelin fan

Steeplechase water jump

Hammer circle

Discus circle

Javelin runway

Lane

Shot-put fan

Shot-put circle

Discus fan

One lap is 400 m

High-jump fan

High-jump mat

Hammer fan

Triple-jump take-off board

Triple-jump take-off line

Indicator board

Triple-jump runway

Long-jump take-off board

Landing area

RELAY BATONS

Hollow plastic tube

TYPES OF SHOE

Lightweight construction

Reflective side strip

Wedge heel

Spiked sole

TRACK SHOE

Air-cushioned sole

RUNNING SHOE

DISCUS THROW

Swing · *Shift* · *Twist* · *Release*

HIGH JUMP

Drive · *Arch* · *Take-off* · *Approach* · *Landing*

SHOT PUT

Crouch · *Shift* · *Thrust* · *Release*

HAMMER THROW

Swing · *Entry* · *Lift* · *Release*

JAVELIN THROW

Withdrawal stride · *Half turn* · *Step* · *Drive forward* · *Release*

POLE VAULT

Handstand · *Push-pull* · *Release* · *Rock-back* · *Hang* · *Take-off* · *Plant* · *Landing*

LONG JUMP

Take-off · *Flight* · *Hitch-kick* · *Stretch* · *Landing* · *Take-off board*

TRIPLE JUMP

Take-off · *Hop* · *Skip* · *Jump* · *Take-off board* · *Land on foot used for take-off* · *Land on opposite foot*

Racket sports

PROTECTIVE
EYEWEAR

THE OBJECT OF ALL RACKET SPORTS is to make shots the
opponent cannot return. Games are played by two players
(singles) or four players (doubles). Racket shape and size is
tailored to each sport, but all rackets are constructed of wood,
plastic, aluminium, or high-performance materials such as
fibreglass and carbon graphite. Racket strings are usually
synthetic, although natural gut is still used. Tennis is played on a court divided
by a low net. Opposing players serve alternate games. At least six games must
be won to gain a set, and two or sometimes three sets are needed to win a match.
Tennis courts may be concrete, grass, clay, or synthetic, each surface requiring a
different style of play. Badminton is an indoor sport that is played with light, flexible
rackets and a feather shuttlecock on a court with a high net. Players can score points
only on their serve. The first to reach 15 points (11 points for women's singles) wins
the game. Two games are needed to win a match. Squash and racketball are both played
in enclosed courts. One player hits the ball against the front wall, and the other tries to
return it before it bounces on the floor more than once. Squash rackets have smaller,
rounder heads and stiffer frames than badminton rackets. In America, the game is played
on a narrower court than an international court using a much harder ball. Squash games
are played to nine points (international) or 15 points (American). In racketball, players
use a ball that is larger and bouncier than a squash ball. The racket is thick and sturdy,
with a large head, short handle, and a thong that loops around the wrist. Points can
be won only when serving, and the first player to reach 21 points wins.

TENNIS RACKET

Synthetic string

Frame

Head

Logo

Throat

Grip

Butt

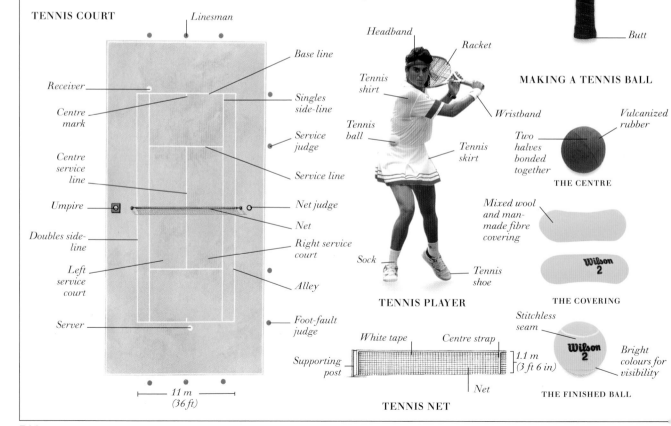

TENNIS COURT

Linesman

Base line

Receiver

Singles
side-line

Centre
mark

Service
judge

Centre
service
line

Service line

Umpire

Net judge

Net

Doubles side-
line

Right service
court

Left
service
court

Alley

Server

Foot-fault
judge

11 m
(36 ft)

TENNIS PLAYER

Headband

Racket

Tennis
shirt

Wristband

Tennis
ball

Tennis
skirt

Sock

Tennis
shoe

MAKING A TENNIS BALL

Vulcanized
rubber

Two
halves
bonded
together

THE CENTRE

Mixed wool
and man-
made fibre
covering

THE COVERING

Stitchless
seam

Wilson
2

Bright
colours for
visibility

THE FINISHED BALL

TENNIS NET

White tape

Centre strap

Supporting
post

1.1 m
(3 ft 6 in)

Net

BADMINTON RACKET AND SHUTTLECOCK

Synthetic string

Flexible frame

Shaft

SHUTTLECOCK

Feather crown

Cork tip

Handle

RACKET

SQUASH RACKET AND SQUASH BALLS

Protective strip

Frame

Synthetic strings

Logo

Open-throat head

SQUASH BALLS

YELLOW DOT (VERY SLOW)

WHITE DOT (SLOW)

RED DOT (FAST)

BLUE DOT (VERY FAST)

Shaft

Handle

RACKET

AMERICAN SQUASH COURT

Outer boundary line

Front wall

Side-wall line

Service line

Telltale

Floor

Side wall

Half-court line

Service box

Short line

Server

Receiver

Right service court

Left service court

⊢ 5.6 m (18 ft 6 in) ⊣

INTERNATIONAL SQUASH COURT

Outer boundary line

Front wall

Service line

Tin

Side-wall line

Floor

Side wall

Short line

Service box

Half-court line

Server

Left service court

Right service court

Receiver

6.4 m (21ft)

BADMINTON COURT

Service judge

Receiver

Doubles side-line

Singles side-line

Linesman

Umpire

Net

Short service line

Server

Back boundary line

Alley

Long service line (doubles)

White tape

Post

Net

6 m (20 ft)

1.5 m (5 ft)

BADMINTON NET

RACKETBALL RACKET, BALL, AND GLOVE

RACKET

Synthetic string

Frame

Logo

Leather treated to make it sticky

Throat

Short handle

Wrist thong

JAGUAR

RACKETBALL

GLOVE

RACKETBALL COURT

Front wall

Side wall

Service line

Server

Service zone

Service box line

Receiving line

Service line

Centre court

Floor

Receiver

6 m (20 ft)

Golf

GOLF BALL
AND TEE

THE GAME OF GOLF was first played in Scotland some
400 years ago. Players are required to hit a ball, using
a wooden or iron club, from a smooth level point or "teeing
ground", down the "fairway", and on to a putting green where
the target hole is located. The fairway is a strip of clear land
along which there are natural hazards – such as ponds and streams,
man-made hazards – such as bunkers (sand-pits), and rough (areas
of uncut grass). Championship golf courses have 18 holes. The object
of the game is to hit the ball into each hole in turn, and to complete
the "round" using as few strokes as possible. Players compete
individually or in teams, playing the course together in
groups of two, three, or four. The two basic forms of
competition are match play and stroke play.
In match play, the side winning the majority
of holes over a certain number of rounds
wins the match. In stroke play,
the winner is the player who
finishes a certain number of
rounds having made
the fewest strokes.

GOLF BALL WITH BALATA SURFACE

Dimpled
surface

Wound yarn

Liquid

Balata
cover

Membrane
to contain
liquid

Water
obstacle

Putting
green

Dog-leg
hole

Bridge

Pond

Hole

Teeing
ground

Pathway

Fairway

Screen
of trees

Elevated
green

Putting
green

Clubhouse

Bunker

Practice
area

Rough

**AUGUSTA NATIONAL
GOLF COURSE, AUGUSTA,
GEORGIA, U.S.A.**

A TYPICAL HOLE

Teeing
ground

Water obstacle | Bridge | Fairway | Wood | Rough

MAKING A WOODEN CLUB

Close grain of wood

Persimmon wood

Outline of head

RAW MATERIAL

Streamlined back

Slot cut for plate

CREATING THE BASIC SHAPE

Plastic insert on face

Metal sole plate protects the wood

ADDING THE LEAD WEIGHT

Sand, stain, and varnish finish

THE FINISHED CLUB HEAD

PUTTER, WOOD, AND IRON

WOOD

Textured vulcanized rubber grip

IRON

PUTTER

Shaped pistol grip

Stainless steel shaft

Steel shaft

Steel shaft

84 cm (33 in)

94 cm (37 in)

109 cm (43 in)

Angled neck

Heel

Toe

Blade

Neck

Heel

Toe   Groove

Neck

Face

Toe

Sole

Heel

RANGE OF WOODEN CLUBS

10 degree loft

DRIVER

15 degree loft

3-WOOD

21 degree loft

5-WOOD

RANGE OF IRON CLUBS

22 degree loft

3-IRON

26 degree loft

4-IRON

30 degree loft

5-IRON

34 degree loft

6-IRON

38 degree loft

7-IRON

42 degree loft

8-IRON

46 degree loft

9-IRON

50 degree loft

PITCHING WEDGE

56 degree loft

SAND WEDGE

GOLF ACCESSORIES

GOLF SCORE RECORD

SCORECARD AND PENCIL

BALL MARKERS

TEE PEGS

PITCHMARK REPAIRER

PRACTICE BALL

Spiked sole

LIGHTWEIGHT SHOE

Flag pole or pin

Green

Bunker (sand-pit)

547

Archery and shooting

TARGET SHOOTING AND ARCHERY EVOLVED as practice for hunting and battle skills. Modern bows, although designed according to the principles of early hunting bows, use laminates, fibreglass, dacron, and carbon, and are equipped with sights and stabilizers. Competitors in target archery shoot over distances of 30 m (100 ft), 50 m (165 ft), 70 m (230 ft), and 90 m (300 ft) for men, and 30 m (100 ft), 50 m (165 ft), 60 m (200 ft), and 70 m (230 ft) for women. The closer the shot is to the centre of the target, the higher the score. The individual scores are added up, and the archer with the highest total wins the competition. Crossbows are used in match competitions over 10 m (33 ft), and 30. m (100 ft). Rifle shooting is divided into three categories: smallbore, bigbore, and air rifle. Contests take place over a variety of distances and further subdivisions are based on the type of shooting position used: prone, kneeling, or standing. The Olympic biathlon combines cross-country skiing and rifle shooting over a course of approximately 20 km (12½ miles). Additional magazines of ammunition are carried in the butt of the rifles. Bigbore rifles fitted with a telescopic sight can be used for hunting and running game target shooting. Pistol shooting events, using rapid-fire pistols, target pistols, and air pistols, take place over 10 m (33 ft), 25 m (82 ft), and 50 m (165 ft) distances. In rapid-fire pistol shooting, a total of 60 shots are fired from a distance of 25 m (83 ft).

CROSSBOW AND BOLT

Laminated fibreglass bow

Bolt

Bolt rest

45 mm (1¼ in)

Bolt

Stirrup held between feet when drawing bow

CROSSBOW TARGET

Sight

Hardwood laminate limb

Dacron string

Sight

MODERN BOW

Plastic fletch

Nock

Forearm guard

Finger hole

Aluminium shaft

BRACER

FINGER TAB

Strap

Pressure button

Quicks SUPER-QS

Wristband

ARCHER'S GLOVE

Grip

Velcro fastening

Weight

V-bar stabilizers

Magnesium riser

Waistband

Accessory pouch

ARCHERY EQUIPMENT

QUIVER

SMALLBORE BIATHLON RIFLE

Rifle sight without magnifying lens

Barrel

Fore sight

Trigger

5.6 mm (0.22 in) calibre bullet

Trigger guard

Magazine

Extra magazine stored in rifle butt

155 mm (6 in)

SMALLBORE FREE RIFLE TARGET FOR 50 M (165 FT) RANGE

BIGBORE HUNTING RIFLE

Bolt

Telescopic sight

Bolt handle

Open sight

Open sight

7.62 mm (0.3 in) calibre bullet

Sling fixing point

1 m (39 in)

BIGBORE RIFLE TARGET FOR 300 M (100° FT) RANGE

AIR PISTOL

Cocking lever and barrel

Wooden grip shaped to fit the hand

Piston

TARGET PISTOL

197 mm (7¼ in)

155 mm (6 in)

Back sight

Fore sight

Hammer

Sight pin

Firing pin

Trigger

Air-pistol pellet

Sight ring attachment

PISTOL TARGET FOR 18 M (60 FT) RANGE

AIR-PISTOL TARGET FOR 10 M (33 FT) RANGE

Magazine

9 mm (0.35 in) calibre bullet

Nock

FIELD ARROW

Metal tip

Feathering

Wooden shaft

Straw butt

White inner 2 points

Aluminium longrod stabilizer

Blue outer 5 points

Yellow inner 10 points (bull's-eye)

ARCHERY TARGET

Ice hockey

ICE HOCKEY IS PLAYED by two teams of six players on an ice rink, with a goal net at each end. The object of this fast, and often dangerous, game is to hit a frozen rubber puck into the opposing team's net with a ice hockey stick. The game begins when the referee drops the puck between the sticks of two players from opposing teams, who "face off". The rink is divided into three areas: defending, neutral, and attacking zones. Players may move with the puck and pass the puck to one another along the ice, but may not pass it more than two zones across the rink markings. A goal is scored when the puck entirely crosses the goal-line between the posts and under the crossbar of the goal. A team may field up to 20 players although only six players are allowed on the ice at one time; substitutions occur frequently. Each game consists of three periods of 20 minutes, divided by breaks of 15 minutes.

GOALKEEPER

Helmet
Face mask
Throat protector
Butt end
Team shirt
Pants
Catch glove
Blocking pad
Goalkeeper's pad
Skate
Blade
Blade
Goalkeeper's stick
Heel

ICE HOCKEY RINK

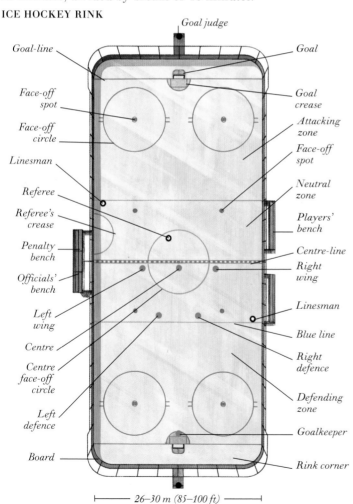

Goal judge
Goal-line
Goal
Face-off spot
Goal crease
Face-off circle
Attacking zone
Linesman
Face-off spot
Referee
Neutral zone
Referee's crease
Players' bench
Penalty bench
Centre-line
Officials' bench
Right wing
Left wing
Linesman
Centre
Blue line
Centre face-off circle
Right defence
Left defence
Defending zone
Board
Goalkeeper
Rink corner

26–30 m (85–100 ft)

THE FACE-OFF

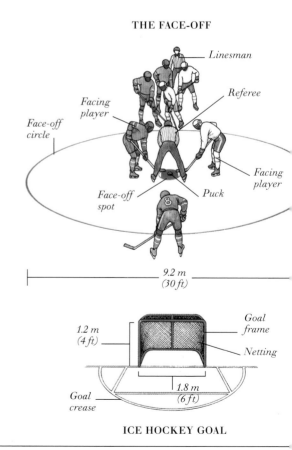

Linesman
Facing player
Referee
Face-off circle
Face-off spot
Facing player
Puck

9.2 m (30 ft)

1.2 m (4 ft)
Goal frame
Netting
Goal crease
1.8 m (6 ft)

ICE HOCKEY GOAL

GOALKEEPER'S HELMET

Customized paintwork

Face guard

Chin protection

JOFA

PLAYER'S BODY ARMOUR

Air vents

Rigid plastic shell

Manufacturer's logo

CANADIEN

Chin strap

Foam padding

PLAYER'S HELMET

ICE HOCKEY STICKS

GOALKEEPER'S STICK

SHOULDER AND CHEST PADDING

OUTFIELD PLAYER'S STICK

MADE IN FINLAND

TORSPO

Pro 5000

TORSPO

Pro 500

147 cm
(4 ft 9 in)

Shoulder padding

ELBOW PADS

Strap

Chest padding

Wrist protection

Thin shaft

TORSPO

TORSPO

Heavy padding

Flexible gusset

Rigid finger cap

GLOVE

LEG PROTECTOR

Rigid plastic casing

D'R Daignault-Rolland

Knee protection

Vulcanized rubber

7.6 cm
(3 in)

FROZEN PUCK

16.5" 43cm CENTURION-J

Thick foam backing

Wide lower shaft

Ankle support

Leg pad

Safety heel tip

501

Blade

SKATE

Puck stopper

39 cm
(15 in)

32 cm
(12½ in)

Thick blade

Heel

Alpine skiing

COMPETITIVE ALPINE SKIING is divided into four disciplines: downhill, slalom, giant slalom, and super-giant slalom (Super-G). Each one tests different skills. In downhill skiing, competitors race down a slope marked out by control flags, known as "gates", and are timed on a single run only. Competitors wear crash helmets, one-piece Lycra suits, and long skis with flattened tips to minimize air resistance. Slalom and giant slalom skiers negotiate a twisting course requiring balance, agility, and quick reactions. Courses are defined by pairs of gates. Racers must pass through each pair of gates to complete the course successfully. Competitors are timed on two runs over different courses, and the skier who completes the courses in the shortest time wins. The equipment and protective guards used by slalom skiers are shown opposite. In Super-G races, competitors ski a single run that combines the technical challenge of slalom with the speed of downhill. The course requires skiers to complete medium-to-long radius turns at high speed, and contain up to two jumps. Clothing is the same as for downhill, but slightly shorter skis are used.

DOWNHILL SKIER

Ski goggles
Helmet
One-piece lycra ski suit
Wrist strap
Ski pole
Basket
Ski boot
Safety binding
Tail
Ski glove

ALPINE SKI SLOPE COURSES

Downhill start
Downhill racing control flag
Super-G start
Pine forest
Giant slalom start
Giant slalom gate
Slalom start
Slalom gate
Safety barrier
Finish line

SKI BOOT

Polyamide inner boot
Tongue
Upper cuff
Upper strap
Buckle
Energy-distributing bonnet
Power bar
Adjusting catch
Tension control
Sole
Lower shell of boot
Heel grip

SAFETY BINDING

Toe-piece
Wing
Housing
Anti-friction pad
Heel-piece
Blind release lever
Release adjustment screw
Base plate
Brake arm

SLALOM CLOTHING AND EQUIPMENT

Anti-glare lens

Elasticated strap

GOGGLES

Hard nylon shell

Padding

Strap

Chin guard

SLALOM HELMET

Extended cuff

Wrist strap

Rigid pad for hand protection

SKI GLOVE

Tail

Adjustable shoulder strap

High collar

Double-knit wool and polyester fabric

Wrist strap

Grip

Ribbed cuff

Zip pocket

Front zip fastening

Shock-absorbing platform under boot

Edge

Moulded polypropylene

PADDED SWEATER

HAND GUARD

Waterproof fabric

188–203 cm (74–80 in)

Tough polypropylene shell deflects the shaft of the slalom gate

Shaft

Velero strap

Basket

Cuff fits over ski boot

LEG GUARD

SLALOM SKI POLE

PADDED SKI TROUSERS

SLALOM SKI

Tip

Equestrian sports

EQUESTRIAN SPORTS HAVE TAKEN place throughout the world for centuries: events involving mounted horses were recorded in the Olympic Games of 642 BC. Showjumping, however, is a much more recent innovation, and the first competitions were held at the beginning of the 1900s. In this sport, horse and rider must negotiate a course of variable, unfixed obstacles, making as few mistakes as possible. Showjumping fences consist of wooden stands, known as standards or wings, that support planks or poles. Parts of the fence are designed to collapse on impact, preventing injury to the horse and rider. Judges penalise competitors for errors, such as knocking down obstacles, refusing jumps, or deviating from the course. Depending on the type of competition, the rider with the fewest faults, most points, or fastest time wins. There are two basic forms of horse racing – flat races and races with jumps, such as steeplechase or hurdle-races. Thoroughbred horses are used in this sport, as they have great strength and stamina and can achieve speeds of up to 65 kph (40 mph). Jockeys wear "silks" – caps and jackets designed in distinctive colours and patterns which help identify the horses. In harness racing, the horse is driven from a light, twowheeled carriage called a sulky. Horses are trained to trot and to pace, and different races are held for each of these types of gait. In pacing races, the horses wear hobbles to prevent them from breaking into a trot or gallop. Breeds such as the Standardbred and the French Trotter have been developed especially for this sport.

SHOWJUMPING SADDLE

High cantle
Deep seat
Pommel
Forward-cut flap
Knee roll

SHOWJUMPING FENCES

Standard
Foot
Plank

UPRIGHT PLANKS

Standard
Foot
Pole

UPRIGHT POLES

Back pole
Standard
Foot
Pole

TRIPLE BAR (STAIRCASE)

Standard
Pole
Foot

HOG'S-BACK

Pillar
Wood block paint to resemb a bri

WALL

Hard hat
Riding jacket
Browband
Throat-latch
Rein
Jodhpurs
Cheek-piece
Showjumping saddle
Hindquarters
Dock
Running martingale
Noseband
Brushing boot
Sheepskin numnah
Girth
Stirrup iron
Riding boot
Gaskin
Hock joint
Hoof
Fetlock joint
Pastern
Coronet

SHOWJUMPING HORSE WITH RIDER

RACING SADDLE

Cut-back head

Cantle

Surcingle loop

Forward-cut flap

Lightweight steel stirrup-iron

Rawhide stirrup-leather

RACING SILKS

Plain cap

Spotted cap

Quartered cap

Plain sleeve

Plain sleeve

Striped jacket

Plain jacket

Spotted sleeve

Jacket with sash

Paddock

Clubhouse

Finishing line

Grandstand

Dirt track

Home stretch

Far turn

Clubhouse turn

Tote board

Grass track

Start of straight

Barrier

Back stretch

SARATOGA RACE COURSE, SARATOGA, NEW YORK, U.S.A.

Browband

Rosette

Cheek-piece

Bridle

Noseband

Driving saddle

Rein terret

Shaft

Crupper

Skullcap covered with racing silk

Goggles

Quartered racing silk jacket

Whip

Rubber bit-guard

Driving rein

Lightweight harness

Thimble

Girth

Seat

Racing sulky

Stirrup

Over-reach boot

Belly-band

Pacing hobble

Pneumatic tyre

Wheel

HARNESS RACING WITH A STANDARDBRED HORSE

Disc covering spokes

Judo and fencing

COMBAT SPORTS ARE BASED ON THE SKILLS used in fighting. In these sports, the competitors may be unarmed – as in judo and boxing – or armed – as in fencing and kendo. Judo is a system of unarmed combat developed in the East. Translated from the Japanese the name means "the gentle way". Students learn how to turn an opponent's force to their own advantage. The usual costume is loose white trousers and a jacket, fastened with a cloth belt. The colour of belt indicates the student's level of expertise, from white-belted novices to the expert "black belts". Competitions take place on a mat or "shiaijo", 9 or 10 m (30 or 33 ft) square in size, bounded by "danger" and "safety" areas to prevent injury. Competitors try to throw, pin, or master their opponent by applying pressure to the arm joints or neck. Judo bouts are strictly monitored, and competitors receive points for superior technique, not for injuring their opponent. Fencing is a combat sport using swords, which takes place on a narrow "piste" 14 m (46 ft) long. Competitors try to touch specific target areas on their opponent with their sword or "foil" while avoiding being touched themselves. The winner is the one who scores the greatest number of hits. Fencers wear clothing made from strong white material, which affords maximum protection while allowing freedom of movement, steel mesh masks with padded bibs to protect the fencer's neck, and a long white glove on their sword hand. Fencing foils do not have sharpened blades, and their tips end in a blunt button to prevent injuries. Three types of swords are used – foils, épées, and sabres. Official foil and épée competitions always use an electric scoring system. The sword tips are connected to lights by a long wire that passes underneath each fencer's jacket. A bulb flashes when a hit is made.

JUDO HOLDS AND THROWS

SIDE FOUR QUARTER HOLD

SINGLE WING

BODY DROP

ONE ARM SHOULDER THROW

SHOULDER WHEEL

SWEEPING LOW THROW

STOMACH THROW

KNEE WHEEL

JUDO MAT

16 m (52 ft 6 in)

Judge

Scorer

Holding time-keeper

Time-keeper

Danger area

Contestant

JUDO KIT

Draw-string

Contestant

Referee

Contest area

Safety area

Cotton trousers

Black belt

Heavy-duty cotton jacket

FENCING PISTE

Rear limit line

14 m (46 ft)

Sabre and épéé warning line

Scorer

Electrical scoring apparatus

Centre line

President

Time-keeper

On-guard line

Body wire

Reel

FENCING EQUIPMENT

Steel wire mesh

Padded bib

MESH MASK

Woven metal thread

METAL JACKET

Cuff

Glove

GAUNTLET

TARGET AREAS ON THE UPPER BODY

Wire mesh

Mask

Bib

Under plastron

Tierce

Sixte

Quinte

Gauntlet

Quarte

Seconde

Prime

Octave

Septime

Metal over-jacket

Breeches

Fencing shoe

Stocking

THE SABRE

THE FOIL

Martingale

THE EPEE

Button

Blade

PARTS OF THE SWORD

Guard

Tang

Leather pad

Alternative pistol-grip handle

Brass screw

Steel foil pommel

FENCING TARGET AREAS

SABREUR

FOILIST

EPEEIST

Swimming and diving

SWIMMING GOGGLES

SWIMMING WAS INCLUDED in the first modern Olympic Games in 1896 and diving events were added in 1904. Swimming is both an individual and a team sport and races take place over a predetermined distance in one of the four major categories of stroke – freestyle (usually front crawl), butterfly, breaststroke, and backstroke. Competition pools are clearly marked for racing and anti-turbulence lane lines are used to separate the swimmers and help keep the water calm. The first team or individual to finish the race is the winner. Competitive diving is divided into men's and women's springboard and platform (highboard) events. There are six official groups of dives: forward dives, backward dives, armstand dives, twist dives, reverse dives, and inward dives. Competitors perform a set number of dives and after each one a panel of judges awards marks according to the quality of execution and the degree of difficulty.

STYLES OF DIVES

Starting position

Hands above head

Legs fully stretched

Flight

Arched back

Toes pointed

Entry

Feet together

Hands close together

FORWARD DIVE

BACKWARD DIVE

SWIMWEAR

Latex rubber moulds to shape of head

CAPS

Rubber-covered wire

NOSE CLIP

Moulded rubber

EARPLUG

High neckline

Man-made stretch fabric

Drawstring

High-cut leg

Strong seam

SWIMSUIT

TRUNKS

SWIMMING POOL

Swimmer

Chief time-keeper

Lane number

Starting block

Lane time-keeper

End wall

Placing judge

Starter

Recorder

Side wall

Backstroke marker 15 m (49 ft) from end of pool

Anti-turbulence lane line

Referee

Stroke judge

Backstroke turn indicator 5 m (16 ft) from end of pool

Bottom line

Turning judge

Turning wall

Lane

23 m (75 ft 6 in)

Perfectly steady armstand

Arms and legs align throughout flight and entry

ARMSTAND DIVE

Arms spread wide apart

Body and legs straighten for flight and entry

TWIST DIVE

Pike position

Height of dive

Shoulders fall backwards for vertical entry

REVERSE DIVE PIKED

Pike position

Hands touch toes

Feet lift up for straight entry

INWARD DIVE PIKED

FRONT CRAWL
Flutter kick

Arm pulls like a paddle

Arrow-like position

Body rolls on a central axis

FULL BODY STRETCH

LOWER ARM PULL

STREAMLINED ARM ENTRY

SIDE-TO-SIDE BODY ROLL

BREASTSTROKE
Straight leg

Knees together

Elbows tucked in

Arm fully extended

BODY GLIDE

DOUBLE ARM PULL

SQUEEZING THE WATER

FROG KICK

BACKSTROKE
Little finger enters first

Arm comes up straight

Recovering hand

Shoulder exits water first

BODY ROLL

PULLING THROUGH

STRAIGHTENING OUT

SHOULDER LIFT

BUTTERFLY
Palm turned outwards

Legs ready to kick down

Head clears the water

Shoulders power the stroke

CATCHING THE WATER

DOUBLE ARM PULL

KICKING DOWN

WHOLE BODY UNDULATION

Canoeing, rowing, and sailing

Wᴀᴛᴇʀʙᴏʀɴᴇ ꜱᴘᴏʀᴛꜱ are as varied as the crafts used. There are two disciplines in rowing; sweep rowing, in which each rower has one oar and sculling, in which rowers use two oars. There are a number of different Olympic and competitive rowing events for both men and women. The number of rowers and weight classes vary. Some rowing events use a coxswain; a steersman who does not row but directs the crew. Kayaks and canoes are used in straight sprint and slalom races. Slalom races take place over a course consisting of 20 to 25 gates, including at least six upstream gates. In yacht racing, competitors must complete prescribed courses, organized by the race committees, in the shortest possible time, using sail power only. Olympic events include classes for keel boats, dinghies, and catamarans.

SAILING GEAR

Sleeveless long johns · Buoyancy aid · Long-sleeved jacket · Neoprene material · Belt · GLOVE · Bootlace · Ribbed top · Non-slip sole · BOOT

ONE-PERSON KAYAK AND PADDLE

Blade · Rim · Shaft · Nose cone · Right rail · Cockpit · Back strap · Stern · High density polythene · Toggle · Bow · Left rail · Seat · Cockpit rim

SINGLE SCULL AND OARS (WITH CLOTH DECKING REMOVED)

Neck · Shaft · Stroke-side oar · Spoon · Blade · Colours · Gate · Adjusting screw · Gate clamp · Grip · Bow-side oar · Button · Loom · Rigger · Sycamore beam · Stretcher · Water shoot · Bung · Aft shoulder · Shoe · Keel · Sternpost · Spruce beam · Diagonal frame · Aluminium beam · Kelson (kelson)

LIFEJACKET

Backstrap rescue strap

Reinforced seam

Neck opening

Whistle

Topping-up valve

Lanyard

Waistband

SAILING DINGHY

Elastic control line

Boom

Rudder

Mast

Mainsheet

Standing rigging

Spreader

Stern

Bow

Tiller

Toestrap

Centre-board

Cockpit

Shroud

Jib fairlead

Non-slip deck surface

SCULLS

DOUBLE SCULL

SINGLE SCULL

SWEEP-ROWING BOATS

COXLESS FOUR

COXED PAIR

COXLESS PAIR

EIGHT

COXED FOUR

Slide track

Wheel

Sliding seat

Main deck

Saxboard

Wheel spacer

Forward deck

Hatch

Breakwater

In-board

Bowball

Bowpost

Angling

ANGLING MEANS FISHING WITH A ROD, reel, line, and lure. There are several different types of angling: freshwater coarse angling, for members of the carp family and pike; freshwater game angling, for salmon and trout; and sea angling, for sea fish such as flatfish, bass, and mackerel. Anglers use a variety of methods of catching fish. These include bait fishing, in which bait (food to allure the fish) is placed on a hook and cast into the water; fly fishing, in which a natural or artificial fly is used to lure the fish; and spinning, in which a lure that looks like a small fish revolves as it is pulled through the water. The angler uses the rod, reel, and line to cast the lure over the water. The reel controls the line as it spills off the spool and as it is wound back. Weights may be fixed to the line so that it will sink. Swivels are attached to prevent the line from twisting. When a fish bites, the hook must become embedded in its mouth and remain there while the catch is reeled in.

Keeper ring

Handgrip

Drag spindle

Disk drag

Drag washer

Disk spring

Gear retainer

Dual click gear

Retaining screw

Check pawl cover

Check pawl

Check slide

Check spring

HOOKS, SWIVELS, AND WEIGHTS

REELS

Spool-release button

Reel foot (reel scoop)

Plate-nut

Click mechanism

Mechanical brake

Side plate

Centrifugal brake

Spool

Handle

Star drag

Level-wind system

MULTIPLIER REEL

Eye

Shank

Bend

Gape

ANATOMY OF A HOOK

Throat

Point

Barb

TREBLE HOOK

ABERDEEN HOOK

REVERSED BEND HOOK

Line

Reel foot (reel scoop)

Unskirted spool

Handle

Tension nut (drag adjustment)

Ratchet (anti-reverse device)

Handgrip

EXAMPLES OF BARREL SWIVELS

HILLMAN ANTI-KINK WEIGHT

Reel

Bail arm

FIXED-SPOOL REEL

FLY ROD AND REEL

Intermediate ring

TIP SECTION

Reel seat

Screw locking nut

Tip ring

Disk drag housing

Reel foot (reel scoop)

Line

Butt cap

Drag knob screw

Butt extension

Clicker plate

Drag knob

DragonFly 100

Disc Drag

Release lever

Spool screw

Spool cover

Release spring

Spool-release button

Handle

ARTIFICIAL FLIES

Line guide

DUNKELD WET FLY

Body

Tail

Cheek

Head

Line guide cover

Hackle

Retaining screw

Ribbing

ARTIFICIAL LURES

DEVON MINNOW

Fin

Eye

Treble hook

Swivel

Tulip mount

DEER HOPPER DRY FLY

Front hackle

JOINTED PLUG

Eye

Tail

Adjustable vane

Joint

Hook

Treble hook

Head

Wing

563

THE MODERN WORLD

Personal computer

PERSONAL COMPUTERS (PCs) fall into two main types: IBM-compatible PCs, known simply as PCs, and Apple Macintosh PCs, known as "Macs". They differ in the way files and programs, and the user's access to them, are organized, and programs must be tailored for each type. However, in most other respects PCs and Macs have much in common. Both contain microchips, or integrated circuits, that store and process data. The "brain" of any PC is a chip known as the central processing unit (CPU), which performs mathematical operations in order to run program instructions and receive, store, and output data. The most powerful personal computer CPUs today can perform more than a billion calculations a second. Data can be input via CDs, USB memory sticks, and other storage media. Highly portable laptop and network PCs are also in widespread use. Most PCs are able to communicate with many other devices, including digital cameras (see pp. 580-81) and smartphones (see pp. 588-89).

LED-backlit glossy wide-screen

Keyboard

Mouse

iMAC

USB ports (4)

Audio in jack

Headphone jack

Firewire 800 port

Ethernet port

Mini display port

Powercord connector

REAR OF iMAC

Webcam

LCD display

Keyboard

Touchpad

Fingerprint reader

Left touchpad button

Right touchpad button

Headphone jacks (2)

Audio in jack

HP PAVILION DV4 LAPTOP

Optical drive

Power connector

USB ports (2)

Expansion port

Remote control

Display

Digital media slot

Security cable slot

RG-45 (network) port

HDMI port

eSATA/ USB port

External monitor port

SIDE VIEW OF HP PAVILION DV4 LAPTOP

COMPONENTS OF A SYSTEM UNIT

CD drive

DVD drive

RAM chips

COOLING FAN

RAM BOARD

Floppy drive

Power button

Reset button

Chassis

CD DRIVE

SYSTEM UNIT OF A PC

Circuit board

Video out connectors

Cooling fan

Graphics processor

GRAPHICS CARD

Edge connector

SIDE CABLE

Expansion slot

Back-up battery

Microprocessor socket

MICROPROCESSOR

Cable connector

HARD DISC DRIVE

BIOS chip

Graphics card slot

RAM board sockets

MOTHERBOARD

POWER SUPPLY

DATA CABLE

Tablet computer

By the early 1990s electronic circuitry had been miniaturized to such an extent that it was possible to make small handheld computing devices. The first of these was the Personal Digital Assistant (PDA), which offered features including an address book, calendar, and notepad. In recent years, PDAs have been overtaken by smartphones with Internet and email access (see pp. 588–589). A related product is the e-book reader, which stores books in digital form and uses "electronic paper" to mimic the appearance of ink on real paper. An e-book reader no bigger than a thin paperback can store several thousand digital books in its memory. The most recent handheld computing device is the tablet computer. This looks like a thin flat display, but it is actually a complete computer. Tablet computers are typically controlled by a touch-sensitive screen and have a wireless link to other computers and the Internet. They run software applications, or apps, downloaded from the Internet. The most popular tablet computer currently is the Apple iPad. It has a multi-touch interface that enables its screen to detect the movements of fingertips. As well as selecting options and apps by touching the screen, images can be enlarged or shrunk by moving fingertips apart or together on the screen.

Sleep/wake button

APPLE IPAD

Home button

App icon

Touch data is sent as a list of finger positions to the controller where the information is used to zoom in and out of a web page

LCD with buttons displayed

Fingers alter the electric field around nearby sections of the grid

User touches clear protective screen

Touchscreeen electronics interpret the outputs from the grid to work out exactly where the fingers are

Controller

MULTI-TOUCH INTERFACE

15-cm (6-in) screen

Next page button

Previous page button

Joystick controller

ACER LUMIREAD E-READER

ELECTROMAGNETIC
INTERFERENCE SHIELDS

Cable
connector

Back panel

*Wi-Fi
card*

OUTER CASE

Battery casing

Digitizer

Cable
connector

DOCK CONNECTOR CABLE

SPEAKER ASSEMBLY

A4 processor

LOGIC BOARD

POWER, VOLUME, AND
SCREEN ROTATION
LOCK CONTROLS

*Antenna
cable*

WI-FI ANTENNA 1

HEADPHONE JACK

WI-FI ANTENNA 2

LIQUID CRYSTAL DISPLAY

LITHIUM-POLYMER BATTERY

DISPLAY DATA CABLE

COMPONENTS OF AN APPLE IPAD

Headset jack

Camera lens

Touch sensitive screen

*Previous
page
button*

*Next page
button*

Keyboard

*Five-way
controller*

Back button

Home button

Menu button

*Touch
sensitive
screen*

*Control
buttons*

AMAZON KINDLE E-READER

BROADCOM PERSONA TABLET

OTHER TABLET COMPUTERS

SAMSUNG GALAXY TAB

Flatbed scanner

SCANNERS CONVERT physical images into electronic form, allowing them to be sent over the Internet, displayed on a website, stored on a computer, and manipulated using specialized software. Scanners work by detecting and analysing light reflected from an opaque image, such as a photographic print. Some can also scan photographic transparencies by analysing light that has passed through the image. Flatbed scanners contain a unit, called the scan head, that contains a lamp, mirrors, a lens, and an array of CCDs (Charge-Coupled Devices). The carriage passes beneath the image; the lamp shines light on to or through the original; the mirrors reflect the light on to the lens, which focuses it on to the CCD array. Each CCD detects the brightness of light from a particular pixel (picture element) along a· horizontal strip and converts this data into an electric signal. For colour images, the light is usually passed through red, green, and blue filters and then directed to the CCD array so that it can be broken down into its component colours. This information is then converted to digital form. The quality of the image depends on its resolution, measured in dpi (Dots Per Inch).

SCANNER

Integrated transparency unit (TPU)

Reflective document mat

Glass plate

Start button and indicator light

Photo print button

Scan to email button

Scan to Web button

Power supply cable

Direct current (DC) inlet

Lock

TPU connector port

Inverter board

Lamp power supply connector

Shield plate

Panel board connector

Cover support

FILM AND SLIDE HOLDER

35mm-slide holder

35 mm film strip holder

HOW A FLATBED SCANNER WORKS

Original image (photograph or artwork)

Lamp

Lens focuses light on to CCD array

Glass plate

The electronic image is converted to digital form and transmitted to a computer

CCD array builds up electric charges that vary according to the brightness of the light beam

Light beam is reflected from the original to a series of mirrors

Carriage is moved beneath the original by a stepper motor in a rapid series of tiny steps

UNDERSIDE OF SCAN HEAD COVER

COMPONENTS OF A SCANNER

TPU connector

Hinge

LID ASSEMBLY

Underside of lamp housing

Glass plate

Lens assembly

Universal serial bus (USB) port

Ferrite core

Integrated transparency unit (TPU)

Scan head

Reflective document mat

Mirror

FCC cable

Carriage shaft

FCC cable slot

Finger recess

UNDERSIDE OF COVER

OVERHEAD VIEW

Idler pulley

Underside of control panel

Control panel circuit board

THE EFFECT OF SCANNING AT DIFFERENT RESOLUTIONS

Pixel

15 DPI
Lowest resolution at which you may scan.

72 DPI
Used for websites and screen images.

300 DPI
Used for printing books and magazines.

Airbus 380

CROSS-SECTION OF FUSELAGE

THE AIRBUS A380 WAS CONCEIVED in the early 1990s to compete with, and if possible replace, the Boeing 747. Work began in earnest on what was then called the A3XX in 1994. Its maiden flight was in April 2005. The A380's shape is subtly moulded to minimize drag from its ovoid fuselage. The structure makes extensive use of composite materials, such as thermoplastics and GLARE (aluminium and glass fibre). Its engines are very powerful, but also very efficient. It is claimed that when carrying 550 passengers, the A380 uses only 2.9 litres (¾ gallon) of fuel per passenger per 100km (60 miles).

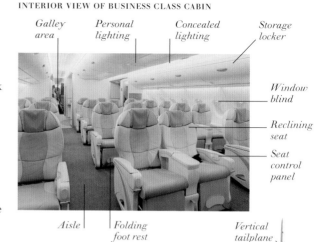

INTERIOR VIEW OF BUSINESS CLASS CABIN

Galley area
Personal lighting
Concealed lighting
Storage locker
Window blind
Reclining seat
Seat control panel
Aisle
Folding foot rest

Obstruction light
Swept titanium fan blades
Vertical tailplane
GLARE upper fuselage
Horizontal tailplane
Wing landing gear

FRONT VIEW

Company logo
Split rudder
Jupp-Reese winglet
Upper deck windows
Overwing emergency exit

F-WWOW

A380

Auxiliary Power Unit (APU) exhaust
Horizontal tailplane
Aft door
Belly fairing
Flap track fairings
Tailcone fairing

SIDE VIEW

Body landing gear

INTERIOR VIEW OF GALLEY

Counter

Bar area

Storage unit

Non-slip flooring

COCKPIT

Engine warning display

Overhead control panel

Sun blind

Windshield

Folding table with integral keyboard

Primary flight display

Navigation display

Onboard information terminal

Fly-by-wire side stick

Rudder pedal

Pilot's seat

Pylon forward fairing

Wing leading edge

Headrest

Seatbelt attachment point

Flap track fairings

Air intake duct

Navigation light

Cursor control device (CCD)

Multifunction display

System display

Power levers

Antenna

Fuselage

Upper deck passenger door

Main deck passenger door

Flightdeck door

Flightdeck windscreen

A380 AIRBUS

Wing landing gear

Engine cowling

Sculpted wing-root fairing

Main deck windows

Nose landing gear

Inkjet printer

INKJET PRINTERS EXPEL ink droplets from hundreds of tiny jets, or nozzles, on to a medium, such as paper, to print an image. Each droplet corresponds to a single pixel (picture element). Black-and-white printers use only black ink, while colour printers overprint combinations of the printing colours (cyan, yellow, magenta, and black) to create a full colour range. The printhead containing the nozzles moves sideways across the paper, creating a line of pixels, before the paper moves slightly forward so the next line can be printed. Two basic methods are used to eject ink: thermal, in which ink is heated to form an expanding bubble that expels a droplet from the nozzle, and piezoelectric, in which an electric current expands a crystal causing it to push out the ink droplet. The printer shown here can print digital photographs directly from a memory card.

EPSON STYLUS PHOTO 895 COLOUR INKJET PRINTER

Printer cover

Colour ink-cartridge clamp

Black ink-cartridge clamp

Output tray

Output tray extension

Carriage drive belt

Settings display

Settings control panel

Power button

PC card adapter

Ink-cartridge replacement button

Roll paper manipulation button

Maintenance button

OVERHEAD VIEW WITH OUTER CASING REMOVED

Paper hopper

Head data cable support

Preview monitor socket

Motor assembly

Paper thickness adjust lever

Colour ink-cartridge clamp

Spur gear

Head data cable

Paper output stacker

Black ink-cartridge clamp

Ink outlet hole

Colour ink cartridge

Ink outlet hole

Black ink cartridge

INK CARTRIDGES

PC CARD ADAPTER

PAPER FEED COMPONENTS

Attachment clip

ROLL PAPER HOLDER ADAPTER

ROLL PAPER HOLDER

Attachment clip

PAPER SUPPORT

OVERHEAD VIEW OF CASING

Left edge guide

Sheet feeder

Right edge guide

Printer cover

Preview monitor slot

Settings display

Photo select button

Cancel button

Start print button

Processing light   *Setting select buttons*

EPSON

HOW A PIEZOELECTRIC INKJET PRINTHEAD WORKS

Uncharged piezoelectric crystal

Charged crystal expands, increasing pressure in reservoir

Ink sucked into reservoir by lowered pressure

Uncharged crystal contracts, lowering pressure in reservoir

Ink reservoir

Ink droplet forced out of firing chamber by increased pressure in reservoir

Firing chamber

INKJET NOZZLE

DROPLET EJECTED

CHAMBER REFILLED

The Internet

THE INTERNET CONSISTS OF TENS of thousands of computer networks linked together to form one huge global network, allowing any computer on one network to communicate with any computer on another. The two main services used on the Internet are email and the World Wide Web. Email allows text messages to be sent – along with attached computer files, images, or video clips, for example – to other computers on the Internet. The Web consists of billions of pages made up of digital files that are stored on computers across the world and can be viewed using a Web browser. The Web also provides interactive access to various services, for example banking and shopping.

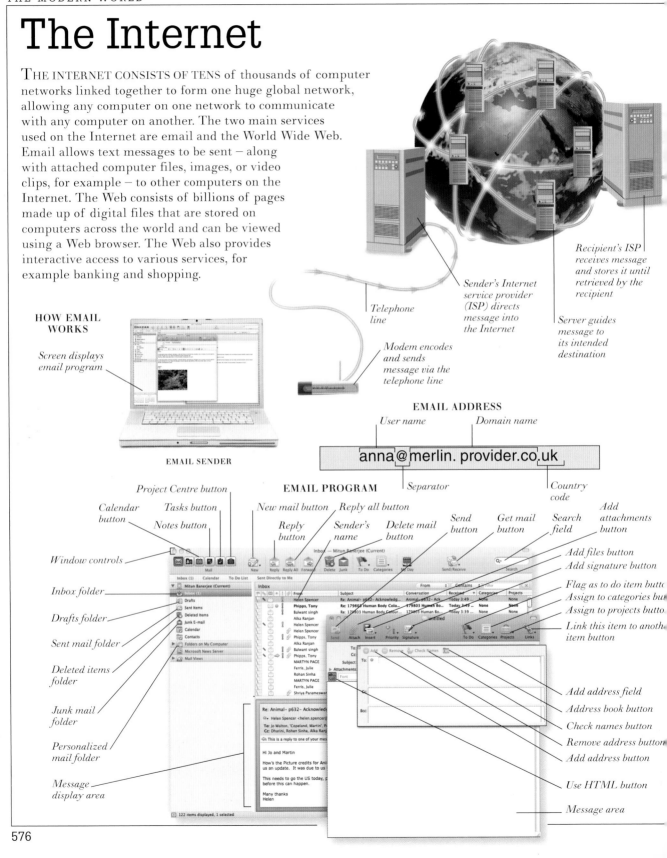

Recipient's ISP receives message and stores it until retrieved by the recipient

Sender's Internet service provider (ISP) directs message into the Internet

Server guides message to its intended destination

Telephone line

Modem encodes and sends message via the telephone line

HOW EMAIL WORKS

Screen displays email program

EMAIL SENDER

EMAIL ADDRESS

User name *Domain name*

anna@merlin. provider.co.uk

Separator *Country code*

EMAIL PROGRAM

Project Centre button *New mail button* *Reply all button* *Add attachments button*

Calendar button *Tasks button* *Reply button* *Sender's name* *Delete mail button* *Send button* *Get mail button* *Search field*

Notes button

Window controls *Add files button* *Add signature button*

Inbox folder *Flag as to do item button*

Drafts folder *Assign to categories button*

Sent mail folder *Assign to projects button*

Deleted items folder *Link this item to another item button*

Junk mail folder

Personalized mail folder *Add address field*

Address book button

Check names button

Message display area *Remove address button*

Add address button

Use HTML button

Message area

EMAIL RECIPIENT

Modem

Email program on screen displays received message

Computer with email program installed

Mouse

STREAMED INTERNET VIDEO ON-SCREEN DISPLAY

Program name

Window controls

Born To Be Wild

Screen

Volume slider

Rewind button

Fast forward button

Full screen button

Play/pause button

Seek bar

Web browser displaying item link

RSS (REALLY SIMPLE SYNDICATION) FEEDS

Site icon

Feed name

Feed list

NewsFire

Mac OS X Tip of the Week: Where Does Tha...
New Items

Israel seizes Hamas legislators
BBC News

Edelman – Emirates Stadium almost ready fo...
Arsenal.com – Arsenal FC News Headlines

Eriksson defends management style
BBC Sport | Football | World Cup 2006 | Teams | Engl...

Mac OS X Tip of the Week: Where Does That ...
Apple Hot News

Apple Hot News

"Back in black: MacBook world's best laptop?"

Published: Yesterday, 19:09

Reviewing the MacBook for MSNBC, Gary Krakow writes, "Quite frankly, this notebook computer is the best I've ever used." [Jun 28, 2006]

Search

Pull-down edit menu button

News reader window

News item summary

Search field

Feed add button

STREAMED INTERNET RADIO ON-SCREEN DISPLAY

Programme display

Window controls

BBC World Service

real

Status indicator

Stopped

0:00/0:00

Pause/play control

Elapsed time display

Volume control

WEB PAGES

Browser menu with navigation buttons

Dorling Kindersley – Illustrated Reference Publisher

http://www.dk.com

Google

Search field

Universal Resource Locator (URL), or web page address

DK www.dk.com

Click on a flag to visit a chosen country

United Kingdom   United States   Canada   Australia   Germany

India   South Africa   China   Spanish Language

Navigation area contains links to other parts of the site

Home page

Rollover button provides links to subsidiary page

United States

UNIVERSAL RESOURCE LOCATOR (URL) ADDRESS

Prefix

Page locator

http://www/dk.com/store_select.asp

Main website address

dk.com

Thursday, April 07, 2011

Home   New Books   App Shop   Children's Books   Eyewitness Travel   Browse   Services

Discover more at dk.com

STAR WARS   DK

DK In The News

VINO

Subsidiary page

Hyperlink text allows direct access to another web page or website

Electronic games

MARIO SPORTS MIX WII

VIDEO GAMES HAVE BEEN around since the early 1970s. They are played on PCs, arcade machines, on a TV using a home console, and on portable hand-held consoles. Players use devices such as joysticks and control pads with buttons to control movement and action on screen. The latest generation of consoles uses motion sensor technology to allow players to manipulate objects on screen by simply moving the controller. The most advanced game systems respond to gestures and commands spoken by a player, without any need to use a hand controller. The game itself is stored in the form of digital information on CD, DVD, or microchip – which may be integral or stored in a removable cartridge – or on an internal hard disk. A central processing unit (CPU) (see pp. 566–567) is needed to process commands from the players, while specialized graphics chips are used to process the complex mapping and texturing functions that make modern games appear so realistic.

MICROSOFT KINECT AND XBOX

- X-box 360
- Eject button
- Disc tray
- Ring indicator
- Cooling vent
- Power On/Off button
- Infra-red projector
- Colour camera
- Kinect
- Infra-red camera
- Status LED indicator

KINECT (FRONT PANEL REMOVED)

NINTENDO 3DS

COMPONENTS OF NINTENDO 3DS

- Inner camera
- 3D screen
- Speaker
- 3D depth slider
- Touch screen
- Control buttons
- Motherboard cable
- Stylus holder
- Motherboard cable

LOWER CASE BASE

- Select key
- Home key
- Start key
- Power On/Off button
- Circle pad
- Control pad

NINTENDO 3DS (OPENED UP)

- Ribbon cable
- SD card slot
- Circuit board

SD CARD READER

- Power connector
- Game card slot
- MEMS gyroscope
- Headphone jack

NINTENDO 3DS MOTHERBOARD

NINTENDO Wii FIT PLUS

Wii FIT PLUS BALANCE GAME

Hand controller

ACTIVITIES ON A BALANCE BOARD

Foot/hand area

Wii

Bumper

Power LED

Wii BALANCE BOARD

Power On/Off button

Power On/Off button

D-pad

Home button

Preset −

Effects buttons

Player LEDs

Preset +

Wrist strap

Wii HAND CONTROLLER

Wi-fi antenna

Control pad

Power On/Off button

Control button pad

Touch-sensitive screen

LOWER CASE TOP

Circle pad

LOWER LCD ASSEMBLY

WI-FI BOARD

INFRA-RED BOARD

Fixing screw

Positive terminal

Negative terminal

3.7 volt Lithium-ion battery

VOLUME CONTROL

BATTERY COVER

RECHARGEABLE BATTERY

CIRCLE PAD

Digital camera

FOR MORE THAN 200 YEARS, CAMERAS recorded pictures as chemical changes in silver-containing substances, on a strip of flexible, celluloid film. The digital camera records pictures in electronic form. At its heart is a specialized integrated circuit known as a charge-coupled device (CCD). This has millions of micro-units known as pixels. It works in the opposite way to a miniature computer or TV screen. Instead of electric signals making pixels shine, when light hits a pixel it generates a tiny electrical signal, according to the light's colour and brightness. The signals from the CCD's millions of pixels are analogue: they vary continuously in a wave-like fashion. They are converted by a microchip to digital codes of numbers, represented as on-off electronic pulses. The digital signals are processed and fed to the camera's internal memory or a removable memory device such as a data card or memory stick. Photographs can be downloaded from a digital camera to a computer via a cable or in some cases a wireless link. Some digital cameras automatically reduce blurring caused by camera shake or fast movement, some can record video clips as well as still pictures.

6.8cm (2.6in) liquid crystal display

Flexible ribbon cable

MONITOR

Protective steel panel

CHASSIS

Keypad

HOW A DIGITAL CAMERA WORKS

CCD turns light into electronic signals

Lens focuses light

Light from scene

Analogue signals

Analogue to digital converter microchip

Microprocessor

Digital signals

LCD screen

Memory stick

In-camera memory chip

Connector cover

Eyelet for camera strap

CHROMED PLASTIC SIDE COVER

Flash lamp

Infrared receiver (rear)

Speaker

Shooting mode button

Playback button

Delete button

REAR CASE

Menu button

OK (Select) button

Speaker mounting bracket

Speaker

SPEAKER ASSEMBLY

COMPONENTS OF NIKON COOLPIX S1000PJ

Shutter release button

TOP PANEL

Projector button

Focusing lens

Filters

Projector LED

Ribbon cable

PROJECTOR ASSEMBLY

Projector assembly cover

CODEC with speaker driver and video buffet

Display controller chip

LOGIC BOARD

Projector window

Flash window

Lens

Infra-red receiver (front)

Self-timer lamp

Camera module connector

Nikon

COOLPIX

NIKKOR 5X WIDE OPTICAL ZOOM VR 5.0-25.0mm 1:3.9-5.8

FRONT CASE

CCD image sensor

CAMERA MODULE

Nikon LITHIUM ION BATTERY PACK EN-EL12 3.7V 1050mAh 3.9Wh JFBC NIKON CORPORATION, JAPAN

Lithium-ion battery

EN-EL12 RECHARGEABLE BATTERY

Lens cover motor

LENS COVER

TYPES OF DIGITAL CAMERA

Mode selector

Shutter button

Nikon

Lens release button

DIGITAL SLR

18–55mm zoom lens

On/off button

Shutter button

Lens release button

SONY

16mm interchangeable lens

DIGITAL CAMERA WITH INTERCHANGEABLE LENS

Water-resistant case

Shutter button

Electronic flash

Strap mount

Canon PowerShot D10

Lamp

12.1

Microphone

Lens

UNDERWATER DIGITAL CAMERA

Shutter button

Microphone

Left lens

Right lens

Flash

Lens cover

3D HD

FUJIFILM

3D DIGITAL CAMERA

Digital camcorder

A CAMCORDER records a scene as a sequence of 25 or 30 still images per second, along with sound. It comprises a video camera to capture light from the scene, a viewfinder through which the scene may be viewed, a screen on which the recorded scene may be viewed, a charge-coupled device (CCD) to convert the visual data into an electric signal, and a means of storing the signal. Digital video cameras convert the signal into digital form – a series of separate measurements of the initial analogue (continuously varying) signal. They record the digital signal, usually on a chip or hard disk. Camcorders often have a slot where a memory card can be inserted to expand the memory and store longer recordings or more still pictures.

COMPONENTS OF A JVC EVERIO CAMCORDER

MONITOR SHELL

MONITOR MOUNT

MONITOR FRAME

Screen connector

6.8-cm (2.7-in) LCD screen

MONITOR SCREEN

Speaker

Play button

Auto/Manual recording button

Info button

Menu button

AV terminal

LEFT SIDE

OK button

Grip belt

Battery

Power/ Charge lamp

Access lamp

Zoom select lever

Power/charge lamp

Access lamp

LEFT OUTER SHELL

Lens cover

Microphone

LCD monitor

TOP VIEW

LENS COVER ASSEMBLY

SPEAKER CIRCUIT BOARD

Speaker

Monitor frame

USB terminal

DC terminal

Start/Stop button

MOTHERBOARD

LCD monitor

Battery

REAR VIEW

Grip belt

CHASSIS

RIGHT OUTER SHELL

Lens cover switch

Grip belt release lever

SDHC CARD

LENS UNIT MOUNT

Lens

CCD mounting peg

LENS UNIT

CCD chip

SENSOR BOARD

Start/Stop button

3.6-volt lithium-ion battery

GRIP BELT FASTENER

JVC

GRIP BELT

REAR PANEL

Zoom select lever

OK button

CONTROL UNIT

RECHARGEABLE BATTERY

Home cinema

HOME CINEMA REPLICATES a real "movie theatre" using pictures displayed on a high-quality widescreen television set, such as a plasma TV, and surround sound from strategically sited loudspeakers. The source for sound and vision is a DVD (Digital Versatile Disc). Its player uses standard CD (Compact Disc) digital technology, but with a higher density of laser-read microscopic pits – more than 20 billion such pits in multi-level spiral tracks that, stretched out, would extend nearly 40km (25 miles). Blu-ray is a high-quality DVD system that fits much more data on its disc than standard DVDs, allowing High Definition video files to be stored. It is hard for the human ear to discern the direction of low-pitched sounds, so these emanate from a central bass speaker, often built into or below the screen unit. High-pitched sounds, the direction of which is easier to detect, emanate from mid- and high-frequency speakers positioned around the viewer. Plasma screens use fluorescent tube ("strip-light") technology. Tiny three-cell pixels, each about one millimetre across, contain red, green, and blue phosphor chemicals and a gas mix. Where electric pulses coincide for a split second in the criss-cross matrix of wire electrodes, the gas energizes and emits ultraviolet light, which in turn makes the phosphor glow.

BLU-RAY PLAYER

Ventilated case

Display panel

Open/close button

On/standby button

Disc tray

Play button

Stop button

HOW SURROUND SOUND WORKS

DVD player under screen

Centre sound channel

Subwoofer (bass unit)

Plasma screen

Front left sound channel

Front right sound channel

Rear left sound channel

Region of most realistic sound reception

Rear right sound channel

WIDE-SCREEN PLASMA DISPLAY

Mid-grey bezel

Damped anti-shock swivel base

16:9 (width:height) screen proportions fit human field of vision

HOW A PLASMA SCREEN WORKS

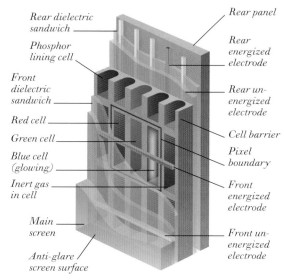

Rear dielectric sandwich

Rear panel

Phosphor lining cell

Rear energized electrode

Front dielectric sandwich

Rear un-energized electrode

Red cell

Green cell

Cell barrier

Blue cell (glowing)

Pixel boundary

Inert gas in cell

Front energized electrode

Main screen

Anti-glare screen surface

Front un-energized electrode

INTERNAL VIEW OF SONY DAV-S300

Mains electricity supply lead

Internal fuse overload protection

Voltage reduction and regulation circuits

Power transistors

Power transistor heat sink (dissipator)

DVD/CD drive turntable

DVD/CD laser-reader (within compartment)

Enclosed DVD/CD compartment

DVD/CD sliding tray

Tweeter speaker connectors

Woofer speaker connector

VCR (video cassette recorder) connections

Radio tuner aerial socket (FM)

Internal radio tuner aerial (AM)

Video input/output circuit board

Tuner settings memory microchip

Tuner/amplifier link cables

DVD/CD processor microchip

Display screen and control circuits

Display screen

Ribbon connectors transfer DVD/CD signals

Control buttons

Enter button activates menu choices

Volume control

Access slot in tray for reading underside of DVD/CD

FRONT VIEW

Mains power on/off switch

DVD/CD sliding tray

Vibration-reducing damper foot

Remote control sensor

Display screen

Radio tuner FM/AM selector

Muting button

DVD/CD control buttons

Volume control

Headphones socket

Power button

Sleep button

TV power button

Function button

Display button

Previous/next track buttons

Play button

Enter button

DVD display button

REMOTE CONTROL

Personal music and video

THE FIRST BATTERY-DRIVEN PORTABLE source of sound and music was the transistor radio of the 1950s. In the 1970s, the magnetic audio cassette tape allowed recordings to be played on portable tape players. Also, new metal alloys permitted the tiny but high-power magnets needed for lightweight earphones. In the 1980s, compact discs brought music into the digital era. Sony's MD, or minidisc, introduced re-recordable CDs that used magnetic and optical technology. From the mid 1990s, music could be stored in all-electronic digital form in a microchip, usually in the MP3 file format. These files can be transferred between devices and via the Internet. Today, a variety of portable media gadgets can record, play, and store video, photographs, and music in electronic form.

MP3 PLAYERS

Headphone jack

Mode switch

Volume control

Power/Play/Pause button

Headphone jack

Next/Previous track control

USB port

LED

CREATIVE ZEN STONE

ZEN

Back/Home button

Record/Stop button

Volume control

Display

Zap button

Bass/Play mode

Earphone

On/Off/Pause button

Shuttle switch

SONY B-SERIES MP3 PLAYER

Subwoofer

Volume controls

Neck band

Satellite speaker

SONY

USB jack

Shuffle button

Volume controls

Jog lever

SONY W-SERIES WALKMAN

JBL SPYRO SPEAKERS

Satellite cable

Standby button

iPod

Speaker enclosure

ZEPPELIN IPOD SPEAKER DOCK

Remote control

COMPONENTS OF MICROSOFT ZUNE HD

Power button

Digitizer

Home button

Front panel

Base plate

FRONT PANEL

Power button cover

CHASSIS

3.7-volt battery

Media button bezel

Audio codec chip

EEPROM memory chip

Headphone jack

Sync port

LOGIC BOARD

MICROSOFT ZUNE HD

8.4 cm (3.3 in) OLED display

Back panel

Tri-wing screw

Back panel

Media button

Ribbon cable

DISPLAY

REAR VIEW

Bottom backplate

Media button

SIDE VIEW

Power button

Touchscreen

Media button

music
videos
pictures
radio
marketplace
social
more

Headphone jack

Sync port

Home button

Mobile phones

IN THE EARLY 1990s, THE MOBILE PHONE (or cellphone) was a rare luxury, but in recent years it has outsold almost every other electrical gadget – as a professional tool, domestic convenience, and even a fashion accessory. Mobile phones have also generally shrunk in size, due to improvements in rechargeable batteries, which now store more electricity for longer in a smaller package, and to smaller, more efficient electronics that use less electricity. A "mobile" is basically a low-power radio receiver-transmitter, plus a tiny microphone to convert sounds into electrical signals, and a small speaker that does the reverse. When the mobile phone is activated, it sends out a radio signal that is answered by nearby mast transmitter-receivers. The phone locks onto the clearest signal and uses this while within range (the range of each transmitter is known as a cell). The phone continuously monitors signal strength and switches to an alternative transmitter when necessary. The phone's liquid crystal display (LCD) shows numbers, letters, symbols, and colour pictures. Newer models have a larger screen for more complex colour images, and commonly incorporate a camera, radio, and MP3 functionality. Smartphones, which are increasingly widespread, contain additional software and more may be downloaded. Smartphones typically offer Internet and email access, PDA-like functions (see pp. 568–569), and may even contain GPS navigation software.

Top microphone
Front camera
Receiver
Status bar
Earpiece
Bottom microphone
Home button
Speaker

I-PHONE 4

Menu key
Home key
Back key
Search key

LG OPTIMUS 2X

HOW A MOBILE PHONE WORKS

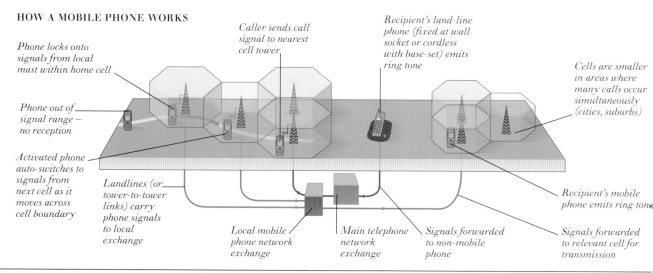

Phone locks onto signals from local mast within home cell

Caller sends call signal to nearest cell tower

Recipient's land-line phone (fixed at wall socket or cordless with base-set) emits ring tone

Cells are smaller in areas where many calls occur simultaneously (cities, suburbs)

Phone out of signal range – no reception

Activated phone auto-switches to signals from next cell as it moves across cell boundary

Landlines (or tower-to-tower links) carry phone signals to local exchange

Local mobile phone network exchange

Main telephone network exchange

Signals forwarded to non-mobile phone

Recipient's mobile phone emits ring tone

Signals forwarded to relevant cell for transmission

COMPONENTS OF BLACKBERRY CURVE 8520

BLACKBERRY CURVE 8520

LCD screen

Ribbon connector

Front housing

DISPLAY

Locating tabs

Keypad keys

KEYPAD

Bezel

FASCIA

Screen connector

Camera

Trackpad

Keypad circuit board

LOGIC BOARD (FRONT)

Trackpad module

SIM card slot

LOGIC BOARD (REAR)

SCREEN LENS

BATTERY COVER

Headphone jack

Volume control keys

REAR HOUSING

Lithium-ion battery

Negative terminal

Positive terminal

RECHARGEABLE BATTERY

Headphone jack

Screen lens

Micro USB port

Left convenience key

Trackpad

Send/call key

Menu key

Left shift key

Volume control keys

Right convenience key

End/power key

Escape/ back key

Delete key

Speakerphone key

Right shift key

BlackBerry

(3) Messages

589

Global positioning system

THE GLOBAL POSITIONING SYSTEM (GPS) is a network of
24 navigation satellites orbiting the Earth that people can
use to pinpoint their position. The satellites orbit at a height
of 20,000 kilometres (12,500 miles). A GPS receiver picks up
signals from any of these satellites that are above the horizon.
It uses information in each signal to work out how far away it
is from the satellite. It can calculate its position on the Earth's
surface when it has information from at least three satellites.
A basic GPS receiver shows the latitude and
longitude of its position on its screen. More
advanced receivers, especially those designed
for use in vehicles, show their position on a
digital map. These receivers often show extra
information, such as the vehicle's speed and
the length of the journey. Some receivers
warn drivers if they exceed the speed limit
for a road and even tell drivers which
traffic lane to use at the next junction.
Directions are shown on the screen and
also spoken by a synthesized voice.

*Cigarette
lighter
adapter and
speaker cable*

Antenna

IN-CAR GPS

Page key

*On/off and screen
control button*

Enter key

Quit key

Rocker pad

Menu key

Speak key

*Liquid crystal display
(LCD) screen*

Find key

Zoom keys

Route key

HOW GPS WORKS

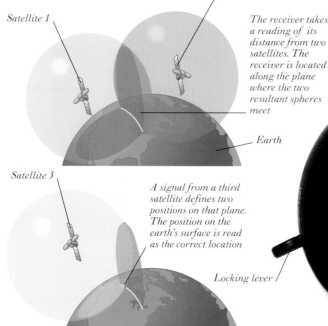

Satellite 1

Satellite 2

*The receiver takes
a reading of its
distance from two
satellites. The
receiver is located
along the plane
where the two
resultant spheres
meet*

Earth

Satellite 3

*A signal from a third
satellite defines two
positions on that plane.
The position on the
earth's surface is read
as the correct location*

**IN-CAR MOUNTING
BRACKET ASSEMBLY**

MOUNTING BRACKET

QUICK-RELEASE BASE

Locking lever

Release catch

*Ratcheted
base*

Speaker
plug

Power plug

Waterproof
case

Sling

COMPONENTS OF AN IN-CAR GPS

High-contrast
liquid crystal
display (LCD)
screen

Data plug

Antenna

GARMIN ETREX HAND-HELD GPS

Memory
battery

Data plug
socket

Main printed
circuit board
(PCB)

Rear case

USB PROGRAMMER ASSEMBLY

Shielded
receiver

Data
cartridge

Universal serial
bus (USB)
programmer

SPARE FUSES

Front case

Liquid crystal
display (LCD)
assembly

Underside
of control
pad

Vacuum cleaner

IN A CONVENTIONAL VACUUM CLEANER, an electric motor spins a fan that sucks in air carrying dust and debris. The air is forced through tiny pores in a dust bag, trapping most particles. In the 1990s, James Dyson's dual cyclone "bag-less" design did away with the dust bag – and the reduced airflow caused by clogging of its pores. An electrically driven fan creates a partial vacuum within the machine. This sucks air into the machine past a rotating brush that loosens dirt. The air flows into a cylinder-shaped bin. As the air whirls around the bin like a miniature storm, or cyclone, larger particle are flung outwards and fall to the bottom of the bin. The air then passes through perforations into a cone-shaped inner bin and then into a series of smaller cones, spinning faster all the time and flinging smaller and smaller particle out. The nearly clean air exits the machine through micro-filters that trap the tiniest particles. Some Dyson vacuum cleaners run on a large ball instead of wheels. The ball makes it easier to steer the cleaner.

Wand handle and brushbar controls

Upper wand

Lower wand

Motorized brushbar floor tool

DYSON DC05 MOTORHEAD

CYCLONE ASSEMBLY

Air intake from hose

Air exit to bin/cyclone cover

Hose electricity connector

Hose slider

Inner cyclone cone

WASHABLE PRE-MOTOR FILTER

Microporous filter

Bin upper seal seating

Perforated shroud

Bin handle clip

DUST COLLECTION BIN

Hose slider seating

Hose electricity supply

Post-motor micropore filter

Central retaining screw

Filter rim casing

Inner bin fin

Bin upper seal

Bin base

Bin lower seal

Inner bin dust collection area

Bin handle

Polycarbonate plastic bin body

Bin cover retaining clip

OVERHEAD VIEW OF DYSON DC05 MOTORHEAD

Suction reduction control

On/off and brushbar motor control

Hose cuff electrical link

Flexible hose shrouding

Tool or wand cuff

Accessory holder

Electricity connector to brushbar motor

ACCESSORIES

Tool/ brushbar connector

Nozzle

Textured scraper

STAIR TOOL

CREVICE TOOL

Wand telescopic link

Brush tool articulation

UPHOLSTERY BRUSH

WAND

Hose base

Main motor casing

Hinged bin/cyclone cover

Air intake to bin/cyclone cover

Bin cover retaining clip

Flexible hose shrouding

MOTORIZED BRUSHBAR FLOOR TOOL

Wand/handle connector

Bin cover handle

dyson

Motor air intake

Wheel guard and flex rewind

Main wheel

Handle connector

Brushbar drive motor cover

Roller

Sole plate roller

Brushbar drive belt cover

Rotating brushbar

Sole plate

Iron and washer-dryer

IN THE DAYS BEFORE WASHING MACHINES, laundry was done by hand – washed in a barrel, squeezed in a roller-mangle, hung on a line, and smoothed with an iron heated on the hob or stove. In the 1880s electrically heated irons were one of the first home electrical appliances. Today's iron still applies heat, sometimes moistened with steam, to dampen and flatten garment fibres. Machines with electric heaters and motors took the strain out of washing from the 1910s. Up to the 1960s, three machines were needed to wash, spin, and dry. Now clothes are swirled in a rotating ribbed tub of hot water, then spun fast to throw off most of the water, before slowly tumbling in electrically heated air to dry – all in one appliance.

FRONT VIEW OF A MIELE WASHER-DRYER

Detergent tray

Control panels

Door

Filter access flap

COMPONENTS OF A STEAM IRON

Steam control knob

Spray nozzle aperture

Spray barrel

Spray pump

Nose

Spray nozzle

Steam barrel

Steam release activator

Water tank

Soleplate surround

Handle

Temperature and steam control dial

Nose

Heating elements

Pilot light

Mains spade contacts

Earth wire

Mains supply lead

Pilot light supply wire

Mains flex

SIDE VIEW OF STEAM IRON

Flex kink guard

Steam control knob

Spray and steam knobs

Temperature and steam control dial

Water tank

Soleplate

Securing screw mounting

Heel moulding

Mains flex clamp

COMPONENTS OF A MIELE WASHER-DRYER

Waste water anti-siphon pipe hook

Detergent tray holder

Water inlet valves

Drum suspension springs

Water inlet hose

Water inlet connector

Waste water pipe

Detergent tray recess

Control panel

Control panel wiring

Water inlet pipe

Drum and door seal

Drum inlet elbow

Stainless steel rotating drum

Door catch with safety cut-out

Door metal cap

Door porthole

Filter seal

Fluff filter impeller

Drain tap

Door wiring loom

Detergent tray

Fabric softener section

Water-softener dial

Filter screw cover

Filter

Hinged front panel

Tray fascia

Miele

Water hardness adjustment and filter flap lever

Microwave combination oven

CONVENTIONAL OVENS use electrically warmed elements or a flame to heat food. In a microwave oven heat energy is created by electromagnetic waves produced by a magnetron and led by waveguides into the oven compartment. These microwaves cannot pass through the compartment's metal casing, being reflected within and spread evenly by a fan. But they do pass through most types of plastic, ceramics, and glass. Therefore platters or containers made from these materials are suitable for use in microwave ovens. A combination oven also has conventional heating elements, to grill and "brown" in the traditional fashion, either alone or in conjunction with microwaves.

MICROWAVE COMBINATION OVEN

Turntable rotator

Door lock

Display screen

Control panel

Metal cook/grill tray (non-microwave)

Rollers

Glass cooking turntable

Metal turntable cover (non-microwave)

Metal grill/griddle (non-microwave)

Under-turntable roller ring (non-microwave)

HOW MICROWAVES HEAT FOOD

Hydrogen atom

Oxygen atom

Each water molecule in food has two hydrogen atoms and one oxygen atom

Water molecules spin with energy from microwaves

Microwaves make water molecules vibrate

Making the molecules move generates heat

SIDE VIEW OF MICROWAVE COMBINATION OVEN

Wiring loom

Magnetron assembly

Waveguide

Voltage regulators

Mains earthing wire to case and chassis

Door

Control panel circuitry

Rigid metal chassis

Fan electricity supply

Main fan

Magnetron cooling fan

Door safety cut-out mechanism

Low-voltage supply for control circuits

Voltage transformers

Thermal/electrical insulation

Mains electrical lead

Circuit board plug

Electricity supply to magnetron

High-voltage magnetron supply

TOP VIEW OF MICROWAVE COMBINATION OVEN

Waveguide backing

Heating element cover

Heating element terminal cover

Electric heating elements

Oven compartment casing

Outer casing fitment

Microwave-proof door seals

Door

Thermal/electrical insulation

Overheat cut-out sensor supply

Chassis earth terminal

Voltage stabilizer

Magnetron assembly

Voltage circuitry

Control panel fascia

BACK VIEW OF MICROWAVE COMBINATION OVEN

Main fan electrical supply

Magnetron cooling fan

Magnetron cooling fan mounting

Magnetron perforated heat sink (dissipates warmth)

Mains electrical lead

Thermal/electrical insulation

Fan transformer

Vibration-reducing fan mounting

Cooling perforations for heating elements

Back of oven compartment

Fan dust shield

Main fan (scatters microwaves and circulates hot air)

Rear chassis plate

Toaster

MOST ELECTRIC TOASTERS not only grill slices of bread, they also pop them up when ready. While the slices rest on a spring-loaded rack, electric heating elements toast the bread. At the same time, a bimetallic strip heats and expands. One of the two metals in this strip expands more quickly than the other, causing the strip to curve. As it bends, it completes an electrical circuit and activates an electromagnet. The magnet attracts a catch, releasing the spring that holds the rack down in the toaster. The elements switch off, and the toasted slices pop up.

Connecting wire

Ejector bracket

Time switch

Variable time control knob

Selector switch

Screw

Switch end casting

Crumb tray

Screw

End baffle plate

Screw

Earth connection point

Screw

Cable entry point

End element connecting link

End element

Foot

Baseplate

End element wire guard

Screw

Washer

Screw

Mains input lead

Cable retaining gland

Ejector knob

Screw

Nut

Spring

Ejector bracket

Ejector assembly

Plain end casting

Switch end casting

Stainless steel cover

Selector switch

Ejector knob

Variable time control knob

Foot

Crumb tray

Fixing screw

Screw

Foot

Inner cage assembly

Centre element wire cage

End baffle plate

Foot

Screw

Plain end casting

Stainless steel cover

Screw

Element retaining stop

Nut

Washer

Screw

Element connecting link

End element

Nut

Washer

Screw

Centre element

End element wire guard

Drills

THE ELECTRICALLY POWERED MOTOR OF A POWER DRILL, cooled by a fan, turns a shaft at high speed. The shaft connects, in turn, to a system of gears that rotates a chuck even faster. Clamped by the chuck, a sharp bit cuts out the hole, and at the same time the bit's screw-shaped grooves channel the waste out of the hole. For drilling hard materials, many power drills have a hammer mechanism: when this is operated a ratchet in the gearcase causes the chuck and bit to pound in and out as they drill. A hand drill, although slower and less forceful than a power drill, is easier to control. For cutting wide holes, carpenters often prefer a brace-and-bit. This acts like a lever: the bowed handle of the brace moves a larger distance than the bit, turning the bit with extra force.

MOTOR ASSEMBLY

Commutator

Armature

Armature spindle

Fan

Motor case

Field coils

Motor case

Spring

Brush

Screw

Washer

Lead wire

Brush holder

Electromagnetic induction capacitor

Chuck key holder

Triac device

Screw

Top insert blank

Hammer mechanism actuator

Screw hole

Hammer actuator position

Gearcase position

Motor position

INTERNAL VIEW OF CLAMSHELL

Trigger position

Lock button

On/off trigger

TRIGGER MECHANISM

Washer

Spring

Cable

GEAR MECHANISM

Thrust plate

Ratchet mechanism

Spindle

Gearcase cover

Chuck key

Jaw

Bit

Gearcase

Washer

Spring washer

Gearcase cover screw

Chuck keyhole

POWER DRILL

Hammer mechanism actuator

Chuck

On/off trigger

Chuck key holder

Cable

HAND DRILL

Main handle

Turning handle

Side handle

Drive wheel

Pinion

Chuck

Jaw

Bit

Gearcase screw

EXTERNAL VIEW OF CLAMSHELL

Screw hole

Exhaust vent

BRACE-AND-BIT

Quill

Head

Crank

Handle

Ratchet

Chuck

Jaw

Bit

Air inlet

Clamshell screw

House of the future

HOUSES IN THE FUTURE are likely to be more environmentally friendly and energy-efficient than older dwellings, by making better use of materials and intelligent control systems. The Integer house was designed by Cole Thompson Associates, Bree Day Partnership, and Paul Hodgkins Associates, and built in conjunction with the Building Research Establishment in the UK. One of its key features is a large conservatory that warms one side of the house. Extensive use is made of recycled, natural, and renewable materials and energy. The walls are made from timber and insulated with fibre from recycled newspaper; waste water from the bathrooms is saved and used to flush the toilets; and a wind turbine and solar panels contribute some of the electricity requirements. Many elements were prefabricated off site for ease of construction. The Integer house uses only half the energy and a third less water than a traditionally built house.

WALL CONSTRUCTION

Cellulose fibre insulation

Vertical batten

Plasterboard

Red cedar boarding

Vertical batten

Noggin

Breather paper

Skirting board

Floating floor

Cables and ducting

Wooden boarding

SIDE AND REAR VIEW OF THE INTEGER HOUSE

Single-glazed conservatory

Gutter collects rain water for use in the garden

Composter for recycling kitchen waste

FRONT VIEW OF THE INTEGER HOUSE

Turfed roof helps to regulate temperature

Passive stack vents from bathroom and toilet

Automatic louvres cool conservatory

Small windows reduce heat loss

Red cedar walls that do not require painting or staining

Intelligent electronic door-lock

Hatch for home deliveries

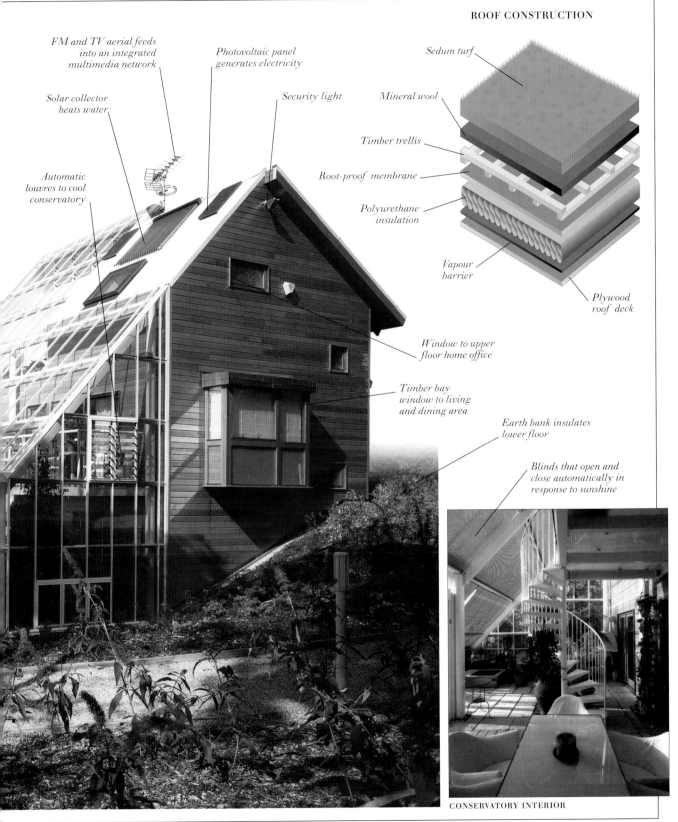

ROOF CONSTRUCTION

Sedum turf

Mineral wool

Timber trellis

Root-proof membrane

Polyurethane insulation

Vapour barrier

Plywood roof deck

FM and TV aerial feeds into an integrated multimedia network

Photovoltaic panel generates electricity

Security light

Solar collector heats water

Automatic louvres to cool conservatory

Window to upper floor home office

Timber bay window to living and dining area

Earth bank insulates lower floor

Blinds that open and close automatically in response to sunshine

CONSERVATORY INTERIOR

603

Renewable energy

RENEWABLE ENERGY COMES from sources that do not become depleted as we use the energy. When a fossil fuel such as coal is burned, it is gone forever, but a renewable source remains available no matter how much is used. The tides, waves, flowing water, sunlight, and the wind are all renewable sources of energy. Wind and water energy are captured by a device called a turbine. The turbine spins and drives an electricity generator. Energy from sunlight, or solar energy, is changed into electricity in two main ways. One uses mirrors to concentrate solar energy and magnify its heating effect which is used to change water into steam to drive turbines. Photovoltaic cells change sunlight directly into electricity. A cell is made from two layers of silicon. One gives out electrons (negative particles) and the other receives them. Sunlight knocks electrons out of atoms where the two layers meet, separating them from the positive particles. The electrons are attracted to one layer of the cell, the positive particles to the other layer. Electrons are naturally attracted to the positive particles, but to come together again, the electrons must flow out of the cell, through an external electric circuit, or load, and back to the other side of the cell, creating a charge. The cell supplies electric current for as long as light keeps falling on it.

VESTAS V47 WIND TURBINE

Blade

Blade pitch control

Hub controller

Aerodynamic hub cover

Blade bearing

Blade hub

Rotor lock

TIDAL POWER

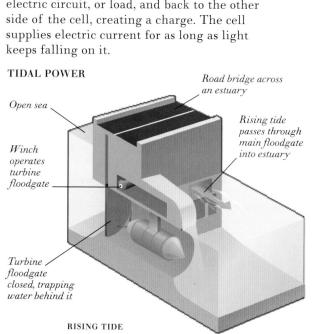

Open sea

Road bridge across an estuary

Rising tide passes through main floodgate into estuary

Winch operates turbine floodgate

Turbine floodgate closed, trapping water behind it

RISING TIDE

Turbine floodgate opened by winch allows trapped water to flow out to the open sea

Main floodgate closed as tide falls

Escaping water drives turbine

FALLING TIDE

Gearbox

Oil cooler

Generator

Anemometer

Wind vane

Service crane

Hydraulic unit

Electronic controller

Yaw ring

Yaw control

WIND TURBINES IN A WIND FARM

HOW A GENERATOR WORKS

Slip ring collects current from coil

Carbon brush collects current from slip ring

North magnetic pole

Wire coil rotates inside magnet

Wind or water flow through turbine rotates shaft

South magnetic pole

Moving the wire past a magnet makes a current flow through it

FIRST HALF TURN

North magnetic pole

Coil makes half a turn

Direction of current reverses every half turn

South magnetic pole

SECOND HALF TURN

SOLAR POWER

Anti-reflective coating

Glass

Electrons flow out of cell

Electric current powers external load

Sunlight

Contact grid

N-type silicon

Junction

P-type silicon

Back contact grid

Light knocks electrons out of atoms

Electrons flow back to cell

HOW A PHOTOVOLTAIC CELL WORKS

Solar panel containing photovoltaic cells

Power lead-out wires

Waterproof cable connector

SOLAR PANEL

Cloning technology

IN A LIVING CELL THE GENETIC MATERIAL DNA (deoxyribonucleic acid) contains thousands of units called genes that carry instructions for development, growth, and repair of the living creature. During normal reproduction, half the mother's genetic material contained in an egg cell joins with half the genetic material from the father carried in a sperm cell, to form a unique new genome (set of genes) for a new life. During the early stages of embryo development, the fertilized egg divides into stem cells, which have the potential to become specialized into the hundreds of cell types in a body. Through therapeutic cloning, stem cells can be produced in a laboratory. It is hoped that in the future this technology can be used to grow new tissue that can be transplanted back into the donor to treat illness, without fear of rejection – when the body recognizes a transplanted part as "foreign" because it has different genes, and tries to destroy it. In another form of cloning, performed experimentally using animals, genetic material from a donor animal has been inserted into an egg from another animal that has been emptied of its own genetic material, to produce an animal genetically identical to the donor.

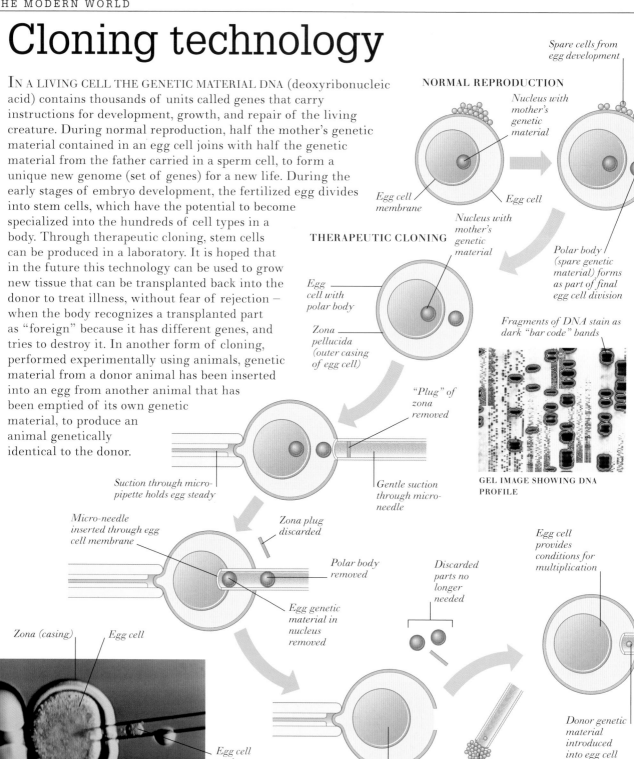

NORMAL REPRODUCTION

Spare cells from egg development

Nucleus with mother's genetic material

Egg cell membrane

Nucleus with mother's genetic material

Egg cell

Polar body (spare genetic material) forms as part of final egg cell division

THERAPEUTIC CLONING

Egg cell with polar body

Zona pellucida (outer casing of egg cell)

Fragments of DNA stain as dark "bar code" bands

GEL IMAGE SHOWING DNA PROFILE

"Plug" of zona removed

Gentle suction through micro-needle

Suction through micro-pipette holds egg steady

Micro-needle inserted through egg cell membrane

Zona plug discarded

Polar body removed

Discarded parts no longer needed

Egg cell provides conditions for multiplication

Egg genetic material in nucleus removed

Zona (casing)

Egg cell

Egg cell nucleus containing genetic material

GENETIC MATERIAL REMOVED FROM EGG

"Enucleated" egg cell (lacks nucleus with genetic material)

Stem cells (unspecialized or undifferentiated cells) collected from donor

Donor genetic material introduced into egg cell

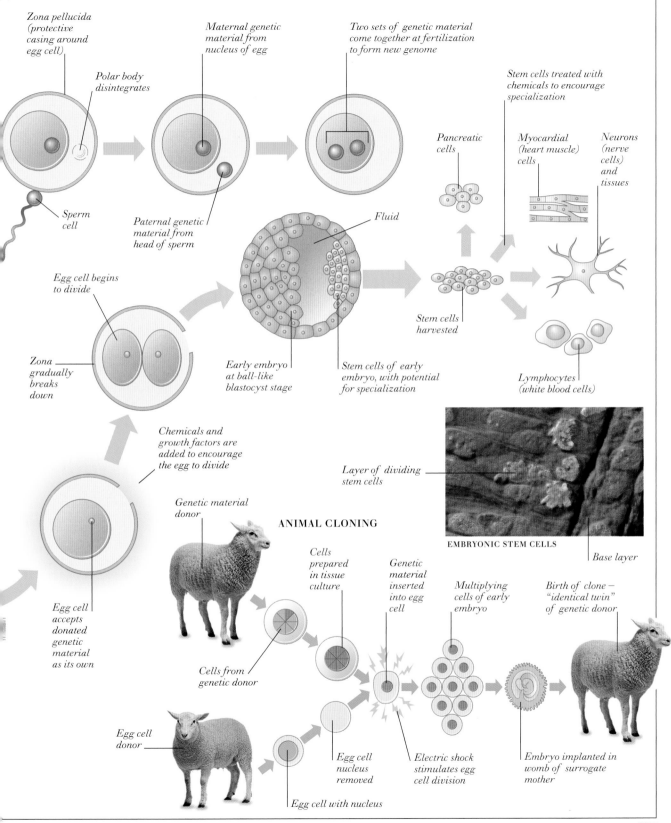

Zona pellucida (protective casing around egg cell)

Polar body disintegrates

Maternal genetic material from nucleus of egg

Two sets of genetic material come together at fertilization to form new genome

Stem cells treated with chemicals to encourage specialization

Pancreatic cells

Myocardial (heart muscle) cells

Neurons (nerve cells) and tissues

Sperm cell

Paternal genetic material from head of sperm

Fluid

Egg cell begins to divide

Zona gradually breaks down

Stem cells harvested

Early embryo at ball-like blastocyst stage

Stem cells of early embryo, with potential for specialization

Lymphocytes (white blood cells)

Chemicals and growth factors are added to encourage the egg to divide

Genetic material donor

ANIMAL CLONING

Layer of dividing stem cells

EMBRYONIC STEM CELLS

Base layer

Egg cell accepts donated genetic material as its own

Cells prepared in tissue culture

Genetic material inserted into egg cell

Multiplying cells of early embryo

Birth of clone – "identical twin" of genetic donor

Cells from genetic donor

Egg cell donor

Egg cell nucleus removed

Electric shock stimulates egg cell division

Embryo implanted in womb of surrogate mother

Egg cell with nucleus

607

Robots

ROBOTS ARE MACHINES THAT CAN carry out a variety of tasks on their own, with little or no human control. Most robots are mechanical arms used to build things in factories. The end of the robot's arm can be fitted with different tools for gripping, drilling, cutting, welding, and painting. Robot toys have become popular, too. They incorporate sensors that respond to sounds and sometimes touch. Some of them can even understand spoken words. Scientists are also trying to create more advanced, human-like robots that can see, hear, learn, and make their own decisions. ASIMO, a robot developed by the Japanese car manufacturer Honda, is one of these advanced humanoid robots. ASIMO stands for Advanced Step in Innovative MObility. It looks like a small astronaut wearing a backpack. ASIMO can walk, talk, carry things, recognize familiar faces, and respond to its name. It was the first robot that could walk independently and climb stairs. There are robot toys too, in the shape of animals with simple artificial intelligence.

Motorized fingers

Neck joint

Shoulder joint

Battery backpack

Battery charge indicator

Rigid torso

Hip joint

Knee joint

Ankle joint

Padded foot

ASIMO HUMANOID

ELEMENTS OF ROBOT ACTION

CENTRAL PROCESSING UNIT (CPU)

Information from sensors

Pre-programmed instructions

Information from sensors interpreted by CPU to modify actions

SENSORS

LIGHT

SOUND

TOUCH

PROXIMITY

SMELL

TASTE

MECHANICAL ACTIONS

Motorized
fingers

Wrist joint

Elbow
joint

Floor mounting

CAR-BUILDING ROBOTS

Vehicle body

Welding tool

Arm up-down
joint

Wrist joints

End
effector

Arm out-in
joint

Arm
rotation
joint

Kawasaki

ZX165U

KAWASAKI INDUSRIAL ROBOT

Floor-mounted
base

Head touch
sensor

Nose touch
sensor

Back touch
sensor

Eye LED

Tail
LED

Camera

ROBOT DOGS

Battery

Flexible neck

Touch sensor

Infrared
sensor

Whipping tail

Sonic sensor

Leg joint

ROBOREPTILE

609

High-performance microscopes

OPTICAL MICROSCOPES FORM A MAGNIFIED image by using lenses to bend light. Some special-purpose optical microscopes used in industry and research are designed for observing particular materials, such as living cells. They produce magnifications of up to about 2,000. Electron microscopes produce magnifications of as much as 50 million, although 2 million is more typical. Their images are formed by means of electrons focused by magnetic lenses. There are two main types: scanning electron microscopes (SEMs) scan electrons back and forth across the surface of a specimen; transmission electron microscopes (TEMs) transmit electrons through a thin slice of the specimen.

FEI TECNAI G² TRANSMISSION ELECTRON MICROSCOPE

TEM IMAGE OF A VIRUS

OPTICAL MICROSCOPE IMAGE OF DYING NERVE CELLS

Video camera

Right eyepiece

Filter turret

Left eyepiece

Objective lens

Manipulator

Manipulator

Specimen stage

Specimen

Electron gun housing

Evacuated column

Condenser aperture

Condenser housing

Objective lens and specimen stage

Objective aperture

Imaging system housing

Vacuum valve

Detector

Binocular eyepieces

Viewing screen

OLYMPUS BX51W1 OPTICAL MICROSCOPE

HOW A TEM WORKS

Electron gun

Electron stream

Aperture plate

Aperture creates electron beam

Condenser focuses electron beam

Specimen stage

Specimen

Objective lens refocuses image formed by electron beam

Projector lens enlarges and projects the image

Binocular eyepieces

Specimen airlock

Phosphor imaging screen glows when hit by electrons to create the image

Cooling device

Camera

TECNAI

Screen

Image controls

Mouse

Keyboard

HITACHI S-3500H SCANNING ELECTRON MICROSCOPE

Evacuated column

Image controls

Screen

Vacuum pump cabinet

S-3500H

Keyboard

HOW A SEM WORKS

Electron stream

Electron gun

Aperture plate

Aperture creates electron beam

Scanning coils direct electron beam across the specimen

Condenser lens focuses primary electron beam

Screen

Objective lens refocuses electron beam

Specimen stage

Electron detector assembly

Secondary electrons from the specimen surface

Specimen surface hit by primary electrons

Underside of caterpillar body

Caterpillar foot

SEM IMAGE OF A CATERPILLAR

Space telescope

SPACE TELESCOPES ORBIT THE EARTH hundreds of kilometres above the ground, their instruments collecting light from stars and galaxies. Telescopes in space have a clearer view than those on Earth, because they are unaffected by the Earth's atmosphere, which absorbs or distorts much of this radiation. There are a variety of types of space telescopes designed to observe different types of light. The Hubble Space Telescope observes infra-red, ultraviolet, and visible light. It can detect objects that are 100 times fainter than those any telescopes on Earth can see. When this 11,000-kilogram (12-ton), 13-metre (43-foot) long telescope was launched by the Space Shuttle in 1990, it was found that its primary mirror was faulty and its images were blurred. Astronauts fitted extra optics to correct the problem in 1993.

IMAGES TAKEN BY HUBBLE

Pillar of gas

CONE NEBULA

VIEW FROM COLUMBIA SPACE SHUTTLE

Space shuttle remote manipulator system (robot arm)

Solar array

Axial instrument unit

Central deflector

High-gain radio antenna

Rotating joint

Crew handrail

Aft shroud

Guidance control sensor

2.4-metre primary mirror

Aperture door mounting

Light shield

33-centimetre secondary mirror

Secondary baffle

Epoxy resin frame

Crew handrail

Aperture

Aperture door

Door hinge

Light shield

Aluminium shield

EXPLODED VIEW OF HUBBLE SPACE TELESCOPE

Hydrogen gas emissions

Young star

"WHIRLPOOL" GALAXY

"Tadpole" galaxy

DRACO CONSTELLATION

Newly formed stars

OMEGA NEBULA

"Spirograph" nebula

LEPUS CONSTELLATION

Instrument bay

Batteries

Space shuttle remote manipulator system (robot arm)

Space shuttle astronaut

Instrument module

Space shuttle astronaut

Interstellar cloud remains

PLEIADES STAR CLUSTER

Young star – LL Ori

GREAT NEBULA, ORION

High-gain radio antenna for communication with satellites

Aperture door acts like a camera lens cap

Aperture allows light into the mirror housing

HUBBLE SPACE TELESCOPE

Primary mirror housing

Solar array supporting arm

Solar array collects solar energy for operating instruments

Crew handrail for astronauts to hold during maintenance operations

Light shield blocks out peripheral light

Thermal insulation to protect against extremes of temperature

Solar array

Aft shroud

Crew handrail

High-gain radio antenna

Probing the Solar System

SPACE PROBES HAVE VISITED every planet in the Solar System. They take photographs and gather data that cannot be collected using Earth-based equipment. Some probes fly past or orbit around planets or moons, while others land. Two Voyager space probes flew past the outer planets in the 1970s and 1980s. Two Viking spacecraft landed on Mars in 1976. The Magellan spacecraft orbited Venus from 1989 and mapped its surface. The Pathfinder spacecraft landed on Mars in 1997 and released a rover vehicle to explore the surface. The Mars Exploration Rover (MER) Mission landed two rovers in 2003. The Cassini space probe reached Saturn in 2004, and in 2005 its mini-probe, Huygens, landed on one of its moons, Titan, and became the first probe to land on a moon of another planet.

A MAP OF JUPITER'S VAST MAGNETIC FIELD PRODUCED BY CASSINI'S INSTRUMENTS

DIONE, ONE OF SATURN'S MOONS, ORBITING ABOVE THE "A" RING

High-gain antenna

Sun sensor

Helium tank

Visible and infrared spectrometers

Remote sensing pallet

Wide-angle camera

Radio-isotope thermoelectric generator

Magnetometer

Fields and particles intruments

Huygens mini probe

Attitude control thruster

Main engines

Propulsion module

Heat shield

Reaction wheel

Lower equipment module

CASSINI SPACE PROBE
AND HUYGENS MINI-PROBE

PANORAMIC VIEW OF TITAN
TAKEN AS HUYGENS DESCENDED

THE ROCK-STREWN SURFACE OF TITAN,
PHOTOGRAPHED BY HUYGENS

Panoramic camera (Pancam)

Navigation camera (Navcam)

Pancam mast assembly

Low dain antenna

Magnet array

Ultra-high frequency (UHF) antenna

Rover equipment deck

COBBLESTONES LYING IN TROUGHS BETWEEN DUST RIPPLES ON THE MARTIAN SURFACE, PHOTOGRAPHED BY ROVER "OPPORTUNITY"

Thruster cluster

Heat shield

Star scanner

Propellant tank

Cruise stage

Backshell contains lander craft and rover

MARS EXPLORATION ROVER SPACECRAFT

High gain antenna

Cruise electronics module

Third stage motor

Delta II launch vehicle second stage

Solar array

Aft bogie

Bogie wheel strut

Warm electronics box

Front hazard avoidance camera

Aft rocker

Forward rocker

Instrument deployment device

Rocker deployment actuator

MARS EXPLORATION ROVER (MER)

Aluminium wheel

Political map of the world

This map depicts the political boundaries of the world's nations. There are currently 196 independent countries in the world – a marked increase from the 82 that existed in 1950. With the trend towards greater fragmentation, most recently with the creation of Southern Sudan in July 2011, this figure is likely to increase. The largest country in the world is the Russian Federation, which covers 17,075,400 sq. km (6,592,800 sq. mi.), while the smallest is the Vatican City, covering 0.44 sq. km (0.17 sq. mi.). Under the Antarctic Treaty of 1959, no countries are permitted territorial claims in Antarctica.

ABBREVIATIONS	
AFGH.	Afghanistan
ALB.	Albania
AUT.	Austria
AZ. OR AZERB.	Azerbaijan
B. & H.	Bosnia & Herzegovina
BELG.	Belgium
BELO.	Belorussia
BOTS.	Botswana
BULG.	Bulgaria
CAMB.	Cambodia
C.A.R.	Central African Republic
CRO.	Croatia
CZ. REP.	Czech Republic
DOM. REP.	Dominican Republic
EST.	Estonia
HUNG.	Hungary
KYRG.	Kyrgyzstan
LAT.	Latvia
LIECH.	Liechtenstein
LITH.	Lithuania
LUX.	Luxemburg
MACED.	Macedonia
MOLD.	Moldavia
MON.	Montenegro
NETH.	Netherlands
PORT.	Portugal
ROM.	Romania
RUSS. FED.	Russian Federation
SLVK.	Slovakia
SLVN.	Slovenia
S.M.	San Marino
SWITZ.	Switzerland
TAJ.	Tajikistan
THAI.	Thailand
TURKMEN.	Turkmenistan
U.A.E.	United Arab Emirates
UZBEK.	Uzbekistan
VAT. CITY	Vatican City
ZIMB.	Zimbabwe

Time zones

The world is divided into 24 time zones, measured in relation to 12 noon Coordinated Universal Time (UTC), on the Greenwich Meridian (0°). Time advances by one hour for every 15° longitude east of Greenwich (and goes back one hour for every 15° west), but the system is adjusted in line with administrative boundaries. Numbers on the map indicate the number of hours that must be added to, or subtracted from UTC to calculate the time in each zone. Thus, eastern USA (−5) is 5 hours behind UTC.

TYPES OF CALENDAR

GREGORIAN
The 365-day Gregorian calendar was introduced by Pope Gregory XIII in 1582 and is now in use throughout most of the Western world. Every four years (leap year) an extra day is added. Below are the names of the months (and number of days).

January (31)	July (31)
February (28, 29 in leap years)	August (31)
	September (30)
March (31)	October (31)
April (30)	November
May (31)	December (31)
June (30)	

JEWISH
The Jewish calendar is a lunar calendar adapted to the solar year. It normally has 12 months but in leap years, which occur seven times in every cycle of 19 years, there are 13 months. The years are reckoned from the Creation (which is placed at 3761 BC); the months are Nisan, Iyyar, Sivan, Thammuz, Ab, Elul, Tishri, Hesvan, Kislev, Tebet, Sebat, and Adar, with an intercalary month (First Adar) being added in leap years.

MUSLIM
The Muslim calendar is based on a year of 12 months, each month beginning roughly at the time of the New Moon. The months are Muharram, Safar, Rabi'I, Rabi'II, Jumada I, Jumada II, Rajab, Sha'ban, Ramadan, Shawwal, Dhu l-Qa'dah, and Dhu l-Hijja.

CHINESE
The Chinese calendar is a lunar calendar, with a year consisting of 12 months. Intercalary months are added to keep the calendar in step with the solar year of 365 days. Months are referred to by a number within a year, but also by animal names that, from ancient times, have been attached to years and hours of the day.

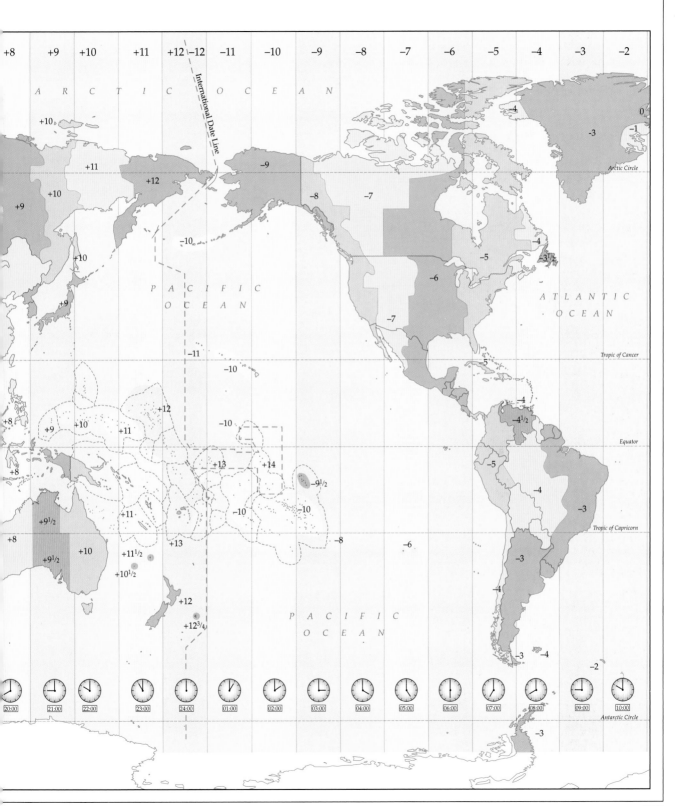

Useful data

UNITS OF MEASUREMENT

METRIC UNIT	EQUIVALENT
Length	
1 centimetre (cm)	10 millimetres (mm)
1 metre (m)	100 centimetres
1 kilometre (km)	1,000 metres
Mass	
1 kilogram (kg)	1,000 grams (g)
1 tonne (t)	1,000 kilograms
Area	
1 square centimetre (cm²)	100 square millimetres (mm²)
1 square metre (m²)	10,000 square centimetres
1 hectare	10,000 square metres
1 square kilometre (km²)	1,000,000 square metres
Volume	
1 cubic centimetre (cc)	1 millilitre (ml)
1 litre (l)	1,000 millilitres
1 cubic metre (m³)	1,000 litres
Capacity (liquid and dry measures)	
1 centilitre (cl)	10 millilitres (ml)
1 decilitre (dl)	10 centilitres
1 litre (l)	10 decilitres
1 decalitre (dal)	10 litres
1 hectolitre (hi)	10 decalitres
1 kilolitre (kl)	10 hectolitres

IMPERIAL UNIT	EQUIVALENT
Length	
1 foot (ft)	12 inches (in)
1 yard (yd)	3 feet
1 rod (rd)	5.5 yards
1 mile (mi)	1,760 yards
Mass	
1 dram (dr)	27.344 grains (gr)
1 ounce (oz)	16 drams
1 pound (lb)	16 ounces
1 hundredweight (cwt) (long)	112 pounds
1 hundredweight (cwt) (short)	100 pounds
1 ton (long)	2,240 pounds
1 ton (short)	2,000 pounds
Area	
1 square foot (ft²) (in²)	144 square inches
	1 square yard (yd²)
9 square feet	
1 acre	4,840 square yards
1 square mile	640 acres
Volume	
1 cubic foot	1,728 cubic inches
1 cubic yard	27 cubic feet
Capacity (liquid and dry measures)	
1 fluidram (fl dr)	60 minims (min)
1 fluid ounce (fl oz)	8 fluidrams
1 gill (gi)	5 fluid ounces
1 pint (pt)	4 gills
1 quart (qt)	2 pints
1 gallon (gal)	4 quarts
1 peck (pk)	2 gallons
1 bushel (bu)	4 pecks

NUMBER SYSTEMS

ROMAN	ARABIC
I	1
II	2
III	3
IV	4
V	5
VI	6
VII	7
VIII	8
IX	9
X	10
XI	11
XII	12
XIII	13
XIV	14
XV	15
XX	20
XXI	21
XXX	30
XL	40
L	50
LX	60
LXX	70
LXXX	80
XC	90
C	100
CI	101
CC	200
CCC	300
CD	400
D	500
DC	600
DCC	700
DCCC	800
CM	900
M	1,000
MM	2,000

METRIC - IMPERIAL CONVERSIONS

TO CONVERT	INTO	MULTIPLY BY
Length		
Centimetres	inches	0.3937
Metres	feet	3.2810
Kilometres	miles	0.6214
Metres	yards	1.0940
Mass		
Grams	ounces	0.0352
Kilograms	pounds	2.2050
Tonnes	long tons	0.9843
Tonnes	short tons	1.1025
Area		
Square centimetres	square inches	0.1550
Square metres	square feet	10.7600
Hectares	acres	2.4710
Square kilometres	square miles	0.3861
Square metres	square yards	1.1960
Volume		
Cubic centimetres	cubic inches	0.0610
Cubic metres	cubic feet	35.3100
Capacity		
Litres	pints	1.7600
Litres	gallons	0.2200

IMPERIAL - METRIC CONVERSIONS

TO CONVERT	INTO	MULTIPLY BY
Length		
Inches	centimetres	2.5400
Feet	metres	0.3048
Miles	kilometres	1.6090
Yards	metres	0.9144
Mass		
Ounces	grams	28.3500
Pounds	kilograms	0.4536
Long tons	tonnes	1.0160
Short tons	tonnes	0.9070
Area		
Square inches	square centimetres	6.4520
Square feet	square metres	0.0929
Acres	hectares	0.4047
Square miles	square kilometres	2.5900
Square yards	square metres	0.8361
Volume		
Cubic inches	cubic centimetres	16.3900
Cubic feet	cubic metres	0.0283
Capacity		
Pints	litres	0.5683
Gallons	litres	4.5460

RULES OF ALGEBRA

EXPRESSION	COMMENTS	EXPRESSION BECOMES
a + a	Simple addition	2a
a + b = c + d	Subtract b from either side	a = c + d - b
ab = cd	Divide both sides by b	a = cd ÷ b
(a + b) (c + d)	Multiplication of bracketed terms	ac + ad + be + bd
a^2 + ab	Use parentheses	a(a + b)
$(a + b)^2$	Expand brackets	$a^2 + 2ab + b^2$
$a^2 - b^2$	Difference of two squares	(a + b)(a-b)
1/a + 1/b	Find common denominator	(a + b)/ab
a/b ÷ c/d	Dividing by a fraction is the same as multiplying by its reciprocal	a/b × d/c

POWERS OF TEN USED WITH SCIENTIFIC UNITS

FACTOR	NAME	PREFIX	SYMBOL
10^{18}	quintillion	exa-	E
10^{15}	quadrillion	peta-	P
10^{12}	trillion	tera-	T
10^{9}	billion	giga-	G
10^{6}	million	mega-	M
10^{3}	thousand	kilo-	k
10^{2}	hundred	hecto-	h
10^{1}	ten	deca-	da
10^{-1}	one tenth	deci-	d
10^{-2}	one hundredth	centi-	c
10^{-3}	one thousandth	milli-	m
10^{-6}	one millionth	micro-	u
10^{-9}	one billionth	nano-	n
10^{-12}	one trillionth	pico-	p
10^{-15}	one quadrillionth	femto-	f
10^{-18}	one quintillionth	atto-	a

Note: The American system of numeration for denominations above one million is used in this book. In this system, each of the denominations above one billion (1,000 millions) is 1,000 times the preceding one.

BIOLOGY SYMBOLS

SYMBOL	MEANING
O	female individual (used in inheritance charts)
□	male individual (used in inheritance charts)
♀	female
♂	male
×	crossed with; hybrid
+	wild type
F_1	offspring of the first generation
F_2	offspring of the second generation

TEMPERATURE SCALES

To convert from Celsius (C) to Fahrenheit (F): F = (C × 9 ÷ 5) + 32
To convert from Fahrenheit to Celsius: C = (F − 32) × 5 ÷ 9
To convert from Celsius to Kelvin (K): K = C + 273
To convert from Kelvin to Celsius: C = K - 273

Celsius	-20	-10	0	10	20	30	40	50	60	70	80	90	100
Fahrenheit	-4	14	32	50	68	86	104	122	140	158	176	194	212
Kelvin	253	263	273	283	293	303	313	323	333	343	353	363	373

MATHEMATICAL SYMBOLS

SYMBOL	EXPLANATION
+	addition
-	subtraction
×	multiplication
÷	division
=	equals
≠	does not equal
>	greater than
<	less than
≥	greater than or equal to
≤	less than or equal to
∞	infinity
%	per cent
π	pi (3.1416)
°	degree
≈	is approximately equal to
∠	angle
∏	parallel to
∑	summation
u, u	vectors
f(x)	function
!	factorial
√	square root
ξ	universal set
A ∩ B	intersection
A ∪ B	unison
A ⊂ B	subset
Ø	null set

PHYSICS SYMBOLS

SYMBOL	MEANING
α	alpha particle
β	beta ray
γ	gamma ray; photon
ε	electromotive force
η	efficiency; viscosity
λ	wavelength
μ	micro-; permeability
ν	frequency; neutrino
ρ	density; resistivity
σ	conductivity
c	velocity of light
e	electronic charge

CHEMISTRY SYMBOLS

SYMBOL	MEANING
+	plus; together with
−	single bond
●	single bond; single unpaired electron; two separate parts or compounds regarded as loosely joined
=	double bond
≡	triple bond
R	group
X	halogen atom
Z	atomic number

SCIENTIFIC NOTATION

NUMBER	NUMBER BETWEEN 1 AND 10	POWER OF TEN	SCIENTIFIC NOTATION
10	1	10^1	1 3 10^1
150	1.5	10^2 (= 100)	1.5 3 10^2
274,000,000	2.74	10^8 (= 100,000,000)	2.74 3 10^8
0.0023	2.3	10^{-3} (= 0.001)	2.3 3 10^{-3}

TRIGONOMETRY

Angle A (degrees)	sin A	cos A	tan A
0	0	1	0
30	1/2	√3/2	1/√3
45	1/√2	1/√2	1
60	√3/2	1/2	√3
90	1	0	∞

Shapes: Plane

Two-dimensional shapes are termed plane (or flat) shapes. Plane shapes constructed with straight sides, as illustrated here, are called polygons. They are categorized according to the number of sides they have – for example, three-sided polygons are known as triangles. A polygon that has sides of equal length and internal angles of equal size, such as a square, is said to be regular.

SCALENE TRIANGLE
A triangle (three-sided polygon) with no equal sides or angles.

ISOSCELES TRIANGLE
A triangle with only two sides and two angles equal.

RIGHT-ANGLED TRIANGLE
A triangle with one angle as a right angle (90°).

EQUILATERAL TRIANGLE
A regular triangle. All angles are 60°.

SQUARE
A regular quadrilateral. All angles are 90°.

RHOMBUS
A quadrilateral with all sides equal and two pairs of equal angles.

RECTANGLE
A quadrilateral with four right angles and opposite sides of equal length.

PARALLELOGRAM
A quadrilateral with two pairs of parallel sides.

TRAPEZIUM
A quadrilateral with one pair of parallel sides.

PENTAGON
A five-sided polygon. A regular pentagon is shown above.

HEXAGON
A six-sided polygon. A regular hexagon is shown above.

OCTAGON
An eight-sided polygon. A regular octagon is shown above.

AREAS AND PERIMETERS

The formulae for calculating the areas and perimeters of simple plane shapes were devised by Classical Greek mathematicians.

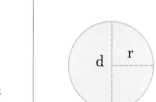

CIRCLE
r = radius
d = diameter = $2 \times r$

Circumference = $2 \times \pi \times r$
Area = $\pi \times r^2$
($\pi = 3.1416$)

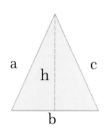

TRIANGLE
Height = h
Sides = a, b, c

Perimeter = a + b + c
Area = $\frac{1}{2} \times b \times h$

RECTANGLE
Sides = a, b

Perimeter = $2 \times (a + b)$
Area = $a \times b$

Shapes: Solid

Three-dimensional shapes are known as solid shapes, and include spheres, cubes, and pyramids. A solid shape with a polygon at each face is called a polyhedron.

TETRAHEDRON
A four-sided polyhedron. A regular tetrahedron is shown.

CUBE
A regular hexahedron. All sides are equal and all angles are 90°.

OCTAHEDRON
A polyhedron with eight sides.

PRISM
A polyhedron of constant cross-sections in planes perpendicular to its longitudinal axis.

PYRAMID
A polygonal base and triangular sides that meet at a point.

TORUS
A doughnut-like, ring shape.

SPHERE
A round shape, as in a ball or an orange.

HEMISPHERE
Formed when a sphere is cut exactly in half.

SPHEROID
An egg-shaped solid object whose cross-section is a circle or an ellipse.

CONE
An elliptical or circular base with sides tapering to a single point.

RIGHT CYLINDER
A tube-shaped, solid figure. A right cylinder has parallel faces.

HELIX
A twisted curve. The distance moved in one revolution is its pitch.

SURFACE AREAS AND VOLUMES

Volume refers to the amount of space that a solid object occupies. Its surface area is the sum of the area of each of its faces.

CYLINDER
Surface area =
$2 \times \pi \times r \times h + 2\pi r^2$
Volume $= \pi \times r^2 \times h$

Height = h
Radius = r

CONE
Surface area =
$\pi \times r \times l + \pi r^2$
Volume $= \frac{1}{3} \times \pi \times r^2 \times l$

Height = h
Radius = r
Side = l

RECTANGULAR BLOCK
Surface area =
$2 \, (a \times b + b \times c + a \times c)$
Volume $= a \times b \times c$

Sides = a, b, c

632

648

654

658

664

Acknowledgments

Dorling Kindersley would like to thank (in order of sections):

The Universe
(consultant editors – Sue Becklake, Gevorkyan Tatyana Alekseyevna):

John Becklake; the Memorial Museum of Cosmonautics, Moscow; The Cosmos Pavilion, Moscow; The United States Space and Rocket Centre, Alabama; Broadhurst, Clarkson and Fuller Ltd; Susannah Massey

Prehistoric Earth
(consultant editors – William Lindsay, Martyn Bramwell, Dr Ralph E. Molnar, David Lambert):

Dr Monty Reid, Andrew Neuman, and the staff of the Royal Tyrrell Museum of Palaeontology, Drumheller, Alberta; Dr Angela Milner and the staff of the Department of Palaeontology, the Natural History Museum, London; Professor W. Ziegler and the staff, in particular Michael Loderstaedt, of the Naturmuseum Senckenburg, Frankfurt; Dr Alexander Liebau, Axel Hunghrebüller, Reiner Schoch, and the staff of the Institut und Museum für Geologie und Paläontologie der Universität, Tübingen; Rupert Wild of the Institut für Paläontologie, Staatliches Museum für Naturkunde, Stuttgart; Dr Scheiber of the Stadtmuseum, Nördlingen; Professor Dr Dietrich Herm of Staatssammlung für Paläontologie und Historische Geologie, München; Dr Michael Keith-Lucas of the Department of Botany, University of Reading; Richard Walker; American Museum of Natural History, New York

Plants
(consultant editor – Richard Walker):

Diana Miller; Lawrie Springate; Karen Sidwell; Chris Thody; Michelle End; Susan Barnes and Chris Jones of the EMU Unit of the Natural History Museum, London; Jenny Evans of Kew Gardens, London; Kate Biggs of the Royal Horticultural Society Gardens, Wisley, Surrey; Spike Walker of Microworld Services; Neil Fletcher; John Bryant of Bedgebury Pinetum, Kent; Dean Franklin

Animals
(consultant editor – Richard Walker):

David Manning's Animal Ark; Intellectual Animals; Howletts Zoo, Canterbury; John Dunlop; Alexander O'Donnell; Sue Evans of the Royal Veterinary College, London; Dr Geoff Potts and Fred Frettsome of the Marine Biological Association of the United Kingdom, Plymouth; Jeremy Adams of the Booth Museum of Natural History, Brighton; Derek Telling of the Department of Anatomy, University of Bristol; the Natural History Museum, London; Andy Highfield of the Tortoise Trust; Brian Harris at the Aquarium, London Zoo; the Invertebrate Department, London Zoo; Dr Harold McClure of the Yerkes Regional Primate Research Center, Emory University, Atlanta, Georgia; Nielson Lausen of the Harvard Medical School, New England Regional Primates Research

Centre, Southborough, Massachusetts; Dr Paul Hopwood of the Department of Veterinary Anatomy, University of Sydney; Dean Franklin

The Human Body
(consultant editors – Dr Frances Williams, Dr Fiona Payne, Richard Cummins FRCS):

Derek Edwards and Dr Martin Collins, British School of Osteopathy; Dr M.C.E. Hutchinson of the Department of Anatomy, United Medical and Dental Schools of Guy's and St Thomas' Hospitals, London. Models – Barry O'Rorke (Bodyline Agency) and Pauline Swaine (MOT Model Agency)

Geology, Geography, and Meteorology
(consultant editor – Martyn Bramwell):

Dr John Nudds of the Manchester Museum, Manchester; Dr Alan Wooley and Dr Andrew Clark of the Natural History Museum, London; Graham Bartlett of the National Meteorological Library and Archive, Bracknell; Tony Drake of BP Exploration, Uxbridge; Jane Davies of the Royal Society of Chemistry, Cambridge; Dr Tony Waltham of Nottingham Trent University, Nottingham; staff of the Smithsonian Institute, Washington; staff of the United States Geological Survey, Washington; staff of the National Geographic Society, Washington; staff of Edward Lawrence Associates (Export Ltd), Midhurst; John Farndon; David Lambert

Rail and Road
Rail (consultant editor – John Coiley)
Michael Ashworth of the London Transport Museum

Road (consultant editors – David Burgess-Wise, Hugo Wilson)
The National Motor Museum, Beaulieu; Alf Newell of Renault UK Ltd; David Suter of Cheltenham Cutaway Exhibits Ltd; Francesca Riccini of the Science Museum, London. Signore Amadelli of the Museo dell' Automobile Carlo Biscaretti di Ruffia; Paul Bolton of the Mazda MCL Group; Duncan Bradford of Reg Mills Wire Wheels; John and Leslie Brewster of Autocavan; David Burgess-Wise; Trevor Cass of Garrett Turbo Service; John Corbett of The Patrick Collection; Gary Crumpler of Williams Grand Prix Engineering Ltd; Mollie Easterbrooke and Duncan Gough of Overland Ltd; Arthur Fairley of the Vauxhall Motor Company; Paul Foulkes-Halbard of Filching Manor Motor Museum; Frank Gilbert of I. Wilkinson and Son Ltd; Paolo Gratton of Gratton Museum; Colvin Gunn of Gunn and Son; Judy Hogg of Ecurie Bertelli; Milton Holman of Dream Cars; Ian Matthews of IMAT Electronics; Eric Neal of Jaguar Cars Ltd; Paul Niblett, Keith Davidson, Mark Reumel, and David Woolf of Michelin Tyre plc; Doug Nye; Kevin O'Keefe of O'Keefe Cars; Seat UK; Ian Whitley, Raj Johal and Andy Faiers of the Honda Institute; Roger Smith; Jim Stirling of Ironbridge Gorge Museum, Staffordshire; Jon Taylor; Doug Thompson; Martyn Watkins of Ford Motor Company Ltd; John Cattermole, Customer Services Manager at London Northern Buses; F. W. Evans Cycles Ltd; Trek UK Ltd (Bicycle); Sam Grimmer; Colin Uttley

Physics and Chemistry
(consultant editor – Jack Challoner)

Sea and Air
Sea (consultant editors – Geoff Hales and Harvey B. Loomis):
David Spence, Gillian Hutchinson, David Topliss, Simon Stephens, Robert Baldwin, Jonathan Betts, all of the National Maritime Museum, London; Ian Friel; Simon Turnage of Captain O.M. Watts of London Ltd; Davey and Company Ltd, Great Dunmow; Avon Inflatables Ltd, Llanelli; Musto Ltd, Benfleet; Peter Martin of Spencer Rigging Ltd, Southampton; Peter Rowson of Ratseys Sailmakers, Southampton; Swiftech Ltd, Wallingford; Colin Scattergood of the Barrow Boat Company Ltd, Colchester; Professor J.S. Morrison of the Trireme Trust, Cambridge; The Cutty Sark Maritime Trust; Adrian Daniels of Kelvin Hughes Marine Instruments, London; Arthur Credland of Hull City Council Museums and Art Galleries; The Hull Maritime Society; Gerald Clark; Peter Fitzgerald of the Science Museum, London; Alec Michael of HMB Subwork Ltd, Great Yarmouth, and Ray Ward of the OSEL Group, Great Yarmouth; Richard Bird of UWI, Weybridge; Walker Marine Instruments, Birmingham; The International Sailing Craft Association; The Exeter Maritime Museum; Jane Wilson of the Trinity Lighthouse Company, London; The Imperial War Museum Collections; Thorn Security Ltd; Michael Bach

Air (consultant editor – Bill Gunston):
Aeromega Helicopters, Stapleford; Aero Shopping, London; Avionics Mobile Services Ltd, Watford; Roy Barber and John Chapman of the RAF Museum, Hendon; Mitch Barnes Aviation, London; Mike Beach; British Caledonian Flight Training Ltd; Fred Coates of Helitech (Luton) Ltd; Michael Cuttell and CSE Aviation Ltd, Oxford; Dowty Aerospace Landing Gear, Gloucester; Guy Hartcup of the Airship Association; Anthony Hooley, Chris Walsh, and David Cord of British Aerospace Regional Aircraft Ltd; Ken Huntley of Mid-West Aero Engines Ltd; Imperial War Museum, Duxford; The London Gliding Club, Dunstable; Musée des Ballons, Calvados; Noel Penny Turbines Ltd; Andy Pavey of Aviation Scotland Ltd; Tony Pavey of Thermal Aircraft Developments, London; the Commanding Officer and personnel of RAF St Athan; the Commanding Officer and personnel of RAF Wittering; The Science Museum, London; Ross Sharp of the Science Museum, Wroughton; The Shuttleworth Collection; Skysport Engineering; Mike Smith; Solar Wings Ltd, Marlborough; Julian Temple of Brooklands Museum Trust Ltd; Kelvin Wilson of Flying Start

Architecture
(consultant editor – Alexandra Kennedy):
Stephen Cutler for advice and text; Gavin Morgan of the Museum of London, London; Chris Zeuner of the Weald and Downland Museum, Singleton, Sussex; Alan Hills and James Putnam of the British Museum, London; Dr Simon Penn and Michael Thomas of the Avoncroft Museum of Buildings, Bromsgrove,

Worcestershire; Christina Scull of Sir John Soane's Museum, London; Paul Kennedy and John Williamson of the London Door Company, London; Lou Davis of The Original Box Sash Window Company, Windsor; Goddard and Gibbs Studios Ltd, London, for access to stained glass windows; The Royal Courts of Justice, Strand, London; Charles Brooking and Peter Dalton for access to the doors and windows in the Charles Brooking Collection, University of Greenwich, Dartford, Kent; Clare O'Brien of the Shakespeare Globe Trust, Shakespeare's Globe Museum, Bear Gardens, Southwark, London; Ken Teague of the Horniman Museum, London; Canon Haliburton, Mike Payton, Ken Stones, and Anthony Webb of St Paul's Cathedral, London; Roy Spring of Salisbury Cathedral; Reverend Gillean Craig of the Church of St George in the East, London; the Science Museum, London; Dr Neil Bingham; Lin Kennedy of Historic Royal Palaces; Katy Harris of Sir Norman Foster and Partners; Production Design, Thames Television plc, London; Dominique Reynier of Le Centre Georges Pompidou, Paris; Denis Roche of Le Musée National des Monuments Français, Paris; Franck Gioria and students of Les Compagnons du Devoir, Paris, for access to construction models; Frank Folliot of Le Musée Carnavalet, Paris; Dr Martina Harms of Hessische Landesmuseums, Darmstadt; Jefferson Chapman of the University of Tennessee, Knoxville, for access to the model of the Hypostyle Hall, Temple of Amon-Re; staff of the Palazzo Strozzi, Florence; staff of the Sydney Opera House, Sydney; staff of the Empire State Building, New York; Nick Jackson; Ann Terrell

The Visual Arts
(consultant editor – Pip Seymour):
Rosemary Simmons; Michael Taylor of Paupers Press, London; Tessa Hunkin and Emma Biggs of Mosaic Workshop, London; John Tiranti, Jonathan Lyons of Alec Tiranti Ltd, London; Chris Hough; Dr Ashok Roy; Satwinder Sehmi of Alphabet Soup, London; Phillip Poole of Cornelissens, London; George Weil and Sons Ltd, London; The National Gallery, London; Chris Webster of the Tate Gallery, London; China Art Cultural Centre, London; London Graphic Centre, London; A.P. Fitzpatrick, London; Flowers Graphics, London; Intaglio Printmaker, London; Falkiner Papers, London; Edgar Udny and Co, London; John Green

Music
(consultant editor – Susan Sturrock):
Boosey and Hawkes Music Publishers Ltd, London, for permission to reproduce extract from The Prodigal Son by Arthur Sullivan; The Bass and Drum Cellar, London; Empire Drums and Percussion, London; Argents (part of World of Music), London; Bill Lewington Ltd, London; Frobenius organ at Kingston Parish Church, Surrey; Yamaha-Kemble Music (UK) Ltd, Tilbrook, Milton Keynes; Yamaha Atelier, London; Akai (UK) Ltd, Hounslow, Middlesex; Casio Electronics Co. Ltd, London; Roland (UK) Ltd, Fleet, Hampshire; Richard Schulman; Andy Brown of Musictrack

Sports
The Sports Council Information Centre, London; The British Olympic Games Committee; Brian Crennell of Black's Leisure Group (First Sport); Lillywhites of Piccadilly, London; Mitre Sports International Ltd, Huddersfield; David Bloomfield of the Football Association; Denver Athletics Ltd, Norfolk; Greg Everest and Keith Birley of the British League of Australian Rules Football; Peter McNally of the Gaelic Athletic Association; Jeremy Garman of James Gilbert Ltd.; Rex King of the Rugby Football Union, Twickenham; Neil Tunnicliffe and John Huxley of the Rugby Football League, Leeds; Wayne Patterson of the Basketball Hall of Fame, Springfield, Connecticut; Brian Coleman of the English Basketball Association; All American Imports, Northampton; George Bulman of the English Volleyball Association; Julie Longdon of Mizuno Mallory (UK) Ltd; Juliet Stanford of the All-England Netball Association; Jeff Rowland of the British Handball Association; Cally Melin of Adidas UK Ltd; Patrick Donnely of the Baseball Hall of Fame, Cooperstown, New York; Ian Lepage and Stephen Barlow of the Hockey Association, Milton Keynes; Alison Taylor and Anita Mason of the All England Women's Lacrosse Association, Birmingham; David Shuttleworth of the English Lacrosse Union; Les Barnett and Jock Bentley of the British Athletic Federation Ltd, Birmingham; Mike Gilks of the Badminton Association of England; Gurinder Purewall for advice on archery; Chris McCartney of the US Archery Association; Geoff Doe of the National Smallbore Rifle Association, Bisley, Surrey, for information and reference material on shooting; Fagan Sports Goods Distributors, Surrey; Konrad Bartelski for advice on skiing; The British Ski Federation, Edinburgh; Mike Barnett of Snow and Rock of London; Sally Spurway of Mast-Co. Ltd, Reading; Sarah Morgan for advice on equestrian sports; Steve Brown and the New York Racing Association Inc, New York; Danrho of London; Alan Skipp and James Chambers of the Amateur Fencing Association, London; Carla Richards of the US Fencing Association; Hamilton Bland and John Dryer of the Amateur Swimming Association, Loughborough; Cotswold Camping Ltd, London; Tim Spalton of Glyn Locke (Racing Shells) Ltd, Chalgrove; Terry Friel of the US Rowing Association; House of Hardy; Leeda Fishing Tackle

The Modern World
John Lewis, Brent Cross, for the loan of products for photography; Apple Computers UK; Palm Inc.; Epson UK; Naynesh Mistry of Brother UK; Nintendo; Sony UK; Nokia Mobile Phones Ltd; Sony Ericsson; Tony Broad of Garmin Europe; Dualit Ltd; Black and Decker Ltd; James Honour of the Buildings Research Establishment; Craig Anders of Cole Thompson Associates; Vestas Wind Systems; Bryan Adams of MIT; Dr Julian Heath of *Microscopy and Analysis*; Fei UK Ltd; Steve Parker; Ian Graham

PHOTOGRAPHY:
M. Alexander; Peter Anderson; Colin Bowling; Charles Brooks; Jane Burton; Peter Chadwick; Simon Clay; Gordon Clayton; John Coiley; Andy Crawford; Geoff Dann; Philip Dowell; John Downs; Mike Dunning; Torla Evans; David Exton; Paul Forrester; Robert and Anthony Fretwell of Fretwell Photography Ltd.; Philip Gatward; Steve Gorton; Anna Hodgson; Gary Kevin; J. Heseltine; Cyril Laubscher; John Lepine; Lynton Gardiner (American Museum of Natural History, New York); Steve Gorton; Michelangelo Gratton; Judith Harrington; Peter Hayman; Anna Hodgson; Colin Keates; Gary Kevin; Dave King; Bob Langrish; Brian D.Morgan; Nick Nicholls; Nick Parfitt; Tim Parmenter and Colin Keates (Natural History Museum, London); Tim Ridley; Dave Rudkin; Philippe Sebert; James Stevenson; Clive Streeter; Harry Taylor; Matthew Ward; Jerry Young

PHOTOGRAPHIC ASSISTANCE:
Kevin Zak; Gary Ombler; Govind Mittal

ILLUSTRATORS:
Julian Baum; Rick Blakeley; Kuo Rang Chen; Karen Cochrane; Simone End; Ian Fleming; Roy Flooks; Mark Franklin; David Gardner; Will Giles; Mick Gillah; David Hopkins; Selwyn Hutchinson; Mei Lim; Linden Artists; Nick Loates; Chris Lyon; Kathleen McDougall; Coral Mula; Sandra Pond; Dave Pugh; Colin Rose; Graham Rosewarne; John Temperton; Halli Verrinder; John Woodcock; Chris Woolmer

MODEL MAKERS:
Roby Braun; David Donkin; Morrison Frederick; Gordon Models; John Holmes; Graham High and Jeremy Hunt of Centaur Studios; Richard Kemp; Kelvin Thatcher; Paul Wilkinson

ADDITIONAL DESIGN ASSISTANCE:
Stefan Morris; Ulysses Santos; Suchada Smith; Niyati Gosain; Jomin Johny; Ridhi Khanna; Amit Malhotra; Payal Rosalind Malik; Anamica Roy; Ira Sharma; Balwant Singh

ADDITIONAL EDITORIAL ASSISTANCE:
Helen Castle; Colette Connolly; Camela Decaire; Nick Harris; Andrea Horth; Stewart McEwen; Damien Moore; Melanie Tham; Pragati Nagpal; Suparna Sengupta; Anita Kakar; Divya Chandhok

INDEX: Kay Wright; Lynn Bresler

Picture credits:

The publisher would like to thank the following for their kind permission to reproduce their photographs:

2011 Research In Motion Limited 589tr; Action Plus 530tc; Alamy images David Kilpatrick 581tr, 581cra; Nikreates 586ca; NordicImages 591tr; Oleksiy Maksymenko Photography 568cra; Arthur Turner 579cla; Martin Williams 569bl; Anglo Australian Telescope Board 11cl, 11cra, 11cbl, 12tr, 12bc, 13tl, 13bl, 14tl, 16b, 17tc, 17bl, 22tl/D.Malin 16tl, 26tr, 27tl; Austin Brown and the Aviation Picture Library 426tl; Baptistery, Florence/Alison Harris 453r; Biophoto Associates 217ca, 217cra, 228cbc, 228cbc 230tr; BRE Imaging 602bl, 602r, 603tl, 603br; Paul Brierley 311bra; Bowers & Wilkins: B&W Group Ltd 586b; British Aerospace/Anthony Hooley 412tl, 415tl; British Aerospace (Commercial Aircraft) Ltd 416tl; By prmission of the British Library 432tl, 445bl; British Museum 459tl, 459tr, 460tr, 460tc, 460tb, 489b; BP Exploration 299; Duncan Brown 25t; Frank Lloyd Wright, American, 1867-1959, Model of Midway Gardens, 1914, executed by Richard Tickner, mixed media, 1987, 41.9 x 81.3 x 76.2, 1989.48. view 1. Photography courtesy of the Art Institute of Chicago 495t; J.A. Coiley 331cr; Bruce Coleman Ltd/Andy Price 272tl; Canon Europe 581crb; Corbis Jon Stokes/Science Photo Library 576cl; Paul Sounders/Terra 328b; Wu Ching-teng/Xinhua Press 568br; Haruyoshi Yamaguchi/Sygma 608r; Courtesy of the Board of Trustees of the Victoria and Albert Museum, London 454-455b; Creative Labs, Inc. 586tc; Dorling Kindersley Owen Peyton Jones 566cr, 582-583, 589; Dyson 592tr; European Passenger Services 329tl; ESA /PLV 11bl; European Southern Observatory (ESO) 53tl; Fei Co. 610cr, 610r; French Railways 329c; FUJIFILM UK 581br; Garmin Europe 590c; Geoscience Features 311cla; Robert Harding Picture Library 62tl; Getty Images Bloomberg 569bc, 569br; Tony Cordoza 584tr; Hannah Johnston 588ca; Photodisc/Ryan McVay 577tl; Harman International Industries, Incorporated JBL 586cl; Hitachi High-Technologies Co. Ltd 61 1tr; Michael Holford/British Museum 372bl, Michael Holford 374tr; Honda 354tr, 355b; Hutchison Picture Library 60cl; iFixit Miroslav Djuric 580-581 (Nikon Coolpix S1000PJ), 587 (Components of Microsoft Zune HD); Brett Hartt 578cra; The Image Bank/Edward Bower

306tr; Jet Propulsion Laboratory 11cbr; 30bc; 31bc; 31bcr; 38tl; 42crb; 44cb; 44cbr; 44bc; 46tl; 46cr; 46cb; 46bc; 46br; 50tl; 50cra; 50cl; 50c; 50cr; 50br; Kawasaki (UK) 609bl; KeyMed Ltd 248bl, 249bl, 249cbl; Department of Prints and Drawings, Uffizi, Florence/Philip Gatward 431tc/Uffizi, Florence/Philip Gatward 433tl; Robin Kerrod/Spacecharts 615br; Dr D.N. Landon (Institute of Neurology) 228bl,br; LG Electronics 588cr; Life Science Images/Ron Boardman 244bl, 244br; The Lund Observatory 15bc; Brian Morrison 329tl, 329tr; © The Henry Moore Foundation 455tr; Used with permission from Microsoft 578tr, 587br; Musée d'Orsay, Paris/Philippe Sebert 437tc, 441tc; Musée du Louvre, Paris/Philippe Sebert 453tl, 453l, 453be; Musictrack/MOTU Digital performer 521bcl; NASA/AUI 13tr; NASA and The Hubble Heritage Team (AURA/STScI) 44tl; NASA Dr. R. Albrecht, ESA/ESO Space Telescope European Coordinating Facility 31fbr; CXC/ASU/J. Hester et al 28cra; JPL/DLR 44br; JPL JHUAPL 42br; JPL-Caltech/University of Arizona 42fbr; NASA/JPL 11 cbr, 11br; 30tl; 30bl; 30br; 30bc; 31bc; 31bcr; 31bl; 34cr, 38tl, 40tl, 40cr, 42cr, 44cb, 44cbr, 44bc, 44cr, 46crb, 46tl, 46cr, 46cb, 46bc, 46br, 48tl, 48cra, 48bca, 48bc, 48br, 50tl, 50bc, 50bc, 50cbr, 50br, 50cr, 52cr, 612cr, 612tr, 613tl, 613tcl, 613tcr, 613tr, 613c, 613cr, 614tl, 614tr 614cl, 614bl, 614c, 615tr, 615cr, 615c; National Maritime Museum 373br, 392-393b; National Medical Slide Bank 217cr; Nature Photographers/Paul Sterry 286tl; Newage International 317bl; Nintendo 578tl, 578clb, 579tl, 579tr, 579cra; Olympus 610cl, 61 0bi; Oxford Scientific Films/Breck P. Kent 166tl; Planet Earth 274tr; Press Association Images AP 609cr; Quadrant 326tr; Margaret Robinson 332tl; Giotto The Expulsion of the Merchants from the Temple Scala 435tc, 435bl, 435br; RapidRepair.com Ben Levy 569ca (iPad Components); Rex Features Jonathan Hordle 609br; Roland UK 521tl; Science Photo Library 10bl, 13tr, 214bcr, 214bl, 236tr/Michael Abbey 225tc/Agema Infrared Systems 318tl/AGFA 220tl/Alex Barte 605tr/David Becker 607cr/Biophoto Associates 217crb/Dr Jeremy Burgess/ Science Photo Library 132tl; Dr Jeremy Burgess 255bcl/CNRI 214tl, 214cl, 214c, 214cr, 214bl, 214clb, 214crb, 214blc, 214br, 217cb, 255bcr, 238tl, 249bcr, 253tr, 253cra, 256tl; Science Photo library /Earth Satellite Corporation 288cl, 293br/Dr Brian Eyden 228cbr/Professor C. Ferlaud 245bl/Vaughan Fleming 311tl/Simon Fraser/U.S. Dept.of Energy 214bcl,

266tl/Eric Grave 217br/Hale Observatories 32br/Max Planck Institute for Radio Astronomy 15tl/Jan Hinsch 225tc/Jodrell Bank 11tr, 13c /Manfred Kage 217c, 235br, 237br/Dr William C. Keel 13br/Keith Kent 564c/James King-Holmes 316tl, 606bl/Russ Lappa 310bra/ John Mead 605br/Astrid & Hans-Freider Michler 217tr/ Dennis Milon 52bl/NASA 11cla, 12tl, 15tr, 30c, 32tl, 35tl, 36tl, 36cl, 36cr, 36bc, 42tr, 52tl, 291cr, 300tl/National Optical Astro Observatory 52tr/NIBSC 253crb/Omikron 244bc/David Parker 63bl, 304-305, 308br/ Alfred Pasieka 606cr/Philippe Plailly 308tl/ Quest 611br/Roussel-UCLAF/CNRI 217tc/Rev Ronald Royer 32cr/Royal Observatory, Edinburgh/D Malin 11tl, 11cr,12c, 16cl, 16cr, 17br/David Scharf 235bl/Dr Kaus Schiller 248bcl, 248bcr, 248br/Secchi-Lecaque/Koussel-UCLAF/CNRI 253br/H. Sochurek 214cb/ Stammers/Thompson 230tl/Sheila Terry 234tl/ US Department of Energy 310bc/US Geological Survey/Science Photo Library 8-9, 30bcr, 42tl, 42bl/Tom Van Sant/Geosphere Project, Santa Monica/Science Photo Library 273tr, 281tr, 296tr, 297tl/Dr Christopher B. Williams/(Saint Marks Hospital) 249br; Oxford Scientific Films/Animals/ Breck P. Kent 167tl; Pratt & Whitney Canada 418-419b, 419t; Science Museum 306bl, 306bcl; 306 bcr, 324t, 326-327b), 330tr, 331ct, 331 cb; Sony Corporation 586tr, 586cr; Sporting Pictures 524tl, 544cr; TechRepublic Bill Detwiler 578-579b; Tony Stone Worldwide 280tl; David Bomberg St Pauls and River 1945/Dinora Davies-Rees/Tate Gallery 431bc; David Hockney A Bigger Splash 1967/© David Hockney/ Tate Gallery 443tc; J.M.W. Turner The Burning of the Houses of Parliament Tate Gallery 439tc; Vision 26tr, 27c; Jerry Young 306tl; Dr Robert Youngson 241cr; courtesy of Vestas Wind Systems 604t; Zefa 217bc/Janicek 276tl/H. Sochurek 210tl, 250tl, 254tl/G. Steenmans 292tl

(t=top, b=below/bottom, a=above, l=left, r=right, c=centre, f=far)

All other images © Dorling Kindersley For further information see: www.dkimages.com

Every effort has been made to trace the copyright holders. Dorling Kindersley apologizes for any unintentional omissions and would be pleased, in any such cases, to add an acknowledgment in future editions.

Some pages in this book previously appeared in the Visual Dictionary series published by Dorling Kindersley. Contributors to this series include:

Project Art Editors: Duncan Brown, Ross George, Nicola Liddiard, Andrew Nash, Clare Shedden, Bryn Walls

Designers: Lesley Betts, Paul Calver, Simone End, Ellen Woodward

Additional design assistance: Sandra Archer, Christina Betts, Alexandra Brown, Nick Jackson, Susan Knight

Project Editors: Fiona Courtney-Thompson, Paul Docherty, Tim Fraser, Stephanie Jackson, Mary Lindsay

Editorial Assistant: Emily Hill

Additional editorial assistance: Susan Bosanko, Edward Bunting, Candace Burch, Deirdre Clark, Jeanette Cossar, Danièle Guitton, Jacqui Hand, David Harding, Nicholas Jackson, Edwina Johnson, David Lambert, Gail Lawther, David Learmount, Paul Jackson, Christine Murdock, Bob Ogden, Cathy Rubinstein, Louise Tucker, Dr Robert Youngson

Picture Researchers: Vere Dodds, Danièle Guitton, Anna Lord, Catherine O'Rourke, Christine Rista, Sandra Schneider, Vanessa Smith, Clive Webster

Series Editor: Martyn Page

Series Art Editor: Paul Wilkinson

Managing Art Editors: Philip Gilderdale, Steve Knowlden

Art Director: Chez Picthall

Managing Editor: Ruth Midgley

Production: Jayne Simpson